SEARCH FOR PARADISE

A Patient's Account of the Artificial Vision Experiment

Jens Naumann

To order additional copies of this book, contact:
Xlibris Corporation
1-888-795-4274
www.Xlibris.com
Orders@Xlibris.com
118093

[handwritten] ... I hope you enjoy

the book,

thanks for being my

empowerer !

SEARCH FOR PARADISE

[handwritten] 27-9-2012

CONTENTS

CHAPTER 1

February 23, 1981

As I lay in that hospital emergency ward, I could not stop thinking about how careful I was going to have to be from now on. Not even the hourly shots of Demerol could slow down my mind, which was going around and around in the same pattern, as if caught in a trap. I had lost things before in my life, like the time I forgot my wallet containing a freshly cashed paycheck left lying on the counter in a gas station, or like that time I had rolled my math teacher's Datsun trying to spin doughnuts in the Chetwynd Elementary Secondary School's parking lot.

"This time," I thought miserably as the reality hit me, "this loss will be a tough one to absorb." Time heals, or so they say, and I will depend on that this time more than ever. The doctor came to look at my eye again. I do not recall his name, just his face. He had a very serious expression. I mused in practical desperation in an attempt to reduce the seriousness of the situation if he even knew how to smile.

"Doctor," as I called him, looked at my left eye for a minute, and then at my right. "This one is fine," I explained to him. "It is the left one that cannot see. The left one has the metal in it." I was a little concerned about his looking at my right eye, which was perfectly fine. I had heard a bit on the news once about the wrong operation performed to a person in a hospital, and I just wanted to be sure he did not operate on the wrong eye. Imagine that—having the left one knocked out and then the right one blinded by a screw-up. There would be nothing left. No driving. No faces on people, and no stars in the sky. I'd be better off dead.

Doctor kept looking at my right eye. "Yeah," he started, in his preoccupied manner that I swear is taught in medical school, "I just wanted to reconfirm this before wheeling you into the operating room." He looked at me again for a second, and then continued, "I have to admit, though, that your right eye does not look perfect either. There is quite a bit of bruising around it."

I insisted to clarify the situation. "Yes, I had been in a bit of a scuffle last week, but I can see perfectly out of the right one." I used whatever terminology I could recall from high school biology. "It is just the socket around the outside that is a bit stressed, but the cornea, retina, and other components of the functional part of the eye are working perfectly." I had to add again, as if he was a schoolchild I was talking to. Perhaps my manner seemed a little disrespectful with regards to his competence as a doctor, but what the heck, it was my future at stake here. "It's the left eye," I said as I pointed to it, "that does not see because of the metal in it."

Doctor looked in the left eye again, this time circling the eye with a felt marker. He said in a voice even gloomier than before. "Yeah . . . we'll work on it in a few minutes. We'll put you under . . ." Then he added, as an afterthought, more to himself than me, "It's going to be difficult to get that one out."

I lay there, solitary again, except for the noises of pain and suffering around me. I looked to my left, where the curtain surrounding my compound was not pulled fully so as to confine me visually. I had to turn my head further than before, as now my left eye was out of commission. I saw other people lying on their bunks, awaiting emergency care as well. This was not a good day for any of us. Nurses were busily fussing with everyone, attempting to comfort us as best as possible. I envied them for their ability to just go home after work, leaving these problems behind them.

Being in here was sure a different world. The beauty was gone from it in here. The world was made for the lucky and the fit. At this moment, I was depending on this doctor as if he were God. He would remove the metal from my left eye and then repair it so I could see again. The pangs of doubt, however, were ever present, and no dosage of Demerol could ease my mind.

I let my thoughts drift to the doctor's comment about my right eye being bruised. It was just a few days ago when that took place. It was Friday night, or more the late afternoon, when my buddy Steve Hardwick and I sat at Steve's uncle's place playing cribbage as usual. The railway camp for which we worked was mostly inhabited by Portuguese workers who were great guys, but several years my senior, and spoke only their tongue between themselves.

Therefore, Steve, the only other English-speaking employee in the camp, and I kept to ourselves. Steve was a nice enough guy, and having ten years on my seventeen years, I expected, naively enough, some adult insight at times from him. I did receive it in the form of instructions of how to play cribbage. Steve did not have a driver's license, or even a car, so my having a pickup truck was an asset for Steve to escape the confinement of the Chetwynd railway camp with me.

I could not imagine being without a driver's license. Steve seemed to handle it in stride. I asked him once about it, and he merely replied, "Oh, I got a few too many fines, and I had to give it up . . ."

I thought it a bit bizarre, as living without a driver's license was like living without rhyme or reason for me. I had mine for only a year and a bit then, but its importance was beyond that of anything else in my life—signifying the very essence of life—independence, mobility, and freedom.

The cribbage game dragged on, when I suggested we go to Dawson Creek, a town of about twelve thousand inhabitants, situated sixty miles or so east of Chetwynd. Why not, as it was a Friday night, and section work for the British Columbia railway camp would not commence until the next Monday. Therefore, we had money to spend and time to waste.

We headed out to the driveway of Steve's uncle's where my pickup truck was parked. I liked the looks of it—two tone blue and black, with all the indications of freedom surrounding it. All I had to do was get in and drive. Steve got in the passenger side, and I in the driver's. It was a special feeling of power and control to have the steering wheel in front of me, and the gas pedal under my foot. Furthermore, a man ten years my senior was sitting beside me, rendered powerless by his misdemeanors.

I fired up the old '71 Ford and headed out to Dawson Creek.

We arrived an hour later in the town, looking for whatever nightlife looked most appeasing to us. Steve mentioned that we should look for "chicks," and I agreed, as the company of the opposite gender often adds to the beauty of the evening. With us both being single, it only made sense for both of us to socialize with some great gals.

We decided on a bar which was right on main street, or at least what looked like main street in Dawson Creek. I had no problems getting in, underage and all, as my height and appearance fooled the majority of receptionists and bouncers alike. Steve, wearing his cowboy hat, sat down with me and together had a couple of draft beer—the kind one can buy for a dollar a glass.

But it wasn't more than two or three draft later that I noticed a change in Steve. His personality seemed to take an about-turn to the aggressive. Having arrived late, the bartender had insisted we "drink up" and go on as it was approaching one in the morning. I finished mine, being conservative for the purpose of driving, but Steve turned to me in a manner I had never seen in him before.

"The hell with him," he drawled. "We stay until we're good 'n ready . . ."

We were the only ones left—the others had already left, and all that remained was a worried bartender, anxious to get home, with his "please get him out of here" look in his face when looking at me. I had slightly nodded in his direction at his unspoken request, upon which turning to Steve, I said,

"Steve." I pretended to look and see out of the darkened window facing Main Street. "Drink up. I think there are some chicks out there for us . . ." I had not seen anyone, except for the traffic light, as the street outside the window was dark. Nevertheless, to my relief, the mention of more excitement got Steve drinking up and heading for the door. I paid the bill and joined him on the sidewalk, glancing over my shoulder to see the silent "thank you . . ." in the eyes of the bartender before I left.

Once outside, the air was crisp, and the view was good as the traffic lights lit up the street. To my astonishment, there had been some "chicks" outside, but they did not look like they were interested in us. In fact, I thought they frowned rather profusely when Steve said, in a rather deliberate and belligerent voice, "Wow! Look at those two chicks!"

I had no idea as to what to do at that point. I had never seen a perfectly normal human being become so unhinged by alcohol before. Steve was actually running after these gals, whereas they had made it quite obvious that they had no interest in the whole affair. No telling Steve, though. I followed close behind, not as an accomplice, but rather as that of an observer. I saw three burly guys standing at the wall of a building, shadowed from the streetlights.

They advanced on us, and despite my efforts to warn Steve, they were on us. One grabbed me in a headlock, and two were working on Steve. Little did these guys know about our daily wrestling with 150 lbs. railway ties, 16 lbs. spike hammers, and setting 1,000 lbs. rail whenever there was a derailment.

Needless to say, they did not have much success with us. I broke free with little effort, however, did bruise my right eye socket a bit where the man had attempted to retain me in a headlock. I glanced at him, who had no idea what to do next. I stole a glance over my shoulder, and seeing that Steve was sitting on one of the men, while knocking him in the face repeatedly, he did not see the approach of the "red-and-blues"—the telltale mark of the police cruiser, which I took as my queue to get out of there.

I was around the corner of the building, ducking in and out of the parked cars in the lot. It was a dark Friday night, giving plenty of cover and shadow. It looked to me like Steve was going to spend the night in the drunk tank, and I had no intention of joining him. I looked through the side window of a parked car I was hiding behind and saw the three men from in front of the building dispersing in all different directions, except for the one I had taken.

I guessed they had Steve in a cruiser already and were looking for me. Over my shoulder, I saw my '71 Ford pickup. Outlined against the streetlight of the road on the opposite side of the block, it looked like a promise of freedom to me. It was just fifty or so feet to go. I snuck in that direction, keeping low between the parked cars. The men were dispersed throughout the lot, but not in the area where I was hiding. I wondered how I would start the truck and not be noticed, until I realized that the men were nowhere near a vehicle, so they would have to guess which direction I was going before being able to follow me. Whatever the case was, I had to get out of here. Trying to explain the situation to them would have been fruitless—they wanted blood.

I slid into the driver's seat and closed the door, making as little noise as possible. The key went in the ignition with my left hand, and in seconds, I was heading out of town to the west. I was on the open road—Highway 97—toward Chetwynd. No Steve with me this time. I doubted I would ever drink with him again unless we were well positioned in a BCR camp, away from civilization.

Worriedly, I glance over in the rearview mirror periodically during the one-hour drive home. Should these guys follow me, I would have to either outrun them or make a stand. I had plenty of power under my foot, as I had inherited this machine from Don Lasser, the son of the Mayor of Chetwynd, who had a passion for power and speed; and with the small-town RCMP knowing his father's stature, Don would only score a "warning ticket" rather than the real thing should he be caught in a radar trap. He would have laughed at the situation I was in today. I decided, despite all, to keep within the speed limit to avoid having to make another generous donation to the police.

They seemed to be out in full force tonight. They were truly scary, as they could pull my freedom at any time they chose—just four speeding tickets and I'd be doing time in the passenger seat just like Steve.

That was Friday night. The following Monday morning, I met Steve at the camp again. He was fully recovered, and his old mature self again. He mused at the proceedings of the previous Friday, with no idea of why the men we met from the side of Main Street were so hostile.

We stood together, early in the morning of the cold Northern British Columbia winter, watching while the Portuguese workers stick the heads of the pickaxes in hot cinders inside of forty-five-gallon drums and pulling them out with heavy tongs while pounding their tips to a sharp point with a hammer and anvil.

What I found bizarre was that they dunked the tip in the snow after sharpening them, and then replacing the handles, considering the axes ready for use. According to Rex Cameron, my former metalwork teacher in John

Peterson Junior High School of Kamloops, that method of hardening steel only hardened it, rendering it brittle, and in order to make it ready for use, it would have to be tempered—that is, it had to be reheated until the purple color of the heat rings forming on the work reaches the outer boundary of the axe, and then one must quench it in oil.

Such an explanation would have been impossible to convey to the Portuguese workers, who not only spoke their own language, but should I have been able to convey the information to them, would have laughed me out of town as, to them, I was just a "young punk," whereas they were older and much wiser.

But that all did not matter, as no one, including us, had any intention of working so hard with those archaic tools that we would risk breaking them.

In due time, we were all on the speeder, a small maintenance vehicle on rails, heading out on the rail line between Chetwynd and Fort St. John. The foreman, George Cardinal, bearing a very serious expression upon his face drove the speeder carefully, paying close attention to the possibility of an oncoming train or obstructions on the rails, while all the time looking for track in need of repair or something boring for us to do. George was a native from the area, and I heard he had eight children. What kind of a fool would deliberately build a wall around his free life in such a manner? I never did go right out and ask him, as there might be more to it than I knew.

Then we came on the area of George's choosing. It was obvious to see why, as there was a section of rail almost completely submerged in ice. By the looks of it, snow had melted nearby the tracks, and the resulting water had run across the track and re-froze. The result was one section of ice in front of us, with no difference in grade between the rails and the ice. The speeder was too light to continue, as it would have rode on top of the ice with its flanges, and then gone right off the tracks. All we had to do was clean about six inches of ice from the inside of either track to make room for the flanges.

Out with the picks. They were sharp and fresh and quite effective for the job. George came by with a pair of safety glasses for each of us.

"Here," he said as he held them out, "just to keep ice from flying at you." I tried them on, but after three hacks with the pick, they slid to the end of my nose, blocking my view and being a general nuisance. I put them in my pocket.

It was just before our lunch break when I gave a good swing at the ice and missed the small area beside the rail, hitting the rail head-on. One would expect the pick to buck in the hands give a sharp crack and flatten out its tip slightly from the hard impact. Not this time. The pick felt like it gave a bit—almost like it penetrated the rail somewhat—and I felt a sharp stinging in my left eye at the same time the view on my left side went foggy. I could hardly see large shapes out of that side now, as if looking through the frosted glass of a privacy window. I inspected the end of the pick, and my heart stood still when I saw, with my remaining functioning eye, the neat break off the area where the sharp end of the pick used to be. That metal had to be in my eye.

I approached George, who was working on his own section of track. He was always admired by the fellow workers for not just giving commands to the workers while sitting in the speeder drinking coffee. This policy, however, did not go over well with the other foremen from different sections.

"George," I started. He stopped and turned toward me. "I hit the rail by accident, and I think a piece of metal from the pick flew in my eye." I stated in a voice that made George stop what he was doing and look at me. George and I seemed to respect each other well, so when I spoke, he took me seriously.

"Can you wash it out?" George did not yet understand the scope of the situation. George was leaning on his pick handle, scanning my face.

"No, it's right in there, and I cannot see out of it either."

I closed my right eye, and, indeed, all there was to see was a blur where George stood. The trees, shrubs, snowbanks and all; the beauty of the world disappeared into a meaningless fuzz. I quickly opened my right eye.

George walked up close, and I saw his face change as if he had seen an oncoming train while driving the speeder. The other workers, including the men who sharpened the picks that morning, sensed something wrong and came over. The eldest, an immigrant from Portugal, who spoke no word of English, picked up my pick, inspecting its end.

"We'd better go into town," George radioed in for an ambulance. I stepped into the Chetwynd hospital upon returning to town with the ambulance, and the general practitioner on duty took only one look before ordering an air ambulance to take me to Prince George, a town of fifty thousand citizens, located two hundred miles south of Chetwynd. I was already nervous before, but now I realized it was not going to be an easy fix. Knowing about the eye from biology in high school, I suspected the cornea and the lens was penetrated, therefore allowing no focus. If that was the case, I would have to wear heavy glasses from here on. I knew about the retina too, which is the fine film of tissue and nerves at the back of the eye that does the seeing. I did not dare think that it could be damaged.

I asked the doctor, who ordered the ambulance, about the details of my injury. He did not say much. Demis Liete, the road master from that area of track of BCR, came in. He and the doctor talked some, and then Demis came to me to sign papers. The letterhead read "Worker's Compensation Board of

British Columbia." I stared at it for a few seconds with my good eye, almost in denial. "It couldn't be that serious," I told myself. But Demis just looked at me, beckoning me to sign the papers.

"For just in case," he explained, "we hope you won't need it."

Little did I know that someday I would have to live from the small percentage worker's compensation board awards the loss of one eye.

I boarded the chopper, which had landed right in the parking lot of the Chetwynd hospital. An attendant accompanied me but did not say much as there was a lot of noise on the chopper. We flew across the Rocky Mountain pass at an altitude just clearing the mountaintops. The beauty was astronomical, as the Rockies unfolded before us like a carpet of paradise. Even in spite of the circumstances, the view was absolutely breathtaking. The sun was out that day, revealing the true beauty of the landscape before us. The caps of the mountains were covered with white snow and ice, spreading out like a blanket before us for hundreds of miles. Looking straight down through the glass section of flooring in the chopper, I could see the small, deep green pools of water in the valleys.

We had landed on the designated section of the lot in Prince George just after two thirty in the afternoon, but now it was near seven in the evening with no further progress. Two nurses came and wheeled my bed to a X-ray room. They took some pictures of the side and front of my head, and then wheeled me to the operating room. There in the operating room, the staff was nice and kept telling me how everything would be all right. At that time, I believed them.

I awoke in the recovery room, with a terrible headache. All around me, there were the moaning sounds of human suffering. I figured that I was all right in comparison to someone attempting to recover from a major surgery. Heck, the eye was such a minor thing physically, with seemingly very few nerves that actually feel pain. But, man, it sure changed my world to have only one.

The left eye was securely bandaged. I went back to sleep, and when I awoke for the second time, I found myself in the ward with three other beds in the same room. I got up out of bed and looked at the sunny day outside, as my window overlooked the parking lot. The sunny day seemed to hit harder on my right eye than it ever had before. I shielded it, taking in only a bit of the lot at a time. I saw people out there, driving around the lot, in search of a parking space. Others were walking, and the world looked, once again, alive. I remember clearly the absence of sight from my left eye and how it seemed to irritate me. I looked around the room, moving my head more than usual in order to see the full scope of it with the restricted field of one eye. I couldn't wait to get the bandage off my left eye so I could see again with both of them.

Doctor came into the room. I was lying down, trying to lose the aftereffects of the anesthetic of five hours of surgery. He took another close look at my right and put in a drop. I was still curious as to why the fascination with the eye that had no damage, but I did not worry as I had yesterday, about him possibly confusing the hurt eye with the good one. He took the bandage off the other eye, and I could feel the cool air of the room on my eyelid. But I saw nothing. I said nothing, but my mind was wheeling. "It must be really bad," I told myself. Doctor got out a small light and shone it in, holding what looked like a magnifying glass in one hand.

"Do you see anything?" he asked, not moving his mouth much as we were close, and he was trying to hold still while peering in my eye. I could see the small glow of the light in my left eye. In spite of the low quality of vision, I felt a bit of relief that there was some optical connection. The yellow light I saw was grainy and spotted, with some areas totally black in my visual field.

"A bit," I replied with some apprehension. Is this the best it will do? I paused in mid-sentence to stress my disappointment. I had still hoped that perhaps there was some magic trick, or an obvious and easily solved explanation for the lack of vision in that side. It seemed to me that I could see the blurred images a lot better out of it before having the operation to remove the metal.

"We had to dig for the metal," the doctor explained. He continued. "Not only did it go through both sides of the eye, but into the socket and lodged itself just short of the brain. It must have flown like a bullet. I have removed the bullets of air rifles out of eyes before, but this one went deeper than that."

I remembered the impact of the pick on the rail. It did not bounce or jar in my hand. All that energy harnessed in the swinging pickax must have gone straight in my eye.

"Had I only worn those safety glasses . . ." I felt a sinking, sickening feeling in my heart. With that, the doctor looked again at my right eye and replied.

"I don't think that would have stopped that kind of a force.

In fact, the only way we got the metal out was by lining up the three holes it left and using a magnet to pull it out. Now imagine the complications posed with bits of glass in there as well. He let that sink in and added, "We'd have to open the skull and look for the pieces from there, and that is risky for the optic nerve, which could compromise the other eye as well." Doctor didn't have to say any more. I forgot about my left eye and thought of the right one. There was the

15

person across the room, reading a magazine. I could read the cover from where I was sitting, see the sun shining into the window onto the floor of the ward, the worried look of the doctor, the visitors streaming along the corridor outside the open door of the ward. My mind flashed briefly to a scene when I was fourteen, sitting on the school bus, looking out the window on my way to high school in Kamloops. We had been stopped in a traffic jam on Columbia Street, and upon looking out of the window of the bus, we saw a blind man walking with his guide dog along the sidewalk. "What a life that could be!" I remember thinking at the time. No colors, no shapes, no light, no nothing.

I shuddered at that scene now, while sitting in the ward of the hospital, with Doctor working to make things better. I figured I had lost one-third of my sight, as there is a kind of overlap where both eyes see the same thing. Then again, how could one, I mused, say there is any reduction, as when I move my head around a bit more, I can see the same thing as those with two eyes. Perhaps we can get that other side going later on, I hoped. Whatever the case was, it was not me on that sidewalk being dragged by a dog alongside Columbia Street.

I was discharged a few days later. The doctor gave me some eye drops to put in my right and left eye periodically. At this point, I questioned the logic of wasting drops on the good eye, which had even lost its bruised look around the socket. The doctor explained that often when there was an impending infection forming on one eye, it will carry over and ruin the other as well. This time, I did not attempt to graphically imagine the consequence. I obeyed, to the letter, his instructions regarding the drops.

My folks came to pick me up and take me up to Chetwynd via Route 97, the only highway going to that region. It is a beautiful three-hour drive through the heart of the Pine Pass, which is the winding road crossing the Rocky Mountain ridge. The view was still breathtaking, even after having crossed it many times before when I was driving alone. I feasted what remained of my sight on the beauty of the nature. One could not tire of seeing the mountains. I noticed that when looking out of the side window of the car, my depth perception was back, as the objects closer to me moved by faster than those further away. The blank spot on my left side bothered me. Occasionally, I closed my right eye and aimed my left into the full stream of sunshine just to see light out of that side for some form of relief. To see out of that side gave me a feeling inside like laying a cool, wet cloth on a burn. The next several weeks I did not work at the railway. The more I thought of it, the more reluctant I was to ever pick up a pick again—or even to that matter, a sledgehammer often used to drive spikes. That was a principal part of being a section man, however, and one would have to trust that this would not happen again. Even wearing safety glasses would not be a comfort. The image of the man using the guide dog became more and more frequent in my imagination. I have to be careful now.

Upon returning to Chetwynd, I could not wait to go for a drive with my old '71 Ford. It had been a week since driving, and where my father had parked it after bringing it back from the camp, it was necessary to back it out, past the house and my mother's parked car alongside the driveway. I fired it up, the familiarity of the controls comforting me. I put it in gear, cranked my head to look behind me, and was suddenly back on the brakes hard.

To my astonishment, I could not tell how far away I was from the house. I rolled down the side window and used the space of gravel between the neighbor's property boundary and the side of the Ford to judge my location. I saw my mother looking out the window of the house at me, and my progress. Never once, between us, did we discuss the possibility of me not being able to drive after losing an eye. That idea was unthinkable.

I progressed down the road, more timid than usual even though the town was small and traffic was next to none. I pulled carefully into a parking space in front of the local post office, just off the South Front Street. There was a car behind me, the driver doing the same. Suddenly, I hit the brakes real hard and screeched to a halt. I was going to hit the post office! I came to a quick stop, as I was really not going fast. A horn blared angrily behind me, and looking out the side window, still breathing a sigh of relief, I realized I was only halfway in the parking lot. The back bumper of the vehicle beside me was right at the side door of the '71. What a disaster, I figured. No depth perception at this range is quite a hassle. I slowly had to advance, using the back bumper of the vehicle alongside me as a guide. I spent many other parking experiences in a similar dilemma, at times getting out of the truck just to see the distance I had left before connecting with the other vehicles.

I still drove a lot, however. The motion gave me the third dimension of sight, and so long as I kept my head tilted a bit to the left, I could cover enough space on the left side for safety. I was more dependent upon the mirror on the left door, as that gave me the view of cars coming up beside me in either lane changes or during cornering. I was inclined, however, to revisit my friend Don Lasser, who had originally doctored up this truck to go real fast, to take out the performance parts and replace them with stock components. The value of speed, somehow, wore off from this event.

Having been in the surveying business for summer jobs, I occupied myself during my convalescence looking for other work. A man I knew well, Dave McIntyre, with whom I used to work during the summer holidays in between school grades, was searching for help as he had just started up his own company. Not only did he offer to hire me, but also to train me on the operation of the land survey instruments. This was a welcome change, as even though there was a quantity of physical work involved, there was a great responsibility associated with the accuracy of the mathematics and precision of the operation of the instruments. Luckily, the theodolite required only one eye to operate. This skill, being extremely visual oriented, seemed to strengthen my right eye until I hardly seemed to notice the lack of the sight in the left.

My recovery went well. I learned to drive more effectively, discovering other methods for judging distance that did not depend on the angle between the two eyes as it does traditionally. For example, upon entering a parking stall, I judged the height of the vehicle I would be facing, and when I felt that the point of that vehicle almost corresponded with the height of mine, I must be close enough, as there was always a downward angle of sight when sitting in a pickup truck. When driving a car, however, the angle of sight was almost straight, and I did not feel so comfortable. I never did consider purchasing a car just for that reason. I lucked in when I found work for a legal surveyor, the owner being called Mr. Alex Daniluk, who operated an office for legal survey work not only in Chetwynd, but also in Prince George. At the time I was accepted for the company, I mentioned to him that I had but one eye, and he indicated that it would not be a problem.

Demis Leite, the road master from British Columbia Railway, approached me one day in a restaurant.

"Hello, Jens," he began, advancing toward my table.

"It looks like you have recovered all right. Too bad, however, that you lost that one eye." I sensed the sincerity in his sympathy. He had always been a fair man to work for. Once someone had suggested to me to take the company to court for having used an inappropriate method to sharpen the picks, but I had figured that unless the intentions of those sharpening the tools had been malicious, there was no justification for a pursuit.

I pondered over the offer of Demis for a minute. Presently, I was an instrument man on a survey crew, driving around the company vehicle, making decisions, playing with all the expensive instruments, commanding the other party members, and on top of that, being paid almost twice that I was paid at BCR. How could I possibly get back in the speeder just to pick up a shovel and pick all day, and worst of all, risk losing my other eye? My reply was based on this deduction.

"Sorry, Demis, but thanks anyway. I did find better work that pays more and which is more interesting. Best of all," I had to add, "it does not endanger my other eye." Demis understood, especially the last remark.

"Yeah, you are right. Should that happen, you'd be cooked." Just cooked—the words echoed in my mind as I shuddered inwardly at the thought of the unthinkable.

We exchanged other pleasantries, and I felt that he must have been somewhat relieved upon leaving. Neither of us had expected this to happen on what seemed like such an ordinary day to start, when I lost my eye, and I would hold no one responsible. But it sure added up to a loss, nonetheless.

Life became better. Alex had obtained a contract with a pipeline company to do a legal survey on a pipeline route traversing the Bullmoose Mountain region, a beautiful area of nature situated many miles northwest of Chetwynd. The only way to access this region on a daily basis was by flying in by helicopter. Thus, every day of work comprised of arriving at the airport with the other two crew members and boarding a chopper just to fly into the heart of the wilderness. The flight took almost an hour there, and another for the return. We were over the Rockies again, and with it unfolded the breathtaking view. Unlike my last chopper flight, this time I had no metal in my other eye or the worries associated with it. Occasionally, the pilot let us take turns at operating the helicopter, when he felt we were safely in the air. It became a passion for me to fly the thing. The freedom it offered was incredible. A person could touch down anywhere in the paradise below at a moment's notice. At that point, I vowed to get my pilot's license as soon as finances permitted. In my opinion, this must have been the best offer from the Creator himself as a means of finding happiness.

Life only became better by the month. I took to motorcycling, having purchased a Yamaha XT250 Enduro bike, which was not much bigger than a bicycle, giving me the freedom to use either the highway or cut my own trail in the woods. This size of machine took little to no fuel, allowing a lot of traveling by only spending the change in the pocket. Only a few months later, I met a lovely girl, Lorri, who shared with me the same enthusiasm for life, adventure, and freedom.

Lorri and I enjoyed life to the fullest. I had bought her her own motorbike, because, I pointed out, life is all about being in the driver's seat. I couldn't help feeling sorry for her when she sat on the back of my bike, riding shotgun while I had all the fun. Rolling down the highway, the warm wind in our faces and stopping at the occasional trail just to follow it to see where it went was about as close as one could come to heaven. In winter, we spent our time at the ski hills, one of them called Azu Mountain, which was in the heart of the Pine Pass, about 150 kilometers south of Chetwynd. We both carried cameras and often paused to take pictures of one another while flying over a jump, or better yet, when wiping out, with all our equipment flying through the air. It was a precious time for us.

Early in the spring of 1983, Lorri and I found out we would be parents soon and decided to get married. I remember the doctor approaching us hesitantly as we sat in the waiting room of the clinic, bearing news he figured would shock us. When he announced the news that we would be parents, in a manner as if it was a terminal illness we were facing, we both surprised him by smiling gleefully in response as we had just won the lottery. The start of a life, according to us, could only be good news. I, however, had not reflected fully upon the situation. Nonetheless, I knew, without even the contemplation, that this would not be a sacrifice to my freedom as had been the loss of my left eye. Certainly, one had to make compromises, such as trading the motorbike in for a station wagon and skiing only occasionally as money was needed elsewhere, but the pleasures in return were infinite. The child was ours, and ours to raise. Lorri shared the same enthusiasm, if not more, if that was even possible.

We were married in May of that year. Because neither of us belonged to a faith, and since we felt closest to the Creator in the midst of nature, we decided that our wedding would take place on Submarine Mountain, a hill of about thousand feet in altitude, a few miles south of Chetwynd. I often visited that place when I was still single, and today, we were perched upon an outcropping of rock at the side of the mountain, repeating our vows. It was spectacular. From up here, one could see for many miles over the rolling hills toward the south, a vast expanse of uninterrupted nature. Afterward, the preacher who married us threw snow at us, explaining it was the missing confetti, and that started a full-fledged snowball fight. We all had a wonderful time.

The summer following our marriage was filled with warmth, excitement, and hopes. Dominating our thoughts were the challenges of us now being on route of being parents, when just around the corner behind we had been parented ourselves. My boss, Alex, was extremely generous and integrated Lorri into some of the responsibilities as chainman on the survey crew, allowing us to be together as much as possible. In our leisure time, Lorri and I spent our time cruising through the landscape on our motorbikes, trying out every trail or dirt road that branched off the highways, just for the thrill of being there and seeing where they would lead. We enjoyed stopping in coffee shops, where, more often than not, there would be another couple with one or two small children of their own. Instinctively, we would observe with unprecedented interest at the proceedings between the parents and children, musing with wonder that in only a few months we would have a major change in our lifestyle.

As work was slow at the start of July, we decided it would be fun to go out to Ontario to see Lorri's family, as she had grown up in the Kingston region. I had never been west of Alberta myself, so this idea of driving four thousand kilometers seemed very exciting indeed. We loaded whatever we had into our pickup, including the motorbikes, and started the journey. Lorri was content to view the passing landscape, and since I enjoyed driving the most between the two of us, I drove all the way across the country, while we shared the beauty of the world unfolding before us together. The crops were in full maturity that summer as it had been a very good year for farming conditions. Miles and miles of golden fields spanned before us as we traversed the Praries. Many times we pulled over at the points of interest just to try to absorb the full magic of the sight. When we did move on, we did so reluctantly, vowing to return sometime soon, perhaps this time on our bikes, for another look.

Our first stop was Edmonton, a good day's drive from Chetwynd. Since we both had friends here, it only made sense to visit them on passing through. I had to visit my friend Alden Meier, a good friend since our childhood. Alden had been pursuing an office job in computers at the time, making for some good conversation when talking about our careers, which seemed to stretch out before us in an unlimited sea of opportunity. We couldn't resist, either, to visit the Edmonton shooting range. Both he and I had an unmatched passion for guns. We really should have joined the Canadian Armed Forces after finishing high school, but after contemplating all of the possibilities in life ahead of us, we both had decided against it for the reason that once again, we would "be told what to do" by our superiors in the organization. Unlike work, one couldn't just "go home" from the armed forces after the workday was over. We always insisted that once we left our parents' home, we would be free.

But we enjoyed shooting nonetheless. Off we went to the shooting range in Alden's Toyota, which he seemed to take great pride in driving. I was, of course, the passenger, but without regret as this was but a temporary situation, and at the same time, it granted Alden the opportunity to demonstrate his autonomy.

We arrived at the range with a few guns, a couple hundred dollars' worth of ammunition and several small wooden blocks. I had brought along my own rifle, and together we blasted the wooden blocks until we were out of ammunition. Occasionally, I would walk over to the range beside us in order to let the other shooters go to check their targets during our cease-fire, only to be met by shooters grumbling about all the noise we were making. Having had great balls of fun, and with our ears still ringing, we vowed to do this again on the way back from Ontario.

We entered Ontario on the third day of travel, and as I was a little concerned about spending too much money on hotel rooms, as we had no idea as to what faced us in Kingston, I decided to drive through the night crossing the heart of Ontario in the night. I had no idea how much I would regret having made this decision in the years to come.

For the time we did cross Ontario, the most beautiful sight I remember was that while approaching Lake Superior from a hill. The sun was in the process of setting, reflecting off the lake at us. Surrounding the lake were the rolling hills with their outcroppings of rock and beautiful green trees of species unfamiliar to me. Lorri took several pictures and just had to comment, "This would be the perfect place for a house." I had to add, "Don't forget about the dreamboat!" while imagining us taking long, serene cruises into the vast sunset on that lake which was so big, so calm, promising total peace of mind. This, too, was a place on our list to return to, so that our child could play in the sand on the beach while we looked on.

We merged onto the 401 highway, the last leg of our journey, after the second day of driving. I was tired and found it difficult to control the vehicle on the rutted highway while the transport trucks attempted to bully us off the road if we did not maintain a speed well beyond that of the legal limit. I noticed the absence of nature, the landscape having more that of an industrial appeal, giving nothing to really feast my eye on in comparison to the previous segments of our trip.

"We'll have to avoid this highway on the way back," I reasoned with Lorri, who was eyeing the precarious nature of the traffic around us instead of the landscape.

"Yeah, you'd better believe it. There really never was much to see here when travelling on this road." I agreed, but at that time, I didn't have a clue as to what "not seeing much" really meant . . .

I met Lorri's family and looked around Kingston with awe. Never before had I seen such an old town, as the areas in British Columbia, where I spent most of my life, were all relatively new in construction and design. I found the layout of the town confusing but did not regret becoming lost while motoring throughout its streets, as there were so many new things to see. The Kingston Harbour was especially interesting with all the massive cruise ships coming and going. Lorri and I figured it would be nice to take a cruise with our child instead of biking, just for a change. The thought of crossing from one lake to the next, including the great Lake Superior, which was especially close to my heart upon remembering the view from the road, gave me chills of excitement in anticipation.

It was only two weeks after arriving in Ontario that my buddy Dave McIntyre from Chetwynd called me at Lorri's folks' house and asked me to come and help out as a company called Patrick Pipeline needed an instrument man. The pay was going to be good, and the job was expected to last about two to four weeks maximum. I did not refuse the work, as money is mighty handy with a new family to support, I thought. As the job would be out in the newly settled area of Tumbler Ridge, British Columbia, there was no facility for having babies, so it made sense for Lorri to stay in Ontario. Besides, I had planned to return well before the due date of our child's birth.

Lorri drove me to the bus station where I would catch the bus headed for Toronto airport. As we sat there waiting, there was a couple beside us with their toddler of perhaps fourteen months or so, taking his first steps. We both watched with the same fascination as did the parents. As we looked on while the youngster balanced clumsily, a great look of surprise on his face in seeing the world from such a different position in comparison to that of when crawling, both of our thoughts were steered toward that event which would come to us in only a few short weeks. I noticed the parents of this child peering so intently at this precious moment, nothing could have unglued their eyes to compromise the magic of this moment, which they were determined would stay with them for the rest of their lives. Lorri turned to me and spoke her words in what seemed like a musical tune. "Soon it will be our turn . . ."

I spent the first three weeks working in Tumbler Ridge, a town under construction for a coal mining project, with no vehicle of my own. What a change from the paradise of my wife's warm embrace, the Kingston Harbour, the beauty of nature! The nature around Tumbler Ridge could have been nice enough if one managed to look beyond the damage done by all the bulldozers and earthmovers. I could not escape this setting as I had no vehicle, so I concentrated on making money and toughing it out. No car for three weeks was just like a jail sentence to me.

My break came when there was a company truck available for me. The foreman told me it was not a very good truck and that I may not be happy with it. Little did he realize just how deprived I was as a result of having no transportation for three weeks, and I embraced the freedom offered by this machine. It ran, and that is what mattered. That steering wheel seemed to hold magic for me.

The work took six weeks instead of the four as predicted by Dave. I returned as quickly as possible to Ontario once finished, but I missed the birth of my first daughter Danielle by one day. Rats, I thought, and then, with perhaps a little loneliness for my wife attached to the next thought, I would maybe have another chance in the future. I remember upon returning, marching up and down the corridors of the Kingston General Hospital trying to find the room number where Lorri was staying. I saw her sitting in a bed through the opening of the door at the same time as she saw me, and her face literally lit up upon recognizing me in such a beautiful manner I'll remember forever. Our baby was beside her in a little crib. I peered at her with extreme curiosity. What a cute little thing she was! Judging by how tiny her little feet were, I figured she would not be taking her first steps just yet. "We'll have to wait," I thought.

We decided to stay the winter in Ontario and return to British Columbia the following spring. We rented a small apartment just a few miles north of

Kingston. Motorbiking weather was still in full swing, but Lorri was a bit beat up from the birth of Danielle, and preferred traveling in our truck. Besides, we had to take Danielle along. She loved the traveling, and in spite of being cranky in the house, as soon as we got rolling, she would go right into a contented sleep. We guessed it had something to do with all the traveling we did during the pregnancy. We drove to Ottawa one day late in November, passing by the Calabogie Ski resort, wondering if that hill would be as much fun as Azu Mountain.

"Well," said Lorri, after we took a long look out of the truck window at the mediocrity of the runs, "it is better than nothing. It will still be fun." No doubt, it will still be fun. One does not need a golden plate to enjoy a good meal, we figured, and besides, we had lots to do now. We'd probably take turns playing with Danielle during the times that the other took an hour to ski. She would only grow too fast, and neither of us really wanted to leave her with a babysitter. On the way back, we stopped to cut a Christmas tree from the right-of-way of a hydro line. Three of us would have Christmas together this time.

We decorated the tree at home the next day. It was pretty enough, and it was topped with a star that read: "Baby's first Christmas." This was different from our last Christmas, which seemed to be lacking the audience required for such an event. Life was settling down a bit for us now. We spent more time inside, as it was becoming too cold to take out Danielle, who was approaching two months. To pass the leisure time, we rented a piano, and since I already had accomplished grade 6 in the conservatory program during my childhood, I proceeded to teach Lorri what I knew, and I went on to study for the next grade. I figured it would be a kind of surprise for my mother to hear me play the piano again for her upon returning to Chetwynd the following year, as I had practically abandoned this activity in trade for the carefree adventure of traveling. Lorri was interested in starting a career in music, and this seemed a great time to begin.

I did not want to sit around, in spite of the good times we were having. I looked for work in town, only to find the wages ridiculously low in comparison to those of British Columbia. I saw an advertisement in the newspaper about a snowmobile for sale for only a few dollars that needed some work. Figuring on the possibility of making some cash on the side, I looked at Lorri, who was holding Danielle in her arms, about to feed her the bottle, and announced, "I think I'll buy the snowmobile advertised in the paper if it's any good and maybe fix it up for extra money." I grabbed the keys to my pickup. Little did I know that this was the last time I'd see the pretty face of Lorri or that of my child—our child—held tightly in her arms.

I arrived at the home of the vendor, checking out the machine, and found it ran but needed work on the clutch mechanism that engaged the track. I purchased it, with the hopes of repairing it and reselling it for a few hundred dollars.

I brought the machine home and unloaded it on the front lawn of our ground floor apartment. Lorri and Danielle were inside, as it was a chilly day with some snow already on the ground. I started the machine, standing beside it. I revved up the motor somewhat, peering at the clutch, attempting to comprehend why it did not close around the belt. I did not dare sit on the machine lest it engage suddenly and I risk colliding with something within the confines of the front yard. Suddenly, I felt a sharp, stinging pain in my right eye at the same time as the world went black. I lifted my hand to my face, and my hand was suddenly wet. There was something running down my cheek, and when feeling my eye, there was nothing, just like it had popped. I should have died right there, if God had had any mercy at all. But there was no mercy. Lorri saw the horror of the situation to its entirety from the window of our apartment. She came out to help me get inside. I sat there at the kitchen table, awaiting the ambulance, but more awaiting the end of this nightmare. A thousand thoughts went through my mind, as someone who just stepped off the edge of a cliff during the tumble to the ground. I knew far too much about eyes to think I would get away with this one. I could not imagine life from here on. My mind kept returning to the hunting rifle I had in the bedroom, and how that would finish the job and stop the suffering and humiliation I faced. But what about Lorri? she was so happy being married, with all the love and security it offered, and my mind shot back to a documentary I had seen about a widow in mourning after losing her husband. I couldn't do that to her. So I waited, hoping for a miracle, while Danielle, whom Lorri had placed on the kitchen table on a blanket, cooed beside me. I heard her, and I instinctively turned to look at her but saw nothing.

CHAPTER 2

What Now?

The ambulance crew led me out to the awaiting emergency vehicle and laid me down on its bed, one attendant applying a makeshift dressing and the other driving to the same town that our daughter was born in just two months before. Lorri came along, with nothing to say, having left Danielle with neighbors in the apartment. The driver made heroic moves to arrive at the hospital as quickly as possible, but I could not understand the hurry. The attendant applying the dressing kept telling me "everything will be all right," but who was he fooling? I did try to believe it, however, as more of an act of desperation than that of logic. Considering that my first eye had been in much better shape, maintaining not only its roundness, but also being able to see light and rough shapes after the accident, yet could not be saved, my right eye was totally collapsed, with not a trace of light entering it. All I could see was the swirls of red, blue, and brown going around and around in my visual field as if someone had taken a pallet of liquid paint, dumped it into a mixing bowl and stirred it slowly, all the while peering at it closely. Often people approached me later upon hearing of the accident, remarking,

"It must have really hurt!" Only for me to reply it really did not, that is, physically. I did feel a dull ache that was masked by my worry about the lost future and the bewilderment of the pressing darkness around me. The world was dark now, yet on the drive down with the ambulance, I could visualize all the streets and its surrounding buildings as I had driven this route many times before. I was laying down in the vehicle, and perhaps that is why I could not see the buildings, and therefore, with this in my subconscious, I did not feel the full scope of the disaster that faced me.

In the hospital, referred as the "Hotel Dieu," the staff was extremely compassionate with regard to my situation. I did not have to wait for treatment this time as I did in Prince George—I was immediately given an intravenous and carted to the operating room. All I remember of that time was the voices of the staff, as they asked Lorri questions such as, "Did he have lunch yet?" To which I noted with anguish, my intentions of taking Lorri and Danielle out to lunch that day to the small hamburger joint just down the road from us as I had passed by, driving the truck with the snowmobile in the back of it. The nurses had trouble inserting the intravenous tube, and they repeatedly asked me to relax. "How can someone relax under these conditions," I asked myself. "And what are we trying to save anyway?" I could not come up with an answer.

I came to in the recovery room with Lorri by my side, as I recognized her voice. There was a terrible sadness in it, which she tried unsuccessfully to cover up. She told me of the metal that was removed, its size being about half the size of the knuckle of an adult's little finger.

"They didn't have to remove the eye—they managed to take out the metal and close the wound up with stitches." She had intended this to be consoling, and I suppose it was, in a way, as the totality of my loss of sight would have been concreted had the eye been removed. This left, still, a glimmer of hope, as after all, my bandage was firmly over my right eye and the doctor had apparently "repaired" my eye.

I heard approaching footsteps as Lorri said, "Here's the doctor now . . ." in a voice lacking optimism. Yet she too was hoping for a miracle.

A hand touched my shoulder, and a man's voice spoke out of the dark above me. "Hello, Jens, I'm Doctor Willis. I took the metal out of your eye this afternoon." It must have been close to midnight now. Lorri had to go back to our apartment and tend to the baby. She said she'd be back. The doctor continued,

"Can you see anything out of this eye?" He tapped the socket of my left eye.

"No," I started to explain, "I had lost it three years ago when a piece of metal went into it working at the railway, and even though we tried to fix it, it did not hold." I hoped that was not significant now, as it was the right eye that was bandaged. Perhaps, I hoped, we'd take off the bandage and all will be fine.

Dr. Willis took off the bandage. I could feel that Doctor Willis was using an instrument that was used to look at things up close, as he supported his hand on my forehead while attempting to take a better look. I held still, giving him the best chance to do his job. I could feel some heat against my eye, but only saw the same swirls of color in my visual field as I did when first losing the sight.

"Can you see any of this light?" Dr. Willis seemed to ask in a doubting voice, as if he already knew the answer. I saw nothing, and my heart sank to a level it had never been to before. Why was I still alive? I asked myself. I could not believe that life could be this cruel.

Lorri returned, having found a better place for Danielle, leaving her with her grandmother, while she accompanied me in the hospital. I was given a private room, and Lorri could stay with me even during the night. This gesture of compassion from the nurses comforted me a lot, and probably Lorri as well. When holding her with my eyes closed, everything seemed like it was going to be all right, but then when I opened them, the shock returned. I remember going to the bathroom, and, upon finding it, instinctively running my hand up the inside wall, finding the light switch, but there was no gratifying luminosity when turning it on. Just the "click" and still darkness.

Family members called from home to my hospital room as the news circulated. My father, after hearing about the news, had spoken to several friends of his back in Chetwynd, who all elaborated upon the situation and what to do about it.

"Listen," he explained, "I talked to my friend Luke, who said that he knew someone who had a pig's eye transplanted and now can see, but only in black and white. You should look into it. Perhaps ask your doctor." My father was very much into the science shows on television, and I took it for granted that these were all true programs he was watching. I knew Luke, with whom I had drinks, on occasion, in the bar in the Chetwynd Motor Hotel on Friday nights. He worked with my father as a mechanic, and I had a lot of respect for him. I would have to discuss this with Dr. Willis when he returned, I thought. I mentioned this all to Lorri, who took it in with great interest and hope.

"Well, I figure, Jens," she started to say, "that if that is not possible, I would give up one of my eyes for you to have for an implant." She was serious. I could not believe I was hearing her properly. What a generous gesture of sacrifice she was proposing to me! She made this remark in all honesty from the full sweetness of her heart. I tried to imagine the sacrifice she was proposing: two bright eyes and voluntarily giving up one for me. I had once heard that in Brazil, there were people who were giving up one eye of theirs to the price of $20,000, just for the feel of money, but this was different. Lorri did have one eye that was not as good in comparison to the strong one, but still very close to perfect.

"I will have to take the bad one of yours," I reassured her that it would not cost her so dearly that it would blind her instead. But, Lorri, are you sure you want to do that? "Even if I have to wait a few months for a pig's eye, I would rather do that than risk your future."

With that, Lorri replied, not surprisingly touching on an issue ever present in our minds.

"What is there for me in my future if you cannot see? There is no way we can share the same, or even a fraction, of the happiness that we have done in the past if one of us cannot see. I won't feel like motorbiking, or skiing, or anything if you can't." Neither of us mentioned the word "blind" or even brought up the raising of the kids in this manner. That was unthinkable.

Doctor Willis came in, and even before the greetings were over, I brought up the subject, Lorri close at my side, her head directed toward him in great anticipation.

"Dr. Willis," I began, and then continued right into the heart of our solution.

"Why not just implant a pig's eye directly into one of my sockets, or, better yet, replace both of them?" It did sound logical, and the thought of seeing the images I had seen on black-and-white television seemed like an option I could live with. Sure, I would not see the beautiful colors of the changing leaves in fall, the blue of the sky, the richness of the colors of the crops ripening in the farmer's fields on the vast Prairie landscape during the planned trip back to British Columbia. But I would be driving, with the only disadvantage being the traffic lights had certain colors, however, one could go by their positions rather than by their color. I might even see a bit better, as I would have two eyes again, complete with depth perception. I hoped that it would not take too long to acquire those pig's eyes, as I dreaded having to stay in the dark for weeks on end.

Dr. Willis stood still for a minute, and then tried to put things in perspective as gently as possible.

"There is no such thing as eye implants, or transplants, for that matter." He was apologetic, as he continued, all the while that our newly found hopes were shattered into pieces too small to recover. "The only part of the eye that can be transplanted is the cornea, which is the transparent skin at the front of your eye. The lens may be, also, but that won't help you." Dr. Willis was telling me what I already knew about that.

"As for the retina, it just is not possible. Maybe . . ." he added, as the expressions of extreme disappointment on our faces must have taken him aback, "maybe several years in the future. One cannot transplant an eye because there is no way, so far, to connect the optic nerve." There was nothing at all to say now. I heard people walk by in the corridor outside of my room. Unlike the last hospital stay in Prince George, this time I did not see them go by. They all were going somewhere, seeing their target, whether it was the way in front of them, a doorway, a person they recognized, or whatever it may be, they knew where they were heading, yet, if I stuck my head out into the corridor, it was just pitch black. I felt terribly trapped.

Lorri and I just had a bit of small talk between us, commenting on the food, the weather outside, having no idea as to how to proceed from here, or what to say. Our big plans were gone again. The nurses came and went and, on occasion, attempted to reprimand Lorri for not helping me eat, or rather, not feeding me. I insisted on doing it myself, as clumsy as it looked, as it gave at least some feeling of control, which seemed to be in short supply since I came here.

Lorri left later that day to check on Danielle, leaving me alone with my thoughts. They weren't good, so I tried not to think. Dr. Willis had made some mention about the fact that I was now registered with the Canadian National Institute for the Blind (CNIB), which was the blind support agency in Canada. I cringed at the mention of it and did not share it with Lorri. I envisioned a few old men playing checkers under a tree in a park, their gnarled hands feeling for the telltale signs on each game piece, in trying to identify its color, while their sightless eyes, shrouded by dark glasses, stared into oblivion before them, with no recognition of the beautiful sunny day before them. No, I would never fit into that setting; I just would never be able to play that role . . .

There was a brief knock on the door of my hospital room, and a nurse identified herself and announced she had a visitor. I welcomed him, as maybe he held the solution for me, which I was in desperate need of.

"My name is John Warren," he introduced himself, "I hear you have been having trouble with your eyes, and as I have lived through that already, maybe I can help you in finding other things to do."

As my knowledge of the world of darkness was at zero, except for the fact that one avoids that situation at all costs, I did have a genuine interest in the plight of this man, although, I was not at all ready to assume that the eternal darkness was my destiny.

"How did you, John, lose your sight?" Not that it really mattered, I figured, but then again, I had to know what happened next.

"When I was twenty-six," explained John, "I started losing my sight little by little as a result of being diabetic. By the time I was thirty-one, it was all gone. I am forty-two now." I tried to imagine waking up one day with a little less vision than the day before, then being told by the doctors that it will disappear, little by little, until I was plunged into darkness. The first thing to give up would be the driver's license, and that would be a big blow right there." I gave a fleeting thought about my own driver's license, and a sick feeling sprouted from deep within me. "I've been totally blind for about eleven years," he finished.

"And what are you doing now?" I was hoping he would present to me a glamorous and exciting lifestyle that I could envy him for, if only for the purpose of having a possibility of attaining the same in my future. "Like, for example, John, what are you able to do, can you do, how do you get around, and all that?" After more than ten years of this kind of life, surely he would have a good idea of what the future holds.

"Well, I can cook meals at the house, clean it, and do all of the domestic stuff to take care of our son." He was trying hard, as he knew I had a daughter, and he tried to focus on the positive. "Heck, I even bought my son a wagon the other day, and since it came in pieces, I figured out how to assemble it. And as for getting around, I walk to the stores around my place, and even to the bars, and all that. I had a guide dog until recently, but now he is dead, and I use my cane again."

At the mention of the dog, an image of that man I had seen as a child looking out of the school bus window came to me, immediately giving the voice of John a face—that of the blind man walking alongside Columbia Street in Kamloops a few years back. I shuddered at the cruelty of that picture.

"But, John," I pleaded to him, as if he had something up his sleeve he could use to resolve the situation. "Lorri and I always motorcycled together. It is so beautiful, the freedom and all. I cannot bear to think of all that coming to an end!" John pondered over this and replied, a bit on the side of futility, I thought.

"Can Lorri not drive?" This question only made matters worse, and I felt like I was being condemned to chairman of the Granny's knitting club as a tradeoff for riding my motorbike through the Rocky Mountain pass.

"John," I started to explain something I realized later he already was familiar with, "if you are going to be a passenger on a motorbike, you may as well stay home."

John tried again. "You could be a bit innovative, perhaps connecting the bikes together with some metal bars, so that if Lorri leans into a corner, you will too. That way, you'd have your own bike still." "Nice try," I thought, but no dice. "What good will that do?" I kept my tone polite, as none of this was John's fault, but he obviously did not know where I had come from. Only later did I find out he really came from the same background as I did, and despite his show of optimism toward me at this moment, he, too, was still suffering from the loss as well.

At my last remark, he added, "Well, you'd be on your own bike, feeling the wind in your face, and all that . . ." I laughed a bit at that, lacking all mirth nonetheless.

"I may as well sit on a chair with a blower fan blowing in my face." John was not getting anywhere with me, and later I figured he was quite a saint for having come there in the first place. He got up out of his chair and walked to the door, pausing for an instant.

"Good luck," he said, struggling to find words which suited the situation, but finding none. "We'll keep in touch."

I heard his tapping cane, the door open and close. He did not seem trapped completely as I was there, and if he did anything at all for me, the fact that he went out and found his way home alone was probably the best that his visit had done for me. But at the time, I was only thinking of the skiing, the motorbiking, the driving, flying over the Rockies, with the beauty of nature stretching out before me. I needed it all back.

Then, three days later, a nurse came to give me my eye drops for the prevention of infection. It was early in the morning, and she turned on a bright overhead light while I was lying on my back. To my surprise, the "click" of the pull chain for the switch was accompanied with the trace of light.

"Hey!" I exclaimed, "I can see that light!" Lorri was just as excited and rushed to my side, forgetting about the breakfast that was wheeled into my room at that moment. It was faint, very faint, but still there. I covered and uncovered my left eye just to verify its presence. Even the nurse, despite her haste in tending to other patients, paused to share the obvious exhilaration coming from both Lorri and I. I fumbled for the pull chain and kept turning the light on and off for the next several minutes, new hope sprouting all the while in our minds. The presence of light after two days of darkness was refreshing, as if stepping into a cool shower on a very hot day. As the day progressed, I turned to the window and noted the same kind of light, although, after a couple of minutes of looking at the window, I could no longer discern the window from the wall until I covered up my eye for a bit of time. Dr. Willis came in the room, and judging by his more cheery "hello", he must have been tipped off by the nurse that I was seeing something.

He shone the little light, with which he had to inspect the stitching on my right eye, into my left, and this time, I saw the dim yellow light. It was just like a glimmer of hope, after having lost all from my conversation with John, compounded with that of Dr. Willis about the testimony surrounding eye transplants.

Dr. Willis straightened up from leaning over me as I lay in the bed.

"That's real good news for you to be able to see that light. I imagine your right eye has been so strong that the bit of sight you had in the left side was more or less cut off by the brain, only concentrating on the best one. That tends to happen with people who have nothing wrong with their eyes, and we often cover one eye for a set period so the brain realizes there is more than one eye there." His manner of speaking suggested that there was so far no limit on the improvement available on my left eye. I could hardly believe my ears while my mind raced in elaborating over the possibilities. If I could see again, even if it took months to get to that point, I told myself, life would be so much sweeter yet than before. Not that it hadn't been already.

The following day, the light appeared stronger when it was turned on by the nurse. Moreover, I noticed, that night following my discussion with Dr. Willis, the presence of a nightlight on the wall near my bed when the main light was out. I still wrestled with the elements of not seeing what I was doing and also the torture of being trapped in this room. I could not comfort myself by looking out of the window at the people moving around as I had in Prince George or by reading magazines as I had done before. Lorri read to me, as now our despair was lifted by the boundless possibilities surrounding the recovery of my left eye. It bothered me profusely that I could not see the face of Dr. Willis. He was becoming somewhat of a friend, as he was extremely compassionate and I really expected more from my encounters with him than just a voice in the dark. Maybe soon, we anticipated, that would change.

We checked out of the hospital on December 12. I was looking forward to getting out, as I had now attributed my stay there with my misery. That sentiment, however, did not last long. Upon opening the exit door leading to the parking lot, I was in for a big disappointment when the bright, cheery feeling associated with coming out of a building just did not materialize. The cold wind of December hit me at the same time as did the noise from the streets signifying I was outside, but it was still dark. I tried desperately to look out of the remains of my left eye, only to see a bit of light. There was no way I could ever find my way around out here. It was bewildering, to say the least, not to see all the optional paths available in front of me and being able to thus choose the one I wanted. I was used to and expected to see my truck out in the lot, along with all the other parked automobiles, to choose the path there, to sit in the truck, and to drive it either home, to a store, to a restaurant, or wherever I chose. Not this time. The bit of light offered by my left eye might as well have been nothing. I held onto Lorri's hand like a child learning to walk and, in full humiliation, crossed the lot to our parking spot.

I felt the familiar handle for the door, but this time it was the one for the passenger. My mind was blank with distaste for the whole affair. I had committed no crimes against humanity, yet I felt as if I was a prisoner, with my hands shackled powerless, led to the paddy wagon with a bag over my head. The truck started, and the sounds were familiar. As it was stick shift, and Lorri's experience in it was limited, she wrestled a bit clumsily with the controls. I began to reprimand her, only to catch myself. Would I be able to do better? Not this way, that's for sure. That left eye would have to get a lot better before this situation would be resolved. I bit my lip and suffered the way home, a trip several miles north of town.

I was wrong about the hospital having been a cooped-up place for me and that there would be major relief when getting out. In my own home, a small apartment of only five rooms, I could walk around without problems, but I could do that in the hospital as well. I noted that visitors came to my door and complimented me on the progress I was making, but I had different opinions. Of course, I retorted to their overly optimistic remarks, it was easy to get around in here, just like it was easy enough to play hide-and-seek in the dark as a kid. It's when one wants to get out, and see new things, that one has the problems. There is just no way to have adventure in this manner.

Over the course of the next few weeks, we stayed mainly inside, trying to figure out what to do next. There were many tricks to be learned in doing the daily activities like washing dishes, cooking, pouring coffee, tending to the baby, and cleaning that really weren't difficult to learn. With the exception of cooking, an activity I never had mastered even with sight, all the things I did I must have not been using my eyes for to begin with, as there was practically no period of adjustment involved in doing dishes, or even cleaning, for that matter. I suppose that I was well practiced at cleaning the floor from my childhood days when my mother insisted the basement be vacuumed weekly even though I saw no speck of dirt on the floor. Just pace off the room and move over a bit with every pass of the broom just to go through the motion to keep everyone happy. I used the bit I could see whenever I could, for instance, when peeling potatoes; however, often it proved more effective just to feel for the remaining skin needing to be removed.

Danielle proved to be the greatest comfort, in spite of the fact that her crying irritated me, as I really did not appreciate a bunch of noise around me while trying to figure out what was going on by the faint queues offered by the noises from about me. Taking care of her in every manner a father can offer posed no problem at this age of a child. She couldn't move, and whether or not one can see, it was always difficult to dress or undress a baby. I could comfort her and hold her and, still remembering her facial features, completely imagine her as my constant physical contact with her updated her image in my mind.

Little by little, my left eye became stronger, as if in answer to our prayers. However, after about two months, it stopped progressing. Now I could see, very dimly and with many contortions in the picture, larger objects like trees from several yards, a vehicle, if parked so that the background contrasted the color of the vehicle at several yards, and with the help of a magnifying glass, painfully read one letter at a time from large-print books. I was playing the piano again, barely able to make out the groups of black and white keys upon the keyboard. Most of the music was played by feel, but that is not unusual to do as a pianist. I had been able to play a couple of pieces by memory, so the reading of the music was not needed in this case. Temporarily, yes, one could get away with it. I tried several times to read music with a magnifying glass, but there was just not enough vision.

Was it better than nothing? For sure it was. The Lion's Club had donated to me a pair of cataract glasses, which helped bring things into focus. However, the view was so dim that often everything appeared either black or white, rendering me totally blind for minutes at a time, forcing me to keep my eye closed for several minutes. It was on cloudy days that I could get the most out of the vision. I could not recognize faces but could discern the presence of someone in front of me. Electric light seemed the most beneficial to my faded vision, allowing me to see traffic lights from across the street, even the color of them. I could see oncoming traffic by the headlights and the direction of roads by the streetlight rows above my head.

This, however, did not allow me to drive, get back to my job, or see what my growing daughter looked like. In fact, I noted one day when she started to crawl, I would never be able to share those precious moments of Danielle's first few steps if I did not straighten out my vision soon. I consulted again with Dr. Willis, who had, in the meantime, determined that my vision was 2/120, meaning that what a person with good eyesight sees at 120 feet, I could see at 2. That meant I could see the big "E" of the eye chart at arm's length.

Dr. Willis was looking again into my left eye.

"The retina is severely detached, and that is why everything is so dim. It just can't get enough revitalization from the tissue of the back of the eye to regenerate cells quickly enough. Moreover . . ." he announced, attempting to convince me that this was the best that I could expect, "there is a lot of scar tissue pulling it toward the center, not allowing it to reattach. That is probably why the first attempt at reattaching the retina in Vancouver did not work."

I did not take this for an answer, as it looked like there was still a chance. I insisted.

"But what am I to do? I have to get back to work, drive, and lead a normal life. What is left of my life if I cannot see better than this?" I did not expect an answer but rather a referral to another specialist who may be able to help. Dr. Willis gestured at Danielle, who was starting to crawl on the floor, and Lorri sitting in a chair next to her. "You have that, the family." He had a point. Without this family, I would have terminated this life, ridding myself of the humiliation and disappointment that was facing me for years to come. But still, if there is a referral available, why not?

"Dr. Willis," I tried again, in a patient, polite voice that I knew I needed if I was to get anywhere. "You are right—I have the family. But just imagine. How can I be a good father and husband if I cannot pull my load? I need to be able to help the child, walk the child, and drive her to the hospital if she was sick. I need to be able to look at her report card, talk to her teachers face-to-face, and correct her handwriting . . ." I stopped at that, as my own speech brought to light all the things I would not be able to do, and I could not go on.

Dr. Willis got the point.

"Just being there is not enough," I added bitterly, surprising even Dr. Willis with my graphic description. "You have to be able to do something."

Dr. Willis had his head turned away from me when he replied, "I've been in this business for a number of years now, and with my experience, I think you will only lose what you have." By that, he meant I would end up totally blind. "Let's just think about that, all the options, and meet again in a month." A month couldn't hurt any more. Not being in this deep, we left it at that and went back home.

The CNIB became more involved in our lives. I did not want to accept them with open arms but appreciated their assistance nevertheless. It was not the kind of help I wanted—it was sight I wanted back. They came with a warm, greeting manner, bringing along my first lessons in braille, with the promise that braille music was available as well. I figured that would make for a good distraction while I awaited the magic operation that would restore my vision in my left eye.

My right eye was not able to see anything at all, and moreover, it was smaller than it was before, indicating severe trauma had been inflicted. All my hopes lay with the left. It was just a matter, according to us, to convince Dr. Willis that I should see a specialist, have the retina reattached, and then all will be well.

With this in mind, we went to see Dr. Willis again, this time near the end of winter. I had to come to a conclusion about this matter, given that with the spring came the idea that I should return back to work. I was anxious to see this through.

Dr. Willis greeted us in the eye clinic again, and as usual, we measured the progress of recovery of the sight in my left eye. It was more or less the same than it was the last time when we tested it a few weeks ago. With that, Dr. Willis turned to us and brought up the subject directly:

"Do you still want to look into surgery on this eye?" His voice was blank, lacking all expression as he asked.

"Of course." I reiterated the logic surrounding my decision. "I'm living a blind man's life right now, and it is high time to return back to the real world." I winced at the mention of the word *blind*, which both Lorri and I have been avoiding using. It had a destructive, condemning ring to it that signified the ultimate ignorance to reality. This word was often used to describe lovers' negative behavior traits in love songs referencing total ignorance and misunderstanding, ultimately leading to the demise of their relationship. Thus, the expression "visually impaired" seemed far more appropriate, according to us, to describe my situation.

Dr. Willis must have expected my answer, and continued, to our surprise.

"I found two places that would be interested in seeing you. One is an eye clinic in Boston, which performs a procedure I am not at all familiar with. The other is in Toronto, in the St. Michael's Hospital, which will generally be a standard retinal reattaching procedure. "He did not want to take any responsibility regarding the risks involved. "I can give you the contact numbers, and you can set up appointments to talk with them directly."

According to us, that sounded great. We had been prepared for another round of prodding and commiseration at this office to further convince Dr. Willis of the necessity of an operation, and he just came out and gave it to me with no further trouble. He did not even repeat the fears he had about the possible loss of my current sight. Perhaps he tried to put himself in my spot, only to ask himself what he would do. Whatever it was, we were heading home, with every intention to pursue the next and, hopefully, the final step to recovery.

Back at the apartment, we weighed our options. No doubt, the fellows in Boston would want cash, as it is out of the country. We had some saved, but now with not only having no work, I was also cut off unceremoniously by the unemployment insurance department because, according to them, I was considered "non-employable." The way the policy works is rather mysterious. On the form accompanying the benefits is a space one fills out should one have a disability. Lorri had filled this out for me, as we had assumed it would be in our best interest, as perhaps benefits such as retraining programs would be made available to us. Instead, to our dismay, the opposite happened. The policy is that should one have such a condition, benefits are reduced from some fifty weeks to a mere fifteen, as one is considered "non-employable." One would assume that those people would have to eat too, as do their families, but someone had other ideas, having just collected about sixteen weeks myself, that cut us right off our income. It sure was a sharp blow to be dealt by them, we thought, kind of like being kicked when you are already down. This was a policy in bad need of review. We did not know, however, how much they would charge in Boston. We could always sell the bikes and truck, we figured, and when I started to work again, buy different ones, as they were kind of useless without the eye anyhow.

"Heck, Lorri," I had remarked to her on that subject, "it would be fun just to be able to ride a bicycle, or even to walk, while seeing the world around me." I was imagining a bright, sunny day, with all the beauty of spring around me as far as the eye could see, walking alongside the road, while others passed by on their motorbikes and cars. As a child, I did not have a car and was still happy. Being placed back into the real world of sight seemed to take priority now, making the idea of putting on hold the driving for a while not such a painful scenario.

Our other option, the hospital in Toronto, seemed most likely and perhaps most affordable. Moreover, Dr. Willis had seemed more positive about it than the one in Boston. First, I would call Boston, we decided.

I had no trouble getting through, and the secretary of the clinic, unlike the usual ones, seemed to know enough of the procedure that I got what I wanted from her as far as information was concerned. She proceeded to illustrate a picture of the proceedings:

"When you come here, you will be expected to pay the cost of the operation up front. Together with the stay in our hospital, it will be $25,000 US." This was the first topic brought up by her after the initial pleasantries. I made a quick calculation in my head and determined the cost to be about $35,000 in our pesos. We had saved up some, and together with the possible help of friends and relatives, I could pay it back no problem once I started the surveying job again. She continued, only after I quickly, as matter-of-fact as possible, replied, "No problem. What about the surgery?"

"We have a procedure that is called "open-eye surgery," in which we open the eye right up and thus have all the functional parts exposed so we can do a good job, and do it right." She had a few other descriptions about this subject, basically supporting their controversial method of surgery. My mind raced back to the time I had my left eye operated on by Dr. Harris in Vancouver. He had been adamant that I be careful with the eye following the operation, as any jarring or sudden change in internal pressure of the eye could detach or damage the retina. I bade her good-bye, all the time hoping for a break in my next call. Boston was going to charge whether or not it would be successful, and that was risky on its own. The voice of the secretary, moreover, did not strike me as sophisticated or belonging to that of a physician, making me a bit wary of what would really happen to my eye there. I voiced my concerns to Lorri, who hoped, in turn, that Toronto would pan out for us instead.

I wasted no time in calling the St. Michael's Hospital in Toronto. The secretary had also expected our call, but unlike the one in Boston, refused to comment about anything but the availability of a consultation with Dr. Shea, the surgeon who would first see me and advise me on my options personally. I guessed that they were trying to be very professional about it. I was thus scheduled to go down, somewhere in the middle of spring, for my consultation with him. We counted the days.

Spring was just around the corner now, and with it came the desire to get out and the sounds of the passing motorcycles on the road in front of our apartment. The sounds of them passing by was painful, to say the least. The world seemed to continue doing what was right, with only me being knocked out of it. Lorri and I tried to console ourselves with the thought of how it would be next to impossible to do with Danielle now anyways.

"That would be all right, if that was the case," I had to add in reply, hoping she would further support her point of view and finally convince me, "if we'd do other things instead with her. But we are doing nothing." And that was a fact. We just did not know where to start.

One day, Lorri came from the small town of Sydenham, which was just a mile or so from us, with a garage-sale stroller. "Look," she said proudly, "we can take Danielle and go out for walks." That sounded all right, better than sitting around the house, and perhaps I could get into the real world instead of this imprisonment. I walked alongside Lorri while she pushed the stroller into town. I could see a few larger shapes of things like trees and building tops with the heavy glasses I wore. We met some people, most of them relatives or friends of Lorri as she had grown up in this vicinity. I had never met these people before, and so their faces to me were as obscure as those whom one meets for the first time while talking on the telephone. Should I have met up with them on a later date, I would not have recalled talking to them unless they verbally identified themselves. Not everybody tried to take this into consideration, and often, for years to come, when I met someone, I would talk to him or her, often not having a clue as to who they were. We then met up with an acquaintance of Lorri's that listened intently to the reply upon asking how we were. We weren't about to kid everyone by telling them all was fine, so Lorri briefly explained our predicament. "It has been real tough for us this year." She proceeded to explain, "Having lost most of his sight," she said, gesturing toward me, "we want to try to get that back, to get our old life back, to be happy again." The woman with whom Lorri was talking took it all in and replied, to our amazement,

"I know this doctor in town that would help you." Her very suggestion of a doctor helping us sounded like music to our ears. "His name is Dr. Stevens—he would help you. You should see him. I know him, and I can arrange a quick appointment." We imagined, in our desperation, a surgeon, wearing his scrubs, ready to help us, and then coming out of the clinic, with the old life back.

We wasted no time, and within days, we were comfortably sitting in his office. He was a quiet-talking man, and the first thing he requested was our Ontario Health Insurance Plan (OHIP) cards, with which we were naturally armed, to ensure there was no obstacle between us and the confidence of the surgeons, who held all the cards. Dr. Stevens slowly wrote out the information from our health insurance cards and then looked at his watch. I figured this would be the consultation, and he was probably about to see other patients after us.

He began to speak. "So, tell me, what seems to be the problem between you two?" I thought it a bizarre question, but in all reference to the eyesight dilemma, anything will do to start on the topic. Lorri and I graphically described the loss of sight, the medical conditions surrounding the event, and made reference to Dr. Willis in case he needed more information about the present condition of my eyes. With that, he replied, "So, tell me, do you both love each other?" meaning Lorri and I. Had I been able to see, Lorri and I would have stared at each other, puzzled by the question. She must have thought what I did—that he was only interested in the kind of support Lorri would give me to see me through a possibly long and involved eye surgery. We both, thus, retorted as favorably as possible. "Well, yes, very much so." I said in full confidence, "Lorri has always been right by my side, and I know she will do anything to help me through this." Lorri must have been nodding her head convincingly while I was talking, because the doctor seemed to be satisfied.

"Well then," he replied, getting out of his chair and moving toward another door, "it appears there is no problem. You guys have a good day now." He left us at that.

Lorri and I got out of there with very little to say but lots to think about. We marched disappointedly up Main Street in Sydenham to the main road that would take us home. "That was a shrink." I did not mince my words. "Here we thought he was an eye doctor." Lorri was at least as disappointed as I was, not even having Danielle to distract her as we had left her with a babysitter, preparing in preparation for this big event. "I have no idea how that could have happened." She added bitterly, "What a waste of time!"

"Yeah," I agreed, "and hope."

The days went by slowly while we waited for our consultation in Toronto. We met our neighbors who lived in a house about a hundred or so yards to our east in their own house—Barb and Ken Sigsworth. They were related to our landlord, who had asked Ken to come over to tune our piano, as well as hopefully giving us comfort and help through these troubled times. Ken was a great guy, and while he tuned our rented piano, he insisted I try to do it myself, as he figured it was entirely possible to do with one's eyes closed. I did try it sometime later, and even though it took thirteen hours to tune it when I tried, and it did not sound quite right, I did not run into problems on account of not seeing during the task. Therefore, I did not lose interest as any barrier encountered not related to eyesight loss was a barrier that one could overcome.

Barb Sigsworth was, to our pleasant surprise, a piano teacher, and had been for many years before. She was a sweet woman, full of warmth and love for Danielle; she and Ken often invited us over to play Trivial Pursuit while munching on chips and drinking ginger ale. Barb spent many volunteer hours teaching Lorri and me about playing the piano, and she was the greatest contributor in making it possible for Lorri to launch a career in teaching music some years later.

The CNIB came over again, this time bringing along a girl who was a bit younger than me, to teach me how to use the cane. "You could walk into town yourself," I was told, "and do all you did before." Well, that was going to be really something, I thought. I imagined holding on the cane and walking comfortably down the road to Sydenham, going into a store, picking out my groceries, checking out what is new in the tools section, and perhaps picking up a bottle of wine for us on the way back. I was all ready to go.

My first encounter with this method of travel seemed suicidal, to say the least. Here I was, walking alongside the same invisible pathway that was shared with invisible two-ton objects whizzing past me many times faster than one can swing a hammer. My only method of ensuring I was on the so-called safe area was the slight spongy feel the cane gave when touching gravel instead of pavement, which felt a bit more firm. There was a crunchy sound of the gravel as well, but that was masked by the noise of the traffic when it became continuous. Things got especially tricky when crossing a paved driveway that joined to the main road. All the signs, and there weren't many of them, told me I was really in the middle of the road, as there was nothing to shoreline with. Yet I heard cars coming up behind me at their usual break-neck speed while I took a good guess as to which direction to keep going. I found this extremely stressful. The word *precarious* should be, in my opinion, defined as just what I was doing. I paid attention mostly to the instructor who was behind me, ready to bolt into the ditch at the first sign of her shout of warning. If the idea was to do this alone after a few lessons, I would have to find comfort in the fact that if I got hit, I probably would not have to endure this torture anymore. So I just kept on going, more like a Japanese pilot during the attack on Pearl Harbor than someone going out for an enjoyable afternoon stroll.

Upon reaching the town, which was just a main road with a few stores alongside, we proceeded to enter some of the businesses. There was a type of general store in which we went first. I remembered the last time I had been there. It was shortly after Danielle was born, and I had come to buy diapers for Danielle. I had been on my motorbike and felt a bit sheepish walking through the aisles of baby stuff, wearing my black leather motorcycling jacket, while the young mothers wondered what on earth I was doing there. I had felt proud, nonetheless, to be a father and to be trusted in caring for a new life.

Not this time. There was no such feeling of pride in what I was doing today. My instructor showed me how to drag the cane alongside the door to find the handle, and then, upon entering, to listen for the sound of the cash register and the general commotion associated with the counter where the transactions are finalized. Usually, however, she pointed out, someone will see you and come over and ask if you need help. That did not happen in this case, however, as the people in the store saw my instructor there as well and assumed I was taken care of.

"Well," she began, turning to me, "here we are in the store now. What do you want to get?"

I almost looked around, and then the truth hit me. It was just all black around me. I could not identify anything with the low quality of sight I had, so there was nothing to see. Shopping to me meant entering a business and scanning all that they have to offer for the pleasure of choosing something that looks catchy, or useful, or like something I may want to eat for a meal, etc. Certainly, it was possible just to ask the staff to get me a bag of milk, or an article I already knew existed because I had seen it during my sighted years. But I couldn't look at anything new. On top of it all, most things that were for sale were well wrapped in solid wrapping, rendering useless the sense of feel. Should I have been here with someone who shared the same interests as I, perhaps we could have looked at some tools together, provided I took them, against the approval of the staff, out of the packaging, but here I was with a young woman who was as interested in tools as I was in what may have interested her. It wasn't her fault, though, and realizing the futility of the experience, I let the idea of shopping fall to the wayside.

It did not take long to discover that the cane is no more than a stick that one feels the ground with while walking, using the sound of traffic and most of all, knowledge of one's environment, to direct one's self. The only difference between the white cane and a broomstick is, unfortunately, that the cane tells the rest of the world that you are hooped as well. "Look out if you see anyone holding this thing!" It seemed to scream out at everyone. I preferred a broomstick.

My suspicions were only substantiated when I passed by the small hamburger joint just down the road from us one day, ironically, the one I had planned to take Lorri and Danielle out to lunch on the day of my last eye accident. The mobility instructor was a few steps behind me, and I was busily tapping the highway with one tap of the cane, and the next on the graveled shoulder so as to ensure I was not on the road, when suddenly there was a screeching of tires beside me as if there was about to be an accident.

"What's that all about?" I asked the instructor once I noticed the traffic resuming its normal rhythm.

"Oh," she said, having had fled from her original position in case there was a collision, "someone was so busy looking at what you were doing, they didn't see the car in front of them stop until the last minute." I reflected miserably on the time I saw the blind man walking with his dog on Columbia Street in Kamloops. Maybe I did not notice then, but no one seemed to be staring at him. I supposed that in a small town like Sydenham, anyone not quite the same as the others becomes a spectacle to entertain the mainstream. I lost some of my desire to continue walking with the cane at that. "Hopefully," I thought, "this will resolve itself, and I can throw this confounded cane in the trash after my surgery in Toronto."

I had another visitor from the CNIB come over one afternoon. It was an older man named Jack, who worked all his life at DuPont, a synthetics manufacturing company in Kingston. I thought it quite admirable that someone who was totally blind had a job paying a wage comparative to that of the land surveying business.

"So what is your job, if you don't mind saying, Jack?" I inquired, hoping for one of glamour and prestige such as the one I had with Alex Daniluk Surveying back in British Columbia. "Well, you see," Jack started to explain, "I sand bobbins. The company manufactures its own bobbins for its products, such as thread, yarn, rope, etc., and they need to be sanded. They spin on a lathe, and I sand them so they're smooth." My thoughts went back to high school woodworking class, and I imagined holding a piece of sandpaper against the spinning bobbin from now until eternity.

"I suppose I should keep practicing tuning pianos!" I commented, and Jack was not sure what to make of it. "If you can do it, you may as well," he commented at that. The only problem was, I reflected, that I would not be able to drive around to the customers who had the pianos. I practiced more on the tuning aspect anyhow, figuring it would be a good way to make extra money when I was back in business after the anticipated surgery in Toronto.

Then came that day to go. Barb volunteered to watch Danielle, so Lorri and I took the train to Toronto. The last time I had taken this trip was when returning from the airport in Toronto after working for Patrick Pipeline Ltd. in Tumbler Ridge, full of anticipation for seeing Lorri and the new baby. The mood was not quite so cheery this time. I could only see a few rough shapes out of the window as we passed through the towns, which were practically meaningless except for telling me there was a world out there just beyond my reach. It was still better than sitting in the vehicle driven by Lorri, however, as I was one of many passengers here, and it was not as bad as being the one who had to sit alone on the sidelines. People moved about in the train, speaking of their plans for the day, etc., giving me a bit of input that did not only center on what was going on outside the window. That now, was a world closed off to me.

We arrived in Toronto without event, and I held onto Lorri's hand having no idea where we were; we boarded a taxi which took us to the hospital. We waited anxiously in the waiting room. Judging by the activity around me, it did not seem like there were any blind people other than myself there. I had thought there would be more people in my shape. The others seemed to be reading, and even driving them here, having seemingly no business in an eye clinic. I could read braille, now, slowly and laboriously, but read nonetheless. I asked Lorri if she saw any such material among the magazines, but there was none.

Then came our turn. Judging by the voice, and what Lorri told me later, Dr. Shea was in his late forties, or early fifties, or maybe not that old. Whatever he was, it seemed, by the way he was talking, like he really knew his job. He looked several minutes into my left eye, then the right, but quickly back to the left. We paid close attention to what he said next.

"You have a badly detached retina, with a lot of scar tissue attached to it. The best time to reattach a retina is within a few weeks of the injury, and with you, it has been more than three years now." He was downgrading our expectations. "I can try my best to reattach it, and based on my experience, you have a 10 percent chance of improving the eye, and due to some unexpected risks, there is about a 5 percent chance of losing what little sight you have during the operation." We were mauling it over. If the retina was reattached, it would mean quite functional vision. That would be a dream come true after these long months of near complete darkness. He added, just as an afterthought, but seemingly important to him, "I do bill extra for my services. It would be about two thousand dollars after the operation." We were only too eager to reply, almost simultaneously, all the while considering the USD $25,000 demanded by Boston. "That's fine." We announced, with the next big question: "How soon would you be able to do it?"

"Somewhere around the start of July. Be prepared to stay in this hospital for a couple of weeks, and maybe a couple of weeks more if we decide to do two operations spaced apart by a couple of weeks." That would be a long stay, we figured, but once out, it would be like starting over. The secretary established the surgery date to be near the end of June, and once established, we counted, once again, the days to go.

On the way back from Toronto, we planned out what to do next. Lorri would have to stay in Toronto close by, so she can visit me every day, and we would have to find a place for Danielle during that time. She would be nine months old, and it will be hard on us to not have her close. But look at, we told each other, what it will be all for. After this, we would go back to British Columbia and lead a good life. Even if we decided to stay here, I would find work, Lorri would do whatever she wanted, and together we would be happy while Danielle grew up. We were even starting to think about another child in the future. That would be grand.

Back at home, I had to make the painful decision to call Alex Daniluk, my boss from the survey company in British Columbia. I would have to tell him I would not be able to work this year.

"Hello, Alex," I greeted him, hoping he would be as optimistic as me about the success of the upcoming operation. "As you probably heard, I have lost the sight of my right eye, but there is a good chance that I will get the sight back in my left with a planned surgery for it this summer."

Alex astonished me somewhat by his reply.

"You know, Jens, if you go to Toronto, there is a place called '100 Huntley Street' in which there are people who will pray over you and you will see again." I thought he was kidding, but no, he was not.

"How do you figure that?" I had no idea this guy could be serious, but I did have a lot of respect for him, and I was not about to play smart, that is, too smart for my own good. "Jens," he said in all seriousness, "I used to be a raving alcoholic. I could not stop drinking, no matter what. I was ruining my marriage, my career, my life. They prayed for me at 100 Huntley, and now I am healed!"

I knew about his alcoholic past from his nephew. I listened as he continued:

"I am not like the other healed drinkers either. Those who go to Alcoholics Anonymous have to make sure they don't touch the stuff once they are off, or else they fall back into the same pit. I can go, in retrospect, to a bar and have a couple of beers without any worries, and just walk out." He repeated in all enthusiasm of a child having seen Santa Claus, "I am truly healed. And they will heal you too."

At this, I did not know how to react. Lorri guessed there was something weird about this conversation too, but she could never have guessed this sort of talk coming from wise, scientific Alex who I have seen painstakingly building his own boats on his front lawn, with the precision of a mastermind.

I was relieved when he said, "You should still go to the hospital first, as God helps those who help themselves. However, if that is not successful, he wants more from you than that, and you must go to him directly to be healed. They will do that for you at 100 Huntley."

I repeated the details of our conversation to Lorri after hanging up, and neither of us could make head or tail out of it. We weren't about to give up on Alex as a mere dreamer coming unhinged. His comparison with losing sight of an eye with the explanation as obvious as the metal that flew into it could not, in my opinion, be compared with the uncontrollable habit of drinking booze.

We both figured, at that time anyways, that it is mostly a psychological phenomenon which is sometimes overcome in the most bizarre manner. And yes, religion could very possibly solve that; but not the brute reality of blindness as a result of having no retina to transmit the image to the brain. We tried to forget this conversation and make more plans for the hospital stay in July.

Naturally, our expectations grew considerably between the date in April that we saw Dr. Shea for the consultation and the expected date in July for the surgery. Thinking back some time later, a 10 percent chance is really not much at all, considering that the chance of failure made up the remainder of that percentage. We had hoped, however, that perhaps luck was on our side, or that Dr. Shea had gravely underestimated his capabilities. While waiting, we made arrangements to leave Danielle with Barb and Ken Sigsworth during our stay in Toronto. Danielle was making quite obvious efforts to learn to walk, holding onto furniture and trying her best to stay on two feet. We kind of hoped she would hold off on her finishing touches to the art of walking until after we returned.

Then came the day when Lorri and I boarded the train once again, heading out to Toronto, with all the splendor of high hopes. The leaves had come out of their buds and all flowers were in full bloom. The leaves were mainly just a rustling sound for me now, but I could make out the colors of flowers if they were close enough, and in the right quantity of light.

The colors, however, resembled but a slight tint on a grayish-white background, robbing them of most of their beauty. We counted on that changing, along with the expectation to share the spectacle of Danielle's first few steps upon returning.

We arrived on schedule, where I was admitted to a ward, and Lorri checked into the YWCA. She planned to walk to the hospital every day and stay with me during visiting hours, which would be practically all day.

My first surgery took place the very next morning. I was once again wheeled into the operating room, where I would undergo about three hours of surgery. Dr. Shea explained I would have two small holes cut into the front of my eye to insert tools that would cut the scar tissue away from the retina, the same scar tissue that was presently pulling the retina off the backing of the eye. I would also be given medication to control the formation of new scar tissue.

I awoke in the recovery room, my eye bandaged, and in total darkness. I had very little discomfort in my eye, and other than for the aftereffects of the anesthetic, I felt fine physically. I heard the usual moans and groans in the recovery room and the busy staff members moving around to help wherever they could. They spoke to me briefly, in their usual polite and compassionate manner, but did not dwell over my condition as they seemingly were preoccupied with more serious cases.

A few hours later, I was wheeled to the ward where I anxiously awaited the removal of the bandage. There were three other patients in my room.

To my right was a man in his fifties, referred to as "Mr. Ostrocock," who was awaiting eye surgery as well. He could see perfectly fine—how I envied him—but needed minor corrective surgery, which had him so terrified he was actually crying like a baby. Across from me was a middle-aged man named Lawrence Fines, a farmer who hit wrong on a nail which ended up flying into his eye. He was still good with the other eye and was here for retinal repair surgery on his first. I spoke to him about my situation, upon which he agreed the loss of his second eye would spell catastrophe beyond imagination. The third person lay beside Lawrence, but a young man of about thirty, known as Jim, who had been out windsurfing on Lake Ontario, and when he returned, had very itchy eyes to the point where it was impossible to keep them open. He had checked into the hospital to find out he had developed a bacterial infection which could, according the doctors, attack his optic nerves at any moment, rendering him totally blind. Presently, he was on antibiotics, not only in eye drops but through intravenous administered as well. Every half hour a nurse took test samples from his eyes, and all the while Jim admittedly prayed for his sight to be spared. It seemed to me that the three other patients were looking at me like I was an example of the worst-case scenario they were all trying hard to avoid at all costs.

Dr. Shea came in later that day and took off the bandage. I did not get the rewarding glare of light I had hoped for, but all was not black either. I could almost see as much as I had the night before, but things were fuzzier.

"That's normal," pointed out the doctor, "we did stir things up a bit in there, and your eye fluid is not clear now. That should clear up in a few days."

I inquired as to the success of the operation.

"So what happens now?"

"We don't have the retina attached just yet. If it was, you'd see a lot more now." And just to make me feel better, he added, "It might take in a few days. If not, however, we will have to operate again. I think I already had told you that." Indeed he did, and I did not let it get me down. One thing was for sure—we did not hit that 5 percent chance of losing the sight I had. Now with the bandage off, it did feel better to get in some light and see some shapes again. I could even see the red "EXIT" signs in the corridors of the hallway, where Lorri and I often walked for exercise.

The other patients in the ward kept us all company. Jim and Lawrence talked a lot, and their visitors were quite social as well. Jim's bacteria level was diminishing, to his relief, and he was to be discharged soon. Lawrence had his operation to his nail-torn eye, and only two days after the operation, he was seeing well out of it. I had no idea how Mr. Ostrocock was doing—he did not talk much, but did survive his operation. When he had come out of the anesthetic effect, he had taken sick, and a nurse was yelling rather loudly with every heave coming from Mr. Ostrocock,

"Mr. Ostrocock! Your eye!" followed by another very noisy heave from Mr. Ostrocock. This went on several times in a row, seeming rather comical at the time to us. A few days later, I overheard his doctor ensuring him that his operation, too, had been successful. This must be the lucky ward. It should be my turn soon.

My next surgery was scheduled on July 13, a Friday. "Not really a lucky-sounding day." I had remarked to Dr. Shea, who gave me the option to delay, which would be absolutely impractical. Lorri was anxious to get back to Danielle, as with every sound of a crying baby coming from the hospital corridor as visitors came and went made us both long to get back to Danielle. I took the date for the surgery, which would be a procedure in which a plastic band is put around the outside of the eyeball, and in tightening it, would narrow the shape of the back of the eye, and if all went well, forcing the back of the eye against the retina, thus providing the nourishment the retina required. Dr. Shea described it as being considerably more involved than the first operation.

As I waited to be wheeled away, Lawrence was discharged, seeing somewhat out of his injured eye again, but not as good as new. He could, however, walk with it and see good light and color, but reading and driving would have to depend on the other. How I envied him! Jim was out too—his bed empty. "I bet now he wears goggles when surfing on the lake," I commented to Lorri.

Mr. Ostrocock was in the process of telling Lorri his brother's telephone number so she could dial the number as he seemed to have trouble managing tasks with one eye bandaged. His brother was going to pick him up at the hospital. What Lorri did not know was that Mr. Ostrocock also had a stutter, which Lorri only realized after dialing some two dozen numbers for a local call. Nonetheless, when his brother finally did arrive, the doctor of Mr. Ostrocock received a lot of praise for a job well done. I hoped I would be able to do the same for Dr. Shea soon.

Once again I was wheeled to the operating room. When coming out of this one, though, I did have pain in my left eye. This was normal, the nurses told me, as the band around my eye would cause some pain, as well as the scope of the operation, which involved removing the first layer of skin around the eyeball. Most discomforting, though, was the darkness, as my eye was once again bandaged. Just temporary, I figured, so I can easily tough it out.

I was back in the ward. This time, I had a splitting headache which only decreased to a minor discomfort for the half hour that the codeine tablets worked. However, the nurses only let me have one pill every four hours. At the time, at least, I thought this was a big headache. It was only eighteen years later, however, that I found out what a real headache was.

The empty beds were refilled in my ward. Lawrence Fine's bed was now filled by a no-name man who seemed preoccupied grumbling about the smoking ban in the ward. On my right was now an eighty-year-old Russian man who had lost all of his sight from glaucoma and was hoping he could get some restoration. In the remaining bed was a man who knew no English, or any other language I have ever heard. He was older, and the surgery he required would have to be done through a series of local injections as his lungs were too far damaged from smoking to handle the general anesthetic, the doctors explained to family members who did the interpretation.

Then came Dr. Shea into the room. He took off the bandage, and all looked the same to me. No improvement, no degradation to the little sight that I had. Dr. Shea seemed somewhat disappointed but did not want to conclude anything as it was still too fresh after the operation. I still had an irritating headache, and after the two anesthetics in close proximity, I did not feel so good. The no-name man across from me had visitors come in, who spoke very loudly among themselves for hours in French, of what I did not understand much at the time. I could not figure out why they did not have their discussion elsewhere, as the patient they were visiting was not even participating in the conversation. I knew enough of their conversation to realize they were talking about the McMaster University, which was spoken so often and loudly at that it just kept on ringing in my ear long after they left.

"I just wish that they would take their blasted mixmaster out of here!" I exclaimed one day to Lorri, who was getting kind of irate by the whole thing as well. The stress was showing on us. I ate only a bit of the hospital food, and even the sandwiches Lorri bought me from the cafeteria tasted like dog food now. With every passing day, my vision did not improve. The disappointment was slowly wearing on us as we marched up and down the corridors of the eye ward outside of our room.

Two weeks after that Friday, I was discharged. Nothing had changed. I could still see the "EXIT" sign from five paces. We had wasted four weeks, plus a few thousand dollars on the extra billing from the doctor and the expenses for Lorri and the travel here. Worst of all, however, was the thought that I may have to do for the rest of my life with this little bit of vision. The room hadn't been so lucky after all. I asked Dr. Shea about my options on the day I was discharged.

"It is not over yet." He was still hoping, and so I dropped the initial idea of having to remain almost blind.

"We'll schedule an operation in six weeks, if you are still interested." My head was nodding with unconditional approval before he even finished his sentence. He continued,

"We are going to take off some more scar tissue. I don't think we got enough the first time."

We wasted no time getting out of the hospital, but not before scheduling an operation for September 14. Getting out was somewhat of a relief, as we were anxious to get back to our child and to be a little closer with each other as well. We did not let the disappointment get a hold of us with the hope for success in the following surgery. Dr. Shea had not given us any figure on what the success rate would be this time, so we assumed it must be pretty high given he had been the one suggesting a return to the hospital. By the time we boarded the train, my headache was under control, but the effect of the bad eyesight was ever pressing on my daily happiness, as that meant, too, that the trip back by train was as mediocre as that of the previous one.

Back home, we discovered that Danielle was now able to walk with no problems at all. Lorri admired her with awe, and I tried my best to get what I could out of the signs of motion through a dark haze, practically unrecognizable as a moving child. There was only a very small section of my visual field that allowed any kind of vision that was not distorted. This lay at the bottom left corner of my left side, making concentration on the object quite a challenge. I could recognize the shape of a hand, foot, or arm from about a meter away from me, but only if the movement of these limbs were very slow. Try as I might, however, it was not possible to get in my visual field enough of a person's face to piece together the puzzle and figure out what that person looked like. I would have to wait for September.

In the meantime, we kept ourselves busy in doing what would benefit us regardless of the degree of success of the upcoming surgery. I put up my truck and motorbike for sale, an event I remember by the pain it caused. In both cases, the sale was so different from the usual. Once the prospective buyers discovered I was selling them for the fact I could not see to drive now, they had no trouble paying the asking price, or believing there were no ulterior motives for getting rid of the vehicles. I listened in anguish and envy as they drove off my prized possessions, prized not only by the memories they gave but by those great expectations I had in using them in the future. I was only comforted by the idea I would purchase a family station wagon to replace them after my surgery in September. I envisioned watching my kids in the backseat while together we cruised throughout the landscape, covering the better part of North America in leisure while sharing all the moments together.

September came. Due to, in part, the Sigsworth's commitments they had in their private lives which made the task of watching Danielle difficult for them, and in part Lorri's reluctance to leave Danielle again for a long time during my stay in Toronto, Lorri took the next train back to Sydenham upon helping me check in to the Toronto St. Michael's Hospital the day before my surgery—September 13. I did not feel abandoned, as I was sure to be able to use my anticipated vision to walk around in the hospital alone, perhaps in making new friends and acquaintances at the same time. Whatever it was, I was going to be far too busy making plans for the future, such as what to change in our lifestyles to accommodate the family. The thought of being a father was still new to me, and the reality of it, I figured, would hit home so much more once I could see the "product" with my own eyes, just like that couple we had watched a year ago did in the bus station when they were sharing the sight of their child taking his first few steps.

A nurse came by early the next morning and asked,

"I have a pill here for you to put under your tongue so that you get relief from anxiety prior to your operation. We really want you to be as comfortable as possible."

I replied, straight from my thoughts,

"Really, I don't think I'll need it. I am looking forward so much to this operation." I had to really astonish her. "I would ask for it even without the anesthetic!"

At first she was somewhat astonished, but after describing to her the story I had lived through so far, together with the torture of spending eternity in darkness, she suggested instead that I take the pill just to relieve the symptoms of stress caused by blindness until my eye regained sight.

The moment came where I awoke in the recovery room once again. The place was starting to get on my nerves. The sounds were quite familiar to me now, but the total darkness still bothered me, as my eye was, as usual, bandaged. The nurses knew nothing of the course of my operation, and I did not even bother asking them about it. Time would tell when that bandage was removed. I was wheeled back to my ward in short time, as this operation had been only for the removal of scar tissue, and that is rather minor in terms of the aftereffects such as discomfort or nausea. Besides, I was getting to be an old pro at this. What was different this time, though, was that the doctor did not come in to visit me a few hours later to remove the bandage. I was getting impatient, but then again, I told myself, "These are the professionals."

The following morning, September 15, I was again wheeled to the eye ward. The nurses preferred controlling the totally blind with a wheelchair. I did not like that myself, but what was the sense in protesting, I asked myself. Maybe I'll walk back after the bandage was removed. I sat in the ward on a bed while I heard Dr. Shea's voice rambling on to others as he looked at their eyes, as many of his patients were in the same ward, looking forward to his care. Dr. Shea seemed to have a man accompanying him, a doctor by the name of Fraser. They both kept discussing between themselves the condition of the eyes of those patients they investigated.

Then they came to me. I could feel they had removed the bandage by the coolness of the air. Dr. Shea clicked on his little combination light-magnifying glass. Instead of being rewarded by a bright glow which usually made that eye blink, I saw about two tiny specs of very dim light in the bottom left corner of my visual field. There was no comprehendible dialogue between Dr. Shea and Dr. Fraser, and in a minute, they moved to the next patient while instructing a nurse to wheel me back to my room. I was stunned. A nurse came in a few minutes later and asked what I wanted for lunch. I responded by explaining, as best I could, that I really don't have a clue why the doctor never talked to me about my surgery. She understood and said she would tell the doctor that I wish to speak to him.

In short time, Dr. Fraser came alone to my door, and standing in the doorway of the ward, which was so far occupied only by me, identified himself. An attendant from the kitchen came almost simultaneously with the tray of breakfast, but I took no notice of her.

"Dr. Fraser." I wasted no time getting to the meat of my concerns. "I can't see a thing now, except for a couple of dim spots of light. What is going on? How did the surgery go?" Dr. Fraser did not sit down or make himself comfortable. I suppose it would have been a lost cause if he did try.

"We ran into problems," he started in a manner that was a miserable attempt to soften the gravity of the situation. "We had to remove all the scar tissue from the retina before any restoration of sight would have been successful. In doing so, the small machine we use, which is somewhat like a rapidly spinning saw blade, snagged the retina."

The attendant who was fussing with my breakfast interrupted, "Sir, excuse me." She was actually assuming I still had an appetite. "Would you like your fork on the left side, or the right? There is some tea here on the right, and if you want, I can put in the sugar . . ."

"*Never mind*!" I spoke to her brutally as my bottled-up rage from the loss of my future was directed rather unjustly toward her. I could have pushed her out of the room.

"This man is telling me, as you perfectly well are able to understand," I gestured exasperatingly at Dr. Fraser, "that I will be condemned for the rest of my life to blindness, and you think I am worried about eating? Just leave it!"

She left at that. Mr. Fraser was still there, as I heard him quietly sighing.

"Is there nothing else that can be done now?" It came out more like a plea than a demand.

"I'm afraid not." He was grasping for things to say. "There is always the chance that technology will help us in the future." There was nothing left to say.

I was in trouble now, and I felt it all over. I tried to make small talk with a new arrival that came into the ward. This man was a schoolteacher who suddenly lost sight in one eye as his retina had detached and "rolled up like a script," as he had put it. I sensed a tremble in his voice, as he was notably worried. I now felt this same tremble in myself all the time since talking to Dr. Fraser. The very first time I had felt this way was a long, long time ago during childhood when I had committed some sort of ruckus in grade school and the teacher had said she would call my parents. My parents were hard on punishment when talking about problems in school, and all day in that school I was trembling, even when not thinking about the issue, as I knew what awaited me in my subconscious. I imagine that criminals feel this way when, upon committing a serious crime, they spot an approaching policeman. I could not shake the feeling. It was just too much to try to assess—the degree of what kind of trouble this spelled, what the repercussions will be facing me for decades to come. Even the criminals who committed the most hideous crimes have a chance for parole after one-third of their sentence was completed. It did not look as rosy for me; this could very well be a full life's sentence.

I had to spend two more weeks in the hospital while my eye, or what was left of it, healed. The two specs of light diminished until I could not even see those. I did not walk around in the corridors of the hospital, and it was a long and miserable stay in the hospital for that time. The man whose retina had become detached had it deftly reattached by Dr. Shea, and he could practically read normal print with it before he left. The tremble was out of his voice, yet I imagine he now looked through that eye in a different manner. As he left, walking with both of his eyes viewing the path of life in front of him, I could not help but think how the world was just for the lucky.

I had called Lorri only a day or two after the operation, and judging by her sigh of resignation, suspected she had already come to grips with this eventuality since I did not call right away after the operation. There was really nothing more to say. I was to be discharged September 29, three days after Danielle's first birthday.

On the train back home, I could not get my mind off how I should have paid more respect to the blurry, dim shapes of the world outside the windows of the train, those images I still had on the way here, which were now gone. I had never expected this to happen. Five percent was the only chance the doctor had given me for the possibility of losing what I had, and here it was. I felt shaken, like some sort of confidence was taken from me. I once talked with a man who had narrowly escaped death in a car accident that should have been catastrophic to him. He described the feeling like nothing he ever had before, and even though he had not been hurt, he could not just go about life as if it was business as usual. I shared that feeling now, as if there was a deep, nagging trouble facing me that was insurmountable. Up to this point, except for the few days following the loss of my second eye, I had never been in the situation where I did not know what to do next.

It occurred to me, then, in reciting my story to an interested passenger on the train, that I had lost my sight three times, even though I only had two eyes. "Well, at least this is it now, and there is no more sight to be lost now . . ." we had concluded our conversation on that negative note. This is it now; I heard the echo in my head . . . I didn't know at that time, though, that there was still more for me in store to hope for an "lose all over" again.

CHAPTER 3

Attempting to Do Without

I arrived home empty-handed, like a gambler who had bet his life on a hand of cards only to lose. While trying to figure out what to do next, it only made sense to call the people I knew in British Columbia and tell them I would not be coming back. I knew that was the right decision to make, as there was nothing left out there for me. I knew the areas of British Columbia in which I had lived as being practically as unfriendly for a visually impaired man as the moon's atmosphere would be for humans attempting to breathe. In Chetwynd there were practically no sidewalks, no CNIB office, no opportunities, and definitely no tolerance for a profoundly blind man looking to continue his life. In fact, in my years there, I never saw a single person walking with a white cane. Ontario seemed like a friendlier place for me. I did not know anyone here that had known me as I had been before, and I figured that would help as I would not appear like someone who fell right on his face and could not get back up. I sure felt like that, but I did not need anyone around to remind me.

Dave McIntyre, the man who had taught me how to run the land survey equipment, called me after getting wind of the situation from my parents. He had called rather for the purpose of helping me in finding an alternative way to make a living rather than just to say that it was too bad that I could not come back to the old life. Dave and I had spent many afternoons in his house playing around with his new Apple 2 computer, which proved to be very useful in solving surveying mathematics, as those were principally done only with a pocket calculator. In fact, I clearly remembered the time when Dave called me up on a quiet weekday, announcing his newest discovery,

"Jens," he sounded like he had discovered a new flavor of ice cream, "I read in this book I have here that plants feel a sort of pain when they are traumatized."

I thought that interesting.

"What do they do instead of scream at us?" I imagined the ruckus that would create during haying season.

"Apparently," Dave replied, "there is a change in resistance in their main trunk for a given time until they recover." "I'll be right over," I had said, looking for the keys to my old Ford. "Maybe we can do something with your computer."

It took only five minutes to get to Dave's, and by the time coffee was ready in the percolator, Dave had made a makeshift "BASIC" program, which was the basis of the Apple II, and was testing it. He had used the joystick input for a resistance measurement and rigged the screen output to give a continuous scroll of digits corresponding to the resistance between the leads for the joystick. I had brought along some alligator clips from my inventory of electronic junk, which was basically a toolbox full of transistors, capacitors, inductors, and many other odds and ends I had unsoldered from old circuitry. "Take these," I said to Dave, holding out the clips. He grabbed them with one hand, full of anticipation for the results of this experiment.

"Now what about the plant?" I had looked around, noting several potted plants, which appeared to have been nicely taken care of.

Dave motioned in the direction of my glance, pointing out a large, beautiful plant of about three feet in height, which had large, shiny leaves. He took it by the pot back to the computer desk, being careful not to topple the plant.

"Serene has quite a few here, and a leaf less on this one will never show." Dave justified this while connecting one alligator clip on the top of the plant stem, and the other on the stem of a large leaf near the bottom of the plant. Serene was Dave's girlfriend, who was conveniently out for the day.

We were both in a room which had a window facing the road, and both of us passed the occasional glance out the window just to observe any new arrivals.

"May as well start rolling," I said, waiting for the computer to stabilize its digits. We sipped on coffee while watching the screen, which was now scrolling a four-digit number that no longer changed but for the last digit. Dave sipped his coffee with one hand, while rummaging in the desk drawer for a pair of scissors with the other, his eyes never leaving the screen. "Well, here goes . . ." he announced, snipping off a large leaf from the middle of the plant. I could see it out of the corner of my eye sailing gracefully to the floor, all the while watching the screen with anticipation.

Nothing changed. The scrolling numbers were the same as before. "Might as well do another one," Dave snipped again. As I watched the screen, I listened for approaching cars. I was determined to stay an observer, not an accomplice in this matter. Still no change. Dave cut off two more leaves.

By now an obvious pile of leaves collected on the floor. I suggested to Dave, in haste, as we still needed some leaves on the plant to conduct the experiment.

"You know, Dave, I did once talk to a man who accidently cut off three fingers with a circular saw." It was one of our neighbors in Kamloops, who had used a circular saw, and while holding the work he was cutting with one hand, cut off three fingers as he had not seen them under the plywood he was cutting. I continued, "He said he did not even notice he had cut off the fingers at first, as there was no pain. The scissors may be too sharp. Remember," I pointed out, "should you hit your finger with a hammer, it really hurts even though there really is not much damage."

Dave took no time thinking about it. He put down his cup of coffee, and using two hands, rolled up a leaf and started squishing it, the green juice oozing out first over his fingers, then dripping onto the floor.

Dave went to the washroom to wash his hands. Upon returning, we glanced once at the screen, and then he saw the plant. "Whoa! Look at the plant!" Sure enough, even though the plant appeared large at first, full of an indeterminate number of leaves, it looked like a picture puzzle with half the pieces missing now.

"At least you had the sense to cut them off all on the same side," I commented. "Just put that side against the wall and offer to water the plants for Serene for a few days." "I'm kind of disappointed we had no change in resistance." Dave scooped the leaves up off the carpet and stuffed them in the trash, covering them with some loose paper.

"May as well go for coffee at J's Place," I suggested, making reference to our favorite truck stop. We both liked J's Place, as it was a few miles south of town and the drive there gave us time to think about whatever we wanted to discuss. We both took our own vehicles. It was better that way.

But I wasn't going anywhere today. Back in Sydenham, in total darkness, it was just Dave's voice on the telephone, and while listening, I vainly expected a major solution from Dave. "I read up in a science article," Dave said, trying to cheer me up, "that IBM is coming out very soon with a computer program that gives speech to a computer."

I remembered seeing Alex Daniluck, my former boss, forced to stay in his office, fussing around with papers and digits while the sun was out and the vast world waited for me outside. How glad I had been that it wasn't me who had to sit in that office! The idea of a talking computer would mean I'd be eternally confined to an office chair. This was not going to be any fun. "I can't say that will really solve much," I remarked, pointing out the obvious. "A talking computer won't get me out, driving, going places, doing things like before, or show me what is around me." Dave was out of ammunition now, and we had little more to say. Little did I know how much the talking computer, later known as "screen reader software," would become an important part of my life. I never did hear from Dave again.

Next, I had to call Alex Daniluck so as to give him an update on the situation. While dialing his number, the content of my last conversation with him came to me. He had talked about being prayed over by a religious organization in Toronto and seeing again. I still doubted he had been serious. Maybe he just had a bad day or had been extremely tired or just had not understood the full scope of the situation. Nonetheless, I had to tell him I would not return to surveying, and that alone was going to hurt. It had been such a great job.

Alex was home, so it did not take long explaining the current situation with my eyesight.

"The working parts of both of my eyes are totally gone now." I hated the sound of my own voice for the words that were being spoken. "There is nothing more that can be done." It was final.

"You'll have to go to 100 Huntley," Alex announced this as a mother would command a clumsy child to clean up spilled milk. "What could they possibly do?" I tried to clarify the situation further by drawing a comparison. "The eyes are totally ruined, with all the pieces missing. It would not be any different than having an arm or leg missing."

"You'll grow a new eye!" Alex retorted, as if it was me who was not understanding a simple concept. He continued, "That's exactly what will happen. I've seen it on TV. People come there, having been stuck in a wheelchair for years and years, and after the prayer, they get up and walk! Blind people, deaf people, you name it—they come out with all they asked for. I saw it with my own eyes on television."

In the background, I heard his lovely wife, Mary, whom Lorri and I loved and respected dearly, requesting the telephone. "Here," said Alex, "Mary wants to talk to you."

Mary got to the point. "Jens, just put your hands on your baby daughter now." Danielle had been curiously beside us, and to keep her from playing with the telephone, that gesture was already in progress.

"Yes, Mary," I replied, attempting to figure out what she was trying to get at. "She's right here."

"Now just remember," Mary began in total persuasion, "She was not there several months ago. Now she is, in totality, and in perfection." I agreed, all the while having a good idea what would come next.

"She is here because of God, and for no other reason," she continued on the same path. "She came about, with two good eyes and all, as God approved of the love between you and Lorri. If God does that, with a living example of proof in your hand as you hold Danielle, he can give you new eyes too."

The telephone went back to Alex.

"So, tell me," he put it right to me. "Do you want to see or not?"

I knew what I had to say to this, as I had no other choice, considering how directly Alex put it. The Danilucks were, unlike the majority of Northerners, sophisticated, intelligent, and sympathetic people and extremely honest. I had no doubts they contributed a large quantity of their wealth to charities. Alex was the model boss when it came to flexibility and employee treatment in general, often giving generous hikes in salary and making work conditions as comfortable as possible.

"You know that a person has to see to live," I pointed out to Alex, and then, for his satisfaction, "I'll contact 100 Huntley."

I had promised it, so I had to follow through. I did, however, mull over it for a while, concerning the strategy of approach. I found the number without problem through long-distance directory. All that remained was to figure out my approach. If not approached correctly, it could be a humiliating experience. I just could not imagine a business downtown

Toronto calling down God to do favors for them. But Alex insisted, and I had promised.

I waited until Lorri and Danielle were out for the afternoon shopping with Barb Sigsworth in Kingston. Not only was the silence good, but I did not want to share this potentially humiliating experience with anyone. I dialed the number, and after confirming the right number was indeed reached, I presented myself, using my full name, address, and other personal information to verify my sincerity. I had learned early on in life that those who want to remain anonymous will get nowhere when talking to other people. People expect more than just a "voice in the dark, coming from out of nowhere."

I briefly explained my situation, with the details of my attempts of eyesight restoration, etc., and added,

"Through a good friend of mine, who was cured of alcoholism by your organization, I was referred to you in search of help for the help of God to restore what I have lost." I could not put it any more diplomatically, without seemingly sounding desperate and unreasonable.

The voice on the other end of the line, which was that of a man I was guessing in his forties, excused himself.

"Could you just excuse me for a minute? I'll be right back," he said this very gently and politely.

I had a telephone issued by Bell Telephone service that, for an extra five dollars, could be turned up in volume, a special design for the hard-of-hearing population. I found it worth the money as at times long-distance calls were hard to hear over the cries and chatter of Danielle. It was very quiet in the apartment today, however, and I turned up the volume as I heard the sound of receding footsteps in the background.

"There is some nut on the phone wondering if we can get God to make him see." The man had obviously gone off to discuss the situation with someone else in the building. I listened to this, somewhat expectedly, but at the same time in dismay for the blatant way they were presenting it.

I heard other murmurs in reply, and then the footsteps again. "Well," the voice was back, "there is no doubt that prayers would certainly not hurt. We'll certainly keep thinking about you. Good luck."

That was the end of that. At least, I consoled myself that I did as I had promised to Alex. I could not, however, ever imagine calling him and recounting to him what had happened. I brought the conversation up during supper to Lorri while she was attempting to get Danielle to eat her vegetables.

"I called 100 Huntley today." I was glad Danielle was too little to understand, as I would never want my kids to think I was clinging to prayer for the future of the family. "And?" was all Lorri said, somewhat relieved, I took it, that at least now if Alex calls back, we did not look like we were not interested in seeing again. That would truly be crazy.

"When the guy I told my story to put the phone down to talk to someone else, I clearly heard him referring to me as a 'nut.'" It was no surprise. "What do you think they really do there?" We thought it over in no time and concluded,

"I figure that there are people on camera with nothing wrong with them, masquerading as people with disabilities or otherwise, and then getting up and pretending to be healed upon queue." It could have been either of us who said this, as there was no room for dispute in the matter. "This, of course, looks good on TV and a lot of people, who have some money and belief in the goodness of all people, send them good contributions."

Hopefully, I thought, we were wrong.

"What would stop them?" I mused, trying to put things in logical perspective. "I can't think of any law that could prosecute them. They are not stealing or imposing upon anyone, as it is just a TV show. All one has to do is turn off the television." Lorri brought up the next argument.

"And if you really think about it, if this is what it took for Alex to stop drinking, then I guess one could not even call them all that immoral. It just does not apply to the issue of eyesight recovery."

I pondered, and then remembered how the word *blind* was often used to describe the ignorance of perfectly sighted people simply not wanting to comprehend a reality in front of them, rendering them "blind" in an abstract manner.

"Maybe it's for those who don't want to see despite having good eyes," I added, feeling the occasional spray of Danielle's half-chewed vegetables flying in my direction, "and as for those getting out of their wheelchairs, perhaps they were in pain from something and needed extra motivation to get up from the prayers!" It was hard to imagine this could be really the case, but I had still a lot to learn. This line would come back to me much later on in life.

Lorri finished, or rather, gave up on feeding the vegetables to Danielle. We must have been thinking the same thing, as she said, "What are we going to tell Alex if he calls?"

The truth was all we could say; as we really could not deny the fact we called 100 Huntley, as we would appear as not being interested in seeing again. Then we would truly look like we've lost it.

"I hope he doesn't call," I said, as that would be the easiest for all of us.

"Just imagine how that would hurt Alex to find out that this outfit is really a scam. It could ruin him."

Alex never did call back.

Life continued, but not in the same manner. I advertised in the classifieds my downhill ski package of boots, skis, and poles with the grief of one selling the possessions of a loved one that just died. My hunting rifle went the same way, and my friend Alden from Edmonton already knew I would not be coming back to have another round with him at the local shooting range. It was such a peculiar feeling to do all this. Had I died instead of being blinded, it would have been Lorri selling my things, grieving the loss of her husband, and preparing to face the world either alone, or after given healing time, in search of a partner with whom to share the world. That would have been clean and simple, leaving plenty of opportunity for her to start over, with the potential of obtaining the same level of happiness if she did not let the memories get in the way.

But this was different. I could still stand on the skis, hold the rifle, and sit on the motorbike. But the world was gone. Yet, everyone around me said "look at that!" pointing to all that was visible to them, like the roads, the ski hills, the shooting ranges. They just weren't there for me. With most other disabilities such as missing limbs, one probably would feel like being in the same world, but being able to do less, or if the same activities, only with greater difficulty. That had been the case upon losing my first eye; I could still drive and see people's faces, but playing tennis definitely wasn't as easy to do with the limited depth perception. But now the world was gone. Everyone was still talking about it being there, though. I tried to draw a comparison to those who had troubles understanding. They could see me here, in very good physical condition, beside my lovely family, on a beautiful autumn day.

"You really have nothing to complain about," they would point out, "just get out in the beautiful sunny day with your family and enjoy yourself. Stop complaining, for heaven's sake." Then, as one acquaintance continued, "I, on the other hand, just had a rotten day. Imagine, my car broke down, and when I showed up late for work, I was fired! You don't have those kinds of problems."

How I wished I did, instead of this. I tried again to draw a comparison to simplify the matter.

"Just imagine," I said in reply, "if suddenly your family became invisible to you. Now you could feel them, hear them, but when you looked, there is nothing. And all the people who approached you were invisible. And imagine, also, that the whole world was not there, so if the man who is repairing your car tells you to come and pick it up, you could not even find it, or the road in order to drive it. And I cannot even forget the past," I added in despair, "no easier than someone can forget a deceased loved one if everyone around you is talking to that loved one as if he were still alive."

And that is what it really was all about for me. There was no moving on and forgetting the past as long as the rest of society could just walk around without any barriers, all the while saying, "Look at that!" while pointing out things of interest they saw.

I thought briefly, in explaining the phenomenon to the acquaintance, of a movie I had seen as a child called *Now You See It, Now You Don't* in which a magic chemical was developed that could render articles invisible. What havoc that created! Now I was living that havoc. There was nothing left to do now but to wait. Around me, the world continued to turn, the family continued to support me as best they could, but what I needed they could not provide. The most I could do was to assume this would not be a permanent problem, but rather one that will take a few years to resolve. The older folks who spent time in front of television, such as my parents, were convinced, upon watching all the science shows and how the technology advanced, that it would be only a few years before there will arrive a solution for me in the form of artificial vision.

"Computers," my father had said in the most persuasive manner, "is the thing that will save you. Everything is computers now, and it won't take long before a computerized eye will come out for you."

I cannot say I was fully as convinced as he was. After all, these words came from a man who had said, upon seeing my brother and I during our childhood assembling painstakingly salvaged electronic components for whatever project we were pursuing, "What are you two doing with all that junk on the table?" He was referring to the assembly of components we had assembled with spring clips, as soldering was not allowed in the house. Both my brother and I learned a lot about analogue electronic circuitry, as our parents did not, at the time of our upbringing, approve of television, it was up to us to discover the world in constructing our own radios. Interestingly enough, when listening to the shortwave radio bands, we were much better informed of the world situation in comparison to our friends at school who had access to television. Therefore, the words coming from my father only had a limited amount of merit, as I knew better than to believe that a computer was a Pandora's Box holding unlimited possibilities. All the while, though, I wished it did.

By the approach of Christmas, Lorri and I knew there would be another family member by next summer. At this time, I was quite well adapted to caring for Danielle with or without eyesight. Babies always made noise, and as long as there was a reasonable amount of quiet around me, I had no problems locating Danielle even from a distance. The idea of another one coming was only good news for us. I was a little disturbed at the fact that I would not be able to drive Lorri to the hospital when it was time for the birth, as that is what the "hero" type of dad-husband would be doing—or at least that is what I thought at the time. It was hard on my ego to accept that Ken Sigsworth would drive us to the hospital. Ken, however, was such a nice, respectful neighbor, and his manner about the suggestion was nothing for me to feel inferior about.

We had an even better break concerning the upcoming birth, as we met a female doctor Jane, who announced that the Kingston General Hospital now had a family birthing center, and that meant both Lorri and I would be together during the entire birth, and moreover, I would be there to support Lorri during the birth and be able to hold the baby shortly after the birth. Jane was ready to go, but she did warn me.

"I had done this before, and so have my colleagues, and there are times often when the dad just blacks out during the process." She certainly did not want that, as I was not a small guy. "Are you sure you can handle this?"

I tried to imagine grown men losing consciousness upon seeing their own creations being brought into the world. I assured her that no, I would not react like that, as this would be one of the few examples of real beauty being there for me to observe, despite of my loss of sight. The word *beauty* had not been used much in my daily vocabulary since that disastrous day in 1983, but it was applicable nonetheless during the nights with my wife, and now, it will be sought again during the birth of our child. I couldn't wait.

While waiting for the following summer, Lorri and I buried ourselves in our music studies. It was either her or I playing the rented piano in our apartment, pausing only to drink coffee. As we were close to a main road, the traffic continued, and hearing it, I was constantly rendered homesick for the traveling life. Only much later did I realize that I would have had less pain had we moved to a much quieter area, especially where the constant buzz of motorcycles going by was not audible.

Reading the music became an issue for me, as there were new pieces to learn for the conservatory exam I was studying for. I tried the concept of braille music, but it was only legible when using my fingers, meaning I had to memorize the music before playing it. Moreover, the pieces I sought were not available, adding to the problem. Lorri and I worked slowly on impounding the notes into my brain, one bar at a time, with a lot of playing time in between to memorize them. Lorri's music reading capability improved dramatically from this. It took me a few weeks to memorize a classical song in this manner, and I often asked myself the question as to what I could possibly do to make a living with music if I cannot read the script. Even if I found someone who would always be there to read the music to me, I commiserated, "How would I possibly memorize every piece the students or church choir or funeral processions, you name it, expected me to play?" I counted on, I concluded, a solution to arrive by the time I was finished with my musical education, which would take a few years yet.

In fact, I counted on time to do a lot of healing. I reasoned that there had never been someone I had met who was still traumatized by an incident after a set amount of time, say, five years. Meeting many people who had lost loved ones, they appeared to me to have overcome the grief, even in talking about the incident, just two years after the incident. I would give myself five, or even ten, years and no doubt, it will be business as usual after that. Or so I hoped. The day came in July when Lorri had to go to the hospital, she this time instead of me. Unlike the usual hospital gloom, this would be a happy occasion. Ken drove while Lorri and I sat in the back of the car. Lorri was in physical distress as a result of the contractions and depended on me for comfort. That was the least I could give. Upon arriving at Kingston General Hospital, Ken led the way while Lorri leaned heavily on me, and I followed the voice of Ken. By now I had attained the ability to walk in a corridor and "feel" the presence of walls or other large objects by the pressure felt on the eardrums as I approached them, and I had no trouble following Ken and avoiding obstacles at the same time. Lorri was not able to walk much more, and I had to lift her into the bed in the birthing room. Jane arrived, and Ken left, wishing us luck.

As the pregnancy had progressed normally, Jane did not foresee any trouble in the birth about to happen. "It can always still stop, though," she had said, warning us not to expect the golden moment until Lorri's body was ready for it.

"If that's the case," Lorri said, being in no hurry, but did want the big belly to disappear, "we will just have to try again another day."

Over the course of the next few hours, the contractions did slow down, and we were beginning to wonder if we really had a false alarm. I was impatiently pacing the room, and Lorri was falling asleep, as she had not slept much the night before. Then in came Dr. McKenzie, a "specialist" in the maternity ward. He prodded around somewhat on Lorri, who did not like it a bit. She had hoped to stick to the female doctor of our choice, as modesty was a big part of Lorri's life's values. For some reason, the fact that Lorri's contractions had slowed down had caused somewhat of a panic in here, yet we figured we should just have gone home.

"We really should have," said Lorri sometime later, "we would have avoided so much trouble."

But at this point, we did not know any better. Doctor after doctor came and prodded and poked at Lorri. I felt helpless, but this time it had little to do with my eyesight. Jane, too, was seemingly pushed out of the way while the "professionals" did their thing. It was about three in the afternoon when Dr. McKenzie announced to us in a manner lacking compassion, "If you don't have the delivery by 4:00 p.m., you will be taken in for a C-section operation."

Our hearts sank. Where was that beautiful moment we were anticipating? Lorri wasn't sick; the baby was fine, judging by his/her heartbeat, so this made no sense at all. Lorri was now very scared. She would be sliced open like a watermelon, the baby unceremoniously ripped out, and subsequently she would hurt for weeks to come. This was not what we wanted. I felt a wave of guilt, as it had been my fault that she was pregnant. How can something as special as the love between two people result in such a nightmare? Lorri would get over it eventually, I figured, but this is not what the start of a new life should be all about. Something was wrong with this picture. Even Jane, sounding dispirited and disillusioned, could not find anything to say.

Lorri's contractions stopped. We should have run out of there, taken a taxi, and never come back. At 4:00 p.m., an hour before the staff would go home for their Friday night supper, Dr. McKenzie came, along with supporting staff, and carted Lorri to the operating room. I was not allowed in. Jane was, but only for observation. I held Lorri's hand, just as she'd done with me on my countless eye operations gone by. They carted her away, but I had to stop when approaching a line imprinted on the floor, on the other side of which no one but hospital staff was allowed. I listened intently to the sound of the retreating posse, noting the direction they took down the corridor.

A half hour later, I was still in the recovery ward, waiting for Lorri. There was not much going on here, and there was no staff around. This procedure was to take, according to the "experts," an hour at best. I went out in the hall, hearing only the faraway sounds of activity but nothing in the direction they had carted Lorri. I started to walk quietly in that direction, turning left as I had noted the group had made when they took Lorri away. I walked quietly for another several meters and came to a door, which, by the sounds of the noises escaping from it, was slightly ajar, and I recognized the voices within.

"Here it comes . . ." the sound of a man, probably Dr. McKenzie. "Oh yes, a boy!" Then the sound of Jane.

At least, I thought, I was there. A boy, I mused, is so grand, complementing the girl we already had.

"You should not be here, you know." A voice coming from an irate staff member accosted me, with obvious irritation in her voice. "No one is allowed on the other side of that line." She was gesturing in the direction I had come.

I waved my cane, commenting that it should have been marked in braille.

"What are you doing here anyway?" I could hear her snorting as she breathed heavily through her nose. I did all I could to remain pleasant, explaining that it was my son that was just born and I was looking forward to holding him. It was only a few minutes later that they came out of the room with the little boy, and I met them in the corridor. Holding out my hands, they gave him to me, and I did all I could to comfort him. He was quite distressed, as the birth had not been pleasant for him either. As I held him, they told me it would be a little while before Lorri would be out. It was a shame she was not conscious for this precious moment.

I spent the next day at her bedside, listening to her suffer as she moaned and complained about pain. She found herself almost totally immobilized, as she could not even sit up by herself. For her comfort, I had requested a private room, which allowed me to explore it beforehand without having to worry about what the other patients would think of my methods of orientation. Thus, when Lorri did require assistance, I was just as well oriented for giving her a hand as someone would that could see. The staff brought in our son, whom we named Ryan, and together we took care of him, although any work that involved physical movement was left up to me. That gave me a golden opportunity to explore the finer features of my newborn son.

I returned home the next day with the Sigsworths, as they had been taking care of Danielle but needed a rest from that ever-demanding task. I took her back to my apartment, and for the first time since the loss of my sight, I had the full responsibility of taking care of someone. Having the full weight of the task on my shoulders, I was able to push the pressing obscurity of the darkness to the side and concentrate fully on being the dad and the provider. I found it admirable that I had the full confidence of the Sigsworths, as well as that from Lorri, in taking care of this child who was not even two years old, whereas many people who knew me had their doubts I could even tie my shoes by myself. I had noticed this phenomenon early on, but dismissed it as a temporary situation, because, after all, those who questioned my abilities realized that I had just lost my sight at the time, justifying their doubtful manner. As time progressed, however, if someone doubted my ability to fulfill a task I knew I could do, it was irritating and condescending as it conjured up memories of my childhood as the youngest of three children, and anything that required the slightest sense of responsibility to complete was always left to my older siblings.

"I'll show them some day," I'd whisper to myself, wondering if the doubters would actually believe what they saw if I did. But presently, I had little Danielle to nurture, feed, and play with all to myself here in the apartment. I forgot about my pain as I absorbed myself in the task.

Lorri returned in a few days from the hospital, with Ryan, this time cradled in her arms rather than her abdomen. The house was fuller now, and it was always quite lively. Rarely, to my relief, was there enough silence for me to hear the passing motorcyclists on the road in front of our apartment. The place was now quite crowded, and we were thinking about moving to a bigger place.

"We really should get into a town of some sort," I had insisted, imagining the sidewalks I regularly scaled with my cane in Kingston during my mobility lessons with the CNIB instructor. "I would really have it much easier, and also, could do some of the shopping."

Remembering my last excursion in Sydenham, I quickly added, "Provided I know what I want to purchase."

It still would be better than being here. I could not think of anything I could do from this location. Ken Sigsworth, the man who taught me how to tune and repair pianos, already had all the nearby clients in this area, so I wouldn't really be able to tune pianos without being in competition with him. Moreover, either you had a car out here, or you were as trapped as someone serving time in a federal penitentiary.

Lorri understood my point, and we made inquiries about available real estate in various areas and came to the town of Napanee, situated just a half hour west of Kingston. A real estate agent going by the name of Vicki showed us many different rental units, but none seemed appropriate. Upon entering, I would feel the soft, uneven floors, the musty smell of rotting wood, and upon running my hand across the ceiling would notice the sagging tiles and collapsing structure.

"There's got to be something better," one of us said to Vicki, who did not even bother with any sales strategy. "This is just junk." I pointed out the rotting bathroom tile, lifting floor, and mushy window frames. "Really, Vicki," I turned to her, holding out pieces of disintegrating wood in my hand, "there are shacks in better shape than this."

"Nothing can be hidden from you!" Vicki was seemingly amazed at the fact that I was not just walking in a nonobservant trance throughout the buildings. I wished what Vicki said was really true. Not being able to assess my environment was always a sore spot of mine since the loss of sight, and this was no exception. I could not, at least not without climbing on the roof, tell if the structure had a collapsing roof. My world was now much smaller, and if I thought of it, I could ask someone to look at things like tearing shingles or water stains on the ceiling, but the basic power of observation was seemingly out of my control. For a temporary measure, nonetheless, I was doing all right.

We were going through more real estate ads in the classifieds one late summer day when Barb Sigsworth called.

"You should read this article on John Warren," she said excitedly. She was holding the paper, reading out loud. "This man has guts." She announced the headlines. She went on reading the article, which gave details of how John Warren, the blind man who came to see me in the hospital when I first lost my right eye, took up the sport of skydiving. John had gone up for the first time and, like all beginners, was paired up with a professional skydiver, who would ensure the landing and deployment of the chute was done right.

Barb finished the article and asked, "Isn't that absolutely amazing?"

I knew what Barb was getting at. My ego had taken a serious blow upon losing my independence, and it showed. I imagined myself jumping out of the airplane at ten thousand feet and tumbling to the ground, attaining speeds of 150 miles per hour. A minute later, one would pull the cord, opening the chute, and sailing slowly to the ground. At that point though, I wondered for a fleeting moment, "Would I pull it? Provided there was no instructor, would I? Oh, this is not healthy." But the idea toyed softly with my mind. It beckoned me. How Lorri would suffer! The poor, poor girl. But I wouldn't. Not like this. I had to change the subject, but not because I was scared. I just did not want to blurt this new thought of mine out to everyone. It would have to stay a secret.

"I think I'll give John a call and congratulate him." I thanked Barb and dialed John's number.

He answered the telephone in his usual polite voice. He had the voice of a lawyer confident his case would succeed. "How's Flying John!" I had to congratulate him in an unusual manner. We had talked to each other on occasion ever since my loss of sight, so he recognized my voice immediately.

"Back with both feet on the ground" was his reply. He was curious as to how I got wind of this newest venture of his. "How'd you hear of this?"

I told him, and he said, "I've got the paper here. When my wife comes home, no doubt, she'll have to read it."

I inquired how he liked the ride down.

"It was awesome!" He was rather excited in recounting the event, as if he could feel it all over again. "When I jumped out of the airplane, you wouldn't believe all the G-forces you get! I thought my guts were going to come out of my mouth." He thought for a second, and then added, "Then I tumbled down, going faster and faster. After several seconds, it did not even feel like I was gaining any speed. In fact . . ." he pondered, looking for the right words, "except for the sound of the wind, it did not even seem like I was moving anymore. It was just as if . . . as if I was laying on a carpet, as the air under me was just like a mattress. It was the air," he continued to explain, "which kept me from going faster. So I was literally lying on it!"

I tried to imagine it. Jump out at first, and there is the initial acceleration, then the wind, which will make quite a bit of noise. If one wore earplugs, then that would not really be a factor. At ten thousand feet, it could take a minute and a half to come down. With enough to drink, and no sleep the night before, one could practically fall asleep in that time. What a life!

"Then what, John?" I kind of knew it would be the landing routine next.

"The instructor pulled the cord, and we slowed down in a hurry. With both of us on the same chute, you'd think it would just rip wide open." This event must have scared John somewhat. I imagined, as I had since childhood, the picture as it would if one could see. One stands on the edge of the airplane, and with all confidence in a frail piece of cloth, which is precariously folded in the backpack, jumps out with everything to lose. There are the children waiting at home, either learning to walk or perhaps preparing to graduate from school, proudly holding their certificate, scanning the crowd of onlookers to see if their dad is watching. There is the wife, in all her beauty, preparing a meal for the family to share at the evening hour. Never mind the beautiful day below, with the birds singing, the flowers blooming, and an open road upon which one would cascade through the gears on the motorbike in total serenity, just like paradise. With all this to lose, one would have to pray, and pray again, that the chute will open and hold, so all that would not be lost. It is said the first minute of free fall, the time before opening the chute, would be the most fun. With all these worries, and all there is to lose, I could not see how it really could be.

But for John and me it was different. Well, maybe John does not feel that way. He seemed well healed, not complaining one bit about the loss of his sight.

"It was really hard for some time," he had said, with all the insinuations that he was over it just as I had been over the loss of my first eye after which life just continued as normal, in spite of it all. I envied John, but not in a negative manner, as his attitude of being healed from blindness gave me the strongest hope, yet I would overcome this. "In fact," I mused, "perhaps John doesn't care all that much now if he could see in the future or not." But that assumption later proved to be wrong.

Vicki telephoned us a few days later, sharing the news that she had a solution for our housing problem.

"You could buy a house instead of renting one, you know." She was ignoring a vital problem.

"But, Vicki, I wanted to rent as that would mean the landlord would have to maintain the property." It would pose problems for me to mow the lawn or work on any major projects, like hanging a door, changing a carpet, etc."

"I have one here which is really in good shape," Vicki was not one to give up, and it was a good thing, as we found it was cheaper to buy the place and pay the mortgage than to rent. Moreover, it was a good place situated a block from the main street in Napanee, with a garage, although unfinished inside, to accompany the property. I mused over the fact that there was room here for a guide dog. John had spoken well of those he had, and I may as well try one.

The move here was definitely an improvement. There were sidewalks to follow with the cane, and after a mobility instructor came in from Kingston, I could walk in town, although still very uncomfortably. I had to memorize the number of steps between blocks, listen for the traffic to tell if the intersection was safe to cross, and remember how many steps were from the last street corner to the door of the business I wanted to visit. The south end of town was compact and cozy, with the businesses fronting on the sidewalk. On the north end of town, however, it was a different story. Halfway up the road heading north, the sidewalk stopped abruptly, and the cars consisted of a constant stream of extreme noise, making it impossible to hear the sounds of people around me. Once at the shopping mall, I would have to cross a large parking lot before being alongside the building, making it virtually impossible to find the door. I avoided that place. John suggested I apply for a dog, so I did. I was in luck when I applied for the guide dog at the Seeing Eye school in Morristown, New Jersey, as they had had a cancellation, and there was room for me the following month. Classes lasted a month, allowing a circulation of students every thirty days. Lorri and I were a bit excited, not really knowing the limitations of a guide dog. We figured it would give us more freedom and more things to do together that resembled the life we had left behind.

As I was waiting for that day to go to the United States, I decided to give John a ring, telling him of the good news. The way he spoke of dogs was as close as one could get to the steering wheel of a car, which by now, I had an almost uncontrollable craving for. My own mobility, my own control. What heaven that would be!

"Hello," said the voice of John on the end of the line, somewhat drawled out this time. I could not imagine him drinking, as the alcohol would not do much for stabilizing his diabetes.

"John, what's up? You sound spaced out," I commented. Nothing wrong with a party, I thought, and besides, John certainly deserved a good time for a change in his life.

"I'm on cloud nine!" John was happy about something, no doubt. He continued, "I was over at the doctor's last week, and guess what they want to do?"

"I don't have a clue, John." I didn't. "Is it a new drug for the sugar control, or maybe," I had to joke, "a new fertility pill?"

"Better," announced John, chuckling slightly, and then becoming serious. "Last week my eye doctor told me they wanted to try a new treatment for my retinas. They said they had a chance to get some sight back in them, by doing a bit of surgery and laser treatment, and I would see a bit again!" He paused, letting it sink in. "But I will be on an on-call basis, so if the facility becomes free, I have to be ready. No drinking, in other words, starts tomorrow. That's why I'm having a bit of a party now!"

That wasn't like John at all, I thought. I felt terrible astonishment. How could it be that John was telling me all this time that even though he had it rough at first, now all is better, that blind people can do anything they set their mind on, and in giving all the while the impression he was healed, suddenly wanting to undergo surgery for sight recovery?

"That's very nice." I felt a bit shaken, but not at all like John had cheated on me. Rather, I felt envious that he had this opportunity.

I continued, "Wouldn't it be nice if it worked? What would be the first thing you would do?" I was sure he had already thought of it, along with the second thing he'd do, the third, etc.

"Would it ever!" The drinks he had was not clouding his judgment or changing his character; it only shed his guard, which had been in place ever since I met him for my benefit. "The first thing I'd do, Jens, is look at my son. Even if I could see only as much as Debbie can, I would be so happy." Debbie, his wife, was partially visually impaired to the point where she needed a closed-circuit television arrangement to read. She could, however, distinguish between their seven-year-old son and other children if she dressed him in bright clothing. "That's all I need to be able to do. Anything else is a bonus." I was about to comment about all he had said since we met, like the wonderful things blind people can do, the life without limits in spite of the loss of sight, and all the talk surrounding the fact that his life was progressing just as normal now that he got over it. But what else could he have said? What would it have done to me if he had said the truth? If now I was faced with a person who had just lost his sight, I, too, would be forced to think of something positive to say about the whole thing as well, if only just for that person's benefit.

"I wish you the best of luck, John." I really meant it. He had said this to me just before I had gone to Toronto. "Let me know how it goes."

Even though it would not affect me, I still thought it would be neat if he did succeed. No doubt I would be green with envy, but I would be able to see the effect that sight recovery would have on John. He deserved this break that goes without challenge. Everyone deserves to see. After all, even the prisoners in the United States on death row have adequate lighting in their cells where they spend their final hours. Many, many years ago, psychologists have unanimously determined that total darkness constitutes cruel and unjust punishment.

The Seeing Eye guide dog school had issued me the tickets for the bus ride to the Toronto airport, from where I would fly to New Jersey. When I first thought about going down there alone, I remembered the confusion of the airport, along with all the possibilities of getting lost and missing the flight. Even when I could see, it was an overwhelming experience, with my anxiety level subsiding only slightly when finally on board the aircraft, only to dread the chaos attempting to find my suitcases, and then the challenge of getting out of the airport. Now I was to do this in the dark. No wonder blind people sat around at home lots, I mused, as the thought of the upcoming feat was disconcerting at the least. Nonetheless, I could not duck out of this one. I had to make the trip, and perhaps, I hoped, things would be easier on the return, as I would have my new form of mobility—the guide dog.

I called a taxi to pick me up at 3:30 a.m. as my bus left at 4:00 a.m. He brought me to the doughnut shop where the bus stop was, and I asked the driver to lead me to the door, for which I tipped him. After all, special service does not come for free. I was at the front counter and asked a staff member to be on the lookout for the bus, and to please let me know when it arrived. She replied, "Sure thing, I'll hear it before I see it, as it makes quite a ruckus."

I suppose I was thinking everything was done by sight these days and had to laugh at my insecurity. I was shown a seat where a few other people were also awaiting the bus. I couldn't really miss it now, and moreover, the bus driver had been aware that a visually impaired passenger was expected at the stop, so he in fact met me in the shop and helped me on the bus.

Upon arriving at the airport, I reminded the driver I was going to New Jersey, and he said he would help me into the correct terminal. There was all sorts of confusion in the airport. People were everywhere with their suitcases, crying children, and talking in many different languages among themselves. I thought of the stress on the workers, and how it would be so much more relaxing to work outside in the forest, perhaps in surveying a pipeline cutting through the heart of the wilderness. Would I ever have that chance again?

Once at the "special assistance" counter, I really had nothing to worry about. There were employees who were assigned the task to only help the disabled passengers, of which there was only myself and a man beside me, who seemed to be unable to move. He was accompanied by a nurse, and as I heard the conversation between the nurse and the staff, I realized that there was still much more left for me to lose.

I arrived in New Jersey in about two hours, where I was deftly met by staff from the guide dog school. They wasted no sympathy by attempting to "baby" me or any of the other arrivals destined for the same class as me. Holding onto my guide's arm, I did my best to demonstrate my control and balance as the man leading me marched out of the terminal and, weaving in and out of parked cars, discussed my expectations from a guide dog. "I just need to get around more effectively." I had to have a purpose for the dog. "Right now," I stated to him, "if I don't immediately find the door of a building, I have to feel around for it, and that is quite a hassle. Everyone around seems to want to pounce on me in their attempts to help me, just making the situation worse." And that was really a summary of my problems in getting around. If I had the town to myself, I am sure it would be under my control, with nothing out of my reach. But with the others there, I generally got pushed this way, pulled that way, and yelled at from all sides if anyone thought I may be "lost." There were many times when I was not sure where the door was of a building, or perhaps I had just missed it during the first approach, and before trying to find it, I would stand beside the wall, pretending to wait for someone who was to meet me. Once sure the sidewalk was void of pedestrians, I would be free to try again.

I arrived at and entered the school, which was a large building with many hallways and stairs, many rooms as it housed thirty students at a time plus staff. Here I met many other blind people, mostly all coming from the surrounding area in USA, who held all sorts of interesting jobs and seemed to lead more interesting lives than I did. There was a women's ward and a men's ward, between which there was a large recreation room. This was always a lively place to be.

On the second day, we each received our dogs. Mine was a long-haired Shepherd named Ozzy. He was quite a lively creature, always wanting to outpace the others. This tendency of Ozzy to be a speed demon got us in trouble one day, as he ran me into a lady who had just finished putting her money into a parking meter, and as she stepped backward into my path to read the meter, we collided. She did not get hurt but cursed me profusely for the humiliation it caused her. It was always up to the unfortunate instructors who followed us to try to smooth over incidence like this.

A few days into the four-week training session, the school staff called a meeting in the recreation room. We were to watch a movie, I was told. "Kind of bizarre," I thought, "for blind people to sit and watch a movie." Perhaps the instructors were going to fill us in on the pictures, as that worked to a limited degree for me. I did not mind sitting through the documentaries or other non-fiction shows on television, as the sound track played a major role. However, the entertainment shows often had long quiet spells in which the images played the full role of informing the viewer as to what was happening, rendering the experience too frustrating to be considered as "pleasure." This movie, however, did utilize the sound track a lot, and what was missing for us was quickly filled in by the staff member who called the meeting.

The film started interestingly enough, which was all about the life of a young man enjoying himself, active, with all the ingredients of a good life—the lovely girlfriend, meaningful job, and with all the hopes for the future. He liked boxing too, just for pleasure and the thrill it brought. Then there came a part where he was struck the wrong way and suddenly went blind. All the students in the recreation room were listening to the suffering of the actor on television while the staff member continued to speak of the images seen, which complemented the misery of the soundtrack. Memories of the last instances I saw the snowmobile before me seconds before the metal knocked out my treasured remaining eye, the wail of the approaching ambulance siren, the horror in Lorri's voice upon seeing me staggering around in the yard, blood running down my face, all came back to me in an instant. I had to leave.

There was a grand piano downstairs, on the other side of the building, where I went to try to forget these newly conjured memories, fresh as if it was only yesterday when it happened. I really was doing well here up to this point. With all the other students around, together with the straightforward and respectful manner of the staff, I could almost forget the past. But to show this film to people who were already traumatized by blindness was in such poor taste that it made me queasy. I made the piano sing in an effort to blot out the echoes of the movie's sound track in my head.

"Why aren't you watching the movie?" It was an instructor at the door, interrupting my piano playing. He was a man about twice my age, I judged by the voice and mannerisms, whom we respected well as students.

I was still disturbed and would not be shy talking about this issue to him.

"At first I thought it a bit absurd to expect blind people to watch television." I did not mean to really butter him up, but it always helps to introduce positive aspects about a situation before delving into the point. "But the way you are presenting it is really quite effective."

The instructor made a grunting noise just to show me he was still there, listening, awaiting the answer to his question. "Yet I do not understand why you would show a movie to us with such a beginning. I cannot speak for those who were born without sight, but for those of us who could once see and lost it, this conjures up memories which, to me, are unbearable. As was written on my application before coming here, I lost my second eye three years after my first, all the while knowing the value of it. Now the world as I knew it is gone, and I guess it is time to move on. But showing me this kind of a movie, forcing me to relive the experience is painful, to say the least."

I tried to think of some examples which may be easier understood. "Suppose you lost a child, or your wife, whom you loved dearly, would you appreciate seeing this all over again in a movie, even if they are only actors?"

The instructor pondered for a moment, and then replied, without attempting to defend the school's policy.

"I have been working here for fifteen years, and we must be training at least three hundred students a year. I have never been told this before, even though everyone here gets to watch the movie." I found that unbelievable. What were the others doing to heal so fast? Perhaps they were just too shy to say it out loud but felt it inside just like me. I had my doubts on that theory, though, as the students did not seem shy at all.

"The rest of the movie deals with the young man having paved the road for allowing guide dogs in public domains," explained the instructor. "It is really quite an important contribution this young man made for us, which is why we show this movie to everyone." Then he added, "The latter part of the film is a lot more positive."

I agreed to come up, and the rest of the movie was a lot gentler on the viewer. The actor, however, never did recover the original liveliness in his voice, maintaining a trace of resentment and bitterness until the end. The young man in question had indeed done a lot for us, as he had to demonstrate the effectiveness of his dog in front of a court judge by avoiding the obstacle path before him. The movie ended by the narrator announcing that the young man lived only ten more years afterward. I wondered if the eternal darkness just drained the life out of people.

The latter part of the school went well. Twice a day, we would all go out for long walks in the city, as well as in the country, for those who were interested. Even though the dog helped in finding the way, it was still up to the owner to show the way. The dog would pause at intersections, pause at drop-offs on the sidewalk and avoid obstacles with great effectiveness. Oozy loved to go into buildings, making finding the entry doors an easy task. He would even put his nose right on the door handle, if it was not too high for him. Once inside, if I heard the sound of a cash register, I would motion toward it, and Ozzy was only too happy to find the shortest way there. I could suggest another direction and feel by the response of the harness that Ozzy had doubts about the suggested direction. If the route suggested, however, was passable, there was an unmistakable eagerness in his manner of advancing. This was a pleasant change from using the cane.

Near the end of our stay in the school, the instructors wanted to verify that we were ready to go home by expecting us to walk, paired up with another student, through the city following a designated route while perhaps stopping at some businesses for making a purchase, if desired. It sounded like a complicated and crazy venture at first, but I did like the idea of going out with a partner and without sighted assistance. Up to now the instructors had stayed behind several steps, a little further behind with every day that passed. This time, they told us, they would not even stay on the same block as we'd be. The idea was that the dogs had no direction from anyone but their new masters. I knew very little of Morristown, as it was a big city with a lot of traffic noise and other forms of activity. I felt a kind of excitement in heading out on this venture. "I should really do more traveling," I thought to myself.

I was paired up with a young woman, Crystal, who came from a Southern state, complete with a drawl in her speech. We set out together on the route we had memorized by feeling the raised print map of downtown Morristown. The route would take over an hour to cover, leaving plenty of opportunity of getting totally lost or even squashed by the traffic like those unlucky skunks on the surface of the Canadian highways, flattened to a pulp that covered a dozen times the area of pavement than the original size of the deceased animal.

Carrying on a sometimes meaningless conversation, I kept in communication with Crystal while we walked, a bit tentatively, paying close attention to the traffic and the movements of the dog. By now, I had become accustomed to the movements of Ozzy, who had a unique manner of reacting with each situation that arose. The dog was trained to stop when approaching an intersection, awaiting the master's command of "forward," "left," or "right." This time we were in a strange part of town, one not even familiar to Ozzy. He was obviously having trouble distinguishing the sidewalk ramps leading to parking lots from intersections. He therefore hesitated slightly at every ramp, leaving it to me to make the final decision. I would base mine upon the degree of drop-off onto the road, or the traffic pattern, using the approximation that each block in this district would be between one hundred and one hundred and fifty paces.

"Any idea where we are?" Crystal was close behind, as the sidewalk was too crowded to go side by side.

"Not a clue!" I had to yell to be heard over the traffic. "I think we need to go three more blocks before we turn!" "Good thing you know!" I said, having already forgotten the details of the map in my concentration of my environment. Ozzy jumped off a curb, and I followed, knowing a split second in advance by the tilt of the dog that the step was there. I heard the traffic, at the same time, slowing down on my left, signifying the traffic light had changed to red and that we really should not be crossing this road. I pulled back on the dog, retrieving him back to the curb, instructing him to sit while scolding him softly.

"Dogs will get sloppy in their work, and it is up to you to remind them of their responsibilities," the instructors always had repeated to us during our training. Crystal came up behind me, her dog stopping for me and for the curb.

"Just had to correct Ozzy here," I said to her, and just then the light changed, as the motors in the vehicles accelerated beside us in unison. We crossed, once again smoothly mounting the steep curb on the opposite side of the street, as the tilt of the dog's body, when he used his front paws to mount the curb, gave away its position, along with the height of the curb.

Crystal and I paused on the sidewalk, pondering as to where to go from here. A man's voice, belonging to a pedestrian who had been watching us, mistaking me for an instructor, said to me, "If you'd been blind, that dog," he gestured to Ozzy, who looked up at the man, "would have killed you. Imagine being blind and having your dog walk you out in the middle of the road like that on a red light!"

The traffic was very heavy, making this an unlikely place to hold a discussion.

I smiled and said, "He'll be all right. Just a little new at it."

I petted Ozzy, repeating almost the exact words that the instructor had used to comfort the woman I had mowed down a couple weeks ago due to Ozzy's haste. I thought of the picture I may have posed from an observer. A man seemingly in control steps off a steep curb, as if he could see it, the dog takes two steps into oncoming traffic, the man pulls the dog back to the curb, scolds it, all the while using visual gestures to the dog, and then proceeds to tell the dog when the light changes back to green. How could I have explained the situation in a few short phrases over the noise of the traffic to this observer? In spite of Ozzy's faults, if he can make me look like I can really see, he must be doing a good job.

Crystal and I continued on our way. The sidewalk was wide, covered with people and outdoor sales furniture, such as tables and clothing racks set up all over the place. Our dogs slowed to a mere crawl as we negotiated the obstacles, occasionally brushing past them, allowing us to identify the obstacles. I heard the sound of two people talking loudly beside me, one of them obviously trying to sell the product, while the other asking about the price. I called to Crystal.

"Crystal, I'm just going to ask this person what all is for sale here. I wouldn't mind something to take back home." She stopped beside me, and I motioned to Ozzy to go in the direction of the salesperson, which he did, squeezing us between two tables.

"Excuse me," I began, "are you responsible for selling this merchandise?"

"Yes, I am," replied the female voice, "is there anything you are looking for?"

"We'd like something that reminds us of this town when we go back home." Crystal had followed me. Guide dogs are good at following and know the command very well.

Crystal bought some shirts, but I had not brought American money, which was a shame. There was a lot of good stuff there, by the description of the sales lady, who boisterously announced the type of merchandise she had, not only to us, but to all who were there.

We had to weave out of the crowd just to get near enough to the traffic to tell where the road was. If we had not first advanced toward the traffic, the dogs would have assumed we wanted to buy the whole store. I noticed early on that guide dogs seem to love going shopping.

We continued on our journey, using each other's fragmented memory of the raised map we had access to back at the school before leaving on this excursion, to orient ourselves. We couldn't say we were really lost, as the activity around us signified we had nothing to fear. There were coffee shops, bakeries, hamburger vendors frequently approaching us as we passed by, asking if we wanted to buy their product. It was obvious that guide dogs were a major presence in this town, as no one seemed to think twice about us being there. It was easy to tell what went on in the minds of people by how the children talked to their parents as we walked by. We seemed to fit right in, being served and generally treated by the business and populous as if there was nothing wrong with us. I could have stayed here just for the sake of this fact alone.

Crystal and I made it back a full half hour past our expected time. There was only one other couple that had returned so far. The instructor was delighted.

"How'd you like it?"

"Just great!" I imagined living here, calling up a friend, saying "I'll be right over," and walking through this maze of activity, meeting in a coffee shop. I could probably make good living repairing pianos, teaching music to the visually impaired, or perhaps as a German-English translator. With this mobility, there was no reason to sit still.

"It's going to be hard to go back to Canada," I stated, describing the discovery of the freedom associated with this town.

"It probably has more to do with the area you are in," noted the instructor, who must have experience from his encounters with other students, "they generally have much more accessibility in the big cities, as well as the accommodation of people with different needs. Being a minority for whatever reason is harder in a small town." I thought about that as the rest of the pairs of students arrived. No one got lost, no one got squashed. They all had tales to tell about their routes, which were different for each pair. We all went home on a happy note, as the school had not only promoted the use of dogs, but had also introduced a lifestyle for the blind that was definitely worth considering adapting.

I arrived back in my small hometown without incident. Ozzy was quite accustomed to traveling in the trainers' vans back in Morristown, so the flight did not cause any anxiety. By now I felt quite at home in the busy Toronto airport, using the sounds of the masses of people to orient myself. "If I'm lost, being among all these people, that must mean everyone here must be lost," I figured. The security staff was always around anyhow and never wasted any time presenting themselves.

Back in Napanee, winter was very close, as the temperature was considerably lower than in New Jersey. Everyone in the family liked the dog, and later, when the kids went to bed, I suggested we go out to have supper in a restaurant nearby. The streets were rather quiet in this little town, giving me fewer clues to go by in directing Ozzy. When Lorri walked too close to me, he was expecting to follow her instead of going the way I wanted. It was a little rough at first, but I did find the restaurant. I entered, with Lorri coming in behind me, and almost immediately, I was confronted by the owner.

"You have to get out with that dog!" She was hysterical. "It is a guide dog," I said, taken by surprise. "He is allowed in all public places, and I'll make sure he behaves himself." That was not enough. "I'll call the police if you don't get out!"

"I think that is a good idea," I said, noticing the room suddenly turning quiet. There had been several customers chatting among themselves when first entering the room.

She started madly flipping through the pages of the telephone book in search of the number for the police. The owner was obviously not aware of the law obligating business owners to allow service animals in their premises; the beneficial result of the work of that tormented blind man acted out in the television video played back at the guide dog school.

After only a minute on the telephone, she begrudgingly ushered us into a room over to a table away from other customers. It was hard to enjoy the meal after that, but we tried anyways. This was definitely not Morristown, where, on the last day, the staff had invited all of us students out to a fancy restaurant, dogs and all, where I had the best of times since losing my eyesight, staggering somewhat out of the premises having consumed enough drinks to attain a good night's sleep.

But not here, now, in this enterprise where the owner, uneducated about the concept of a well-disciplined service animal, feared that Ozzy would jump up and take other clients' steaks off their dinner plates.

Lorri and I worked together on memorizing the town, and before long, the town was far more accessible with Ozzy than it had been with the cane. I did not feel uncomfortable walking with him as I felt with the cane, although there were frustrating moments. That seemed to go with the package of being visually impaired. I spent many hours walking every day, discovering businesses and homes of piano tuning clients once Lorri gave me a rough description where they were. I got brave once and attempted to cross the large parking complex between the main road and the Napanee Mall, only to end up right in front of one of the two sets of doors leading into the building. It was quite rewarding, even though I still had the problem that I had no clue what was on the shelves. I skirted this issue somewhat by selecting hours that were relatively quiet for business and then going to the smaller stores where the owners were only too happy to tell me what they had. Naturally, it meant I had to buy something before leaving, whether I wanted it or not, as it would not have been right to put someone through this trouble without rewarding them afterward.

I was getting out and around, but not like before. As long as I compared what I gained by the dog, the retraining, to what I had in Sydenham at the apartment right after the eye accident, I could safely say I recovered somewhat. While in town, the traffic was slow and erratic, suggesting the drivers themselves were dealing with the frustration of the detours and obstructions encountered on route. Being away from the open highway and the sounds of the freedom it once offered dulled the pain of the effects of the prison of darkness. I understood now why prisoners in the penitentiaries often chose to work while serving their time: it simply kept their mind off what they were missing.

But then there were the dreams. They started back when I first lost my sight—dreams of doing very little at all out of the ordinary—just being able to see. They are like a nightmare, with the only difference being that the frightening part is the knowledge that soon I would wake up. I would be doing simple things in them, like walking through the woods or target shooting at the Kamloops shooting range, accompanied by my father. The full beauty of the world would be there. Even those things that really weren't considered beautiful were now beautiful—the dark clouds suggesting rain was arriving, the morsels of garbage scattered along hiking trails, the dried-up landscape surrounding Kamloops—they all resembled paradise now. The strangest thing was that I was conscious enough during the dreams that I knew this was a dream, and soon I would wake up to the nightmare of life. It was the dreams that kept me from getting better, from carrying on. In these dreams I would do all I used to do—ride a motorbike, feeling every move, counterforce, and the controls in doing so. I would be flying in a helicopter or a small plane under my control over the landscape, rich with the awesome beauty of the wilderness, knowing that any moment I would wake up and it would be lost.

They came in bursts, one night after another, for a few days in a row, and then stopped for weeks at a time. During the dreamless weeks, I began to recover. I'd make plans of graduating from the Royal Conservatory of Music with an associateship in piano, performing before a cheering crowd, recording, maybe even making it to New York. Perhaps I'd buy a thousand-acre plot of land in the hills, hiking in the hills with my kids for adventure and excitement. But then, when the dreams came, I'd wake up shaken, powerless, and depressed. My will was gone, and it took all I could to walk the dog, let alone think of the future. Once again, I'd telephone friends and family, asking if they may have seen something on television that would make me see again. Yet the answer was always "no" or at times there would be a vague reference to possible research being done; however, it would not apply to my situation as part of the eye still had to be intact for the experiments in question.

The following spring arrived, and with it, another problem. Lorri was expecting again, and this time, she was scared. Upon first visiting the local Napanee doctor, she was told she was considered "high risk" as she had had a cesarean section with Ryan. She came back from the doctor in obvious distress.

"I'm not going there again," she stated with no sign of relenting on that decision. "They are just going to butcher me again."

"Did you talk to Jane?" I had to ask, as she was a very nice doctor whom we both liked. I tried not to think of the last birth, during which Jane had just been pushed to the sidelines. "She could have handled it," I figured, "had she been given a chance."

"I went to her just recently," recited Lorri, referring to her latest visit with her, as Jane was still looking after the needs of our children. "I asked her if the cesarean was really necessary, as after all, she had been there during the operation, and she told me 'probably not.'"

"So why did they do it?" I asked, knowing Lorri would have asked Jane that during her visit.

"Who knows?" Lorri thought about it, recounting the magic hour of 4:00 p.m. Dr. McKenzie had stated for the operation time, with all being done by 5:00 p.m.—just in time to get home for supper. "Probably a convenience thing." She was getting angry just thinking of it. I suggested she go to the library and find some literature on this matter.

Lorri came home the next day with a book titled *Silent Knife*, an information text, critical of Western culture obstetrics practices, harboring claims that the cesarean section procedure is used in Western society for the sake of convenience rather than for a warranted medical emergency. The author claimed that perhaps one case in two hundred births would benefit by being conducted as cesarean, however, in some localities across North America, the frequency is as high as one out of four births. The testimony was clear, and the reasoning made perfect sense. The proper and the improper birthing procedures were described within in detail. Lorri read the book out loud, often repeating chapters in order to understand every last detail. Reading the book made us both feel better. I was glad to know it was really not my fault after all. We had figured a married couple, committed not only to each other but to the family, should only rejoice upon learning they have a new arrival on the way, not grit their teeth in fright in anticipation of another debilitating surgical procedure.

We read the book many times over the next few weeks. Lorri also signed out a book titled *William's Obstetrics*, a rather frightening book to read, as the beauty and fragility of childbirth was totally undermined, it seemed, by the medical community. The approach of the two authors was totally contrary. The one of *Silent Knife* suggested that it was the muscles of the mother's womb, coupled with the help of gravity, which allowed the baby to be born. It reiterated on several occasions that one must never force out the child, as that would injure both child and mother. The approach in this book was that the mother had the final veto as to what position to assume during childbirth. It was the mother who would feel exactly which position to assume during the labor, and it was the assistance's duty to oblige to every one of her demands, supporting her in any way possible.

The *William's Obstetrics* manual, on the other hand, had the mother strapped down in the "stirrups," rendering the mother in what the other book referred to as the most awkward and unlikely position to be for a child to be successfully born.

As we read, we understood more of the procedure. Lorri bought a fetoscope, an apparatus which allowed us both to hear the tiny audible heartbeat of the baby inside Lorri. We could also hear the placenta, which made a roaring sound like that of being close to the ocean while the waves mounted the shore. The first thing we noticed was that the placenta was close to Lorri's side, a good sign, according to the texts we read, that there was no problem with the placenta possibly blocking the birth canal. The heartbeat of the baby was healthy, and its rate was within the boundaries of the norm.

"Maybe we should wait until the baby is practically born before going to the hospital," I suggested one day over dinner. Danielle was feeding herself by now, and Ryan was trying his hand at it too, splattering us both.

"In that case, why bother going at all?" was Lorri's countersuggestion. "It is my baby. You can do everything that I need done, like hold me up, help me move into whatever position I want, and catch the baby. After that, it's all over and we just clean up. You can do that too."

She had a lot of confidence in me, and that was for sure. I was doing quite a few things around the house, like cooking, cleaning, taking care of the children when Lorri was out. I had also learned to master the renovations necessary to keep up the old house and garage that I had insulated and fixed up for a piano repair workshop; the fact that I once had pointed out to Vicki that home repairs would be impossible for me to do back when I first considered buying a house in Napanee now seemed a silly thing to have said. Somehow, nature had set in my life to show me I could do a lot of things without really needing to see with my eyes. My piano tuning/repair job was going better than expected, as Lorri had purchased a car and was driving me around to whoever responded to my classified ad in the newspaper, advertising the service of reincarnating old junker pianos back to life.

The idea of catching a baby, supporting and massaging Lorri's body, and offering security was going to be a breeze in comparison. "Sure thing! That would be the best thing for all three of us!" I responded, imagining a little baby slipping into my hands, with no doctor, nurse, or other busybody pushing me out of the way seemingly believing that obstetrics "experts" roamed the earth before the first child was born lest the child could not be born without their presence; carting away the fragile newborn, only to return sometime later with the baby, casting doubt on the fact that this one is really the one Lorri had. Lorri expected no other answer from me, and I did not flinch at the responsibility. Lorri continued, "It really is a private affair anyhow. I mean, there was no one here when we made this baby, so there is no reason to have it any different when it is born."

We discussed it some more over the next days, ironing out the details. Lorri continued to see Jane, but neither of us shared the intentions with her. That could be troublesome if the medical community got wind of this one. Lorri mentioned that her mother had seven of her brothers and sisters at home too, but now times have changed. Childbirth was a business. It seemed that it was sometimes deliberately complicated by the often unwarranted interventions of the medical society. Moreover, the mother's body was impaired by her nervousness from functioning properly when among strangers. In the animal domain, an animal that is in the birthing process will stop having contractions if it senses imminent danger, allowing it a chance to escape to a safer environment to bear the young ones. It only made sense that it would be the same with people, this hypothesis being reinforced as Lorri's contractions had altogether stopped when, back in the Kingston General Hospital, learning of the possibility of having to undergo surgery should Ryan not be birthed by 4:00 p.m. One day there was a knock on our door. There stood a representative from the local health unit, all ready for a discussion.

"I heard you two are planning not to go to the hospital for your next baby?" She sounded like someone's mother upon learning her children had planned to skip out of school.

It did not take long for me to conjure up an answer. Lorri was standing behind me, and I answered,

"Oh heavens, no. Where did you ever hear that? We are presently seeing fame, our doctor, and all will be as it should. Don't you worry." I turned to Lorri, who very clearly knew how to respond, as my voice indicated. "We are going to the hospital, right, Lorri?"

Lorri must have been nodding as she replied, "Yeah, we are going right to the hospital when the contractions start."

The health nurse left, and for a few minutes, making sure we were in total privacy, I said,

"How did she get wind of that?"

"I just happened to mention it to whom I thought was a friend," said Lorri, obviously feeling cheated by the break in confidence. "I was sure she'd keep her mouth shut."

"I think it is hilarious. I mean these busybodies with nothing better to do than to stick their noses into other's affairs. They do as if it is some crime to have a baby without first allowing the state to put their hands all over it and you as well."

Lorri added in a tone of disgust, "Yeah, I guess that means we are having a contraband baby!"

Through a connection, we came across a club that wrote journals about home birth experiences of other couples, called "The New Nativity," which was circulated in the United States. We subscribed and with great interest read the articles. The journal was filled with the most interesting recounts of home births, told by none other than the participants. The husband was always there to support the birthing woman, sometimes with a few close family members of their choice in attendance. The policy dictated in the journal, by its editors, was such that those pregnancies which were healthy and normal would be candidates for home births, and those with signs of impending trouble would be considered as a possible sickness and conducted in the hospital. It made perfect sense to both of us, as we had no intentions of having the baby at home while knowing it could be disastrous, any more than we would try to do an eye operation at home. But a normal birth, according to our research, was not a sickness, yet could be potentially inhibited from progressing normally when conducted by professionals who would treat it as such. Now we were more careful yet in keeping our plans to ourselves.

My dreams of seeing had subsided for several weeks leading up to the big day of the birth of the third child. Not a day went by without listening intently to the heartbeat of the child, verifying its location and its head-down position within Lorri which ensured an easy birth. When Lorri was relaxed, lying on her back on the sofa, I could feel the head of the baby nestled at her belt line, a small, hard ball which bobbed slightly to the pressure of my fingers. I could feel the child's movement with my hands resting gently on her. Lorri felt the baby kicking all the time, often threatening to upset her stomach, as the child's feet were just below her ribs.

On the first day of December, we left the dog and the kids behind, as we were only a couple of blocks from the grocery store. Lorri felt like she wanted a special food to eat, and together we went, Lorri feeling especially heavy that day. We picked out a couple of articles when Lorri announced to me she was having what felt like contractions, and we should head home. Upon returning home, we both laid down as Lorri wanted to rest. She was not her usual self that day.

Suddenly she sat up in bed, announcing, "I think my water broke!"

I pulled off the blankets, and sure enough, she was right. She continued to labor and complained a bit of the stress of many contractions in a row, all the while holding onto me. She suddenly announced, "I have to stand up!" upon which I did just that with her, as she could not do more than use her hands. I supported her in this position, leaning over to allow her to have a good grip and someone to lean on. She could not quite straighten her legs, and I thanked God I had a good back.

She changed her position again, using more gestures than words now, as the moment was becoming more overwhelming for her. She was breathing heavily, with a constant rhythm. She had one knee on the bed, her other foot still under her, while she held tightly onto my neck and shoulder. I heard her faintly whisper, "Get ready . . ." I had my left hand for her to assist her grip, while I monitored the progress of the birth with my right. I could literally hear the baby descend down the birth canal as she pushed. She gave a cry of pain as the baby forced itself past the scar in the uterus, left there by the malpractice of the previous birth. I thought I heard her whisper something about wanting an ambulance, but when I asked if that was what she wanted, mentioning she seemed to be pushing out the baby, she whispered, "Never mind . . ." as she pushed on.

Then I felt the head. It was unmistakable, and at that moment, Lorri insisted on lying down. I just about had her in that position when she suddenly changed her mind. In fact, she was almost in that position assumed in the "stirrup" setting used in hospitals, when she changed her mind.

"I have to stand up!" I wasted no time, noticing the haste in her voice. Now I had her in full standing position, and with her holding onto my back as I bent over, I had both hands free as the head of the baby fully exited. It was the most peculiar feeling, as the eyes of the baby were moving under my fingers, and the mouth was pursing its lips. Lorri whispered, at the same time as I noticed, "The cord's around the neck."

I ran one finger under it from where it came up out of Lorri, and it fell loosely downward. One push further and the slippery, wiggling baby squirmed into my hands. It was unbelievable. This little baby, still attached to Lorri by the rather long cord, was crying softly in my hands. As we never had an ultrasound while Lorri was pregnant, I quickly ran my hand over the child, noting no imperfections. Moreover, I noticed the baby was a girl. "A girl!" We both noted at the same time, although her voice was a little lower when crying than that of her sister. "Hi, little Leah!" We both welcomed her officially into the world, and I passed the jewel to her mother as she let her feed, just like a real baby back in the old times, off her mother.

From Leah's feeding, Lorri immediately had more powerful contractions. In the book *Silent Knife*, it was described as a necessary reaction to further contract the womb, allowing the placenta to detach and, at the same time, closing the tiny capillaries that fed it, preventing dangerous blood loss. When Danielle had been born in the hospital, she had been immediately carted away by the staff, not allowing for this procedure, and consequently Lorri lost a lot of blood, rendering her into an extremely fatigued state for many days afterward.

I skirted downstairs and began to boil the scissors and string I had prepared for cutting the cord. This would be the easiest of the procedure, as it was really not necessary to do. If one did not cut the cord, it would eventually fall off the navel of the baby anyhow. The popular notion that the blood of the baby would run back into the placenta was a mere myth.

Shortly after the birth, Lorri birthed the placenta, and we inspected it, as dictated in the texts, to ensure it was completely intact. There was no reason it wouldn't be if it had not been stressed.

I balled up the mess consisting of the soggy bedding and spread out new bedding for Lorri. She had lots of energy, moving around with greater agility now that the baby was out of her tummy. We chatted excitedly among ourselves, all the while admiring the new arrival.

I opened Danielle's bedroom door. We did not want the kids to be in the way during the birthing, but now it was time to make new introductions. Ryan was still a baby himself, but Danielle could already say a few words and understood some concepts. "Daddy!" announced Danielle, "baby . . . crying!"

She had noticed too. Lorri heard this and laughed out loud from the other room. Danielle entered the room and paused for a long moment, peering at the baby. She had no idea where it came from.

We never did go to the hospital with Leah. She had not been sick, rendering that idea unnecessary. Moreover, we were made aware of the fact, in reading the *New Nativity* journals, that considering those who are sick go first to the hospital, it is equally possible to catch a sickness in the hospital as a result of this phenomenon. When Lorri reflected on the events that had passed during the delivery of Leah, she noted, not to my surprise, "Do you remember when I said I wanted to lay down?" "Oh, yes," I replied, "I had been relieved to get some rest from holding you up, and then you weren't happy at all I had to pick you right back up."

"As soon as I got close to lying down," she explained, "I could feel my tailbone digging upwards against the baby. It was as plain as day there was no way she would have come out." I believed it, as Leah was a full pound heavier than Danielle had been and a good two inches longer.

Lorri was back to teaching music a couple days later. It was not so much for the money, but rather for the pleasure of showing off the baby. We did say we had the baby at home. No one said anything about that.

I composed an article for the *New Nativity* journal and sent it off. I avoided mentioning my blindness, as I was not proud of it.

We were busy as the winter dragged on. I often wished we were in Morristown, where the sidewalks were vibrant with life, the people welcoming, and where many other guide dog users roamed the streets, like me, in search of company. When I went out, people stepped aside, seemingly avoiding me, probably as a result of the public campaigns for guide dogs instilling attitudes such as:

"Don't interfere with a guide dog and its owner" or "Let the dog do its work—they're a team, so don't talk to them."

These attitudes may be practical but resulted in a very lonely existence. I remembered a book I had read about an invisible man, who was tortured by the fact that everyone would just look right through him, as if he weren't there anymore. I felt that way now. This was not the setting for longevity, I concluded. Yet Lorri liked it here, and we had just settled the family here as well. Things weren't going to change any time soon. The following spring, Ozzy suddenly was sick. Maybe just a flu, we thought. I took him out to the porch, giving him a place to lie down, and he suddenly died. The day before I had been walking with him, and now it was over. I had prepared myself for the eventuality of his death, as the fact remains that dogs do not live as long as humans, so attaching one's self to an animal as one would to a human was futile. Nonetheless, I was again without the freedom, or at least the bit the dog gave me. I called the "Seeing Eye" school.

"Sorry to hear that," replied the instructor, who had been the same one I had in the school. "That sometimes happens. We have an opening in about eight months coming up."

"Eight months!" I exclaimed. Having to wait until the next year was too much to expect from me. "I'll try to find another school that has a shorter waiting list."

"Good luck," said the instructor, and I needed it.

There were no other openings. Demand was outdoing supply in this department. Lorri read an ad in the paper to me that night. "Two-year-old German Shephard for sale," she announced, and then, as an afterthought, "Fifty dollars."

I thought about it. If I had not kept correcting and reminding Ozzy of what he was doing wrong during our walks, eventually he would become useless. When attending a guide dog school, the dogs are pretrained, but they do not work much for anyone but the trainer who had trained him. It was more a school of training the students how to train a dog than the matter of the dog being trained. Well, the fifty dollars was worth a try. I can always sell the dog again. I just wanted to make sure it was going to be friendly, given we now had three small children who'd always be in close contact with the dog.

I bought the dog. It did not take much to determine it was friendly and hospitable to everyone it met. A protective animal as a guide dog would be a disaster. After all, the idea of having the dog was to have access to public places, which were often crowded with people.

I strapped the harness on the dog, and with the white cane in my right hand, began to walk down a familiar part of the sidewalk in front of our house. I started to lead the way, keeping the dog close to my side, and scolding him when he stepped off the sidewalk. I made him sit at the curb, before crossing the street. The dog was quiet, much calmer than Ozzy. He was not sure where to go, and I made him sit on the other corner of the curb after crossing the street. We retraced our steps, this time hitting the curb at the right place. I petted and caressed the dog, which he enjoyed profusely. Upon retracing our steps to the original curb, he pulled more positively on the harness and proudly stepped up on the curb, turning his head toward me in full expectation of a reward. This dog, I said to myself, was going to be good.

Two weeks later, I was once again walking all through town with our new dog, whom I named Baby, as he sometimes acted like one, crying for his seemingly special rubber toy when we wouldn't give it to him right away. Baby was a short-haired Shepherd, whereas Ozzy had been a long-haired Shepherd. This made for some possible confusion if one wasn't aware of the fact that Baby was not Ozzy.

One day there was again a knock on our door. This time it was an animal control representative, who announced the latest,

"We had a complaint that you were starving your dog."

"How so?" I had no idea how anyone could look into my home to measure the rations I was feeding Baby.

"For the past year you had passed by this person's house, and he saw your dog well-filled out, and now, since the past two weeks or so, your dog appears extremely thin in comparison. In other words," she summed up, "you must be starving him."

I explained the situation. "I had just bought this dog, which is a short-haired dog whereas the old one was a long-haired one." She did not seem to believe it, as she did not relent on her position.

"Did you get him tested for worms?"

"No, why should I?" I had no idea what that would solve. Dogs with worms made it quite obvious that they had them. I knew Baby had been thin when I received him, as he had been in a kennel with other dogs, and the competition for grub must have been fierce.

"If you don't," the animal control officer threatened, "we'll have to take him away. I'll give you a week to get him tested, and I want the results in my office before then." At that, she marched off and got in her car.

I heard her drive off as I stood there in the doorway of my house. I did not have to guess as to what went on in her mind as she positioned herself behind the steering wheel of her car, the whole world in front of her for the taking. For me the world was pitch black, yet this lady thought it appropriate to yank out the little freedom the dog offered me. I felt a strange sensation inside, as if humanity had betrayed me. For the first time since acquiring Ozzy, I thought of the man I had seen as a child walking along Columbia Street in Kamloops with his guide dog. What absurdity it would have equated to had someone, with a perfect set of eyes, suggested taking the dog from that man for any reason at all. I turned to Lorri, who was taking it all in, defeated in the attempt to explain that we always had food available for Baby.

"What is lacking in her," I said, referring to the animal control officer "is that what distinguishes a human being from an animal."

The following day I asked for a test for worms, as well as a letter from the veterinarian confirming Baby was in a good state of health. The next stop was the animal control office. "There were no worms," I announced this in a manner bordering on impolite. "As well, this dog is a full fifteen pounds heavier than the previous one was." I handed over the papers. All she said was "OK" and turned back to her desk. I had troubles imagining her caring for children or doing any more than pretending to love a man. I got out of there, the words "you learn something new every day" ringing in my ear from something my father would have said many years ago. This, however, was something I did not want to learn.

Following the birth of Leah, it did not take long for the dreams of seeing to haunt me again. Just like the images of those who one had loved but are now gone, the world would reappear in full color and detail during the night. Unlike the claims of scientists who equate pictures seen in dreams as those stored in the memory, I did not recognize the majority of what I saw. There would be very little action involved, just the motion of traveling through the world, while taking it all in. Even though I seemed unconscious, I would still be aware of the fact that this would soon end, replaced by the relentless black of everyday existence. The dreams hurt, setting me back, but I did not want them to stop. When I awoke, I concluded that heaven and hell does exist, however, but not in the way the Bible dictated. One did not have to go elsewhere, after death, to find either of them—one could find them right here, during this life, on this Earth. The most confusing part about it was that my life seemed to be good—if any observer saw the wealth in my kids, the fact that we were just in our early twenties and had our own home, the fact that we had our businesses that thrived—there was no argument that I was doing well . . . but I wasn't there to see it—somehow, the darkness made it seem like I was attempting to watch the best of all movies but with a burnt-out light in the film projector.

Before long, we were anticipating another addition to our family, this time without the anxiety we felt when expecting Leah. We knew what would happen and how to ensure a trouble-free birth. We followed all the procedures of last time with regards to monitoring the pregnancy, which progressed normally. This was going to have to be another home birth.

I had by now finished fixing up the one-car garage that came with the house for a woodworking shop, as well as for repairing old pianos I purchased at bargain prices and resold after the repairs. Lorri enjoyed using the wood lathe for making crafts such as wooden canisters when she was not teaching music. It was during one of these afternoons she spent, leaning over the lathe table, when she came into the house with a worried expression in her voice.

"For some reason I feel a bunch of activity from the baby where it normally isn't." She was gesturing toward her lower abdominal area where one would find the baby's head. As Lorri had been carrying this baby for over seven months, there was no doubt it was fully developed.

"Just relax on the couch for a bit, and we'll see what's up," I suggested. We needed to keep calm, I figured. It was not unusual for her to get tired of feeling the baby move inside of her, especially if she wanted to concentrate on something.

She relaxed, and as I searched about her abdomen for the heartbeat with the fetal heart monitor, I found it in an unusual location—close to where Lorri's ribs began. Next we had to find the head. Using our fingertips, we both gently prodded around until we found it—around the eleven o'clock position.

"What's it doing here?" was Lorri's question, which was not really directed at anyone. "It must be the feet kicking that I am feeling in my lower abdomen."

"Do you suppose that is from working in the shop?" I wondered how this could happen so quickly. We did not really want to deal with a breech birth if at all possible. Nature's idea of having the head of the child come out first, according to the texts we read, was to ensure the lungs stay compressed and unable to breathe in the fluid as a result of the pressure from being in the birth canal until the child's mouth and nose was out and in the open air. In the *New Nativity*, there had been a home birth done breech, successfully, however, it would be worrisome. In *William's Obstetrics*, the procedures recommended for assisting in a breech birth resembled more a wrestling match than a birth.

"I suppose that when I leaned on the table, the baby's head may have become dislodged from between my pelvic bones, allowing it to turn," Lorri stated, remembering the relief she felt when allowing the baby to rest a little up on the bench instead of her supporting the entire weight.

I reasoned with her, grasping at logic which I hoped would prevail. "Well, if it is that easy to turn out of position, why not use the same method to turn it back?"

This only made sense. During Ryan's birth, which had led to a cesarean section, there had been absolutely no effort made by the "professionals" to turn the baby. I remember them looking at the shape of the baby inside Lorri using ultrasound and just standing there, helpless, despite all their education, rendered helpless by the fact, I figured, that they could not "see" as to what they were doing.

"I suppose it should be possible," replied Lorri, opening one of the childbirth texts. "I did not stress my abdomen very much at all, so it shouldn't take much to turn it back."

We reviewed some of the information while Lorri winced every time the baby kicked. What we knew for certain was that the baby could only be turned in one of the two directions it took to return it to the head-down position. Signs of the baby being stressed were an increase in the heartbeat. The most probable direction would be the one that took the least amount of turning. The most important risk in turning the baby would be the stressing of the umbilical cord that nourishes the baby. If it is pinched in any way, the manuals told us, the baby's heartbeat would increase rapidly, just like us trying to hold our breath.

"I'll be really gentle," I assured Lorri. "I should not have to push down at all—just use the weight of my hand." It was amazing how much Lorri trusted me, but then again, who else was there, I asked myself. She had fully given up on the medical professionals as they tried to muscle their way through childbirth, using forceps, cesarean sections, episiotomies, and other invasive methods of intervention, all the while imposing movement restrictions on the mother in the most illogical manner.

I was poised over her, listening attentively to the rhythm of the baby's heartbeat. Lorri held the receiver of the fetoscope, peering at her watch.

"Give me fifteen seconds," I requested, for the start and stop of this duration, while I listened to the heartbeat. I quadrupled my result, which gave the rate per minute. It was about 180, and that was average. I placed my left hand at the eleven thirty position on Lorri's abdomen, and my right at the six o'clock position, pushing up slightly in order to get the legs of the baby out of Lorri's pelvic area. I waited, letting the weight of my left hand do the turning. The hand slowly descended, and I could feel the little bulge the baby's head move downward. I nudged my hands counterclockwise after a minute and waited again. I knew the baby was moving because the heartbeat was no longer as loud, and Lorri had to reposition the receiver. I continued to move my hands counterclockwise, pausing a minute or more in between the repositioning, until finally my left hand was at the six thirty position, and my right near the three o'clock position. I could feel the head of the baby under my hand, now reluctant to movement. The heartbeat did not change.

The baby kicked, and Lorri announced, with triumph in her voice, "That's better! The feet are right where they should be!" Lorri had not complained of any discomfort during this procedure. I listened further to the heartbeat but noticed no difference from the usual.

"It looks like this baby has free travel between this position and the one he just came from," I pronounced, judging by the ease of movement it had between this position and the former, "and I figure it could be pushed out of position again."

"We'll have to check and make sure it is in the right position when I have the contractions," Lorri stated, obviously worried about the probability of a breech birth if this precaution was not taken.

"No problem moving the baby," I said in reply, "it was so easy, I could have had a beer while doing this, provided I had someone to hold the bottle for me."

Lorri's fingers ran over the scar on her abdomen, left there by the cesarean section performed during Ryan's birth. "I wonder why the doctors wouldn't have tried this when Ryan was turning." There was a hint of dismay in her voice.

"I don't have a clue," I said. But I did. The doctors were bewildered because they could not see what was going on inside of Lorri at the time of Ryan's birth. The ultrasound did not make a reliable enough image for them to work with, and they lacked the ability to make a picture of the clues provided by the heart monitor and the feelings in their fingers. I, on the other hand, formed an instantaneous and accurate image of the baby the minute I laid my hands upon Lorri's abdomen. This method of childbirth, if applied to the majority of mothers who had healthy pregnancies, could spare them from so much misery and pain. Yet, I did not want to give any merit to the loss of my eyesight. By no means should the loss of eyesight be attributed to anything positive. It only constitutes of torture and anguish. Those specialized trades one learns from being in the dark can be learned equally effectively by those who can see if they only had the will to temporarily close their eyes in order to learn. That would be similar to learning a second language by prohibiting the use of any maternal languages during class time. Therefore, I concluded, the only problem is the lack of will. No one wants to spend even a few minutes a day in the world of a blind person. "No one would ever believe us," I said to Lorri, who only nodded in agreement.

The next two months passed in anticipation of the next birth. It was a bit like waiting for Christmas. Surely, we knew it would be a baby, but it would still be unique. The baby kept turning breech, and we kept turning it back. The trick was, as we had agreed, to make sure it would be head-down just before delivery. That would have to be verified between contractions, as that is the only time Lorri's stomach muscles would be relaxed enough for me to get a picture of the baby with my hands.

Kyle's birth was serene and beautiful, as was Leah's, happening right on a hot summer afternoon. His head came out first, as expected, and his body followed, dropping into my awaiting hands. This time, Danielle was old enough to understand that another baby would join us soon, giving us someone to share the new arrival with.

Kyle started to grow, as did the others, and I, once again, craved the sight of my family, the world, and all that there is to be seen. Leah was walking now, and Kyle would soon be doing the same. I was walking in town with Danielle now. She was able to follow me, at four years old, if I made sure she did not daydream during the wait for the lights at the intersections. I would talk to her all the way through town just to make sure she was still following me. She was great company, as she talked a few words here and there in reply, mainly in reference to what she saw. This was a welcome change as, in spite of all I tried to convey to the people in the street, they still were convinced that I should remain "alone with my dog." Maybe, I hoped, the kids, upon growing older, would be even better company.

In 1989, when we were expecting another child, Lorri indicated she would want to move somewhat out of town, as our place was getting too crowded. It wasn't so much the house, but rather the land, which was tiny at best. The kids had nowhere to go but in the street, which was becoming busier with automobile traffic with each new land development. I agreed, knowing all the while that my personal mobility, or the little I had, would be sacrificed. Personally, for me, it could be a step backward. For everyone else, it did the opposite. The kids had more room to play, and Lorri attracted a new roster of music students while being able to retain most of those from the previous location, as we only moved a few kilometers. Unlike when we had first contemplated buying our first home in Napanee, this time I had no worries about all the renovations that the old farmhouse and outbuilding would need—that part was now easy to do as I somehow felt that very clear pictures of my work projects, such as the doorframes and walls for repair—fixed a perfect image in my head for me to work with. Even nailing with a hammer was now easy, a feat I once figured impossible to do without eyesight.

Since arriving to the farm we bought, my dog Baby was never again used as a guide. I thought I'd use him to walk the five kilometers into town when I needed something, but I never ended up doing this as my life just became busier with the property. There was, despite my original fears of losing out from the move, a tradeoff for me in being out in the countryside. Behind the house, spanning for miles was a wilderness that included fields, hardwood and coniferous forests, and swamps which belonged partially to us and in most to the surrounding neighborhood, but which stood virtually uninhabited. The bush was filled with wildlife, bringing back memories of when my father and I would go on hunting expeditions. I had hiked many times as a boy and a young man while being sighted, and once in the bush, the only use for one's eyesight was to appreciate the nature. All the trees and landmarks generally looked alike, rendering useless the sense of sight to retrace one's steps. One would be forced to use the location of the sun in respect to the time of day, the direction of the wind, third-dimension landmarks such as the general direction of a slope, and audio clues to find one's way. Having purchased a simple braille compass, and knowing that the major road cut westwards south of our house, I had no qualms about exploring the woods. The most remarkable part of these excursions was that I had no restrictions on me as to what I could touch here. I had marked the main path traversing our property with a wire strung on posts, and if any time I desired to "see" what was where, I could use a stick or just my hands to explore the area. I would never have had this opportunity in town. For four years, I walked the sidewalks, knowing by heart every street in Napanee, but never was I allowed to just go on someone's property and touch a tree or a flowerbed or the side of a house. That would not conform to expected human behavior. In the world of humans, one only touches that what does not belong to you with the eyes. One can look at anything that is visible, whether it is a person, place, or thing, but to touch it is prohibited. Nature, on the other hand, doesn't mind to be touched.

It was shortly after buying the farm that I heard news on the national radio station that sounded like the best music heard in a long time. I was in the process of preparing a meal, Lorri was teaching piano, and I had the radio on a low-volume setting on the kitchen counter. I listened intently.

" . . . the institution dedicated to this research has been working with volunteers for several years on this project, which promises to help the profoundly blind. The engineers have described the resulting sight to be similar to that seen on sports scoreboards, in which individual lightbulbs are used to display each of the segments of the image. The resulting crude image will not be adequate for driving a car; however, it promises to address the majority of patients who were blinded as a result of extreme retinal trauma." My ear was practically on the radio speaker when the last sentence escaped, before the subject was changed by the radio announcer. "The scientists believe it will take about seven more years to perfect this technology prior to distribution to the public."

Seven years, I thought it over. It was 1990, and that would mean in 1997 all should be better. I wondered how much it would cost, and if I'd ever be able to get in. Surely there'd be millions of people standing in line. But I had to get this—there was no other choice now. My blindness was now transformed from a once permanent situation to a temporary one—one I just had to bear a few years longer until life would, once again, return to what it should be.

CHAPTER 4

Hope Once Again

We all sat around the kitchen table that night, testing out a new meal I had prepared. Cooking was an old routine for me now, as I had practiced and perfected the trade over the course of a few years, ever since Danielle was two months old. She was six now, and along with her sister Leah, brother Ryan and Kyle, who was still in his high chair, they made all the usual noises associated with eating around the kitchen table at the old farmhouse.

"I heard something interesting on the radio today," I began, not raising my stare from the plate in front of me. I seldom looked up at the family, as when I heard them around me, without looking, I felt they were just another normal family. It was when I tried to look at them that I was in for the disappointment, as they were always completely invisible to me. How much I craved to see them before they all grew up!

"What's that?" asked Lorri in a tired voice. She was not only teaching music during the day, but also studying music, which consisted of hours of daily practice, in order to further her education.

"This place in the States claims to have ready in about seven years a crude form of artificial vision for people who lost function of their eyes," I announced, not daring to explore the prospects that may bring to us.

"Wow . . ." was all Lorri could say after a moment of contemplation.

"The vision is supposed to be about like that seen on those sports scoreboards which have all those lightbulbs lighting up the scores and the names of the winning teams." I did not find it hard to imagine what things looked like, using hundreds of little lights to make a picture.

Lorri reflected upon something she had seen. "That is pretty good vision. The numbers and letters are quite easy to read. Wow! Seven years, you said?"

"Yeah," I replied, thinking of the 2,500-odd mornings I would still have to get up in the dark. "Danielle would be a teenager, and the youngest would be seven. That still would not be too young to do fatherly things with them, like the other dads can do." That was one of my dreams—to do with my kids what other people's dads can do with theirs.

"Wow . . ." said Lorri again, obviously thinking about the possibilities. I imagine she was tired of having a blind husband too. Her friends had the security of their man showing up out of nowhere when they got into trouble, just to help them out. The husband would share the responsibility of going to the parent-teacher interviews, graduations, and perhaps taking the kids to the doctor's when they got sick. But here, it was always her who did these things, even when buying groceries, paying bills, no matter what needed to be done. She had the car. Now that we were out in the countryside, she had no help. I did not like that one bit either. Out here, without a car, a person was nothing.

"What do you think it will cost?" was her next question. This operation would be offered, more than likely, in the United States, and it wouldn't be for free.

"I figure, based on the price of the Boston clinic that we had been interested in taking," I was dating back to the options of having surgery on my left eye when we were still in Sydenham, "it would be about $25,000 US."

"We'll have to save some up" was Lorri's reply. Money was not a commodity which was in abundant supply now that we had not only a family, but with me out of the land surveying picture, my contributions were not as pronounced. That, too, was hard on my ego.

"It would almost be worth just selling this place for it," I said, calculating the advantages. It was my turn to explore the possibilities, a dangerous move. "I could recover the dough in no time. Just remember how quickly we had saved money when we were first together. At that time, we did not even try!"

We had all sorts of hopes from here on up. Dormant thoughts, like those of skiing downhill on Azu Mountain, biking together in the Rocky Mountains, flying an airplane over the vast expanse of nature in Northern British Columbia, all came back to me in an instant. Now we would include the children. That conjured up an image of a child learning to walk, teetering through its first steps with that grand expression of astonishment and surprise upon its face.

"You'll have to have one more for me to see grow up," I said this slyly to Lorri, who must have been reading my mind, as her response came instantaneously.

"Only if you are the one who has him!" was her reply, with a hint of mirth in her voice. I knew she would, just one last time, not only for me, but for her to have to share with me from beginning to end.

The dreams started up again in earnest. Gone were any fragile barriers I may have set up over the course of the last eight years of blindness, protecting me from the thoughts of seeing. One cannot look for a new spouse if he believes the one he loves is still alive, looking for him. This was a national news radio station I was listening to, giving it full credibility. It was not a scam, nor an operation which may or may not work. It had to work. It was designed for people who had no eyes left.

Every night I was on my old motorbike, peering at all that the world had to offer. When approaching the end of the dream, I had no fear. Soon, soon I will be able to see. The past eight years of my life were almost like they had never existed. When I thought of what all happened in my life between the ages of twelve and twenty, the amount of pictures and steps of progression would take novels to write. But when thinking, in retrospect, of what happened since the loss of my sight, it seemed to me that there was very little in my memory worth remembering that made sense. There were no pictures. And the sounds, like those made by the kids when small, were long since forgotten. There was no doubt that my mind functioned on the pictures seen. I couldn't wait for that to change. I had to have something to show for this life.

In seven years, I reasoned, I would have been blind for fifteen years. Even the criminals in this country who are condemned to life imprisonment are eligible for parole after a third of their sentence is served. Maybe I am not on my best behavior. Whatever the case is, it will take seven more years, and then I had better be ready. I will have a lot of catching up to do once I finished doing time. Lord only knows what the crime was that I had committed.

I buried myself in the task of farming. Never having done this before, I dealt not only with the difficulty of doing this in the dark, but also with the problems associated daily with the animals, fencing, building upkeep, and machinery breakdowns. I developed a crude method of driving a tractor, which allowed me to traverse the fields in a grid-like pattern, allowing me to cover the land while planting or harvesting the crops. I had little idea of what I was doing, but there was room to learn. Once things were set up, which I was able to do on my own, I was free to deal with that what all other farmers deal with. With bells tied to the collars of the cows and a radio playing quietly in the barn, I had no more problem in rounding up the animals at night than did the others. As this was not a job I would have engaged in if I could see, the fact that I was suffering from a disability mattered little in this case. Several years ago, I remembered cruising along the deserted country highways with my motorbike, watching in wonder at the men and women slaving in the fields, seemingly wasting the beautiful summer's day in doing a job that appeared entirely unrewarding. "Why would anyone," I mused to myself, "waste such a nice summer doing that, sweating and cursing in the fields, when they could be roaring around on a bike having a ball like I was?" Little did I suspect, at that time in my life, that if everyone had done that, we would have nothing to eat; I guessed it was time to grow up . . .

The farming task not only gave me a sense of purpose and allowed me to apply my hillbilly countryside upbringing, but it gave me something to look forward to doing once I had my sight back. Thus, as I traversed the fields using my strung guide wires on posts to help me keep the tractor on line, I played with the future possibility of removing the wires and driving like everyone else—just around in circles and thus covering the field without having to turn around after every pass. That would save so much time, and I could then keep up to my neighbors.

We heard nothing more of the artificial eye for quite some time. I talked to my friend Alden Meier, who was always up to date on the new software and hardware packages available in the monopoly of the computer domain. Surely he would know if something came out. He promised me he would be on the lookout for any such development if it did arise. I also decided to call my friend John Warren, the man who first met me after my loss of sight, posing for role model, in my hospital room. I had lost his number, and so I called one of his friends, the rehab instructor from the CNIB—Armando.

"Hey, there, Armando," I began, as I often talked with him about any new technologies out there for the blind. "Would you have John's number handy?"

Armando paused, and then replied soberly, "He died last year." I did not know what to say. He would have been in his mid-forties and blind for about eighteen years or so. It was so unexpected, my thoughts went into a jumble. John, so cool about having lost his sight, so seemingly recovered and content, with everything under control. But then I remembered the time he phoned me, telling me of how he was due for an operation to try to make him see again. Maybe that is what did him in. Once the barriers are removed, the barriers that you set to protect yourself from grief, there had better be on the other side what you expected to catch your fall. If not, you'll keep going down. But now it was over for him. When one dies, all is equal. There is no such thing as a disabled dead man. I felt a moment of envy for John when thinking about this, just like I had when first encountering him in the hospital—the John with everything under control while I had suffered miserably in the hospital bed, wondering how dismal the future was that faced me.

Time moved on quickly as I had buried myself further in work, as well as in doing some courses through a correspondence school. Despite my total lack of interest in computer technology for the blind at the time, Dave McIntyre made me aware of it upon the loss of my second eye; the talking computer I purchased in 1992 was a good investment, allowing me to read via scanner and voice output for the text on the computer. Every day I listened to the CBC news, the radio interviews, the scientific presentations, with no further news about artificial vision. Occasionally, a friend would call up with the news I have since learned to touch with only the little part of my little finger in jumping to any conclusions.

"I saw on TV that there are blind people now seeing!" would be the typical start of such a conversation. Naturally, they expected an enthusiastic reply from me. Most people were so badly educated in the field of vision and eyesight that they figured if there was a blind guy on TV that could now see, it would be the solution for me too. In all cases, the news was about the idea of new technology applied in resolving cataracts in either the lens or the cornea. None of that would do me any good, I would try to explain, but that would fall onto deaf ears. I hoped they would not get the impression that being blind no longer bothered me, as that would be entirely false.

The year 1993 marked a decade since that fateful day when my second eye was taken by the part of the clutch from the old snowmobile. Ten years once meant to me the ultimate time needed to be passed in order to overcome the most troublesome of problems in one's life. I had reasoned that practically any problem, no matter how severe at a given moment in one's life, would surely be resolved if given ten years to either resolve itself, or the effects of it would simply disappear. But now I knew different; some things just don't go away, no matter how much time is given. I thought of Dr. Michael Shey and decided to give him a phone call, hoping he may know of any new advances in eye technology which could help me.

Dr. Shey's office quickly scheduled an appointment for me to see him later that fall. I tagged along with a friend, who drove me the three hundred-kilometer distance to Toronto. The eye clinic seemed to be the same by what I could remember of the layout as I waited for Dr. Shey, now sounding older, talking to other patients. He came to me, briefly looked at the remains of my retina, talking medical language to whom I suspected as an intern and giving the intern the opportunity to look into my eyes as well. What Dr. Shey discussed with him didn't seem like it made for good news. Finally, he turned to me.

"Jens, you can travel around the world as often as you like, but you will not see again." He was blunt, too blunt, with his approach as he continued, "You just have to accept that your life will be spent in blindness, and you'll have to make the best of it."

I never visited the St. Michael's eye clinic again.

The seventh year since initially hearing of the miracle invention, 1997, came and went. John Hopkins University in Utah was launching a campaign regarding their research in eye technology, and once again, I received all the phone calls. But nothing from Alden, who had the knowledge in eye biology, to assess what would possibly apply to me. Another institute in the United States, as well as a foreign one, had launched publicity regarding their research in retinal chip implants. Even a blind pop star was interviewed on TV for the possibility of seeing again using one of these systems. My neighbor telephoned me, all excited, and once again ripped away what remained of my barrier that separated my life from the harsh reality of being blind.

"There is someone, a celebrity, I think," she began, "who is going to be interviewed about seeing again using an electronic eye. You should come over and watch this on my TV." We had no TV, as it would just annoy me too much to have the sound without the picture. I did not need any more stress like that. I could never understand some of the blind friends I had who would seriously say they were appreciating television, depending entirely on the sound track of the television just left too many blank spaces in the program for me.

"Do you have any other details?" I asked the neighbor, who did not.

"It's an electronic eye, that's all I know. Probably something that would help you." The neighbor was offering to help, and I just had to go, as it could have been just what they had been talking about in the radio broadcast in 1990.

But it was not that at all. It was all about a retinal implant, which helped only those who still had an intact retina, with only the top layer of the nine that constitutes the retina destroyed. Moreover, it would take several years of laboratory tests to get into the commercial trial stage. I went home with my hopes back on the drawing board. I still won't have the key to get out of this prison.

I had no idea how much longer I could wait this out. "Perhaps," I mused, "I would not have been so anxious to see if the reports did not always get thrown at me every time there was hope." Hope can be good, but also destructive. It was becoming just as hard to adapt to this situation if every time I made a bit of progress in distancing myself from the reality, someone came up and blurted out: "You should see what I saw on TV today!"—still another scientific breakthrough! Yet, I could not ignore it. These were, after all, well-educated people attracting the attention of some very prestigious news agencies, who would not risk reporting on false news. This had to be real, and it had to be close. "But how much longer do I have?" I would think.

By now Danielle was a teenager and tried, as most adolescents, to distance herself from the proceedings of the family. Our youngest, Aaron, was now two, learned to walk already, and was the last Lorri would agree to carry. I couldn't blame her, as we were both getting older. The worst was that we seemed to have put everything on hold, that is, our personal lives, waiting for the big event when everything would start up just as we had left it in 1983. The stress was evident in our relationship, as we resembled two people pretending to walk down a path which didn't really exist.

The children, however, grew and prospered. They were all healthy and as happy as any other child in the district. According to them, there was nothing at all wrong with either Lorri or me. I was just as much Dad as Lorri was Mom. I belonged just as much the way I was as Lorri belonged as she did. The children accepted it and never once questioned it. In fact, they did not even know how I had lost my sight and did not seem to care. One day, about three years later, our neighbor had offered to give Ryan, who was then fifteen years old, an old snowmobile they had laying around for him to fix up. Most parents would have suggested he wear a helmet and watch his speed once it gets going, but not I.

"I don't really appreciate Ryan being offered that snowmobile," I had said to my neighbor, to whom I must have appeared as a crusty old man who deliberately wanted to be difficult for no reason at all. "I lost my second eye from a piece of metal flying out of one of those things."

My neighbor paused, searching for words, and remarked, "What would be the chance of that ever happening to Ryan?" Ryan, being old enough to understand the context of the conversation, stood at the side, seemingly retranslating my anxiety to a negative response he did not want to hear. To him, all that mattered was that the neighbor would succeed in convincing me he would be fine, just for the purpose of acquiring the machine. By no means was the possibility of him losing an eye on his mind.

That day the snowmobile did not get delivered to our house; however, within a year Ryan had one anyhow. Lorri had no objections, and Ryan did not care. As I heard the motor revving up on the thing, parked at the barn with Ryan at the controls, I shuddered, trying my best to blot out the sound. The horror of the last encounter I had with such an invention was as fresh to me as if it had happened yesterday. Yet, no one else was affected by it. Lorri was truly healing from the experience. Somehow, I had been left behind.

I was continuing to tune and repair pianos for a living, even though I had started up a firewood processing business. One of my regular customers for piano work, a middle-aged man by the name of Carmen, took special interest in my search for sight recovery, as he had lost the function of one of his eyes, virtually overnight, as a result of glaucoma.

"I can't believe it," he was saying one day when he was helping me repair my ancient farm machinery, "I awoke a few days ago, and my eye was right out of commission. I get the other one checked every five days at the eye doctor's in Kingston just to make sure the same thing does not happen to that one."

"How are you doing with one eye?" I inquired, suspecting I knew the answer.

"I am doing all right," he recounted, "I am still able to drive. There is really nothing that changed, except that I am really worried."

Then he added, as a kind of afterthought. "I've been thinking about you a lot lately."

Carmen was a nice guy, even though when I first met him, he was a sort of worrywart toward me, being concerned about me hurting myself with every move I made. Now, however, he did not seem so worried. He seemed to have taken on an interest in my life like never before. I did not have to guess what he was preparing himself for.

I wondered what I could say to him. I felt like blurting out that I hoped, just for his own good, that he would sooner die than be subject to a life of total blindness. I said instead, "I sure hope your other eye outlasts you." That seemed like a gentle way of saying it. Perhaps he was more interested in hearing me say that blindness was not a big deal, or that one gets so accustomed to it that it doesn't mean anything anymore after a couple of years. I could not do this as I am a terrible liar.

In 1999, I decided to do something fun with the money I had set aside all these years to see again, as it looked like it just wasn't going to happen. Following the ice storm which had torn down all the electrical lines in the area for miles and leaving most of Eastern Ontario and Western Quebec without power, I decided to invest in a sort of electrical power "certainty" with a new concept I had often dreamed of as a child but never had the funds to do. I was in the store in Kingston called "Renewable Energy of Plum Hollow" where mainly woodstoves and other gadgets for natural energy conversion were sold, when I was made aware of a huge solar panel on display. It put out seventy-five watts in bright sunlight, so I asked the store owner, Chuck, what it would take to get right off the electrical grid for my household.

"It's not possible to get off the grid with just solar panels." Chuck was warning me not to think that it was so easy. "Just look at all you are using and think that if you now bought a few of these panels, you would be able to get off the grid—that's a lot of power you need."

I thought about it back home. The biggest panel available at the time was hundred watts, of which only an average of 350 watt hours per day was possible to get in this region of Ontario, thanks to the cloudy days along with those with sunshine. So, I figured that if I had enough of them, and cut down the power consumption through more energy-efficient devices, it may work. What would be a shortfall, I'd use a generator for.

The experiment ended up working. I had built a windmill as well which later looked like it may fall to pieces in a strong windstorm, strewing pieces on top of my treasured panels, so I bought a couple of small turbines as well. After investing in sixteen of the hundred-watt panels and a couple of small wind turbines, I built a structure to hold all of them, along with a couple dozen batteries and other necessary components—and behold, our house was on solar and wind power only.

The new solar system was the talk of the town—even the children's elementary school asked for tours for the student's benefit. The *Napanee Weekly Guide* took some pictures and made an interview, and to top it off, when we needed a woodstove installed the following spring, the same company who sold me the products and claimed my experiment wouldn't work, had to use my same system in order to run their power tools for the installation of the woodstove. However successful the experiment proved, I still could not see the lights when I turned them on to show off the system.

Then, one evening in late spring of the year 2000, the telephone rang. It was Alden, my friend from grade school, with whom I used to goof off, and later in 1983 when passing through Edmonton on our way to Ontario, I spent the day target shooting with at the Edmonton shooting range.

"Jens, I found something on the Internet," he stated in a matter-of-fact manner, yet with a hint of it being tentative in his voice nonetheless. "The Web site is called 'WWW.artificialvision.com.'"

"Really . . ." I had replied, not needing to ask what it was all about, considering the self-explanatory nature of the Web site name.

"It comprises of a method of restoring vision to those who are profoundly blind and have no function of the eyes." Alden began to skim through the site, talking all the while on the telephone. "An array of sixty-eight surface electrodes is implanted onto the surface of the visual cortex, and when any one of these electrodes is given a current, they produce a small dot of light to appear in the visual field of the patient, its location being dictated by its corresponding electrode location upon the surface of the brain."

I listened intently. Alden knew computers, electricity, and understood enough of the function of the eye that whatever he said was not based on false assumptions. Moreover, he knew me from when I could see. He was one of the last two people who really knew me. The other was Steve Demarni, a man who had grown up with me and had been, and still was, acquainted with Alden. Lorri, unfortunately, I began to think, perhaps knew me as a sighted man for such a short time in her life that I noticed she was starting to forget who I really was.

Alden had more to say.

"Jens, they are looking for patients to try their new commercial system in which they want to implant two of such arrays. They want to do this early next year."

This was it. I couldn't believe my ears for a minute. It had been over seventeen years now since I saw the last time. What would all be involved for me to be accepted? How long would it take for me to be in there? I wasn't even worried about the cost. I would find the money.

"This sounds too good to be true!" I had to mention it to Alden, who replied, "It is a New York-based company. Right on

Broadway! It is led by Dr. Dobelle and his team of engineers and surgeons. It mentions here there are about three hundred people involved, including scientists, surgeons, optometrists, you name it. I even did some research on that William Dobelle character. It seems he is quite a brilliant guy."

Brilliant, that must be the word for him. I imagined him, dressed in scrubs, wearing small, round spectacles, looking over the shoulders of all the staff in his research and development department, giving out orders, nodding his approval while the smartly dressed engineers continued diligently with their tasks. Making the blind see was William's job. "That is as close to divine intervention as one could find on this planet," I thought. Now it was Bill's turn. It crossed my mind for a fleeting moment what had been mentioned in the Good Book, how the year of 2000 would offer great revelations, one of them being that "the blind would see." Is that coincidence?

"I've got to have this," I said to Alden, who only agreed. "This just makes too much sense. It is not a shot at an idea that may or may not work."

Just to substantiate my conclusions, Alden replied, quoting from the Web site: "It says in here that a few volunteers have already been tested with this system, some of them having this system since 1978 installed in their heads. They are still alive, so that is good news!" He had to add that.

I thanked Alden, and then set about the task of worrying about the possibilities of getting in. Hopefully, I thought, there would be a price attached, and thus not every blind person, some of them very poor, would not take my place, making the waiting list last to the end of my life. There must be millions of blind people in the world, and the chances of getting in would be next to none. He had said "some patients" in the write-up Alden had read from, insinuating perhaps a dozen or so. This was an international Web site, and considering the sheer number of blind people in Canada alone, now topping 120,000 registered with the Canadian National Institute for the Blind, what would be the chances of getting in? My protective barriers were gone now. All I could do was think of everything around me, the children's faces, the house, the trees, the world, displayed in the sports-scoreboard style portrayal. Man, that has got to be beautiful!

The next day, Lorri went over to the neighbor's house, who had the Internet hookup, to find the Web site and print it off for me. Yes, it was ten years, not the seven years as expected after hearing of the first initial report in 1990 on CBC. This must have been the same company. Lorri had a lot of respect for Alden's judgment and immediately searched the details of the information. Not surprisingly, she was as excited about it as I was. For me, that was a good sign. She hadn't forgotten what life had been like when I could see after all.

She entered the house, holding the papers of printed material, all the while reporting, "There are some awesome pictures in here! There is one picture here where the volunteer is looking at an electrical outlet!"

I was curious as to the acuity of this apparatus. "Can you actually see where the prongs enter the wall?" I remembered clearly how an electrical outlet had looked when I was sighted, and this was a good source of reference, as they had not changed, unlike everything else, since the last time I could see.

"Yes, I can!" announced Lorri, obviously assessing the potential of the vision offered by this device. I wondered how that could be, considering there were only sixty-eight electrodes in the array of electrodes. But then again, I reminded myself, this is a *doctor* who is writing this. It would have to be accurate.

"Well, let's have it." I had to hear what it all said. "I'll scan it later and read it again with my computer. You may as well read it to me first."

Lorri started to read:

State-of-the-Art

ASAIO Journal 2000

Artificial Vision for the Blind by Connecting a Television Camera to the Visual Cortex

Wm. H. Dobelle

Blindness is more feared by the public than any ailment, with the exception of cancer and AIDS. We report the development of the first visual prosthesis providing useful "artificial vision" to a blind volunteer by connecting a digital video camera, computer, and associated electronics to the visual cortex of his brain. This device has been the objective of a development effort begun by our group in 1968 and represents realization of the prediction of an artificial vision system made by Benjamin Franklin in his report on the "kite and key" experiment, with which he discovered electricity in 1751.* ASAIO Journal 2000; 46:3–9.

This new visual prosthesis produces black-and-white display of visual cortex "phosphenes" analogous to the images projected on the lightbulb arrays of some sports stadium scoreboards. The system was primarily designed to promote independent mobility, not reading. We have also provided a battery powered, electronic interface that is radio frequency (RF) isolated from line currents for safety. This interface can replace the camera, permitting the volunteer to directly watch television and use a computer, including access to the Internet.

Because of their potential importance for education, and to help integrate blind people into the workforce, such television computer and Internet capabilities may prove even more valuable in the future than independent mobility. In addition, the image from the camera or interface and an overlaid simulated real-time display of the phosphene image seen by the volunteer can be rebroadcast from the system over an RF link to a remote videotape recorder and viewing screen. This allows real-time monitoring, as well as post-trial analysis, by the experimental team.

The television camera, which is built into a pair of sunglasses, is shown in figure 1; the prosthesis, worn by the blind volunteer is pictured in figure 2, and the complete system is described schematically in figure 3, including both the television/computer/ Internet interface and the remote video screen NCR monitor, neither of which are shown in figure 2.

These efforts were inspired by a seminal paper published by Giles Brindley's group in 1968.[1] Our first human experiments

From the Institute Dobelle AG, Zurich, Switzerland, and the Dobelle Institute Inc. at the Columbia-Presbyterian Medical Center, New York, NY.

Submitted for consideration September 1999; accepted for publication in revised form November 1999.

Reprint requests: Dr. Wm. H. Dobelle, New York, NY in 1970–72[2] involved cortical stimulation of thirty-seven sighted volunteers who were undergoing surgery on their occipital lobe under local anesthesia to remove tumors and other lesions. In 1972–73, we then stimulated the visual cortex of three blind volunteers who were temporarily implanted for a few days with electrode arrays passed through a Penrose drain.[3] Our subsequent experiments have involved four blind volunteers implanted with permanent electrode arrays using percutaneous connecting pedestals. Two volunteers were initially planted in 1974.[4] One array was removed three months after surgery and the second after fourteen years.[†] The first five volunteers were operated on at the University of Western Ontario in London, Canada. Two additional blind volunteers, including the subject of this article, were implanted in 1978 at the Columbia-Presbyterian Medical Center in New York City.[6] They have both retained their implants for more than twenty years without infection or other problems.

[*] From Watson W: An account of Mr. Benjamin Franklin's treatise, lately published, entitled Experiments and Observations on electricity, made at Philadelphia in America. Philos Trans R Soc London 47: 202–211.

[†] The first implant was removed, as planned, after three months. The second volunteer agreed to continue participation but his implant was removed due to a blood borne infection that did not originate with the implant.

The Volunteer and Implant

The sixty-two-year-old subject of this article traumatically lost vision in one eye at age twenty-two and was totally blinded at age thirty-six by a second trauma. He was continuously employed, before and after losing his sight, as an administrator by the State of New York. He retired in 1997 after thirty-two years of service. The electrode array was implanted in 1978 when he was forty-one years old. Because of discomfort during surgery caused by mechanical impingement of the teflon electrode matrix on the volunteer's falx and tentorium, his electrode array is posterior to the position of the arrays implanted in our six other blind volunteers. We have been using this implanted pedestal and intracranial electrode array to experimentally stimulate the visual cortex, on the mesial surface of the right occipital lobe, for more than twenty years. However, the fifth generation external electronics package and software are entirely new, taking advantage of cutting edge technology that has only recently become available. An X-ray of the implanted visual cortex electrode array is shown in figure 4, and the numbered electrode layout is detailed in figure 5.

A platinum foil ground plane is perforated with a hexagonal array of 5 mm diameter holes on 3 mm centers, and the flat platinum electrodes centered in each hole are 1 mm in diameter. This ground plane keeps all current beneath the dura. This eliminates discomfort due to dural excitation when stimulating some single electrodes (such as number 19) and when other arrays of electrodes are stimulated simultaneously. The ground plane also eliminates most phosphene interactions[3] when multiple electrodes are stimulated simultaneously and provides an additional measure of electrical safety that is not possible when stimulating between cortical electrodes and a ground plane outside the skull. Each electrode is connected by a separate teflon insulated wire to a connector contained in a carbon percutaneous pedestal. Fabrication techniques for these electrodes[6] and pedestals[7] have been previously described. The original surgery in 1978 was performed under local anesthesia, and implants in future patients can probably be performed on an outpatient basis by most neurosurgeons.

Phosphenes and their Map in the Visual Field

When stimulated, each electrode produces —one to four closely spaced phosphenes. Each phosphene in a cluster ranges up to the diameter of a pencil at arm's length. Neighboring phosphenes in each cluster are generally too close to the adjacent phosphenes for another phosphene to be located between them. These "multiples" are unlike the phosphenes described by our other blind volunteers, or those reported by Brindley's volunteers.[1] They may be due to the use of a ground plane array, although we have used a similar ground plane array in one temporarily implanted blind volunteer without producing multiple phosphenes. Other possible causes for these multiples include the fact that the volunteer lost vision in his two eyes at different times or that we may be stimulating visual association cortex (areas 18 and 19) rather than primary visual cortex (area 17).

All phosphenes flicker at a rate that seems unrelated to the pulse, repetition frequency, or any other parameter of stimulation, or to cardiac pulse, breathing rate, or other physiologic function.

Using a variety of computer and manual mapping techniques, we determined that the phosphene map occupies an area roughly eight inches in height and three inches wide, at arm's length. The map and the parameters for stimulation both appear to be stable over the last two decades. The map of some of the phosphenes in this volunteer's visual space is shown in figure 6, and is more nearly a vertical line than the larger, more two-dimensional maps reported by our earlier volunteers, or by the volunteers of Brindley.[1] We suspect, but cannot prove, that this unusual map, like the clusters of multiple phosphenes, is due to placement of the electrodes on visual association cortex (areas 18 and 19) rather than primary visual cortex (area 17). in the future, we may implant up to 256 additional surface electrodes, particularly on the left occipital lobe of this volunteer, to increase the resolution of this system.

However, trying to place additional electrodes within is impractical, at least at this time. Our anatomic studies in cadavers 8 indicate that primary visual cortex (area 17) would permit placement of 256 surface electrodes on 3 mm centers on each lobe in most humans (512 electrodes total). However, stimulating adjacent visual association cortex—as we believe we are doing in this volunteer—would substantially expand the number of possible electrodes in the matrix. The organization of the stimulator is modular, and the system described here is being expanded to allow us to stimulate 256 electrodes on each hemisphere.

The Electronics Package

The 492 × 512 pixel charge coupled devices (CCD) black and white television camera is powered by a 9 V battery an connects via a battery-powered National Television Standards Committee (NTSC) link to a sub-notebook computer in a belt pack. This 14.5 camera, with a 690 field of view, uses a pinhole aperture, instead of a lens, to minimize size and weight. It also incorporates an electronic "iris" for automatic exposure control.

The sub-notebook computer incorporates a 120 MHz microprocessor with 32 MB of RAM and a 1.5 GB hard drive. It also has an LCD screen and keyboard. It was selected because of its very small size and light weight. The belt pack also contains a second microcontroller and associated electronics to stimulate the brain. This stimulus generator is connected through a percutaneous pedestal to the electrodes implanted on the visual cortex. The computer and electronics package together are approximately the size of a dictionary and weigh approximately ten pounds, including camera, cables, and rechargeable batteries. The battery pack for the computer will operate for approximately three hours, and the battery pack for the other electronics will operate for approximately six hours.

This general architecture, in which one computer interfaces with the camera and a second computer controls the stimulating electronics, has been used by us in this, and four other substantially equivalent systems, since 1969.[9] The software involves approximately 25,000 lines of code in addition to the sub-notebooks' operating system. Most of the code is written in C++, whereas some is written in C. The second microcontroller is programmed in assembly language.

Stimulation Parameters

Stimulation delivered to each electrode typically consists of a train of six pulses delivered at 30 Hz to produce each frame of the image. Frames have been produced with —one to fifty pulses, and frame rates have been varied from one—to twenty frames per second. As expected,[4] frame rates of four per second currently seem best, even with trains containing only a single pulse. Each pulse is symmetric, biphasic five hundred microsecond per phase (thousand microsecond total). Threshold amplitudes of —ten to twenty volts (zero peak) may vary +/−20 percent from day to day; they are higher than the thresholds of similar electrodes without the ground plane, presumably because current shunts across the surface of the pia-arachnoid and encapsulating membrane. The system is calibrated each morning by recomputing the thresholds for each electrode, a simple procedure that takes the volunteer approximately fifteen minutes with a numeric keypad.

Performance of the System

We know of no objective method for comparing our "artificial vision" system with a cane, guide dog, or other aid for the blind. For example, there is no standard obstacle course on which such devices, or the performance of volunteers using them, can be rated. Indeed, even the vision test for drivers' licenses in most jurisdictions uses only static Snellen tests. Furthermore, there are really no analogous low vision patients with parafoveal tunnel vision, plus scattered field defects (due to gaps between phosphenes), no color vision, and no depth perception to provide models for testing.

Initially, the volunteer was unable to recognize letters or numbers. Based on extensive personal experience in the 1960s with corneal transplant patients whose vision had been restored after many years of blindness, I expected that it might take the volunteer more than a year to learn how to use our new artificial vision system. This expectation was reinforced by the work of Valvo[10] and others. However, within ten one-day sessions, the patient learned to use the system, and he has continued to practice three to four hours per day two or three days per week.

With scanning, he can now routinely recognize a six-inch square "tumbling E" at five feet, as well as Snellen letters, HOTV test, Landolt rings, and Lea figures of similar size. These psychophysical tests are summarized in figure 7. He can also count fingers. With the exception of finger counting, these acuity tests have been conducted using pure black characters on a pure white background at an illumination greater than 1,000 lux. Six-inch characters at five feet corresponds to a visual acuity of approximately 20/1200. A frequency-of-seeing curve for the "tumbling E" and for Landolt's ring is shown in figure 8.

Paradoxically, larger characters are slightly more difficult for this volunteer because they extend well beyond the limits of his visual "tunnel." The rapid fall-off with characters smaller than 20/1200 is also quite reproducible, but the explanation is uncertain. In the future, more sophisticated psychophysical experiments may compare this volunteer with normal patients, separating effect due to processing at the retina and lateral geniculate from those occurring at cortical levels or beyond.

Similar acuity results have been achieved with the television/computer/Internet interface replacing the camera, although scanning is slower because a keypad is currently used for control, rather than neck movements. The volunteer believes that his performance will continue to improve with additional experience, particularly practice in scanning. The resolution of the system itself is ultimately limited by the analog-to-digital conversion in the NTS link between the camera or other source and the computer and thus can be improved by a better link, a different camera, or both.

Of course, visual acuity is normally measured with optima correction. Adding a lens to the existing camera is one possibility;

however, because of size, weight, and cosmetic considerations, we have chosen to accomplish magnification "correction" in software, which proved very difficult to write and is still being debugged. In addition, we are exploring use of image processing techniques, including edge detection. This additional computer processing required for edge detection slows the frame rate to approximately one per second, but the volunteer is practicing use of such displays for mobility. In a larger (benchtop) development system, with a different camera, no NTSC link, and a 300 MHz processor of slightly different design, frame rates can be increased up to seven per second.

We had expected that the patient might have trouble with apparent changes in size or shape of the phosphene image, particularly because the electrodes seem to be on visual association cortex. However, at this point, there are no signs of either metamorphopsia or dysmetropsia, and corrective image processing has not been necessary.

As we have reported with earlier volunteers,[2] brightness can be easily be modulated by changes in pulse amplitude.[11] However, provision of "gray scale" has not proven very valuable so far, probably because of the combination of tunnel vision and limited resolution. The phosphene display is planar, but is of uncertain distance, like the stars in the sky. We, therefore, plan to add an ultrasonic or infrared "range finder"[12] in which the brightness of an easily identifiable phosphene, probably the one produced by electrode number 14 in this volunteer, is a function of distance. This is analogous to the "heads up" displays used by military pilots.

Although stimulation of visual cortex in sighted patients frequently produces colored phosphenes, the phosphenes reported by this volunteer (and all previous blind volunteers to the best of our knowledge) are colorless. We speculate that this is the result of postdeprivation deterioration of the cells and/or synaptic connections required for color vision. Consequently, color vision may never be possible in this volunteer or in future patients. However, optical filters could help differentiate colors, and it is also conceivable that chromatic sensations could be produced if future patients are implanted shortly after being blinded, before atrophy of the neural network responsible for color vision.

Contrast is entirely a function of the software, with adjustment by the experimental team depending on the experimental situation.

The system also allows "reversals" in which the world looks much like a black-and-white photographic negative. Reversal is particularly useful when presenting black characters on a white background. These characters are then reversed by the computer so they appear as a matrix of white phosphenes on the patient's (otherwise dark) visual field.

The phosphene map is not congruent with the center of the volunteer's visual field. Phosphenes also move with eye movement. However, the volunteer's ability to fixate with this artificial vision system is a function of aiming the camera using neck muscles, rather than eye muscles. It helps that the camera image is displayed on the remote video screen for monitoring by the experimental team. In addition, we use a laser pointer in the temple piece of the volunteer's glasses so the experimental team can tell at any moment where the camera is aimed by looking for the red dot.

Low-vision patients often follow lines, including the junction between the wall and the floor, and/or lines of lights on the ceiling, and this volunteer has been practicing this approach. People with very limited vision can also achieve excellent mobility by following people. The volunteer has been practicing use of the system for this purpose as well and can easily follow an eight-year-old child.

The volunteer frequently travels alone in the New York metropolitan area, and to other cities, using public transport. He believes that one of the most dangerous errors in mobility is to mistake the space between subway cars for an open car door. He has been using the artificial vision system to practice this differentiation while we monitor his performance with the remote VCR and viewing screen.

Discussion

In the United States, there are more than 1.1 million legally blind people, including 220,000 with light perception or less.[13] Similar statistics are thought to prevail in other economically developed countries. Unlike some other artificial vision proposals, such as retinal stimulators, cortical stimulators are applicable to virtually all causes of blindness. Our device may also help some legally blind low vision patients because the cortex of sighted people responds to stimulation similarly to the cortex of blind people. We believe that some blind children will be particularly good candidates for this new artificial vision system, because of their ability to quickly learn to use the system. In addition, without visual input, the visual cortex of blind children may not develop and this would prevent their use of artificial vision in the future. For example, the second patient implanted on the same day in 1978 as the volunteer reported here, was blinded in an accident at age five and implanted at age sixty-two. Although he has retained his implant for more than twenty years, he has never seen phosphenes. However, our device is contraindicated in the very small number of blind people with severe chronic infections and the even smaller number blinded by stroke or cortical trauma.

None of the seven blind volunteers in our series have ever exhibited epileptic symptoms or other systemic problems related to the implant. Based on our clinical experience during the last thirty years, implanting thousands of patients in more than forty countries with other types of neurostimulators (to control breathing, pain, and the urogenital system) we believe the principal risk of our artificial vision device is infection, which might require removal of the implant in addition to antibiotic therapy.

To control costs and ensure easy maintenance, our design uses commercial off-the-shelf (COTS) components. The computer, stimulating electronics, and software are all external, facilitating upgrades and repairs. However, despite ongoing software improvements and use of larger numbers of electrodes in the future, it is unlikely that patients will be able to drive an automobile in the foreseeable future, much less get legal approval to do so.

Development of implanted medical devices such as this artificial vision system progresses in three stages. First, there is speculation, then there is hope, and finally there is promise.

Given our considerable experience with neurostimulator implantation, we believe that we can promise a 512 electrode system that will be cost-competitive with a guide dog. More important, that cost can be expected to drop dramatically in the future, while performance should continue to improve.

Acknowledgments

I thank W. J. Kolff, the mentor and friend who enabled me to begin this project from 1968 to 1976. I also thank this blind volunteer and his family, as well as the more than fifty other sighted, blind and deaf volunteers who have been involved as surgical subjects in our sensory prostheses research, as well as the thousands of patients in more than forty countries who have been implanted with our clinical neurological stimulators since 1969. I also thank (alphabetically) R. Avery, G. Brindley, M. Dobelle[†], M. D. Dobelle, C. Eyzaguirre, D. Evans[†], H. K. Hartline[†], B. Lisan, E. F. McNichol Jr., W. Partridge, W. Penfield[†], K. Reemstma, D. Rushton, and T. Stockholm, for reasons best known to each of them. J. Girvin has been our principle neurosurgical collaborator since 1970. He implanted all seven of our blind patients assisted by J. Antunes, D. Fink, M. McDonald, D. Quest, T. Roberts, and T. Stanley among others. D. Dohn, C. Drakest, P. Gildenberg, M. G. Yasagil, and many others have also provided neurosurgical advice and assistance. M. Mladejovsky and, more recently, P. Ning have guided our computer engineering efforts during the past thirty years with programming assistance from a group including D. Eddington, J. Evans, A. Halpert, M. O'Keefe, and J. Ochs. More than three hundred other scientists, physicians, engineers, and surgeons have been involved in our experiments since 1968, including K. Aron, B. Besser, M. D'Angelo, G. Dulmage, S. Fidone, B. Goetz, R. Goldbaum, J. Hanson, D. Hill, R. Huber, D. Kiefer, G. Klomp, T. Lallier, L. Pape, B. Seelig, K. Smith, L. Stensaas, S. Stensaas, and M. Womack III[†]. J. Andrus and L. Homrighausen (Surdna Foundation, New York, NY), Max Fleischman Foundation (Reno, Nevada), H. Geneent (IT&T Corp., New York, NY), E. Grass (Gross Instruments, Boston, Mass.), Wm. Randolph Heart Foundation (San Francisco, CA), E. Landf (Polaroid Corp., Cambridge, Mass.), S. Olsen (Digital Equipment Corp., Maynard, Mass.), D. Rosef (New York, NY), M. Shapirof (General Instrument Co., New York NY), Wm. Volker Fund (Monterey, CA), and more than hundred other individuals and foundations provided financial support prior to 1981 without which this program would have been impossible. During this period we also received equipment donations from dozens of corporations, including Phillips Electronics, Fairchild Inc., Siguestis Inc., Soldran Inc., Bell Telephone Laboratories Inc., Hughes Aircraft Corp., Sanyo Corp., General Atomic Corp., Thermionics Inc., and TRW Inc. Since 1981, all financial support has been provided by the Dobelle Institute, Inc. and its United States and Swiss affiliates. Financing our R&D on artificial vision entirely by sale of related neurological stimulators was consciously modeled on the Wright Brothers, who developed the airplane with proceeds from their bicycle factory. Like the airplane, the artificial vision project has entailed a high risk of failure, and a long development time, which are incompatible with conventional venture capital horizons. Advice and assistance in this respect has been provided by P. Baldi, P. Conley[†], R. Downey, D. Ellis III, C. Giffuni, A. Gutman, E. Heil, 1. Lustgarten[†], J. McGarrahan, P. G. Pedersen, S. Sawyier, L. Towler, T. Young, and L. Weltman among others.

References

1. Brindley GS, Lewin WS: The sensations produced by electrical stimulation of the visual cortex. *Physiol (Lond)* 196: 479–93, 1968.
2. Dobelle WH, Mladejovsky MG: Phosphenes produced by electrical stimulation of human occipital cortex, and their application to the development of a prosthesis for the blind. *J Physiol (Lond)* 243: 553–76,1974.
3. Dobelle WH, Mladejovsky MG, Girvin JP: Artificial vision for the blind: Electrical stimulation of visual cortex offers hope for a functional prosthesis. *Science* 183: 440–44, 1974.
4. Dobelle WH, Mladejovsky MG, Evans JR, Roberts TS, Girvin JP: "Braille" reading by a blind volunteer by visual cortex stimulation. *Nature* 259: 111–12, 1976.
5. Dobelle WH, Quest D, Antunes J, Roberts T, Girvin JP: Artificial vision for the blind by electrical stimulation of the visual cortex. *Neurosurgery* 5: 521–27, 1979.
6. Klomp GF, Womack MVB, Dobelle WH: Fabrication of large arrays of cortical electrodes for use in man. *J Biomed Mater Res* 11: 347–64, 1977.
7. Klomp GF, Womack MVB, Dobelle WH: Percutaneous transmission of electrical energy in humans. *Trans ASAIO* 25: 1–7, 1979.
8. Stenaas SS, Eddington DK, Dobelle WH: The topography and variability of the primary visual cortex in man. *Neurosurg* 40: 747–54,1974.
9. Mladejovsky MG, Eddington DK, Evans JR, Dobelle WH: A computer-based brain stimulation system to investigate sensory prostheses for the blind and deaf. *IEEE Trans Biomed Eng* 23: 286–96,1976.
10. Valvo A: Sight restoration after long-term blindness: The problems and behavior patterns of visual rehabilitation. New York: *American Foundation for the Blind*, 1971.

11. Henderson DC, Evans JR, Dobelle WH: The relationship between stimulus parameters and phosphene threshold/ brightness, during stimulation of human visual cortex. *Trans ASAIO* 25: 367–70,1979.

12. Dobelle WH: Artificial vision for the blind: The summit may be closer than you think. *ASAIO J* 40: 919–21, 1994.

13. Leonard R: Statistics on vision impairment: A resource manual. *Lighthouse International*, February 1999.

14. The Dobelle Group. Available at: http:www.dobelle.com.

15. Watson W: An account of Mr. Benjamin Franklin's treatise, lately published, entitied Experiments and Observations on Electricity, made at Philadelphia in America. *Philos Trans R Soc London* 47: 202–11, 1751–52.

16. Sobel I: Camera models and machine perception. AIM-21. Stanford Artificial Intelligence Laboratory, Palo Alto, California, 1970.

Afterword

Our team has continued to develop the hardware and software of this artificial vision system. Five key developments have occurred in the two months since submission of this paper for publication in September, 1999.

Development of a New Technique for Phosphene Mapping

Phosphene mapping is complicated by the fact that all phosphenes are produced in a relatively small area, which makes pointing difficult. This is compounded by the fact that phosphenes move with eye movements. In the refined technique, two phosphenes are selected to provide a vertical scale. The volunteer is then asked to estimate the vertical distance between each phosphene and these two references, as well as the distance to the left or right of an imaginary line connecting the reference phosphenes. This approach resulted in some small changes in the map described in figure 6, but the principal result was to "compress" the map horizontally from three inches across to about two inches across.

Use of a More Powerful Computer

During the last two decades, many improvements in our hardware and software have developed because of rapid technological advancements in computer technology ("Moore's Law"). Shortly after submission of this paper, we were able to obtain a new computer in an almost identical small package. This more powerful system uses a 233 MHz processor, 32 MB of RAM, and a 4 GB hard disk. After debugging the software, the extra computing power proved important in two areas: (1) magnification in software, and (2) image preprocessing, particularly edge detection.

Electronic Magnification

The pinhole camera we have been using is small, light, and inconspicuous. However, it has a 69' field of view. Conventional optics would be heavy and conspicuous. Moreover, it is difficult to conceive a "zoom' version without using a motor drive. Using the more powerful computer, we were able to implement software magnification algorithms that were not possible with the initial portable system discussed above. The ray value for all pixels (120 × 160) were recorded and then 2, 4, 8, or 1 6 pixels were combined to create a single pixel for transmission to the patient. Using magnifications of four (and sometimes eight) times, the patient's resolution improved to the point where he can now recognize a two-inch high letter at five feet, as opposed to a six-inch high letter at the same distance. This represents an acuity improvement from roughly 20/1200 to 20/400. Less magnification (e.g., 2x) was insufficient. Due to the patient's tunnel vision, at 16x the image far overlapped the tunnel, with effects similar to the acuity degradation described for letters larger than sixinches at five feet in figure 8 above.

Edge Detection

In 1969–70, our team (M. Mladejovsky and W. Dobelle, unpublished data), at the University of Utah began exploring computer simulations of artificial vision displays using a head-mounted display (originally designed by Ivan Sutherland) attached to a "single-user" PDP-L computer. This research was part of a much larger (unclassified) program on computerized image processing sponsored by the Advanced Research Projects Agency of the Department of Defense. Edge detection clearly extracted important information and removed "noise." However, this computer (which occupied approximately eight thousand square feet) required hours to process a single frame. The 120 MHz system described above was able to process approximately one frame per second, which is too slow for mobility. The new 233 MHz system, using Sobel filters 6 for edge detection, can process and transmit images to the volunteer at speeds up to eight frames per second. A mannequin as pictured by the television camera (figure 1) is shown in figure 9A. The same scene is also shown after edge-detection processing in figure 9B. We believe that such processing will be an integral part of all clinical visual prostheses.

Ultrasonic Range Finder

Using edge detection, it is particularly helpful for the blind patient to know how far the wall is located behind the mannequin (figures 9A and B). Ultrasonic range finders for the blind have been known for many years; however, they have typically translated distance into audio signals that interfered with the ability of blind patients to use their hearing. (Indeed, this writer almost fell down a stairway at the University of Utah while blindfolded and trying to use an ultrasonic-to-audio conversion device. I did not hear the warning of a companion.) However, by placing an electrostatic transducer on the left lens of the patient's eyeglasses (lateral to the camera and below the laser pointer), we have begun exploring the supplementary information that can be provided by modulating brightness, blink rate, and identity of selected phosphenes.

Discussion

The blind volunteer is now able to navigate among a "family" of three mannequins—standing adult male, seated adult female, and standing three-year-old child—randomly placed in a large room, without bumping into any of them. He can then go to the wall and retrieve a cap that has been placed on the wall at a random location. Navigating back in the direction from which he came, he can find any of the three mannequins and place the cap on the head of whichever one we request. As the volunteer gains more experience, and we make further refinements in the system, rapid progress can be expected. Even more rapid advances can be anticipated with larger electrode arrays, more powerful computers, and more sophisticated image preprocessing algorithms.

Wm. H. Dobelle, PhD

December 1, 1999

New York, NY

Lorri was finished reading, stressing slightly the "PhD" and the "New York." It all sounded too good to be true. Yet, all of this fit in a perfect puzzle, leaving little left for doubt.

"Amazing . . ." I said, shaking my head at the simplicity of the concept. "It is obvious Dr. Dobelle knows what he is doing. Just from judging by the selection of words, the sentence structure, and the ease in which he expresses himself in this article speaks highly for his abilities."

Lorri scanned the sheets of paper again. "Just looking at the people he has collaborated with is enough for me. Looking at all these PhDs and MDs is enough for me to assume that half the brain power in the world is at work on this project."

We discussed the volunteer, the one shown carrying the first prototype, the one who moves among the mannequins in the picture, placing the hat upon the selected figure.

"The chosen one . . ." I had such envy for this man. "He is the chosen one, from millions of blind people in the world, he now can see. I wonder what it must be like. I wonder how he must feel—posing for the cameras, showing to the world that, yes—it is not just hope or speculation. This is promise." I couldn't help myself from quoting directly the words of Dr. William H. Dobelle.

How I envied the volunteer! He deserved the electronic eye, nonetheless. He had lost his sight in a similar bizarre fashion as myself—first one, then the other. He had had a little more time in between, though, so at least he could have seen his kids starting to grow.

"I wonder how that volunteer must feel when having to give the equipment back after using it the three or four hours it is given to him for the day." I tried to imagine the scenario. All night he would toss and turn in bed, anticipating the relief from the pressing blackness. No doubt he had all his protective barriers, those shielding him from the reality of blindness, disassembled, along with all their foundations precariously built over the years of being blind, the first time the vision system was turned on. Yet, I imagined, for the three hours of using the system he would look at everything that there possibly was to see—peering contentedly in the faces of passers-by, the buildings, the parks, and perhaps doing his best to sneak the system to where he wanted a permanent picture for future recollection. For three hours, he would be in heaven. He would look at his watch, only to see that he had but five minutes to go, and the pain would sear in his brain as did the times I dreamed, in full color and beauty of imagery, knowing the nightmare will come the minute I wake up. But this volunteer, unlike myself, knew he would have another three hours in a day or two and would treasure every moment and memory of what he had seen until the next time. He would talk about everything he saw that day when sitting with his family around the dinner table that night, all the while the family members nodding their heads in amazement, commenting on how great it was that their father, her husband, was able to see again. All of this, thanks to Dr. William Dobelle and his wonderful team. How I wished that volunteer could be me!

Lorri and I reviewed part of the Web site that dealt with the possibility Dr. Dobelle would implant a few test patients with his new "bilateral" system, one that used two implants instead of the single one that the volunteer had. There were forms one could fill out on the Net, but knowing the attention that "Net" interactions usually led to—totally ignored—I was looking for a more personal contact. "Besides," I had said to Lorri, "we have to make sure that it is actually real people that are involved in this." The Internet, an area of information mainly unpoliced by the law, had as much bad and shady as it had good on it. It was a "lookers and believers beware!" type of region.

But there it was, a person responding to the name of Lisa, to be called at the Columbia-Presbyterian Medical Center, right on 3960 Broadway, New York.

"I'll give her a call first thing in the morning," I announced this, all the while doubting I would even have a chance to get in.

"The price is stated here at being about $50,000 US," Lorri stated in a matter-of-fact manner. "What would that be in Canadian currency?"

I did a rough guess. The exchange was about 72 percent at the time. "It would be around $70,000." That was not good, as it was far above the $25,000 that Boston clinic wanted from me in 1984, when arranging to perform open-eye surgery. We had a family to take care of, with lots of kids that had their needs. I wasn't making nearly the salary I used to when I could see. At that time, I had worked one shift in the sawmill and the next in the surveying business. That had meant two paychecks of almost nine hundred dollars every two weeks. No such luck now, however. Blind people just cannot clinch the good jobs, generally speaking. As one older gentleman had put it to me in New Jersey at the Seeing Eye guide dog school: "Should there be two contestants standing before an employer, both equally qualified for the job in question, and one of them can see, bright eyed, looking at the employer, while the other is blind . . . who is it that gets the job?"

"It's a lot of money . . ." I didn't know what else to say. When I had first lost my sight, I felt the sensation that I was in deep trouble. I still felt it, but stronger now. I am but one person out of a family of ten—Lorri, the eight children, and myself. How much will the family bend to accommodate a very personal desire of mine? What difference would it make to the kids if I should now see? They were doing fine. They knew me only as that what I am now. Lorri, on the other hand, had a better future to face with me. After all, once the diversion of child-rearing is passed, what will she and I have in common? She had been originally attracted to me on the pretense that I was the adventurist, the leader on the seat of a bike, the one who took her by the hand through the world, pointing out all the good in it to her. No such luck now. But with this machine of Dr. Dobelle's . . .

Then it hit me. I did not have to worry, as I could borrow, beg, remortgage the house, whatever it took, as I would, once again, return to the workforce as I had been at age twenty, once clenching this invention of Dr. Dobelle's, and make all the money right back, giving it back to all who had helped me. It was so simple. I had almost forgotten what it really meant to see again. I had once heard of prisoners, incarcerated for two decades, having forgotten entirely that their prison sentence would be over some day. Yes, for the first years they would count every passing hour and what was left to serve. Then somewhere in the middle, the hope vanished. Then the warden would tell them it was their turn to leave, as the sentence was served. The warden, anticipating a holler of joy and a mad dash to the exit door of the prison made by the prisoner, would be astonished to find the prisoner looking at him with an expression of blank misunderstanding. "What are you talking about . . . ?" would be the weak, noncompliant reply. "You're free! You're now free! You can go now!" the warden would try to break the trance, hoping any minute the prisoner would catch on with the expected enthusiasm. But the prisoner just stands there, blankly looking at the warden, as if suggesting to a fish that it should jump out of the water and live on land. "What is that—that 'freedom' you are mentioning? What am I to do with it? I don't know anybody out there. I wouldn't know what to do." And sure enough, a lot of them come right back. That is called life imprisonment. One doesn't need locks and chains to stay inside the walls anymore. Once one is totally demoralized, there is no way out.

It shocked me to realize that this was happening to me. This process of demoralization must have taken hold of me over the course of the last few years. I had been very engaged in all sorts of activities, especially since I had acquired a computer with scanner and voice card in 1992, allowing me to read, study courses, as well as write. The computer had allowed me to record new electronic circuits that I had enjoyed designing since childhood. At that time I had drawn schematic diagrams, and now I could do the same using literal descriptions of the circuit design instead. Together with the firewood processing business I was operating, I had little time to think about what I could be doing if I could see. That would compare to taking on jobs in prison while serving a sentence; however, its intention is to assist in passing time, leading up to the great moment of being released. Now it appeared to be my turn to be released coming up in short time, and I had better be prepared.

"How about we do whatever we can to get the money, and then I'll make it back?" I had no doubt Lorri would be convinced. "I'll sell the firewood without replenishing the supply for next year's sales, which would give quite a bit. I'll sell the snowplow, farm equipment, and anything I have that I can sacrifice." I meant it, attempting to display how far I would go to make this a reality.

"I could sell my piano," said Lorri. Now that was a sacrifice. She needed that piano to teach music, and it was her prized possession as well. She had bought it from her own earnings several years ago, a brand-new grand piano. As we both played, and every now and then the kids, too, would make an effort to play, the investment was more than justified. Now that Lorri suggested selling it so I could get this apparatus clearly demonstrated to me how much this meant to her. "We'll find the money," she continued. "It may be hard, but we'll find it."

The kids were at school and Lorri at work when I called Lisa—the famed Lisa that was to be at the other end of the line, on route to paradise. I dialed the New York number, and to my surprise, I was greeted by a voice:

"Dobelle Institute, Lisa speaking. How may I help you?"

My heart was in my throat when I struggled to find the right words.

"My name is Jens Naumann. I am calling from Canada. My friend saw your Internet site, and as I have been blinded since I was twenty, I am really interested in acquiring the artificial eye offered by Dr. Dobelle. I am fully prepared to pay for this, and am very happy to find this on the market." I was glad I could actually mention I would be able to pay for this invention. After all, I reasoned, Dr. Dobelle has to be paid for his efforts. He certainly deserves it.

"Well, if you were blinded as an adult, Dr. Dobelle figures this really should work for you," Lisa said, her voice ringing like that of an angel's in my ear. "I'm really happy too, for all the blind people, that there is now a solution for them. It must have been awful being in the dark all this time." She was such a compassionate girl. I couldn't wait to meet her, along with the rest of the team, and of course, Dr. Dobelle. But when would that be?

"How do I get into this program?" I inquired, and then repeated, "I am fully prepared to go, to pay, and I understand the whole concept behind this, as I work with electronics myself." This was starting to sound like an attempt to get a job more than an inquiry about a surgical procedure, but I had to get on that list. I just had to.

"There is an application online," began Lisa in her musical voice, "if you download it, print it off, and fill it out, just send it to us. Once we get it, we'll contact you and ask for any details we need. And by the way," she added, "we'll send you more literature on the Dobelle Eye when we receive your form."

I thanked her, verified the mailing address, and waited for Lorri to return that night. I had telephoned the neighbor's to see if we could come over to get a printed copy of the application form, but no one was home. Lorri did find a student of hers that had Internet to print out the application form later that night. I was anxious to see what it said and what it demanded of me.

The form was three pages' long. Apart from the usual questions such as name, languages spoken, cause of blindness, amount of present vision in each eye, any other medical considerations, etc., there was an interesting one asking if I still dreamed, and whether or not it was in color. I thought this a bit bizarre. Sometimes I did dream during which I had sight, but often I dreamed when I could only hear and feel. When this happened during my childhood, it would constitute a nightmare, as I would expect at any minute a monster to appear out of the darkness, ready to eat me. But yet, Dr. Dobelle assumed that any event consists of an event during which there are real images to be seen. But, then again, I consoled myself to excuse his lack of knowledge in this department, Dr. Dobelle is not blind, so he would not know this. The fact that he asked about the presence of color during the dreams, however, looked promising. Perhaps, I mused, he expected to give color vision to those who still dreamed in color. I toyed with that idea for an instant, and then concluded I was getting too greedy.

In the middle of the form was a question regarding how this would be paid. Would it be either in payments, full payment, or through medical insurance? Even though I had every intention to get this paid by the Ontario Health Insurance Plan, we decided to make it look the most impressive—fill in the "cash up front, in full" selection on the form. Little did we know, at that time, how important that move was.

We sent the application form via registered mail and waited in anticipation. Many questions were running through our heads, many of which were shared with each other and with friends. I had made a few friends in this vicinity who were genuinely excited about the prospects. We did not get ourselves in over our heads in expecting this would happen in short time. It may take years, we concluded, before the backlog of patients is at the point where I will be accepted as one of the next roster of patients. We now had time to think, time to dream, and time also to prepare for the event. I had to make sure I sold my possessions for what I could to have the money ready. Many years ago, as part of our marriage arrangement, Lorri and I had decided it best to keep our finances separate from each other, giving each one of us a sense of control, as one would not have to be accountable to the other when deciding what to do with the money. We also shared the expenses of the family, and with whatever we had left, we had to ask no one what to do with it. I, therefore, tried my best to not depend upon whatever Lorri may have saved. She, after all, was the person responsible for the food and clothes for all of us, whereas I had the responsibility of paying house-related issues. Lorri needed her money so we could eat, and I had no intentions of dipping into that for my own purposes. Throughout our wait, there was never a question as to whether or not this invention of Dr. Dobelle's would work; it was only a matter of how long we had to wait to get in. Neither did we ever question the future of the existence of either the company or the availability of the procedure. I had always considered the requirement of eyesight as essential. This sentiment was readily shared by the Ontario Health Insurance Plan, which I assumed readily paid for any surgical procedure essential for either restoring or maintaining vision. Thus, from our point of view, it was logical to compare the essentiality of the artificial vision system to that of other medical devices such as the cardiac pacemaker. No human being would ever force another to remain in the dark if a solution was available to relieve that situation. After all, I reminded myself of previous times I had thought this, even the prisoners awaiting execution on death row in the State of Texas were given adequate lighting in their cells.

This argument, in fact, convinced me that I had to approach the Ontario Health Insurance organization should I be accepted into this program as a patient. It would not be just to serve my own purpose—it would make this country aware of new advancements in sight recovery. In fact, I could easily demonstrate that my last stay in the hospital in 1984, consisting of at least six weeks of ward time as well as the three surgeries would tally up a cost to the government much higher than the $50,000 US demanded by Dr. Dobelle. And to further support the idea, it would be worth my trouble to point out that I had only been given a 10 percent probability of improvement in eyesight resulting from that expenditure. Dr. Dobelle's, in retrospect, would be close to a surefire venture. Thus, no decision making panel consisting of individuals of sound mind would ever be compelled to reject this argument. It turned out, though, that I had more to learn on this subject.

We waited some more. It really was not a long time, but it seemed endless nonetheless. In the middle of August, I decided to write Dr. Dobelle another letter. I did not address it directly to Dr. Dobelle, as surely he would not waste his time reading all the mail that arrived in his prestigious office daily. The reasoning for writing this letter was simple—I was, in whatever way possible, trying to get on the top of the pile of applications of other blind potential patients coming from all over the world. Having already made appointments for the requested physical checkup and eye status assessment, which would be conducted in September, I fired up the computer and began to write, just as one would to acquire a new job.

August 17, 2000

Dobelle Institute Inc.
3960 Broadway
New York

Dear Staff,

Upon having read the entire write-up on your Dobelle visual prosthesis, I was even more impressed by the results so far achieved than I ever imagined possible. Having personally invested thousands of dollars in visual aids like the Mowat Sensor, Milarm audio infrared detector, a guide dog from Morristown, New Jersey, to name a few, I feel this Dobelle eye cannot be compared to any other aids on the market, as all previous aids required the user's senses that are already stressed to the limit without such devices. The idea of the Dobelle eye using the dormant sense of vision for operation is beautiful, to say the least, as this indeed changes the blind person's life to one with visual input, which means the user is, in effect, no longer blind. I must confess I have been in the process of investigating the idea of stimulating the cortex myself ever since a friend of mine, who was exposed to an electroencephalograph while being tested for epilepsy, claimed he saw light and colors at random during the test without his eyes being used as the receiver. This got me thinking about how the relentless darkness could be overcome by such a device, which can be triggered by the Mowat Sensor. This would enable me to approach an object and thus be warned of its presence with the light flickering in my cortex instead of beeps or vibrations to concentrate on. Moreover, it has been common knowledge among psychologists that the absence of light can result in severe depressions in humans. In Toronto, there is actually a clinic that offers helmets to depressed patients (suffering from seasonal affective disorder) which have a florescent light in the visor which cures depression during the gloomy winter months. I had asked a friend to surf the Internet and try to find out the voltage and type of electric impulses required for this experiment when he came across your Web site. Boy, what luck!

I have been fighting blindness and its terrible effect on a person's quality of life ever since I lost my sight. My accomplishments have been rewarded many times. Let me name a few:

- successfully completed grade 10 piano with the Royal Conservatory of Music.
- devised a method of farming and gardening without eyesight, including driving and operating a tractor with hay cutting and baling equipment attached with no sighted assistance.—first blind person to ever receive a license to carry a restricted firearm after successfully completing the chief provincial firearm officer's pistol handling and shooting test. In this test, I scored on my target at twenty-five yards, using a sound target and an attached level on the pistol barrel for insurance I am not overshooting the backstop. Previous to this test, the Ontario Provincial Police told me I would never be allowed to even own a gun as it would be unsafe. Please see enclosed a letter from the vice president of the Napanee Rod and Gun Club—successfully became an entrepreneur in piano tuning and repair and firewood cutting, splitting, and selling and making a living. I cut and split the firewood without any sighted assistance, with the exception of delivering the wood to customers. I successfully completed a St. Lawrence College (in Kingston, Ontario) course in computer programming in C++ and subsequently writing the National Foxhunter's assoc., a program called Houndmaster that allowed the masters of hunts to enter the scores of hundreds of hounds at one time and get flawless score calculating as this was done manually up to that point in time.

In spite of what I so far accomplished in trying not to live a blind man's life, I cannot help but wonder how much better things would go with the 20/400 vision that the Dobelle eye offers. For any person with a certain amount of imagination, logic, and optimism, the Dobelle eye would expand the horizon to an unprecedented limit for those presently in total darkness. I cannot help but muse at how nice it would be to "see" the cut hay from the standing hay, or to be able to guide down a country road that is too messy and unorganized to properly follow with a cane, or to locate a parked object in the field like a wheelbarrow, etc., with ease. In the rural environment, I can bet the Dobelle eye will make even more of a positive difference to a blind person than it does in an urban environment. The fact is that in the country things are not clear cut with sidewalks to follow, car noise to use as guides, and definitely no sighted people around at random to offer assistance. In fact, I use my braille and talking compass should I get disoriented and head straight for the direction of the main highway before I can be reoriented again. This could happen when being just a couple of steps off the beaten path as a cane is often useless in the country. I can imagine that if I had some limited sight such as what the Dobelle eye offers, the concept of sport shooting at a target that you can actually locate visually would sell the Dobelle eye to any of my shooting counterparts who may be losing their vision themselves.

I find it fascinating that the Dobelle eye software was compiled in C++ programming language. Even though I enjoyed and was successful in the programming field, I found it increasingly difficult to continue in the field as the move from the DOS operating system to the Windows environment more or less put blind people out of business. Computer users now expect pretty pictures and fancy fonts that speech synthesizers simply cannot deal with. The Dobelle eye, however, promises to help out for those who really want the help in this field.

What I am trying to say, dear staff, is that for seventeen years I have lived in a cloud of relative despair, if you want to call it that, where I was resigned begrudgingly to an uninteresting and confined life of darkness, and now I finally came across a team who is dedicated to helping me, along with thousands of others, out of this void. Should I be lucky enough to be selected as a patient, I would dedicate my life to promoting this product to every person I come across. Having once been sighted myself, I am convinced that every sighted person in the world is a potential blind person with the wrong turn of events. I would demonstrate the usefulness and necessity of such a product and lobby the government to fund this Dobelle eye for those who qualify, in the same way that the government presently funds the purchase of talking computer and scanner equipment for the blind. There are presently many clubs, such as sporting and recreational organizations, who donate a set amount of proceeds to charity causes and other organizations for better public relations. I am sure if I demonstrated this Dobelle eye the Dobelle institute would be number one on their list. I would like to see your Dobelle eye to be as universally acceptable and accessible to a blind person as would be a pacemaker for those with heart trouble.

On the personal finance issue, I am prepared to pay whatever necessary to acquire the Dobelle eye technology. My wife and I have five hundred American dollars spare a month to dedicate to the payment, or we could get a loan, or even liquidate our farm if necessary. However, if I should be able to use the technology while making payments, I would be able to lobby the government organizations much more successfully in funding not only my unit but other blind people's units as well. After all, the government may say that if I already paid for it, why should they help me? With this move I figure I'll pave the way for all blind people to get funding for the Dobelle eye in the future. Please consider my application seriously. Thank you so much.

Sincerely yours,
Jens

Now we had to wait. Every day we checked the mailbox in anticipation, and every evening we discussed the new future we may be lucky enough to face. Hope was there, and in full vigor. This was not just a radio broadcast in which a reporter talked vaguely of some invention coming about sooner or later—this was the real thing. I reviewed the Internet information on the Dobelle Eye, which I have come to refer to it as, on a daily basis. I just had to get this thing.

I reviewed the letter I wrote to Dr. Dobelle dated August 17. Within it, I had pointed out my knowledge in electronics and computer software for the reason that he would not have to worry about me having a simplistic approach to the concept as if it was powered by magic. If Dr. Dobelle had a choice as to which patients to start with, those most knowledgeable in these fields would be easiest to deal with, considering their cooperation and tolerance to minor glitches usually associated with prototypes. Moreover, they would have adequate dexterity to be left to their own devices for connecting the various components to one another.

I made a point of my competence by describing what I have been up to for the duration of my blindness, even though Lorri thought it inappropriate to include the part about having acquired the permit to convey and shoot restricted weapons. "He's going to think of you as a kind of nut who likes shooting at everything." She was obviously concerned about the fears shared among big-city dwellers.

I had replied to her concerns over the issue, "I want to make sure he understands I don't just sit around here twiddling my thumbs, but rather, I do what I can to make things happen. This permit is issued by the law and is only available to those with a clean criminal record and to those who are safe and competent. Besides," I had to add, "there is a 50 percent chance he is a Republican, and they all *love* their guns anyways!" I found out later that I was correct.

In this letter, I felt it necessary to push the point that blindness was not an option for me, provided there was a choice. At first glance, the contents of the letter gave the impression to the reader that blindness was practically overcome upon judging my successes in acquiring work, having fun, and dealing with practical everyday problems during life. I was afraid that Dr. Dobelle, being faced with a massive pile of requests for the vision system, would come across my letter and application, just to say, "This guy is doing all right—he doesn't really need this thing! Considering all he does, he's leading a good life and seems happy." Concluding this, he might just disregard my request and concentrate upon those who were suffering more. I had to make sure he knew I was suffering in spite of what I had engaged myself in. So I waited, having little doubt I did anything wrong in sending the letter.

The reply came one day in early September, during the time we normally were preoccupied with the preparations for sending the kids back to school. Lorri came charging into the front door, just having returned from the mailbox situated at the front of our driveway.

"We got a letter from Dr. Dobelle!" She was out of breath, yet in spite of her rush to make her point, she was still careful in referring to him as "Doctor" Dobelle. She wasted no time in opening the letter and commencing to read slowly so as to allow our brains to absorb and understand every last detail of its contents.

Dobelle Institute, Inc.
Avery Laboratories, Inc.

August 25, 2000

Jens Neumann
Napanee, Ontario
Canada K7R 3L1

Dear Mr. Neumann:

Based on a preliminary review of the form you submitted to us, you would probably be a candidate for implantation with a visual prosthesis.

This would involve shaving your scalp and inserting an electrode—-through a small hole in the skull—in contact with the visual area of your brain. The operation would be done under local anesthesia. It could probably be done on an outpatient basis, although we would probably prefer that (at least for the initial cases) you stay in the hospital overnight. Of course, exchange of considerably more information would be necessary before either of us could make a final decision.

When payment will be required has not been decided. We are now developing plans for implantation with the new "commercial" system, which is scheduled to be ready later this year. However, no final surgical sites have been selected. I will be back in touch with you from time to time in the months ahead as our plans develop.

Sincerely,
Wm. H. Dobelle, PhD
Chairman & Chief Executive Officer at the Columbia-Presbyterian Medical Center
3960 Broadway, New York NY 10032-1543
Phone: (212)927-4000 Fax: (212)927-6300 www.dobelle.com

CHAPTER 5

Fighting the Odds

"Let's read it again," I said to Lorri, who was holding the paper in front of her, more than likely rereading the contents quietly to herself. Upon completing it, she said " . . . signed: Dr. William H. Dobelle, PhD."

"Does it look like a stamp was used, or does it look like a real signature?" I had to know this. I calculated that if Dr. Dobelle had the time to sign each letter individually, it must be down to a few hundred applications for him to process rather than a few thousand. Should it be a stamp however, who knows how many there are, thus rendering my chances to be one of the first to almost nil.

"It's his own signature, all right," Lorri replied, peering closely at the scribble on the paper. "Not all that neat, and it is for sure written in ordinary pen, as the stamps generally are accompanied by some smearing around the writing."

"I don't suppose doctors such as he has the time to spare in writing their name neatly." I justified the hurried manner the letter was signed. "Most importantly," I reminded Lorri, "he took the time to sign mine personally, which must mean I passed the first step!"

I could not subdue my excitement. I took the letter to my computer and scanned it, giving me the luxury to review it several times, until I had it memorized. I reviewed each point made, elaborating upon each with Lorri.

"First of all," he says, "you would probably be a candidate for implantation, which is excellent news!" I continued, quite pleased with the comment which came next:

"This would involve shaving your scalp and inserting a small electrode array . . ." And then it says, "The operation would be done under local anesthesia. It could probably be done on an outpatient basis . . ." I turned to Lorri. "It sounds like it is not much more involved to implant than getting a root canal at the dentist's!"

"By the sounds of it, like the part about the shaved scalp, the idea that you are getting shaved must be what Dr. Dobelle wants to make sure you won't object to," replied Lorri. "I cannot imagine anyone worrying about something like that when given the opportunity to see again."

It looked so simple and logical on paper. I imagined a small hole, like the size of the end of my finger, having to be drilled in the skull to install this outfit. I would be sore for a bit, as the hole would have to heal, and also the small section where the scalp had to be punctured would be tender.

"I wonder where we will have to go," I asked Lorri, who had no idea either.

"It will be kind of fun, though," said Lorri. "We are due for a good vacation."

I thought about it for an instant, and then jumped to the most amazing conclusion.

"I'll be able to do sightseeing with you on the next day out of the hospital!" I imagined castles, palm trees, and strange-looking foreign people wearing funny clothes in black and white, their faces appearing grainy on account of the pixel-graphics vision offered by the Dobelle eye.

Then, for a fleeting moment, the memory of our last train trip to Toronto in 1984, with all of its hopes of seeing the return trip, and how cruelly they were dashed, came back to me. I quickly shook it off. This was different, I told myself. This was science, technology, with a surefire success rate. This was not a situation in which success was dependent upon delicate retinal tissue healing a certain way.

Lorri responded, after a brief delay, "That would be great . . ." Was she thinking the same thing? We both did get badly stung back then in 1984, making it unlikely we would ever forget the events. Yet it would be different if we could look back upon it as a problem we finally resolved. Then the pain of it all would disappear.

"I'll get right on the telephone and hurry up those doctor's assessments of my health and eye condition he requested," I referred to the last part of the letter. "I'm sure Dr. Willis will be thrilled to hear about this idea of vision restoration."

"I bet he'll be surprised," said Lorri, still remembering Dr. Shea in Toronto telling me that I was going to have to accept my blindness and get on with it. "You can travel around the world as often as you want, no one will be able to make you see again . . ." he had said in 1993, leaving me grasping at thin air for support. How I looked forward to the day I would march into his clinic, look him in the face, and announce that with enough perseverance, anything can be accomplished. But first I have to get all the way in.

"There is some more information they sent with the letter as well." Lorri pointed out, "There is a type of resume about Dr. Dobelle, as well as a question-and-answer document."

"I'll start with the questions and answers," I said, "just to make sure we know what we're getting into."

I took it, scanned it, and began to study it.

Dobelle Institute, Inc.
Dobelle Laboratories, Inc.
Institute Dobelle AG (Zurich)
Avery Laboratories, Inc.

Frequently Asked Questions

1.   Employment Opportunities

Like the United States Marine Corps, we are always looking for a few good men and women.

We have always been particularly interested in employing gifted students—many of the most important contributions to the artificial vision project have been made by people less than twenty-one years of age—including my own eight-year-old son who invented the TV/computer/Internet interface. Please send a resume by mail to our Long Island

Administrative Headquarters:
The Dobelle Institute, Inc.
Attn: Artificial Vision Personnel
61 Mall Drive
Commack, NY 11725–5703

-It would be helpful if all applicants to work in New York City or Long Island are US citizens or already hold a "green card." It would be helpful if all applicants for employment in Zurich are already eligible for permanent residency there.

We are particularly interested in electrical/computer engineers and technicians with a strong background in both hardware and software.

2. Physicians and Surgeons

If you are interested in referring or implanting patients, please send your CV by mail to:
The Dobelle Institute, Inc.
Attn: Artificial Vision Physicians and Surgeons 61 Mall Drive
Commack, NY 11725–5703

3. Investments in the Dobelle Institute and Affiliated Companies

-All entities are held by my wife and me. Between 1968 and 1980, we spent about USD $7,000,000 at the University of Utah and at Columbia-Presbyterian Medical Center in New York City. About USD $225,000 came from NIH, the rest from private benefactors. Since 1981, all support, totaling about USD $18,000,000 has been provided by the Dobelle Institute and its affiliated companies.

4. Visits to the Institute

We shuttle among three locations in Zurich, on Long Island, and in Manhattan. Sorry, but it is just impractical to try to schedule visitors except under the most unusual circumstances.

5. Why did it take so long to get Jerry to this point?

-When he was first implanted in 1978, the computer system was ten feet wide, five feet high, three feet deep and weighed several thousand pounds. Today it weighs ten pounds and is about the size of a dictionary.
-In addition to size and weight, the present system is five hundred times faster than the 1978 model.
-Electronic components that we needed for this stimulating circuitry only became available in the last eighteen months.
-Including operating systems, there are about fifteen million lines of code. Two decades ago, the necessary software did not exist.
-We needed to demonstrate long-term percutaneous implants without infection.
-We needed to demonstrate long-term stimulation without causing epilepsy.

-We needed to demonstrate long-term stimulation without damaging the visual cortex.

-We needed to demonstrate long-term implantation and stimulation with stable phosphene displays.

6.   What is the next step?

-Putting larger arrays of electrodes. We now have more than fifteen thousand patients around the world with other systems, and our electrode-building technology is far more sophisticated than it was in the 1970s.

7.   What kind of collaboration do you seek with agencies for the blind?

-My colleagues and I are experts in medical devices—their design, manufacture, and implantation. Blind patients are going to need help in learning how to use the visual prosthesis, and that is where I think established agencies for the blind can make a real contribution.

8:   Frequently asked questions by potential patients:

Q: Will your device work for those patients who are blind since birth?
A: We don't know if it will work in patients who are blind from birth. In general, this group has been the least interested in the visual prosthesis, and they constitute only a few percent of the blind. However, patients who are visually impaired from birth can suffer anomalous development of the visual cortex, which may be avoided by early stimulation. The youngest patients with our breathing pacemakers were implanted when they were less than two months old.

Q: What blind patients would not be able to use your device?

A: We believe the device will be applicable to virtually all patients who are blind or who have very low vision. The only ones contraindicated would be a few blinded by serious brain damage, or who have chronic infections, etc., that preclude surgical implants.

Q: How complicated is the implant surgery?

A: All of our blind patients to date have been implanted under local anesthesia. I believe that this will continue in the future with most clinical implants occurring on an "outpatient" basis.

Q: When will your device be available?

A: We presently have more than fifteen thousand patients who have been implanted in more than forty countries around the world with other neurostimulators. We hope to make the visual prosthesis commercially available throughout the world starting later this year outside the United States.

Q: Why will your device not be available in the United States initially?

A: over the last twenty years, all our clinical devices have been introduced abroad then brought back to the United States. In fact, de novo introduction of new drugs and devices in the United States is very rare.

Q: Is your device indicated for patients who are blind in only one eye?

A: Unilaterally blind patients can qualify for a pilot's license in the United States. I don't know any reason why they would need a visual prosthesis.

Q: I have cataracts. Can your device help me?

A: If you have cataracts, they should be removed surgically. This is a lot less invasive than implanting a visual prosthesis.

Q: I have low vision. Does this device only benefit those who are completely blind?

A: Patients who have a small amount of vision are not contraindicated. Visual cortex stimulation seems to work the same in both sighted and blind patients.

Q: How much will this device cost?

A: The system has been deliberately designed to take advantage of commercial off-the-shelf components. This cost-saving approach is sometimes known by the military acronym COTS. A few years from now I believe the cost of the procedure, including medical charges and the device, will be in the neighborhood of USD $50,000 although it will be much more expensive in the immediate future.

Q: Will my insurance carrier pay for your device?

A: We have secured reimbursement authority from Medicare and analogous private and government insurance plans around the world for our other devices. We believe this will also be true of the visual prosthesis, but it will undoubtedly take a number of years.

9. Technical Questions

Q: I would like to know more about the technical details of your system. Where can I find more information?

A: All releasable technical details are in the ASAIO Journal article and in other publications cited in the bibliography. If it is not covered in the paper, it is probably proprietary because of patent applications, etc.
Q: I have some ideas which I would like to discuss with you. How do I reach you?

A: Sorry, because of legal constraints, I cannot talk to you about your ideas. If you have a granted patent or published article, please send it to me.

Q: Why are you using surface electrodes?

A: Of course I have thought about intracortical depth electrodes and other penetrating electrodes (for example, the geniculocalcarine radiations). In fact, I originally proposed those approaches to the National Institutes of Health in 1970. Since that time, I have realized that the occipital lobe can move as much as two centimeters, and such penetrating electrodes are an invitation to fatal hemorrhage.

Q: Have you considered other approaches which would not require surgery?

A: Of course I have also thought of magnetic stimulation and other noninvasive techniques. I simply don't see how to employ arrays of such stimulators.

Q: Why have you chosen this approach over retinal stimulation?

A: Retinal stimulation is technically very easy. I even conducted experiments on myself in 1977. However, only a limited number of blind patients have intact retinas.
Cortical stimulators could be used by virtually all blind patients.

Q: Why haven't you developed your device to be completely implantable?

A: Using a percutaneous connector and keeping all of the hardware and software outside the body allows for easy service and easy "upgrades." For example, Jerry has already used six different systems over the last twenty-one years. Experienced bioengineers try to avoid implanting microelectronic circuitry, particularly custom chips, anywhere in the body. I believe a "total implant" would be a step backward.

I read and reread the questions and their corresponding answers, all the while forming a picture of my mentor—William Dobelle. I had already formed a picture of a man who had exceptionally logical problem-solving abilities, along with a well-rounded knowledge of electronics, biological issues, as well as the physical principles of vision. In reading these questions, not only was my former impression of him reinforced, but an element of human compassion was obvious. For instance, in answering the question of why this system took so long to come about, he responded by suggesting great concern with respect to the possibility that prolonged stimulation of the visual cortex may cause side effects. He could have been rich and famous years ago if he hadn't taken all of these precautionary measures, which were only for the benefit of the patients. Other examples to substantiate his apparent empathetic character lay in the fact that he saw hope in developing infants' visual cortex via stimulation so they may profit with sight in the future, as well as in the case wherein he commented about the inevitable involvement of blind agencies to assist in the rehabilitation process.

"He really couldn't be doing this for the money," I commented one day to Lorri. "Just look at the investment he already put into this, and considering his age, it is unlikely he will recover this before the end of his time." I hated to think of the end of his time. Someone so dedicated to bettering the plight of humanity deserved to revel in his accomplishments for many years. It did not seem right for someone to work so hard, hold up his accomplishments for the world to see just to die soon afterward.

"Let's hope he'll live for a while," Lorri replied. "He really couldn't be doing this for cash, as he would surely not deter those with one eye or with cataracts from investing into the system."

How true, I thought. I could not help but read between the lines about the cataracts.

"If you have cataracts, they should be removed surgically. This is a lot less invasive than implanting a visual prosthesis." In this sentence, he was suggesting that the logical reason for removing the cataracts is purely practical from the standpoint of the surgery. By no means did he suggest the vision was superior coming from one's own retina. He seems to leave the vision produced by the removal of cataracts and that offered by the prosthesis on an equal level. Looking back, I recall that my landlady in Sydenham had been almost blind from cataracts, and after having them removed, she could drive her car if she wore the heavy glasses, which magnified her eyes to the size of saucers when facing her.

I couldn't help but toy with this idea. The farm upon which we lived had been set up by me so I could drive a pickup truck, tractors, and anything else on four wheels, but I was restricted to our property. It was a nice jail here, but still a jail. I fantasized briefly of perhaps cheating on the eye test, perhaps in using digital magnification, and thus reacquiring my driver's license, once I had this implant in my head. In the area where I lived, a man without a driver's license was really stuck, with nowhere to go. This was evident by how everyone's children in my neighborhood put every effort into attaining their right to drive the day they were of age. I couldn't wait to get back into it myself. "Hold on," I told myself. "Not so fast. You're not in yet."

Just out of interest, I scanned the literature describing the life of William Dobelle.

Curriculum Vita William H. Dobelle, PhD

Founding Fellow American Institute for Medical and Biological Engineering

Dr. Dobelle has been accorded one of the highest honors available to an American scientist with election by his peers as a Founding

Fellow. Formal induction ceremonies were held in 1993 at the National Academy of Sciences, Washington, DC.

Chairman & Chief Executive Officer The Dobelle Institute. Inc. Columbia-Presbyterian Medical Center. New York. NY The Dobelle Institute was the first tenant in Columbia University's Audubon Biomedical Science and Technology Park. This facility was dedicated by New York's Governor George Pataki in 1995. The institute is involved in collaborative efforts with physicians at the Medical Center to surgically implant neurological "pacemakers" developed by Dr. Dobelle to control breathing, intractable hiccups, and chronic pain. It also continues long-term educational programs and efforts to improve—and develop new types of neurological stimulators, including development of artificial vision for the blind (TV camera connected to the brain by a computer).

President. Dobelle Laboratories. Avery Laboratories. & Institut
Dobelle AG Commack. NY and Zurich. Switzerland 1982. Present Avery Laboratories was founded by others in 1969, Institut Dobelle AG (Zurich) was organized by Dr. Dobelle in 1983, and Dobelle Laboratories in 1993. These companies have been pioneers in the manufacture and distribution of permanently implanted electronics for the stimulation of the human brain and central nervous system. Avery Laboratories was a founding member of the Health Industry Manufacturers Association, a three hundred-member trade association whose affiliates produce over 90 percent of the diagnostic and medical equipment manufactured in the United States. Avery Laboratories was also a founding member—and Dr. Dobelle has been a board member—of Medmarc, Ltd., a Befmuda company (now reincorporated in Vermont) which is an acknowledged leader providing product liability insurance to medical device manufacturers. Dr. Dobelle financed his transition from academia to industry by organizing companies that developed a revolutionary family of large sail-assisted catamarans for commercial and recreational purposes, a number of which remain in service in the Caribbean.

Director: Division of Artificial Organs. Columbia-Presbyterian Medical Center New York. NY 1976–81
The division, which Dr. Dobelle organized, involved about fifty full—and part-time investigators. including collaborative programs with colleagues at other institutions in the United States, Japan, Canada, and Europe. Research included artificial vision for

the blind—the project with which Dr. Dobelle is most publicly identified—as well as cardiac assist devices in man, organ banking including human heart transplantation, hybrid and mechanical artificial pancreas for diabetics, and artificial hearing for the deaf via electrical stimulation of the skin. Dr. Dobelle also organized and directed the Presbyterian Hospital Organ Bank (heart, kidney, skin, bone, cornea, etc.) and helped reorganize the New York Regional Transplant Program, transferring it from the Blood Center to the auspices of the New York Academy of Medicine. Funding for these efforts was provided by grants and contracts from the National Institutes of Health, National Science Foundation, and about hundred private foundations and industrial benefactors. He also organized and directed a program for gifted students from the Bronx High School of Science and other selected public and private schools. Alumni achieved recognition in the Westinghouse Science Talent Search and Rhodes Scholarship competition, and some have continued to work in Dr. Dobelle's laboratories.

Associate Director. The Institute for Biomedical Engineering, The University Of Utah—Salt Lake City. UT 1969–75 Initiated and directed research on artificial vision for the blind (electrical stimulation of the visual cortex), and artificial hearing for the deaf (intracochlear stimulation) as well as planning and administrative responsibilities for several other projects including total artificial heart. Completed a PhD in Physiology while working as a full-time faculty member. He also organized and directed both the university's Microelectronics Laboratory and the Intermountain Organ Bank. The Johns Hopkins University Baltimore. Maryland 1960–67, supporting himself with a full-time job on the Hopkins' research staff. Dr. Dobelle completed BA and MA degrees in biophysics. During this period, he coauthored an important series of papers characterizing human cone pigments thus elucidating the physiological basis for human three-color vision. To provide human retinas for this research, he organized the Medical Eye Bank of Maryland which quickly became the world's largest. He also led a series of scientific and historical collecting expeditions; quarry ranged from iguana gall bladders in South America's Orinoco river basin to sperm whale hearts in the North Pacific. These expeditions subsequently resulted in his election as a fellow of the Explorer's Club. In 1987, after a series of expeditions which began in 1962, Dr. Dobelle finally succeeded in tracing Balboa's route of discovery through the jungles of Panama, rediscovering the famous lost peak from which Balboa first sighted the Pacific Ocean (" . . . silent on a peak in Darien").

Executive Director. Republican State Central Committee of Maryland 1968

While at Johns Hopkins, Dr. Dobelle became interested in the applications of computers to political campaigns and served as a campaign aide to Maryland Governor, Spiro T. Agnew. In 1968, he took a sabbatical from science and served as Director of the Maryland Republican Party coordinating campaigns for the US Senate and eight seats in the US House of Representatives with the national Nixon-Agnew campaign. He also served as a consultant to other federal candidates throughout the United States and later worked on campaign in England and in France.

Early Education and Research 1941–59

Born on October 24, 1941, in Pittsfield, Massachusetts, and raised in Massachusetts and Florida. Earliest research on artificial hip, conducted with his orthopedic surgeon father, resulting in a series of patents at age thirteen. A Vanderbilt University senior at age eighteen, Dr. Dobelle dropped out of school to do independent research on visual physiology, supporting himself as a Porsche mechanic and commercial fisherman.

Publications and Professional Activities Dr. Dobelle has published many articles on artificial organs, biotechnology, organ transplantation, microelectronics, and regulatory affairs in professional journals and has twice received the Kusserow Award from the American Society for Artificial Internal Organs (ASAIO). He has served on the editorial boards of the Journal of Artificial Organs, the International Journal of Artificial Organs, and Medical Device and Diagnostic Industry. He also serves on program and administrative committees for a number of professional societies in the United States and Europe and has been a grant reviewer/site visitor for NIH, NSF, the VA, and several private foundations. Long involved in regulatory affairs, he formulated the "IDE Application Form" now widely used for investigative applications to the FDA, chaired Food & Drug Administration liaison activities for ASAIO, and served on the executive committee of the American National Standards Institute's medical device panel. (His father. Dr. Martin Dobelle, took several sabbaticals from private practice. First, as director of a crippled children's hospital on a New Mexico Indian reservation. Later, as chief surgeon for the Missile Test Center at Cape Canaveral. In 1964, he joined the FDA to organize the predecessor of today's Bureau of Medical Devices).

Personal
Married to Claire Louise Atkinson, a writer and TV producer. She cofounded the Press and the Public Project, an independent production company that has won a number of national Emmys for their documentaries on PBS/TV, including the weekly press series Inside Story with Hodding Carter. The Dobelles commute between an apartment in Lincoln Center and a home on Long Island with their three young children, Martin David (b: 10/2/90), Molly Laura (b: 1/31/92), and Mimi Lillian (b: 11/4/93). Martin David may become a third-generation medical device developer. At age nine, he has filed his first patent for the idea of providing a TV/computer/ Internet interface for the artificial vision device. Dr. Bill Dobelle's other interests include opera, ballet, and sailing.

"I'd better practice up the Mozart and Chopin on the piano," I said out loud upon reading the last sentence. Opera, ballet and sailing! This was no hillbilly from Napanee.

I had to read this literature several times just to be able to absorb it all. Not only would this man be of superior intelligence, but also of astounding physique, possessing an infinite supply of energy always being translated into obvious productivity. I was certainly too old to believe in heroes, but this guy was coming rather close to the example of a perfect human being. It was difficult to imagine one person could accomplish this much in one lifetime, considering the diverse nature of all of his accomplishments—medical device engineering, exploration, politics . . . Yet, the most pertinent of all was his claimed success in the development of his neurostimulator devices described in the first few sentences of his curriculum. "He has what it takes," I told myself, as all there was left to do was to make sure I did my share as well and not disappoint him.

The next step on the venture was to secure my physical and eye exams. The physical was routine, with the exception of the question printed on the form which read: "How much alcohol do you consume?"

I scratched my head about this one. I had no idea about the medical pertinence of this query, yet knowing the "perfectionist" culture that Eastern Canada was becoming more and more known for, I was tempted to write in that I did not drink. This could, however, backfire as New Yorkers come from far too diverse a background to masquerade as "nonsmoking, sober, and celibate" model citizens. I decided to fill in the blank the "1 per day" selection, as that was a happy medium between the model citizen, the sociable drinker, and most of all, giving Dr. Dobelle the impression that I am not a liar, and therefore he can safely believe the other answers I had responded to on the questionnaire.

My family doctor, however, had different ideas. "One drink a day?!" she said exasperatingly. I had no idea if that meant it was too much or not enough. I was about to admit that it was closer to two to four a day, when she continued, "You're an alcoholic by medical standards!"

I did not think it was that bad and hoped that Dr. Dobelle would be a more open-minded individual.

Next on the list was Dr. Willis. I decided to go to him not so much for the eye exam, which I could have acquired elsewhere, but more to discuss the idea of artificial vision. Having been there from the start of my blindness, his insight would play a role in my quest for vision.

We met in the same clinic we sat in eighteen years ago when I first lost my last eye. Dr. Willis sounded considerably older, and I imagine I did too. He had, nonetheless, remembered the details of my case as he had once stated that very rarely does he encounter a situation in which a patient is blinded so suddenly and so totally at the threshold of their life.

"So you are giving it another shot," he stated in a tone insinuating total support for my involvement and my ambition to see once again. The warmth in his attitude was ever-present. If Dr. Dobelle shared an equal personality, I once said to Lorri, we would have all we ever wanted in New York.

"I've done quite a bit since we last met," I said to him, referring to the family, the work, even the fact that I survived eighteen years—a feat which hadn't been entirely anticipated when I had lost my sight. "But I still have not even come close to living the way I once did."

Dr. Willis needed no convincing. He was an active man, living in total independence out in the rural district of Kingston, and he loved driving his car.

"No doubt it would be nice if this worked," he said, scanning the letter I received from Dr. Dobelle, along with the literature attached, describing the details of the project.

"Do you think OHIP may pay for this?" I asked him, not knowing what to expect for an answer.

"It's hard to tell," he said, picking up a form off his desk. "I can certainly assist you in recommending this procedure once you are sure you are going," he offered. "I will have to investigate it further, however, in order to ensure the legitimacy of this company, and make sure the players are qualified physicians."

"I really wouldn't want to go if they aren't," I said. "The last thing I need is to have my head opened up in someone's basement!"

"You mean, just like Dr. Frankenstein?" joked Lorri.

That name *Frankenstein* came back to haunt me later. I don't know if Lorri felt what I did when speaking my last sentence, considering that our "basement" obstetrics actually served us better than did the "legitimate" doctors at the Kingston General Hospital when it came to birthing our children. But this time is different, I thought, as unlike childbirth, brain surgery is, after all, a medical procedure.

The help from Dr. Willis would be vital in receiving support from the Ontario Health Insurance Plan. If we did get approval, however, Dr. Willis warned us they may not agree to pay in advance. In that case, we would have to pay for it first, making the quest for money important in spite of the reimbursement. If the Canadian Dollar kept its value of $72 US and the price remained at $50,000 US, we should be able to do it.

I sent off the forms from the medical exams, fully in anticipation of a reply. I occupied myself in my business, cutting vigorously the firewood, hoping for a cold winter so that lots of this would be sold, giving us enough money to pay Dr. Dobelle. October was a busy month in sales, and with every cord of wood sold, I was another $180 closer to a world of light and pictures. It was on one of these afternoons that Lorri charged out of the back door, yelling, "Someone from the Dobelle Institute wants to talk to you!"

I was still dripping with sweat and sawdust when I charged into the house, still wearing my rubber boots and removing the earplugs while I grabbed the phone.

"Hello, Mr. Naumann?" It was a young man, sounding fresh, enthusiastic, and educated. "It's Lou Coleman from the Dobelle Institute."

"I'm really glad to hear from you," I said with equal sincerity. "What can I help you with?"

Lou began his explanation: "We'd like to get a better idea of what you expect from the vision system we are offering. We have composed a questionnaire which suggests various scenarios encountered in life, and we'd like you to choose the one which best describes your preference."

"That seems simple enough," I retorted, anxious to hear the questions as they may provide me with a better idea as to the potential of the artificial vision system.

"First question, then," began Lou. "Which is more important to you: to drive a car, to walk down the street unassisted, or to pick out your own products in a supermarket?"

I had to think this one over. It was obvious that the best vision was demanded in driving a car and the least was required for walking unassisted down the sidewalk. I worried about the fact that if I chose the "to drive a car" choice, perhaps I would give the impression I would not be satisfied if the vision was slightly inferior than required for attaining a license. However, should I choose the one requiring the least vision, perhaps I would appear as lacking ambition in returning to the real life of the visual, and thus bringing little merit to the efforts of Dr. Dobelle.

"I would love to be able to drive a car," I chose my words with care, "nonetheless, should I attain vision which is less than required for that, I would still be very happy to pick out my products to purchase, or even just to be able to walk down a sidewalk without assistance." I hoped I wouldn't spoil my chances to get in by how I answered to this interview.

"Next," continued Lou, "would it be more important to you to drive a car, walk unassisted, or watch television?"

Again I pondered. "I'm not much of a couch potato, so the TV is hardly my priority," I started, adding quickly, "It would be great to be able to do, especially in looking at the monitor of a computer. But I still say that the mobility concerns are the most pertinent for me." I did not draw distinction between the driving or the walking this time, as my main goal was to give the impression I would be tolerant of imperfections with the system, yet promote its merits to the maximum.

Lou went on with the interview. "Which is more important to you: to walk unassisted, pick out your own products in a supermarket, or watch television?"

I was somewhat puzzled at the course the questionnaire was taking. Lou kept using three of the same four scenarios, mixing them up in all manners possible with each question. I kept on answering them without specifying any concrete demands from the vision system offered. All the time, however, I was worried about giving the wrong impression, risking falling into a trap, yet found it overwhelming to hear him mention doing activities such as driving a car, watching television, or picking out my own products in a supermarket. It had been a half a lifetime since I did those things that the rest of society seems to take for granted.

"You have to admit, though," I had to interrupt Lou to clarify myself, "if a person had enough vision to drive a car, which would constitute 20/40 in acuity, he'd have no problem doing anything else, like those other choices you suggested. But that does not mean," I had to reiterate, "that should I not have the required acuity that I would be dissatisfied."

"But you'd have a hole in your head with a cable coming out," replied Lou, abandoning his prewritten script.

"That's no big deal," I returned as convincingly as possible. "You have to remember that I am totally in the dark right now. Just to see a bit would be priceless, even if it means a wire comes out of my head and electronic components are strapped to me. Being totally in the dark is not a healthy way to live."

"I can only imagine," Lou replied in total understanding. "I'll certainly tell Dr. Dobelle how you feel and what you are hoping to gain. Thanks for the interview."

I hung up the telephone with the certainty that I had given myself the best chance to get into this project. Lorri could not help commenting, "That's really something! You were talking about driving a car, watching TV and all that. Is that really what this will do?"

"I suppose so, or they never would have posed those kinds of questions." I thought hard of how these activities could be possible to do with only sixty-eight points of light, as implanted in the volunteer. "Perhaps they really improved the system since the original article was written in year 2000. Whatever it is, though, there is no sense doubting the word of Dr. Dobelle, considering his education. If he says I'll be able to drive, then it must be so."

There was no more news from the Dobelle Institute for the rest of the year. When Christmas came, we refrained from spending much, demanding from the children that they sacrifice this Christmas's fruits for those of the future, when we can recommence a life of fun and adventure, as we had once planned when Lorri and I first got married. "Next year I'll see the tree you are decorating," I had said one day while the tree was being erected in the living room. It still sounded too good to be true.

We waited, somewhat impatiently, for the next news from Dr. Dobelle.

Near the end of January came another letter from Dr. Dobelle. There was even more excitement accompanied with its discovery in the mailbox than with the last one.

January 26, 2001

Dear Mr. Naumann:
In Re: Implant of Visual Prostheses

Please excuse my delay in following up on your questionnaire. I had emergency open-heart surgery in October (coronary artery bypass grafts), and I just returned to the laboratory full time last week. I am recovering rapidly and feel fine.

We have now made arrangements to implant the next series of patients in Lisbon, Portugal. There are three reasons for this. First, Joao Lobo Antunes, MD, who will be doing the surgery, implanted Jerry while Joao was a faculty member at Columbia-Presbyterian

Medical Center in New York. He is now dean of the Medical School and chairman of the Department of Neurosurgery at the University of Lisbon. Joao attended medical school in Lisbon—where his father was professor of neurology—then trained in neurosurgery at Columbia Presbyterian. He is board-certified in the United States and serves as president of the European Neurosurgical Society.

Joao Antunes will be assisted by Prof. John P. Girvin, former chairman of the departments of neurology and neurosurgery at the University of Western Ontario in London, Canada. John is a past president of the Canadian Neurological Society. Prof. Girvin also trained in the United States and is board certified in the United States. Drs. Antunes and Girvin have done the surgery on all blind volunteers implanted by us since 1968; therefore, we are highly confident of the skills of the surgical team.

Second, the private CUF Hospital—where surgery will be performed—is now completing a new office building as part of their complex, which will house the Dobelle Institute (Portugal) Lda. Third, the regulatory situation in Portugal is favorable. As you may know, almost all drugs and devices are introduced abroad before permission is sought from the FDA for sale in the United States.

Prior to surgery, Professors Antunes and Girvin will do a complete physical exam, including radiological studies. Beth Seelig, MD—Director of the Psychoanalytic Institute at Emory University in Atlanta—will conduct psychiatric screening in Lisbon. Beth is an ophthalmologist as well as a psychiatrist, and she screened the previous patients, including Jerry.

The price for the implant has not been established yet, because we do not know the number of patients who are interested. There are substantial fixed costs that need to be offset, and the more patients that are interested, the lower the cost per patient. You can expect to spend only one night in the hospital but will have to remain in Lisbon for about a week so we can be sure that you are free of infection before you return home. This will be a pleasant experience, since Lisbon is a lovely, modern city. It is also very inexpensive by international standards. Although we do not anticipate any particular problems, it will also be wise to involve your local physician to provide follow-up after you return home.

I am enclosing a copy of the article about Jerry, two stories from *Business Week*, and a summary of the video/audio clips which can be accessed on the Web (www.artificialvision.com). While you may already have this material, I am sending a second set to be sure.

Jerry—the blind volunteer has been implanted for twenty-three years—and I will call you within the next month to follow up on this letter. If you have any questions, feel free to e-mail me (whd@ dobelle.com). I look forward to further discussions in the near future.

Sincerely,
Wm. H. Dobelle, PhD
Chairman & Chief Executive Officer

The contents stuck in my head like glue.

"He must be taking my application seriously," I said, adding, "and he's really getting serious about getting this done!"

Lorri reread the part about his heart surgery. "Imagine if this guy got a heart attack now and died. What terrible timing this is for heart trouble."

"I'd hope he has a backup team should that happen. Just look at the hotshots he has listed in this letter, such as Professor Girvin, Dr. Antunes, and Dr. Seelig. Surely they would carry it right on."

"Right," said Lorri, "I remember his previous information he gave us saying that over three hundred scientists from all different facets of technology were involved in this project. There is no way it can die now."

At least I hoped not. There certainly were some impressive players—a director of a psychiatric institute and two presidents of national neurological societies. What more could one ask for, I asked myself.

I just have to get in as a patient now. It seemed like I had passed all the tests so far. The next thing to wait for will be the telephone call from Dr. Dobelle. I already prepared some questions for him and hoped I would be in the house when he called.

On February 15, 2001, I had the flu and spent my time in bed, feeling miserable while the cold wind howled outside. There were a lot of customers purchasing firewood from my business, and due to my condition Lorri managed them between those arriving at the door and those calling on the telephone. In the early afternoon, I was awakened by the ringing of the telephone. I heard Lorri's side of the conversation.

" . . . no, I'm sorry, but he is sick in bed today. Can I take a message?"

Suspicious of who it might be, I struggled out of bed, just to hear the next part of Lorri's dialog. " . . . did you say Dobelle?"

I was in the kitchen, reaching for the receiver. "Just a minute," Lorri continued, "he is out of bed now and wants to talk to you."

I pressed the receiver to my ear, forgetting completely about the side effects of my flu.

"Hey . . . ! How's it going, Jens," drawled a voice on the line, resembling that of a roughneck inquiring about firewood with the intention of dealing me down, wearing a torn plaid shirt and blue jeans. "I hear you're a bit under the weather today!"

"Is this you, Dr. Dobelle?"

"Hell, just call me Bill!" was the comeback, just like those truckers I spoke to often on the Citizens' Band radio. "Your application got my attention from the unusual number of children you have!" explained Dr. Dobelle. I chuckled, wanting to make a comment on that, but thought better of it.

"I'm hardly sick when comparing it to your heart condition you spoke of in your last letter." I then added in his language, "It looked like you were going to push daisies instead of getting the vision project going." I heard a sign of disapproval from Lorri as she attempted to tell me that one does not talk to a doctor like that.

"Yeah, damn right!" said Dr. Dobelle. "I had just come from a trip from abroad, when I felt this pain in my chest and arm. A doctor friend of mine took only one look at me, and before I knew it, I was in the operating room for the surgery. He figured I was almost lost. But I'm fine now."

"Bill, that sounds good. It would be a shame to go now. I'm really interested in this vision system and want to get in as fast as possible. I have the $50,000 and read all the information, so I have an idea of what to expect."

Dr. Dobelle started on that subject right away. "The price is going to be $66,000 US. That'll cover everything including the warrantee, testing, etc." He let it sink in, to which I immediately replied, "OK. That's fine, no problem." But I knew it would be a problem.

"You do want this money all up front, do you?"

"Well, yeah," he said in his slow, deliberate manner of speaking, "Once this stuff is in the patient's head, and he doesn't want to pay, you can't rightly pull it back out!"

I imagined a berserk doctor in scrubs, wearing small spectacles chasing after a patient down the corridor of a hospital while holding a pair of vice grips, intent on recovering the implant from the patient delinquent on his account . . .

"What would you say about what I can expect to see?"

"I've got Jerry, our first volunteer, on the line too," began Bill. I was not too anxious to talk to Jerry, as I read lots of him in the articles sent, and as well, he did not have the new "bilateral" system, in which two implants are used. "You should be able to recognize faces with the new system, wouldn't you think so, Jerry?" Dr. Dobelle was turning to Jerry, who was sharing the line in New York with him.

"Maybe" was Jerry's reply following a notable pause.

"Yeah, you should be able to recognize faces with this new system, Jens." repeated Dr. Dobelle to me.

"Wow!" was my reply, imagining the faces of my children in dot-matrix format. "Tell me, Bill, am I really a patient now?"

"Hell, yeah," said Bill in an "of course" manner, "I wouldn't waste my time calling if you weren't!" He then added, "I'd already gone through some 1,200 applications and am getting kind of tired of it."

That was music to my ears. I had other questions. "When do you figure on doing the implantation?"

"No later than April, or at the latest June. Count on April." I took that at face value. That would not leave much time to find the extra money. But the wait, at the same time, would not be so painfully long.

"You have no doubts it will work for me?"

"I see no reason why it wouldn't work," said Dr. Dobelle "Well, count me in, Bill," I said in total conviction, "just let me know when you want the down payment."

"Very well, then," said Bill, showing no sign of doubt in having me as a patient. "Real nice talking to you, and should you have any questions, just give me a shout."

"By the way," he added, "I'll send you an official invoice with the breakdown of the equipment on it."

"That should let me get the application for OHIP funding," I replied, hoping this would make up for the shortfall now that the price just went up another $16,000 US.

"I wouldn't count on it," said Dr. Dobelle, "I've dealt with OHIP before, and they're not all that imaginative. But you can always try to get a refund on some later date."

That was it for my first meeting with Dr. Dobelle.

After I hung up the telephone, Lorri turned to me.

"I first thought it was some roughneck wanting to buy firewood." He did not sound all that highly educated, I thought to myself, but then again, look at all he has done.

"First impressions aren't always accurate. It must be the New York accent," I responded, the next issue on my mind. "It's going to be another $16,000 American bucks more than we first thought."

"Not good news," said Lorri, then suggested, "maybe the exchange went up for the American dollar."

I telephoned the Bank of Montreal hotline for exchange rates, just to find it had done the contrary.

"It's below sixty-eight cents now," I said, a sinking feeling setting in. This meant another $5,000 more in Canadian dollars to come up with. I had no idea how far I could push Lorri's support in this venture. There were, after all, other people in this family whose needs had to be met as well.

Then, remembering I was really "in" the project, I said, "Dr. Dobelle said I will really get this come April or June."

We thought long and hard about the cash situation. While I had talked to Dr. Dobelle, Lorri sold another $50 on firewood. However, in the course of the last few months, the exchange rate of the Canadian dollar dropped more yet, costing us yet another $5,000, and on top of that, Dr. Dobelle now announced that we needed another $25,000 in our dollars more. Now we were at well over $100,000 Canadian, and there was no way we could get it together before June. What a mess!

"We will have to raise it somehow," began Lorri. I was hoping she would have ideas. "We'll have to go to the different clubs, the Canadian National Institute for the Blind, and try all we can with OHIP."

"I'll phone the CNIB in Kingston and see what they can do, as well as start the application with Dr. Willis for the OHIP application," I said, firing up the computer. There was a lot of work to be done.

My first step was to call the Canadian National Institute for the Blind. It only made sense, as this group was dedicated to helping those who couldn't see. To me it made just as much sense to call on them as it would to call a mechanic should one have car trouble. It was Armando I reached, the same man who taught me how to read braille eighteen years ago. He himself had lost his sight while he was a young teenager and thus had understanding toward my situation.

"Just imagine how this would help everyone should this work out," I said to him, figuring he would also profit from the availability of the system in Canada for all the blind to have.

"No doubt it would be nice," he said, then reminding me, "but remember that for the forty or so years that I have been blind, many promising newscasts with so many promises and predictions made by 'scientists' have come and gone, all of which promised to make the blind see or the crippled walk, and yet the number of people registering with the CNIB is ever increasing, and as you know, wheelchairs are still in use today."

I thought of John, the man who had first met me to attempt to cheer me up when I had first lost my sight. Having been blind for eleven years at that time, he had portrayed himself as the ultimate model of rehabilitation as he spoke of how his life continued as normal despite his blindness. Yet, when he was invited to participate in that experimental retinal surgery a few years later, the very hint of a promise of vision caused all of his tediously constructed barriers against depression from blindness come crashing down as he spoke to me on the telephone of all that he will experience once he can see again — only for the operation to fail.

But it was too late for me now—my barriers were long gone. Armando knew that, as he did not elaborate further on that point.

"I can give you the name of the E. A. Baker foundation for the Prevention of Blindness's representative, and you may also want to try the Lion's Club, the Rotary, the Knights of Columbus, the Trilium Foundation, even try to tap into the unclaimed lottery winnings fund. There is also the 'assistive devices' program funded by the provincial government, but I have no idea about their policies regarding this system you want."

First I had to do all I could from my end. I advertised anything I could get my hands on that actually belonged to me. Lorri had offered to put the piano up for sale, but I protested. "You need that to earn money. Besides," I added jokingly, "maybe I have to use it to practice up and play piano for donations!"

"That may be an idea," said Lorri, not taking it as a joke. In the meantime, I sold what was left of my farming equipment and anything I had to provide some sort of personal entertainment which could be sacrificed. I had a few pistols I had used for target shooting, a four-wheel drive truck with a snowplow I enjoyed driving around the property, and various other gadgets I figured were worth the sacrifice. Nothing would be as good as seeing, so there was never a doubt. If I can avoid selling the house then that would make these sacrifices all for the better.

I called around to the former piano tuning customers I had on list for the possibility of making a bit extra in the work department. Any extra revenue would be welcome. One of those on the list was the Napanee Grace United Church, for whom I tuned their pianos. I knew the secretary who worked there as a compassionate woman who really enjoyed the fact that after tuning a piano, I would try it out by playing a classical tune.

Sharon, the secretary, listened to my story and said, "You know, Jens, you can play really good on the piano. Maybe you can hold a concert here at the church and we'll advertise it for you. Let me talk to the minister, and I'll get back to you."

I hung up the telephone, wondering if I really had enough to offer for a concert. I played a few of my Royal Conservatory of Music exam repertoire from time to time, but since I was not occupied with making a living from the piano playing, I had not played much. I did, however, insist in playing enough times the pieces I had memorized and liked, as it took a lot of effort to memorize a song. In the process, Lorri would read note-for-note a single bar of music, giving details regarding the octave and duration each note is played in a single bar. Generally, we could only cover a bar of music at a time, and I would play that bar over and over again until it stuck in my memory. When learning the following bar, I would keep playing the former bar or bars already learned lest I forget them. The process is painfully slow and inefficient, but effective nonetheless for learning a composition to its exact detail, a requirement of the Royal Conservatory of Music. Together Lorri and I hammered the repertoire for the grades seven to ten in my head plus a few extra compositions in order to allow me to complete the exams. Disappointingly, at the end of it all, I never could apply my abilities in this field as the small-town mentality toward blindness in Napanee made it impossible. I had tried, only to have an individual call up one day, inquiring about music lessons for her child:

"I heard you are blind and pull the shades and teach the students in complete darkness," she had said, conveying to me the rumors that circulated through town about this absurd idea.

I could not understand how anyone could think that I'd get away with it even if I had such strange teaching methodology. Thus, even though Lorri had, at that time, a lower level of musical education, I encouraged any students I had to join with her instead. I could not afford, if not for my sake but for my children's, a reputation as a weirdo in this little town. I had kids that were going to school, and the last thing they needed to contend with was to be made into a laughingstock.

Sharon, the secretary of the United Church in Napanee, called back within a day and gave me the news that I would have the opportunity to play in the church, and as well in that of the United Church in Newberg, a small town about a half hour's drive east of Napanee. The congregation would be told of this event in advance, and it was up to me to convince them of the merits of this venture and to ask for their donations to make this possible for me. I accepted.

This was the beginning of my fund-raising venture, and it was difficult. I practiced the piano in the evenings, cut and sold wood in the daytime, and also took the time to lobby other clubs to be supportive. As I practiced my classical compositions, I thought hard of the speech I would have to make to the crowd. That would be the most difficult of all. I would feel like a beggar, my pride down on the ground while I pleaded for support. That was going to be contrary to my beliefs, no matter how supportive the crowd would be. Moreover, the ministers had mentioned it would be appropriate if all my kids accompanied me to the evenings where I played. Danielle now was seventeen, Ryan fifteen, Leah thirteen, and the others younger, yet not too young to understand what was going on. It would be hard on them too. I hoped, for their sake more than for mine, it would all be worth it.

One day the telephone interrupted my music practice. It was Carmen, the man who had lost one eye recently through glaucoma, all the while visiting a doctor in Kingston every five days to make sure the other remained intact.

"I heard of you and your quest for the artificial vision operation through Armando at the CNIB," he said, sounding older than the last time I spoke to him.

"Are you a volunteer driver for the CNIB now?" I asked him, figuring he would do that as he had recently retired.

"No, not me. I'm a client now. My other eye went recently," he said in disgust, adding, "here I went to the doctor every few days, and I figured they had everything under control. Then I woke up one day and saw practically nothing."

I felt miserable suddenly. I did not even know what to say. Now I knew what it felt like to be on the other end—like those who visited me after I had lost my sight. There was no way I was going to be able to console him on this one. I had so much more ammunition to do so in comparison to what John had when he visited me in the hospital eighteen years ago, and all of this Carmen had seen for himself, but there was no denying it—it was a miserable situation compared to the beautiful world of sight. "Carmen, I think this artificial vision can work. If it does, I'll do everything in my power to let you get a crack at it too. I'm sure I will have clout down there when I get my operation and this way be able to convince them to take you on next." That was the best I had to offer, and it was more than was offered me eighteen years ago when I had first heard that blindness would be a part of my life forever.

"I can't wait, although my heart is weak, and I may not qualify for the operation. In the meantime, I have been doing some stuff around here, like splitting wood with the axe. I walk some with the cane too and drive my truck in and out of the garage. My wife told me one day," he told me, rather proud of her, 'since you saw what Jens did despite being blind, you have no excuse to sit around feeling sorry for yourself. Get out and do something!' And so I just had to get out and do something!

I laughed at this. "Carmen, there is nothing worse for a blind person to have than a companion that gives you no room to maneuver. I imagine if my wife was overly protective of me, I would have left her first thing!"

Carmen reassured me. "I'm sure the CNIB will help you, and with me being a member of the client board, I'll bring up the issue again at our next meeting. In the meantime, do let me know what progress you will have."

I couldn't wait for the chance to show Carmen, to walk up to his house alone, knock on his door, and say "let's go in town" and then engage in all the activities left only for the lucky in the world. I had no doubt he would be a candidate for this operation as well, considering the operation had such minor side effects that Dr. Dobelle considered it as "day surgery."

It was all the Carmens, the people presently suffering in darkness or those who will be in the future that I thought of when speaking to the congregation at the Newberg United Church the evening I played piano for money. The minister, a compassionate lady called Georgia, briefly introduced me, then it was up to me to do the talking. I stood in front of the audience, feeling their expectant expressions upon my face. I thought of a time long, long ago how nervous I was when, in sixth grade school, I had faced the entire class in giving a science presentation about the principles of nuclear fission, or at least how I perceived it back then. How much easier that had been compared to this.

"Thank you for taking the trouble to come out here tonight." I began uneasily, then continued, "As Georgia said, I had lost my eyesight in two separate industrial accidents during my youth, and in spite of all efforts to rehabilitate, I only had nominal success in integrating with my sighted counterparts. I had no choice up to now in living with this situation, as I know you understand that it is difficult and unrewarding to say the least."

I didn't like the sound of the negativity I had in my dialogue, as this seriously undermined all what I had accomplished, such as my kids and all I had done in spite of the hurdles. I realized then that the kids never had listened to me talk this negatively about myself before. But, I told myself, one has to do what is necessary if one has a mission to accomplish. This time, the mission was wrenching the hearts of the audience for the justification of supporting this newest venture.

"Recently there has been a lot of research in various parts of the world in combating blindness, and, to my surprise, I was accepted to such a research institute in the United States as a patient for an artificial vision implant. With this system, electronic components such as those used in computers are used together with other components installed on the surface of the patient's brain so that small dots of white light can make up a picture equal to what is in front of the patient. I'd be able to see where I am going, where other people are, and read large text, which would be an enormous improvement in my life."

"Unfortunately, the price is set at $66,000 US, about $100,000 in Canadian dollars, and even though I am doing all I can in attaining this sum, I am still short, as OHIP will most likely not pay for this procedure. I have therefore prepared a musical evening for you to enjoy, and I hope to one day be able to see your faces while you watch my fingers move on the keyboard."

I continued as the silence was accompanied by a few distant murmurs.

"There are many blind people in Canada who are presently hoping to have the opportunity to see, and in having the vision system available to demonstrate, I am sure that I can convince the authorities at OHIP to integrate the vision system from Dr. Dobelle as part of their mandate to combating blindness, thus allowing all Canadians to profit from this."

Thanks again for coming. I have some documents here to show to you afterward, should you be interested, or maybe even have a friend or relative who is struggling with the loss of eyesight."

I had brought along my letters from Dr. Dobelle along with any other papers on the issue. I then sat down and played Chopin, Shubert, Beethoven, and a dozen other masterpieces on the rickety old church upright piano, hoping it would at least hold out intact until the end of the concert. I had been able to play piano before I had lost my sight, and even after eighteen years, I still thought it easier to play while being able to see the keyboard. I couldn't wait for that to be, once again, a reality.

The evening went well—the turnout was good, and my fingers weren't too rusty. Lorri and I spoke to many people before leaving, all of whom wished us luck and were excited to have me see their faces in June. "Would you be able to recognize me?" was the typical question, upon which, remembering my conversation with "Bill" on February 15, I would answer: "According to this Dr. Dobelle, yes, I should be able to, but you will look a bit grainy."

Georgia called me the next day and announced that the donations totaled $4,469 that night. She was going to hold it in an account, and when I needed it, I would have access to it.

I couldn't resist the urge, in my excitement, to tell Lorri.

"Guess what! We just collected almost $4,500 last night! Isn't that great?" Upon which Lorri replied, "Sure is! By the way, there is another letter here from Dr. Dobelle. I'll read it to you . . ."

Dobelle Institute (Portugal) Lda.

February 20, 2001

To: Jens Naumann

From:
Wm. H. Dobelle, PhD
Chairman & Chief Executive Officer

Sub: Our Telephone Conversation

Jerry and I enjoyed our telephone interview, and we look forward to further discussion in the months ahead.

Most of the patients we have spoken with preferred that surgery be done in June rather than earlier, and that is now our plan. Other details remain as discussed.

As I told you, prices have now been set and a list is enclosed. However, do not send any money until and unless you are asked to do so.

Jerry and I will be talking to patients in the "pool" from now until sometime in April—there are several hundred of you. Once we have gotten a "handle" on the group, we will be back in touch.

If you have any questions in the interim, please e-mail, fax, or call me.

Regards!

Introductory Price List—Delivered in Lisbon, Portugal, Effective February 1, 2001

Visual Prosthesis System (discounted): USD $66,000 consisting of:

-one miniature camera mounted on glasses, one frame grabber, one microcomputer
-one stimulus generation module
-two implanted electrode arrays with percutaneous pedestals, three sets of rechargeable batteries, and one charger

This price includes:

-all psychiatric evaluation and testing—five years' full warranty (not including travel or freight)—five years' annual follow-up examinations in Portugal (not including travel)
-five years' access to all upgrades and accessories (such as a TV interface) as developed, at "company cost"—Unlimited telephone consultation. Customer responsible for replacement batteries, as needed

Medical/Surgical Fees (payable to physicians) USD $4,000

Hospital Expenses (payable to hospital CUF): USD $5,000 This includes all hospital expenses

Personal Expenses (payable to miscellaneous vendors): USD $5,000 (or less)
This includes our estimate of:
-Airfare to and from Lisbon for two people; hotel for one week for two people; food for one week for two people

-Miscellaneous expenses (such as taxicabs)

> We require prepayment of a USD $20,000 deposit, and the balance in advance of surgery. This deposit will be immediately refunded if the patient is found psychiatrically or medically unsuitable for surgery. However, the patient will remain responsible for travel to and from Lisbon and other personal expenses. The deposit and the balance should be wired to . . .

Lorri slowed down when coming up to the price list. There seemed to be some confusion in her manner as she neared the "surgery" and "hospital stay" prices, but all seemed too clear when the letter was completed.

"It looks like we need another $9,000 US on top of the original $66,000" was the dismal conclusion.

"Just when we thought we were getting somewhere in our fund-raising!" I said with a sinking feeling, the words of one of Bruce Springsteen's hits echoing through my mind: "One step forward—and two steps back . . ." I used to listen to this song many years ago, eighteen years old, the music ringing out of the speakers of my pickup truck stereo, not having much of a clue at that time what he was really talking about. Maybe Bruce himself did not have such an intention for his music when he had recorded it, but it sure described the present situation right here.

"Well, the price is on paper now, and it shouldn't change anymore," I said, hoping for many more fund-raising events to follow, in the hope of making up the shortfall.

The reality faced me, however, that maybe I would just not be able to get this kind of cash before my surgery was due. The uncertainty was troublesome, to say the least, as I felt like a chance was slipping out of my grasp. Should I fail the financial test, I would ruin the confidence Dr. Dobelle had in me, probably wiping me right off the list. The line in his letter—"there are several hundred of you"—clearly illustrated that there was only a 1 percent chance at best to be one of those to get in first. Dr. Dobelle had promised me during our telephone conversation that I would be implanted for sure within this summer, and now it was up to me to hold up my end. I had to try every trick in the book.

One of Armando's suggestions had been to contact a provincial government organization called "assistive devices" in an effort to gain support financially. This organization already approves a percentage of financial assistance for the purchase of talking computers and other aids for the blind. "What the heck," I thought, "they just may be in for this one, as it would surely be an excellent example of an 'assistive device' for the blind." How more directly could one solve the problem of blindness than by curing blindness itself? I did not hesitate to call once finding their number. A man by the name of Faz

Hassan acted as spokesperson for the organization. I explained my situation, sent copies of the letters and other information from the Dobelle Institute I had received thus far, and his reply was:

"Assistive devices does not even consider approval for any devices involving an implant in the body, and also only would consider approving the funding of devices sold in the province of Ontario. For further confirmation, contact . . ."

I did not have to hear more. One down, and a few others to go.

The dreams of seeing again came back in full force every night. It must have been the uncertainty which started them—one dreams of those things he is least likely to attain. The images, strangely enough, had lost their color, and the resulting black-and-white images resembled those seen when looking through brush or weeds that happen to be in the way, segmenting somewhat the picture seen. It was in one of these dreams I found myself sitting at a large table, looking into the face of a doctor I have never seen before, wearing his scrubs, asking me if I could see anything yet. At that, I did not answer—I merely glanced around the room, then proceeded to walk to a large trash bin resting in one corner, and after folding up my white cane, threw it within. I awoke, trembling at the thought of not having enough money to pay for this system.

I had to call Dr. Willis again. He was my hope in clinching the health insurance approval. Should I get written approval, I reasoned, it would be easy enough to get a loan from a financial institution in the interim.

"How's the OHIP application coming along?" I asked Dr. Willis when I called his office. He had gone through a lot of trouble already, and now I counted on him to waste more of his professional time on paperwork.

"I just managed to contact Dr. John Girvin in Saudi Arabia," he replied, seemingly satisfied to have accomplished this feat. "I wasn't going to sign any request that wasn't legitimate." "That's great," I said, equally pleased, "I wouldn't want to have just anybody stick their fingers in my brain!"

Dr. Willis continued, "Dr. Girvin and I had a long talk about this. It does sound risky, no doubt. But I did tell him about you, Jens, and said that if there was anyone in the world who would give this a good try, it would be you."

"Thanks a lot!" I had to say, as maybe that would give me more of an edge when arriving there.

"In the meantime, I'll send off the request for OHIP funding for an out-of-province procedure, and send you a copy as well. After this, it's between you and them."

Prior approval for full payment for out-of-country funding, signed March 24/01 by Dr. Willis Clinical diagnosis:

Right eye has two-degree trauma

Left: old trauma related proliferative vitreoretinal vitreoretinopathy.

Other surgeons: Dr. Willis, Dr. Micheal Shea

Proposed treatment for approval:

Insertion of artificial vision device for bilateral blindness.

Services not performed in Ontario

Is the treatment generally accepted in Ontario as appropriate for a person in these medical circumstances?
Yes, none other available.

Is it considered experimental?
Probably, yes.

Is this treatment performed in Ontario by an identical or equivalent procedure?
No.

Comments:

This is a very specialized service offered only by the Dobelle Institute incorporated.

I have discussed this procedure with Dr. John Girvin. He will be glad to give you more information on request.

Details for follow-up care:
This info will be provided by the attending surgeon.

This procedure required for work-related accident.

It looked simple enough to me—there was no other option for me; the prosthesis would be implanted by a certified neurologist, and should their rules dictate that I have the procedure done before the reimbursement, I would qualify for a loan without doubt, or so I hoped.

In the meantime, I had more fund-raiser events planned by the many supporters living in this little town of Napanee and the neighboring villages. There were more musical events wherein I did all I could to appease the supporters; there were small but significant donations from private individuals, organizations, and clubs. Some were more substantial, like those coming from the Lion's, the Toccacelli Foundation, Roblin Women's Institute, and some very significant donors in which one individual donated $10,000 and yet preferred to remain anonymous. A lady by the name of Ethel went through a lot of trouble distributing donation requests to the local businesses and organized a yard sale in which we would inherit used goods to sell on the next sunny day. This all added up, yet as I watched the bank account, the value of the Canadian dollar kept dropping into an abyss of worthlessness.

"Try the CNIB!" said Ethel one day, as she always stopped at our place to see how the effort was going. "If anyone is going to help you, it would be them."

"I did ask them for help via telephone," I said, vaguely remembering the conversation. "Maybe I should try that again. Thanks for reminding me!"

I was back on the telephone and was informed that a response was being drafted and would be sent to me in the mail. I had made direct reference to the "E. A. Baker Foundation for the Prevention of Blindness" which Armando had mentioned during our first conversation on the subject of fund-raising. Imagining success, I waited impatiently for the mail to arrive.

In the meantime, since it was April 12, I figured I would call the Dobelle Institute as I had heard nothing from them at all since my last letter from the end of February. The number was no longer available in the Columbia-Presbyterian Medical Center which I had previously dialed to reach Lisa and Lou. I was given a new number in Commack instead.

The voice of a man answered the telephone, "Avery labs, Dobelle Institute, Dobelle labs and affiliated companies . . ."

I introduced myself as a patient for the artificial vision, asking for Dr. Dobelle, and there was a pause as I heard him say to someone else in the office.

"Can you take this call, Chris?" upon which a woman took the telephone, and I started all over again.

There was a pause, and in an uncertain voice Chris responded, "Well, Dr. Dobelle is out for now and won't be in for a couple of weeks. Maybe you can call back then . . ."

That is all I got out of her. I was kind of mystified. Where was Lou Coleman? What about Lisa? I hoped they were on holiday. It just seemed a bit mysterious, the fact that out of three hundred scientists and engineers and doctors, there was no direct representative for patients to talk to in the absence of Dr. Dobelle. I marked the date on my calendar and decided to call back in two weeks.

Through the efforts of the fund-raisers, the local newspapers and a television station in Kingston became aware of my quest and asked me for interviews. CKWS TV even had me playing the grand piano for them, which I welcomed as this allowed more awareness of the project, and perhaps would apply more pressure onto the CNIB and OHIP to be more supportive. I had no idea what Dr. Dobelle would think of all this, as the publicity surrounding the fund-raising would have been one of my topics of conversations when talking with Dr. Dobelle. One very interested agency was CBC, the Canadian National news agency. CBC TV brought over Janice McGregor, the reporter, along with her film crew and engaged in an extensive interview, with every intention of having "follow-up" filming in the future. I was being as cooperative as possible to these agencies and had special interest in pleasing the requests of CBC as they were investing a substantial effort in propagating my story.

"If you have to argue any with the OHIP," Janice had indicated, "I wouldn't mind being informed about the general proceedings." I promised her I would be as open as possible, provided all parties agreed. Never once did I suspect I would encounter any resistance to the press from Dr. Dobelle.

On April 25, I made another call to the Dobelle Institute in Commack. I had my finger crossed to get through this time, as that would certainly allow me to answer more questions to the public who were donating to my cause. I needed to have more info for them, especially considering I had nothing coming since two months ago.

"Dr. Dobelle is presently ill," the voice said on the telephone, this time not Chris, but the same man who had answered the first time. "But he should be back in a couple of weeks. His illness is not major."

That was all I received. Together Lorri and I worried. The kids had their own troubles and concerns and did not appear to be affected one way or another by the events. I just had to learn to be patient. I marked another two weeks off on the calendar.

Lorri came in holding a copy of the local *Napanee Guide* newspaper. "You should see how famous you are," she announced. I was a little too worried at this point, as the publicity only meant I had to explain why I was making such a fuss about getting funding when there is no Dr. Dobelle to get a hold of, let alone direct the master plan to restore the world's blind's eyesight. "It says: 'Napanee Man Receives Brain Implant' for the headline!" Lorri continued, obviously amused by the wording just as I was. The kids crowded around to look.

"Does it say that this has anything to do with restoring vision?" I had to ask. Surely the idea of receiving a "brain implant" would seem strange at best to the majority of people reading this article.

The telephone rang, and upon answering it, I found myself talking with a representative from TVO (TV-Ontario).

"We were wanting an interview with your doctor, Dr. Willis, regarding your vision system implant, and he refused!" The man sounded angry, expectant of a negative reaction from my side. "It really has nothing to do with Dr. Willis," I explained, "it is only the request for funding from OHIP that Dr. Willis is helping me with, as I have no business talking about my medical condition to OHIP. You would have to interview Dr. Dobelle . . ." I paused. How can he do that if I can't even talk with Dr. Dobelle either? TVO left me at that, saying they would try that next time but were still disappointed they could not get Dr. Willis to talk in detail about the system. I really needed to get a hold of the Dr. Dobelle.

At the start of May, we attended a fund-raiser dance in a hall south of Napanee. It was well organized, and many friends came to help and enjoy themselves. I sat down at the piano to play a few tunes, just to find that one of the black keys had been broken off. It was almost impossible to play the thing, as the clusters of two and three black notes making up the individual octaves were vital for me to orient my fingers with the keys. That dance brought us another $900 closer to our dream.

I reviewed again my letter to the CNIB. I wanted to give them a call again but thought better of it. They could ask "So when was the last time you talked to the Dobelle team?" and I would be fumbling for an adequate answer. I reread the letter, hoping it would magically solve the problems we were having with the funds.

CNIB (Canadian National Institute for the Blind)
1929 Bayview Ave.
Toronto, Ontario
M4G 3E8

Attn: A. E. Baker Foundation for the Prevention of Blindness

Dear Staff,

I, being a client of the CNIB since 1983, heard of your organization from the Kingston CNIB office and would like to ask for your help if it is at all possible. Please let me explain my situation, if I may.

In 1981, when I was seventeen years old, I lost my left eye during work at the tracks of British Columbia Railway, which could not be repaired in spite of numerous operations to the retina. Then, quite unfortunately at the end of 1983, I lost my right eye while repairing a snowmobile, and thus was completely blinded, and had no further chance to see according to all retinal surgeons around the globe. My resulting life was not fulfilling by any means as a result of this, but as all desperate people do, I still hoped for a miracle.

My break came in July 2000, when a friend told me of the Internet Web site "WWW.Dobelle.com," which described the visual prosthesis developed by Dr. William Dobelle of the Dobelle Institute, a company devoted to making pacemakers and other neurological stimulators. This Dobelle Eye would use a video camera and computer which sends electronic signals directly to the brain, bypassing all optic nerves and retinas, thus solving a vast majority of blindness problems encountered in adults.

I immediately applied to the Dobelle Institute, giving all necessary information along with reports from Dr. Wendell Willis and also my family physician. As the Dobelle Eye had already been tested successfully on six patients, I was excited to hear of the commercial implants this institute had planned for the following year (2001) and was determined to receive one. I received a reply shortly afterward from Dr. Dobelle, indicating that I was a likely candidate for the implant. Then about two weeks ago, I received the letter enclosed which confirmed the beginning of these commercial implants. I also received the promised phone call from Dr. Dobelle on February 15, 2001, in which he told me I would be ready for implant this summer.

As you can imagine, I am extremely excited at the prospect of seeing again. Dr. Dobelle indicated there was no doubt this would work in my case, and he also shared the final price as being $66,000 US, which is to be paid before the implant can be performed. I am not surprised at the price, as so many years of research was necessary for this to become a reality.

I would like to ask you for some financial assistance for this Dobelle Eye to be made possible for me. I have eight children, ages five to seventeen, own a house, and am privately employed tuning and repairing pianos and processing firewood for sale. My wife, Lorri, teaches private music lessons, and we get by to pay the bills and rear the children, but to come up with the amount of money equivalent to another house by rural standards is not possible on such short notice. Since I am convinced I will have far more opportunity to get better employment, I offer to pay back the amount donated over a long period of time. Moreover, I would be very willing to demonstrate and assist anyone interested in this product once I have it so other people encountering blindness may be made aware of this new product.

I am currently attempting to contact "assistive devices" and any other government agencies to try to establish funding. However, I would be one of the first Canadian citizens to receive such an implant, so I am skeptical about the government having a quick response. I do, however, plan to lobby the government full tilt into providing funding for this device once I can demonstrate its practicality so all Canadians may benefit from this product.

I would be very pleased if you would consider my request. I am going to receive more documents from the Dobelle Institute that indicate the exact price and the breakdown of the costs. I will send you a copy as soon as it arrives so you may use it in your quest to prevent blindness.

Thank you for considering my situation, and I will wait anxiously for your reply.

Sincerely yours,

Jens Naumann
Napanee, Ontario

I realized then I should send the next letter off I had received at the end of February in which the price list was written. That may be why I had not yet received an answer. In the meantime, I figured I would check the state of the Canadian dollar versus its American counterpart. It was shockingly low—just over 61 cents US for every Canadian buck. Now we would need about $125,000 just to get that $75,000 US, and then have to worry about the travel expense as well. One step forward and two steps back. If this dropped any more, we would surely never make it.

I called the Dobelle Institute on May 10. Mario answered the telephone, a man who must be one of the engineers. "Dr. Dobelle is not in, but call back in a couple of weeks. He is having some complications with his bypass surgery."

This meant I could not unload the down payment, which would have looked good. The equivalent of the $20,000 US down payment had by now been collected, and if I could unload it to the institute, it would look like I was actually using the cash for the project—not just hoarding it for God knows what! On a daily basis, passers-by would ask us "So, when is the surgery?" and we would not have a date. The money was just sitting there, and it was starting to feel uncomfortable to live here. I had kept a record of all donors who were willing to identify themselves, but there were some I did not ever get to know. It would be difficult to return all the money, although most of the larger donors could have theirs returned. This was not a healthy way of thinking. I needed that operation.

On May 26, just before the planned garage sale in which we would sell all the donated items, I tried the institute again. A man with whom I had never spoken before told me . . .

"Bill has been in and out of the office every couple of days. I'll get him to call you when he is here the next time." I asked about the vision project. "Dr. Dobelle had said that he wanted to start visual prosthesis implants in June. Do you know when he is scheduling them?"

The reply was disappointing to say the least. "No, I have no idea. You have to talk directly to Bill about that. He is the one doing the vision project."

The yard sale went well, yet I felt ill at ease. I tried my best to sound positive and hide my worried disposition to not only the public but to Lorri as well. "I should hear from Bill any day," I told her, not believing it myself. It was not so much the content of the conversations I had with the so-called staff at the Dobelle Institute that gave me the anxiety; the manner in which the employees spoke was one of: "Oh, Bill Dobelle, and well, what was that? Oh, yeah, the vision project . . . well . . . that's his baby . . ." Lisa was so upbeat about the whole thing the first time I called her last year. Lou Coleman was equally enthusiastic, yet these people I was talking to every two weeks may as well have been employed as undertaker's assistants. There was no spirit or even recognition of the project.

I had converted all the collected money into US dollars, along with our assets. We secured a line of credit which brought us close, but still about $12,000 US from the magic number.

It was then that Lorri charged again into the door, holding a letter from the Ontario Health Insurance Plan, directly coming from Kingston.

"Maybe you got the approval for the funding, which would mean we'd be able to return all the donated money," she said, tearing open the envelope.

"Wouldn't that be nice," I replied to that, imagining the psychological freedom that would give us. "We'd be able to assess this whole thing a little better, take our time, and not feel so pressured by the town to go for it, even though Bill isn't ready yet."

"You're right about that," Lorri answered, remembering her last trip into town. "Every time I want to buy groceries, or pay the bills, everyone asks about you and your surgery date. It's getting kind of embarrassing."

With that, she started to read:

Ministry of Health and Long-Term Care

P.O. Box 48
Kingston, Ontario

May 31, 2001
Dr. Wendell Willis
Hotel Dieu Hospital
166 Brock St.
Kingston, Ontario

Dear Dr. Willis:

Re: Jens Naumann,

This will acknowledge receipt of the Prior Approval Application for full payment of insured out—of-country health services that you submitted on behalf of Mr. Naumann.

Full funding was requested for insertion of "artificial vision" device for the condition of bilateral blindness.

The original application and the additional information provided by Mr. Neumann has been thoroughly reviewed by ministry staff. As a result of this review, it has been concluded that the treatment requested is considered experimental in Ontario. Experimental out-of-country medical treatment is not eligible for reimbursement as an insured benefit under the Health Insurance Act of Ontario. This request for prior approval of full payment for health services outside of Canada has been denied. The denial pertains strictly to the health services requested. I regret that I am unable to provide you with a more favorable response. If there is additional information that you and/or your patient have not provided and which you wish to have reviewed, the ministry is prepared to reassess this application. Supplementary information supporting your request may be submitted to the director, Provider Services Branch, at the following address:

Ministry of Health and Long-Term Care
PO Box 48, Kingston, ON

Should your patient elect to obtain treatment outside of Canada without prior ministry funding approval, please be advised that elective out-of-country hospital and/or physician services would not be eligible for reimbursement. Under the current out-of-country payment policy only emergency health services provided in connection with an acute, unexpected condition, illness, disease, or injury that arises while the individual is outside Canada, and that require immediate treatment, may be eligible for reimbursement at limited unapproved rates.

The original decision regarding this request may be subject to appeal before the Health Services Appeal and Review Board. Consequently, if there is no additional information which you or your patient wish to submit in support of this application, your patient may wish to have a hearing before the Health Services Appeal and Review Board. The procedure of the board requires that your patient (within fifteen days of receiving this letter) mail or deliver a written request to the Health Services Appeal and Review Board, 151 Bloor Street West, 9th Floor, Toronto, ON.

At the time of mailing, a copy of your letter should be sent to the director, Provider Services Branch, Ministry of Health and Long-Term Care, PO Box 48, Kingston, ON.

Yours sincerely,
Hugh Langley, MD, CCFP
Medical Consultant
Out-of-Country Unit

"Well, that sure helps!" I couldn't hide the sarcasm. It was hard to believe that OHIP readily spent at least an equivalent sum on the retinal reattachment attempts in 1984, with only a 10 percent possibility of success yet did not offer even a percentage of funding for this system, which was so much more apt to be a success.

"I'll have to appeal it," I said to Lorri. I looked hard for a bright side in all of this. "At least now we can show this to Ethel and other people who are helping us fund-raise in order to prove we are still in need."

I started the process of appealing the decision, which was my responsibility as I was still going to partially depend upon the pocketbooks of others to get this procedure done. The citizens of Napanee were, after all, also paying taxes toward the "OHIP" fund, and thus every opportunity should be taken to put it to work. After contacting the Health Services Appeal and Review Board, I was instructed to prepare my case as I would be obliged to argue my points, as well as have a chance to cross-examine the OHIP representative before a decision-making panel. That gave me a lot of work to do. On the positive side, the review board's representative told me only 2 percent of funding denials are contested before this panel, and out of those, three-quarters of them are given a favorable response. The odds were in my favor.

On June 7, I called Commack again.

"Dr. Dobelle is in and out of the office regularly, but is still visiting the clinics to monitor his health situation," the man's voice said. It was not Mario, the man I had spoken to before. And then, of course, the familiar line I got to know so well came next:

"Call back in a couple of weeks."

I had no idea what was going on down there. If there were really "several hundred" patients in the pool of recipients-to-be, as Dr. Dobelle had originally implied in his last letter, would they all be calling with the same frequency as I was? He had said "June" was the month for the implants, yet, here it was, well into that month with no response from Dr. Dobelle. If he was really going in and out of the office regularly, why was there no concrete response from the company representatives?

Janice from CBC TV called again, wondering if I had a surgery date yet. It was easier to deal with her, as she had not invested her own money into this venture, and thus I was not really accountable to her. She would have a good story, even if the whole thing fell to the wayside. My fund-raiser friends however needed an explanation. At least I had the rejection letter from OHIP for them to feast upon, as that left me a bit of time. I knew there was one more fund-raiser concert in which I would play the piano scheduled at the Anglican Church for the end of the month, and I hoped that the next time I called Dr. Dobelle, I would get a favorable response.

June 21 marked the "couple of weeks" since my last call to Commack on June 7. Mario was on the telephone this time.

"Dr. Dobelle has some serious health problems, and I really have not seen him or heard from him in over a month," he informed me, contraindicating the idea that Dr. Dobelle was "in and out of the office" just two weeks ago. He continued, "He is going to have to reschedule the implants once he returns to the office."

This was bad news. We were so close to having the funds now. We had the entire town cheering for us, but as is always possible in a "cheering crowd" scenario, those cheers can turn to "boos" at any given moment when things go wrong. There wasn't even a suggestion from the part of Mario to call back in a "couple of weeks" this time.

A couple of days later, I had to play, as scheduled, in the Anglican Church. As the few people seated themselves, I said to Lorri under my breath, "This will have to be it . . . if this is what life is all about, I'm not interested."

She understood, feeling the strain upon our reputation, and this unexpected turn of events seemed more and more like adding insult to injury. My speech was dry, although I tried my best to sound positive. Three months ago, this was a lot easier, as the possibilities looked bright. Now, I had my doubts. There were some serious indicators that screamed at me from underneath the words spoken on the telephone. Why was there no client representative for the artificial vision project? Why did it seem that Dr. Dobelle was the only spokesperson of this project? Why was there no apparent infrastructure already in place to manage the project in spite of the absence of Dr. Dobelle? If Dr. Dobelle was not performing the surgery, his presence should not be vital for this project.

But it was too late to back out now. If only I had had all the money for this in the first place. I had not paid yet and could still back out, if it did not mean disappointing the entire town. If the money was all mine, I would only risk disappointing Lorri. Even disappointing her would be a hard choice to make, as I had complained bitterly all these years about the blindness I was living. Right now, though, in light of the absence of the surgery schedule, it would be much easier to live with the uncertainty if I did not have to explain it to every visitor that came by our house or passed us in the street.

These thoughts ran through my head as I played in the church that evening. It did not make for an emotional performance, even though the piano was of superior quality compared to the others I had played elsewhere. As I played, I realized that it was no longer the dream of seeing again that was first on my mind, but it was the mess I found myself in. It was a letter in the mail I needed from Dobelle, not necessarily to say I would get surgery, but rather to explain the delay, or even if there was a definite cancellation, I would have it easier than this. I felt a wave of anger at Dr. Dobelle. "What is it with this guy anyway," I asked myself. Surely he did not think that blind people, placed practically at the end of the list of "employable" people, would just open their wallet and pull out $75,000 in American funds? He must have some idea that we had to scrounge the money, and thus were accountable to the donors.

Lorri came in near the last day of June with a letter in hand. It came from the CNIB, straight from Toronto, probably a reply from my funding request, I thought. Lorri opened the letter with less than the usual excitement. She must have scanned it in advance before reading out loud, as I could tell just by the sound of her voice what it was about to reveal.

The Canadian National Institute for the Blind Toronto, ON

June 27, 2001

Mr. Jens Naumann
Napanee, Ontario

Dear Mr. Naumann,

The following statement clarified the position of CNIB with respect to medical and technical experimentation and treatment in the area of eyesight. Please feel free to share this with anyone who inquires.

If I can be of further assistance, please do not hesitate to contact me.

Medical Advancements Core Message

The Canadian National Institute for the Blind (CNIB) welcomes all advancements, whether medical, technological, or pharmaceutical, that prevent blindness or enhance or improve the quality of life for people who are blind, visually impaired or deaf-blind. However, we do not comment or endorse any specific tests, products, or procedures and suggest that anyone who is considering undergoing any medical procedure should discuss all options fully with an eye care professional. Whenever we are asked to comment on specific medical procedures, we refer inquiries to the appropriate eye care professionals.

The (CNIB) specializes in rehabilitation services and working with people who are blind, visually impaired, and deaf blind so they can lead independent and productive lives. Through our E. A. Baker Foundation for the Prevention of Blindness, the institute supports research we hope will lead to curing, arresting, or minimizing the impacts of vision loss.

The CNIB has been providing rehabilitation services to Canadians since 1918.

Sincerely,
James W. Sanders,
Vice-President of Client Services and Technology

"Useful," I commented in a flat tone of voice. "Yeah . . ." agreed Lorri, folding the letter and holding it out to me.

"How much is the check?" I inquired sarcastically. "You'd better give me that letter so I can show it off to the CBC should they ever inquire about what kind of support I am getting," I continued, quoting a sentence on the letter, "after all, they want me to 'feel free to share this with anyone who inquires'."

It was only much later, when completing a Social Services Worker program through Loyalist College that I understood that a human services agency must be strict in compliance with the given mandate which was, for better or worse, assisting the visually impaired with daily living, for the CNIB. The EA Baker Foundation did, however, seem to have a misleading name.

July was a difficult month to pass. The kids were home, glad to be out of school and avoid the questions by curious teachers about my "surgery." A bright spot in the month occurred when Alden, my friend who told me about the Dobelle Institute Web site in the first place, called up and asked how things were going. I relayed some of my frustrations, to which he offered to loan me the cash remaining to be raised. The news was wonderful, as that meant the fund-raiser friends of mine could say that there was enough money now, and no more donations needed to be made. That was a bit of a relief anyways. I promised Alden I would pay back the money in three installments every Christmas until I was paid up.

Janice from CBC TV called again. I had to be careful that I did not let my worries show. I stated that "Dr. Dobelle is sick and needs to reschedule the surgery and will call me when it is time . . ." with no indication of the small signs of pending disaster I discovered. Judging by how cruelly the press treated politicians, I had no doubt that the slightest bit of bad publicity would ruin my chances of ever getting on the "patient list" should Dr. Dobelle get the program off the ground. I did tell her about my attempts to appeal the OHIP decision, upon which she inquired if it was all right for her to attend the hearing. "Sure thing, if they will let you," I replied, counting on the idea that should a media representative be present, there is more of a chance in receiving a favorable response.

I e-mailed Dr. Girvin, as I had his e-mail address from Dr. Willis. I introduced myself and then asked him if he had heard anything from Dr. Dobelle and how his illness was proceeding. Dr. Girvin replied the next day.

"I had no idea that Dr. Dobelle was sick. I'll have to inquire about that, and I'll get back to you."

The waiting game continued. People were on summer vacations now, leaving us to ourselves somewhat. Firewood sales were only for those campers coming from out of town, minimizing the necessity for explanations about the "surgery." There was no more talk about the vision system or Dr. Dobelle around the dinner table. I dropped my line—"Once I have my vision system . . ." with which I had started a sentence in the past few months when planning future activities and tried to forget all I could about this whole thing. I made backup disks of the list of donors and how much they contributed, as it looked like the chances were that I would have to pay it all back soon. "If nothing happens by September," I indicated to Lorri, "this all goes back to the people."

I didn't call Commack anymore. They had my number, so all I could do was wait for September. I had already made the plans of returning the money. Donations received in the yard sale and benefit dance, where no specific donations and amounts were recorded, would be given to local charities with all of the local media involved in writing this up for the public to see. Every cent would be returned. It was only two weeks to go before the end of August when we, to both our surprise and astonishment, received a letter from "The Dobelle Institute."

Dobelle Institute (Portugal)

Dear Mr. Naumann:

I'm sorry for this delay in contacting you. After we spoke I was rehospitalized for an extended period for treatment of a diabetic ulcer on my foot—and I only recently returned to the office.

Meanwhile, colleagues moved the Artificial Vision Project forward, (albeit, at a greatly reduced rate). Surgeries will be performed in Lisbon, Portugal, beginning the third week of January, 2002. We are now preparing to purchase the components needed to assemble each system. This includes platinum and special connectors for the electrode/pedestal combination, and all of the electronic components including the chip computers and TV cameras.

However, as I told you when we last spoke, the Dobelle Institute (Portugal) Lda. is unable to finance these and other purchases without taking deposits from patients. If you are still interested in being implanted, I must ask you for such deposit which is fully and immediately refundable if by some chance we find, at the last minute, some reason not to proceed. (Our cortical stimulation device is applicable to virtually all blindness.)

I am enclosing agreements for your down payment, as well as a copy of the price list and wire transfer instructions. It is very important that you send us a copy of the wire transfer receipt—as well as the down payment agreement—so we can trace payments in Portugal. If you have any questions, I can usually be reached here at the office. Nights and weekends, I am usually home (not published).

In any case, I expect to call you in the near future.

Regards,
Wm. H. Dobelle, PhD
Chairman & Chief Executive Officer

Dobelle Institute (Portugal) Lda. Artificial Vision for the Blind

Introductory Price List—Delivered In Lisbon, Portugal, Effective February 1, 2001
Visual Prosthesis System (discounted): USD $65,000 consisting of:
-one miniature camera mounted on glasses, one frame grabber, one microcomputer, one stimulus generation module
-two implanted electrode arrays with percutaneous pedestals, three sets of rechargeable batteries, and one charger. This package includes:
-five years' full warranty (not including travel or freight); five years annual follow-up examinations in Portugal (not including travel)
-five years' access to all upgrades and accessories (such as a TV interface) as developed at "company cost"
-unlimited telephone consultation. Customer responsible for replacement batteries, as needed Evaluation as a Patient: USD $2,000—Psychiatric Evaluation
-All Other Testing
Hospital Expenses (payable to hospital CUF): USD $8,000. This includes:
-All Surgical Fees
-All Hospital Expenses
Personal Expenses (payable to miscellaneous vendors): USD $5,000 or less
This includes our estimate of:
-Airfare to and from Lisbon for two people; hotel for one week for two people
-Food for one week for two people
-Miscellaneous expenses (such as taxicabs)

We require prepayment of a $20,000 deposit, and the balance in advance of surgery. This deposit will be immediately refunded if the patient is found psychiatrically or medically unsuitable for surgery. However, the patient will remain responsible for travel to and from Lisbon and other personal expenses. The deposit and balance should be wired to . . .

You have been provided two (two) copies of this agreement signed by Dr. Dobelle on behalf of the institute. Please sign both copies. Retain one (1) for your records and mail the other copy with the wire transfer receipt (see below) to:

The Dobelle Institute (Portugal) Lda. c/o 61 Mall Drive
Commack, New York 11 725-5703

Simultaneously arrange with your bank to wire transfer the $20,000 deposit to the institute according to the instructions in Section no. 4 below and in the price list. The bank will issue a receipt showing the transfer ID, number, due date, and other information. A copy of this document should be attached to this form so we can "track" your payment in Portugal.

AGREEMENT made and entered into this day of between The Dobelle Institute (Portugal) Lda. of Lisbon, Portugal ("Seller") and JENS NAUMANN ("Buyer") of ONTARIO, CANADA

(1) Seller hereby agrees to manufacture a visual prosthesis system for this Buyer, consisting of a miniature eyeglass—mounted camera, a microcomputer, a stimulus generation module, two implanted electrode arrays, two percutaneous skull pedestals, three rechargeable batteries and one battery charger.

(2) Buyer hereby agrees to purchase said specially manufactured visual prosthesis system from the Seller.

(3) The total purchase price to be paid to the Seller for the visual prosthesis system is $65,000 USD, which shall be paid as follows: (a) a nonrefundable deposit of $20,000 USD upon signing this agreement; and (b) the balance of $45,000 USD in advance of delivery and surgical implantation of the visual prosthesis system.

(4) All payments under this agreement shall be made by wire transfer to: Dobelle Institute (Portugal) Lda.

(5) Buyer agrees that the surgical implantation of the visual prosthesis system will only take place at the CUF Hospital, Lisbon, Portugal. Seller has negotiated a fixed price with the hospital of $8,000 USD for the surgical implantation of the visual prosthesis system, which is the Buyer's responsibility to pay directly to the hospital. In addition, Buyer shall pay to Seller $2,000.00. Buyer shall pay the hospital in full prior to the Buyer's admission to the hospital.

Seller makes no representation to the Buyer with regard to the surgical, presurgical, postsurgical, medical and/or hospital services to be provided to the Buyer by CUF Hospital.

(6) In the event that Seller is unable, or unwilling, for any reason or no reason, to manufacture and/or deliver the said visual prosthesis system within one year from the date of this agreement, the Buyer shall only be entitled to a return of all funds paid to the Seller hereunder, without interest.

(7) If Buyer wishes to terminate this agreement prior to surgery, Seller shall be entitled to retain the contract deposit of $20,000 USD as liquidated damages.

(8) If, at the time of admission to the hospital, the Buyer is found to be psychiatrically or medically unsuitable for the contemplated surgery, the Seller will return all funds paid by the Buyer under this contract. Buyer, however, shall remain responsible for travel to and from Lisbon and other personal expenses associated with same.

(9) The provisions of this contract shall be governed by the laws of Portugal. The Courts of Portugal shall have exclusive subject matter and personal jurisdiction to determine all disputes between the Buyer and Seller hereunder or otherwise.

Buyer's Signature_____
Buyer's Name_____
(Please Print)

CHAPTER 6

Dr. Dobelle Back in Office

We reviewed the letter with extreme interest. The highlights included the explanation for his absence, the request for money, and the tentative surgical dates to be in January 2002. I scanned the letter onto my computer and studied carefully the details of the contract.

"Unbelievable!" I commented, "The prices are the same. I thought perhaps they would go up again!" There was no doubt that my confidence in pulling this one off had begun to dwindle from the events of the last few months.

"I suppose we should send off the down payment tomorrow," Lorri's idea sounded good, as that would give us proof that we were indeed applying the collected money to the cause.

"I may as well call Dr. Dobelle right now, as it seems he wants to talk to the patients anyhow." If anything, my intention was to confirm to him that I did indeed have the cash ready to send off.

A pleasant-sounding female voice answered the line, "Dobelle Institute . . . Louise speaking. How may I help you?" This sounded a lot more promising than the previous few months had. I introduced myself and asked for Dr. Dobelle.

"That you, Jens?" said a gruff voice in the labored manner of speech that seemed to be a trademark of Dr. Dobelle. "I hear you're back in business," I said, adding, "since when do you have diabetes anyways?" I was referring to the "diabetic ulcer" that had been mentioned in his latest letter.

"I never knew! In fact, I'm not really, as I don't take insulin or anything like that. I think I picked up a damned germ in the hospital when I was in for my heart bypass. It lodged under my toe, causing an infection they couldn't control."

I found Bill's language selection interesting, and a bit un-doctor-like.

"That's rotten," I sympathized, thinking back to the time I was in the hospital for four weeks in a row. Dr. Dobelle was in for a few months. That must have been hard. "So what did they do about it?"

Dr. Dobelle explained, "First they put me on antibiotics, then they cut the end of my toe off. When that didn't stop it, they cut part of my foot off. And that still didn't stop it, so they cut off my leg below the knee!"

I felt a pain in the pit of my stomach in hearing this. Murphy's Law states that all that can go wrong will go wrong, but this is pushing it. It did not seem normal that this much bad luck would engulf a man who had passed sixty years of his life without any injury prior to accepting me as a patient. Thinking back on the circumstances surrounding the loss of my sight, which were equally bizarre, I couldn't help but wonder if someone was out to keep me in the dark. In the last few years, I had taken many chances with fate, for instances in using the machinery with which to cut and split firewood, which were responsible for injuring the majority of operators who had perfect eyesight. Then there was the farm machinery, the cows I had dealt with every day, and also the antennas I installed for those people who were too afraid of heights to climb the rickety antenna towers. Nothing ever happened to me while I did these things, yet every chance there was for my eyesight seemed to be jeopardized.

Now I was starting to wonder if maybe my involvement with Dr. Dobelle might be pulling him into the same rut. I hoped I was wrong. The physical and psychological torture he went through must have been near unimaginable. First to be told to lose a toe, the idea already taking some getting used to, then to be told it would be the foot—the foot is rather important and hardly something to get used to however, when this reality is still difficult to face, then to be told it would be the leg—this had to be horrible. But now, only a few months later, when most of us would still grieve the losses, Dr. Dobelle was pushing right ahead with the work on artificial vision—to solve a disability that wasn't even an issue with him personally. I had to admire this man more than I did before.

"Oh no!" I sympathized with Dr. Dobelle. "What rotten luck! I bet you are more than worried about the other one."

"Yeah," he replied, "I'm sitting here, looking at it right now. I'll need that one in order to have any success in using a prosthesis. I'm due for one to be fitted next week, and then I'm going to go fishing with my son. All that hospitalization has been getting to me."

I imagined his boat capsizing and Dr. Dobelle drowning during his fishing trip. So much more opportunity for bad luck to strike! "Sounds like a good idea. By the way," I got to the reason for the call, "I have the cash for the down payment for the vision system. I'll wire it off tomorrow and fax your office a copy of the transfer."

"Sounds great! We'll let you know when we get it. Do you have any questions about the contract?"

"No," I said, even though I could have asked about there being no Dobelle Institute representative during his absence. I did not really want to annoy him however, and after all that he went through during that time I was annoyed at not getting a hold of him—while he was suffering so much in the hospital—it didn't seem right now to say anything more. His battle was a tough one, no doubt.

"You pretty well covered all the details with your literature you sent."

There was nothing else to be said for the time being. Lorri and I went to the Bank of Commerce in Napanee that afternoon. We did not normally deal with this bank, as geographically it was out of our way. We were closest to the south end of Napanee, and the Bank of Commerce was at the north end. However, they had the best price for sending off a wire transfer, and we needed to economize as much as possible.

A lady by the name of Paula took the details written on Dr. Dobelle's contract, our money order of $20,000 US, and pushed several buttons on the machine used to send off the loot. "All done!" she announced a couple of minutes later. "It should be there in a few days at best." We went home that day feeling like the first real step was done in realizing a dream. I sat down at the computer and proceeded to write Dr. Dobelle a letter just to keep my foot in the door as far as I could. Of course, I would include the transfer slip to prove my loyalty to the company.

August 22, 2001

Dobelle Institute Inc.
61 Mall drive
Commack, NY
11725-5703
USA

Dear Dr. Dobelle,

I enjoyed our telephone conversation today and hope you manage to make up for such an awful start to a new year by having good luck adapting to the prosthesis which will replace your foot. Hopefully you can find comfort in still being able to take your son fishing. I have six sons and have so far not been able to do that;

however, this visual prosthesis you developed sounds extremely promising to help me start a new life.

I have enclosed the transfer slip of the $20,000 US I had the Canadian Imperial Bank of Commerce wire to the destination in Portugal as instructed on the contract. I also signed and enclosed the contract and retained one for myself.

I discussed the $45,000 remaining balance with the CIBC, who told me if I get a bank draft, retain the receipt for it, I could take it with me to Portugal, and if I had a mishap (the plane crashed, before arriving in Portugal) then there would be no problem in my wife recovering the money. (I wouldn't need the implant then!) But that is putting paranoia at its best. The remaining $10,000 I could tote along in cash and thus pay the hospital and psychiatrist up front. However, these are minor details we still can ponder over.

We just have to make sure neither of us get into trouble between now and January. I cut and split firewood here for a living and could remove major body parts from one wrong move, or could electrocute myself with my home-built solar wind electrical station. However, neither of these incidents are in my plans, so I look forward to hearing from you in September regarding exact travel details to Portugal. Take care and get your fishing in before the snow flies.

Sincerely yours,
Jens Naumann
Napanee, Ontario

I had to throw in the "wind and solar electrical station" experiment that I was engaged in just to comfort him that I was electronically competent, and thus a better choice for a patient. Everything counts. Dr. Dobelle had been through a lot since our talk in February, therefore it was possible he forgot who I was or what was written on my application form. Now that he was getting the money, I hoped he would be happy.

Ethel came to visit a day later. I heard her car pull up through the open window of my office, and she walked up to the house with less of a spring in her step than before. It was obvious she was under pressure as well, as campaigner for my cause, to come up with an explanation for the delay.

Before I even said "hello," I greeted her by saying "Good news, Ethel, Dr. Dobelle is back in business." I waved the letter under her nose. "I even called him yesterday." She took the letter and began to read it to herself, mumbling some of the words as she did. She read louder and more clearly when coming to the phrase—"If you are still interested in being implanted, . . ." upon which she scoffed. "Yeah, right . . . Imagine not being interested anymore?" She left happy to have the explanation, the tentative date, and the bank slip that I had sent off the down payment. The down payment spoke for practically all of the collected funds which did not come out of my own pocket, leaving us, luckily, looking good for the rest of the community. The money was non-refundable if it was me who chose to change his mind. I realized then that I was trapped—I had little choice but to participate in the surgery, lest I disappoint the citizens. The pressure was not hard to take, as I did really want to get this operation. Yet, some of the pieces of the puzzle did not quite fit. Why was I always talking with Dr. Dobelle? I would have expected a sales or medical representative instead, as Dr. Dobelle would be far too occupied to deal with every patient on his own. I certainly did not want to risk receiving the implant only for the company to go "belly-up" a couple of years down the road. No one around here would have a clue what to do if this stuff in my head ever got infected, or be able to repair the equipment when it failed. I couldn't pose either question to Dr. Dobelle, as that would clearly demonstrate a lack of confidence in the company. That may mean he would drop me like a hot potato. I did not share these concerns with anyone.

At the start of September, I received the following letter which I found a little curious, as it should really not take much to send a wire transfer to a bank. It was, after all, not a physical transaction; it was merely an instruction to change a number in another computer terminal.

Dobelle Institute Inc.
Dobelle Laboratories

August 31, 2001

Mr. Jens Naumann
Napanee, ON

Dear Jens:

We received your agreement and wire transfer form. When we have confirmed that the money was actually received in Portugal, I will contact you again, but this may take a few weeks.

Sincerely,
Wm. H. Dobelle, PhD
Chairman & Chief Executive Officer

On September 10, 2001, I called Commack to see if the transfer had arrived in Portugal. Louise was on the telephone, and Dr. Dobelle took over.

"Hang on, Jens," he said slowly, and then barked something at Louise. "These damned secretaries are so damned slow!" he pointed out irritatingly as Louise rummaged around for the latest faxes. "If Banclo Espirito received it, they would fax me right away." Bill pointed out. I figured he was holding a cordless receiver, as I could hear him laboriously wheeling himself around in his wheelchair.

"How is the prosthesis coming along?" I made some conversation while we waited for Louise. If I hadn't, I figured, then she would have been barked at some more by him.

"The fucking thing hurts too much," grumbled Dr. Dobelle. "I just paid $15,000 for it just so it can sit on the filing cabinet."

"You may have to heal up a bit better," I tried to console him. Hearing a doctor swear like that was certainly new to me. All the eye doctors and obstetricians I had met so far in my life had a much more professional selection of vocabulary.

"No, Jens, it's not there yet," he announced, adding, "It really should be, as it takes me about a day to get cash from here to there. Then again, I am in New York!" as if that explains everything, I thought.

"I'll have to see what my bank has to say tomorrow, as they are closed today," I said, concerned that the cash was not arriving, perhaps giving Dr. Dobelle the impression I was incompetent after all. I'd have to call them tomorrow after opening hours at 10:00 a.m. to see what was going on.

The following morning started out just like all Tuesdays—the children prepared their lunches for school, and I started a pot of coffee and sharpened up the chain saw while I waited for the coffee to percolate. Lorri planned her workday in teaching music, which was still rather disorganized as it was the second week of the teaching year and all was in disarray. I had planned on working until just before lunch, then calling the CIBC in Napanee to find out what was taking so long with the money transfer.

I was cutting away at the never-ending woodpile when a long-time customer pulled up with his pickup truck in preparation for winter. In spite of the hardship of the delay with the implant surgery, it did allow me to sell another round of firewood prior to going to Portugal, meaning more cash to deal with the unexpected. I shut off the saw and greeted my client.

"I guess you aren't aware of what is in the news," he began, not waiting for an answer. "New York is under attack. Some terrorists took over a bunch of passenger jets and are doing major damage to the city."

It took a bit for me to understand what he said. The radio of his truck was murmuring in the background, and I opened the truck door to hear the details.

"Yeah," the client continued, not aware of the stakes I had in that city. "They took down one tower of the World Trade Center, and the other's on fire. Thousands of people are dying as we speak." He began to load his truck.

I kicked off my boots at the house, too disturbed to continue a job which required the utmost in care to avoid injury. Lorri was listening to the radio, of which every station was barking out the graphic horror taking place in a city I had depended upon for my salvation. Together we felt a sense of despair, which took no words to share. I imagined Dr. Dobelle, trapped in a burning building, sitting in his wheelchair while the elevators were rendered inoperable, the flaming tomb collapsing around him as millions of blind people listened to his final screams, powerless to help, their only chance to flee the oppressive blackness gone forever. Somebody—something, was trying, once again, to stop me from seeing again, and whatever it was, was going through extreme measures to do so. I didn't worry about the wire transfer that day.

I just had to wait it out, but my curiosity got the best of me, and I had to call the next day in Commack. It took many tries in order to get through. When Louise answered the telephone, I felt relief that at least their place was still intact. My next question was about Dr. Dobelle, as he had spent a lot of time in Downtown New York in his life, and who knows if he was now still alive.

"Oh yes," she said, "here, I'll let you talk to him." "Oh yeah, what a mess," he said with obvious remorse. "No, I wasn't in those buildings yesterday. Had I have been, I'd just be a pile of smoldering dust by now."

And that would mark the end of the vision project, I thought to myself. I was still in contact with Dr. Girvin through e-mail, but it seemed that whatever news Dr. Girvin received was that what I knew already. For instance, about a week after I talked the first time to Dr. Dobelle after he returned back to the office, Dr. Girvin wrote me a message in which he indicated that Dr. Dobelle's life was in balance during the summer, but that he now is accelerating the vision project. It seemed unlikely to me that Dr. Girvin had the geographic capacity to take over the project should Dr. Dobelle fail to be able to continue for whatever reason. There never did seem to be a shortage of these reasons. I crossed my fingers and hoped for the best.

On September 22, it was Louise that called me. "Jens, I just noticed that the account number written on your wire transfer slip is wrong!"

"How so?" I asked. "There should be a routing number and an account number."

"Well, listen to this," Louise began, reciting the account number for the institute. It's supposed to be 014-4797-20002, and what's written here is 014-479-20002."

I could tell that the curse to stop me from seeing was still in full force, this time scoring again. If this money is lost, there is no way I could get another $35,000 Canadian together. We were stretched to the limit as it was. The price of this thing added up to more than our house as it was. I was sweating when I hung up the telephone.

"That's ridiculous," commented Lorri bitterly, "you'd think with a transfer of that size the bank would pay a little more attention to what they are doing." I couldn't agree more. As the majority of transfers were of only a few hundred dollars at best in this little town, this one should have been checked by more than one person before sending off. I hoped the bank would clear this up in a hurry.

We approached the bank the following day, bringing along the routing information written on Dr. Dobelle's contract. "Oh dear," Paula was apologetic. "I'll send out an amendment right now. Just give me those papers and I'll get on it right away." She went back to the machine and did some typing again. I crossed my fingers and attempted to incite a caution on her part. "Check it before you send it, OK?" This was the most I could do, as it would seem rude to do any more than this.

"It will take a few days to get a response on the amendment." Paula was not making me feel much better. All the other patients' money is probably in by now. "Due to the terrorist attack in New York, as the main transfer for international transfers is in Manhattan, it may be a bit longer than before this all happened."

We took our slip of paper and went home. Together we worried about the money. Carmen, my friend who had lost his sight a couple years ago due to glaucoma, telephoned me. "Ready for the surgery?" He was waiting in anticipation as if it was he himself that was going to get it.

"Not yet," I remarked, adding, "everything that can go wrong is going wrong. First, Dr. Dobelle gets sick, almost dying from a heart attack, and then again he just about drops out from diabetic complications. Now the bank misdirected my down payment. It doesn't look too promising at the moment."

"He made it through the terrorist attack?" asked Carmen. This was a rather big issue on the media, and New York was right in the middle of it.

"It's a wonder he did," I said, thinking of what else will come up. "But when I get it, I'll come over and see you." I sounded confident but did not feel that way. The missing money was a problem, all right. The bank had already made it clear they would not pay it back. All they could do was look for it. I got out the amended transfer slip issued to me by the bank and scanned it for my own records. I figured I would fax it to Dr. Dobelle next just to confirm that I was doing something about the missing cash.

The scanner finished the scan, and the computer spoke in its usual expressionless voice the details. My heart stopped when it spoke the account number.

"Lorri!" I ran out of my office, holding the transfer slip. "What is the account number written here?"

Lorri repeated the bad news. "014-4797-200002" She did not catch onto the panic right away, as it was me who had that number memorized. She compared it to the latest letter from Dobelle. There was an extra "0" in it this time. I couldn't telephone the bank, let alone go there to straighten it out right away. I felt that I would have furiously insulted Paula for her carelessness. Yet, it wasn't her fault either. Something was making this happen—something out of my control.

Another amendment was made on September 27. I had no more qualms of demanding care on the issue. Paula had nothing left in her to defend herself either.

"Once you're done entering the number," I insisted, "have another employee check the figures before sending it off." The second employee obliged. "Read it out loud, right from the machine," I instructed. "That way it will be my fault as well if it is wrong." This suggestion made for good cooperation. She did, and it was right this time. That figures, I thought. There was no comfort however, as a mass confusion now faced the bank transfer.

Two days later, we received another letter from the Dobelle Institute.

> Dobelle Institute (Portugal) Lda.
> Artificial Vision for the Blind
>
> DATE: September 27, 2001
> To: All Blind Surgical Candidates
>
> Fr: Wm H. Dobelle, PhD
> Chairman & Chief Executive Officer
> Re: Notify Me by the October 19 Deadline
>
> As you know, we have set an October 19 deadline for deposits. Once I have a final list, and know exactly how many people are involved, I will proceed:
>
> 1. To buy and begin assembly of computers, chips, TV cameras, custom connectors for the skull pedestal and platinum for the electrodes, among other things.

2. To schedule surgery for each patient, giving you a date around the third week in January. This date is subject to change, of course, especially if you have a schedule conflict.

3. To explore discount hotel accommodations, although "rack rates" are already very low in Lisbon and the city is compact so geography is not important.

4. To explore discount airline arrangements, although, once again, "off-season" rates are already very low.

If you have not already done so, could you call me on our no-charge "hotline," which is:
1-800 . . .

Outside the United States, this is usually accessed through "USADirect." If you have trouble, call me "collect" (e.g., reverse the charges), at my office: (631 . . .)
Nights and weekends, I can usually be reached at home.
Alternately, particularly if your answer is negative, e-mail me at: whd@dobelle.com

This didn't look good.

"I think he's putting the pressure on us to pay," Lorri commented, noting the last line " . . . particularly if your answer is negative . . ." as if he still doubted we were really serious about having the surgery.

"Money talks," I said, "anyone could have concocted this transfer slip and faxed it to him, and it has been a month and a week to send a three-day money transfer. You can't blame him for his doubting us."

"We'll have to send off another transfer if we want his confidence. The nineteenth of October is not far away," I suggested, thinking about the miserable situation in depth. We were certainly at another dilemma. We had the line of credit and some of our own saved money that would be good for another transfer. This would mean, however, that should the first transfer not be found, we wouldn't be able to afford the operation anyhow. Yet, we would not be able to get our second transfer reimbursed, as the contract precisely stated that the down payment stays with them for damages. The second down payment cash could be used to pay back the citizens of Napanee, swallow our losses, and get on with it. On the other hand, if the first transfer was located after reimbursing the donors, the golden chance to see again would have been thrown to the wayside.

We pondered over the problem. It was impossible to console myself that everything would be all right. The donors had so generously given a helping hand just for the entire effort to be wasted. I could not sleep that September night. Back in 1983, when first having lost my sight on that ominous day of December 7, I had dragged down my little family of Lorri and the baby Danielle with my misfortune. Now, eighteen years later, it is happening again. All this money, most of it not directly mine as Lorri and the rest of the family had equal claim to what was not donated, is going to be wasted, menacing to throw us into poverty just to attain a dream that has little chance of coming true, as there was something out there working against me. It was then that I resolved this would be my final attempt for eyesight recovery.

With that resolution secretly made, the only logical step would be to send off another transfer the following day. I had enough paranoia to realize that another transfer of the equal amount would create additional confusion to an already chaotic situation. We decided, therefore, to send off $21,000 US just in order to be able to distinguish between the two transfers. We also decided on going to another bank to make this transfer.

We decided on the Toronto-Dominion Bank, as that was the bank we had dealt with since 1985, when first arriving in Napanee. It was Penny who made the transfer.

"Now be really careful to get the correct digits in the machine," I warned her. "The CIBC had screwed up the first transfer, and a month later, they fouled up again on the amendment! This is all from not double-checking."

"That must be awful," she said, typing in the digits, "especially since you still don't have the money back."

She typed the final digits, then announced, "All ready. I just have to send it off now."

"Wait a minute," I halted her, insistently, "just reread me the numbers that are in the machine. I have them memorized." She did not show that she was irritated by my mistrust in her and started.

"Account number is 014-4797-2000 and the routing number is . . ." I couldn't believe it. Who was doing this to me? Surely the banks were better than this at sending off money, as there would be no way the economy would have a chance this way. I spoke calmly despite my turbulence inside. After all, I did not want to startle her and have her hit the "send" key by accident.

"You forgot the last digit, the '2', of the account number," I said quietly, in a manner suggesting I felt sorry for her. I did so, in fact. This wasn't her mistake; this was the way it was supposed to be, according to whatever was following me around.

Penny looked at the letter from Dr. Dobelle again. The missing numeral must have been slightly separated from the others, as she said in a puzzled expression, "Oh yeah, there it is . . ."

We went home with the heaviest burden on our shoulders since we experienced the loss eighteen years ago. We had just spent $41,000 US with absolutely nothing to show for it. I recalled the time we purchased the farm we were presently living on; the price was high, but after spending the money, we had so much to show for it. Moreover, we could always sell it again if we didn't like it, we had told ourselves, and thus losing any flicker of doubt that we were doing the right thing. Not this time. This was not at all the way I expected the dream to unfold.

Lorri and I buried ourselves in our jobs. While Lorri had her music lessons to attend to, I buried myself in the firewood business. More and more customers were buying now, a welcome change from the summer, which was spent working like a slave, spending thousands on logs, with only the odd ten dollars' worth of wood sold to a camper wanting wood for a fire to keep the mosquitoes away. The work was hard, boring, and dangerous. The most dangerous part of it was rolling the logs, which could weigh over five hundred pounds, down from a pile which sometimes was twice my height. "If one of those ever hit me," I thought to myself, "I would either be dead if God had mercy on me, but with my luck I would be in a wheelchair as well as blind." I had lost all confidence in mercy. I did realize as well that I would have to quit this job soon. The gasoline/oil mixture used in the chain saws was building up in my lungs. I spent some nights choking for air, wrestling with the feeling that someone had their hands around my throat and was slowly squeezing. In spite of all the physical exercise I was getting, I was badly out of shape. When I tried to run, my knees hurt and I was completely out of breath after a hundred steps. Yet I had no extra weight to carry. There was no doubt in my mind that this job had to stop soon. "Once I can see," I told myself, "I would start a business installing solar/wind electrical installations for private and commercial clientele." I would not need perfect vision, as I could already work with electronic components with no vision at all. It would come in handy, nevertheless, to see the client's house, the location of large objects like trees, etc., which could block the sun or wind, when assessing the location of the installation. Most of all, if the people thought I had a bit of vision, they would be under the impression I was in control and knew what I was doing, even if I didn't have the vision system turned on. It was the confidence that others had in me that lacked the most when being blind, I concluded a long time ago, and I believed that this invention of Dr. Dobelle's would change that.

It was halfway through the second week of October that I received the letter from Dr. Dobelle, the first bit of good news in a while.

Dobelle Institute
Artificial Vision for the Blind

October 10, 2001
To: Mr. Jens Naumann
Napanee, Ontario

Canada

Fr:
Wm. H. Dobelle, PhD
Chairman & Chief Executive Officer
Re: Wire Transfer

We have received your paperwork, and the bank in Portugal has confirmed receipt of your deposit.

They have no trace of any earlier transfers, which I understand is due to the fact that your bank fouled up the routing/account information. I would raise holy hell with your bank to get this money returned to you.

Thanks!

Holy hell was what would be needed to get things moving again. I called Paula at the CIBC just to hear the usual response—"We have a search out, and we haven't heard back from them yet . . ." which was more than useless to me. There was a constant feeling of helplessness in the process as no one was prepared to take responsibility and promise an eventual reimbursement if the money was not relocated. Paula referred my case to "customer service," another voice to which I had to explain the situation all over again. "We'll look into it" was the typical response, and I feared the worst. I remembered then that my sister, Petra, was a branch manager of an Abbotsford CIBC, and even though geographically the branches were a few thousand kilometers apart, it appeared the branches worked through a common network. Petra referred me to an employee in the branch to whom I quickly corresponded via fax.

November 7, 2001

CIBC (Clearbrook)

Attn: Christine

Re: Lost wire transfer for Jens Naumann, original transfer number 4010335, for 20,000 dollars US from Napanee, Ontario, CIBC branch to Banco Espirito Santo, Lisbon, Portugal.

Dear Christine,

On November 2, the CIBC (Napanee) sent information via fax to the Customer Care Center, Toronto, into the hands of Debbie Storie (ext 5921), and this morning, I got a hold of her as she was not in the office yesterday. Upon talking to her, I discovered she was not given the second amendment for the transfer dated September 27/01. She only had the first amendment (September 23) which has the wrong account number. Therefore, she now has to recontact Napanee to get the right information.

As a result, I wonder if you could see if the last trace (October 17/01) was conducted using the correct account number. Chances are it was not, but instead was based on the first amendment, which still had the account number wrong. I will give you the correct number again:

account number: 014 47972 0002 routing: 00070 014 00 47972 000 298

Please note that originally, the August 22 transfer was missing the second "7," and the first amendment from September 23 had an extra "0" just before the last digit. If indeed the trace was conducted using the wrong account number, that could be the problem all the way along. Since Paula from Napanee CIBC initiated the trace in the first place and then sends only the first amendment to Toronto, it looks suspicious.

Thank you for your help.

Sincerely,

Jens Naumann

After reviewing the fax before sending it, it seemed to me that unfortunately I was again undermining the thinking capacity of the professional employees of our financial establishments. Why did Debbie from customer service not get information about the second amendment? This was unfolding more like a circus with every passing day, constantly shedding uncertainty upon the possibility of receiving that implant. In the meantime, however, we had received more credit from two credit card companies, and it looked like we could give up on this money and scrape through anyways if we were really careful about Christmas. It was going to be hard on the kids, as we did the same thing last year. That explanation of the vision implant being "just around the corner" has now been with us for almost a year and a half.

We were within three weeks of a scheduled hearing at the Health Services Appeal and Review Board, which meant I had to prepare my arguments to present to the panel. I had a good idea what the arguments were against my funding request by the general manager of the health insurance plan (OHIP) since receiving a copy of the case prepared by him.

Ministry of Health and Long-Term Care
Health Services Division, Provider Services Branch Kingston, ON

November 1, 2001

Ms. Abby Katz Starr
Chief Operating Officer
Health Boards Secretariat
151 Bloor Street West, 9th Floor Toronto, ON
 and copy to
Jens Naumann
Napanee, ON

Dear Ms. Katz Starr:
RE: Jens Neumann vs. General Manager, Ontario Health Insurance Plan
HSARB File# 01-HIA-0061

Enclosed is the Summary of Grounds of Response concerning the above-noted subscriber as requested.
A copy of the Grounds of Response has been sent to the appellant at the address above.

Yours sincerely,
W. G. G. Fisher, MA MB FRCSC
District Medical Consultant Coordinator

Enclosures

Health Services Appeal and Review Board Grounds of Response
Appellant: Jens Naumann,
HSARB File #OI—HIA-0061
Payment of Artificial Vision System

The appellant in this case is Mr. Jens Naumann of Napanee, Ontario, who is seeking a specialized service to be provided by the Dobelle Institute, Inc., which is currently based in Portugal where it is associated with a private hospital. The appeal in this case is for the funding of a visual prosthesis, the provision of which has been described as a very specialized service only offered by the Dobelle Institute.

A prior approval application form was completed on behalf of the appellant by Dr. W. Willis, specialist ophthalmologist at the Hotel Dieu Hospital in Kingston, Ontario. The proposed out-of-country treatment is noted to be the insertion of artificial vision device for bilateral blindness. The proposed out-of-country facility was the hospital CUF Trav Do Castro, Lisbon, Portugal, under the care of Dr. W. H. Dobelle, who is not a physician.

Part 4B of the prior approval application form indicating that the services are not performed in Ontario was completed to show that the treatment is generally accepted in Ontario as appropriate for a person in the same medical circumstances, that it was probably considered experimental and was not performed in Ontario by an identical or equivalent procedure. The additional note was added that "this is a very specialized service which is only offered by the Dobelle Institute Inc."

The request for the funding by prior approval was considered by Dr. Hugh Langley, medical consultant to Provider Services Branch of the Ministry of Health and Long-Term Care in Kingston, Ontario. Dr. Langley wrote to Dr. Willis on May 31, 2001 to acknowledge receipt of the prior approval application noting that "full funding was requested for insertion of "artificial vision" device for the condition of bilateral blindness.

The original application and the additional information provided by Mr. Naumann has been thoroughly reviewed by ministry staff. As a result of this review, it has been concluded that the treatment requested is considered experimental in Ontario. Experimental out-of-country treatment is not eligible for reimbursement as an insured benefit under the Health Insurance of Ontario. This request for prior approval of full payment for health services outside of Canada has been denied.

The appellant has provided copies of correspondence that he received from the Dobelle Institute. In a letter written to Dr. Langley dated April 7, 2001, Mr. Naumann indicated to Dr. Langley that "At present, I am attempting to find a way to fund this procedure out of my own pocket. However, I hope that you may assist me in establishing funding from the medical insurance department, as the quality of life improvement resulting from a successful implant would be greatly welcome for both me and my family."

The payment of insured medical services outside Canada by the Ontario Health Insurance Plan is subject to the provisions of the Regulations under the Health Insurance Revised Statues of Ontario, 1990, Chapter H6. The criteria for full funding by prior approval are those found under Section 28.4 of Regulation 552 under the Act, which reads as follows.

2&4 (1) In this Section, "Preferred provider arrangement" means a written agreement between the minister and the operator of a hospital or health facility outside of Canada for the delivery of specified insured services to insured persons, and "Preferred provider" means the operator.

(2) Services that are part of a treatment and that are rendered outside Canada at a hospital or health facility are prescribed as insured services if (a) the treatment is generally accepted in Ontario as appropriate for a person in the same medical circumstances as the insured person; and b) either, i) that kind of treatment that is not performed in Ontario by an identical or equivalent procedure; or ii) that kind of treatment is performed in Ontario, but it is necessary that the insured person travel out of Canada to avoid a delay that would result in death or medically significant irreversible tissue damage.

(3) If insured services prescribed by sub-section (2) are covered by a preferred provider arrangement, the amount payable is the amount provided in the preferred provider arrangement.

(4) If insured services prescribed by sub-section (2) are not covered by a preferred provider arrangement, the amount payable

is the usual and customary amount charged by similar facilities under similar circumstances to major insurers for services provided, to persons they insure in facilities located within the jurisdiction where the insured services are provided.

(5) The following are conditions of payment of amounts for services prescribed in this section:

1. An application for approval of payment must be submitted to the general manager by a physician who practices medicine in Ontario on behalf of the insured person, and the application must contain a written confirmation from that physician that, in the opinion of the physician, one of the conditions set out in clause 2(2) (b) is satisfied 2. The general manager must give written approval of the payment of the amount under this section before the services for which approval has been sought are rendered.

3. The services must be received within the time limit set out in the approval described in paragraph 2.

4. The services are covered by a preferred provider arrangement; they must be received from a preferred provider. There are also certain exclusions to insured services which are set out in Section 24 of Regulation 552. In part, section 24 reads as follows. 24. (1)

The following services rendered by physicians or practitioners are not insured services and are not part of insured services

Subpart 17

Treatment for a medical condition that is generally accepted within Ontario as experimental

The documentation that provides further information about the requested service in this case raises a number of issues. The prior approval form completed by the Ontario physician indicates that the service is probably considered experimental.

The documentation from the Dobelle Institute written to the appellant clearly indicates that the provision of the visual prosthesis and the implantation surgery is intended to be provided in Portugal because the regulatory situation there is favorable. As you may know, almost all drugs and devices are introduced abroad before permission is sought from the FDA for sale in the United States.

The Dobelle Institute has made it clear that they require prepayment in the form of a $20,000 deposit, and the balance is paid in advance of any surgery. The provision of the visual prosthesis has been based on a volunteer population. The insertion of the visual prosthesis does not constitute a standard and generally accepted medical treatment.

From the Web site of the Dobelle Institute comes an article entitled "Frequently Asked Questions." Question number 11 refers to the possible insurance payments for the device.

With respect to insurance payments, the answer given is: "We have secured reimbursement authority from Medicare and analogous private and government insurance plans around the world for our other devices. We believe this will also be true of the visual prosthesis, but it will undoubtedly take a number of years." In other words, there is no insurance coverage for the visual prosthesis, and it is unlikely there will be for many years to come.

It is the Grounds of Response, therefore, in this case that the visual prosthesis device is in a developmental stage, subject to implant only in chosen volunteers. It is clear that the Dobelle Institute expects advance funding for the provision of the device. It is not a generally accepted treatment. Although the use of the visual device involves a medical service of intracranial implantation in the visual cortex of the brain, such a procedure is not listed in the Ontario Schedule of Benefits or prescribed as an insured service. Dr. Dobelle is not a physician but is a medical device engineer. The services requested by the appellant in this case are not services that are generally accepted in Ontario, are services which are in an early stage of development and have not yet been subjected to controlled clinical study. As the press release entitled "Artificial vision system for the blind announced by the Dobelle Institute" has described Dr. Dobelle's first human experiments in the artificial vision project took place beginning in 1970 and involved cortical stimulation of thirty-seven sighted volunteers undergoing surgery on the occipital lobe under local anesthesia to remove tumors and other lesions. Three blind volunteers were then temporarily implanted with electrode arrays to stimulate the visual cortex. Subsequent experiments involved four blind volunteers who were implanted with permanent electrode arrays and plain percutaneous electrode pedestals. It is clear from these descriptions that Dr. Dobelle's work can be considered research and experimental at the present time. The services requested by the appellant are not prescribed as insured services of the Ontario Health Insurance Plan.

W. G. G. Fisher ND MB FRC
District Medical Consultant

attachments:

Visual Prostheses

Center for Neural Interfaces, Department of Bioengineering. University of Utah, Salt Lake City, Utah 84112.

The development of man-made systems to restore functional vision in the profoundly blind has recently undergone a renaissance that has been fueled by a combination of celebrity and government interest, advances in the field of bioengineering, and successes with existing neuroprosthetic systems. This chapter presents the underlying physiologic principles of artificial vision, discusses three contemporary approaches to restoring functional vision in the blind, and concludes by presenting several relevant questions to vision prostheses. While there has been significant progress in the individual components constituting an artificial vision system, the remaining challenge of integrating these components with each other and the nervous system does not lie strictly in the realm of neuroscience, medicine, or engineering but at the interface of all three. In spite of the apparent complexity of an artificial vision system, it is not unreasonable to be optimistic about its eventual success.

Department of Bioengineering, University of Utah, Salt Lake City Journal

The development of a cortically based vision prosthesis has been hampered by a lack of basic experiments on phosphene psychophysics. This basic research has been hampered by the lack of a means to safely stimulate large numbers of cortical neurons. Recently, a number of laboratories have developed arrays of silicon microelectrodes that could enable such basic studies on phosphene psychophysics. This paper describes one such array, the Utah electrode array. and summarizes neurosurgical, physiological, and histological experiments. The clinical summary suggests that such an array could be implanted safely in visual cortex. We also summarize a series of chronic behavioral experiments that show that modest levels of electrical currents passed into cortex via this array can evoke sensory percepts. Pending the successful outcome of biocompatibility studies using such arrays, high count arrays of penetrating microelectrodes similar to this design could provide a useful tool for studies of the psychophysics of phosphene perception in human volunteers. Such studies could provide a proof of concept for cortically based artificial vision.

Related Articles/Books
Altruism and the volunteer: psychological benefits from participating as a research subject.
Seelig BJ, Dobelle WH.
Emory University Psychoanalytic Institute, Department of Psychiatry and
Behavioral Sciences, Emory) University School of Medicine, Atlanta, Georgia
30306, USA.
Privacy Policy

Psychiatric assessment of potential volunteers for hazardous biomedical experimentation should include an assessment of the motivations underlying the altruistic action of volunteering. Screening goals include evaluation of informed consent as well as screening out experimental subjects who would be likely to be psychologically harmed by participation. This discussion of psychological issues to be considered, beyond those of informed consent and screening for severe psychopathology, originated in the psychiatric screening of the small group of original volunteers for the "Dobelle Eye" Artificial Vision Project. These individuals entered the project over twenty years ago at a time when they could expect no tangible benefit from participation. Superficially altruistic behavior, such as volunteering for this project, serves multiple psychological functions, and in a given clinical case, the determinants are often complex. A spectrum of altruistic behavior is suggested, based on interviews with these original subjects as well as from extensive evaluation of patients studied in the setting of psychoanalytic treatment with one of the authors (B.J.S.). We suggest that adaptive altruism can explain the finding that some volunteers gained actual psychological benefit from their participation. This unanticipated finding, that participating in research as an experimental subject can result in lasting improvement in self-esteem, is discussed. Suggestions are made for increasing the likelihood of such benefit. Ethical ramifications are addressed.

Brain chip offers blind chance at "sight." Whether the device will work with patients blind from birth, who may lack a fully developed visual cortex, remains a question, Dobelle says.

"It's important not to oversell this," says Bioengineer Richard Normann of the University of Utah in Salt Lake City after reviewing the study. But Normann, who has researched artificial vision devices for more than fifteen years, says the results "suggest this line of research might be fruitful."

With other researchers, from our archive: Dobelle has worked with his vision chips in a sixty-two-year-old patient since 1978. Neurosurgeons slipped a one--inch square grid containing sixty-eight electrodes onto the brain's visual cortex. Stimulating the electrodes produced "phosphenes," bright flashes of light perceptible to the patient. Results from that work, reported in the journal of neurosurgery, sparked public interest in artificial eyes twenty years ago.

It has taken that long for computers to fulfill those hopes, Dobelle says. After getting the TV signal, more powerful computers now can trigger the brain electrodes in a regulated pattern in real time. "The fact the electrodes have survived for twenty years is a positive result," says William Heetderks, head of the neuroprosthesis program at the National Institute of Neurological Disorders and Stroke. "If—and I stress if—the patient's mobility dramatically improves, it would be the first demonstration of an artificial vision system," he says. According to the study, a carbon plug in the patient's skull connects wires to the brain implant. No infections have developed, chiefly because of heavy blood flow throughout the scalp, which constantly brings immune cells near the plug connected to the implant. One other facet of a brain vision implant, Dobelle says, http://www.usatoday.com/life/cyber/tech/review/crg8l4.htm Page 2 of* 3
07 10/31/2001

Brain chip offers blind chance at 'sight' is that it may allow a blind person to receive input from a computer screen, providing access to the Internet. A sighted person with such a connection would see the computer image "superimposed on their environment," Dobelle says.

In related work, Normann has developed a silicon chip-based electrode system that would insert wires one-tenth the thickness of a human hair into the visual cortex of the brain. Such a refinement allows much closer spacing of the electrodes, he says, and thus a more finely resolved picture. He expects that at least six years of testing would be required before such a device faced human experiments.

A spokesperson for the Food and Drug Administration says a high-risk medical device, such as a brain implant, would probably require long clinical study and expert committee review before gaining sales approval. Knowledge of phosphenes emerged from early brain surgery reports on epilepsy patients. They reported light flashes whenever the visual cortex, in the back of the brain, was prodded.

Artificial vision systems that connect directly to the brain would offer advantages over recently publicized technologies that try to send visual signals to damaged retinas, Normann says. Relatively few blind patients have intact retinas capable of adapting digital signals. Brain implants would entirely bypass damaged eyes to generate imagery in the mind.

"Both types of devices may eventually coexist as aids for the blind," he says. "But it's not right around the corner."

I read the arguments, as well as the additional research clips attached to the end with interest. I had heard of Richard Norman before in various newscasts in which the possibilities of artificial vision was discussed. I found it rather curious that William Heetderks would define the existence of an artificial vision method as successful "if, and I stress if—the patient's mobility dramatically improves, it would be the first demonstration of an artificial vision system . . .," suggesting that a dramatic improvement in mobility is the criteria determining the feasibility of the system, and thus its availability for the patients. It is obvious that Heetderks has *no idea* what it is like to be profoundly blind after once having had full eyesight. I would think the ability to see light would be the determinant for providing a vision system to a patient.

Another astonishing surprise came when reading the article titled "Altruism and the Volunteer" in which B. Seelig mentions that one of the principle reasons for participating in a project such as the artificial vision experimentation is for the purpose of building up self-esteem and perhaps serving a useful purpose in life. There was no mention at all in the article that the volunteers may have been so deprived of light that the idea of seeing a few "dots of light" would be analogous to a person dying of thirst in a desert sipping the few drops of water in the bottom of an abandoned flask. It was plain to conclude that B. Seelig, W. Heetderks, and Richard Norman had no problems with their eyesight. It appeared from first glance at the attitude propagated by reading between the lines of the researchers was one that suggested there would be no involvement of the blind community when making the decisions as to what quality of vision is adequate. The danger existed, undoubtedly, that only once the sighted community of "researchers and experts" were satisfied with a certain quality of vision would the technology be made available. In the meantime we, the blind, stay in the dark. They were the ones holding the cards, waving them at us every now and then, smiling all the way, while we faced each day in blackness.

Dr. Dobelle, however, was not like that. There must be a quality about this man that set him apart from the others. He was sighted as well, yet he seemed to understand the plight of the profoundly blind. He certainly stood the chance to make money from this venture, but he would deserve it. After all, the researchers mentioned in the general manager's articles were more than likely not living in poverty either.

I reviewed the arguments posed by Godfrey Fisher, which seemed equivalent in nature to those posed by Hugh Langley previously. These include the fact that cortical stimulation for vision is experimental, that Dr. Dobelle is not a physician, and that the money is demanded in advance of the surgery. The pertinent sections of the Health Act were mentioned, which gave little room for argument. I still felt the odds were with me, as it would be difficult for sighted individuals to look a blind person in the face and say "even though this will make you see a bit, we don't think you should get it . . .," or would it? I would not, however, want to bank too strongly on the sympathy issue. Considering that the term "experimental" is not precisely defined in the Health Act, as well as the fact that in the ASAIO Journal 2000, it was stated that the visual cortex atrophies when not in use over many years, suggesting urgency in attaining this implant. I had to try my best not only for my own funding initiative, but for the eventual introduction of this procedure in Canada for all of my blind counterparts to profit from. Dr. Dobelle was, after all, not a young guy anymore, and should he retire from this project before it is properly publicized, it stands a chance of once again being entrapped within the walls of the research laboratories.

I decided to fax a copy of Godfrey's arguments to Dr. Dobelle in the hope he would have other suggestions, as well as explaining to me the importance of the "radiology" mentioned in his second letter to me in January. His response came within that day.

Dear Jens,

I don't think any insurance carrier will support artificial vision in the next ten years.

In my experience, OHIP is one of the less imaginative carriers, but I wish you good luck.

The radiological studies are routine prior to neurosurgical intervention, nothing special is anticipated.

Regards,
Dr. Bill Dobelle
The Dobelle Institute (Portugal) Lda.

It was a good thing that Godfrey Fisher did not have a copy of this letter, as that would signify immediate defeat. If even Dr. Dobelle doubted this should be funded by OHIP, it would be a hard sell for me to convince the general manager otherwise. Good luck is what I needed.

In short time I received another letter from Dr. Dobelle, this one evidently sent to all blind patients who had previously corresponded with him.

Dobelle Institute (Portugal) Lda. Artificial Vision for the Blind

October 22, 2001
To: Mr. Jens Naumann
Napanee, Ontario, Canada

Fr:
Wm. H. Dobelle, PhD
Chairman & Chief Executive Officer
Re: Implant of Visual Prosthesis

We have extended the deadline for a number of people until November 2.

I know you may be thinking about the aftermath of September 11.

By coincidence, my new secretary and her husband were in Portugal and Madeira last week on a trip that they had planned long before I hired her. They had a great time and you can contact Louise at (USADirect 800 797-5244) or call the office "collect" at this office. Her e-mail address is: LMC@dobelle.com. Incidentally this is a new e-mail address, and it may take a day or two to get activated.

Once I have a final list, and know exactly how many people are involved, I will proceed:

1. To buy and begin assembly of computers, chips, TV cameras, custom connectors for the skull pedestal and platinum for the electrodes, among other things.

2. To schedule surgery for each patient, giving you a date around the third week in January. This date is subject to change, of course, especially if you have a schedule conflict.

3. To explore discount hotel accommodations, although "rack rates" are already very low in Lisbon, and the city is compact so geography is not important.

4. To explore discount airline arrangements, although, once again, "off-season" rates are already very low.

I will be back in touch with you in a couple of weeks. Meanwhile, thank you for your confidence.

It looked like Dr. Dobelle still had some work to do in assembling the components. I would have expected them to be already finished, considering that Christmas is not a particularly productive season, as well as the complexity of the components requiring adequate time to assemble. Perhaps this could be viewed, I figured, as proof that there were indeed many workers in the laboratory and that Dr. Dobelle is just the acting spokesperson for the patients. The best news was that the dates for surgery were still in the neighborhood of January 2002. I did not know how many more delays I could take.

Janice from CBC called me again. She was confirming my attendance at the appeal hearing on November 20, as she had attained permission from the board to be able to sit in provided she did not use a camera during the proceedings. Whatever the verdict would be, it was going to be broadcast on television. I had to make sure I was well prepared and not appear to be fumbling for words.

I decided to answer Dr. Dobelle's latest letter for the purpose of assuring him that I was not going to experience a "schedule conflict" at the time of surgery. It would be hard to picture someone delaying the chance to see again by doing something more important. I also wanted to demonstrate my commitment in promoting the vision system via the CBC reporter during my hearing.

November 5, 2001

Dobelle Institute
NY

Dear Dr. Dobelle, Louis, and staff,

I received your latest letter last week dated October 22, in which you extended the deadline for the down payments. I am sure Louise had a nice time as it is getting kind of frigid here and goofing off in Portugal beats working in an office. Since the hijackers are fried to a crisp, they will pose no more problems anyhow, and as for me, I definitely would not let a couple of hooligan welding boxcutters deter me from accomplishing my dream of the past eighteen years. Thank you for the e-mail you sent in response to my fax describing my attempts to appeal the funding rejection. I figure if your ten-year prediction is right, I can only make this year 1 by bringing this to their attention.

Today I received a call from Janyce McGregor, a bigwig at the CBC National Current Affairs program. She was already very interested in following up on this visual prosthesis development and now wants to be an observer at my hearing with the Health Services Review Board. Maybe that will boost the imagination of OHIP.

My missing cash dilemma was referred to the CIBC customer care center in Toronto as of today, and tomorrow I get to correspond with them. CIBC Napanee complained that Portugal is not responding to any of their traces and that they cannot get through to them on the phone. Well, if I do not have this straightened out by January, I can use my new Dobelle Eye to look for a large wad of cash in a Portuguese gutter! The bank is sure this will be resolved, but they are not sure when. All sorts of things can still happen in the next ten weeks, so no big deal about that.

My family and I am sure looking forward to receiving the exact date to arrive in Portugal for the implant. Any day is fine with me, as I have put any important issues on hold for the weeks surrounding January. I do have a couple of questions, the latter probably better answered by Louise:

1: Is it imperative that I travel with an escort? My wife has to attend her work and the seven children, and I am having a bit of trouble finding a companion.

2: Supposing the above question is answered "no," is there assistance at the Portugal airport to help those with a visual disability, such as the assistance available in Canada and the United States?

An answer on e-mail is fine. I sure hope the program is sailing smoothly at your end. Thank you and all the best.

Jens Naumann

The problem of finding someone to take care of the family during our absence was so far unsolved. We had no family members in the position to do this for us. Even though the two older kids could have managed fine by themselves, they could never supervise the younger ones. Moreover, we had the woodstoves to look after—nothing to be entrusted to children. When we had originally been told that the surgeries will take place during the summer holidays, the possibilities of finding help would have been more favorable. In the absence of a babysitter, I decided to go alone.

It took little time to get a reply from Dr. Dobelle.

Dear Jens,

I would try to keep publicity down to an absolute minimum. We will not cooperate in any way with the woman from CBC National Affairs Program until after your system is up and working. I can explain better by telephone.

I would really suggest having a companion. It's not just the airports that are a problem (in fact they are relatively easy) but all the associated travel within Lisbon. I don't know how old your kids are, but even a responsible ten-year-old can do the job. In fact, Craig's daughter was only eight when she began to serve as a guide dog for her mom and dad.

As far as I am concerned, your bank is making excuses for absolutely unprofessional work on their behalf. I would get an attorney to go after them for immediate return of the extra money. Meanwhile, as I told the girl from the bank who called me some weeks ago, she can contact Antonio Vieira at (351) 21 799 0528. He is not directly responsible for wire transfers, but he can tell them who to talk to, although they should have this information through their own wire network service.

Regards,
Dr. Bill Dobelle
The Dobelle Institute (Portugal) Lda.

I was surprised at the opposition Dr. Dobelle voiced regarding the CBC reporter. I had assumed that the media interest would be a good thing. Dr.

Dobelle's opposition to publicity seemed to suggest a lack of confidence in the product. I was concerned by this, as was Lorri, as we had originally dealt with Janice from the CBC in the hopes that Dr. Dobelle would cooperate. Janice had spent considerable time and effort into the reporting thus far, and it was necessary to continue the coverage. It was this coverage that had started the fund-raising effort, and it will be the coverage of the final product that will reward the donors. I thought I'd call Dr. Dobelle.

"Look, Jens," Dr. Dobelle began in his sluggish speech, "I don't want to mess around with reporters when I have a job to do. Do you know how much trouble they can be?"

I tried to calm him down. "All she is doing is a documentary about my situation and wants to use the vision system to give it a happy ending." I hoped that would console him.

"I don't really give a damn what she wants," he said in a perfectly undoctorlike manner. "I've got a job to do, and she can wait until I invite her."

I thanked Dr. Dobelle and left it at that. His letter had been more civil than this conversation, that was for sure.

"What did he have to say about Janice?" asked Lorri, having heard only my side of the conversation.

"He doesn't want to mess around with reporters." I used his words to give Lorri more of an idea of the problem.

"Oh," she said. "What are we going to tell Janice?" Janice had been very nice to us, and extremely supportive, and the last thing we wanted was this to hit her. "Not this," I said affirmatively. None of this and neither that last letter. I suppose we can tell her that Dr. Dobelle is a little eccentric and has some press paranoia."

That did not sound good. Good thing that he wasn't going to stir around in my head, I thought. If he was taking on the responsibility of representative for this project, it was going to be a hard sell. I tried to shrug it off as a bad day. Perhaps Dr. Dobelle thought that Janice was out to bad-mouth the project, looking for any little fault in order to make it fall to ruin. I knew that wasn't the case. Neither Lorri nor I told Janice about our latest conversation with Dr. Dobelle.

Then came another letter in the mail.

Dobelle Institute (Portugal) Lda.
Artificial Vision for the Blind
November 7, 2001

To: Mr. Jens Naumann
Napanee, Ontario

Fr:

Wm. H. Dobelle, PhD

Chairman & Chief Executive Officer

Re: Surgical Arrangements

1.   Objective: The attached picture (in mailed copies of this memo) from the Guinness Book of World Records clearly shows the system. By merging external photographs of Jerry wearing the equipment, with an artist's conception of the implant components, one gets the whole picture. One lens of the glasses contains a tiny TV camera, and the other lens incorporates the ultrasonic distance sensor. Information from these two sensors is fed down a twisted pair of cables to the computer. After processing the signals, the computerized stimulator in the belt generates pulses that travel up a cable to the pedestal, which protrudes slightly through Jerry's scalp (hidden by hair). The wires which run from the base of the pedestal travel a significant distance under the scalp before penetrating the bone and endura. The electrodes, in turn, lie on the middle surface of the brain. In Jerry they are implanted unilaterally, while new patients they will be implanted bilaterally.

2.   Expected Performance: I will stress again that we cannot expect "normal" vision. Because of the limited number of electrodes, resolution is reduced even while scanning. Moreover, phosphenes are white sensations on a black background. Images will be similar to those you'd expect watching a black-and-white movie negative. I believe that vision will, in general, be good enough to recognize faces and to secure independent mobility. However, no such promise can be made for any individual patient.

3.   Money Due Before February: In addition to your hotel, airfare, and other expenses, you will incur $10,000 USD in fees for the physicians, surgeons, and psychiatrists, and a second payment of $45,000 USD for the equipment. All of these fees have to be paid in advance, since there is no realistic way that we can "repossess" a neurostimulator once it has been implanted. I'm sure you understand.

4.   Surgical Date: We have tentatively scheduled your surgery for: February 20, 2002

However, this has to be confirmed by the surgical team. Do not make any arrangements yet for travel or hotel. It is also important for us to know whether this date is convenient for you, both schedule-wise and economically. Will you have the balance of funds necessary to complete the implant by February, 2002, or do we need to set back a date later in 2002, or even 2003?

5. Hotel & Airline Reservations: Although we have a significant number of bookings to offer, no two people have the same schedule. Therefore, I would suggest you select a competent local travel agent and let them handle this for you. The CUF Hospital is in the old section of the city, a few blocks from the river and near the old bridge. However, Lisbon is a fairly compact city. Cabs are very cheap and almost any downtown hotel will do fine, but try to avoid the periphery of the city.

6. Passports, visas, etc.: Passengers from the United States need a passport but no visa. I am not sure about the requirements from foreign countries to Portugal. In any case, if you do not have your documents in hand, I suggest you get them as rapidly as possible.

7. Accompanying Persons: You must have accompaniment in Lisbon. It is even older—and less handicapped accessible—than New York. If your spouse cannot join you, what about a relative or friend?

8. Arrival: I would suggest arriving a few days early so we will have time for the physical and psychiatric exams, also so you can get over the "jet lag."
    You will have to remain in Lisbon for about one week after surgery to be sure that you are not infected. I will send you more information about all of this when we get your surgical date finalized.

9. Weather: I really don't know the weather in Lisbon, in February, but I will investigate and let you know.

"We have to wait another month" was the first thing Lorri said before reading the letter out loud. It was going to be the third week in February now.

More stuff to show Janice, without Dr. Dobelle's consent, of course, along with another explanation about a delay to the fund-raising crew.

"Did I say I couldn't stand any more delays?" I said to Lorri, attempting to recommence the "countdown" until the actual date of surgery. How much I wanted it, yet it kept evading me. "The fact that it is in the Book of World Records looks good for us." I noted the next point made: "Right there Dr. Dobelle says I should be able to recognize faces!"

I had thought in my previous conversation with Dr. Dobelle that he may have been talking without considering the meaning of actually being able to see faces. But here again, it was in writing.

"That will be rather good vision," I said, recalling that on the poor quality movies it was difficult sometimes to recognize the actors. This vision would be so close to real that one would practically be able to drive a car under less than stressful conditions. I couldn't wait to get this.

Two days later, another letter arrived. This one was filled with good news.

Dobelle Institute (Portugal) Lda.
Artificial Vision for the Blind

November 9, 2001

To: Mr. Jens Naumann

Fr: Wm. H. Dobelle, PhD
Chairman & Chief Executive Officer

Re: Your Wire Transfers

You will be thrilled to hear that Banco Espirito has now found a second wire transfer for $19,985 USD, which was received on October 24, 2001. We had previously received $21,000 USD on October 4, 2001. So far, however, there is no trace of Your third transfer. Am I correct that you made three (3)?

Both the $19,985.00 and the $21,000 have been credited to our account. Because of the wire transfer problems at your bank, I would suggest leaving the extra funds in Portugal and giving you credit at the time of surgery. I will, however, return the money to you, if you need it.

Meanwhile, I appreciate your handling of the woman media representative from Ottawa. We really need to keep things down until the implants are complete and successful. To insure this, as

I'm sure you understand, I plan to proceed on a "staged" basis, incrementally adding features (no charge) to your system.

Regards!

Both Lorri and I breathed a sigh of relief which must have been audible in the entire neighborhood. It took a while for the reality of the discovery to sink in. We would be able to afford it now. We'd be able to have a decent Christmas, handle the small unexpected bills, and not launch ourselves into a catastrophic debt by using the credit cards with their astronomical interest rate charges. We all went out for pizza that night, something we hadn't even dared to do in the last year. I telephoned Paula, who was absolutely ecstatic to hear the news. I also realized that the winning of the appeal for OHIP funding was not as important now. It would still be nice to receive support, nonetheless.

As Dr. Dobelle had mentioned he was on the lookout for a third transfer, I thought it best to call him regarding the issue. He must have misunderstood the second amendment of the first transfer as another transfer. It was past office hours, so the most logical thing to do was call his home.

A woman with a young, vibrant voice answered, "Sorry, but Bill is probably still on his way home. Do you have his cell number?"

"I sure do," I answered, "would you happen to be Mrs. Dobelle?" She chuckled at the "Mrs. Dobelle" and replied, "I am, yes."

"Nice to talk to you," I said, trying not to sound like I was prying into her personal affairs. "I'm one of his patients scheduled for a vision implant. I'm really excited to get it."

"Well, that is great. Bill has been very preoccupied with the project lately and is just as excited to get it going too." This was my first contact with Dr. Dobelle's personal life. It appeared stable, which was important to both Lorri and I, as an unstable personal life often resulted in a neglected business. I still found it difficult to comprehend why Dr. Dobelle did not leave the sales and miniscule details with regards to the organization of the project with an employee. I tried his cell phone number.

"Hello" was all Dr. Dobelle said upon answering. No reference to the "Dobelle Institute."

"Is that you, Dr. Dobelle?" I inquired. I recognized his voice. "If you're driving, I'd better make it short. I imagine New York driving takes all concentration available just to stay on the road."

"I've got my own driver," he replied, then continued, "I'm too much on the phone to be driving."

"Luxury," I thought. Meanwhile, I would have loved to be able to drive myself around. Having a driver would be analogous to hiring a man to take your wife out for the night.

"Dr. Dobelle," I began to explain the money situation. "There was no third transfer. That means all the money is now in your hands that I originally sent. It sure is a relief." Dr. Dobelle reflected for a second, then spoke, "Yeah, it sure is a lot of money to just lose like that. Twenty thousand bucks is a lot of money."

"Well, you've got it now, so you may as well hang onto it and I'll send you the rest. This time I'll be really anal about getting the right numbers in."

Dr. Dobelle laughed at that. I had no problem trusting him with the extra money. It never even crossed my mind that he could be crooked.

Ethel came by the following day to chat about the progress we were making.

"When is your operation again?" She was not sure about the exact date as she never did receive it.

"February 20," I responded, expecting what came next. "You told me it was about the third week in January. What's going on?"

I showed her the letter, as well as the previous ones suggesting a date in January.

"This must be hard on you," she said, pointing out the obvious. It probably wasn't that easy on her either, as she constantly had to change her story to the people she had talked into supporting me.

"You know scientists," she remarked after a pause of contemplation. "They always are so preoccupied with their work, they lose all track of time."

That sure was shedding a good light on things. I figured I was blind for this long, I was just going to have to be patient. It wasn't long before another letter arrived.

Dobelle Institute (Portugal) Lda.
Artificial Vision for the Blind
November 13, 2001
Fr:
Wm. H. Dobelle, PhD
Chairman & Chief Executive Officer

Re: Press Embargo and Final Surgical Dates

1. Press Embargo:
    Over the last forty (40) years, I have learned that you never speak to the press about patients who are "on the table," much

less preoperatively. Results should only be discussed after the data has been analyzed and published in a recognized refereed journal. This is the reason that our current Web site states that "everything I know about artificial vision and am willing to talk about" is contained in the ASAIO Journal article about Jerry. As a matter of irrevocable policy, I will not answer the phone, much less talk to reporters about the upcoming series of cases. You, too, should be silent on the matter. If you have any questions or problems, you can contact me on our toll-free hotline (800 . . .). Nights and weekends I am usually home. My e-mail address is: whd@dobelle.com.

2.   Final Surgical Date:
     Professor John Girvin is teaching a neurosurgical course in Kuwait, so everyone's surgery has slipped one week. In your case, surgery will be done on:
         Wednesday, February 27, 2002

3.   Suggested Schedule:
     You should also allow one day for jet lag recovery. We need two days preoperatively to orient and test you and seven days post-op to be sure that you are not infected. Please realize all dates could change again. Do not buy tickets that cannot be refunded or changed at the last minute. Arrival: Overnight, Saturday, February 23/Sunday, February 24, 2002
         Recover from Jet Lag: Sunday, February 24, 2002
         Orientation and Testing: Monday, February 25 & Tuesday, February 26
         Post-surgical Recovery: Thursday, February 28 through Wednesday, March 6
         Depart for Home: Thursday, March 7, 2002

"I hope he makes up his mind about the date sooner or later," commented Lorri.

I felt a wave of dismay as I recalculated the days to my next surgery. One step forward, two steps back. "I suppose we should make flight arrangements," I said in reply, hiding my dismay. "It sounds like he made up his mind."

"Yeah," started Lorri, reviewing the script. "We should pay the extra for changeable tickets."

We called a travel agent, who wasted no time in furnishing us tickets. For an extra $150 each, we could get them so they were able to be rescheduled within two weeks from the departure date. We also paid for two week's worth of accommodations at one of the cheapest places to stay—the "Pensao Barca Do Tejo," which cost $70 per night, rated as a two-star resort. Any others were not only over $150 Canadian, but required a taxi for getting to and fro as well. We just didn't have that kind of cash.

November 20 was a rainy, cold day when my sister-in-law Vivian and I drove the three hours to Toronto for the hearing regarding my OHIP funding. I had written all of my arguments in braille so I could refer to them during the procession. Upon entering the city, I was again reminded of the big city noise, as there was a constant rumble in the background, even though it was a day when Toronto was relatively quiet. Upon entering the businesses, I was also reminded of my stay in Morristown, New Jersey, wherein I felt completely at ease and not at all discriminated against as a result of my handicap. As Vivian and I strolled downtown, I couldn't help but mention to her that if Lorri really liked the city, I would move here in an instant.

We met Janice at the elevator of 151 Bloor Street, and together we went up the elevator to the ninth floor. We were greeted at the reception desk of the appeal board and then seated in the waiting room to await our time to start. In the meantime, Dr. Fisher arrived, and in listening to him converse with the secretary, he struck me as a civil man who was going to be anything but trouble.

At 11:00 a.m., we were seated at separate tables, one for myself accompanied by Vivian and another for Dr. Fisher, which was located a few meters to my right. Janice took her place at a table near the back of the room. The three-panel members faced us and were deftly introduced to us by the spokesperson.

"Beginning with the appellant, you each may state your case, and following that you are each entitled to a session wherein you may cross-examine your adversary in posing questions. Finally, you may give your final submissions, if you have any."

It was me who had to stand up first and state my case. I introduced myself as well as my situation of blindness, and then proceeded to explain the merits of the Dobelle Eye.

"Considering that I have no other alternative, as pointed out by Dr. Willis on his application for funding, I cannot possibly continue a life in darkness in light of these recent developments in technology."

"Dr. Langley had rejected my request for funding as Dr. Dobelle is not a doctor, as the idea is experimental, and for the fact that Dr. Dobelle wants the money in advance, which goes contrary to the rules of OHIP."

"In starting with Dr. Dobelle's credentials, he is obviously preoccupied in connecting the medical aspect of the endeavor with the electronic one, but leaves both to its respective expertise. Dr. Antunes and Dr. Girvin are performing the surgery. Therefore, it is not necessary for Dr. Dobelle to be specifically licensed to perform surgery if it was never his intention to do so."

This argument sounded good, but while I spoke, it suddenly occurred to me that Dr. Fisher could argue that Dr. Dobelle really should be a neurosurgeon as he was the one deciding what got installed in the brain and what kind of power would be applied to it. I hoped Dr. Fisher was not too sharp this morning to catch onto this counterargument. I continued.

"Next, Dr. Dobelle requires the money in advance for reasons dictated in his letters to me. This is an international effort, the components have to be secured and so does the commitment of the patients. It would obviously be an international nightmare for him to litigate patients that default in payment. I am also confident that an arrangement can be established with Dr. Dobelle regarding the payment if a firm commitment is made by a reputable health insurance company in advance of the surgery.

"And for the third reason of rejection, the term 'experimental' is totally unjustified for use in this case. Typical experimental procedures are those which are founded upon superstitious hypothesis, or no hypothesis at all, with a very minute chance of success. Typically they would be in their first five years of their nascence. This procedure, on the other hand, has been proven effective in a large majority of patients tested, and the operating procedure performed on the brain is similar to that of Jyles Brindley's patients in 1968. What has made this procedure recently available was the availability of portable microprocessors, which is an external system that has no role in the surgical operation."

I figured I would leave further elaboration on that point for my final submission. It was always good to have a strong last word, I figured, as that is what rings in the ear of the panelists, analogous to the last song one hears on the radio before turning it off. It was Dr. Fisher's turn to speak.

"I basically have nothing new to add other than what is written in my written submission to you." He addressed the panel in a voice which did not suggest he should be favored when making the decision. "Mr. Naumann seemed to cover all the reasons for the rejection, and the one most questionable is the definition of experimental. I cannot find any way around the fact that this is not an insured service."

It was evident to me that Dr. Fisher was not really interested in keeping the funding from me; he portrayed the impression on me that he would have gladly offered the funding if he had the capacity to do so. He had nothing new to add.

My turn to cross-examine came next. I had prepared a few nasty questions, which I now did not want to pursue, as the man I was facing was not at all the type of character I expected. Any aggression I had planned to use was not going to be called for. This was going to be a discussion, not a debate.

"Dr. Fisher, I would like to know if you discussed the details of the surgery with Dr. Girvin prior to concluding that this procedure is experimental." I asked this one in a polite fashion, knowing very well he did not.

"No, I did not do that," he responded.

My next question dealt with the experimental definition. "Is there a criteria predefined in the health act as to what constitutes an experimental procedure? In simpler terms, is there a definite cut-off date in which a procedure deemed experimental loses that definition?"

Dr. Fisher paused, then replied, "There is no exact definition of what is deemed experimental and what does not. There is, however, a list of presently accepted procedures, and this procedure in question is not listed."

"Are other similar implants within the skull approved by OHIP, such as the one designed to aid the deaf?"

"Yes" was Dr. Fisher's response.

"Is there presently a cut-off for maximum funding given to an individual patient for sight recovery attempts? In other words, should a person require several very expensive procedures currently listed as covered by OHIP for the purpose of gaining a small amount of sight, would OHIP be in the position to say 'no, that is too costly for what is being gained'?"

Once again, Dr. Fisher said, "No, there isn't."

I had to ask the next question without the malice I had intended to use before meeting Dr. Fisher.

"What would you suggest I do in place of proceeding with this surgery?"

It was kind of a mean one. I did, however, go through pains to appear genuinely interested in perhaps following other suggestions should he have some. His answer was equally humble.

"I really cannot think of any alternative treatment." My final question was one which drew a response I was not looking for.

"Does not OHIP fund other prosthesis for other handicaps?"

"No," Dr. Fisher replied, "it is presently Assistive Devices that funds these prosthesis."

I had already exhausted that one. It was made clear to me by Faz Hassan that no implants would be covered by Assistive Devices.

The panel asked Dr. Fisher if he wanted to pose any questions for the cross-examination, but he declined. I was then given the opportunity to make my final submission. I would like to start by pointing out the fact that both Dr. Fisher and I have the same interests regarding OHIP—neither of us want to see it abused or depleted of resources necessary for the well-being of Ontario citizens. After all, given that any member of my family or myself could face a health crisis in need of treatment, the availability of OHIP is crucial for ailments other than addressing eyesight as well." I wanted to clarify my intentions to the panel as being sincere. "However, in this case, I am convinced it is money well spent considering that the possibility of success is, at first glance, by far greater than those of other presently covered surgeries such as those I had in 1984 which cost the system an equivalent amount, if not more."

I shall dwell upon the "experimental" definition, as the other reasons for rejection have already been assessed as not viable. Dr. Fisher admits there are no precise criteria defining the term. Dr. Dobelle has proven the implant poses no danger to the health of the test patients. Dr. Fisher admits there are other neurostimulator implants presently already funded by OHIP, such as the one used to aid the deaf. "This means that the medical aspect of this operation is well beyond the experimental."

"Moreover, when taking into consideration the high cost of surgical procedures presently funded by OHIP, it is very possible that in the future the Dobelle vision system could prove to be more effective and economical when used to substitute conventional eye surgery should the chances of success for that surgery be extremely remote."

"And finally, when considering a section of the health act dictated the allowance of an out-of-country treatment should there be the threat of irreversible tissue damage from further delay," I was quoting from the written submission received by Dr. Fisher, "Dr. Dobelle's past experimentation proved the reality that the visual cortex has the tendency to 'atrophy,' thus not allowing for chromatic sensations in long-term blinded patients, as well as not allowing patients who lost their sight in early childhood to profit from cortex stimulation. This suggests that I have little choice but to engage in this implantation in order to give my visual cortex the best chance to continue to function in the future."

I knew I had a strong case. The panel undoubtedly had enough of a "gray area"—a margin to maneuver, to pass this one through if they really wanted to. However, the reality was that if the 120,000 clients presently registered with the CNIB all wanted such a system, they would be entitled to it if I was given the green light for funding. The cost would be astronomical.

Dr. Fisher had no final submission. He appeared to be giving me the best chance. The panel went into the room apart from the one used for the hearing for their deliberation.

Janice had said nothing throughout. She was very professional. I remembered the "press embargo" mentioned in Dr. Dobelle's letter and wondered what exactly to do about it. Janice was sincere, but Dr. Dobelle was paranoid about any press. The fact that he had sent a "press embargo" notification to all the patients this time suggested that I was not the only one who had the press involved. It was obvious that blind people are going to look to the press for help in fund-raising. It is unlikely that blind people would be rolling in the dough, considering all the lost employment opportunities at the loss of sight. After all, it was the government-operated employment insurance system which openly wrote me off as "not employable" following the loss of my sight. Now the press was suddenly required to be kept in the background. It was not the interest of the press that was the issue—it was the interest of the donors that mattered. If they wanted to know something about my progress, they would look to the press to find it. "Look, Joe," they would say, pointing at the television, "I gave fifty bucks toward the operation for that guy, and now he can see!" and they would feel so proud of themselves. And quite rightly so. But now Dr. Dobelle wants them out of the picture. It was going to be difficult to do.

The Appeal panel returned with their verdict. The spokesperson turned to me, saying, "What a well-prepared case you presented. We rarely get this kind of professionalism from patients demanding funding."

I hoped that would mean I had been successful. I imagined there would be some nasty brawls during these hearings from people simply depending on the panel feeling sorry for them.

"I would like to remind both the appellant and the respondent that we, the panel, are bound to the provisions of the Health Act and cannot base our decisions upon sympathetic reasons." The spokesperson addressed both Dr. Fisher and myself, then proceeded to read from the prepared script of which I later received a copy.

Health Services Appeal and Review Board
151 Bloor St. West
Toronto, ON

Mr. Jens Nauman
Napanee, ON

AND

Attention: Dr. Godfrey Fisher
General Manager, Ontario Health Insurance Plan Health Services Division
Provider Services Branch
2nd Fl., 49 Place d'Artnes
P.O. Box 48
Kingston, ON K7L 5J3

In response, please quote File 01-HIA-0061 Re: *Jens Naumann vs. the General Manager*, Ontario Health Insurance Plan

Enclosed is a true copy of the Final Decision and Reasons of the Health Services Appeal and Review Board in the above-noted matter.

Any appeal from this decision to the Divisional Court is governed by Section 24(1) of the Health Insurance Act.

Yours sincerely,
Abby Katz Starr
Registrar

FILE NO.: 0 1—HIA-0061
PRESENT:
Bonnie Patrick, Vice-Chair Thomas Kelsey, Vice-Chair Christine Moss

The 20th day of November 2001

IN THE MATTER OF A HEARING UNDER SECTION 20(1) of the Health Insurance Act, Revised Statutes of Ontario, 1990, Chapter H.6—BETWEEN:

JENS NAUMANN—Appellant
—and—
THE GENERAL MANAGER,
THE ONTARIO HEALTH INSURANCE PLAN Respondent

Appearances:
For the Appellant: Jens Naumann Vivian Campbell

For the Respondent,
General Manager, OHIP: Dr. Godfrey Fisher

Final Decision and Reasons
Summary

Jens Naumann, the Appellant, is blind. He applied to OHIP, the Respondent for funding of the insertion of an artificial vision device to hopefully alleviate the Appellant's blindness. The Appellant's request was denied by the Respondent because the treatment requested was considered experimental in Ontario. The Appellant appeals this decision.

Facts

The Appellant had retinal reattachment surgery performed in 1981 following an industrial accident. The surgery was unsuccessful, and the Appellant was left with blindness of the left eye. Following a second industrial accident, the Appellant was left blind in his right eye as well. Three successive surgeries have been performed on the Appellant's left eye, none of which were successful. He spent a total of six weeks in hospital for these surgeries. The Appellant graduated from a school training him in the use of a seeing eye dog in 1985. At this time, all programs currently offered by the Canadian National Institute for the Blind have been exhausted by the Appellant. The Appellant is the father of eight children. The Appellant heard about the work being conducted at the Dobelle Institute, Inc. located in Portugal. The Appellant is of the opinion that the procedure offered exclusively at the Dobelle Institute is the only possibility available at this time for the restoration of his sight. The Appellant does not agree that the procedure is experimental.

Law

Health Insurance in Ontario is governed by the terms of the Health Insurance Act (the Act) and the regulations made under this Act. The Act provides a scheme for payment of medical services provided in Ontario. Section 28.4 of Regulation 552 under the Act outlines the preconditions to approval by OHIP of out—of-country treatment. 28.4 (1) In this section, "preferred provider arrangement" means a written agreement between the Minister and the operator of a hospital or health facility outside of Canada for the delivery of specified insured services to insured persons and "preferred provider" means the operator. (2) Services that are part of a treatment and that are rendered outside Canada at a hospital or health facility are prescribed as insured services if, (a) the treatment is generally accepted in Ontario as appropriate for a person in the same medical circumstances as the insured person; and (b) either, (i) that kind of treatment that is not performed in Ontario by an identical or equivalent procedure, or (ii) that kind of treatment is performed in Ontario, but it is necessary that the insured person travel out of Canada to avoid a delay that would result in death or medically significant irreversible tissue damage.

(3) If insured services prescribed by subsection (2) are covered by a preferred provider arrangement, the amount payable is the amount provided in the preferred provider arrangement. (4) If insured services prescribed by subsection (2) are not covered by a preferred provider arrangement, the amount payable is the usual and customary amount charged by similar facilities under similar circumstances to major insurers for services provided, to persons they insure, in facilities located in the jurisdiction where the insured services are provided.

(5) The following are conditions of payment of amounts for services prescribed in this section

1. An application for approval of payment must be submitted to the General Manager by a physician who practices medicine in Ontario on behalf of the insured person and the application must contain a written confirmation from that physician that, in the opinion of the physician, one of the conditions set out in clause 2(2)(b) is satisfied. 2. The General Manager must give written approval of the payment of the amount under this section before the services for which approval has been sought are rendered.

3. The services must be received within the time limit set out in the approval described in paragraph 2.

4. If the services are covered by a preferred provider arrangement, they must be received from a preferred provider. The payment for insured services by the Ontario Health Insurance Plan is also subject to certain exclusions described in Section 24 of Regulation 552. The parts of this section which relate to the Appellant are: 24(1) The following services rendered by physicians or practitioners are not insured services and are not part of insured services

16. an examination or procedure for the purpose of a research or survey program other than an assessment that is necessary to determine if an insured person is suitable for the program. 17. Treatment for a medical condition that is generally accepted within Ontario as experimental.

Issues

The Respondent has no authority to pay for out-of-country medical services unless the treatment is an "insured service" as that term is defined in sections 24 and 28.4 of Regulation 552 under the Act.

In this appeal, the Board must determine:

1. Is the procedure being offered by the Dobelle Institute generally accepted within Ontario as experimental? 2. Was there an assessment necessary to determine the suitability of Appellant for a research or survey program?

Reasons

Experimental Treatment

The Appellant submits that there is no definition of "experimental" in the Regulations to the Act. Further, Dr. Willis stated that the procedure was "probably experimental" when completing the Application for Prior Approval on behalf of the Appellant. The Appellant submits that when the Regulations to the Act were drafted, the surgery and device for which the application was made was unknown in Ontario, and therefore was not specifically addressed by the Regulations. In addition, the Appellant submits the treatment involves the use of a prosthesis, and the Appellant submits that all prosthesis are experimental as continual advancements to these devices occur. Finally, it is the submission of the Appellant that Dr. Dobelle has been testing the device in question for thirty-one years, a period of time long enough to take the treatment out of the realm of experimental. The Appellant submitted an article authored by Dr. Dobelle entitled "Artificial Vision for the Blind by connecting a Television Camera to the Visual Cortex." The article describes the work of Dr. Dobelle starting with the first involvement with human subjects in 1970 to 1972 to the description of the surgery's effect on one particular volunteer, within whom the electrode was implanted in 1978.

In total, seven volunteers to the surgery were discussed in this paper.

The Respondent submitted an article entitled "Altruism and the volunteer: psychological benefits from participating as a research subject", authored by Dr. Dobelle. The Board notes that the author calls the participants in his work "volunteers" and not subjects, the usual title given to participants in a clinical trial involved in experimental treatment. Further, the article states that "this device has been the objective of a development effort begun by our group in 1968", the use of the term "development" suggesting a treatment which is not yet out of the experimental realm of the research on the treatment. Another article entitled "Altruism and the volunteer;

psychological benefits from participating as a research subject" authored by Dr. Dobelle, the doctor refers to the participants in his research as "experimental subjects." Dr. Dobelle also states that "participating in research as an experimental subject can result in lasting improvement in self-esteem." Clearly, this article supports the submission by the Respondent that the treatment being offered to the Appellant is experimental in nature in the opinion of Dr. Dobelle.

Dr. Dobelle states on his Web site that the reason the device is not available in the United States is because "de novo introduction of new drugs and devices in the United States is very rare." The use of the term "new device" is suggestive of an experimental treatment. When questioned about insurance carriers paying for the device, the doctor states that other devices in use at the Institution have been funded by Medicate and analogous private and government insurance plans around the world, it will take a number of years for reimbursement to be available from these same funders for the particular device in question here.

An article written by Dan Vergano, USA *today* entitled "Brain chip offers blind chance at 'sight.'" The author quotes a bioengineer named Richard Norman of the University of Utah who says the results presented by Dr. Dobelle with respect to his device "suggest this line of research might be fruitful." Again, it is clear that the treatment is still in the research phase of its development and thus experimental.

Based on the evidence before it, the Board finds that the treatment is generally not accepted in Ontario, deemed as experimental and therefore not an insured service.

Suitability for Research Program Since the treatment has been found to be experimental in nature the Board must determine if any services are necessary to determine the suitability of the Appellant for the program. In a letter to the Appellant from Dr. Dobelle dated August 25, 2000, the doctor states that the Appellant would probably be a candidate for implantation with a visual prosthesis. In the "Introductory Price List" effective 1 February 2001 one of the services provided at the Dobelle Institute is called "Evaluation as a Patient, psychiatric evaluation, all other testing." The Board finds that these are an examination or procedure for the purpose of a research or survey program that is necessary to determine if an insured person is suitable for the program and is therefore an insured service. When asked by the Board, the Respondent advised that artificial limbs and other external prosthesis are not an insured service of OHIP. Rather, the Ministry of Health and Long Term Care has an Assisted Devices Program to which application is made for funding or partial funding of the prosthesis required by a person resident in Ontario.

Jurisdiction

The jurisdiction of the Board is defined in Section 21 of the Act. s.2 I (1) Where a person requires a hearing by the Appeal Board, the Appeal Board shall appoint a time for and hold the hearing and may by order direct the General Manager to take such action as the Appeal Board considers the General Manager should take in accordance with this Act and the regulations, and for such purposes the Appeal Board may substitute its opinion for that of the General Manager.

The Board is limited to ordering the General Manager to act "in accordance with the Act and the regulations." The Board cannot, for compassionate reasons, order the General Manager to provide OHIP coverage for treatment of residents of Ontario who do not satisfy the requirements of the Act and Regulations. There is no provision in the Act or the regulations giving the Board the authority to change the conditions set out in Regulation 552. Without express authority, the Board must apply the conditions that are set out in s.24 of Regulation 552.

Decision

The Board has found that some of the services which will be required by the Appellant are part of an assessment. The Board has found that those services which are not part of the initial assessment are experimental in nature, and therefore, not insured services of OHIP under the Health Insurance Act.

Appeal allowed

The General Manager is directed to reimburse the Appellant for those services necessary to determine the suitability of Appellant for participation in this particular research program.

I collected my papers from the table where I had been situated and walked out of the room. Back in the waiting room, I had a few brief words with Dr. Fisher.

"Thanks for the interest in my case," I began, shaking his hand. "I will keep you posted if this is a successful surgery, as I am sure that within a few years this will be offered as an option to those who become profoundly blind."

Dr. Fisher wished me luck, indicating that he genuinely hoped it would work.

Janice approached Vivian and I, wielding a microphone. She was allowed to film there, and insisted on an interview right there in the building. I hoped she wasn't looking for a confrontational scene between myself and Dr. Fisher, because if she did, she'd be out of luck.

"How do you feel things went during the hearing?" I reflected upon the proceedings. "I think it went well, considering that there was little room for a decision based upon sympathetic grounds. I did gain the funding of the preoperative testing, which means a couple of thousand less out of my own pocket. It would have been great to receive full funding. I look forward to showing Dr. Fisher the system when it works. Chances are that the next blind person requesting funding will have better success."

I was saying this on television as I really believed it. It would work, no doubt, I thought. Janice filmed Vivian and I walking to the elevator, and we went home.

"No decision based on compassionate grounds," I said to Vivian. "Humans sure pretend to be more sympathetic than they really are," I quoted from the panel's findings.

Vivian kept driving, saying nothing. I knew what was going on in her head. She had known me before I had lost my sight. I took an immediate liking to her when first meeting her upon coming to Ontario. She and Lorri and I would be all on our own motorbikes, cruising around town. She knew who I really was and how much I needed this system. But as the appeal panel had said, there were no provisions for ordering OHIP to pay based on sympathy for the patient's situation.

I received another letter from Dr. Dobelle. It was accompanied with a Christmas card, in which lay a picture of his three children. My kids looked at them, commenting, "Those running shoes they are wearing are expensive!" Sure, I figured, a man who dedicates his life to making the blind see deserves to be able to afford the best. I read the letter with the scanner, which was a rundown of Dr. Dobelle's personal life.

> 2001 has been an interesting year, which I would not care to repeat. About the only good thing was the fact that the Guinness World Book of Records featured the artificial vision project for the second year in a row and all three children continue to thrive, as

you can see from the picture. Meanwhile, most of my time was consumed by illness and an almost twenty-year-old divorce case.

What started as a tiny diabetic ulcer—about the size of your little fingernail—under my big toe, led to four sequentially aggressive amputations, which culminated in losing my left leg below the knee. I now have a prosthesis and can walk hundred yards or so when assisted by a cane, and shorter distances without one. I can also climb stairs if I have a banister for support. However, I was hospitalized for almost seven months this year, plus November and December of 2000.

Meanwhile, Gladys continues to try to reopen our divorce from the early 1980s (asking $8,000 per month, plus all applicable taxes, for life). Prior to her lawsuit, Gladys babysat Marty on a couple of occasions, although she was identified to him only as a "friend." Everything was quite amicable until the publicity broke last year surrounding the artificial vision project. That apparently triggered dreams of riches beyond the bounds of avarice. Her case resulted in two front-page stories in the *New York Times* and half hour on national TV under the aegis of Dateline USA. As of early December 2001, we are still awaiting a decision from the judge.

Claire and I are looking forward to 2002 with renewed anticipation. The institute's business survived my nine months' absence due to a hard working, loyal staff—and more recently the specter of September 11-—although many surgeons would still prefer to watch the war in Afghanistan on TV rather than take on new patients. In addition, I have been moving forward with the artificial vision effort. I expect you will hear more about the latter in 2002.

It sounded like Dr. Dobelle was undergoing his own fight with a handicap, and winning all the way. I was glad to hear he was already walking again. I looked forward to seeing him in standing position, managing the electronic components in full vigor as a doctor should, demonstrating strength and knowledge in his posture.

I showed the letter to Ethel when she came by before Christmas. She made reference to the divorce case with interest.

"I actually saw that Dobelle case on TV concerning his divorce," she said, then added, "they seemed to make a big deal of it." "Are you sure it was

Dobelle?" I inquired, slightly concerned that the issue would preoccupy Dr. Dobelle and cause another delay.

"Yeah, I think so," she responded.

That gave us, once again, something to worry about. The last letter from Dr. Dobelle arrived just before Christmas.

Dobelle Institute (Portugal) Lda.
Artificial Vision for the Blind
December 18, 2001

To: Mr. Jens Naumann
Napanee, Ontario
Canada, K7R 3L1

Fr: Wm. H. Dobelle, PhD
Chairman & Chief Executive Officer

Re: Update

First, let me wish you and your family a Merry Christmas and a Happy New Year.

Dr. John Girvin, who is now based in Jeddah, Saudi Arabia, will be visiting his home in Nantucket over Christmas. I will meet with him there and then fly to Lisbon on Thursday, January 17, to meet with Dr. Joao Lobo Antunes. The purpose of these meetings is to "rehearse" the planned surgeries.

As of today, fabrication of the implants and assembly of the electronic components are proceeding normally. However, we can always encounter a "glitch." These surgeries are critically important to you and to the program, and if I see anything adverse, I will postpone without compunction.

1. Sunglasses. Could each of you please send me two (2) pair of sunglasses with plastic lenses? The lenses will be drilled by us to accommodate the tiny TV cameras, and having you send us sunglasses insures proper fit.
2. Reservations: Those of you scheduled for surgery in February and March of 2002 should have your reservations by now. Could you please send me details of your air travel to and from Lisbon? Also, where you will be staying with telephone and fax numbers (if known).

3. Office in Lisbon: We are making what I hope are the final arrangements for an office in a building adjacent to—and owned by—the CUF Hospital. These arrangements were interrupted by my illness. I will send you the phone and fax numbers as soon as they are available.

4. Delivery of Electronics: We will test you in Lisbon, but because of postoperative edema, relatively little experimentation will be possible. Because importing the electronics into Portugal, then exporting them with you is a complex and expensive process, we will deliver the system to you at your home after the thirty-day healing period has passed. One of our engineers, will, of course, accompany the system to your home and "customize" it for you.

5. Final Payments: You should bring with you to Lisbon bank or "certified" checks for costs in excess of your $20,000 deposit. These checks are:

Amount Payable To:

Equipment:*1 24,000 USD "The Dobelle Institute (Portugal) Lda. Hospital: $4,000 USD CUF Hospital"

Surgery: $4,000 USD "Joao Lobo Antunes, MD & Associates" Evaluation: $2,000 USD "The Dobelle Institute (Portugal) Lda." Be aware that "certified" checks are almost like cash. If you lose them in transit, it is very difficult to get a refund or replacement check.

Thanks.

*1: Because of second $21,000 USD transfer.

We elaborated somewhat over the contents of the letter. "I hope Dr. Dobelle is not buttering us up for another delay." I said, making reference to the "delay without compunction" phrase.

"I hope not either. We have to find a babysitter for our kids, and I already told my students I will not teach during the last week in February and first week in March," said Lorri, obviously concerned about the possibility.

"We'll have to make the arrangements right after Christmas," I said, "or else I will have to hire an escort to accompany me to the surgery."

It was one or the other, as Dr. Dobelle did not want me to come there alone. It must have been for the supporting of the patient after the operation that an escort was supposed to be there according to Dr. Dobelle. However, considering the surgery was to be minor—"possible to do on an outpatient basis," I found it hard to believe it would be necessary. "I'd like to be there anyways," said Lorri. "Remember that he said I would get the equipment thirty days after the operation," I reminded Lorri. Gone was the idea that I would sightsee with Lorri during my last few days' stay in Portugal. "You should be able to see by the start of spring!" remarked Lorri.

Another thirty extra days, on top of the February 27 deadline! This was really dragging on.

Christmas came with all the usual excitement. The tree was cut from a private farm, and when I went to the proprietor to pay, he asked me, "When's your operation? Or did you already have it?"

"No, not yet," I said, adding, "I had expected it last summer so that I could see the tree this year. It has been a rough year for us. Any more delays and we may go berserk!" I had been planning on spending this Christmas in a brighter environment than the usual black. At the moment, a Christmas tree meant a prickly obstacle in the middle of the room that had to be carefully avoided as the decorations were held onto it by good luck more than anything else. It sure did not get my admiration; however, I never shared this point of view with the family as it would have been negative and only would serve to spoil their happiness. If I could just see the lights on it, I told myself, it would make such a difference.

January was cold, which meant good firewood sales. I tried to get ahead in the cutting and splitting of the logs as I was sure I would want to play with my equipment after coming back from Portugal instead of working. I never did take into consideration that I may not feel well after the surgery. It was, after all, defined as "day surgery." Then came an e-mail on our new computer terminal that we had bought at a garage sale.

From: Louise Castagna
To: Jens Naumann

Subject: Naumann postponement 1–24 Date: Thursday, January 24, 2002 10:42:00-0500

To: Mr. Jens Naumann
Napanee, Ontario
Canada, K7R 3L1

Fr: Wm. H. Dobelle, PhD
Chairman and Chief Executive Officer
Page 1 of 2
January 24, 2002
Re: Brief Postponement of All Artificial Vision Surgeries

I returned to the office yesterday from "rehearsals" in Lisbon, to encounter the first real problem of our undertaking. The connector manufacturer missed the Friday, January 18 deadline for shipment of new parts by a few days. More importantly, his projected production volume is inadequate to begin surgeries on February 18.

The Solution

I have considered a variety of stopgap scenarios, including doing some cases, but not others. However, this leaves little room for error. The safer course is just to postpone things so the connector manufacturer can build volume systematically. This probably means the cases that were scheduled to begin in the middle of February would now go on corresponding dates in March, and cases scheduled in March would go in April. I will be back in touch about rescheduling. I realize the pain—including rescheduling travel—this will cause everybody but can see no truly legitimate alternative. I should reemphasize that the quality of work being done by this manufacturer is excellent, but the only problem is speed. But trying to accelerate matters can only lead to additional problems which none of us need.

Other Developments

During my brief trip to Lisbon this weekend I signed the lease for our new offices, as scheduled. The building is a newly remodeled one, adjacent to, and owned by, the CUF Hospital. Paota de Leon, a Columbia-University trained bioengineer, with a special in Linux programming, is coordinating this office, in part because she speaks fluent Portuguese.

Discuss:

I'm sure some of you will want to discuss all this directly with me.

Thanks.

This was all we needed. All arrangements had already been made with five different families for the children. Lorri's students had all been given notice of our absence, and everyone in town that remotely knew us expected me to have the operation by the end of February.

"Maybe it's time to stop thinking about it for a bit," I suggested, wondering how much more recalculating a person could do like this. "Dr. Dobelle now says another month, but surely there will be another delay somewhere."

It did sound a bit like he was flying by the seat of his pants. How can one possibly have the plans to implant ten thousand patients annually, as indicated in previous information sent to me, when he did not even have enough material for a dozen or so patients? What sense would it make, I asked myself, to have all the computers and stimulators ready to go and yet not implants? But, I told myself, he will figure it out. Besides, it's too late to turn back now.

The other details of the letter sounded promising. By no means would I call up Dr. Dobelle in a fit of frustration. He could, after all, very easily just send back the money and tell me to stay home. Considering his reviews of media reporters, it would be a real possibility. So we just swallowed up the delay, the expense of rearranging flight and accommodations, and the impatience of those friends who had offered to help us. Therefore, when the next letter arrived, it was business as usual at home.

February 7, 2002
To: Mr. Jens Naumann
Napanee, Ontario
Canada K7R 3LI

Fr: Wm. H. Dobelle, PhD
Chairman & Chief Executive Officer

RE: Electrode Implants

The work is proceeding smoothly, albeit slowly because of the handwork involved.

I will be in touch with you around February 21, 2002, to reschedule surgical implantation.

A few weeks later, another letter arrived with a little more information, although it was still labeled "tentative."

To: Mr. Jens Naumann
February 19, 2002
Napanee, Ontario
K7R 3L1

Fr: _____ Wm. H. Dobelle, PhD Chairman & Chief Executive Officer

Re: New Schedule

1. Surgery: About half of the electrode/pedestals have been received and assembled, and the remainders are expected to be completed in the next several weeks. All look and test well, but the hand-assembly required has been very slow. Again, I apologize for the delay in schedule. I have tentatively rescheduled your surgery for:
    Monday, April 8, 2002

2. Other Important Dates:
    Arrival: Overnight, Tuesday, April 2/Wednesday, April 3 Recovery from Jet Lag: Wednesday, April 3 Orientation & Testing: Thursday, April 4 & Friday, April 5 Postsurgical Recovery: Tuesday, April 9 through Tuesday April 16.

Depart for Home: Wednesday, April 17

3. Final Payment: The balance of approximately $34,000 is due and payable before surgery, as I'm sure you understand. 4. Contact: Please contact me to discuss the above. Our toll-free number is (800) 797-5244. Nights and weekends I can be reached at home (. . . My e-mail address is whd@dobelle. com.

Upon receiving this letter, there was the same air of unpreparedness as the previous letter had. Why would only half of the electrode arrays be assembled? It was difficult to put the finger on the cause of this situation. It was undoubtedly a venture which was unprecedented, and that may well be the reason for these delays. It was possible, I mused, that Dr. Dobelle had had no idea if there would even be any interest in the product before advertising it. Therefore, he did not have any idea how much time to invest into the manufacture of the parts required for the implants. It was possible that, for example, he had anticipated only two or three interested patients for implant for this round but was forced to provide more as a result of their pressure to receive it. It was hard to imagine pressuring Dr. Dobelle for anything. Then again, perhaps some patients became bold and protested when they learned they would not get the implant. I speculated on this situation for many days. Neither Lorri nor I took the date of April 8 seriously until we were well into March, anticipating another delay all the while.

It was when we got the request for the rest of the money that we figured he finally had his cards in order.

Dobelle Institute (Portugal) Lda. Artificial Vision for the Blind

To: Mr. Jens Naumann February 28, 2002, Napanee, Ontario

Fr: Wm. H. Dobelle, PhD
Chairman & Chief Executive Officer
Re: Final Invoice

Contrary to my previous statement, I find that it would be much easier to pay the final invoice by wire transfer, rather than by certified check.

Could you please arrange to wire the balance due to: Banco Espirito Santo, SA
Routing # 0007 0014 0047 9720 0029 8
Sede: Av. Liberdale 195
1250-142 Lisbon, Portugal

For Credit to the Account of:
The Dobelle Institute (Portugal) Lda. Account #014/47972/000.2
1. Total Price of Equipment $ 65,000.
2. Evaluation 2,000.
3. Hospital Fees 4,000.
4. Surgical Expenses 4,000.
    Total $ 75,000 USD Less Deposit (41,000) Balance Due $ 34,000 USD
Thank you.

"Another occasion for us to lose sleep in worrying about lost money" was my comment. I would have preferred having the cash in hand. There wouldn't be a lot of time this time to look for a lost transfer as there had been before. Yet we had little choice. It was obvious Dr. Dobelle wanted to have the money in hand before we arrived. He had what I wanted, and I had what he wanted. Somehow, though, I conceived that it was me who wanted his product more than him wanting my cash. More than likely, I mused, he had tons of it already, and my contribution was merely an indication of my good faith. It was, therefore, I who had to make the first move.

We were at the TD bank again, bank draft in hand, scrutinizing the competence of the employees. There was no room for complacency. It was sent off along with the receipt to Dr. Dobelle, with our fingers crossed all the while. I received the following acknowledgement from the Dobelle Institute.

> Thank you for the wire transfer. Let's hope the bank does it right this time.
> Dr. Bill Dobelle

Now we had to wait. I kept in touch with John Girvin through e-mail, indicating I had paid in full for the system and that I was anxious to receive the implant. I was apprehensive about questioning the procedure with him, as I did not want to appear as if I doubted the validity of it, or that I was getting cold feet as the day came closer. The "psychiatric testing" mentioned in the invoices of Dr. Dobelle were somewhat intimidating. I kept, therefore, my conversations via e-mail with John as mundane as possible. His responses, in turn, were equally unrelated to the vision project. He indicated some of his sporting activities of the year, which included canoeing in Quebec. He was a true Canadian, by the sounds of it, and both Lorri and I looked forward to meet him.

We were well into March when we received this letter, which we first feared would be another announcement for a delay.

> To: All Recipients
>
> Fr: _ Wm. H. Dobelle, PhD
> Chairman & Chief Executive Officer
> Re: Telephone Numbers in Portugal
>
> As of a few hours ago (Wednesday, March 13), Dr. Dilys Gore reports from Lisbon that Portuguese Telecom are still having a problem getting their act together. They have promised to come every day this week, but no luck. I will send you the new office phone and fax numbers as soon as they have been installed.
> Meanwhile, our party will be staying at the Marriott Lisbon Hotel
> Phone: 011 351 21 723 5400
> Fax: 011 351 21 723 5440

Steve Diamond and I will arrive on Easter Sunday, and the rest of our party will arrive on Tuesday, April 2. If you need me, please do not hesitate to call the hotel, which has a very reliable message center.

Thanks,

"Imagine that," commented Lorri, "they're staying at the Marriott. Now that's getting ritzy."

"I don't imagine our Pensoa Barca do Tejo will measure up to that kind of standard" was my addition.

"Well, considering what he has to offer us," Lorri said, "I suppose he deserves it."

The letter had further confirmed his commitment to the project. Moreover, we discovered by telephoning Commack that our money had indeed arrived in Portugal. Now there was, once again, time to reflect upon the future. The images of people in dot-matrix form moving about me flashed in my mind as I anticipated the results of the procedure. Everywhere I went, I imagined the objects in front of me in a black-and-white negative form, just as described by Dr. Dobelle. This was going to be beautiful.

Another letter came, only days before our scheduled flight. It was too late for us to change our flight plans now as we surpassed the two-week limit. We opened it, not knowing what it would bring.

To: All Blind Patients

March 28, 2002

Fr: _____ Wm. H. Dobelle, PhD, Chairman & Chief Executive Officer
Re: Update

1. New Office: The address and phone numbers of the new office are:
The Dobelle Institute (Portugal) Lda. Avenida Infante Santo #34, 7th Floor
Lisbon, Portugal 1350-179
Phone: 351 21 394 0473
Fax: 351 21 394 0474
    The building belongs to the CUF Hospital and is located across Avenida Infante Santo from that complex. Because the street runs

in a deep valley at that point, the hospital has built a pedestrian bridge across to the building. However, rather than trying to find it yourself, I would use taxicabs since the parking is very scanty.

As you know, we have had great difficulties with Portuguese Telecom, and I am not absolutely certain about the telephone numbers. The telephone rings but I'm not sure that it is our phone. The fax machines rings, but it has to be hooked up when Steve Diamond and I arrive on Easter Sunday.

2. Contact us: Patients should contact us as soon as they arrive in Lisbon, since the schedule may appropriately change for each of them.

3. Hotel: I will be staying at the:
Lisbon Marriott Hotel
Phone: 351 21 723 5400
Fax: 351 21 723 5440

Please do not hesitate to contact me there, especially if you do not get a live person at the office.

4. Wire Transfer: Please fax the receipt for your wire transfer to our office in Commack, New York: (631) 864-1610. This will be recorded by our Comptroller, and a duplicate faxed to us in Lisbon.

It was all good news. All that remained now was to get there and to pass both the physical and the psychological exams. I had no reservations about the procedure.

Most of all, I looked forward to meeting Dr. Dobelle, who, by now in my mind, had assumed the resemblance of a savior.

CHAPTER 7

Bill

It was April 2, 2002, when the airport bus took the two of us to the airport in Toronto at about 4:00 p.m. I had checked several times in my pocket for our passports and airline tickets. There was no room for goofing up now. The day before we had carted the children in either pairs or one at a time to the respective homes of friends who volunteered their help. It was a lot to ask from them, as the possibility always existed that things would go terribly wrong in the process of the surgery, warranting a prolonged stay in Portugal. But that was all taken care of now, and the next time I met the kids, I would have the implants in my head. It would be all over, and all that will be left will be to wait the thirty days for the computer equipment. It will be a great summer, we thought.

The flight for Frankfurt, Germany, with Lufthansa was to leave at 8:30 p.m. It would have been more convenient to have a flight that went straight to Lisbon, as it would have been shorter and possibly cheaper. However, the year before, a flight by Air Transat had run out of fuel as a result of mechanical failure, and the pilot barely managed to land the craft safely on an island on the outskirts of Portugal. Their license to fly that route was suspended, leaving no other choice but to use connecting flights.

I did not mind the prospect of staying in Germany anyhow. We would have no time to leave the airport; however, I would have the opportunity to visit the country as the last time I did was thirty-five years ago as a small boy.

Lorri and I and a young businessman shared the three seats in a row by the window of flight 471. We chatted about mediocre things for a while, as we did not really want to get into either heated debates or establish a friendship that we would probably not be able to maintain. However, when the young man asked me if I was on a vacation, I really had no choice but to either explain or tell a lie.

"Actually, this is not much of a vacation," I started. After all, it is not much of a holiday to have a hole cut into one's head. "I'm going for an artificial vision implant."

It gave me an odd sense of elevated self-esteem in saying that. It seemed like I was drawing an end to the blindness situation, and thus, because this handicap is now only temporary, I was not really in the category of a "blind man"—an identity I really had trouble with from the beginning of my sight loss, but more so since the learning of this new development from Dobelle. Knowing this felt good. That meant I could freely engage in conversation about skiing, motorbiking, or flying aircraft, as I would soon be back in that world. I had been avoiding talking about interests that didn't apply to my abilities for a while now, as I felt awkward and out of place to only be able to speak of what I did back in the "good old days."

I decided to finish the explanation about the artificial vision surgery facing me, as the man seated beside me was waiting for more, as this was as yet unheard-of. "It's a New York company that is doing the implants in Portugal to avoid trouble from the FDA. It is a project based on the research of Dr. Brindley in England, and Dr. Dobelle is taking it a step further with the microprocessor technology."

I handed him the paper. "I should really have a job with the Dobelle Institute as advertising manager," I thought to myself. He must have read the ASAIO Journal, I had handed him, through a few times, as it was almost landing time when he handed it back to me.

"Fascinating," he said. "I sure hope it works for you." We were dropped off at what seemed like the middle of the runway with giant metal staircases leading us to the ground. I was offered an elevator for special unloading, which puzzled me somewhat. I figured there were many passengers on board much less capable to descend the fifty or so steps to the ground than myself. A defensive feeling came over me as I protested; I felt my dignity was at stake. It was my first opportunity to speak in German when I told the stewardess, "Please, madam! I'm really able to walk! Save that lift for those who need it." I was somewhat worried that if Dr. Dobelle somehow met up with me not trying my best to be in control using a white cane, he'd change his mind about allowing me to have the artificial vision device. My focus was on making the best first impression as a perfect implant candidate.

We were bused to the terminal where we awaited our next flight. We were paranoid about missing our next flight, and even though we had over two hours to kill, we went straight for the gate and waited. Lorri amused herself reading out loud some German tourism literature while I corrected her on the pronunciation whenever I managed to decipher what she was saying.

"We'll have to come back sometime for a vacation," I said, thinking about the excitement of visiting Germany. "Maybe I'll know German by that time," Lorri replied, continuing to read the flyer.

We had big plans, no doubt. I spent the next three hours on the connecting flight, worrying about the psychiatric exam that faced me at the Dobelle Institute. If Dr. Dobelle had plans to implant a dozen or so patients, chances were he would have at least twice that came over to Portugal, and then handpick those who were the most likely to be successful. I understood fully that the first round of patients would be the most critical in determining the future of the project. Should there be even one unhappy camper who liked to make a fuss about it, it would threaten to kill the project. Should that happen after a few hundred successful patients, then the impact would be virtually unnoticed. I would have to be as positive as I could possibly muster without sounding fake. I feared that a psychiatrist who worked in this field for several years would be able to look through a person as if they were made of glass. Dr. Dobelle appeared to take the issue seriously, as this was costing another two thousand dollars. There had been no psychiatric exam preceding my retinal surgeries. Silently I recited answers to possible questions I may be asked by Beth Seelig, concentrating upon the positive and the exuberant.

The aircraft was descending toward the Lisbon airport runway in an erratic and haphazard fashion. Unlike the top-quality Boeing 747 with which we crossed the Atlantic, we were now on a rickety Airbus which felt like its last maintenance check took place in the 1960s. The turbulence bordered on the severe as the aircraft's wings flexed dangerously with each updraft. Lorri was obviously worried as she clutched my arm in fear. Every creak and groan was audible, as all conversation had ceased between passengers. Judging from what I knew from my flying experience piloting a Cessna many years ago, it was evident the pilot had concerns as well, as he accelerated the approach in order to maintain control.

For the past eighteen years, I had the attitude that the prospect of death did not scare me, as that would probably mean I would face a much better situation the next time around. This time I wasn't so sure. With the idea of seeing again after such a long deprivation, it was obvious the experience would be so much sweeter than it would be to those that see every day. It would be analogous to the flare of passion when meeting the long-lost love after several years of living a life of celibacy. Not only would the beauty of seeing again be beyond that ever experienced by anyone, but I also would have the family already in place with which I could share the experience. I couldn't lose all that now—it would be such a loss. Then I remembered the curse against me that made Dr. Dobelle sick, that interfered with the wire transfer procedures, and that more than likely took my sight in such a bizarre fashion to begin with. In this world, one has got to be ready to lose.

We were only a few hundred feet above the runway when the aircraft again dropped, caught only by the cushion of air near the surface. The craft touched down hard and seemed to skid sideways for an instant until it straightened out before the pilot applied reverse thrust. As we rolled to a stop, I could hear the passengers breathe a sigh of relief in unison. The curse didn't get me this time, but it did remind me of its power.

We made ourselves into the Lisbon airport with little difficulty. It was much smaller than the Toronto International. Lorri followed the other passengers as they made their way to the baggage carousel. We had marked our luggage with ribbon, facilitating easy identification. Outside the front doors there was a line of taxicabs parked, and judging by what the other passengers did, we went to the one in front. We approached somewhat apprehensively, as all we heard around us in the airport was the unintelligible chatter of the Portuguese language.

"Can we have this taxi?" Lorri asked tentatively, ready to wait this one out if the response was unfavorable.

"Yes," the driver said. We were in luck—he spoke English. Dr. Dobelle had indicated that most people spoke English in Lisbon, but so far, I had not heard any. Perhaps they were just being culturally correct and were using Portuguese just for the purpose of protecting their own heritage.

I tried pronouncing the address of the Barca do Tejo, but all the driver did was throw me a puzzled look and hold his hand out for the written address. He looked briefly at it and said, "Oh yes, there it is."

So much for my Portuguese!

It was a bumpy ride through the old cobblestoned roads of the older part of Lisbon in the back of the Mercedes taxicab. I could tell it was a diesel by the clickety-clack sound of the motor. It conformed neither to the rhythm of a four—or six-cylinder engine, bringing me to the conclusion it would be the famous five-cylinder exclusively built by Mercedes. As we raced through the streets, the driver chatted in his less-than-perfect English about all the attractions of Lisbon.

The cab driver found the Barca do Tejo with some difficulty, as it was on a street just wide enough for one and a half vehicles in a neighborhood that Lorri described as somewhat medieval. The Barca do Tejo stood five stories high, entirely built of rock.

It was the highest structure in this immediate area. Lorri noted that the buildings did not exceed much more than a few stories throughout the tour of the city—definitely not the skyscraper city like Manhattan, or even Toronto.

"Just one earth tremor and this joint goes down like a house of cards on a windy day," I remarked as we entered the ancient structure. I winced at the thought of all that rock piled above me, held there by good luck and chance.

There was no expansive foyer as there was in the Western-style four-star hotels, that was clear even to me as I noticed there was the dingy, confined feeling as I stood in front of the desk near the door. A man spoke in broken English.

"You have passports?" His English was much better than my Portuguese.

We gave them to him. He seemed to say nothing but look at the passports for a long time. I wondered if he was up to something dire, perhaps he would keep the passports and demand us to get out. I felt vulnerable and noted a change in Lorri indicating her trepidation. I edged myself closer to the entrance leading behind the counter in case I had to work him over. Without these passports, we'd be cooked in trying to get back.

To my relief, he did pass them back. Lorri took them both at once, not waiting for him to pass mine separately to me. I tucked mine in my inside coat pocket. Now what . . . ?

The man grabbed a key off a nail on the back wall and said, "Come." We followed. The key had only two or three bumps on it; a paper clip probably would have tripped the lock. I tried to remind myself to be optimistic, as this was a place much cheaper than the norm. He led us to an elevator, which felt rickety and unstable. It was not much bigger than a double telephone booth. He pressed a button and instructed, "Go to number . . ." He paused to think of the number in English, then pointed at the first numeral on the key. "Then . . . left . . ." He waved his left hand. "And there is the room."

I realized now that he just did not know enough English to have a comfortable conversation, making him appear as unsociable. That reminded me of my mother who did not talk for years to the neighbors as she was timid of using her less-than-perfect English language skills.

The elevator door closed, and Lorri pushed the "4" button. The sound of the small ventilation fan in the elevator stopped. Lorri was suddenly frantically yanking at the door. "Hey! The lights went out!"

We hit some of the other buttons while we banged on the door. Finally, the lights went back on and the door opened. We wasted no time getting out of that cubbyhole.

We approached the manager again, who was puzzled. "The elevator stopped," I announced, adding, "where are the stairs?"

"It stop?" he asked, still puzzled. He looked inside, making us look silly, as everything appeared to work.

"Follow me. I show you stairs," he replied. He probably thought we were nuts.

We had to go through a few narrow stone-lined corridors, with a few steps here and there going up and down in a disorganized manner, before coming to the rest of the flight, which took on a more regular pattern after the second floor. I noticed that the rooms were more like apartments in the bottom of the building, as there were many sounds of family life and activities such as cooking supper going on in the rooms. There were several children playing in the corridors, their mothers talking among themselves. The harmony among the clients suggested they lived here for quite a while and knew each other well.

The manager unlocked our door, an old wooden one, which closed with a loud slam behind me. I thought again of the precarious stack of rocks making up the building, vowing to be more careful next time I closed the door. The room smelled like carpet cleaner.

"See . . . TV," said the manager, proudly turning it on. It babbled away in Spanish.

In the same room where the bed was, there were two doors that opened like garden doors. There was a sizeable gap under them, indicating that in winter this place would be freezing cold—if we had the Canadian winters, that is. Lorri looked out of the glass panes.

"What a beautiful view! I can see the whole harbor from up here." The manager was pleased at the remarks from Lorri and threw open the doors, which revealed a very small balcony that protruded only about half a meter from the side of the building, with only a small and rickety railing keeping one from plunging four stories to the cobblestone road below.

"Better not step on that, Jens," warned Lorri. "It looks like it's going to fall off."

"Very nice!" we said to the manager. "Where is the bathroom?" We had hoped for running water. Chamber pots just wouldn't be quite so cozy.

"Right here." He motioned to the other side of the room, opening a door. There was a small bathtub, a toilet with its flush button on top of the lid, and a small sink. I inspected the bathtub. The showerhead was not attached—it was on a hose, like the spray nozzle on a car wash device. You had to hang it up on a hook in order to have a shower.

"What's this?" I asked, feeling around. "Two toilets side by side?"

Lorri giggled. "No, it's one of those things you wash with after going to the bathroom."

"Fancy . . ." I commented. The fixtures were old and leaking, but the whole thing had such an air of comfort that I just could not imagine going elsewhere. It was so different than to what we were used to, making this special. It was going to be kind of a vacation for sure.

"Leave the key when you go out for the cleaning lady," said the manager, getting better at his English. He probably had all the words in his head but just hadn't used it for a while. He left us then. We sat together on the small bed in the center of the room, close together, musing at the strangeness of everything there. Yesterday we were still in Napanee, and now we were here, thousands of miles between us and the children.

"We may as well find the office," I suggested. I was curious as to what it would be like. It was now the third of April, so it only made sense to "register."

We went back down the stairs, and after a small exploratory session through the back corridors in our attempts to find the way to the front door, we were back outside on the rough cobblestone road. The sidewalks were narrow, making it difficult for Lorri and I to walk side by side. We had no idea where we were going, as neither the name of the road we were on or the intersecting ones seemed to Lorri to have a sign. I suggested we walk to the direction of the heavy traffic noise at one end of the road. If anything, we could find a taxi and give the driver the directions to the CUF Hospital, simplifying the procedure.

We reached the intersecting road, which was heavy with traffic. The sidewalks were even narrower, making it virtually impossible for us to walk together, so I walked behind Lorri, careful not to swing my cane too far out to the curb lest the end of my cane be hooked by an oncoming car. It seemed customary to have big plastic containers on the sidewalk in front of every exit door of the buildings, occupying virtually the entire sidewalk. Upon approaching one, we would stop and wait for a break in the traffic before skirting out into the street around it.

"Bus!" yelled Lorri, barely audible over the sound of the traffic. I could hear it rumbling toward me, and we both flattened ourselves against the side of the stone building boarding the sidewalk. The bus neither slowed nor budged a foot from the curb when passing us at breakneck speed, just to slam on the brakes a hundred yards further down the block.

We carried on for several minutes in this fashion, becoming more and more confused as to where we were.

"It doesn't look like there are any businesses around here at all!" shouted Lorri over the city noise in frustration. "Well, I know that about five hundred steps behind us and then to the right is our way back home!" I reassured her. We could always go back and call a cab from the front desk if we had no luck.

"I can't see a darned name for any road, and all the buildings are just cement houses of some sort. And up there," Lorri gestured further down the road, "is a walled-in complex, kind of like a jail."

Then we got a break. There were two taxicabs parked on the same side of the road we were on. The drivers were sitting on the hoods of their vehicles, conversing in their unintelligible language.

I touched the back door of the closest vehicle. "No! No! No! . . ." The driver was off his seat, approaching us in a frenzy of gestures, followed by a lot of jabbering, which I took as a refusal to drive us.

"I guess he doesn't want to drive us," I said to Lorri, who was backing away from the situation. "Where is the C-U-F hospital?" I queried the driver, who had settled down somewhat now that we were away from his car. I reposed the question, which still gave no response but some gibberish I couldn't decipher.

"He is shrugging his shoulders," said Lorri, "He doesn't understand."

I had my briefcase with me, so I tore out a piece of paper along with a pencil and printed the letters C U F upon it, then showed it to the driver.

"Oh!" He now understood. "Hospital COOF!" He pronounced the letters C U F as if they were a word, then pointed up the road toward the complex that looked like a prison. "That?" said Lorri, exaggerating here expressiveness, to which the driver responded, "Sih! Sih."

"That has to be it," said Lorri as we continued up the sidewalk. We approached the complex, but the iron gate was closed, and we were in no mood to climb in just to be locked into a small cell for eternity.

"The office should be right across the road," I said, fingering my braille notes upon which I had written the addresses of all the places we were to go to.

"Is there a bridge for pedestrians?" Lorri looked around and found it just on the other side of the same road we were walking on.

"It's right here, but I don't see anything like an office building!" We were expecting big skyscrapers with the usual markings of medical centers as found in Canada. We had no luck at all. We were marching up and down the street in vain, and we even circled the hospital to look for other bridges. We stopped for a brief rest at the corner building we started out from, and Lorri said, "Hey, there is a big '34' here!" I had the number memorized by now.

"That's it!" we said, and opened the door.

A uniformed guard immediately stood in our way. Again the Portuguese language bombarded us.

"We are patients here," we tried to explain calmly. The guard spoke a single word in heavily accented English. "Where?" in a rather unfriendly voice, as if we wanted to heist the place.

"Floor 7. The Dobelle Institute," I said as slowly and clearly as possible. I could hear the elevators rumbling only a few meters from where we stood.

"Not here yet, they not open." He gave us the good news of the day.

Luckily I did not believe him and proceeded to pull out the letter from Dr. Dobelle, which stated that I should arrive on April 3. I waved it under his nose insistently, talking firmly all the while.

"Look here! This is from Dr. Dobelle in person! He wants us here today." I ran my finger up the top left corner of the paper, making sure he saw the letterhead. I didn't imagine he had a clue as to what else the letter said.

It worked. He relented and let us go to the elevators. "Some hospital!" I said to Lorri, who was still recovering from the confrontation. "I'd hate to be sick and have to come here to save myself!"

The elevator hit the seventh floor, the door opened, and we stepped out. There were two directions to go: the first one being totally unoccupied, and the second having glass doors upon which "Dobelle Institute" was painted in block letters. We opened the doors and went inside.

It was Louise Kastagna who greeted us. I recognized her voice from our previous telephone conversations. "Hello, how are you?" she said in a warm and receiving manner. We exchanged pleasantries while she busily shuffled boxes of material around in order to clear a path to the chairs in the waiting section of the office. There was stuff everywhere. Louise was dressed in casual clothes, not at all like a secretary of a reputable medical genius. There were more shuffling noises further into the office, but no one came out to see us. We talked some about our flight, our experience in finding the building, and our experience with the guard downstairs. "Yeah," concluded Louise supportively, "he is kind of a crusty guy, that's for sure." She led us into the next room and said, "Jens, Lorri, meet Jerry, the first volunteer who had the implant. You probably read about him."

I raised my hand to Jerry, assuming he wore the system from Dr. Dobelle. He couldn't possibly be without it.

Gerry shook my hand once he found it, greeting us warmly with his New York accent.

"How's it going, Jens?" He sat at a table that resembled a wooden desk. "Welcome to Portugal."

"How's your vision system going?" I asked, very excited to meet this celebrity about whom the news agencies had written about. "Did you take a look at Portugal with it?"

I was curious to know what all he could observe with it. "I don't have it with me," he said to my disappointment. "It's not the easiest thing to carry around, you know!" he said, chuckling.

"I bet you miss it," I said, hoping there was an explanation for his unworried tone as he addressed the situation. I had expected he would be disappointed and depressed by not having it. Perhaps he was just a tough man, I thought to myself.

Jerry took my right hand and pressed my fingers against the back of his head. He relaxed his grip on my hand as I felt the object, which resembled a couple quarters piled on top of each other, stuck to his scalp. I could feel that one section was sagging somewhat toward the scalp.

"That's what will be put in your head too, except two of them," announced Jerry.

"That's no big deal," I said, remembering that since Jerry was with the Dobelle Institute, even if on a volunteer basis, if I showed anything but a positive attitude, it may mean that I would be one of those patients put on the back burner for later. I wanted to see, not look pretty. Not all that many people noticed my looks anyway; they just seemed to notice my white cane. This should change soon.

"Is it sore around the jack?" Lorri inquired. Jerry replied, "No, not at all. For a couple of months after the operation, I had a sore feeling around it, as well as a bit of stuff oozing out around the edges, but now it seems like there is rarely anything. Every now and then, there is a bit of crusty discharge in my hair around it, that's all."

I stood in front of Jerry for a minute while Lorri talked with him. I tried to think about what the news articles said about him and the vision experiment. Somehow I had been thrown off by the difference between what I expected from our first meeting and by what I observed in front of me. I did not have to see to get this picture. Jerry was sitting at a desk, virtually immobile. He was not wearing the vision system, with which I had expected him to walk around, promoting the system to the fullest while making jokes about how I looked just to push the point that it was a good thing. I pushed onward with another question.

"So, Jerry," I interrupted the conversation he was having with Lorri. "What do you see with your system? What did you see when wearing it and walking around in town, or anywhere else?"

"Well," began Jerry, looking for the right wording. "What I'd see would not look like the real object, but more like a sign that there was something out there. So say I want to cross the street—I'd point the camera down the road and maybe see a couple dots to tell me that there is something out there, but it wouldn't look like a car. Just like looking at a tree—I know there is something there, but would have to ask someone or walk up to it and touch it to see what it really is."

That did not at all sound like 20/400 vision. What happened to the idea of reading two-inch high letters at five feet? A little, soft voice of doubt started to whisper in my ear, but I shook it off. I couldn't recover now if I walked out of this one. Moreover, the rest of Napanee wouldn't let me. I pushed onward.

"But this is real light you are seeing, right?"

"Sure it is," said Jerry, "they're all white. The next system might be better too, you know."

He had a point there. I would get two of these in my head. Lorri asked the next question, to which he answered something I never expected.

"Are you here to get your system updated also?" I recognized that question from Lorri came from one of the news releases wherein Jerry was quoted as not being able to wait to get the new system installed so he can see better.

"No, not me," said Jerry, "I have put all of my last twenty-five years into this project as a volunteer. I put my head under the knife so that one day there is no more blindness. This was my contribution. Someday I think there will be a time when perhaps a child or grandchild of my grandchildren say . . .

"Guess what—a kid in my school just lost her sight last week from an accident and now has an artificial eye and is reading again . . ." to which my grandchild replies: "It was my grandfather who had the first such experiment made on him, and now he's helped all blind people to be able to see."

Jerry paused for an instant, then repeated, "That is why I am doing this. I have done my part now. I am well over sixty years old now, and it is time someone else continues from where I left off."

It was for the contribution to society that Jerry did this. It spoke highly for his character, but not so good for the artificial vision system's performance, or its positive impact on Jerry's life.

"But what about seeing?" I was insistent for an explanation. I felt I was witnessing someone throwing a winning lottery ticket in the wastebasket. "You could see with that system you were using every second or third day in New York, and now you're totally in the dark again?"

Jerry came back immediately. "Well, I just don't like the way things look with phosphenes. They just aren't pretty like the world was when I could see with my eyes. I want to remember the world as I had seen it, not in small white dots. The colors, the shapes, the faces of beautiful people, that all changes when you see just the little dots. No, I prefer to just remember what I saw."

I had no idea what to say to that. "I just cannot stand the constant darkness," I replied, to which Jerry said nothing. Jerry had seen, after all, for thirty-six years of his life, and I only 20. Perhaps, I reasoned with myself, had I seen my kids grow and had a chance to experience the world in its fullest for sixteen more years, perhaps I would . . . no, I would still prefer to see, phosphenes or not. I just couldn't understand. It was such a small operation, such a little sacrifice, and with such rewards. "He must really be slowing down," I thought.

"I'd better call Dr. Dobelle," I said, turning to Louise. Louise turned toward the hall, leading into other rooms of the office. "First you might as well meet our engineers—Steve and Jim."

I could tell they were young men in their early twenties, probably fresh out of college, judging from their voices. They shook my hand and greeted me courteously. I admired them for their involvement in the project.

"I look forward to working together with you for years to come," I said, thinking that it is only good that they were young, as they would be able to contribute many more years to the project. There was generally a loss of information and progress in an advancing project every time a key worker retired, quit, or was fired. At least with Steve and Jim, it did not look like they would be up for retirement for decades. I did not want to embarrass them by over-complimenting them; I would have many opportunities in the future to show my appreciation for their efforts. I heard Louise dial the telephone.

" . . . yes, he is here now. He came in just a few minutes ago. Yes, he did come up with his wife. Do you want to talk to him?" Louise gave me the telephone.

"So you came early just to check us out, huh?" was what Dr. Dobelle had to say in his labored, rusty voice, speaking from his hotel room. "Ya had to check us over to make sure we were doing things right, huh?" He said all this in the most undoctorlike manner.

"Yes, I guess you can say that." I laughed politely. I could have made some comments regarding the mess and the apparent unpreparedness of the establishment, but thought better of it.

"I kind of had a rough landing coming in, but now that I'm here, it should be all right. I was expecting my hotel room to be a little more up to standards than it is."

"Well, you could stay here at the Marriott, if you want. It's a good business-style hotel, but only if you don't insist I check your implants every minute of the day just because I'm here."

I thought that comment was a little out of place, but then again, he did not know me. He must have thought I was a real whiner.

"By the way," Dr. Dobelle continued, "I've got your implants in my briefcase."

Very hygienic, I thought. "In your briefcase?" I thought things would be more professional than that. But then again, this was the genius, and there was no need to question that fact any further.

"I just hope you don't get my implants mixed up with the stapler!" I tried a bit of humor on Dr. Dobelle.

Dr. Dobelle chuckled and got back to business. "You should be at the office tomorrow at ten and we'll do the exams."

That would be the psychiatric and physical exams. I would have to prepare for them. Luckily, I had no flu or cough, indicating that there should be no problem with the physical. "See you then," I said to Dr. Dobelle, and then we left the office.

Lorri and I did not talk much on the way back home, as our first mission was to find a place to eat. It was around suppertime now, but there was no Burger King or McDonalds in sight. Lorri searched frantically, but in vain. It took us a good half hour to reach the road that went parallel with the harbor, which looked like the main drag in Portugal. Still there were no high buildings or any recognizable businesses. Men who I took as panhandlers came up to us occasionally, jabbering away in their language, but I ignored them. I just held up my cane and kept walking. We needed our cash. Only later, after revisiting Lisbon a few times more, did I realize that these men weren't panhandlers, but rather street salespeople drumming up business, selling watches and trinkets to tourists.

We were nearing 7:30 p.m. and still found nothing to eat. I couldn't believe it. I heard some clanging of pots and pans and smelled the unmistakable smell of cooking food.

"This looks like a place where they make pizza!" announced Lorri, and then we timidly advanced into the building, which was not much bigger than an average household kitchen.

"Can we have pizza?" Lorri asked, trying to accentuate the word *pizza*, as it may be universal.

"No, no, no . . ." said the man who could have been the owner. Then he jabbered a bit, and then reached to his wrist and reset his watch, pointing at it while continuing his dialogue. "Not until nine tomorrow morning," said Lorri in dismay. It was getting late, the sun was set, and soon the streets would be dark. We had enough trouble the way it was.

I had no idea who, in their right mind, would enjoy pizza at nine in the morning. Moreover, why would one eat pizza which was made the night before? "Let's just go back," I suggested. "We really aren't in the position to get lost if we have to be back to the office tomorrow morning." We returned to our hotel, and by the time we reached our room, we could smell all the tenants on the floors below us cook their delicious meals while we sat upstairs, hungry. "In this town," I said, turning to Lorri, "you could be a millionaire and starve to death."

Through the spacious cracks around the balcony doors, we heard the life from the streets around us. Instead of slowing down, it became more and more lively. It was well past midnight, and the sounds of life did not quieten. There was a dance disco of some sort not more than a couple buildings over from our place, which played very loud music, the drums echoing throughout the surrounding buildings. We tried to get some sleep but spent the evening talking instead.

"Wouldn't it be nice to go out for supper?" I said, the emptiness in my stomach becoming more obvious.

"A bottle of wine would be nice too," added Lorri. Little did we know that Lisbon had everything we wanted; we just had to go out to get it.

"Isn't it weird that Jerry does not want to see with the vision system?" I said, changing the subject as the day's events converged in my mind to something more important than my appetite.

"I can't figure it out," said Lorri. "Just to do this for the sake of science, but preferring the darkness over the phosphene images is very strange. By the way, what did Dr. Dobelle have to say when you talked on the phone to him?"

"He said he had my implants in his briefcase."

Lorri pondered over my response. "I guess we'll meet him tomorrow. In the meantime, you'll have to pretend to be sane in order to pass the psychiatric exam!"

I thought about what she said, then about the guard in the office building, about the fact that Jerry would rather be in the dark, and also about the fact that Dr. Dobelle was carrying what was to be stuck into my brain around in his briefcase.

"I do? Maybe it's the other way around."

The next day came soon enough. We still had no clue where to get breakfast, so we just walked slowly to the office building, hoping that Louise could give us some advice. If worst came to worst, we resolved that we'd take a cab to the Marriott Lisbon where the Dobelle crew was staying and just eat right in their lounge.

The guard let us in without question this time. The elevator opened, and we once again approached the glass door of the Dobelle Institute on the seventh floor, which stood open this time. There was a fair amount of activity inside the office. Louise greeted us, this time being dressed up like the secretary of a genius.

"Hey, Jens, how are ya?" was what Dr. Dobelle said in his unmistakable voice I had heard so many times in the telephone receiver as I approached him. I held out my hand on a downward angle as he was seated in a wheelchair. I clasped his hand, noting the frailty of his grip. I gave him a pat on the shoulder with my free hand, which revealed a small, bony frame. If he had indeed been on the expeditions as written in his CV, then the last years must have taken a lot out of him.

"It is good to meet you," I said tentatively, "and I really appreciate the effort and conviction you have put into this project."

Dr. Dobelle looked up at the cowboy hat I wore. I had borrowed it from a friend as I anticipated looking strange upon leaving the hospital because I was told I would be shaved bald and have two jacks sticking out of my head as well. Later on, I figured, they would be hidden by my hair, but in the interim,

I planned on wearing this hat. I gave Dr. Dobelle my hat, which he held for some time, inspecting it closely.

Louise interrupted with more introductions.

"We also have Dr. Dillis Gore here as well as Dr. Beth Seelig, and here is Dr. John Girvin."

I shook hands with each one of them. Dr. Gore was an intelligent-sounding woman in her mid-thirties, according to my best guess, who certainly showed a lot of promise for continuing the project, as I was somewhat disappointed by the bad shape Dr. Dobelle was in. I recognized the name *Seelig* as the person who wrote the article "Altruism and the Volunteer: Psychological Benefits from Participating As a Research Subject," as well as the psychiatrist who would assess my suitability for this implant. She had a warm, friendly disposition with a hint of authority in her manner of speech. I judged her from the first impression as a great asset to the project. Perhaps, I hoped, I would get a chance to talk with her on a later date regarding the rehabilitation of patients fitted with this device of Dr. Dobelle's.

Finally, I came to John Girvin, to whom I actually had to look up as I spoke, as he was either standing upon a chair or very tall.

"How are your canoeing trips going, Dr. Girvin?" I made reference to one of his e-mail messages he had sent me in which he described his latest canoeing ventures in Quebec. "You know, Jens," he said laughingly, "I think I am getting a bit old for this. I had expected to go paddling down a river but ended up having the portage the majority of the route." "Portaging is but another word for carrying one's canoe along with all the other gear through the most god-awful terrain while all the bugs have a marvelous feast, given both your hands are occupied, and all this while you wish you were situated at a seaside resort, drinking beer and watching Spanish girls dancing."

Dr. Girvin laughed at this. "You're right at that. I'm getting to be sixty-seven years old, and this is just not as much fun as it used to be."

In spite of his age, Dr. Girvin sounded young and vibrant. The engineers were scurrying around in the back of the building, and I paused briefly to greet them. In another room within the office, there were three people seated, talking quietly amongst themselves. It was a blind man with two female companions. I could not make out what they were saying, and neither was I introduced to them.

I got to the point when I retrieved my hat from Dr. Dobelle.

"So, Dr. Dobelle, can we talk about this vision system you have for me?"

"Yeah, let's go into the conference room," said Dr. Dobelle, then looking over his shoulder in the direction of the front desk in the reception area. "Louise! Help me to the conference room."

Louise came over hurriedly, and grasping the handles of Dr. Dobelle's wheelchair, she pushed him in the direction of the conference room, which was a considerable distance away. "I thought you had a prosthesis," I said, hoping for an explanation for his immobility. I had originally expected him to set an example in the use of prosthesis, as, after all, he was asking the same of us, the patients for his visual prosthesis. "I have one—I just paid $15,000 for it, but the damned thing hurts." He said in such a manner that suggested he may not try to use it for some time to come.

"You'll just have to grit your teeth and do it anyway," I suggested. "It's much better than just sitting all day."

"That's easy for you to say," said Dr. Dobelle, sounding impatient at my suggestion. The fact was that it was not easy for me to say. I, too, had to grit my teeth and learn to walk with the cane in spite of the pain, I thought to myself, but better to leave the issue alone. There was no sense starting an argument over something I had little knowledge of. "Yeah, it must be hard," I said, letting the issue fall.

We were seated at the table in the conference room—a room which was only furnished with a large table and several chairs, but nothing else. Louise moved a chair out of the way so Dr. Dobelle could pull up to it, sitting directly opposite me with Lorri beside me. Louise left the room, closing the door behind her.

"Am I the first one here?" I inquired to Dr. Dobelle, starting the conversation.

"No, you're the second." Dr. Dobelle turned to Lorri. "You must have seen those people there in the other room as you came in. Well, the guy, who wanted the operation, shows up here, totally scared and unable to talk or respond to any questions. Meanwhile, the wife and daughter of his were crying as if he was about to go to his funeral."

"Why was that?" I said.

"I got no idea," said Dr. Dobelle in his rusty voice. "We sure don't need patients like that, though. I'm just going to give them back their money and send them home."

I wasn't going to let that happen to me, I thought. I could not imagine going home empty-handed.

"As far as I am concerned, Dr. Dobelle," I started, reinforcing my commitment to the project, "the worst pain that I ever had was when suddenly the world went black. Any physical discomfort that I may have in alleviating the situation, even by the slightest degree, will be minor in comparison to the loss of sight."

"Did you talk to Jerry?" asked Dr. Dobelle, putting the last patient's problems to the side.

"Yes, I did. But I am kind of puzzled as to what he describes as being able to see. He said he could not really identify objects, but rather could only tell they were there. That's a far cry from recognizing faces, I think."

Dr. Dobelle did not hesitate at this, as he may have already thought it out.

"Jerry's pedestal broke some time ago, as it is only made of carbon. He can't see more than seventeen phosphenes in total. You'll be able to see 140."

I let myself be comforted by that explanation. Despite this, I still had troubles believing it possible to recognize faces with 140 electrodes, or even with 1000, for that matter. I remembered reading in a medical journal that the first signs of macular degeneration was that the patients would have troubles recognizing faces, even though everything else in their environment looked normal. To think that several dozen dots of light, which weren't even given a gray scale, as they were either on or off, would directly compete with biological vision was pushing it, even to a novice's mind like my own. Yet I stayed quiet.

"That won't happen to the pedestals that you're getting," continued Dr. Dobelle, figuring I believed everything he said, "you'll be getting the titanium pedestals. They will be held on by six bone screws each. I should be able to lift you right out of your chair by them without them being damaged."

"That's great," I answered, but I did not feel like I meant it at the time. I had had the impression I would be getting what Jerry had implanted, only with one on each side of my head. Now things were being changed. Furthermore, I had difficulty imagining Dr. Dobelle, as frail as he was and unable to stand up himself, being able to lift me off the ground.

"Do you think it will be just as good?"

"Better," said Dr. Dobelle, expecting me to leave it at that. I did.

"Here's one right here," he said, clipping open his briefcase, which was beside him on the floor. He pulled out a crinkly sounding plastic bag and tossed it on the table in front of Lorri.

"Well, that's pretty small," commented Lorri, peering at it. "It's in a bag, so you can feel it," she said as she slid it to me.

I felt a roundish object, which had a diameter of a dime, with a flange of perhaps twice that diameter at one end. There were wires coming out of the end where the flange was. Its length was no more than about seven coins piled on top of each other. At the other end of the wires, which were about fifteen centimeters or so long, there was a small triangular piece of material, with many little bumps on it.

"That's the part that goes onto your brain," said Dr. Dobelle, watching me touch the little triangle, of which one side measured no more than about three centimeters.

"We're going to implant two different sizes of electrodes onto your brain." Dr. Dobelle was explaining the implant that I was still investigating. "One side will have the 1 mm electrode diameters, as Jerry has, but the other side will have 3 mm electrodes. I think they will work better than the 1 mm."

I thought about this for a minute. "Are you sure, Dr. Dobelle?" I was a little mystified at his sense of logic. It had precisely stated in even his own journal that the location of the electrode on the visual cortex corresponded with the location of the phosphene on the visual field. It only made sense to assume that a larger stimulation area would result in a larger phosphene.

"Yeah, trust me," said Dr. Dobelle. I hoped he'd be right. I fingered the objects inside of the bag, continuing to assess the size of the pedestal. It was going to stick out of my head, all right, but there was no way around it. If this was the worst of it, I supposed I could put up with it even if the vision was not perfect. The top of it was not much more than a centimeter and a half in diameter, but the bottom, the part under the scalp, would be close to three centimeters in diameter. "Luckily," I thought to myself, "this does not mean a three-centimeter hole had to be cut into my skull."

I assessed the triangular electrode array, which felt like a thick piece of plastic that was still very flexible. I had no idea that teflon, the material used in Jerry for the implant and what I assumed this was, could be this flexible. But then again, this was modern technology. In fact, it was "state of the art."

"So how do you get this array into the head and ensure it is flat and well placed with just a little hole in the skull?" I was curious to know what instruments they would use.

"Well, the hole will be big enough so we can get our fingers into there and do what we have to. We do have to place it between the faux and the visual cortex, which involves a bit of fiddling, so we need the space."

"So how big is the hole made in the skull?" I was getting worried. All the while I had been reading the literature on this procedure, the description of the surgery was "a small hole in the skull," and with that I imagined a hole no bigger than that of the end of my finger.

Dr. Dobelle held up his hands for Lorri to see.

"Show me," I said to Lorri. Seeming to be speechless, she said nothing but held up her hands, using her index finger and thumb from both hands to form the outline of a hole through which I could have dropped a playing card without folding it or turning it sideways. A tinge of horror gripped my stomach. I shook it off as best as I could, not letting Dr. Dobelle see my true feelings.

"So what exactly are the surgeons going to do?" I turned to Dr. Dobelle, speaking quietly and keeping my voice as controlled as possible.

"Well, let me show you," he replied, attempting to push himself backward from the table in order to come around the table to me. I got up and walked around the table, taking a place on a chair beside him. He talked as he drew his finger across the back of my head to show me what he meant. "First we cut your scalp in three directions, like three sides of a square, leaving it attached only at the bottom of your head." He ran one finger from the place behind my left ear where the hairline was, drawing straight upward to the very top of the back of my head. Then he drew his finger across the top of my head, upon which he returned downward until reaching the hairline at the bottom of my right ear. He had effectively squared off the entire part of the back of my head. "Then we grab the top of the scalp where we cut, and pull it downward, tearing it off the skull until it is like a flap hanging down the back of your neck. That exposes the entire skull at the back of your head."

According to a description later given to me by Lorri, who was watching Dr. Dobelle all the while he talked of tearing down the scalp, he made a grimace during the demonstration equivalent of that made by an undertaker who was attempting to stuff an oversized, uncooperative corpse into a coffin that was too small.

Dr. Dobelle continued his description of the surgery, which was becoming less and less an operation typically referred to as day surgery.

"The next thing is to cut a chunk of bone out of the back of your head. Then we have to cut the dura. That is a membrane which covers your brain. We cut in a sort of triangle so we can tear it off the brain, but still sew it back up later after we slip in the two implants."

I was listening, imagining everything he said in full color, close up. What I wasn't imagining was my own face on the other side of that head, now in pieces, the scalp flapping uselessly down the back of the neck . . .

"We have to cut canals into the surrounding skull in order to house the seventy-two wires coming out of each implant. We then grind flat a part of your skull, upon which we screw the two jacks, one on each side of your head."

He touched the back of my head not far above my ear on either side of my head, localizing the position of the pedestals. "After that, we put the bone back in place and secure it there so it doesn't fall in. Next, we put the scalp back in place, but first we implant a sheet of platinum under your scalp for the ground connection. And that's it."

I could tell Lorri was struggling with the idea of me being butchered like that. I was too. Yet, I had no choice. The dark world was no less threatening to my existence as a tumor would be in the head of a patient suffering from such a disease. To simply return to a world of darkness would mean I would not live a meaningful life well into my senior years, just like a brain tumor would eventually result in one's demise.

I imagined the sounds and the experience this would be to live through. Even if the nerves were adequately dulled through local anesthetic, the sounds of the tearing scalp, the sawing of my skull, the idea that at that moment there would be a man's fingers, along with a knife, deep inside of my brain, the tightening of the screws in the back of my head, the grinding of the channels for the wires, the flap of my scalp dangling between my shoulder blades, a region which would more than likely not be anesthetized . . . it would have been much easier if that airplane had crashed upon landing in Lisbon.

"And all this under local anesthetic?" I refrained from raising my voice. "You'd have to pepper me with so many needles my flesh would resemble hamburger afterward."

Dr. Dobelle spoke in a manner suggesting his main concern was practicality rather than humanitarian considerations. Luckily, the two coincided to the same plan of action. "No, we're going to put you under. The doctors figured that's most practical as we can put you in any position we want without having to worry about your comfort, as it will take at least an hour to do all this."

I had to get away from the subject of the surgery. The other patient along with his family had left, leaving myself and Lorri as the only people in the office other than the staff. I heard the telephone ring in another room, which brought me back to reality. I did not want to discuss the surgery with Lorri in the presence of Dr. Dobelle.

The door of the conference room opened, and Louise came in. "Bill," she began, noticing we weren't speaking for the moment, "there is a patient on the telephone who just came . . ." She never got to finish her sentence, as Dr. Dobelle exploded at her.

"Darn it, Louise, get the heck out of here! I'm busy with patients, can't you see that?"

Louise backed toward the door, her face burning with embarrassment, while she stammered somewhat and then just left, closing the door behind her. Lorri and I were taken by surprise by this totally unwarranted outburst of frustration. Louise was at least my age, possessing an air of friendliness and warmth welcome in this environment of doubt and confusion. I would have loved the chance to unwind somewhat in engaging in small talk, with Louise as a diversion. Lorri and I were embarrassed by the behavior of Dr. Dobelle as well.

Dr. Dobelle turned back to us in a voice suggesting absolutely nothing had ever happened.

"So do you have any questions?"

I had no idea what I would have done had he ever talked to me like that. If he was anyone else, I would do my best to give a stout opinion of my own, but here he was, the man whom I had trusted to unlock my prison door. Perhaps, I reckoned, had Louise stood her ground and simply calmed Dr. Dobelle as one would a rude child, explaining the situation, he would have relented. With her scurrying off as quickly as she did, it only made him feel more powerful. "But maybe," I thought quietly, "this kind of a person is what it took to get this project going." I forced myself to concentrate on the issues surrounding the vision system.

"Yes," I began, trying to skirt around the surgical issues. "Do you have the equipment that we will be wearing?"

"It's right here," said Dr. Dobelle, reaching down to one end of the table and slamming a metal box measuring about a half a foot square in front of me on the table.

"That's the computer," he said, and slamming another box about the same size in front of me, he continued, "that's the stimulator, and this is the battery."

The battery was half the size.

"You get a belt to put that all in." All together it weighed about ten pounds. I thought it may make a person look kind of funny, but then again, it could be hidden under a shirt. Dr. Dobelle passed me a pair of sunglasses wherein one of its plastic lens were drilled out, its hole holding a small video camera no larger than the size of the end of my finger. "That's the camera. That's your electronic eye right there."

I put them on, facing Lorri so she could see me wearing them. This part of the technology was perhaps the cheapest and least complex of the entire system, especially considering the horror of the upcoming surgery.

But the power of the glasses fitted with that little camera was incredible. It felt so good and so right when those glasses sat on my nose. All I needed was that little connection to the brain, and I'd be able to see through this bionic eye as if I never went blind—the images appearing in my visual field as if a television screen replaced the dreary darkness of every day. I snapped out of it, thinking again of the surgery.

"Do you have them all built, for all the patients?" I asked, holding up the stimulator box and the computer, one in each hand. Dr. Dobelle lowered his voice in a reassuring gesture as if he was a car salesman putting the finishing touches on a final deal.

"They're all on the shelf, ready to go."

I took his word for it. On the shelf, ready to go. I certainly did not want to go through this surgery and then not have anything to show for it. Many thoughts were racing through my head, most of them not what I expected before coming here. Right from Jerry's reluctance to have another surgery, Dr. Dobelle's interesting personality to the elevated concern of a surgery, and its possible implications, dulled my mind in an overload mode wherein I understood all the concepts, yet was powerless to stray from the original objective—to see again. What concerned me most about the surgery was that I may wake from it as a raving lunatic with little or no capacity to think, let alone be able to appreciate the vision gained. Yet Jerry was not like that, so perhaps I should be all right too. If anything should go wrong, I hoped it would kill me.

"Where do we go from here?" I said to Dr. Dobelle, who had resorted to small talk with Lorri about how he had enjoyed himself when visiting Disneyland. As I heard him talk about all his life experiences, the last line of his curriculum vita echoed through my head—"Dr. Bill Dobelle's other interests include opera, ballet, and sailing . . ."; he hadn't even touched those subjects yet—we still had a lot to catch up on about his amazing past.

"Come in this afternoon and you'll be given the psychological exam with Beth," he indicated, turning to Lorri. "Can you push me out to the main office from here?"

He had a little wheelchair, which lacked the large back wheels generally used for the patients to be able to push themselves with their hands, so he either had to be pushed by someone else or he attempted to propel himself with his remaining foot. Why he didn't invest in a better chair, allowing more personal independence, remained a mystery to me. Lorri pushed him out as I followed into the main office, being greeted by the other staff members. Lorri and I chatted with Dr. Gore as well as with Dr. Girvin about the details of the surgery. Talking with either of them was so refreshing in contrast to talking to Dr. Dobelle that I put my anxieties aside for the moment in discussing the merits of the operation. Both Dr. Girvin and Dr. Gore were convinced the operation was going to be a success.

Dr. Dobelle was talking with Louise, making no reference to the events which just passed between them. Maybe he did not know he was really being so difficult to her, I thought to myself. But considering his tone of voice, selection of words, and that he was speaking in his native language, it may have been more of a standard communication manner for him with which he saw nothing unusual.

I approached Louise, making sure first of all that Dr. Dobelle was done with her lest I be told to be quiet as well. "Louise, we have no luck in this town finding a place to eat. Last night we were all over town looking for a place, and the best we found was a pizza joint that looked like it was run from someone's garage, only to be told we won't be served until nine o'clock in the morning!"

Louise paused her tapping on the computer and looked up at us. "What time were you out?"

"About seven o'clock," said Lorri, adding, "well past suppertime." Louise chuckled. "Around here suppertime starts at eight, or even later. The

Portuguese culture is different. People are up past midnight eating. They usually close all restaurants from about three o'clock until eight or so."

Lorri turned to me. "So in other words, that guy at the pizza place meant nine at night! It sure would have hit the spot at that time!"

No doubt it would have hit the spot. Louise suggested, "There's a place just downstairs in the same building, run by someone who speaks a bit of English as well. Try that for lunch."

We did. The place was no bigger than a room in a typical household, with seating accommodation for perhaps a dozen people. The proprietor, a middle-aged woman, measuring a good foot and a half less than myself in height, greeted us. There were two selections on the menu, which she recited verbally. It comprised of either a plate of fish or pork. I chose the fish, and Lorri the pork. The fish arrived in less than ten minutes, steaming hot, accompanied by fresh vegetables and rice. The fish was in its whole form, lacking only the entrails. The proprietor, and chef, whose name I could never remember, took the bones out of the fish using only two forks in such an efficient manner that it was unbelievable she took only a minute. The meal was delicious. She then came over and asked if we wanted dessert or even coffee.

"Coffee is the magic word," Lorri said, nodding in agreement. We heard a machine whirring in the back of the kitchen, and shortly she returned with two cups on saucers, which I could hear as they clanked together. Lorri said to me in a strained voice as if she was trying to suppress laughter. "Look at the cup they gave us."

I reached in front of me and started to laugh as well. The cup was the size of what one would give to a baby for playing tea party. It was so small I couldn't have been able to stick two of my thumbs into it at the same time. In it was a sauce that smelled of the rich, full aroma of high-quality coffee. The proprietor held out a packet of sugar for me to add to the coffee, which I normally took black. I tried it black first, only to find it burned my throat. I turned to Lorri, who was trying to figure out what to do with the coffee soup.

"I'll take the sugar this time just to soften it up enough to be consumed." Lorri was stirring her mixture and turned to the waitress/chef/owner. "Thank you very much," she said, and I followed with the same gesture. She was trying hard, and it was good coffee. All it needed was water, but then again, water is free.

The bill came, which was a ridiculously low sum. I placed a two-euro coin on the table, and we walked out the door. A few seconds after starting down the sidewalk, the proprietor chased us down, holding the tip. "You forgot this!" she said, not at all suspecting it was a gratuity.

"It is a tip. It's for you for serving us," we said back to her, smiling a gesture of thanks. She refused to take it, and we took it back, trying not to make a fuss about it.

"I guess one doesn't give tips here," I said, wondering why she didn't just take it and leave it at that.

"I guess it's a matter of pride," Lorri commented at that. I thought of my own situation back home, where no one gave me a tip for cutting all that firewood either. The best tip I could expect was to have a customer who did not try to overload their vehicle in an attempt to get more wood than what they paid for. But I certainly wouldn't have minded a tip every now and then—the pride would have had its place in a job well done.

We walked around Portugal, killing time until my next appointment with Dr. Seelig. The air was fresh, and the weather was beautiful in comparison to that in Canada in early April. There were palm trees growing right out of the sidewalks. I touched their trunks whenever we passed by one, as this was my first experience with these strange trees. There was a lot of life in the streets with an unusual amount of pedestrians. As we walked, Lorri peered into the windows of the buildings lining the streets.

"You know, there are a lot of restaurants that are just like houses on the outside, but inside there are tables and chairs set up. I never noticed them before."

"Well, tonight around midnight, we'll have to go into one and try it out," I suggested, thinking about how the last meal was so good and economical as well.

"I need to go to a bank and exchange my American cash for Euros," I said to Lorri, who was still window-shopping. She spotted one, with the word *Banco* written on it, which was one Portuguese word I understood. We went inside and stood in one of the two lineups. Many people were there, withdrawing cash. There was one man serving a line who sounded like he knew some English. I held out two hundred American dollars, saying as clearly as possible, "Change into Euros?"

I expected him to take the money and charge a percentage for the exchange. They were, after all, a business that specialized in finances, and one must expect to support them for their services. "No, we can't do that for you," said the man in good English. "We only do that for our best customers."

Lorri heard the same as I did, and for an instant we paused, taken by surprise. There were people behind us, impatient to get on with their tasks. We thanked the man at the counter and left the bank.

"Weird," said Lorri. That went without question, leaving me with nothing more to add.

"How do you get to be a good customer, anyhow?"

"Who knows?" was the answer, as I counted the remaining Euros in my wallet. It wasn't much.

We returned to the office for the Dobelle Institute that afternoon. There was a flurry of activity in the office, and Dr. Dobelle insisted on briefing me prior to the scheduled meet with Dr. Seelig.

"So after this," he began, making reference to the psychological exam as if he assumed it would pass without doubt, "I'll be with other patients, so I want you to show up tomorrow at the office, and Steve will take you to the hospital for your physical."

I was relieved he foresaw no problems with the psychological exam and decided to take the opportunity to further show my interest and knowledge in the project. I had been hoping for a more important position in the vision quest than just being a guinea pig, but rather someone with the capacity to contribute in the advancement of the technology. I reached in my briefcase and pulled out a paper I had prepared a few weeks ago.

"I had written up a proposal as an idea to solve the problem of the image moving around with the movement of the eye," I said, handing him the paper. "Since the camera you use only has its very center pixel arrangement used, I thought this out to be practical in the sense that one uses the entire camera to facilitate eye movement. I also have another proposal which would result in better acuity in spite of limited phosphenes, yet not compromise mobility."

April 2002:

Proposal #1—Zoom control (magnification) operated by facial muscles

Written by Jens Naumann

After carefully reading the ASAIO Journal 2000 titled "Artificial Vision for the Blind by Connecting a TV Camera to the Visual Cortex," it became quickly apparent that the full potential of the phosphene grid projected upon the visual field is dependent upon the recipient's ease and speed in manipulating the external hardware and software to project the best image for a given setting. To realize the potential of the phosphene grid, the individual sensations, which correspond with the number of electrodes, may be interpreted as "binary" input to a part of the brain which lays dormant and useless in a profoundly blind person. The binary input provided by the phosphenes are analogous to the binary input, for example, of the typical home computer keyboard. In this example, an 8-bit input provides a maximum of 2 multiplied by itself 8 times (2 exp. 8) and equals 256 possible combinations. Thus, a 68-electrode input to the visual cortex will supply a total of 2.95×10 exp 20 possible images, and a 150 electrode grid provides 1.47×10 exp 45 possible images. In a hundred-year span, utilizing 24 hrs/day, and seeing ten images per second, the maximum number of images possible to see is 3.1×10 exp 10. Therefore, even with a 68-electrode implant, a recipient cannot claim that he "has seen it all." In theory, the electrode array numbering either 68 or 150 should provide unlimited observation power to the recipient.

Magnification

As is typical of any magnification device (telescopes, microscopes, etc.) increasing the size of the image directly compromises the visual field, and vice versa. Also, an image in motion will appear to increase its velocity in direct proportion to the magnification factor. As the advantage in magnification is increased acuity and its disadvantage is the restricted visual field, it is therefore vital that the switching between a magnified state and an unmagnified state of the image be available to the recipient with the least amount of time spent switching between these two options.

Upon reviewing the ASAIO 2000 Journal, it is stated that even though the volunteer taking part in the experimentation could easily identify a six-inch letter at a given distance, paradoxically he could not identify much larger characters, as their size exceeded the range of the volunteer's visual field. This fact makes it clear that if further demagnification was used, this problem would not exist as demagnification results in a corresponding larger visual field.

However, with the above modifications, acuity would be less, and smaller characters would not be identifiable. Should the volunteer, on the other hand, have access to instantaneous magnification and demagnification, he could achieve his navigation with the low magnification setting, and once fixated upon the illegible character, magnify to a preset level and identify the character. Should the volunteer be the least disoriented as a result of moving, or the object moving, he can instantly revert back to the low magnification state. Thus, instantaneous access to magnification will, in effect, provide the recipient with the "best of both worlds," these being high acuity and good navigational visual field.

To draw an analogy with biological vision, having instant access to magnification would compare to having the ability for a driver of an automobile to "glance" into the rearview mirror while maintaining full control of the vehicle and the forward visual field. Should the driver, however, have to spend the extra moment to turn his head to look behind himself, the results could be catastrophic.

Hands Off

The limitation of success of any aid for the physically disabled operator partially lies in how many body parts are used to operate this aid. For instance, a white cane or guide dog effectively results in the loss of one hand while using this aid, and a device incorporating audio signals results in a temporary hearing impairment while using the device. In the case of the artificial vision device, any required use of hands to control the device settings once it is adjusted for the day's work would be disadvantageous. Should the recipient, for example, be in the process of soldering electronic components upon a circuit board, having the iron in one hand and the solder in the other, have to readjust the magnification manually with the hands, production would be compromised. It is therefore necessary to incorporate a method which can allow the recipient to access magnification and demagnification without using his hands.

In the example of biological vision, a person is inclined to "squint," an action which is controlled by facial muscles surrounding the eyes. This action effectively reduces the peripheral vision, resulting in greater concentration of the object scrutinized. Moreover, this action often inadvertently changes the shape of the eye and achieves temporary correction in the case where 20/20 vision is not normally available. If this natural and socially acceptable action were incorporated into the artificial vision device as an option to control a preset magnification macro, the recipient would achieve instantaneous access to magnification or "zoom control" in a hands-off fashion. Using this action may also have positive psychological benefits as the recipient will practice similar actions to those used before the loss of eyesight.

General Layout

The hardware itself would consist of an NO (normally open) microswitch (spst) which activates a macro incorporated into the software. This microswitch would be spliced into the conventional keyboard interrupt vector (0×16) activating the same BIOSKEY(2) function return as is shared with the shift keys. It would be practical to have a selection for degree of magnification provided in the menu upon activating the macro. This level would be set prior to the recipient undertaking a certain task. For example, when soldering electronic components upon a circuit board, the recipient would select near maximum magnification; however, if sightseeing is on the agenda, a smaller degree of magnification will provide a more stable perspective during motion.

The switch would be mounted inside of one of the glasses lens, between the lens and one of the recipient's eyes. Two movable hinged arms would be mounted in such a way that one arm supports the base of the switch and the other contacts the plunger near its fulcrum, and the ends of these arms contact the skin immediately below the eyebrow (close to the eyelid) and the corresponding arm contacts the cheek at the point where the cheek attaches the lower eyelid.

From my observations, a typical squinting action will move these two surfaces together by 1/4 inch with a pressure of approx 2 oz with very little effort. Considering the mechanical advantage offered by the length of the arms operating the microswitch, this should be adequate for ease in selecting magnification levels.

The connection to the computer is made via a two-conductor cable, which may be in the same housing as the camera output cable.

Potential

In theory, full acuity potential is achieved when a direct camera pixel to phosphene representation exists. This means every pixel on the camera activates an electrode on the visual cortex, and thus only the same number of pixels as there are electrodes are being used in the camera. Any further magnification would only cluster the electrodes to represent a common camera pixel, and no further acuity would be achieved. A 492-512 pixel 69-degree diagonal field camera as described in the ASAIO journal were applied to a computer with such a link that each pixel is accounted for, the camera would have eight dots per inch resolution at five feet. Since a 5 × 5 minimum pixel grid is required for a character to be recognized, the maximum acuity of the camera would be approx 20/120. For a 12 × 13 electrode grid, however, this would represent a 1 1/2 square of visual field at five feet; hardly adequate for navigation.

This field of vision would be manageable only if the recipient is able to cycle between the magnified and non-magnified view as often as necessary to get the better of both perspectives. It will also be imperative that the magnification software be so designed that the center of visual field be represented by the same camera pixel regardless of what the magnification factor is. Otherwise, upon magnification, the object desired to be magnified would disappear from the visual field upon activating the macro.

April 2002

Proposal No. 2 for Artificial Vision

Incorporating Eye Movement into Artificial Vision

Written by Jens Naumann

According to the information provided in the ASAIO Journal 2000 titled "Artificial Vision for the Blind by Connecting a TV camera to the Visual Cortex," the present system hardware does not incorporate eye movement as a means to control the direction of visual fixation for the recipient. Therefore, the act of observing images exceeding the visual field provided by the active camera pixel grid (scanning) is controlled by the recipient's neck muscles rather than eye movement. In the case of biological vision, the eye movement does not necessarily replace entire neck movement, but does limit the necessity of moving the head for small changes in the visual field location. For example, a person reading a book will typically move his head to look at another page, but will use eye movement to read the script. If the eye is moved in the case of artificial vision, the phosphenes move with the eye, and as a result the image moves also. This means that if a recipient stands in front of a particular image and turns his eyes to the side, the image will then appear to be at the side rather than directly in front of him.

General Solution

At present, the artificial vision camera has its center pixel corresponding with the electrode representing the center of vision (focal point) of the visual field. All the pixels of the camera are not necessarily utilized, as the 69-degree field afforded by it would result in a very "faraway" (demagnified) perspective, and to increase magnification the outer perimeter of pixels would have to be deactivated. If eye movement and location could be captured by the computer, the center of vision electrode could be moved with the corresponding eye movement to represent a different location on the camera pixel grid. If further eye movement in one direction forces the visual field to become restricted as there are no more pixels available on that side of the camera's field, the result would be similar to that of biological vision, as extreme eye movement to one side restricts the periphrial vision available on that side. In electronic comparisons, the action of the eye movement would be similar to that of moving a joystick in a computer game.

Capturing Eye Movement and Location

As no medical intervention is desired, the most practical way to capture eye movement and the resulting pupil direction is to have the recipient wear a soft contact lens which has its center (pupil) impregnated with ferrite filings. A spherical plate would be placed inside the corresponding eyeglass lens which houses four coils arranged so that the distance between the top coil and the eye pupil is closest when the eye is moved to look up; the left coil is closest to the pupil when the pupil is moved to the extreme left, etc. As a result of these coils, their inductance will be influenced directly with the location of the ferric material in the contact lens. A small electronic package would have to be designed which converts the inductance of these coils into variations in amplitude, which is then fed into the computer in the same manner as joystick input.

Electronic Package

The output of the electronics package would have to provide similar changes in amplitude with eye movement as would a joystick. The typical joystick consists of 25K ohm linear taper variable resistors which provides four separate resistance changes depending upon the location of the joystick. As the computer provides five volts to these resistances, with a typical hundred-ohm min resistance at extremes, the current can range from 1 mA to 50 mA for either the vertical or horizontal axis control. This range can be duplicated in output with the electronics package incorporating inductive reactance as a variable instead. As inductive reactance changes directly with the permeability of the core of an inductor, the closer the ferric powder present in the contact lens is to the air core inductor, the greater the reactance. If this reactance is tuned to resonance by a corresponding capacitance, the AC current flow in the circuit through a series connected load will vary.

The use of reactance warrants an alternating current is present. Therefore, an AC oscillator is constructed to provide an RF frequency of perhaps.5-3 MHz, and with mutual coupling the four coils installed surrounding the recipient's pupil are tuned to resonance at extreme eye movement in the corresponding direction of the coil location. Therefore, if the eye is moved to look up, the upper coil will provide greatest (or least, depending upon whether the capacitance is shunted or in series with L) reactance.

The individual resonant circuits are loaded with a transistorized amplification unit so that a greater response is sent to the computer. With proper circuit design, the change in coil permeability should create a nonlinear change in resistance similar in range to that of a joystick.

The frequency of the AC oscillator would have to be high enough to accommodate manageable inductor/capacitor sizes but low enough that slight changes in capacitive and inductive entities from the cable leading from the glasses to electronics package causes the frame location to shift without eye movement.

Software Modifications

Two minor software modifications would be necessary for this system. A mathematical reassignment of the camera pixel that represents the center of visual field would have to be made depending upon the linear input afforded by a joystick. This is a standard technique utilized in windows cursor movement.

The input, however, would not be linear as a linear taper potentiometer would supply when in series with a voltage. Inductor core permeability alters inversely with the square of the distance from ferrite material (minus the inductance of the air core), and considering adverse entities introduced in construction, cables, and component impurities, the algorithm representing the slope of change with given distance between eye pupil and inductor would require considerable experimentation to perfect. However, if only 50 percent of eye movement was used to alter the focal point in a desired direction, it would still help considerably in scanning and also suffice in allowing the recipient to utilize eye movement to duplicate the sensation that he is seeing with his eyes.

Discussion

I have had experience in experimenting with this technique and realize it is entirely possible to do this without introducing untested theories. Using ferrite-impregnated contact lenses would have the requirement to shield the AC oscillator so as not to interfere with radio reception. A less familiar method would utilize a reflective substance on the surface of the contact lens, a small selected frequency light transmitter mounted in the inside of the glass's lens, and four corresponding receptors mounted in the same manner as the coils would in the inductive unit. This manner would add to the usefulness in allowing the computer output to be interrupted when no light is reflected (when the recipient closes his eye) adding to the normal eye function sensations that recipients who lost eyesight in adult years would probably appreciate.

I hoped Dr. Dobelle would at least look at them, which he quickly glanced at and then set aside.

"I'll have my engineers look at this," he said, then tapping the papers, continued, "But who's going to pay for all this? We're a small company, you know."

A small company was not what I had expected. However, sometimes a small company could be several dozen people. In comparison to General Motors, even a few hundred employees would constitute a small company.

"Well, you just put this in as part of possible improvements in the future so you always have another update available." I was still puzzled why Dr. Dobelle worried about money when he had planned to implant ten thousand patients annually. "Just like big companies like, take Microsoft. I bet they have updates on the shelf for twenty years to come, constantly being able to monopolize the market because of it. They, too, would never put all their improvements on the market at once. That would compromise their monopoly."

Dr. Dobelle thought about this and answered, "Yeah, I suppose you're right. But the difference here is that there's no competition."

"I thought there's lots of research institutions working on this," I said, provoking another round of discussion. "They will be working on it for a while. You probably heard of the Johns Hopkins University, haven't you?" said Dr. Dobelle.

"Yeah, I did. They are working on the same idea, aren't they?" I said.

"They are, all right. But they think the penetrating electrodes are the great thing for the future. Yet they tried implanting a Chinese girl in the 1990s, and she died from it. They killed her as a result of those electrodes, which caused a hemorrhage. They are probably the closest, but even they won't be implanting on a commercial basis for decades to come."

So this was my only chance, at least to Dr. Dobelle. It seemed like a very small world all of a sudden.

"So all the researchers in this field know each other?"

"You bet! And they all know me. They're envious, jealous, all of them." Dr. Dobelle was chuckling to himself gleefully as he spoke. "But we'll show them, all of them. That guy called Richard Normann who is working on those penetrating electrodes doesn't like me one bit. He's going to be fiddling around for a long time because he's really putting himself up for a big challenge with those penetrating electrodes."

"How safe is the stimulation on the brain anyways?" I asked, thinking suddenly about the Journal 2000 article in which there was a comment that the volunteers have so far not had epilepsy from the stimulation.

"I implanted thousands of cats myself and subject them to literally hundreds of thousands of hours of stimulation, and following that looked at their cell structure surrounding the electrodes afterward, with no hint of structural changes or mutation. It's safe," he ended with assertion.

I had to let myself be consoled with that explanation, taking also into consideration that Jerry was seemingly fine. I was still curious as to how the brain chemistry was not affected if electrical current was applied in "pulses" rather than cycles, ensuring the absence of electrolysis.

"How do you prevent electrolysis when you apply the direct current pulses to the brain?" I inquired.

Dr. Dobelle voice showed a hint of arrogance. "Who says I'm using direct current?"

"In your Journal 2000, you mentioned using "pulses" to stimulate the brain in the volunteers. A pulse is a short duration of electrical current which can be of either polarity. In the case that polarity is reversed and an equal duration pulse is applied, that is referred to as a "cycle" in electrical terms. That's why I'm confused, suspecting there could be electrolysis." Dr. Dobelle seemed perturbed at being questioned like this. I would have to drop the issue soon. "Well, we use a capacitive coupling. That'll prevent electrolysis." I wasn't so convinced he knew exactly what that meant, as he did not explain it any further. I refrained from mentioning the fact that even capacitors had trace elements of resistance of various degrees in their electrolyte, which still left room for electrolysis. The engineers would, I figured, be better candidates to discuss this with, and they would make necessary alterations should there be any problems.

"I'll leave you with Beth now," Dr. Dobelle said, calling to her to start with the psychological exam.

Dr. Seelig came in, greeting us cheerily and excusing herself for the moment she took Dr. Dobelle and wheeled him out into another room where another patient and his family awaited him.

Dr. Seelig seated herself beside me, placing a small cassette recorder onto the table along with other note-taking paraphernalia. We were in the process of breaking the ice through small talk, when Lorri asked if she should leave.

"No, not really," stated Dr. Seelig, who insisted to be called Beth. "It is important for you to be equally at ease about the whole idea of the implantation as Jens is."

That did make a lot of sense, but at the same time, it introduced another variable into the equation. It meant that if Lorri was not a good enough actor, it too could mean that I would not be able to go through with it. I anticipated her cooperation, but at the same time, I would have understood her opposition. I could not imagine the dilemma associated with the possibility that this would happen to Lorri. The thought of her head being torn open with a can opener like the top of a soup can for a procedure which could end up giving catastrophic results would make me do anything to change her mind. But, at the same time, the thought of her being blinded would make me sick as well. I did not know how she would react here with me today, or what she was thinking. I had kept secret most of my bad feelings about Bill Dobelle, the reduction in expectations for the usefulness of the vision system, and most of all the sickening prospect of having my head so brutally pillaged. She had heard everything Dr. Dobelle had said to me about the surgery, yet neither of us shared our thoughts with one another.

Beth started the recording of the cassette, remarking "I hope this thing works" under her breath.

"So, tell me, why are you deciding to go through with this?" was the content of her first question. I felt like blurting out that I wanted to see, that's all. I did not want to get tortured, or electrocuted into oblivion, nor made to look like a robot from outer space; I just wanted to see. It is a basic right for all living beings. Had I said that, however, I would have been too honest. She could have used it as a reason to disqualify me. I had to be careful; I really wasn't sure what she was looking for.

"It is an interesting experiment to be involved in, you have to admit." I started stating all my reasons for involving myself into this. "I have a desire to do more with my life other than just to accept things as they are. This opportunity is priceless for contributing to the advancement of humanity, and at the same time it offers its rewards, as I would be delighted to see the world, even if in crude format. By no means can I expect a hundred percent chance of success, but I realize my chances of success is zero should I go back home empty-handed." I had to be realistic enough to be believable, yet not too dependent upon the outcome of the surgery. It was a fine line to walk, but the more I spoke of the merits of my involvement and my tolerance to an unpredictable outcome, the better I was setting the stage for Lorri when it was her turn to speak. I was not at all convinced I was going to come out of the upcoming surgery smiling, yet I did not want Beth to have control of my destiny. I could always refuse to go to the surgery at the last minute if I wanted to. With this in mind, it was easier to talk.

Moreover, I kept in mind Beth's involvement in the literature surrounding the "altruistic" component, taking advantage of her knowledge in this concept without hinting I knew about her write up, lest she thought I was influencing her decision. "I was convinced many years ago that more could be done to combat blindness, but there seems to be reluctance on the part of the researchers to let blind people access the technology. I like the fact that Dr. Dobelle is allowing us to make the assessment as to whether or not existing technology is useful to us or not." I concluded with this sentence, leaving no doubt in Beth's mind as to my suitability as a patient.

"I was about to ask you how you would take it should this operation not render you any sight, but you already covered it. But what about getting sick from this? Do you realize you could contract meningitis from this procedure?" She posed this question at me as if she was trying to convince me staying blind was a better alternative. But I saw through it. She had a job to do, and she was testing.

"Lorri knew of a person who died of the same problem without any brain implant," I said, pretending I knew this risk of the operation. I did not. Nowhere in Dr. Dobelle's literature did it suggest this was one of the risks. But it was too late to turn back. "I can say, however, that it is rather dangerous living in total darkness, both psychologically and physically. A person has a bigger risk of dying of boredom sitting in total darkness!" I said this to be taken partially as a joke, yet there was a lot of truth to it at the same time, depending on attitude, the level of rehabilitation, and willingness to take risks. All I had to do was recall the time I walked with the white cane for the first time, feeling for the side of the road with the cane and forced to guess at the straight-ahead direction to follow when encountering intersecting driveways while the traffic whizzed past me only an arm's length beside me.

"And what about you, Lorri?" was Beth's next question. Lorri was well rehearsed as she lent all the support she could. "He really needs to go through with this," she said. "We had hoped for this kind of opportunity for many years, and if this can help him see, that is what will help him be happy again."

She continued offering her support, convincing Beth there was adequate closeness between us for the possibility of absorbing the unexpected.

There were other questions, but basically the psychiatric exam was just an interview. One could have played the game right and passed it regardless, and I suspected Beth was quite aware of that. In that case, it seemed evident that the patient would have enough intelligence to make the right decision anyways. Beth was such a nice person to have in this project. Her understanding nature concerning the suffering in life and her knowledge in rebounding after a handicap was survived would be priceless once patients who were recently, as in a few days ago, blinded would be introduced to the vision project. It was ultimately those who showed up in a hospital, just blinded and as bewildered as I had been in 1983 who would profit the most from this surgery. It would have been so much more humane had I been offered a crude form of electronic vision the day I was told my retinas were beyond repair. With Beth on board, we could devise a plan to make the prospect as attractive as possible.

"Well, it looks like you are well prepared for this event. Let me talk to Bill for a moment and I'll be back." Beth went into another room, and Lorri and I went to the front desk to talk with Louise and Jerry.

"Louise, can I have a receipt for the $2,000 cost of the preoperative exams? OHIP said they would pay that part of it back." Louise turned to Dr. Dobelle and asked if she could do that for me.

Dr. Dobelle replied, "Sure we can." Then added jokingly, "In fact, if those guys are paying for it, why not write out a receipt for fifty grand."

Beth turned to Dr. Dobelle, a hint of testiness in her voice as if she hadn't noticed his joking manner. "Now, Bill, that would not be ethical, now, would it?" Beth spoke slowly and deliberately as one would talk to a child in need of chiding. Dr. Dobelle said nothing. There was an angry moment of silence before I said, "Well, anyways, not really possible anyhow. I already showed them your bill of two grand, and it's no use dickering with them anyways, as they can get pretty nasty." Lorri started to talk of the arguments we had with them, the appeal hearing and how it was luck to even get a penny out of them. The fifty grand would have helped us, nonetheless. Following that, we changed the subject, discussing our encounter with the Portuguese bank. The standoff was covered up, but a subtle trace of bad air persisted between Dr. Dobelle and Beth.

Dr. Dillis Gore came in the office, exhausted with her day's tasks. "How are you guys doing?" she asked us in her English accent. She sounded cheery and professional in spite of her state of fatigue. "Pretty good," I said, adding jokingly. "Beth here just took out my brain to see if I had one. I hope she put it back. What are you up to?"

Dr. Gore sighed. "I have to move all this furniture into here. On top of all that, all the little appliances I brought over aren't made for the higher outlet power. What a hassle!" Dr. Girvin spoke from one of the desks in the front of the office. "I just found that out too late after plugging in my laptop. It just went 'poof' and that was it."

"I had no idea you doctors wasted your time with such ordinary things. You should be up to your elbows in brains or something like that," I said, enjoying the presence of these committed players in the project. Nothing could go wrong as long as these people were involved, I told myself.

"Oh, we'll do that next week," Dr. Girvin said, laughing. It was my brain he was referring to. I felt a bit ill at ease when thinking about it, but I did not let it show. We left the office in search of something to eat.

We walked around town for quite some time before venturing into a restaurant. It was really just someone's home with the main room on the ground floor decorated as a dining room with a few tables and chairs set out. Lorri had seen a couple of other people sitting at them before entering, giving us the sign that the business was open. We smiled a lot at the woman who was serving the others, sat down, and hoped we'd be able to communicate enough.

"Menus with pictures would help," commented Lorri, trying to figure out the writing. She spelled some words out to me from the posted menu, but none of it resembled either English or German, the only two languages I knew at the time. Sitting there, we looked very Western and absolutely out of place.

The waitress came over, pointing at the menu and uttered one word in English in a warm and receiving voice.

"Fish?"

I nodded at the same time that Lorri said, "Yes, sure, that would be great." At this, the woman turned and went out the door into the street.

"Where is she going?" I asked Lorri, hearing the door close. "I'm not sure. I think she understood what we wanted, but I can see her crossing the street and going into another business over there."

"We'll wait and see, I guess," I said. In North America, or at least in Napanee and area, no one ever trusted people enough to abandon their business like this, not even for a minute. A minute later, our waitress returned, holding a fish on a platter, showing Lorri by holding it out to her beside our table. Lorri nodded enthusiastically, saying, "Yes, yes, I like that." The woman went back into the kitchen area and started to cook. Lorri turned to me in amazement. "That is a fish which she must have just bought live a few moments ago! It has not even been cleaned yet."

"That's as fresh as you can get it," I added, marveling at this cultural difference in comparison to our ways in Canada, where everything is packaged a dozen times, sterilized and preserved with dangerous chemicals and mostly frozen, with no record of when the fish would have been harvested.

"I think this will taste good," Lorri said, seeing our plates being brought to our table only a few minutes later. She was right.

We drank a bottle of wine, which was unbelievably good. Having no obligations to drive, Lorri relaxed along with me in consuming the meal which would have cost at least fifty dollars for each of us had this been Canada. While we enjoyed our meal, I couldn't help bringing up the last day's events.

"So what do you think of all this?" I did not have to explain what I was talking about.

"Kind of interesting. It's really something to meet all those doctors and engineers."

"And Dr. Dobelle?"

"Well," Lorri was choosing words so as not to alarm me. She really couldn't do that, however, as I had thoughts along the same line. "I expected a little more professionalism from him." "Yeah," I added, thinking about the first time I talked to him on the telephone and what Lorri had thought of him before he had identified himself. "He kind of does talk like a backwoods' firewood customer in search of a bargain."

"Did you see how irritated he was with Louise for interrupting our meeting?" I couldn't get the outburst of that event out of my head.

Lorri replied, "If that was me, I'd be out looking for a new job."

"His knowledge about electricity seems to be modest at best," I said, reflecting upon our conversation in the conference room. "He likes to throw around big words, but I am not sure if he really knows what he is talking about."

"But look at the rest of the team," said Lorri, while we both sipped our wine. "John Girvin, Dillis Gore, Beth Seelig, and who knows how many more in the States and in the CUF Hospital. Then the engineers, Steve, Jim, and I bet there are others that are older and not so shy in the States. They'll keep him in check."

I nodded in agreement, consoled by Lorri's testimony. "Yeah, you're right. They'll keep him in check. He's just one guy among hundreds of vibrant players in this project." Or at least, that's what we hoped.

We agreed that Dr. Dobelle had an obvious talent in selecting strong workers for his project. For him to try to know every aspect about the field and then hire substandard workers would have been very problematic in retrospect.

Life became more relaxed at the Barca Do Tejo, as more people took notice of us and smiled in gestures of kindness. We still avoided the elevator at all costs, using the stairs as a way to meet other people. There wasn't much to say to them; however, the language remained a barrier. "We'll have to learn some Spanish or something like that," said Lorri once, as we both would have been able to touch this appealing culture much more intimately had we spoken their language. Our winding corridors had their advantages when using the stairs, as we could smell all the varieties of cuisine that was fabricated at suppertime. The small children playing in the hallway made us become more homesick for our own children with every passing day.

We arrived at 34 Infante Santo the following day, this time being greeted by the guard in a welcoming manner. As we stood in front of the elevators, waiting for one to arrive at the ground floor, we were greeted by Beth Seelig.

"How are things going upstairs?" I asked, shaking her hand. She replied warmly, with an air of positivity.

"Great. I've got more patients to interview, and preparations are made for your surgery."

"Yeah, I'm here to go over to the CUF for my physical," I said, even though she probably knew that.

"How's Dr. Dobelle?" asked Lorri.

Beth answered without precision, "Oh, he's just Bill."

"Kind of rough around the edges, huh?" I had to add this. We were in the elevator now, and soon we wouldn't have the chance to analyze the inner workings of Dr. Dobelle.

"Yeah, he's a little rough, all right. But you know," Beth continued, attempting to shed a positive light on the problem under discussion, "he's meaning good deep inside his heart." Lorri spoke up in support, "He's actually trying to help people."

Beth agreed. "Yes, he's trying to help people. That says a lot for him."

The elevator door opened, and with it the conversation of that subject closed abruptly.

"Jens!" hollered Dr. Dobelle when he saw me. He was still in his wheelchair, sounding tired, as if he had consumed more wine than Lorri and I put together.

"Steve is going to take you down to the hospital. They'll do your physical there."

Steve, one of the young engineers, joined us in the elevator. It was easy to strike up a conversation with him. He had all the markings of a loyal worker, dedicated employee, possessing social charisma. He and Lorri got along great right from the start, both sharing the same sense of humor.

"Are you going to help with the surgery?" I asked Steve.

"No, not me," he said quickly, "I think I'll keep my hands out of that stuff."

"How about Bill?" I asked humorously, making a strained face of concern. "Is he helping?"

"Oh gosh, let's hope not," Steve answered, the tone of his voice indicating serious concern at the suggestion.

We arrived in the CUF Hospital, all of us unsure as to where to go. We stood around a bit, when I asked Steve, "Do you speak Portuguese or Spanish?" to which he replied, "About three words."

"You mean, the translation for beer, wine, and food?" asked Lorri jokingly.

Steve laughed nervously. "Yeah, something to that nature." We were bustled ahead toward a reception desk as people had gathered behind us, assuming we were in the lineup. "We may as well mention the Dobelle Institute and Dr. Antunes," I suggested. "Maybe that gets the ball rolling, and they'll send someone who speaks English."

"It's worth a try," Steve said.

It worked. Steve and I did the talking first, which caused a favorable reaction as the lady at the reception desk motioned to the chairs in the waiting section.

"So far so good," Steve said. "Is this your first time in here?" I asked, turning to Steve.

"Yes, it is," Steve replied. "I met Dr. Antunes before, so I know what he looks like. He speaks English."

A female nurse came over to us, chattering rapidly in Portuguese. It must have been a masterpiece of a run-on sentence, as I detected no pause in speech of any sort for what seemed to be at least two minutes of speech. Steve waited until she was finished, seemingly listening intently. "Can you just slow down a bit? We are here for Dr. Antunes."

The nurse walked away, shaking her head and muttering to herself in frustration.

"You handled that really well," I said to Steve sarcastically. The poor guy was becoming flustered by the minute. "Yeah, you did," added Lorri in a humorous tone. "Give me a break! She's blabbing a mile a minute, and I don't have a clue what she is saying."

We were giving Steve a bit of a hard time, and he realized it was all in fun.

"I think they think you're the patient," I suggested to Steve, "as they are always talking to you. Maybe they will give you an implant!"

"Or maybe a sex change!" Lorri and I couldn't resist bugging Steve.

We carried on with a more mild conversation until a man, most likely a nurse, who identified himself as Pedro came over to us. He spoke English. All three of us were relieved. He led us to another room on the ground floor in which there were eye charts and an assortment of optical equipment.

I was seated before the same kind of instrument Dr. Willis and Dr. Shea had many years ago. Pedro reached over and with his thumb gently lifted my eyelid so the lens of the instrument could contact my eye.

"Not much to see in there," I pointed out as he peered into it. "We get people sometimes coming here from places like Africa who are blind for years as a result of something simple like a cataract. Dr. Antunes won't give you surgery for an implant if all you need is removal of a cataract in order to see."

Pedro shone a very bright light from an angle coming from below my left eye into my left pupil. "Do you see anything?" he asked. "I see a bit of light on my bottom left corner," I replied. It was so refreshing just to see that bit of light. A wave of bitterness overcame me for an instant as I thought about all I could have done with my life had this not happened. "But that's all going to change now," I thought positively.

Pedro continued with his examination, taking blood samples, along with various other procedures typically related to a physical examination. He asked me questions about allergies, being especially particular about my reactions to anesthesia. I did all I could to convince him I was fine with a general. I hoped he'd believe me, as the very idea of being conscious during brain surgery made me queasy. Just like it was futile to remain blind if one had a cataract in light of modern surgical procedures, it constitutes cruel and unjust punishment to be subject to brain surgery with only a local anesthetic when the general was available, I reasoned.

Pedro was finished and then brought in Dr. Antunes along with two other doctors whom he identified as Dr. Domingo Coiteros and Dr. Ken Smith.

I shook hands with them all. Dr. Antunes explained the operation in detail to me. His explanation was no less gory than that of Dr. Dobelle's. I winced again at the thought of having my scalp ripped down until it hung uselessly like an old rag about my shoulders. I felt faint at the thought of the huge hole opened in my skull.

"I am sure this will resolve the terrible problem of not being able to see," pointed out Dr. Antunes after finishing his explanation.

It was reassuring to hear that from him—a lot more reassuring than hearing it from Dr. Dobelle.

Dr. Domingo talked some more with both Lorri and I about the surgery and what to expect afterward.

"You'll be here for about a week, and then you'll be quite tender for a few weeks afterward," said Dr. Domingo. "A week?" I was very surprised to hear this. Judging by Lorri's gasp, so was she.

"But Dr. Dobelle said this could be done as day surgery," I said slowly as I wanted them to understand the meaning of this. "He said we may have to stay a night this time just for observation." I may as well have told them that my mother thought I should be president of the United States, as they took no notice of what Dr. Dobelle had told me, as if his word was secondary at best.

"This is a big operation. It will last about three to four hours. We're opening up your head, we'll be using steel stitches to keep your skull plate in place after the surgery, and you will probably have fifty stitches in your head to keep on the scalp. You'll also be leaking some brain fluid out of the implants, so we'll keep you here until it is healed up." The shock of the immensity of the procedure was just starting to grip us. Lorri blurted out a question I knew we had to know first.

"And how much will all that cost?" We were both thinking about the horrendous cost of hospital bed time in Canada and the United States.

Dr. Domingo was the only one left talking to us as Dr. Antunes had other obligations, his part of the exam satisfied. Dr. Ken Smith was along as an observer, I was told by him, from the United States. I saw that as a great thing as he may be able to continue the push for this procedure to be accepted in North America.

"Not to worry," said Domingo, "you have already paid for a week's stay here."

It was good news to both of us. I was beginning to wonder after finding out about the extent of the surgery if I would feel up to climbing the four stories via stairs in the Barca Do Tejo only a day after surgery. I did, however, wonder what was going on with Dr. Dobelle. He must have known all along that this would mean a week's stay in the hospital, as arrangements had already been made for that prior to my operation. All he had mentioned was that we would stay in Portugal for a week after the surgery for ensuring that we were free of infection before going home. I did not mention this to Lorri, as I figured it would not really change anything anyway. Whether I stay in the hospital or in my hotel room for that week was, at this point in the game, irrelevant. It will be kind of boring, though, I thought, as I'd probably miss getting out in the streets of Lisbon, which had become a rather pleasing pastime for both of us.

"Come back here on the evening of April 7," instructed Domingo, "and we'll get you settled in your room for the surgery on April 8." I shook hands with Domingo and left.

We marched back to the office with a little less of a humorous disposition than before.

"Sounds scary," I said to Steve. "So much for one day in the hospital."

"Did he really say that?" Steve asked disbelievingly. "I have the letter in my briefcase." I quoted as best as I could remember the first letter I received from Dr. Dobelle. "Your scalp will be shaved. The electrodes will be inserted through a small hole in the skull. This could be done on an outpatient basis, but we'll prefer you stay in the hospital for at least one night for the first few cases."

Steve shook his head, said nothing, and kept on walking. In the office, I picked up my receipt for the cost of the psychological and physical preoperative examinations for OHIP and left. Lorri and I had almost three days to kill in Lisbon. They were going to be fun, which they were.

It would be a while before I felt like having fun again.

CHAPTER 8

In the Hospital

The three days prior to my surgery went quickly. We used the little video camera, which had been issued to us by Janice from CBC, to take a few shots of our surroundings, the highlights of Lisbon, and a few shots of myself talking about my feelings prior to the surgery. The three days of exploring Lisbon served only to help my buildup of courage for the upcoming operation, as I was frustrated not to be able to engage in any of the visual interaction with my environment that I knew was attractive. "If I could just think about the happiness that a successful turnout would bring," I told myself, "it makes the pain worth it." I had, by now, let fall the idea this would be a relatively minor surgery or that the recovery would be quick. At the same time, I had no idea how it would affect me, as the injuries I had experienced during the course of life always had involved a muscle that would be either lamed or rendered very painful to use by the injury. In this case, however, the scalp and skull had no real purpose in my daily activities, and other than being tender to lie on, I could not imagine in which other way I would suffer. "I'd have to wait and find out," I told myself.

I arrived at the hospital on the night of April 7 and was deftly assigned to a room on the second floor. To my surprise, I was issued a private room that had all the signs of comfort. The room measured at least twenty feet in length, had a high-tech bed that I could readjust with the push of a few buttons via a console attached to one of the sides, a television and, best of all, a fold-open couch that transformed into a comfortable bed for Lorri, who was welcomed by the staff to stay with me during my convalescence. The nurses were extremely friendly, taking many pains to try to be understood as they explained the food menu, which consisted of five meals daily.

"This is better than our hotel," Lorri pointed out. "Yeah, the bed is sure a lot more comfortable," I said, pushing the controls as it whirred underneath me.

"Imagine the fun it would be to get romantic on this one," I joked to Lorri, continuing the demonstration of the bed's technology. "This thing would do the work for us!"

Lorri laughed, and then reminded me, "You won't feel too romantic tomorrow." She couldn't have been more correct.

Dr. Pedro came to visit me, talking about the planned course of events leading up to my surgery. I was to have my surgery the following morning at ten, which should last about three hours. I would be given antibiotics through intravenous drip to avoid infection, or at least reduce the chances of that happening. If it did infect anyways, I would have to be reopened and have the stuff pulled back out, he said. I tried not to imagine the consequence of that happening. All that trouble and all that pain just to be back to the starting point. The possible disappointment was unimaginable. When Pedro was finished outlining the procedure, he turned to me on his way toward the door and asked, "Are you nervous?"

"No, not really," I said, keeping in mind I had the right to walk out of here right up to the point I am put under.

"You should be," Pedro said, and then left.

Silence hung in the room for a minute as Lorri and I thought about what he just said.

"He sure doesn't sound too optimistic," I said, breaking the silence.

"I suspect he just doesn't know his English well enough to know what the word *should* means," Lorri said, continuing her explanation. "I think he meant 'I would have thought you would be nervous.'"

Pedro's English was pretty good, as I found very few grammatical errors when we had talked, but Lorri could still be right. Through the bit of French I had taken in high school, it was the subjunctive and conditional tenses that were the most challenging to learn in a second language.

As I lay in the bed, Lorri attempting to find a channel on television that did not capitalize upon the misery in the world, I could not help thinking about the numerous times in the past I had awaited a magic cure for my sight recovery just like this—awaiting a surgery with many promises, many dreams that were to follow. "Here we go again," I thought, "and hopefully for the last time." I was becoming too old for this.

I was carted down the aisle of the second floor by way of my bed into a large elevator the following day, destined to the operating room. There I was totally disrobed, lying naked on the operating table. I was grateful they intended to administer the catheter only after I was put under the general anesthetic. The anesthetist poked and prodded my arm and hand but had no success in inserting the needle into a vein, so he then commenced the prodding into my feet instead. It hurt as if I had stepped into the nest of bumblebees, the stinging pronounced and prolonged. "We're going to put you out first and then position you on the table." It was the voice of John Girvin, and even when laying down I could tell he was taller than a normal man—definitely taller than the Portuguese, who seemed to me as if they were all walking around on their knees.

"How are you going to keep my head still during the surgery?" I asked.

"We clamp your head in a kind of three-point vice. It is rather uncomfortable, so that's why we will wait for the anesthesia to take effect."

"How are you doing, Jens?" It was Dr. Dobelle, sitting somewhere near the end of the bed near my head, probably so he can get a good look at what's under the hood, I figured. His voice was slurred as if he was very tired.

"Oh, it's you, Dr. Dobelle," I said, wondering how much he would participate in the surgery. "I guess you're here to make sure everyone does things right?" "You bet," he said quite matter-of-factly. "Since you're our first patient to be implanted with this thing, we might have to make a few alterations during the procedure."

Lorri had been standing by, watching. I was aware of her, even though she said nothing. It must have been overwhelming for her to watch me. I had no idea what she was thinking. This was my last chance to escape. The needles were in place now, but still no anesthesia was administered. If I just got up now, insisted the needles be pulled out, I could take her hand and get out of here. But there would be no place to go except the dark void of blindness. She knew that too. I closed my eyes and waited.

"You can stay and watch if you wear these scrubs," someone said to Lorri. I could not remember to whom the voice belonged, but it was obvious he was talking to Lorri.

"No," I heard her say in a haggard voice. Not a good idea, I thought. These people did not have a clue as to our history, our circumstances of life that led to my being here, or of the stakes involved. I was just a subject to them, an interesting thing to open up, play around with, and then see what happens. To Lorri I was a lover, a man, the one who offered to take her to a new level of happiness and struck down by fate, the one in whom she trusted to assist in childbirth when the system failed her. The people gathered here would never understand, just like Dr. Girvin would never imagine his own wife laying here now, neither would Dr. Dobelle want to imagine his treasured son Marty here either.

I felt Lorri's hand clasp mine for an instant. The entire futility of our existence, our hopes, anxieties, despair, the persisting tenderness between us despite the foreboding future dedicated to vain attempts to correct an event gone wrong, converged upon us in that moment, as more words were spoken between us without making a sound. Her gesture bordered upon that of a good-bye. I heard her walk off, leaving the room.

I awoke under the most torturous circumstances. Every part of my body ached in the most overpowering sensation of agony, my muscular control erratic with the most uncontrollable shaking of every limb threatening to vault me from the bed I was on. My head and body was on fire—I had every reason to believe I had unintentionally awoken during the surgery. "Put me back out . . ." I begged, hoping someone would hear me, but I couldn't make any intelligible sound.

"Why is he shaking like that?" I heard the voice of Lorri, frantically demanding an explanation from the bystanders. "It's just a reaction from the anesthetic . . ." I heard the voice of John Girvin. I wanted to scream out that I have had anesthetics many times before but never felt like this afterward, but all that came from my mouth was a groan. Something had pity on me and knocked me back out.

I was in a sort of trance, listening to a series of noises I could not identify for what must have been a couple of hours before I began to make sense of it. Every now and then, a little device would start up very close to me, sounding like an emergency tire pump—the type one would plug into an automobile's cigarette lighter socket—which would then clasp my arm for a few seconds and then relent its pressure. I heard a few beeping noises as one would hear when first booting up a household computer. Then there were the moans, spaced out screams of extreme suffering as one hears in the best acted out scenes on television horror shows. My head hurt, I felt very light-headed, and my thoughts were a jumble of confusion. I tried to think of simple things, like my right hand opening and closing. I didn't yet try to count the fingers as I may drop into a cloud of confusion again. I tried to sleep, a feat on its own given the automatic blood pressure tester was activating every fifteen minutes, and the screams of my neighbors, whoever they were, were intense at times. I noticed in time that when the screams started, someone would scurry over, and in little time the screaming wound down to an agonized moan. I was quiet—the majority of the pain I felt when first waking up had mostly subsided. Two people who were walking around in this room were talking to one another, but I had no idea what they were saying.

I tried again to count fingers and seemed to manage as I did land on the number five when I was done. I sat up. I did not feel like myself, but it was good to move. By all the sounds around me, and with my head level, I could make out the size of the room—about as large as that of a school classroom,

I judged. Sitting up was quite an effort, and I breathed hard. My head felt uncomfortable. The two people who were talking approached me.

I wanted to speak, but all I thought in was German words. One of the nurses spoke first.

"Lay down . . . lay down . . . you cannot sit." She gently pushed me back, but I was ready to fall over anyways.

"Where am I?" I had finally found my words.

"Intensive care. Now you must rest . . . sleep . . ." She must have given me an injection as I went right back into a troubled unconsciousness, having only a moment to think of what kind of a terrible accident I must have been involved in.

It was the next day when I was back in the hospital room where I originally was wheeled from. I heard the familiar bustle of hospital staff and patients in the corridor and the voice of Lorri at the side of my bed.

"How are you?" she asked, posing the sentence delicately. My thoughts were clearer now, her voice having switched my brain back into thinking the English language was actually in my head. I was once again aware why I was here and what I was doing here. "I'm . . . not . . . sure." I was astonished as to how slowly I now spoke. It was as if my intelligence quotient had dropped from a healthy number to one in the single digits. I tried again, this time to myself, but had no better luck. My head throbbed terribly. There was a bandage around my head, and I slipped my hand in between it and my forehead, but felt little tension.

"You've still got some hair," Lorri pointed out. Sure enough, the first few inches of the front of my head still had my curly hair which Lorri had cut to within an inch or so in length prior to my trip to Portugal. I didn't dare stick my hand further into my bandage to explore the extent of my hair.

"My head hurts," I pointed out laboriously, neither my tongue nor my mouth cooperating with speech. I fell back asleep, yet remaining semiconscious as I heard the mumbled confusion of the activity around me.

I awoke again to the sound of the food carts being brought in. I felt very uncomfortable, as if I had drunk far too much the night before. Accompanying this was a searing pain in my body, with the concentration on the head. I sat up and almost screamed from the pain of the throbbing in my head. I must have caused some sort of ruckus as a nurse came in short time and gave me a healthy injection into my leg. The pain was subdued, as long as I did not move. It hurt to lie on my back as my head throbbed profusely in the area at the back. Moreover, there was a terrible crinkling noise in the back of my head every time I moved, like that made when wrapping up an article with tin foil. I had the impression it was the piece of bone from my skull about to cave in. Yet I could not rightly turn over onto my side because of the presence of various intravenous tubes and the catheter. I was very uncomfortable.

Lorri offered me a bite of food to eat.

"It's really good fish," she said, trying it out. I wasn't going to be any better if I didn't eat, so I tried. To my astonishment, I could not open my mouth further than the width of one finger. That barely left room for the fork.

"You've got to open your mouth when you eat," Lorri reminded me.

"I can't," I said insistently, wondering what was going on. "I just can't open it any further." I sat up slowly, taking my time this time so as to avoid the throbbing in my head, which was always there as a pronounced ache, reminding me that there was something in my head that didn't belong there.

As I was sitting in front of the food tray that had been wheeled up to my bed so that it was on my lap, I noticed a warm liquid dripping out from behind my ears and onto the tray. I moved the food up the tray so as to avoid it from dripping into my meal. "What's this stuff running out of me," I asked Lorri.

"Blood?" Lorri peered at it, then replied in a strained voice. "It's not blood—it's kind of a pinkish sauce . . ."

John Girvin came in and greeted us in his usual flamboyant fashion. I had expected Dr. Dobelle to come, but he was nowhere around.

"How are things with you?" asked John.

"I don't feel quite so good right now. I have a terrible headache." I motioned to the liquid on the food tray. "What's this dripping out from under my bandage?"

John did not even give a close inspection, apparently familiar with the procedure and its consequences.

"That's your spinal fluid," he pointed out. I guessed that meant brain fluid, which really would be the same stuff. I felt sick and lost what little appetite I had.

"I can't seem to open my mouth hardly at all," I complained. "We had to cut into part of your jaw muscles behind your ears as yours seem to grow higher up your head than the norm. That should get better in a couple of weeks," he reassured me, and added, "and the dripping of spinal fluid should stop in a couple of days."

The next day, my headache was worse. The nurses gave me regular pain shots, their efficient, loving manner being the bright spot during my misery. The nurse would slap the part of my thigh where the injection was to be administered, following a brief message, upon which the injection would be entirely unnoticeable. It took that extra several seconds to do that make all the difference in the world, the same several seconds that were lacking in the Canadian hospitals, or at least those where I stayed, where efficiency was the number one, and seemingly only, concern.

Once a day there at CUF were two nurses who bathed me and managed to change the bedsheets without my leaving the bed. Together they would gently move me to one side of the bed, lift the old sheet up on the empty side, lay down in entirety the new sheet in its place, transfer me to the other side, and finish making the bed. The two attendants chatted happily together while at work, giving me the impression that they were enjoying themselves and that I was just as welcome to be there.

"The hospital administration must choose workers who are always in a good mood," I said as they closed the door behind themselves.

"Yeah," agreed Lorri, "I can tell this is a private hospital by the fact that the staff actually has the time for you."

With the catheter gone the next day, it was up to me to go to the bathroom. I had been looking forward to getting out of bed, dragging the intravenous wherever I went. However, I quickly changed my mind when I sat up, my head throbbing angrily. It took another minute to get my feet on the floor. Every move caused a searing pain in my head that threatened to cause it to explode. It took another minute just to stand up, my head hurting beyond anything I had ever felt before. I held onto Lorri while I shuffled painfully to the bathroom. Gritting my teeth, it took all the concentration I had to keep from screaming from the sheer pain of the experience. The trip to the bathroom and back, probably less than twenty-five feet in total, was one of the longest trips I had ever made.

This routine of pain continued incessantly over the course of the next four days. It always took a good fifteen minutes to visit the washroom, the pain in my head multiplying exponentially with every movement of my head. I also noticed that any low-frequency noises bothered me as it increased the pain in my head. It seemed that there was a loading bay underneath my room where a freight truck would be left running, probably in order to keep the refrigeration unit working. The sound was barely audible, but it seemed to vibrate the components within my head. This happened for about two hours every morning, during which I cursed the very existence of it.

It was the second day after my operation when the nurses had to change my bandage.

It was soaked with brain fluid, as was my pillowcase. Lorri watched from a distance as they unveiled the damage, while Lorri held the CBC camera to film the procedure. I hoped Lorri wouldn't faint upon the sight. Luckily, she was tough in this respect, as my head was not a pretty sight.

"It looks like a football with the stitches in it," said Lorri. I didn't dare touch it. I only ventured as far as feeling my hair left at the front of my head, a band of hair perhaps three inches in width starting from my forehead. It was matted and disgusting, making me conclude that we might as well have shaved the whole scalp before the operation, as this bit of hair will be difficult to wash without contaminating the area of surgery. "Can you see the jacks?"

"Yeah. Your scalp is kind of red right now."

Fluid dripped out from around the jacks and ran down my neck as the nurses disinfected the region around them as well as the stitches, which were about a half centimeter apart starting from behind one ear, going up and over the top of the back of my head and down to the other side. Dr. Domingo was there as well, reassuring me that all was going as predicted.

"Then why do I have such a terrible headache?" I asked. Jerry never mentioned having one to me.

"We don't know yet," he said, "we didn't really anticipate it." The pain continued. It still took considerable effort to speak at a less than normal rate. My pillow was still soaked with spinal fluid, and I often had to flip it over just to have a dry spot to lie on while a nurse brought another one. At night I slept uncomfortably, laying mostly on my face rather than the back of my head, which was becoming increasingly tender. The most peculiar event took place when I had a dream that was so realistic I actually thought I was awake. I had always been able to distinguish a dream from reality, but this time I was truly confused. I asked John Girvin about it the next day.

John was sitting in the chair next to the bed. It was the third day after the surgery, and I was not feeling well. "We are going to do a little bit of surgery right here, Jens," he informed me to my dismay.

"That's all I need," I said. "What's wrong?"

"Well, you see," John began to explain. "It had been a good two decades since we did this last on volunteers, and we forgot a little trick. When we cut the holes out of the scalp so that the little jacks can stick through, we use a tool resembling a cookie cutter. In order to ensure the hole is not too big once the scalp is stretched over your skull, one must stretch the scalp tight before cutting in the holes, otherwise the holes will be too large. In your case, we forgot to stretch the scalp. We want to make a couple alterations with stitches around the pedestals right now."

I winced at the thought of more prodding and poking in such a tender place.

"Will that slow down the dripping of brain juice?" I asked, noticeably showing my distaste for that situation.

"It might. That really only stops once the skull heals up." John took off the bandage and closely inspected the scalp. I felt the cool air on my naked scalp. The total lack of a bandage relieved slightly the headache. John noticed my discomfort. "You are scaring us a bit at the office, Jens." He went on to say, "You really shouldn't have a headache like that. We didn't expect this at all." He peered at the jacks, then stood back and announced, "We do have good news—you don't need that surgery. It looks like it may heal on its own."

The nurses started to bandage me up again. I decided to ask John a few things as he had expected to make time for this surgery anyways.

"John, I seem to dream in a peculiar fashion now, more like hallucinations. Is that only temporary?"

"It is apparent in some patients undergoing brain surgery. We cannot explain it, but it should go away," John explained, giving an example of another man who had been a patient of his who had the most vivid hallucinations during his convalescence. "How did the operation go, anyway?" I finally had the desire to talk about it. I had been trying to concentrate upon pain management up to now.

"It took over four hours," began John, reflecting upon that afternoon in the operating room, "but I think we wasted the first hour just trying to figure out how to position you. We had never done a bilateral implant before, so the same angle of approach we used with the volunteers would not be sufficient. We finally decided upon having you facedown, with your head supported in the three-point vice."

He walked over to my bed and showed me the small impressions on my head, one close to each temple. The third was hard to find, as it was underneath the hair on my head. They would have been very uncomfortable to put up with when conscious, as each point poked through the skin and into the bone to ensure stability. "The operation went as planned after that, but we did have to remove and sear some crossover blood vessels joining the left and right visual cortex. They were in the way of installing the implants. We had to make sure they didn't bleed."

It did not sound to me like the procedure was really that simple. There is no way anyone could tell what those vessels actually were supposed to do. I did not bother asking John, as it was highly unlikely he would respond. "Well, you're just going to be a bit less apt to remember something now, or to grasp new concepts, but you'll still be able to walk and talk, except, maybe, a little slower." I wondered if I really would have gone this far if I had known this would be part of the routine. It was too late now.

On the fifth day I was able to move around a bit. I took about five minutes to visit the bathroom now, taking care not to bend down and get back up too fast. Any sudden movement, or even the sudden cessation of a movement, would produce an overwhelming sensation that the top of my head was about to blow off. I was informed I would be leaving the next morning. I didn't feel ready yet, but the surgeons, Dr. Domingo and Dr. Girvin, assured me that since the majority of my dripping of brain fluid stopped, it was safe to get my rest in my hotel now. They did not suspect I had to climb four stories in order to get there.

I was walking past the checkout area with Lorri, slowly so as to avoid restarting the pain in my head, when Lorri said, "Oh, there is a man with a cane, and a woman guiding him. He looks American. Maybe he is one of the patients checking in." We introduced ourselves, the telltale bandage around my head giving away my identity as a patient before I even got to mention it.

"How are you feeling?" asked the man, who was in his early twenties, having lost his sight at age eighteen. His mother Nancy was leading him. His name was Dennis, a seemingly strong man, who was all too ready to see again. His mother was one of the nicest women I had ever met. We engaged in discussion regarding our past and how we ended up here. It was refreshing to talk to someone who wasn't just a doctor, analyzing my condition.

"So, Jens," Dennis asked me, "did it hurt?"

"Yeah, it sure did," I said, reciting the gravity of the headache.

"Dr. Dobelle said it would be a minor procedure when he wrote us," Nancy reminded us.

"Yeah, let's see, 'you will have a small hole in your skull. This could be done on an outpatient basis . . .'" What a joke!" We all laughed at this, Dennis louder than me as my head hurt too much. I didn't think it was all that funny anymore anyways. I had the urge to tell Dennis to run, but then, who was I kidding? He, like me, had no place to go but into a dark void like a life sentence behind bars. We wished him luck with his operation.

Lorri and I walked very carefully out of the hospital's doors, taking several moments when approaching a step that threatened to restart a throbbing pain deep within my skull. I felt weak and uncoordinated, but I was glad to be moving at the same time. I wore the cowboy hat that not only served to cover up the injury on my head, which would surely attract undue attention, but also gave me a bit of comfort as to what may approach me and hit me on the head. The hat had an empty space under it as it did not fit right over the top of my head but rather sat perched on top. Moreover, it had a wide brim that would warn me of an oncoming obstacle should there be one. Normally, hitting my head off a doorframe that was a bit too low would pose a minor inconvenience, but this time it would be catastrophic.

We rounded the corner of the block, heading toward the pedestrian bridge joining the CUF with the office of the Dobelle Institute, and there I found the delivery truck, its motor quietly idling at its low frequency, vibrating the implants in my head like loose components in a child's toy that had been dropped once too often.

"We've got to get out of here," I said to Lorri, tugging at her hand for her to hurry. "The sound of that truck is going to make me go bonkers." Lorri had to pay close attention to what noise I was talking about as the truck was really not very loud at all. It wasn't until we were in the building of the Dobelle Institute that I could blot out the noise.

I was glad that the elevators were slow in the building, as that saved my head from more horrible pain. I was already feeling tired out and ready for a nap when we walked into the office. Dr. Dobelle was there along with Dr. Gore and Dr. Girvin. Steve was gone, more than likely checking in Dennis, the new patient, and Jim, the other engineer, was bustling around with some electronics. Beth Seelig was nowhere in the office. "How are you doing, Dr. Dobelle?" I greeted him. "I had figured you would visit me in the hospital." I had not seen him once while I was there.

"Just been too busy, Jens," he replied. "I left that part in the hands of the surgeons. But now while you are here, we may as well see what you went through all this for."

I had been prepared to make a polite but firm commentary in regards to the underestimation of the extent of the operation I had just received, clarifying the physical hardship that the operation posed in contrast to his description of it. But now that Dr. Dobelle suggested that we see what we really accomplished, I let the issue fall as quickly as it arose in my head. He'd be forgiven for his misleading statements if this worked. "After all," I thought, "I would still have gone through with it had I a better idea of what faced me." That is, if it works.

"What is it that you want to do?" I asked. I had had an inkling he would want to test me but had imagined myself in a lot better physical condition five days after the surgery. Ever since the surgery, I hadn't even thought about seeing again. My priorities lay in survival, in being able to deal with the pain, minute by minute, and in being able to make it to the bathroom and back without the top of my head blowing off. Now I thought again of seeing.

"We're gonna hook you up and stimulate your visual cortex," he said, turning around and yelling, "Jim! Get the equipment ready and start it up!" He turned back to me.

"We're going to see how many of the phosphenes you can see, and which ones are the better ones, given you have two different implants with different electrode sizes in your head. Hopefully it works," he added.

"It had better work, after all this!" I said, noting the sounds of agreement coming from Lorri. "Yeah, it had better work," added Lorri.

"If it doesn't," started Dr. Dobelle, launching himself with his one leg toward the "testing room" at the back of the office, "we'll just pop it out and put a better implant in." Dr. Dobelle was seemingly totally oblivious to the suffering I had endured the last few days. The very thought of someone reopening my head was too much. All I could think of was that that would kill me, and if it didn't, I'd wish it did. All I could think was that if it didn't work, it would stay in there for a long, long time. I said nothing.

John Girvin approached me once I was seated in an office chair, facing a large table upon which the stimulator and computer lay. Jim was seated at my right side, also at the table, mastering a computer keyboard. Dr. Dobelle was being pushed by John Girvin toward the table as well, taking his place at my left. I surveyed the tabletop with my hands while Dr. Girvin was in another room looking for peroxide. In front of Jim, there was a laptop computer that he was using to set the parameters and control the computer of the vision system, which was in turn connected to a stimulator. There was a large, ancient-looking oscilloscope on the table, its noisy fan whirring incessantly. Its purpose was to measure the current flow to each of my electrodes as they were given a stimulation voltage. There was only one switch on the vision system itself—the one I would get to take home. This was only an on–off switch, nothing else.

"What are you looking for?" Dr. Dobelle asked as I felt around on the tabletop in front of me. There was nothing in front of him on the table. I had expected Dr. Dobelle to be actively participating in the entire process, showing Jim how it was done, or at least be sitting in a position whereby he would double-check Jim's settings before proceeding. But Jim was the only one who saw the settings typed on the laptop as he sat at the side of the table across from Dr. Dobelle, the computer screen folded up, blocking any possibility of Dr. Dobelle ever seeing it.

Dr. Girvin came back, holding a small bottle of peroxide. As he unwrapped the bandage, he explained.

"After your surgery, we learned to keep the small plastic covers on the pedestals before doing the implantation. In your case, we forgot, and there is quite a bit of blood and stuff crusted into your implants which we have to clean up before we can hook you up." He opened the bottle and asked me to lean forward somewhat, leveling the implanted pedestals. I hoped this wouldn't hurt.

There was a bubbling noise like boiling water in a teakettle as John applied the peroxide. There was no pain. I hoped it would do the trick, as I had no intention of having this mistake fixed through surgery.

"How delicate is the pedestal?" I asked John Girvin.

"The outside flange is made of titanium, but the inside is a plastic composite. It is actually a jack meant for connecting telephone cables, and it has a limited lifetime. There is a bigger hole in the middle that is threaded for the connecting screw, and there are seventy-two small pin-sized holes in a pattern around that hole into which seventy-two little corresponding pins mate from the cable. That is why you will be wearing small four-inch long cables called 'savers' all the time once you have the system at home. That way you connect and disconnect using these savers, which will eventually wear out, but then we can replace them without surgery. That saves your pedestal."

"I guess since the pedestal and electrode array are connected as one unit, if the pedestal goes, it would mean pull the whole thing out and put in a new array," I said, wincing at the thought of another surgery. More than likely, I'd just be left with one instead of two, I thought.

"Yeah," said Dr. Dobelle, fidgeting with the allen wrench used to hook up my cables, "it would be impossible to solder another jack onto the same wires, so we'd have to pull it back out. But I figure in a couple of years, we will have a bigger and better system that you'd get for free, so you'd have those replaced anyhow."

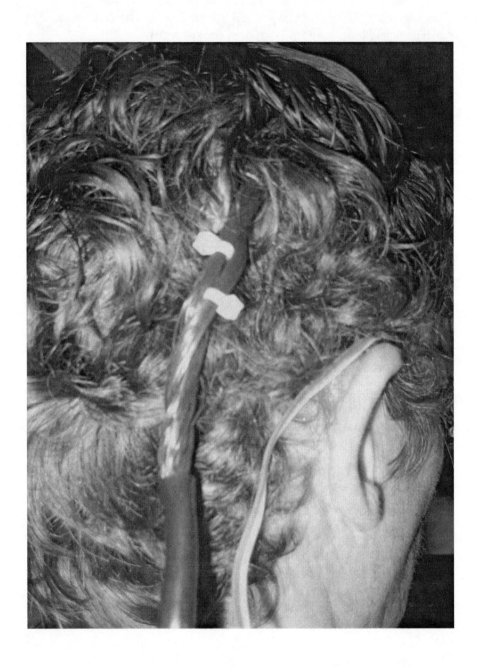

"I'm not so sure about that right now," I said. John was approaching me with a cable, which was a full seven feet long. It consisted of seventy-two 32-gauge wires in a bundle the size of my little finger in diameter, a connector on each end measuring less than a dime in diameter. There was a screw in the center of the jack, well hidden between the wires. This screw was driven by a 1/16 inch allen wrench. John took this wrench from Dr. Dobelle's hands. He searched a bit, peering closely at the connector until the small screw mated with the driver. He placed the connector on my head and started to turn the driver. The sound in my head was a crackling crunching sound, which I found deafening. I held my breath, trying to distance myself from the experience. It gave me the sensation equal to that of someone scratching a chalkboard with a wire brush. Finally, John was done.

"Ready, Jim?" said Dr. Dobelle, sitting in his wheelchair, seemingly doing nothing. Jim had reached over the table and clicked on the computer of the vision system, which beeped a response a minute later.

"What size of processor is that?" I asked Dr. Dobelle, wondering if he really knew. "It's a Pentium 166. It has a 256 megabyte flash disk." "That sounds like a big disk," I commented, thinking of typical computer programs for data management using a mere fraction of that space.

"Yeah, I guess it uses it," Dr. Dobelle turned to Jim. "How much of that does the program use?"

"All but about twenty megabytes," replied Jim, connecting the cable coming from my head to a jack similar to my pedestal on the stimulator unit of the vision system. Jim handed Dr. Girvin another cable.

"Just one side has the grounding cables, so you have to use both cables even to stimulate one side," he explained to John, who was making a wide berth around my chair so as to avoid getting tangled up in the cable already connected to my head.

"Ground cables?" I inquired. "Where are they connected to anyways?"

"You have a platinum plate under your scalp for the ground," explained Dr. Dobelle, obviously feeling important to have at least something to do. I was still wondering why he wasn't checking what Jim was typing into the computer. "Four wires of the seventy-two are attached to one of your jacks, making the ground."

"So that must be why I hear this crinkling sound in the back of my head when I lay down." "They could have at least used a mesh instead of a piece of foil," I thought to myself.

John repeated the procedure in connecting the other cable to my head, this time having more difficulties due to the amount of dirt in the pedestal. The scraping noises of the screw turning in its threads made me shiver. I was feeling faint—the stress of the day was overwhelming. Yesterday, I still had the luxury to lie down after ten minutes of being awake, and today, I was already up for over an hour, having walked for a considerable amount of time considering my condition. My head started to ache more.

"Don't strip the screw!" I warned John Girvin, hearing the "click" every time he rotated the screw, indicating it was just starting to catch and then letting go. I wasn't about to trust his judgment entirely if it was my head in question. "No, I think I'll just leave it where it is for now. It will stay there, and it is probably contacting enough for testing." He turned to Lorri, who was holding a camera. "You'll have to run some more peroxide in there once you get home until it is clean." John walked carefully around the cables, which were long enough to drape onto the floor.

"All ready," announced Jim. Dr. Dobelle remained in his chair, staring at the back of the computer screen that faced Jim. Dr. Gore came into the room, taking a seat beside John Girvin. We were all excited as to what would happen next.

"How many pulses?" asked Jim.

"Fifty," replied Bill.

"That'll give a one-second pulse train," stated Jim, typing on the laptop's keyboard.

"Fifty hertz all right for frequency?" Jim stopped typing. "Yeah," said Bill.

"Negative pulse first?" Jim kept entering values into the program.

"That's what we always did" was the reply.

"Right side first?" Jim asked again, his fingers flying over the keyboard.

"Yeah" was Bill Dobelle's reply.

Jim turned to me, talking in a much less strained tone of voice, "You'll see the dots in your left visual field. The right side of your brain actually controls the left side of your visual field." He continued to type, resorting back to his "yes, sir!" style of speaking in addressing Dr. Dobelle. "Just a couple minutes and we're ready."

I sat still on the chair, wondering what to expect. I was going to make a comment to Beth about this moment, as she was the one I had spoken to the most about my emotions regarding this venture, but she was not in the room.

"Where's Beth?" Lorri asked, just as anxious to see her. "She had to go home early," Dr. Dobelle stated in a matter-of-fact manner. A strange silence engulfed the room, the only sounds being the clicking of Jim's computer keys and the whirring of the fan in the oscilloscope.

"I'd have thought she'd be here for the observation," I went on to say, recalling her recorded studies on this subject in the past. Nobody said anything.

"How many electrodes do you want to test in the right side?" asked Jim, breaking the silence.

"All of them."

"We can only do sixty-four on each side," began Jim slowly, in a manner similar to that of a child expectant of a scolding. "We're still missing a multiplexer on each side in the stimulator."

Dr. Dobelle, who had been busy picking his teeth with the allen wrench used to connect my cables, put it on the table noisily.

"Why didn't you tell me?" Bill accusingly accosted Jim in a voice bordering on hysteria. "Why didn't you tell me?!" He repeated, his voice rising in pitch and volume with every word. There was stillness in the room as even Jim's fingers stopped tapping the keyboard. Jim didn't reply. Not that there was anything to say, either. If Dr. Dobelle had intended to make everyone as uncomfortable as possible in showing his authority, he succeeded.

The words of Dr. Dobelle echoed through my head from our first meeting. "On the shelf and ready to go . . ." is how he described the system. None of them would have the right number of multiplexers installed. "More work to do before I'd be taking this system home," I thought to myself.

"We're ready," Jim said, sounding defeated even though the big moment was about to arrive. This was not really the type of atmosphere I had anticipated in my first encounter with sight after eighteen years of blindness.

"First electrode," said Jim as he pushed a button on the keyboard. I heard a beep coming from the laptop and then sat bolt-upright in my chair, my breathing stopped in mid-breath. A small, black dot appeared on my field of vision, slightly downward and to the left of my center point of focus. It flickered there for a second and disappeared. Its measurement was no larger than that of a penny held at arm's length. It caught me by surprise, the first input to my vision, even though it was a black dot on a gray background feeling unbelievably refreshing, like finally finding the switch of a light in an otherwise black room following many hours of searching in vain.

"That was beautiful! It was a small dot, black in color, just to the bottom and left of my center of vision!" I could hardly contain my excitement. I forgot about my headache.

"You mean you already stimulated that one?" drawled Bill Dobelle at Jim, still in a confrontational voice. "Before you stimulate, say 'now' out loud."

"We have the beep already on the computer," said Jim. "That tells the patient we are stimulating."

Bill leaned forward in his chair, facing Jim and talking in a slow, deliberate manner with an obvious intention of humiliating Jim further. "Before you stimulate, say . . . now . . ."

If Jim had picked up his bags right then and quit, I could not have held it against him; but I thanked my lucky stars that he didn't.

"Anyways, it worked, and that is what's important," I said, breaking the silence. Neither John Girvin nor Dillis Gore was becoming involved. It appeared that Dr. Dobelle was running the show, and successful responses from my electrodes is what he wanted at all costs. Jim's feelings just had to take the backseat for now.

"Now," muttered Jim, pushing another button.

"Nope," I replied, seeing nothing. Jim readjusted the computer, once again muttering the telltale word: "Now."

I saw it this time, at a slightly different place, but still on the left and bottom corner of my visual field. This time the dot was slightly larger, about an inch in diameter at arm's length. It produced a dim, flickering light that lasted for a second. It was beautiful. If I had had control of the button on the keyboard, I would have hit it over and over again. "Yes!" I replied, giving a brief description of the phosphene. "Did you have to increase the voltage on that one?" I asked.

Jim did not answer. He probably did not want any more trouble from Dr. Dobelle, I mused. John broke the silence, saying, "We bring it up, that's for sure." I did know this from his Journal 2000 write-up, in which he stated that voltages ranged right up to 20.

"We start up with 0.5 V." Dr. Dobelle was forced to explain. "Then we try 1, 2, 4, 8, 12, and then 16 V."

I thought about it. That means that the first phosphene called for .5 V, and the next at 1 V.

"You go back and forth then," I said in conclusion, "until you have the threshold?"

"Yeah. We cut it by half every time until you can't see the last value. Then we take the value previous to that one."

"Next electrode," announced Jim, and then, like a good employee, "Now . . ."

"Nothing," I announced. Jim increased the voltage to 1.

"Now," he said again. I saw a very faint flicker very close, but not right on my center point of vision. Jim looked at the screen of the oscilloscope.

"Not really," I said, "it is kind of a flicker that I am not sure was there."

"Bring it up another one," said Dr. Dobelle, once again picking his teeth with the allen wrench, making metallic clicking noises against his teeth.

"Now," said Jim as the computer beeped.

I gasped. There was a bright, white flickering light almost at my center of vision, surrounded by the most beautiful rings of color, as one would see on a perfect rainbow. I wanted to look more directly at it, but the dot of light moved in the same direction as I tried moving my eyes. I remember that when I could see, as a child, my brother and I would look at a lamp and then close our eyelids, and then move around our eyes to see the fading image of the lamp move correspondingly in our visual field.

"Did that one hurt?" asked Dr. Dobelle, noticing my response.

"No, not at all," I said quietly, still reeling at the novelty of the experience. "It was just so pretty. There were colors like the rainbow surrounding the dot this time, making the most beautiful design." In fact, it was similar to letting a drowning man come up for a single gasp of air before pushing him back underwater.

Jim lowered the voltage to 1.5, then to 1.25, then went on with the next electrode. He wasn't writing anything down. "The last current was 5 milliamps or so," Jim informed Dr. Dobelle, who was motioning to the machine on the table. Even the oscilloscope wasn't facing Dr. Dobelle. Jim was in total control. Jim wasn't writing anything down. I hoped the computer was storing the values. This privilege of testing a patient just freshly implanted wouldn't come along too often.

"What are the size of these electrodes again?" asked John, who was still sitting in his chair, some distance away from me. Jim looked over his notes. "These are the 1 mm electrodes."

The testing became more of a routine once the exhilaration of the initial experience of the first few phosphenes was over. Jim would say "next electrode . . . followed by the now . . ." upon which I would say no . . . or yes as Jim readjusted the voltage every time until I could hardly see it, the point considered the threshold. I could tell by keeping track of the number of times Jim would say "Now . . ." as to what voltage we were at when seeing threshold. It became apparent that the color would only appear after voltage was increased well past 25 percent of the threshold voltage. The color did not appear with every phosphene; it only happened with about every four to five or so. The majority of the dots were the size of a smaller to larger coin held at arm's length, although those straying from the center point of vision became larger. They were harder to describe, unless they were big. All the dots were on the left side of my visual field, and all were under the median line of my visual field. The bigger phosphenes were often misshapen, looking like bananas rather than dots.

"There's a banana!" I said, feeling thrilled nonetheless for being able to see. It was pretty in color, showing different colors of the spectrum while giving off a speckled, flickering light that reminded me of looking at a freshly caught rainbow trout when I had been fishing with my father on the frozen ice of the Williston Lake many, many years ago.

"That one had higher current," said Jim. I could not understand why Dr. Dobelle did not have the oscilloscope facing him, as he would be able to tell Jim when to stop raising the voltage, as the voltage was directly responsible in controlling current flow. I couldn't imagine that Dr. Dobelle would be incompetent when it came to reading one; I supposed that he had his reasons for not taking this part of it too seriously.

"How much?" asked Dr. Dobelle.

"12 milliamps," replied Jim.

Dr. Dobelle turned to me.

"Do you have any pain or tickling sensation at the back of your head, right about between the two jacks?"

"No, not at all," I replied. "Why do you ask?"

"We've implanted the ground plane there. If it gets sore, just let me know." I wasn't sure if I would tell him of such little problems, as I was in this program to stay, now that I saw the phosphenes.

"Did you just push the stimulation button?" I asked Jim, not having heard a "now . . ." from him or a beep from the computer. "No," said Jim quickly. He probably thought he was going to get in trouble again. I saw a flickering phosphene that was on for one second, then off for the next, and then on.

"I see a phosphene even without electricity, sometimes on, then off, just to turn back on," I said.

Dr. Dobelle explained, "Those are called residual phosphenes. They happen often when you are first stimulated in your visual cortex for the first time after so many years of nothing. Kind of like a muscle spasm on a person walking for the first time after decades of paralysis. We'll have to wait until it is gone."

We waited while I saw it go on and off for a full minute. It looked nice enough, but its flashing started to make me sick. I felt faint, wondering if I would fall asleep right there in the chair. The day had been a hard one, considering how sore I was from the surgery, but in spite all, I wished that blinking dot would go away, as I associated it more and more with my faint feeling. Luckily, it went away in time. If I had fainted right here, neither Jim, John, or Dillis would be able to catch me in time. And as for Bill helping me, well, forget it, I thought.

We proceeded once the residual phosphene stopped. We were nearing the end of the sixty-four we could try, given the missing component in the stimulator. None of those hurt, even though there were a couple that gave me a little tingling sensation in my right eyeball. This only happened when Jim hit the 12—or 16-V selection.

"That's all for the right visual cortex," said Jim, pressing a few other buttons on the computer. "There were nine with no contact."

No contact meant that there was no current flow detected by the oscilloscope even though sixteen volts were applied. "What are we going to do with the larger phosphenes?" I asked Dr. Dobelle. "I must have had over fifty small ones, like a coin at arm's length, but there were a few larger ones."

"We'll throw them out. We just won't use them," corrected Dr. Dobelle, noticing my quizzical look when he suggested throwing them out. "Those bananas are just a recipe for an epileptic seizure."

The last two words rang through my very sore head. Epileptic seizures were not something I had ever imagined having. I could not imagine myself or anyone else, to that matter, conducting a life with the constant threat of an epileptic seizure looming about, ready to strike at any instant. I had never, never imagined myself having a seizure where I'd lose total control . . . it seemed too much to bear, just the thought of it happening to me. Was that what the faint feeling was when I saw that blinking light?

"Almost fifty phosphenes," Dr. Dobelle was talking to himself, obviously pleased with the success. "You know, Jens, Jerry did not even see phosphenes the first time he was stimulated. We just sent him home and called him back a month later, and then he saw the phosphenes. He never, ever did see color, and neither did Brindley's patients in the 1960s. You're the first one to see color!"

Jerry had walked into the testing room and sat down quietly at the far end of the table. "The old king is dead . . ." he said jokingly. "You're the phosphene king now, Jens." I laughed gingerly, trying to enjoy the events as they unfolded before me despite my fatigue and very dominating headache. My body hurt, and my head throbbed. I wanted to lie down.

Yet, as I assessed the number of dots I saw, all in a rather close cluster on my left visual field, between clock positions 6:15 and 8:45 and from .5 to 6 inches from center of vision at about arm's length away from my face. "I should be able to make some very good pictures with the cluster of dots I saw, considering their small size," I said to Dr. Dobelle. He, along with John and Dillis, voiced their approval to the idea of making pictures with the phosphenes that were, according to them, a bonus, considering that Jerry had seen nothing when tested immediately following the surgery. "Only thing is," I continued, "I don't see any on the top left quadrant of my visual field. Why is that?"

"It's a small implant," John Girvin explained. "It's a pretty small array, which only covers a portion of your visual cortex, and it is easy to miss the center of vision area. Your crossover vessels were enough of a problem to contend with during the implantation, and we did not want to push it, so once the implant was in, we just left it right there. The other side, having larger electrodes, is naturally larger in size and perhaps better located."

"So, in other words," I said, punctuating the obvious, "what I have is what I'm stuck with."

"Yeah," Bill said consolingly. "Your map is a lot better than Jerry's. His are just in a straight line from top to bottom. No lateral dimension to speak of."

Jerry spoke up. "All I have is seventeen anyways. Besides, we're not done yet."

I wasn't about to do anything about it either. If I can see them all like this for the rest of my life, I figured I could learn to do a lot of things with them that I wouldn't have been able to do without sight at all.

"Once you have phosphene fusion," Bill said in a manner suggesting great knowledge of the subject, "your fifty phosphenes will act like several hundred. Trust me. But getting back to what Jerry just said—that it's not over yet—let's try the other side."

In spite of the extreme fatigue I felt physically, along with the throbbing in my very sore head, I felt strangely enlightened by the light I had seen. It was inexplicable, as if a veil had been lifted long enough for me to recover my composure deep within the part of my being that controlled my contentment. There seemed to be a brighter glow to the world, the same glow that gives us the ambition to continue to do what we must in order to survive despite pain and hardship. I hadn't felt this way for a long, long time. I stuck out my head willingly for the next series of testing.

Jim fiddled with the computer for a few minutes. There was no need to hook up new wires as they were already in place. Jim had disconnected the cables coming from my head temporarily from the stimulator case, connecting instead a square comprising of a grid of 8 × 8 light-emitting diodes that would tell him the system is working. The cables were trailing down onto the floor beside me. Their weight kept pulling my head backward, so I felt like I was forced to look at the ceiling. I picked up the cable ends and inspected them.

"I'm hoping you can hook those up yourself eventually," Bill Dobelle said as he observed me. He was still sitting in his wheelchair, shifting restlessly.

"No problem," I indicated, taking the allen wrench and placing it into the hole of the screw head. "This is many times bigger than the components I'm used to working with. Whoever can't hook these up would have to be rather clumsy." Bill's attitude gave me a sense of pride, as the majority of people I encountered had already concluded I would not be able to do the simplest of tasks involving dexterity. But then again, I thought, he was from New York, and in New York the people are known to be much more open to new and sometimes controversial ideas than the small-town folk. Whatever the case was, I welcomed Bill's confidence in my abilities.

"The cables are kind of long, aren't they?" I motioned to the section of the cables I was holding, which were still draped on the floor in spite of the ends being held up in my hands. "That's in case you drop the system. It will fall onto the floor rather than rip the guts out of your head." Dr. Dobelle was not putting it very nicely to me at all. I felt sick at the very thought. Yet he was right, there was nothing to give. 32-gauge wire is not very strong, but with seventy-two strands of it, it is as strong as rope. The connections were screwed together, leaving no weak link in the system to give. The weak link would be the little bone screws holding the pedestals attached to the skull. If they ripped out, the seventy-two strands of 36-gauge wire connecting the array to the pedestal would take the brunt of the force, the weakest link there being the array, attached via an encapsulating membrane to the brain, being yanked unceremoniously out, potentially causing catastrophic damage. To top it all off, even if I did manage to make it alive to a hospital in Napanee or Kingston, given that artificial vision implants weren't on their list of concepts to study during the course of their education, the surgeons would not have the foggiest idea what to do about it.

"It can always get caught on something like a parking meter or hydrant while walking, or get closed in a door," I pointed out, giving Bill something to think about.

"You can't be stupid when you have this thing." Dr. Dobelle minced no words when projecting his thoughts. "Those patients who demonstrate a lack of responsibility just don't get the system. It wouldn't really be a success with them anyhow, as this is a trial system for now. Whoever gets the system now is just going to have to be careful."

I was going to have to be really careful. Dr. Dobelle had a point, I figured, as even automobile manufacturers could not design a foolproof car that would not kill someone should they run it into a brick wall. Owner responsibility was the game in that case, and in the case of the vision system, there was no difference. Now I really knew Bill came from New York.

"Ready for the left side," announced Jim, reconnecting the cables to the stimulator box.

I sat back in the chair, wishing it had armrests, as I was becoming increasingly uncomfortable. Jim replaced the battery running the vision system's computer and stimulator and pulled out the power jack from the laptop, a measure later explained by him taken in order to prevent any chance of getting outlet power channeled to the brain.

"First electrode . . . Now . . ." said Jim, well rehearsed from the practice received during the stimulation of the right visual cortex.

"No," I said, seeing nothing.

"Now," repeated Jim, increasing the voltage from .5 to 1.0.

"No," I said again.

"Now," said Jim, as the computer beeped. I still saw nothing.

"Now," said Jim, having set the voltage to 4.

"Ouch!" I retorted, feeling a deep, searing pain inside of my head that lasted for the full second, which was the duration of the pulse. It felt as though a knife had been stuck in my head and twisted.

"Hurt a bit, did it?" said Dr. Dobelle from where he was sitting. He seemed curious but not particularly concerned. Jim had ceased the stimulation, saying nothing.

"Quite a bit," I replied, trying to hide the effect of the pain. "I didn't see any phosphene either."

"Just leave this one and go on with the next," instructed Dr. Dobelle. Jim tapped the keys in reply, followed by his "Now . . ." indicating he was continuing the procedure. He wrote nothing down regarding the electrode number and the pain it caused. We'd have to come across that one again later.

The next few electrodes hurt, some only slightly, others as searing as the first. My head was not getting any better. On some of the electrodes I saw a bit of light, well dispersed at the right side of my visual field as a speckled shimmer ranging about a foot in size at arm's length. I turned to Dr. Dobelle, my head throbbing profusely.

"You know, Bill, I noticed that it is the jump from 2 V to 4 V, or that from 4 V to 8 V, that seems to be the problem here." I knew I was placing myself in a compromising situation by contesting the big man's authority and knowledge, but it was my head after all. "If we increased from 2 V to 3 V instead of doubling the voltage, just like from 4 V to 5 V, then 6 V, etc., the pain would more than likely be a lot less."

Dr. Dobelle would have none of that. He did not even wait a second before replying, "This is the scientific method. This is the way all testing is done. Any other method had already been tested, but found unacceptable."

"Next electrode," announced Jim once again. I braced myself as he said "now." It was only 0.5 V to begin with, so I felt nothing and saw anything either.

"How are the currents on this side so far?" asked Dr. Dobelle, staring at the back of the oscilloscope.

"They're quite a bit higher than the other side. About 10–20 milliamps, sometimes higher, which makes the signal go off the scale off the scope."

"This is the side with the larger 3 mm electrodes, is it?" Jim nodded his head, increasing the testing voltage and saying "now" as he pushed the button on the laptop. This time I saw a light near the center of my visual field, yet not directly on the center, but rather slightly to the right.

"Yes," I announced, glad to have found one without pain. "It is quite a bit bigger though. It's about the size of an egg at arm's length and slightly speckled, meaning it is made of a bunch of little dots with black spots in between. The outer ring of the phosphene is kind of bluish."

"Does it flicker at all?" asked Bill, seemingly glad to have some success on this side.

"Yes, it does," I answered. "But it didn't hurt, anyways." I figured this as a good thing. If they all hurt on this side, it would mean a very small window of view from only the bottom half of the left visual field. I wanted to be able to do something with this.

"Current is still high," pointed out Jim, preparing for the next electrode stimulation.

We continued with this routine until we tested sixty-four of the electrodes on the left visual cortex, which translates into the right visual field. I saw more phosphenes, although they were bigger than those on my left visual field. I was glad to find out that most of the others did not hurt. There were only about three others that hurt and gave no light either. Bill Dobelle sat through all this in his thoughts, quiet, but seemingly paying attention. John and Dillis were still in the room, but they made no comments. I was becoming more and more tired, fighting the urge to lie down. I had stopped giving details about the phosphenes, but I rather just summed up their value as "good to use" or "too big" in order to hurry up the process. I noticed that this time I saw the phosphenes spread out over my entire field of vision, with some dots on the bottom of center of vision, some on top, and a few on the far right. The dots were larger toward the outer edges of my center of vision, while closer to the center they were smaller and more precise. This electrode array did not give any tiny dots like the one on the other side, but rather gave square-looking phosphenes that would have taken up the place of three of the smaller ones seen on the other side. It was obvious that Bill's idea of having better phosphenes with 3 mm electrodes was wrong. The fact that they took more current seemed logical as well, as more brain tissue would be used to conduct current, just like having more resistors of equal resistance in parallel. It was too late to change that now, though, as this stuff was in my head to stay. Everyone listened while Jim ticked the keys on the computer.

"How do you like the phosphenes?" Jerry spoke up, having been quiet for quite some time.

"They're good to look at," I said. "Did you not see any color?" Jerry thought for an instant and replied, "No, mine are only white. Kind of like stars in the sky."

"Mine aren't really like that." I tried to find an object we had once both seen before, which might clarify the description. I found none. "For me, it's more like a coin, slightly out of round, assuming the colors of the rainbow with the edges a bit fuzzy. Their flickering makes them shimmer like a hologram."

It occurred to me then that for the first time in my eighteen years of blindness, I was sharing an image with another blind man, both of us having seen an image that the others in the room, despite their perfect eyes, could only imagine from the words we were speaking. For all the years gone by, it was me who sat at the kitchen table during the occasions that Lorri brought out the family photos, and while the rest of the family pointed and laughed at the pictures, obviously having a good time, I was forced to try to imagine what they saw but felt I had no right to laugh, as it would be only futile to laugh at my own imagined pictures. But here, now, while Jerry and I spoke, it was the others who had to imagine the pictures. So far, I had nothing to complain about, except the pain.

"We're done," Jim said to my relief, just when I was about to ask how many more were left. I had been keeping track of those that did not work and subtracted them from the sixty-four which were tested.

"We have at least forty good ones on this side," I said, my head hurting almost unbearably now. I realized we still had to walk to my hotel and climb four stories on top of that. I was looking forward to going to sleep.

"How many on the other side?" asked Bill, sounding very tired. "How could he have forgotten," I asked myself, "considering how much work he put into this project?" I would have expected him to be counting every electrode—it was turning out to be a long day for him too.

"Fifty on the last side, forty on this one," I summed it up.

"That's six times more than what I have," said Jerry. Despite my headache, I felt good about that news. Jerry had spoken about his vision quality barely allowing him to see that there was "something out there" rather than being able to identify the object, but with my additional phosphenes, I figured, I'd see enough to recognize objects.

"The phosphenes are better on the side with the small electrodes," I said in a frank voice to Bill.

"Yeah," said Bill slowly, "but the voltages are lower with these electrodes that are larger. That's a good thing." He seemed to have forgotten that the currents were higher. I was in no arguing mood. The stuff in my head would not come out no matter what, so it made no sense to push my point. I was glad to see the phosphenes but would still have preferred to have the little dots on both sides of my visual field, and to have had the right side implanted more precisely so that I'd have the dots spread out over my entire left visual field.

"You're doing all right," Bill kept on talking. "Considering Jerry saw nothing, you're doing fine. Once your encapsulating membrane is in place, which is a thin membrane that entirely surrounds the electrode array, it will be permanently in place. You could still get a different result next time we test you."

"Maybe those that hurt today will be better next time," I suggested. "I'd hate to go through that every time we work with the system." I put my head in my hands, leaning on the table. John came over and took off the cables. They were starting to irritate me as they dangled down behind my ears, rubbing on the tender lesions on my scalp where it was cut during the surgery. John wrapped the bandage back around my head, speaking to Lorri, "When do you leave to go home?"

Lorri put down the camera. "In about four days."

"He'll have to go to the hospital to get the stitches removed," he said, gesturing at my head. There were a lot of them, some of them beginning to bother me.

Louise opened the door of the testing room, and after seeing that Bill was not busy, said, "A patient is here to see you."

"Help me out there, Louise," Dr. Dobelle replied.

"You have more patients to interview?" asked Lorri, surprised.

"Yeah, there's a few others to go, needing interviews, etc. You should come out and meet this guy." Bill was wheeled into the conference room by Louise while Lorri and I followed, my head throbbing harder than usual.

I came over and shook the patient's hand, his name also being Jerry, but with the last initial of "D." Jerry D. shook my hand, greeting me warmly in an ancient-sounding voice.

"Jerry D. is seventy-eight years old!" Dr. Dobelle pointed out. "Jerry, here is Jens, a patient just implanted. He just saw practically all of his phosphenes, and he's quite excited about it." Bill couldn't have had better advertising than this.

"Yes, I did see quite a few of them," I said to Jerry D. "This actually does work, believe it or not," I said jokingly. "I'm not sure if I'll have the acuity to see X-rated flicks, but this is a good start. The only complaint I have is that I have had a terrible headache since I got this operation."

"I've been blind since I lost my sight in a mortar attack in 1945, during the Second World War. I hope this works for me. As for a headache, I've never, ever had one."

Lorri and I nudged each other, saying silently to ourselves, "Here's your chance . . ." There was no way he'd make it through this one without a headache . . . This guy was almost eighty years old, and I wasn't so sure he was going to make it through the surgery.

"I'll talk to you in a minute," said Dr. Dobelle, his chair still out in the hallway in front of the conference room. He closed the door and turned to us. "So you guys are off now?"

"Yeah, I need a rest," I said, sighing. My head hurt terribly. "Who's going to do the psychiatric exam for the other patients if Beth Seelig is no longer here?" I was curious, hoping there might be a replacement. I found people who studied the human mind interesting to talk to.

"I am," Dr. Dobelle said, launching himself effectively toward the conference room door with one foot.

"Wow! You can do a lot of things," Lorri said, helping him to the door. Neither of us were so sure if psychiatric exams were really his strong point.

I was counting the steps as we neared the Barca Do Tejo, ducking instinctively upon entering the foyer.

"Stairs?" asked Lorri, as if there was a choice.

"Yes," I replied, having no intention of being stuck in an elevator in this condition. I kept my talking to a minimum as there was a noticeable grating in my head every time I spoke, my voice seemingly vibrating the implants in my head, giving off a sound like someone had placed an object on top of a loudspeaker while in use.

I treasured the cowboy hat I wore, as on the first turn up the stairs, I encountered a section of the concrete ceiling that was too low for me to stand up under. If I had hit my head here, it would have been right on the spot where I was opened up. I was sure that it would have caved right in. Lorri was over a foot shorter than I, making it impossible for her to really see this coming.

As we approached the last flight of steps, I was breathing heavily, my body feeling unresponsive and almost incapable of finishing the journey. I clutched the banister for support. I had been so healthy the last time I climbed this flight of stairs, but this time I was in a sorry state. Never did I ever suspect that I would be so affected by a surgical procedure considered as "day surgery" as described in my first letter received from Dr. Dobelle. I entered the room, leaving the fiddling with the ancient lock up to Lorri. As I lay down on the bed, I thought to myself that I should really still be in the hospital. I did not feel well at all.

Lorri spoke quietly, realizing my sensitivity to noise. "I'm going to find some snacks for us at a store. I'll be back." As I lay there, I wondered if she really expected me to be alive upon her return. All thoughts regarding seeing again were put aside as I struggled to deal with the pain and general sick feeling from the surgery. I'd been up far too long today.

Lorri returned some time later with yogurt and fruit snacks, which were to be our supper that night. I managed to sit up enough to eat, having had a bit of sleep in the most restless manner. The pillow was damp in some places, as my head was still leaking fluid. My headache was worst from the testing procedure, probably from the stimulation of the electrodes that hurt. I was going to have to work on Dr. Dobelle to get him to understand it is worth the extra time to increase the voltage in smaller steps so as to prevent such violent pain. "Better yet," I thought to myself, "once I have the equipment at home, setting the thresholds myself as Bill had suggested the user does in his Journal 2000, I would be very careful not to raise the voltage too much at once."

"I found some nice-looking restaurants we can visit once you're better," Lorri spoke as she ate her measly dinner. "They're just like a house from the outside, but when you go in, it's really nicely set up."

Lorri had done a lot of exploring while I was in the hospital. She had spent a lot of time with me as well, but during the afternoons when I either slept or groaned in agony from the headache, she needed to get out some. The weather was beautiful in Lisbon, and one would have to spend a couple of years just to see everything that there was to see.

"We'll have to come back sometime later when I'm better," I remarked, still unable to speak at my normal speed. I could not open my mouth very far yet either, forcing me to eat only small pieces of fruit at once.

"Yeah, good idea. When you have the equipment and can see," Lorri said.

"That too," I said, not really having thought about the seeing aspect lately. "I meant when this damned headache is gone." I hoped that would actually happen.

That night I awoke from my restless slumber from the sounds of a freighter leaving the harbor, which was only a mile south of our building. The throbbing engines vibrated the objects in my head, causing searing pains in the area where the surgery took place. I sat up in bed, covering my ears, when the most peculiar-looking white light began to appear in my visual field, which was normally darkish-gray to black in color. It started with a small speck of white just to the right of my focal point and started to grow little by little until it occupied the majority of my visual field. It was stark white, with sharp, precise edges in points around the light just like a broken piece of glass. I stared at it, holding my breath while Lorri slept beside me. I noticed my consciousness beginning to fade as I became dizzy and unable to focus on anything but that white light. The thought of a seizure ran through my head. I tried all I could to shut out that light. I couldn't afford to have a seizure as I could bang my head and that would be the end of me. How does one shut out a light that is held in front of the eyes while the eyelids are pried open? I had to get away from this light is all I knew but had no idea how. I concentrated on the noise of the freighter instead, which seemed to be fading. I wanted to talk so as to divert attention from this light, but the thought ran through my mind that perhaps it was the vibration of the implants caused by the noise of the freighter that started this, and more noise would only add to the problem. I prayed the light would go away for the lack of anything else I could do about it. Eventually, it dissipated, leaving me breathing a sigh of relief. It had taken almost an hour for it to pass.

We spent the last four days within five minutes' walking distance from the Barca do Tejo, visiting the restaurants Lorri had discovered the week before. I spent every afternoon in bed, the nap giving me relief from the headache. It could be kept under control by keeping my head movement to a minimum. The stitches in my scalp were becoming increasingly irritating, leaving me little choice but to ask Lorri if she would take them out.

"Since I helped you in the delivery of our children, I guess you could do this for me in spite of what the doctors might think," I said this jokingly to Lorri, knowing she would oblige no matter what. However, it would still look like we were resorting to a form of vigilantism by not entrusting the doctor's opinion as to when the stitches should be removed. They would have to accept this, I figured, as it was me who had to live with the consequences, just like it was Lorri who had to live with the consequences of the doctor's decisions during childbirth. Lorri got out her dollar-store folding scissors attached to her key chain.

A half hour later, they were out. It felt so much better—just like having a large infected sliver taken from one's foot. The burning sensation was gone from around my scar, which had turned a nasty red color.

"I wonder what John Girvin will say when we go to the institute office the day before we leave?" wondered Lorri.

"We'll find out in a couple of days," I replied.

I had been issued a bottle of pills for pain relief before leaving the CUF. They did not work nearly as effectively as did the shots. On the second to last day in Portugal, we went to one of our favorite dining places situated in a small cafe-style setting just off the main street upon which the Dobelle Institute was located.

"Let's go full out tonight and have a bottle of wine," Lorri suggested.

"It might do me some good," I retorted, wondering what the wine would really do. Lorri went through her now well-rehearsed procedure of gesturing in sign language to order our meals, and then I asked, "Do you have wine?"

Immediately, our host returned with two bottles in hand, one of which Lorri pointed out.

"Here's to what remains of my head," I said, raising my glass. "And artificial vision," added Lorri, concentrating on the positive. The wine did a lot of good, rendering the headache to a practical nonexistence. The quality of the wine was superb, and with Lorri for the first time in years not having the responsibility to drive, she could have more than a mere sip. "I should advise the CUF Hospital officials to make it a policy to have wine on the menu. It would save on painkillers," I suggested. By the time we finished the meal, paid the ridiculously low bill and returned to our hotel, we felt a lot better about Portugal.

The following morning, and our last day scheduled in Portugal, we checked in first to the CUF Hospital, from which we were deftly discharged, as there were no more stitches to remove. Dr. Domingo just took one look at the scar, void of stitches, and laughed at Lorri, saying, "Maybe you should work here!" Dr. Domingo always seemed to be friendly and in a good mood.

Next was the Dobelle Institute at 34 Avenida Infante Santo. I felt pretty good this day in comparison to the last several as I could move a bit faster than that of a snail's pace. It still seemed like I would never be able to work in the business of processing firewood again, however. But today the elevators did not bother me so much as we went up to the seventh floor once again.

There was a fair amount of hollering and confusion in the office when we entered. From my observations, there was a foreigner talking with Dr. Dobelle, attempting to speak to him and understand Bill in the English language, which was quite evidently new to him. I could understand the foreigner's words, but Bill had no idea how to curb his own speech to make it more comprehensible. Bill had a tendency to drawl his words as he spoke, rounding off his pronunciation of his consonants allowing only those who grew up with English to make out what he was saying. Dr. Dobelle heard us enter and turned toward me. "Jens, you said once you spoke some German. I have a patient here whose companion was to translate, but he doesn't speak English worth a shit." Lorri and I hoped he wouldn't be able to understand that either. Bill continued, "Can you speak it at all functionally?"

"No problem," I replied. "I grew up speaking that language at home, using only English in school."

"Can you talk to this patient and his friend for me? I'd like you to explain how the system works and what there is involved with the operation and also what you saw when you were stimulated earlier this week. Can you do that much?" It was surprising to both Lorri and I how much Bill entrusted us in representing his company and project when he knew so little of us.

I turned to the voice of the patient, who was muttering to his companion in German. His companion was somewhat flustered at not being able to understand Bill even though he had been able to function perfectly in English school. He must have expected Bill to be speaking university-style English. He was obviously out of luck.

"Guten tag," I said, introducing myself as a patient who just had the operation, saw the dots of light, and was, of all things, still alive. The patient-to-be was a man in his mid-fifties named Klaus, a businessman from Hamburg who had lost his sight six years ago. Louise situated the four of us, Klaus and his companion along with Lorri and I in the conference room where I explained all I knew about the system and my success to date as a patient. Klaus had not yet made up his mind as to whether or not he wanted to go for the operation. I wasn't going to make it for him, but at the same time I realized he was in the same boat as I—either try this, or stay in the dark.

"I lost my sight totally six years ago as a result of a very rare cancer that attacked my only eye," explained Klaus, his story not much better than mine. "I tried all I could to repair it while I was slowly losing its sight. I was born only with one eye, so this one was rather dear to me. I am in the international trade business, traveling continuously. When I lost my sight, I had two kids, a girl about four years old and a son about ten or so. I am still in business. However, if you want to compare its performance to an automobile, it used to run like a Porsche, and when I lost my sight, it now runs like a bicycle."

"It sure is bad, this whole affair with loss of sight," I said sympathetically. Had this not happened to me, I would not have been able to imagine how it affected everyone in the family. "But I still envy you for the twenty-eight extra years of seeing you had and the opportunity you had to see your kids learn to walk."

"Yeah, you're right there. You lost yours just when you were getting going," Klaus commiserated. "But my kids still have to finish growing up, and so do yours. That's something to see, just like the grandchildren that come afterward. How can we have a good old age while being totally blind?"

I thought of Jerry D., almost eighty years old, statistically living on borrowed time, still giving it a try.

"I have no idea" was all I could say in reply.

We were just winding down our conversation when Bill pushed himself into the room.

As Dr. Dobelle moved himself behind Klaus's chair, I heard Klaus say in German, and in a low voice to his sighted companion.

"Is that him there? What's going on?"

At that his companion, who had been sitting quietly, listening to Klaus and I speak, turned around and looked at Dr. Dobelle and then back at Klaus.

"That's the genius, all right—he's just not looking so well," he said in a frank, matter-of-fact way as one would describe the color of the sky to someone who was not close enough to the window to look out. Klaus said nothing in reply, but his silence indicated he was more than likely thinking just what I was—that Bill Dobelle's health was definitely a major concern for us both. We were not only investing a lot of money—it was our heads that were on the block. The man heading this is not as well as we'd like him to be; his life suddenly being challenged with heart problems and then the diabetic ulcer as he does his best to put his name on the map of human contribution. For us, the recipients, sick of the life of blindness, made our decisions based on those other doctors seen beyond Dr. Dobelle—Dr. Beth Seelig, Dr. John Girvin, Dr. Dillis Gore, Dr. Ken Smith, and the staff of the CUF Hospital. This day I neither encouraged or discouraged Klaus from holding out his head, but upon discussing our situation since we went blind, we had nothing good to say about it. Klaus never did tell me what his decision was, and I never asked.

Dr. Dobelle had brought along the stimulator and computer box, along with the sunglasses equipped with the miniature video camera for me to show to Klaus. As I explained the function of the components, Klaus asked me, "There's only an on–off switch that I can find. Where's all the controls to adjust this thing?"

I translated to Dr. Dobelle, who replied, "Tell him there's a keyboard jack on the side you can plug in, and also, that these systems are only for the next six months or so, after which we'll issue you all with brand-new systems, which will be much smaller and have more options."

I translated, stressing the fact that this was in Dr. Dobelle's opinion, not in mine. I did not mention it to Klaus, but I wondered personally how on earth Dr. Dobelle expected to fabricate brand-new systems along with all necessary software to be ready for issue in six months when the existing systems were still missing components. Perhaps, I hoped, there were several dozen engineers back in Commack, working on the new systems at present.

"How are you feeling?" John Girvin asked me as I left the conference room, wishing Klaus and his companion good luck.

"Better now that the stitches are out," I replied as John removed the bandage for one final look. He admired the job Lorri did in removing the stitches and then asked, "What did you use for this?" Upon which Lorri pulled out her folding scissors from the Napanee dollar store.

"They cost a whole dollar!" announced Lorri, holding them up. We all laughed at that, and seeing we were going to leave soon, Lorri suggested we all group together for a picture of "the team" for us to take home. There was John and Bill and Dillis, along with Jim, Louise and myself huddled together, the only one missing being Beth and, of course, the surgical team of the CUF Hospital.

We said our good-byes, upon which Bill added, "We'll give you a call around the middle of May when we'll be back in New York. I'll have the equipment ready for you then."

"I can't wait!" I said. "Hopefully I'll be all healed up by then and have no more headaches." I was getting tired again from the stress of dealing with Klaus, the throbbing in my head becoming more pronounced. The vibrations of my voice when I talked were beginning to rattle the implants in my head again, so I suggested to Lorri we get some rest, as our flight left at 6:00 a.m. the next morning, meaning we'd have to get up around 3:30 a.m. It was going to be a very long day tomorrow.

As we left, Lorri nudged my arm and said, "Look at that! You were working for the Dobelle Institute as translator and salesperson! What a job!"

I laughed, feeling good to have been useful, toying with Lorri's suggestion.

"Wouldn't that be something? That would be one heck of an interesting job. The only downside would be working with Bill. Considering how he treated Louise and Jim in the short few minutes we were with him, imagine how it would be to have to spend every day together with him?"

"True enough," Lorri said, pulling out some papers from an envelope. "John passed me these papers in case we have problems with security on the way home. There is also one here for our family doctor if we have any problems." She started to read them as we walked.

> The Dobelle Institute (Portugal) Lda.
> Artificial Vision for the Blind
> Information Regarding the Care of the Pedestals

1. Following any operative procedure in which there is incision of the skin, the operative incision requires some passage of time before it can be considered as "healed." The time required for the initial normal scar tissue to form, following an operation, is about three weeks. At this point, the operative incision, although not at full strength, can be considered as healed.

2. In the case of the percutaneous pedestal, there is not, in the true sense, an operative, or surgical, incision. However, the interface between the pedestal and the skin can be considered an artificial incision.

3. Any incision will heal more satisfactorily if: a. It is allowed some exposure to the air; b. There is not repeated adherence to bandages, in which case the incision may continually be made raw by their removal; and c. It is kept somewhat moist.

4. In order to satisfy the foregoing (3b and 3c), it is recommended that any crusting that might occur, never be removed manually, but rather that it be treated with a thin layer of a petroleum-based ointment, like Vaseline gauze wrapping (e.g., Jelonet), betadine ointment, etc., for the first three weeks.

5. Over the initial three weeks following the insertion of the pedestals, it is imperative that the individual adheres to the foregoing recommendations.

(The three weeks is probably a liberal estimate, but it is felt that this simply increases the safety margin for good-quality initial care of the pedestal.)

6. This artificial "incision" between the pedestal and the scalp can be considered to have reached a normal stage of healing when there is no: a. weeping. b. significant crusting. c. bleeding (e.g., blood on the dressings).

7. At this stage, the patient may resume normal activities like shampooing, bathing off the pedestal area itself, swimming, showering, etc. However, vigorous rubbing of the area must be avoided for probably another month. Drying of the area should be done by gently patting it dry with a towel.

8. If at any stage, there is concern about the healing process or any unusual evidence of inflammation, (redness, swelling, or discharge) please contact us.

The Dobelle Institute (Portugal) Lda.
Artificial Vision for the Blind

April 18, 2002
Re: Mr. Jens Naumann

To Whom It May Concern

This is to advise the reader that the above-named patient has been recently operated on April 8, 2002, for the insertion of a new technology for the provision of artificial vision. This technology consists of the following:

1. The insertion of arrays of electrodes against the mesial occipital (visual) cerebral cortices bilaterally.

2. Connectors from the electrode arrays to posterior auricular percutaneous titanium pedestals.
    The only part of this technology which is visible to the observer, and the reader of this notification, is the surface of the percutaneous titanium pedestal. This is the electronic interface to which the

external part of the technology will eventually be connected. It is covered by a "dust cap," which will be recognized as a black, shiny cap with a central allen wrench socket.

The formation of crusting around the interface between the skin and the titanium pedestal is normal. (Our normal management of this interface is to never try to manually remove any crusting that may occur but rather to treat it with a petroleum-based ointment, e.g., Vaseline gauze wrapping, betadine ointment, etc. If the reader of this has any questions or concerns, please contact me or Dr. William H. Dobelle at the address, telephone number, or fax numbers listed below.

It was a Saturday night, which was to be our last in Portugal. We settled down for a sleep when I heard the sound of what seemed to be a freighter leaving the harbor, its engines throbbing. I waited impatiently for it to distance itself from us so that the throbbing wouldn't continue to hurt my head, but it never happened. In fact, it became louder and louder as the night progressed. Lorri was troubled by the noise as well, although it did not translate into a headache for her, just an irritating noise preventing us from sleeping. She looked out the window and said, "It looks like a disco is in full swing across the street from us."

"Hopefully it's over by midnight," I prayed, knowing that if I did not sleep tonight, the trip home facing us would be next to impossible to endure. The noise did not stop. I lay in bed, clutching my head in agony as each beat of the drums coming from the loudspeakers across the street assisted the implants in squishing my brain. This had to be the ultimate form of torture. Had I been under the control of the CIA I would have given them any information they wanted, even that which didn't exist just to put an end to this hell. When I finally dropped off somewhere around 2:00 a.m. from sheer exhaustion, I dreamed of a pair of heavy army-style boots marching up and down a long corridor, each beat of the drums coinciding with the image of the stomping boots.

Shortly after falling asleep, the alarm clock went off, and we struggled out of bed, feeling dizzy from fatigue. "This isn't going to be a good day," I remarked, my head already hurting profusely. It was a bad sign as we weren't even out of bed.

"Next time, if there ever is one," started Lorri, "we really need another week here to heal up better."

"This could be done on an outpatient basis," I slowly recited one of the lines of Dr. Dobelle's first letter, my jaw still unable to open properly because of the cut muscles. There wasn't going to be a next time, I told myself. I could never lie down again for such an operation now that I knew what it involved.

"We'd never have found people back in Napanee who'd be willing to watch the kids another week on top of these last two," I pointed out. Yes, it had been difficult to find these volunteers, but the real reason had to do with the recovery from surgery.

We climbed down the stairs, the suitcase feeling a lot heavier than it did when we had checked in. I reached the bottom floor, my head throbbing as I was overcome by a feeling like I was about to faint. I dropped the suitcase in the makeshift foyer and leaned on the counter. It was an employee who spoke little English that was at the desk, not the proprietor.

"Can you call a taxi for the airport?" I asked, breathing hard and trying to compose myself. I was not feeling well at all.

"You need to pay for the room," he replied as he picked up the telephone and called a cab. I could not believe my ears. I had paid in full the stay in this hotel two months ago through my travel agent. I hoped I could explain it and be understood. We really couldn't afford to pay twice considering the fact that we had thrown all our money at the feet of Dr. Dobelle.

"It's already paid by the travel agent," I insisted. "It was already taken off my credit card a while ago!" This was something we hadn't anticipated.

The young man rummaged through some papers, and then said, "I have no receipt from your payment."

"Call the owner," suggested Lorri. "He'd know we paid." The young man tried but in vain as no one answered. There was a car pulling up in front of the door, its horn blaring. "There's the taxi," Lorri said.

"Look, I already paid it. If for any reason your boss didn't get the money, just give us a telephone call and we'll make sure you get it. But I know I paid it," I pleaded with the young man, ready to just leave via the taxi if he didn't believe us.

"I believe you," he said, doubt still in his voice. I couldn't blame him for his precautionary measures considering how much trouble he'd be in from his employer if he let people sign out without paying. I gave him my telephone number, and we got in the cab.

"Airport . . ." I said to the driver. The word had to be close in Portuguese as he understood immediately. Once out in the main drag, it seemed that the driver became confused and thought that he was a pilot of a jet rather than a driver of a sub-compact sedan. We flew through the streets at breakneck speed, Lorri saying later that his speed exceeded 140 km/h on the curved, cobblestone roads leading to the airport. We both held on for dear life until we pulled up to the airport, the toll charge being half of what it was when we came the other direction two weeks ago. We tipped the driver and dragged our suitcase along with the two carry-ons into the airport.

We sat for two hours at the gate headed for Germany. We had no problems with security, as the implants did not set off the metal detector. I was asked to remove my hat so the security guard could look inside it, but nothing else. We even had the luxury to board directly from the gate rather than being trucked out into the runway, and then having to climb numerous stairs to board the airplane.

At noon we reached Germany. I was rather tired by then, hoping I could get some sleep in the airport in Frankfurt as our wait would be over six hours until our connecting flight to Toronto would be boarded. A glum-looking guard stamped our passports, telling us to line up for security before proceeding to the gate. This time I did not pass through the metal detector without setting it off.

"Halt!" said the guard as the detector wailed. He approached me with his cane-style hand detector, scanning my body. I had no metal on me, so it didn't go off until he touched my hat. He really thought he had something there.

"Give me your hat," he commanded gruffly. I did, and to his astonishment it was empty. He passed the detector again over my head, and it went off again. I bent down so he could see the top of my head. The scalp was still bald except for a small bit of stubble in the center area where the operation was performed was red and puffed up a full centimeter, liquid having built up underneath. The two jacks were on either side of it, pink fluid still dripping out of the cracks surrounding them. I very carefully patted the swollen area of my head with one finger, the scalp underneath quivering like jelly, appearing as if there was no skull at all but only a mass of guck.

The security guard was speechless as he stared at my head from close up. "See?" I said to him, making sure he did. "I had a brain operation, and this stuff was put in my head. I can't really take it out. Do you want to feel?"

The officer was backing away, his voice faltering as he stuffed my hat back into my hands. "No, no . . . it's all right . . . I see now . . . just take your hat and go." Lorri said later that he looked like he was about to faint.

The flight to Toronto was eight hours' long. I tried to get some sleep, but the woman in the seat beside Lorri and I insisted on talking and talking and talking. She knew only German and was on her way to Canada to visit her son. I was not well and didn't really want to talk, but she kept it up, and I had no choice other than to be impolite, which I didn't really want to do. Every time I spoke, there was a terrible grating noise in my brain from the vibration of the implants. I wished I could get some sleep, as we still had to wait for a bus and then take a four-hour bus ride back home. I didn't get any at all during the flight.

It was hot in Toronto when we arrived. I grabbed the carry-on which was the lightest, leaving the heavy one to Lorri. Some gentleman I was. I figured it was still better than Lorri having to carry me out as well as the suitcases. A young man approached us once we were in the airport.

"I'll carry your baggage for ten bucks," he offered. It wasn't a long way to the front doors, but it would have been a few more minutes.

"Ten bucks?" Lorri made it clear she thought it was too much. I reached in my pocket and pulled out the money. "This time I'm not in the bargaining mood. It's either have him carry the suitcases or I will need to be carried too." I gave him the money. It was money well spent. I could hardly walk, holding onto Lorri for support. This trip was adding up to too much for me. The last few days I had not been up more than three hours at a time, and today I was up for close to twenty hours already, and we weren't finished yet. The young man helped us find the bus stop for the trip to Napanee as well. All we had to do was wait.

Lorri was showing signs of fatigue by now. We sat together in our chairs close to the entrance of the terminal, four hours to go before the bus would arrive. Every five minutes, an announcement would be broadcast over the terminal loudspeakers: "Your attention please . . . passengers are reminded that luggage left unattended would be confiscated without notice. Please do not leave your luggage unattended at any moment." This was followed by a repetition in French. Both Lorri and I dozed while the hubbub of the terminal surrounded us. I was tempted to push our luggage out into the aisle just to get rid of it. I was sick of suitcases, headaches, and this announcement which kept waking us up.

"Your attention please. Passengers are reminded not to leave their luggage unattended . . ." I said mockingly shortly after the last repetition, mimicking the announcement. Lorri turned to me.

"Man, that darned announcement is going off more often by the minute." She then realized it was me speaking, not the loudspeaker. "I guess I'm really getting tired," she said tiredly. "I thought it was the loudspeaker again. I hope we can sleep on the bus. Usually it is more comfortable there."

She was wrong. The seats were comfortable enough, all right, and she did sleep, while I gritted my teeth in pain. The bus had one unbalanced wheel, sending it hopping down the 401 highway instead of rolling. It bounced so violently when it reached the speed limit that all the windows and luggage compartment doors rattled. The driver just ignored the problem. The pain in my head reached a new threshold.

Four hours later, we arrived in Napanee, where our eldest daughter, Danielle, the one I saw last when she was two months old, picked us up with her automobile to our relief. She even had the house warmed up with the woodstove, so all I had to do was lie down and sleep.

Early the next morning, only five hours of sleep later, all the kids were dropped off at our house. Some of the people who had volunteered to watch them came in to see me, fully expecting me to be able to look at them. They were surprised at my sorry condition and at the gory sight of my head.

"What about that day-surgery idea?" they inquired in astonishment. I had shown them all the letters I received from Bill Dobelle.

"Can you see me now?"

"Not yet, not yet . . ." I groaned, clutching my head which hurt badly. I really needed much more of a rest. The kids were all excited to see us, and the rest of the day I spent with a pounding headache. It wasn't until the kids went to bed that I found enough quiet to lay down.

It took a few days to recover enough to get out and about again. Just to get out of the house was a relief. I stayed away from town, avoiding having to give explanations to all the curious citizens wanting to see their "money at work." All it was, was a temporary measure until I could see and then the system would speak for itself, I thought.

Ethel, one of my principal fund-raiser friends, came by shortly after we returned from Portugal.

"So you made it!" she greeted enthusiastically, entering the front door and then looking at my head. "My goodness, what did they do to your head?" Her voice had dropped off, losing its enthusiasm as I turned myself once around for her to see. "They did that while you were awake?" She remembered the letters I had received from Bill Dobelle.

"Thank goodness not," I said reassuringly. "It wasn't really what I expected. I did spend a night in intensive care, and then the better part of a week in the hospital. I really should have spent more than that there."

Ethel stared for a moment at my head, saying nothing. "I can't believe the size of that scar," she whispered to Lorri. My hair was returning in the form of a very short stubble, revealing the entirety of the surgical procedure. "Let's hope it was worth it," she added.

"At least you can say to the donors that I didn't have that good a time in Portugal," I pointed out, knowing Ethel had to have something to say to all the citizens who had pitched in. "I did see the little dots of light when they tested me before coming back," I added. I faced her again so she wouldn't have to look at my head anymore.

"Oh, really?" She was pleased as I was. "Won't that be something when you get that equipment in a couple of weeks and can see what I look like!"

"It sure would," I said, but doubting somewhat if that will really be possible after all. Given that the electrodes on my left visual field were somewhat misplaced, and those on the right were far too large to give good vision, and none of the phosphenes landed directly on the focal point, it would be unlikely I'd distinguish one face from another. Yet, perhaps I was jumping to conclusions I had no grounding for. These are, after all, the experts who are doing this, and Bill is a doctor. I still had things to learn regarding this field of science.

"Let me know when you have the equipment," Ethel said, taking one final look at my head. She had a few things to tell her friends now.

It was four weeks later when I ventured back into the wood processing business, working at a very slow pace and using only a small chain saw as the bigger ones were impossible to start without my head getting a shaking from fighting the compression while pulling on the rip cord. I figured on getting done what I could with my work as I'd probably want to "play" with my equipment, doing all the things I had missed out on once I was issued the vision system. I waited impatiently for the promised telephone call from Dr. Dobelle.

CHAPTER 9

The Research Lab

It was May 2, 2002, when Dr. Dobelle rang our telephone in Napanee. I was feeling pretty good again, the headache situation now under control as I could prevent one altogether in modifying my behavior. If I didn't shake my head too much, which meant no running, I felt fine. The back of my head was quite tender still, which kept me from lying on my back at night.

"Are you ready to come down here to New York?" Dr. Dobelle drawled in his now-familiar voice. He sounded rather refreshed in comparison to the last few days I spoke to him in Portugal. I figured it must have been the stress of dealing with the unpredictables that affected him.

"Right now?" I said in a hopeful tone. "My thirty days aren't quite up, but I feel fine!"

"It'll be at least a couple of weeks, as we want to work on a few of you at once, and considering you were the first, you'll have to wait until the others have their healing time complete too."

"So much for my thirty days," I thought. "More waiting. That's been the name of the game right from the start."

"So when do you figure?" I had to stop making plans around this guy, I thought.

"A couple of weeks. Is Lorri able to come down?"

"I doubt it," I said, remembering the cash flow problem that arose every time we both stopped working ever since we spent enough money on my head which could have bought another good house. "Somebody has to work here and make money. The kids have to go to school too. I'll have to come by myself." I knew that Lorri would have loved to come down, just to share the threshold of my life together as I'd see her for the first time after so many long and hard years. We'd never be able to cut it financially, though, and if the kids missed any more school, as some had done during my stay in Portugal since their caretakers lived too far away from their school, they'd be bound to fail their grades. Lorri was going to have to tough this one out and anticipate my return instead.

Bill Dobelle grunted with disapproval. "We'll have a room in a good hotel for you, complete with dining area, but you'll have to take care of yourself when you're not in our office. Can you do that much?"

I was somewhat confused, as the idea of me going there was to see. Of course once I take the equipment to the room with me, I'll be able to get around, just like I used to before I lost my sight. Jerry, the volunteer who had the experimental prototype, was recorded in Bill's journal as having traveled frequently in unfamiliar places with his system, which was only a fraction of what I was going to get.

"I can get around all right with my eyes closed, especially considering I can talk to all the people in the hotel, seeing that I'll speak their language," I was making reference to the situation in Portugal, which was not so convenient when no one spoke either English or German. "But once I have the system, all will be easy anyways."

"Not so fast," Bill interjected hastily. "It'll take a while to get things set up. This is a complex procedure, and you'll be here for about a week or so. I need you to be able to get around to take care of your personal needs in the hotel even without sight."

I was somewhat puzzled at this. He had originally wanted to come up to each patient's house and have an engineer "customize" everybody's equipment. I had envisioned it to take a day at best. Little minor alterations I'd be able to do myself once I was shown how to modify the settings, I thought. Now he wanted me to come down for a week.

"What are we doing down there for a whole week?" I asked.

"Oh, once you're set up, we'll try out a few things."

That sounded good. I imagined myself driving a car, showing the system off to its best. Just to ask Bill's driver to pull over on a deserted country road, saying, "Move over for a few minutes and let me sit at the wheel, Bud, and I'll show you how I can drive" was one of my dreams that had repeated itself on several occasions ever since I was giving the implant.

"That sounds great!" I said in full anticipation. I started to count the days again, figuring the sixteenth of May would be the date, but instead of believing Bill this time, I figured on giving it three weeks just to be on the realistic side.

Bill disappointed me with his punctuality for the first time. "How about coming down tomorrow? I'm sending my driver up to pick you up tomorrow morning first thing. You should be here to see us in the office by the afternoon." It was only the thirteenth. I did not complain. I was ready to go. I gave it some thought about how to get the mapping done. I figured the easiest way would be to describe the location according to its coordinates each phosphene, and once done, would run a straight edge through my visual field, first horizontally and then vertically, observing any misplaced phosphenes. I would ask the engineer which phosphenes to cycle on and off until I found the culprit, which then would have to be remapped. This method would work if we approached the matter logically. If they had a better plan, it would be fine too. I had no idea, after all, who I'd be working with, as there would probably be several engineers working on the project in Commack.

"You should see the car that just pulled into our driveway!" exclaimed one of the children, running closer to the window. "It's really long and black."

"What kind is it?" asked one of the older ones.

"It's a Cadillac!" A man knocked on the door, which I opened. It was the evening of May 13. The man standing at the door held out his hand, talking in a Southern accent. He was big in build and sounded tough.

"My name's Pat from the Dobelle Institute," he said, shaking my hand.

"Man, I'm really pleased to meet you," I replied. "Would you like a cup of coffee? That's quite a drive for one day."

"About nine hours or so," he replied laughing, declining the coffee. "I'd like a place to stay, though. Any hotels around here that are any good?"

"Sure thing," I said, pointing down the way he just came. "Just down the same road you just came from. It's pretty cheap, too. Would you like me to foot the bill for it?" It was probably only about forty dollars, and I figured it was already nice of Bill to foot the price for my transport down there, so I may as well help out here.

"Oh no, don't you do that," Pat said seriously. "Bill's got to be made to pay for this. You just let him pay. He can afford it."

The next morning at six, Pat picked me up. The car was beautiful in the inside, equipped with the most comfortable leather seats, its ride smooth and quiet. As the car was classified as a "stealth stretch," there was a lot of space between the back and front seats.

Is this the car you drive Bill around in?" I asked, admiring the small foldout table attached to the back of the front seat.

"Yeah, and you're sitting right where he normally sits," he said, chuckling.

"Maybe I'll get smarter sitting here," I suggested. Pat laughed.

I had brought my passport along, even though it was common to cross the Canada–US border without such identification. Since the September 11/01 chaos, however, things had been made stricter. I thought it best not to rock the boat. "When we get to the border, Pat," I said as we rolled southward on Interstate 81, heading for the border, "we'll just play it cool, and I'll say I'm visiting with Dr. Dobelle as a friend. I don't have a clue as to their rules regarding being a test patient for a procedure not approved by the FDA."

Pat did not seem concerned at all. "I get what you're talking about, but don't worry. I still have my New York City cop driver's identification. We won't have a problem." Sure enough, we didn't. The border guard in charge took one look at Pat's ID, then at my face and passport.

"How long are you staying?" is all they asked, then waved us through.

"And we're homeward bound!" said Pat, pushing hard on the accelerator, sending the big car vaulting forward down the interstate. I sat back in the seat, relaxing, yet anticipating the big event before me.

"I should be able to see the country on the way back," I mentioned to Pat, who had just spoken about "beautiful America" as he looked at the countryside flying past us.

"Is that what Bill said?" asked Pat. I had expected him to agree, but that didn't happen. Maybe he just didn't get involved with the affairs at the office, being just a driver.

It took four hours as we drove first through Watertown, then Syracuse, then stopping in Binghamton for a bite to eat at Burger King. I had a double whopper, it being all I could manage, while Pat had his with fries and coke. Pat filled the tank with gas, announcing, "It should be another four or five hours at the most." We started up again.

The car phone rang. Pat answered. It had a loudspeaker, allowing me to hear the conversation. "It's probably Bill," Pat said as he answered.

"Where on Earth are you?" It was Bill, talking in his usual brisk manner I hoped was reserved only for employees, not for the patients.

"South of Binghamton," replied Pat.

"Do you have Jens there?"

"Yeah, he's in the backseat. Want to talk to him?" Pat was already passing the phone. I hoped he wouldn't go off the road as he looked over his shoulder at me while driving. Then again, I reminded myself, he is an ex-cop, used to looking back at the backseat of the squad car while managing New York city traffic.

"Jens." Bill was using a different voice now, as if I didn't hear his manner of speech with Pat. "We reserved a room for you at the Sheridan. You'll like it there, as the dining is good. Pat'll bring you here first, but we won't do much today. We might as well start in the morning, get you set up, and then you can start using the equipment."

It sounded great. I'd be able to see by tomorrow night. It was hard to contain my excitement.

"That'll be excellent, Dr. Dobelle." I said, imagining seeing the world with those little dots. I'd have to call Lorri first thing when that happens.

Four hours later, Pat was slowed down to a stop-and-start mode of travel, showing his impatience. "We'll divert into New Jersey, or maybe Pennsylvania to get around this crazy traffic," he said, swinging around the car and stabbing at the gas. We rolled smoother here, but considering from which direction the sun was hitting me now, it was obvious we were not getting any closer to Commack. The car phone rang again.

"Where are you now?" It was Bill, his voice showing a hint of irritation with the apparent delay in my arrival in Commack.

"We're in Pennsylvania," Pat said, proceeding to explain why. "In Pennsylvania?! What the heck are you doing there?" Bill was talking to Pat as he had done to Jim and Louise in Portugal. I hoped Pat wouldn't resign right on the spot and leave me stranded. "We'll be all right, Bill," Pat said calmly. "The traffic's heavy here, and the other way would have been just as slow. It's rush hour now." Pat hung up the telephone.

"What did you do for the New York Police force?" I was curious as to why a cop would be driving Bill around. "I worked there all my life. I was a lieutenant for a number of years before retiring." Pat sounded like an all-right guy who wouldn't give trouble to anyone who didn't deserve it. But then again, I thought, they can be different people when wearing their uniform. It must have been a glamorous position that Pat held before retiring. Now he was bossed around by Bill as if he was a boy going to grade school.

"You mean you were the big boss—holding the cards, telling other people what to do?"

"Sure was," he said, seeming to recall the good old days. "I had it made. Then I retired, but my wife still has to work for a few years, so instead of sitting around at home, I figured I'd do this."

The clock edged up to four hours after noon when the telephone rang again. Pat cursed. "The guy's giving me a headache."

Bill asked to talk to me. He didn't even ask Pat where he was. "Jens, I'm just going to get you dropped off at the hotel. A room's there for you, and Pat'll pick you up at nine tomorrow morning." Then he added, knowing very well about the loudspeaker in the car and the fact that Pat would be listening. "Sorry that we couldn't do anything today. Had you been here sooner, we could have worked on the system some."

I gave Pat the receiver back. "I don't understand the big deal. It's only four o'clock, and we must be close."

"We are," said Pat. "Another ten minutes and that's it. But that's Bill for you."

I would have loved to have been started on right that day—another delay to contend with for such an important project.

Pat helped me into the lobby of the Sheridan, right on Motocross Parkway. The lobby was huge, nothing like the Barca Do Tejo in Portugal was. There was a large water fountain situated in the center.

"Can I please have your credit card?" the attendant asked me at the front desk. I paused in confusion.

"Didn't Dr. Dobelle pay for it yet?" I did not have money trees growing in my backyard, that was for sure. This place must cost over a hundred a night, I thought.

"No, not yet. He said he would, but he still needs to send a check. In order for you to stay here tonight, and for the next five scheduled nights, you need to give us your card."

I reached in my pocket, pulling out a card that I really could not afford to use. What money Bill didn't have of mine already I needed to buy logs for processing into firewood. "How much per night?" I hoped it wouldn't be much. "Two hundred," she said without flinching. That was in American dollars, costing at least $320 per night in Canadian Pesos. I groaned. I had no other choice. Pat was waiting impatiently, trying to distance himself from the affair. The attendant gave me the keys, and Pat, carrying the suitcase, led me down a few corridors until we reached the room.

"Two hundred a night!" I spat out to Pat. "The guy had better be paying for it, because if it was my choice I would have chosen a cheaper one, should it come out of my pocket."

Pat fiddled with the electronic key until it finally cooperated. I put a kink in the card's top left corner so I could tell which way to put it in the lock without having to try it four different ways. "If Bill said he'd pay, he usually means it," assured Pat. I hoped he was right. Lorri would not be amused at $1,600 being gone from the family's dwindling finances in this manner.

Pat left after dropping my suitcase in the room, reminding me of our appointment in the morning. I surveyed the room, noting all its features, including a coffee machine on a small counter. The hotel was first class, no doubt. There was even a radio which I tuned to the old-time favorites station. It was not hard to find a station as there was an infinite selection, unlike Canada, where there was a lot of dead air between stations. I wanted to go for dinner, having a good idea where the restaurant was situated. I mentally prepared myself for the task. What that meant was that I would psych myself into the fact that yes, there would probably be someone in the corridor who, upon seeing my white cane, attempt to immediately run to my rescue as if I was about to hurt myself—this gesture of goodwill perhaps being appropriate should I have just lost my sight the day before, but also a kind of nuisance for someone having worked hard on rehabilitation for the last several years. I had to remind myself whenever I became too irritated with bystanders that the white cane just doesn't reveal the exact time of loss of sight, neither does it have a degree of rehabilitation attached to it—so it is generally assumed that I am in trouble and need help. I stepped out into the hallway, closing the door behind me upon making sure I had the key.

There were people already in the hallways, and I followed them. I had memorized the number of steps going from my door to the next turn and so on until I'd reach the restaurant. To my pleasant surprise, no one paid particular attention to me. Someone was walking beside me, a person I judged as a man by his gait. Men walked differently from women, a fact that took a number of years for me to realize. I seldom errored when I was in a situation where the sounds were not impeded. I was in the second hallway when I asked the person I assumed was a man, "I figure I'm headed to the restaurant. This is my first time in New York."

"Yeah, that's where I'm going too. By the way, welcome to New York!" The man asked me a few questions about my home town, never once referring to my blindness. Welcome to New York, I repeated to myself in full appreciation. How I wished that the small-town folk in Canada would have the same attitude when dealing with someone who was a bit different. But I wouldn't need that once I had my vision system. I'd be just like them, then.

I was seated by a wonderful waitress named Sophie, with whom I conversed and in no time told her why I was here, explaining the quest for vision with the Dobelle Institute.

"My husband was once in a terrible accident that left him completely paralyzed." She began to explain how it happened and how it obviously affected both of their lives. "He believed, however, that he would be able to walk again, and sure enough, it took quite a while, but now he can walk again. I know you'll be able to see again too." She had the most encouraging outlook of which I welcomed every last bit.

I was back in my room when the telephone rang. It was Dr. Dobelle.

"How do you like your room?" he said, sounding a bit like all the other New Yorkers.

"Excellent," I said. "What's up?"

"Look, Jens," he started to explain, "we'll pick you up tomorrow at seven thirty and get you going. Dennis is going to be there too."

"Oh, you mean the young man who checked into the hospital CUF when I checked out?"

"Yeah, that's him. He's just a couple hours' drive from here, making it convenient to bring him back and forth. We'll have two computers going and therefore can do both of you."

I mulled it over, wondering what he was trying to say with the idea of two computers. I thought they were all on the shelf, ready to go. What were all the other engineers besides Jim and Steve doing, I asked myself.

"Then the day after tomorrow," continued Bill, "I've got a press reporter crew invited from *Wired* magazine. You and Dennis can show him what this will do."

I couldn't believe my ears. Whatever happened to all his policies regarding the press he insisted to be followed prior to Portugal? Why would the press embargo, as he called it in his letters to us, suddenly be a thing of the past when there was still work to be done?

"I suppose you're assuming all is ready to go and that I'll be able to use the system when I get it." I was glad of his optimism, even though I would have much rather preferred to adjust to the system for a while prior to attempting to demonstrate it.

"Don't worry, I know what I'm doing," said Bill reassuringly. I left it at that, setting my alarm clock for 6:30 a.m. the next morning.

At 7:30 a.m. sharp Pat knocked on my hotel room door. He led the way out to the parking lot, and I slid into the backseat, right beside Bill.

"Good morning, Jens," he said, holding out his frail hand. "I hope you're ready for getting down to business."

"Never been readier," I said. It sounded like he had everything perfectly under control. Pat drove for only two minutes and stopped the car, opening my door.

"We're here," said Bill, "at the headquarters of the Dobelle Institute. About eleven thousand square feet of floor space." We were at 61 Mall Drive, Commack. I noticed no activity, no traffic. It was as quiet as a cemetery.

"Just stay here for a minute, Jens," Pat said as I climbed out of the car. Pat opened the trunk of the Caddy and pulled out a folding wheelchair. He opened it up and then proceeded to Bill's door. Pat reached in and with his strong arms lifted Bill's frail body out by the shoulders while Bill tried to make it look as though he was helping a bit.

"Follow me," Pat said, and I did, as Pat pushed the genius in the wheelchair. "He really should get practicing with that prosthesis of his," I thought to myself.

We walked a few yards up the sidewalk, and Pat opened double glass doors with a key. I was led through two small rooms when I was greeted by Louise.

"Why, hello, Jens, how are you?" She was friendly as usual. "Did you like your trip back home from Portugal?"

"It was pretty bad," I downplayed the horror of it. "I really wasn't ready to travel that far. Next time I'll stay another week before leaving." What was I saying? There wasn't going to be another time, was there?

"Pat, bring him into the conference room. We'll be there shortly." It was Bill interrupting our conversation. He was the boss.

Pat led me through a couple of other medium-sized rooms, which were perhaps the size of a normal household living room. "This is the kitchen here," he said. I could hear the coffee machine perking out the coffee. I could have used one. The next room we entered was perhaps twenty-five feet by twelve, with a large table in the middle surrounded by chairs. There were no windows, as this was a room in the center of the building.

"No windows in this room," commented Pat, "there's a few like that in here. Make yourself comfortable."

Pat was sitting beside me, making room for Bill to be close to me on my other side. It was hard to believe that I was right in the Dobelle laboratory—the one I had dreamed of all the while I was studying this project on the Internet just a couple of years ago.

"Have you ever been in Portugal?" I asked Pat. I figured as a cop he'd have the means.

"I was there last month when you were there, only a bit after you were admitted, that's why we didn't meet. I liked it a lot. How'd you like the food?" he asked me.

"Great, once we found the restaurants! I bet you had it easier as you probably ate in the hotel." I assumed he was staying in the Marriott Lisbon with the rest of the team, which had a dining lounge.

"To tell you the truth," Pat explained, "I never eaten there."

"How come? The food wasn't good?"

"No, I never got to taste it. I was sitting there with my food just served to me when a man beside me had an epileptic seizure. It caused quite a ruckus. The two women with him, who knew he had this problem, just screamed as the poor fellow was struggling on the floor, looking like he wasn't going to pull through. I had enough and just left. I couldn't eat there now as I'd always think of that day."

"Now that's something that's hard to live with," I said, picturing the agony the poor fellow was going through and how the onlookers, really, had the easy part of the whole affair.

"No kidding," agreed Pat. Bill called him over then and he left. There was no one in the room, so I got up and explored. There was a plain wall behind the chair upon which I was seated with no decor. There was an entrance into another hallway of back rooms at one end of the table. I heard small sounds of activity coming from there. There were a couple of people talking. It sounded like the voices of Steve and Jim. I continued to circle around the table, touching a large plastic plant propped up in a corner opposite of my seating area. I felt around some more. At the end of the table opposite the entrance to the back rooms there was a bookshelf unit, upon which were several books and other unidentifiable objects. I took my seat when I heard the sound of approaching footsteps.

A few people were coming into the room, sitting down and making all the sounds of conscious people yet saying nothing to me. I sat there, listening intently, assuming by their subtle sounds that they were all guys.

Bill's squeaky wheelchair was heading toward us as well. The motion was regular, indicating that someone, probably Pat, was pushing him. Pat pushed Bill up to the table so he was seated at my right. Pat left the room as everyone settled down. There was only Pat and Louise seemingly elsewhere in the building, the rest all in this conference room.

"Now let's get started with morning conference," Bill addressed the group, which couldn't have numbered more than ten in total. It appeared by the reactions, or rather the lack of them, of the employees that this was a morning ritual they would rather do without.

"First of all," began Bill, gesturing toward me at his left side. "We have one of our artificial vision patients here, Jens." A few people said a brief "hello," not so much that they meant it, but rather to make Bill happy.

"So how's the breathing coming along? Ken, Don, Brian?" Bill singled out three workers, who must have been attributed to the breathing pacemaker project.

"We tried stopping those hiccups, but even though it interrupted them, the patient still has them," Don said.

Bill grunted his comprehension, adding, "Doesn't always work the first time," and then, turning to another man at the table, said, "Mario, how are the larger arrays coming along?"

Mario spoke in a well-cultured voice used to dealing with Bill. I recognized his voice as the man I had regularly spoken to during the time Bill was in the hospital. "He's in and out of the hospital, just call back in two weeks," he would say, the same thing two weeks later. Meanwhile, Bill had been inches from the claws of the reaper, never having left the hospital for months on end. I said nothing.

"The arrays are coming along fine, but I've got to find a good pedestal yet. The manufacturer, IT&T agreed to make some for us, but the screw in the middle isn't strong enough. We may have to sacrifice some of the center pins so we can use a larger diameter screw." He seemed to be talking about the larger implants. I wondered if Bill really expected me to get one of those next.

"We'll do what we have to," replied Bill, then changing the subject.

"Steve, Jim, we are setting up Jens and Dennis today. You can both work together on Jens in the morning, but this afternoon one of you work on

Dennis while the other finishes with Jens. Just to remind you, *Wired* magazine is coming tomorrow and want something to write up."

Steve and Jim had been invisible until now. They seemed to try to stay out of the picture as much as possible, succeeding to the point where I don't think a sighted person would have noticed them either. They had been trying to blend into the furniture.

We only have one computer that works right now," Jim said hesitantly, sticking out his neck as spokesperson for the two.

"What? You said they'd be all ready!" There was some uncomfortable shuffling and clearing-throat noises coming from across the table as the others tried to figure out how best to get out of there.

"I guess we may as well get back to work, as I'm expecting an important call from that doctor," Ken said, speaking for everyone except Steve and Jim. It looked like they were the only two actually working in the vision project.

"We can probably have another one ready by this afternoon," Jim said, calming down Bill for an instance.

"Well, you had better hustle," Bill told them, attempting to turn around in his chair. He managed by holding onto the table. He spoke over his shoulder. "Just do the right side of Jens for thresholds, then the mapping. That way we'll at least have something to show the press tomorrow." He started pulling himself toward the door, his progress restricted by the carpeting. Steve and Jim went into the back room area behind the conference table, proceeding to bring out the stimulation equipment.

I sat at my place while Jim and Steve whispered to each other. I doubted it was me whom they wanted to be kept out of earshot; it appeared to be Bill. Just by judging his interaction with the employees during the conference, everyone was scared of him. Meanwhile, I was somewhat stunned as I sat there, thinking about the unexpectedly low number of participants in the vision department. In fact, the breathing pacemaker department wasn't much better. I had expected an R&D department with several employees, including medical doctors, then the technical department, of whom Steve and Jim were only a fraction of the participants. Then there'd be a rehabilitation department, as we were dealing with sight recovery following long-term blindness. Where was Beth Seelig? John Girvin?

"Steve," I called over the table as he was connecting the stimulator to the computer of the vision system. "Where's the rest of the gang, like Beth Seelig, John Girvin?"

Steve stopped and said quietly, "Beth Seelig . . . well . . . left. And John Girvin, I think he is either back in or going back to the Middle East where he has his work. He was never an employee—he was just helping out last month as a favor."

I sat in stunned silence as Jim and Steve continued their work. Beth—gone. John Girvin, being perhaps the most impressive employee—not actually part of the team. Some good he's going to be for us, the patients, by being on the other side of the world. The surgical implant team was just a hired crew, their work being done once the implants are in the head. All that remained of any hope for medical representation for this venture was Dillis Gore in Portugal. That wasn't very much. I wondered briefly what Dr. Willis would think of all of this.

"I am going to hook up your pedestals now," Steve said shyly as he approached with obvious hesitancy.

"Go right ahead," I said, parting my hair from around the first pedestal. Steve carefully unscrewed the small plastic cap that now covered the array of seventy-two tiny holes in the middle of the pedestal. I heard the awful grinding noises in my head, magnified by the fact that the metal pedestal was mounted directly on my skull with no material cushioning the union. Dr. Dobelle had quickly wheeled himself into the room, intent on overseeing the hooking-up procedure. While Steve was reluctantly fitting the cable end into the pedestal fitting, Dr. Dobelle sat and watched from a distance commandingly. It was evident that Steve was not an expert at this as he gingerly fiddled with the cable end, hesitant to apply pressure as he knew what was involved in the surgical procedure.

"Let me give you a hand," I said to Steve, holding the cable end down so he could get a better grip with the screw. The last thing I needed to happen was to have the screw stripped.

"You should put in the savers," Bill instructed from his wheelchair. The savers were just like a cable except they were only four inches or so long. Their function was to allow continuous connections to be made to the pedestal without damaging it. Eventually, the saver would wear out, warranting its replacement, but the pedestal would be saved from the same wear.

The savers were stiff and relatively uncooperative, sticking up like dreadlocks and looking weird. I could bend them down, however, and having curly hair, they would probably be hidden from the onlooker once my hair had a chance to grow longer. Together Steve and I attached the savers.

Dr. Dobelle looked at me and said, "I'm going to send you to your room tonight with those on. You can tell me tomorrow how it was to sleep with them in."

"I guess there's not much choice, as they will keep the pedestals from wearing out," I commented in reply. "The hookup should be easier too as I won't have to worry about the hair getting into the connection."

"Give it a try and see if you can do it," Bill said. I grasped the cable destined for the stimulator box with my left hand, guiding it to the saver hanging off my head. Once lined up, all there was left to do was carefully rotate the cable end while gently contacting the saver end until the two matching flat mating surfaces of the ends were aligned. I gently forced them together and tightened the screw. Dr. Dobelle was visibly proud of the result, assuming all the patients will be able to do this with ease.

"I told you it was easy," he said. "I selected those jacks just so they'd be easy to connect." I was still mystified why he didn't help with the hook-up procedure instead of just sitting in his chair. He could have helped Steve out, not only showing Steve the easy way to connect the cable, but attaining a level of respect as "Doctor Dobelle," which he obviously craved considering his demonstration of power toward his employees. But he decided against this approach—I assumed he had confidence in Steve's judgment.

Jim joined Steve and started to set up the laptop for my session of stimulation, which was supposed to test one of my implants for the thresholds, which was the point where I'd first see the phosphene. It would be a repeat of what was done in Portugal, except this time only those phosphenes recorded as "good," meaning they did not hurt, and did not occupy too much of the visual field, possibly interfering with others.

"Did you get the last component installed in the stimulator so I can get all seventy-two electrodes tested this time?" I asked this even though it would have meant Dr. Dobelle would once again go into convulsions of rage and reprimand if the answer should be "no."

Jim replied, "Yes, we did," and continued with his incessant tapping of the keys. I waited patiently. I had been here since 7:30 a.m., yet now it was past 10:00 a.m., with no testing yet done. The oscilloscope was started, its ventilation fan introducing the only indication of activity in the room. Occasionally, Steve and Jim whispered to one another. Bill left the room with some difficulty, taking a full two minutes just to turn the chair around on the relentless carpet. Once out of the door, Jim and Steve spoke loud enough for me to hear.

"We have to put this file in here for this to work," said Jim to Steve. "Here, I'll show you how to set up the parameters." Jim was the man who knew the program, and Steve appeared to be trying to learn it. Bill wheeled himself back into the room, breathing heavily.

"Ready yet?" was his question. I was sure neither Steve nor Jim really wanted to hear it.

"Just need another twenty minutes or so," said Jim. I knew from experience in programming and electronics that problems could take from a few seconds to a few days to straighten out.

A half hour later, Jim announced, "We're ready now."

"I guess I'll tell Bill," Steve said as he stood up and left the room. Bill came in, being pushed by Steve and took his place beside me at the table. I figured he was already tiring from propelling his chair on his own.

"Well, let's get going. We're going to do what we did in Portugal, Jens. Just the one side today, and then we should be able to map it too."

I knew Dennis was about to show up as Pat had gone out to get him. It was past 11:00 a.m. This was supposed to be my big day; the one I'd been not only anticipating for eighteen years, but also vividly imagining ever since I received my first letter from Dr. William H. Dobelle, PhD.

"Now," said Jim, pressing a button on the keyboard of the computer as it beeped.

"No," I said, seeing only the grayish-brownish-blackish pattern of nothing as I did for eighteen years, except for that time in Portugal when I was hooked up. Jim raised the voltage from .5 to 1, saying again the word "now" that Bill had insisted upon using.

"No" was my answer again. Jim tried again, this time at 2 V.

"Now," he said, a white light shimmering on my bottom left corner of my visual field. It lasted for a second, as I was given fifty cycles of stimulation at a pulse train of fifty. The beauty was similar to that seen in Portugal, this time anticipated and better appreciated as I was not in the pain I had been in when in Portugal.

"Yes," I said, controlling my excitement. I knew this was going to take a while, and I did not want to further prolong the testing unnecessarily. Jim dropped the voltage to 1.5, then up to 1.75, at which point I saw the phosphene again, this time very dimly, lacking all color and shine. That was considered the threshold. Steve wrote down the voltage for the threshold of that electrode number. The oscilloscope showed the current briefly, but that was never recorded.

"Good one?" asked Dr. Dobelle.

"It was kind of big, maybe the size of my hand at arm's length." I was not sure what constituted a good phosphene, but I was going to do all I could to keep my electrodes. Knowing that Dr. Dobelle only wanted to keep the "good" ones, I hoped to keep as many as possible, as that way, I reasoned, I'd be able to see the best.

"We'll keep that one," said Bill. "Next," he instructed. Jim repeated the routine with the next randomly selected electrode, starting at .5 of a volt. The routine became more efficient as the hour passed. I noticed that when the phosphene first appeared and was a dim white, obviously near its threshold. Then when Jim went to double the voltage, which was his only allowed option given to him by Dr. Dobelle, the next time he pushed the button I saw the phosphene in full color; outlined by a rainbow. The bluish-purplish color arrangements were exceptionally beautiful. About one out of every two produced color in this manner. Since I was the only one who could see the phosphene, the engineers, and Bill to that matter, had no choice but to listen to me and take my word for what I saw.

Dennis came into the office before noon. I could hear his voice, recognizing it from when I spoke to him and his mom Nancy who also came along.

"It'll be just a few more minutes," Bill said as they sat down on a couch near his office. They talked for a good two hours before we were done with the thresholds on my right side, which translated to my left visual field. It was the side with the small electrodes, giving fifty-six useful phosphenes. There were nine that had no contact, as Jim had raised the voltage to 16 V without a response. There were some that occupied a large section of my visual field, looking like a banana at arm's length, its light speckled with black spots in between. They were useless, apparently, and I reluctantly made Jim aware of them. He marked them off in turn and said, "We won't put those in the array of useful electrodes."

Bill Dobelle came into the room, pushed by Pat, who had returned after picking up Dennis.

"I'm going to get Dennis up for testing next," Bill said, sounding tired already. "Jens, you disconnect and I'll get Pat to get you some lunch." Steve put the finishing touches on the list of useful phosphenes and said to Bill, "Do you want to look at these results from his right side?"

"Yeah, sure," Bill replied, Pat taking the sheet from Steve and handing it to him. Bill rattled the paper as I disconnected the cables from my savers and stood up. Bill seemed very confident in my ability to handle this job—the engineers having already told me that each cable was worth close to $1,000 and that any carelessness in the connecting procedure could ruin them.

I walked around the conference table to the other side by the bookshelves, making room for Dennis.

Nancy showed Dennis to the chair from where I had just come, and while he sat there and Jim started to set the computer up again, I spoke to Nancy, who had taken her place in a chair beside me.

"How did Dennis fair in the surgery?"

"It certainly wasn't easy," she said, recollecting the extent of the surgery and the recovery. "His head is still not all that well healed. How is yours?"

"Mine seems all right," I said, touching the scalp which was still tender, but nowhere near to what it had been in Portugal. "It still leaks quite a bit of guck out of the place between the jack and the skin," I said.

Nancy was paying attention to the process of testing about to happen to her son, whom she had once raised from a child, witnessed being struck down by blindness and now was to see for the first time. It was supposed to be his big day today too.

"Hurry up and hook him up," said Bill Dobelle from his chair. Steve was standing over Dennis, holding a saver in one hand and gingerly parting Dennis's hair with the other.

"It looks like the skin grew over the pedestal somewhat," said Steve. "I don't think I can put it on."

"Just push the skin back and do it," instructed Bill from his perch. But Steve did not react. Jim came over, probably more out of pity for Steve who was going to take a licking from Bill. Jim looked and practically said the same.

"It doesn't look like we can get it on, Bill, and I really don't want to touch the area with my hands."

"Call Don," said Bill, with a hint of frustration in his voice. Bill was still several feet from Dennis, and even without standing up, he could have wheeled himself to the side of Dennis and looked closer at the implant for himself. Instead, he waited for Don. Only later I realized that the jacks were so messy looking that Bill didn't need to get any closer to see the problem.

Don, a man of about fifty from what I heard while at the morning conference, was an engineer working on the electronics for the breathing pacemaker unit and would usually be present during their implants in the operating room, giving the surgeons advice on the implanting procedure so the device could do its job. Don did not do any surgery.

"What do you want me to do?" he asked Bill, who was still in his chair, holding the results from the stimulation of my right visual cortex.

"Put these savers in Dennis."

Don parted the hair, pondering over the situation for a minute. Bill turned to Nancy and said reassuringly, "Don's one of our bioengineers who implants the breathing pacemakers." It sounded believable.

"Can't be done," Don said finally. "The skin's growing right over, and there's all sorts of oozy stuff under it." Don did not want to get involved.

"Just push away the skin and get this in there." Bill was losing his patients. Don must have been trying as Dennis protested from the pain.

"It's really wet and mushy," repeated Don, giving up. He stepped back from Dennis, placing the savers on the table in a demonstration of resignation. "It's just not something we can do here. It's wet and raw, with all sorts of buildup under the scalp in the region, and I'd just hurt him trying to force them on."

At this point, Bill had to give up on having the jacks connected. Pat came in and handed me my lunch. I hoped it wasn't wet and oozy. Nancy sat beside me, saying nothing. Bill turned to me.

"We'll map you on your one side this afternoon instead." He addressed Pat. "Take Dennis back home. We'll work with him in a couple of weeks after his head is healed a bit better." I heard him and Nancy leave the room silently, Pat in the lead. This wasn't such a big day for Dennis after all.

I ate the burger and fries, which were neatly packaged in a styrofoam container, while Steve and Jim shuffled equipment around on the table, preparing for the mapping. It didn't look like they were about to eat. Dr. Dobelle was still in his chair, most likely thinking about the healing situation with Dennis and what to do if the situation worsened.

I heard him rustle the paper some more, the one that had all my voltages required for each electrode written on it.

"Here, take this back," Dr. Dobelle said, passing the sheet to Steve. "Looks good so far. The currents are low, and you have quite a few that are good. We should be in business by this afternoon." He turned half around, talking to me more than Steve or Jim. He turned back to them. "How much longer before you're ready for the mapping?"

"About forty minutes or so," Jim said. He was giving himself time to deal with more problems.

Bill left the room. I finished my lunch and moved back to the place I had been at when being tested for thresholds. I was impatient to get this part of the procedure going as it would actually give me a picture to look at. Steve and Jim were still fussing around after the forty minutes were up. It was predictable that Bill was going to arrive any minute.

"How are we going to do this?" I asked, breaking the silence that started to resemble a plague in this office. I had heard no sounds from any of the workers in the building all morning, ever since morning conference.

"We are going to map you with a relative mapping program," Jim started to explain politely. "You will see two phosphenes at the same time, although the second one lights up a second after the first. That means the first shines for two seconds, the second for one second. I will use a numerical keypad to indicate to the program in which direction you saw the second phosphene relative to the first. So that means if you see the first phosphene dead center of your visual field, and a second later the second phosphene right above the first, I would press number 8 on the keypad. If the second one is on the top left, I would press number 7."

I thought about it for a minute. This way, if one looked at an object that started coming into view from the left side, the very leftmost phosphenes would light up first. However, they will not necessarily be in a straight line, as the phosphenes are not necessarily spaced evenly. In fact, I had a few that were rather distant from the main group.

"It will work, but it would only give a good map if all phosphenes were evenly spaced in the visual field," I said. Jim agreed. "It's a good start, though."

"For sure," I replied, figuring I'd adjust to it in no time. "Better to have a crooked image than no image at all." I thought of how I'd take the system home and remap it for myself anyhow, taking my time and doing it right. "Tell me, Jim," I asked out of curiosity. "Wasn't it just the voltages of my thresholds you recorded?"

"Yeah," said Jim, plugging away at the keys.

"Then what is Dr. Dobelle saying about the currents being good?"

Jim continued to work, treasuring the time that Bill was in the other room. "I don't know. I can't record the currents all that well with this old scope as it doesn't capture the signal image."

Dr. Dobelle maybe did not know the difference, I concluded. A lot of people didn't know the difference between voltage and current, but they weren't about to claim they did either. It was disconcerting to think that the master behind this project had limited knowledge as to what constitutes electrical entities. Yet Steve and Jim knew, and they were the ones pushing the buttons. Their knowledge, unfortunately, did not have much to do with the brain. I began to wonder seriously how much Dr. Dobelle really knew about the brain. There was John Girvin, but he was in the Middle East. That didn't provide much comfort.

It took another hour before the two engineers were ready to go. They were able to concentrate as Dr. Dobelle did not enter the room until Steve, as instructed by Bill, went and got him out of his office. Steve was helping him into the room as I reconnected the cables. Bill took his place to my right, beside the table as before, smelling sweaty as if he had run a marathon. I hoped it wasn't associated with anxiety over my progress. He really needed a rest, I thought as I heard his exhaustion.

"Ready to go?" drawled Bill. He sounded as if he had just been awakened.

"Yeah, we're ready. I'll start it and you," Jim was referring to me at that instance, "will tell me the direction the second phosphene is relative to the first. It can be either top left, straight up, top right, right, bottom right, straight down, bottom left, left, or on top of each other."

"You press the five key for that one?" I said. "Yeah, that's right. It's quite easy."

"Some of them were rather dim at threshold," I said, recalling that we found the "threshold," which was the point at which the phosphene was barely visible. "You may have to repeat them a few times."

"Just let me know as this is done by pressing the zero." Bill was awake enough to listen in. "Sounds like Jens is ready to do this himself," he commented to my surprise. There would be nothing I'd like more than to play an active role in this process. Bill had a lot of confidence in me. Tired or not, he was shaping up to a fair sport, I thought. If only he wasn't so frail. "By the way," he continued, "we add 25 percent to the thresholds when we do the mapping so you can see it well."

I wasn't sure what to make of that. It seemed like a lot, considering that biological tissue was not guaranteed to have a linear rise in current with respect to voltage. I didn't have to be a doctor to know that. Once in high school, the science teacher demonstrated that fact. "Just because you can't feel fifty volts," he had lectured that day, "doesn't mean that hundred will be only a bit uncomfortable to feel." He then asked us to find a partner who would slowly increase the voltage with a variable power supply while the other held onto the output leads. At sixty-eight volts, I had felt nothing. At seventy-two, it started to tingle. At eighty it was no longer bearable. I wondered if Bill ever did this experiment.

"Is that safe?" I couldn't resist asking.

"Of course. I've been in this business for forty years. I know what I'm doing. Bill shifted in his chair, probably uncomfortable, considering the entire day seemed to be spent sitting down. "Now let's get going."

"Now," Jim said. I saw one phosphene light up in my visual field, sparkling and bright like one would imagine a wishing star, only much bigger and with a ring of color around it. A second later, another appeared above it, slightly larger. Having the two to look at simultaneously was mesmerizing, the appearance of the second phosphene giving a sense of visual motion that captured my attention as would have a frightening movie scene during my childhood. It rendered me speechless until the two stars disappeared from view. I took a deep breath and said, "Straight up."

I then added, "You'd have to press '8' on the pad."

We did a few others, the majority of the phosphenes giving a beautiful display of color. Bill was watching, and then said, "You could probably do that yourself."

I said in response, "I'd love that. The more the patient can do for himself, the more useful the product is in the end anyhow."

"Let him try," Bill suggested to Steve, who slid the keypad to me. I started. It was beautiful. I could play the system like a video game. Each time I entered a number from 1 to 9, the program selected a new pair of phosphenes. If I had any doubts, I could just press the zero key and the last two would repeat.

I was at about the twentieth pair when I noticed the voices of Jim and Steve fading in the distance. Bill had left the room some time earlier, and both the engineers had been scurrying to get the camera system ready, conversing loudly with one another. But their voices had faded, and even my feet seemed like they weren't there. I had been repeating the last pair a few times, no longer able to concentrate, but still fixated onto the display of lights in my visual field. I paused. I was out of breath, as if I had been holding it for too long. I sat back in the chair, the feeling returning in my feet, the voices of Jim and Steve again audible. I had a sudden recollection of what Pat had told me regarding his experience in the Marriott Lisbon's dining lounge. Was this what a seizure was like?

"I concentrate so hard on these dots," I spoke out to the engineers, "that I even forget to breathe!" They chuckled and returned to their tasks. I took it easier from then on, only doing a few at a time. In fact, a lot of the time I couldn't progress at a good rate as the former phosphenes, even without any electrical stimulation, kept coming back. They would shimmer, blinking on and off once every second, making mapping impossible. I took my time, waiting patiently for the residual phosphenes to disappear.

I had the mapping finished when the program no longer spit out any more phosphenes.

"I'm all done, I think," I announced to the engineers. They dropped what they were doing and came over.

"You can disconnect for now until we have the camera connected." One of them handed me the allen wrench. Bill worked himself back into the room. Still in his chair, sitting down, I could smell his sweat and could imagine his cramped position in that little chair must have been uncomfortable. I felt a pang of guilt for having my mobility. "When you're done the mapping on that side, print it out for me and bring it over." Bill rested in the conference room. "We'll get that camera hooked up soon, and then you'll have a better idea as to what this is all about."

"Sounds great!" I was all wired up for that event. I had no idea what kind of an image I'd be able to see. It had to be good, though, as it was already great to look at the sparkling dots during mapping, I thought to myself.

A half hour later, Steve came back from Louise's office where he had printed out the map. On the paper were printed the actual location of each electrode, using the paper as the example visual field. Bill took a look.

"They're all in a tiny group, with a couple of strays. This isn't a good map at all. Jens, what would you say your range of phosphenes is from center vision?"

"About seven inches to the left and six inches low at least, if not more, from center of vision, with a few very close, within an inch, of center vision at arm's length." I knew there was a bit of a group about three inches to the seven thirty polar position, but there was a healthy range spread out as well.

"We'll have to do it again. I don't think that program worked." Bill paused as Steve and Jim abandoned their efforts to hook up the camera. "We'll have to use the polar mapping technique. Jens seems capable of determining the location of the phosphenes he sees, so let's do it that way." He waved the paper he was holding. "This isn't going to work."

"Let me know when you're ready for me," I said to them, leaving the conference room to stretch my legs. It had been a long day already. I couldn't help but think about Bill again, stuck in his chair. Then, reflecting for just a moment on the progress so far with my phosphene map, I began to wonder what this could all bring for me. Logic told me that with only three dozen dots or so, I wouldn't see very much, but my hopes were still high.

"We won't be able to print out the new map we make with that program," I heard Jim say to Bill. "Only this program has the printout feature."

"We'll just do it by hand," Bill said. He called Pat on the building's PA system. "Pat, I want you to go and get some polar graphing paper. Also, bring back a pizza for dinner." It sounded to me like Bill was going to make a long day of it. I didn't mind; sitting alone in the hotel room was not my idea of a good time. "The more we get done today, the more I'll see tomorrow," I reasoned.

I hooked myself up again to the cables coming from the stimulator. An extra twist tie used to hold the seventy-two 32-gauge teflon-covered wires together was installed around the connector for my right side so I would know which went where. If I mixed it up, I risked having a far too high voltage administered to the array, resulting in Lord knows what. I wasn't going to chance it. Steve and Jim also had to select the correct side in the program. It was sometimes confusing as the "right" side could mean either the right visual cortex, meaning the right side of the brain, which corresponded with the left visual field, or the right visual field, corresponding with the left visual cortex. However, if, for some reason, different operators were introduced in the procedure, the two sides could easily be confused. I hoped they made enough notes on their files to clarify the intended reference. Jim continued to punch a few more buttons on the laptop while Steve watched. Jim had been working for the past four years or so with Bill, but Steve had just come on board. Jim was the ace who wrote most of the software, knowing its strengths and weaknesses.

"Ready?" he asked me.

"I am," I replied. "What do you want me to say?"

"I'm going to give you a one-second display of each phosphene, one at a time, and you tell me its clock position and its distance from center of vision."

Jim hit a button, the computer beeped, and a star-like phosphene, still at 25 percent more than threshold, appeared in my visual field. Each phosphene had its characteristics—some were just like the end of a pencil, others had fuzzy edges with a slight out-of-round appearance, others still were larger and slightly speckled, while others yet were a mere glow possessing a dull mixture of colors, analogous to a "black light" used sometimes at discos.

Having seen them now a few times in the last few hours, I was starting to recognize them.

"8:30 at four inches," I answered.

"Now," said Jim after a short delay from entering my previous response.

"A half-inch at 7:30." I liked this phosphene in particular as it was very small, about a quarter inch in diameter at arm's length, crystal clear with sharp, well-defined edges and best of all, close to the center of focus. Seeing this one was just like really seeing as I could focus on it.

The process was completed within an hour. It would be quite a prolonged procedure, I mused, if there were several thousand to do like this. It would take weeks, if not months, to complete, and if something wasn't quite right, it would have to be done all over again. I wondered how Bill had ever planned to implant ten thousand patients a year if he didn't even have an efficient mapping method in place for the few patients he did have. Steve and Jim would be hard-pressed to try to accommodate ten thousand patients.

"We're all done," announced Jim to Bill, handing him a paper that had the coordinates written on it. Pat came in at the same time, holding a pizza.

"I had no luck with the polar graphing paper," he said, placing the pizza on the table in the cafeteria room.

Bill cursed and said, "You'd think in this area, having at least ten square miles of offices, there'd be someone selling polar graphing paper." He motioned to Pat, who obediently pushed him to the table where the pizza lay. We could make our own," I suggested. "All we need is a piece of paper." I reached into my carry bag and got out a blank piece of brailing paper, "and draw twelve lines radiating from the top right corner equally spaced. Those will signify clock positions from six to nine in fifteen-minute divisions. Then we take a ruler and measure in inches the distance from that corner in inches, which will give us a map looking exactly like that I see at arm's length."

"I want the engineers to get the camera hooked up," said Bill. "Good idea, though."

"You can do it," I said. Bill paused, more than likely not anticipating such a request from my part. He probably hadn't picked up a pencil in decades. "Pat, go in my office and get a ruler and pencil."

Bill started drawing lines on the paper. I could hear the pencil scrape along the ruler, going right off the end of the paper and onto the tabletop. Pat and Louise and everyone except Jim and Steve had gone home. The office was even quieter without the whirring of the fan of Louise's computer. Bill had drawn three lines when he dropped the pencil and crumpled up the paper, throwing it at the garbage can behind him and missing. "I messed up," he said, reaching for the pizza. "You want some?" Bill and I sat side by side, eating the pizza while Steve and Jim, having refused pizza by saying they weren't hungry, continued to work in the other room, setting up the camera.

As we sat together and ate, Bill chewing hungrily, I couldn't help but feel in awe of the situation I was in at this moment. Putting aside the raw reality of the task before us, despite its looming uncertainty clearly illustrated by Dennis's implant healing problem, it was still kind of amazing that I had made it this far. So many years I had fantasized about being able to participate in such a powerful experiment, and then, upon hearing of Bill Dobelle, here I was, sitting by his side, the implants in my head, and the dream of what I had dreamed for now coming true. The world has over six billion people, and here I was—the only one for now to have this opportunity. "Pizza tastes a bit like cardboard," I noted its lack of flavor. "Maybe we were supposed to eat the box instead of the pizza."

Bill laughed in agreement. "Yeah, the box is probably better." He took the pizza off the table, box and all, and wheeled to the garbage dispenser, stuffing the package inside. "Let's go to the conference room and get you going." It was well past 6:30 p.m. by then.

Jim was typing away on the laptop when he suddenly stopped, whispering a curse to himself. The computer connected to the stimulator, the one for the vision system, beeped, indicating it was rebooting.

"Lost the connection again," Jim said, shaking his head in disgust. This must have been going on all through supper as Steve said, "Why on earth is it doing this all the time?"

This explained why Jim and Steve didn't come out to eat pizza with us.

"Ready to go?" was Bill's contribution.

"Just another twenty minutes," Steve said, hoping that would solve the problem.

"What's the matter?" Bill was getting impatient for the fiftieth time that day.

"We keep losing communications with the second computer,"

Jim explained vaguely. He restarted everything and tried again. Bill passed a pair of glasses to me. They weren't the ones I had selected several months ago and sent here—they were bulky and far too wide for my head. There was a long connecting cable as well as a second one that had a nine-volt battery dangling off it.

"Here are your glasses," Bill said to me. "These aren't the ones I sent. They're those you showed me in Portugal," I replied, showing Bill how badly they fit.

"Where are Jens's glasses?" Bill asked Steve. "They're still in the back. We don't have the cameras on them yet."

Jim joined in the conversation, waiting again for the computers to reboot. "We'll have to change the hardware somewhat before we can use the cameras as they use a different power source than that available in the stimulator box. We need to install the other power supply for the camera, as the cameras will be run from the battery pack instead of a 9 V like this one is."

"What the hell have you guys been doing all this time?" Bill was getting riled up again. My question to him should have been why did he not look for himself to make sure it was done? I dreaded the answer, which more than likely was that he didn't have enough knowledge as to what the electronics were all about. I would have thought, before I met him, that he would have been right there at the computers, messing with the components and software, assisting Steve and Jim in locating the electronic failure, instead of just sitting there seemingly helpless.

It was past 8:00 p.m., and nothing had changed. Neither engineer could locate the problem as the computer for the vision system kept conking out. Bill was notably worried about the press conference expected the following day. He had hoped I would see the world right in front of the reporters, but now it was going to be kind of embarrassing for all of us.

"The equipment is really not all that reliable," I commented, my hope fading for the eventual return home with my equipment.

"Yeah," replied Bill, sounding very tired. "It might not be ready this time around. I'm disappointed about that too." He turned to the engineers who were still fussing fruitlessly with the junk on the table. "Jim, just leave that for now and set up the VCR over here in this corner, with the screen, with Jerry's video in and ready to go. Since that's not going to work any time soon, we'll just have to show the press what Jerry did when looking for the mannequins in the room, and they can also photograph Jens being stimulated on the other side."

I wondered if Jim and Steve had enough confidence in the system to trust it could do even that tomorrow. After all, if the computer did not continue running without inadvertently rebooting every few minutes during the camera program, it would most likely do the same in threshold or mapping mode. Neither Jim nor Steve said anything. Jim obediently retrieved the VCR, seeming glad to work with something that had a hope in functioning. Dr. Dobelle should really have followed his own advice and kept the media at bay while his electronic "junk" was on the operating table, I thought to myself. It was years later, after running my own renewable energy systems company, that I fully appreciated Bill's strength. It was his level head oriented to problem solving, or more like damage control, while still maintaining composure during a crisis when everyone else felt like throwing in the towel and walking away from the mess. But at this moment, my mind was set on what I hoped for all these years—to see—and to live with pictures in my world.

Steve drove me to my hotel room and went back to get Bill and Jim. They had a long day and were both discouraged, knowing they'd have a problem to come back to in the morning, along with the stress of the media. I did not feel much better, as I had expected to do some seeing here in this hotel tonight. I would have too tough it out, I thought. I decided to call Lorri only after reciting what I really wanted to say.

"How did it go?" asked Lorri, full of hope.

I explained the turn of events of the day, trying to sound somewhat positive, although I did not feel it in my heart. "It could have been worse, I suppose," I said, trying to console myself more than Lorri. "I could have been incapable of seeing the phosphenes. Then I'd be totally out of luck."

"Yeah, I suppose," said Lorri. "It was part of the arrangement, nonetheless, to return with the equipment."

"I couldn't believe how ill prepared the engineers were and how hands-off Bill is when it comes to the components. He doesn't know all that much about the computers, or even the details of electricity—or maybe he does, but is being too modest about it. It's all in the hands of Steve and Jim, and that's all." I spoke harshly, strongly, and only years later, I adjusted my perspective to accommodate the fact that Bill couldn't be an expert at everything—he did know enough to get this project off the ground when no one else did.

"No other employees?" Lorri asked disbelievingly. "We thought there'd be dozens of them!"

"No, those two is all there is, and even there, Steve is just trying to figure out what Jim is doing with the software. If Jim quits, which wouldn't be unlikely, we'd be back to square one." I hoped this wouldn't be a prophecy.

"So how's this going to get anywhere?" Lorri was not prepared for this at all. "Wasn't John Girvin or Dillis or Beth there?"

"No. Steve and Jim said John was either back, or on his way back to the Middle East, Dillis was still in Portugal, and Beth was no longer with us."

The conversation had no other place to go from here. Lorri would have to readjust to the new reality just like I had to. The words "Dobelle Institute" had taken on a new meaning for us now. The extreme sophistication in technology and knowledge was somewhat curbed; the great teams of gifted scientists and researchers were a mere trio of normal people with logical ideas. I did not mention to Lorri about Bill's deteriorating health condition. I had to go easy on her. We both voiced our hopes for an improvement in the situation the next day and hung up. I could have used a drink that night—a good strong one . . . because if I had taken the time to reflect, I may have discovered that perhaps too many researchers could have stalled the project as no one would have dared stick their neck out as Bill did for this dream.

The following day, May 17, 2002, Pat came and picked me up at 7:30 a.m., Bill once again greeting me as he sat in his usual place in the backseat of the Caddy. His clothes were clean and neat from what I could perceive when shaking his hand and holding his shoulder with my free hand. Apparently, he was taken good care of by someone at his home. I noted his favorite place to sit was on the same side where I sat on the drive down there, having proudly stated to Pat "I'm sitting right where the great doctor sits," not knowing what that really meant. I didn't feel quite so childishly excited about the prospect now; I was starting to see him as a normal man, wrestling with challenges, failures, and successes just like I was.

"How was your breakfast?" Bill asked as Pat drove the Caddy toward Mall Drive.

"Orange juice and toast," I said. "I told management I prefer it delivered as I had troubles seeing, so when the porter came up with my tray, he gave me a newspaper as well. Imagine that!"

Pat and Bill laughed heartily. Pat unloaded Bill, placing him into his foldable wheelchair, and I followed as Pat pushed him along a small stretch of sidewalk leading up to the door of the Dobelle Institute. Louise greeted us in her usual polite and enthusiastic manner. We then all sat down at the conference table, where the employees were once again subject to the same routine as yesterday. The topic of conversation coming from the breathing pacemaker group was the possible sale of another machine.

"It wouldn't be bad to have a second sale this month," Bill commented. There was no discussion about the sale or manufacture of any other products. I figured I'd ask Bill about this later, recalling the various stimulators he had boasted about manufacturing and developing in the letters he had sent prior to my investing in this visual prosthesis.

Bill turned to Steve and Jim, who were sitting quietly at the other end of the table. "You guys will have to hustle to find out why the system doesn't work with the camera," Bill commanded, adding, "we have a reporter from *Wired* magazine coming over later this morning, and it would be good to have the thing at least looking like this project is going forward."

"I already found the problem this morning," Jim said, relieved to have something good to say. "There was a short in the battery cable leading up to the stimulator/computer of the vision system. It should work fine now." I found out some time later that morning that the batteries used had been damaged, giving away the secret. The engineers, however, weren't about to share that part of it with Bill. Multiple-cell lithium-ion batteries like those used for this system were expensive.

Once again, the engineers hauled out all the electronics, laptops, and the oscilloscope for the task of the day. I was to be stimulated for the right visual field, being the left visual cortex, and then mapped, basically, a repetition of yesterday except using the other side of my brain. The array in question was going to be the big one—the one with 3 mm electrode diameters instead of the 1 mm electrodes used on the other side.

"Now," said Jim, the computer beeping. I was hooked up and sitting in the same office-style chair as I did yesterday.

"No," I said monotonously.

"Now," Jim said again. But again I replied negatively. Jim increased the voltage to 2.

"Now," he said. Bill was sitting beside me, watching quietly, most likely hoping that nothing else would go wrong before the reporter came.

"Maybe," I replied. "I saw a small flicker near the top of my visual field, maybe. It's hard to tell because my background is not always entirely black." I had noticed that it was blacker today than it had been for a while, however.

Jim increased the voltage setting to 4. "Now," he said, and at the same time I said "*Ouch!*" as there was a deep, angry pain tearing through the inside of my head. That had happened in Portugal as well, probably on the same electrode.

"We'll skip that one," Dr. Dobelle said in a nonchalant manner, suggesting that I should suck it up—but then again, that's really all I could do as stopping the experiment was out of question.

"I had a few on this side in Portugal that produced pain," I said after I recovered. "Why not just skip all those electrodes that caused pain there?"

"We never wrote them down," retorted Jim. Bill started to explain, attempting to justify his oversight in Portugal. "You wouldn't have yet developed the encapsulating membrane that keeps the array in place on the brain. It could have moved in the meantime, making this information useless anyway."

I wasn't too convinced about that. Had he written it down, he would be able to compare this painful electrode to the ones hurting in Portugal, and if they were indeed the same, it would mean we'd have the same problem with the others that hurt in Portugal. But then again, I thought—the more phosphenes, the merrier—so may as well try them out and tough it out. The part of my mind pushing on the project at all costs was still in control.

"How about we just advance much slower than always doubling the voltage?" I suggested. It was, after all, my brain in question. "That way the pain would be only a mere tingle as it surfaces."

"That'll take too long. We'd have to punch in every number manually, and we'd be at it all day. This is the scientific method of doing such an experiment, the same we used in all the volunteers for years. Let's get on with it."

There wasn't much I could say. All the volunteers had smaller electrodes, similar to those I had on my other side, which only produced a minor pain if they were in the wrong place on the brain. But Bill did not seem to understand the fact that a larger electrode would contact more brain matter, and since any matter has resistance relative to its dimensions, a 3 mm electrode could conduct as much as six times the amount of current as a 1 mm electrode. This, coupled with the nonlinear voltage/current relationship (resistance), is a recipe for a painful experience when doubling the voltage applied without limiting the current available. This provision was not installed in the stimulator. Yet, how could I convince Bill of this, I asked myself—he seemed to have his agenda, and his plan would have to prevail.

I gritted my teeth when Jim hit the button for the stimulation of the next electrode, weighing my options in an instant. There was no place for me to go except out of there. That meant I'd be still in the dark, $130,000 down the drain, and a crowd of donors to face back in Napanee who'd demand an explanation. As well, I'd have this stuff stuck in my head without any use for it. I had no choice but to remain there.

"Now," said Jim emotionlessly. It was obvious by his tone of voice he would have gladly gone through the extra trouble of entering small voltage increases so I'd be spared the torture. But the big man was watching; he wrote out the paychecks. The computer beeped. I felt nothing. He had to increase the voltage again. I braced myself.

"Now," he said, and this time I saw a bit of light. I was glad, not only to see the light but to have accomplished this without a searing pain in my head.

This procedure carried on for two hours. The electrodes did not produce a very good phosphene at all—they were larger, the smallest being the size of an egg at arm's length. They all had different shapes; some square, some oblong in either vertical or horizontal directions, some shaped like a half-moon, some like bananas. The light they produced was more speckled than a straight, even-lighted area in the visual field. I did all I could to save as many as possible. There were more painful ones, some of them practically unbearable. By the end of the stimulation session, I was never so glad that this was over with. "Hopefully," I said to myself, "they wrote the painful ones down this time and I wouldn't have to feel them again."

"We're all done," announced Jim as Bill was again wheeled into the room by Pat. He had left to talk with the reporter who had shown up. Now the reporter, Bill, and Pat entered the room.

"How many good ones?" Bill asked, making a good show of the success of the project and making an obvious display of his expectations being met in the preliminary results.

"About forty-five," Jim replied. Steve was still counting again, promising Bill a listing of the results when he had them printed off.

"That's great," Bill said. "I'd like to introduce to you Steven, our observer for the media—Wired magazine—for the next couple of days."

We all shook hands. Steven was a man of average height, of about my age. He sat down at the other side of the conference table. From here he could turn his head and watch the video clip already set up for Bill so all he had to do was push a button on the remote.

"I'll just sit here quietly and mind my own business," he said jokingly to us. "I don't want to interfere with the process, so I'll just observe."

"As of today, we just finished stimulating Jens's left side. He had to tell us the point when he saw the phosphene, that is, the dot of light, as we slowly increased the threshold up to that value." Bill was explaining the process. "If Bill really did what he said," I mused, "I would never have had such pain." He continued, "Now that he's done with that, we're going to map him. We have some good software that relatively maps the phosphenes, placing them in their order so the computer can make images using them. After that's done, he will be able to see for the first time in . . . how many years?"

"More than eighteen," I replied. I knew Bill wanted me to answer that one just to compound the merit to the program headed by him. "If it works, then he deserves it," I thought.

Steve and Jim set up the mapping program. We ran through the first couple together, Steve at the controls, while Jim fussed with the camera arrangement once again. I took over the numerical keypad once we knew all was working as it should. Steve needed the time so he could help Jim.

"So what do you see?" *Wired* magazine asked as I was running the program.

"I see first one dot of light light up, then a second later a second one lights up. I tell the program which direction the second phosphene is relative to the first." I explained the corresponding numerical values to him.

"What do the points of light look like?"

I explained the quality of light, the quivering nature of it, the colors around the edges, especially once the voltage was increased 25 percent for the mapping procedure, the variation of shapes and sizes, and I commented on the size differences in the two electrode arrays and how that affected what I saw. He listened intently.

I mapped a few more, feeling again the out-of-breath sensation as yesterday, along with the feeling of loss of my outer limbs. The voices of Jim and Steve faded, and I heard no more of Steven from *Wired* magazine either. It seemed that the direction the second phosphene was located relative to the first one was often very difficult to determine. I could see them both, clearly, but not be able to tell exactly where they were going. I came across a relatively stubborn pair and repeated the combination several times in my attempt to determine their relative location with certainty. The voices in the room became inaudible now, my entire concentration on only the two phosphenes and my fingers on the keyboard. That was the last thing I remembered of mapping that day.

I came too in an office chair—the same one I had been in earlier, supported by two people, one of whom was massaging my back as I groaned in pain. I did not understand where I was or who was around me. My back hurt many times worse than ever experienced during my career in moving pianos or heaving logs destined for firewood. My head hurt just as much, and there seemed to be a large cut right across my tongue, which was sore and bruised. For several minutes, I heard an unintelligible mumbling around me, recognizing it as no language at all. It took a while before words started to come out of the confusion of sound.

"Can you hear me?" I heard someone say. He must have said that before as I remembered the same rhythm of words but without comprehension.

"My back hurts." This was all I could say and think of. The pain was incredible. The voice talking to me sounded familiar, but I could not place its owner.

"Can you hear me?" It came again.

"Yes," I said. "Where am I?"

"You're in New York, at the Dobelle Institute. Remember?" The voice said again. I thought of New York often, as all the important things for the economy happened there. Even Frank Sinatra sang about New York, but I never had a need to go there. The traffic would be unbelievable there.

"Right. What would I be doing there?" I still had no idea where I was. This could be Canada or Germany, as I've been in both places.

"I'm Bill Dobelle. This is the Dobelle Institute, and you're here for getting artificial vision." So that was who was talking. I remembered him now but had no idea where I would have met him.

"Look, you just had a seizure. You're recovering now, and you're in the office of the Dobelle Institute in New York." Strong hands were still rubbing my back, and I was grateful for that. I did not know what I was doing there, but I knew I must be in New York. I felt like I had entered a time machine and that the world had changed without my knowing it.

"A seizure?" I couldn't believe my ears. That's the last thing I ever wanted to have.

"Yeah, you've had too much stimulation. We're going to have to check out what's going on and change a few things for you."

I felt a wave of panic coming on. I may not be able to get this system now, meaning I lost all the cash, all the hope of seeing again, and have to spend the rest of my life with these useless implants in my head. "Does that mean I can't participate further in this vision program?"

"Oh hell, no. This is just a minor inconvenience, that is, the seizure," Bill said. It sure didn't feel minor to me, but his manner consoled me nonetheless, as I would still be able to go through with this. He continued, "We went through all the phosphenes in Portugal and you never had that happen there."

"I was in Portugal?" I demanded, having absolutely no recollection of going there. "How would I get there?" All I could remember of Portugal were the Portuguese laborers on the section crew at British Columbia Railway, keeping to themselves, not knowing two words in English but feeling lucky anyways as their salary, worth many times more than the present Portuguese currency did back then, ensured their families had a good life back home. I remembered nothing about ever being there. It was as if a block of time was simply missing in my memory.

"Yes, you were in Portugal where you were implanted last month. I think I'll have Pat drive you to your hotel room where you can rest for a while." Bill had nothing else to offer. Pat drove me there, led me to the room. I found it clumsy to walk; the pain in my entire body was so intense I felt I had been run over by a car. It was difficult to talk as my tongue ached, the cut quite evident across the middle.

"You're sure you're all right?" asked Pat. I wasn't so sure.

"My tongue is so sore, and the rest of me is pretty bad too. I feel like I've been in a major fight—and lost."

"Yeah, I understand why," Pat agreed. "You bit your tongue when you had your seizure. It wasn't a pretty sight, that's for sure."

I was starting to remember everything now, the trip to Portugal, and also Pat's description of the man having a seizure in the Marriott Lisbon, the scene of the suffering man taking away Pat's appetite for dining in their lounge forever. I guessed he'd be just as reluctant to eat in the Dobelle Institute now as well.

When Pat closed the hotel room door, the silence and solitude fell upon me like a tidal wave of destruction. The force of this wave came upon me in a strength I had never known before. Even at the time I had lost my second eye, amidst the anguish of the loss, it was the calculated despair of what I could no longer do or see that translated itself into depression and thus emptied the lust to live. Some of its destructive force at that time had been lost in translation, leaving room for some hope, also calculated by prospects which may or may not come true. In this case, however, sitting in total solitude, there was an overpowering force in my being wanting to destroy itself in any manner possible. I had felt it, but could not identify it, ever since my seizure, and now that I was alone with my thoughts, it was on the verge of breaking through. Even the pain in my body from the stress of the convulsions was trivialized by the overwhelming desire to terminate my life. I struggled for control. I knew there was so much yet to live for—the family with whom I'd share the world once I could see it, the reality being just around the corner, the prospect of travel and excitement in the future. Yet there was a part of my mind that had no control, no reasoning, and now it was trying to take over in the most destructive manner possible. Where was Beth Seelig now that I needed her? This was her profession; she could do so much just by being here now. Anybody would have done. I sat on the bed, clutching the covers with both hands, concentrating on each word coming out of the clock radio near the bed. I remembered hearing on the local news in Napanee a resident in some neighboring community, a man with four kids, good wife, and with all his affairs in order, turning suddenly nasty and unsociable to all his friends and family. They did not accept this personally, claiming that "just wasn't like him" to act like this. He took his own life just days later, leaving the community shocked and mystified. I knew now what he had felt in his last few days of life. We are essentially two beings, one our conscious, calculating, and reasoning self, while the other, a force acting upon us without regard for rules, sentiments, or reasoning, yet borrowing from the first the mastery of well-honed tasks. As we grow up, we are taught to control and override the latter being, the one which is potentially contradictory to the survival of the human race. It was that one now that I was trying to control.

Pat knocked on my door just after 5:00 p.m.

"You all right?" he asked. If I wasn't, it would have been too late.

"Bill's just in the dining lounge. He wants to buy you supper and talk to you. Do you feel up to it?"

I met him in the lounge, seated close to the fountain, which had a calming effect on me. My tongue hurt and so did my back, but at least I had the monster in my head under control.

"Are you feeling better?" said Bill. I couldn't begin to explain the circumstances to him. Yet he was the one who gave the psychiatric exams to the last few implanted patients after Beth left in Portugal.

"Jens," Bill started to explain just after we gave our orders to the waiter. "Will you ever forgive Steve for what happened today?"

"Steve?" I was confused. "What did he have to do with it? He was somewhere else when this happened."

"Yes, that's true," said Bill. "But it was the flaw he had in the program that made this happen. Jim checked the mapping program, and it had repeated the same two phosphenes eleven times! Imagine the amount of stimulation that gave you on the same two electrodes. If one of those is in the peripheral vision area of your cortex, that could cause a seizure."

I was no longer confused. Bill did not have enough information as to what constituted the mapping program. He had never used it, never understood

353

any of the operation of the software. He thought it was the program that selected the electrodes to map and repeated them as well. It was me who did the repetitions. Those big electrodes were bad news right from the start, as they gave all that pain that the others didn't. Then, with their larger surface area, the increase of 25 percent for the mapping over the threshold may be a problem too.

"I think it's those large electrodes," I said finally to Bill. "Just think of how many times the electrodes are going to be repeated when looking at a picture? That would mean I'd have a seizure all the time."

Bill was actually giving it some thought. I could tell as he paused a bit before coming up with an answer. "We only stimulate the electrodes for a fraction of a second when using the system," he said in his defense. "In this program you see the phosphene for, what was it, a few seconds?"

"Two for the first, one for the second," I replied. "Yeah, that's not good. I don't think we'll use that program tomorrow."

"Was Steven, the *Wired* reporter, there when this happened?"

"Yeah, he was," snorted Bill disapproving. "He won't have any shortage of material to report on now. He was the one who held you up in your chair." Bill paused for a bite from his dinner and added, "It was a hell of a time to have a seizure."

That's right, Bill, you don't invite the press when the patient is on the operating table, or even on the floor, for that matter, I thought to myself, the "press embargo" idea originally insisted on by Bill still fresh in my mind.

A few months later, when the magazine was published, the seizure was graphically described, as predicted. However, the article did have a positive appeal to it despite all—what Bill said to smooth things over, I still don't know . . . another example of Bill's amazing problem-solving capabilities.

I slept badly that night, spending most of the time in a hot bath, attempting to ease the pain from my body. The savers still attached to my implants were a bit awkward as well as they had annoying little knobs at their ends that sometimes gouged into the still tender area of my head from the surgery. I did not call Lorri that night.

May 17 started late, with Pat picking me up at 8:30 a.m. I felt better in spite of the body aches, especially in my back, and there still was that nasty cut across the tongue. Bill wasn't in the back of the Caddy this time, which meant Pat must have driven him to the office earlier. Pat and I said very little on the way there; he must have avoided talking so as to keep from further discussing the unfortunate incident of the day before. Bill greeted me in the front room of the office when I entered, then asked Pat to take me into the conference room. Steve and Jim were late, so there was nothing to do but sit until they arrived a half hour later.

The engineers, Dr. Dobelle and myself were seated at the table, the others apparently already at work in the breathing pacemaker section, which I had learned was the division called Avery Labs. In fact, in this building, as the sign on the outside of the building suggested, there were three companies: Avery Labs, Dobelle Institute, and Dobelle Laboratories. It seemed impressive enough when reading it, but once a closer look was taken, the observer would find there were only two to four people in each company. Dr. Dobelle, however, would be able to skirt around tax and other regulations by transferring funds, expenses, and responsibilities between them. That wasn't my business, however; I was here to see again. I only found out much later that any financial gains Bill may have from his companies went directly into the artificial vision project.

"First of all, I want to make one thing clear while our friend Steven, the *Wired* reporter, isn't here yet. I deliberately told him we wouldn't start until later this morning so I can tell you all this." Bill was turning his head toward not only the engineers, but also in my direction. "I heard some of you talking yesterday to the reporter about the details of what we are doing, like the power settings, type of current, electrode sizes, etc." I knew he was addressing me more than anyone else in the room as I did most of the talking. Bill continued, but by now I had a good idea of what he was trying to say. "All this information is proprietary. Steven is all ears and can easily sell this information to other companies involved in this research. I'd lose out big-time if that happened. We'd all lose out. We've got to keep quiet about what we're doing. No more discussions about these things when he's around."

I guessed that meant nothing was patented. How could it be anyhow, I asked myself, if Jyles Brindley had done the same thing in the late 1960s? Bill must also have forgotten what all was written in his published and personally distributed Journal 2000, in which details identical to what I gave the reporter were readily available for everyone who was interested in the subject. There was no sense arguing with Bill. He had to have his way and feel like a boss as well.

Steven, the *Wired* reporter, came in as we were setting up the camera. Bill was at the table with us, spitting out the commands.

"How many phosphenes do you want to use and for which side?" Jim asked. Steve, the other engineer, was busy looking over Jim's shoulder so he could participate more actively in the process when more patients were in the office simultaneously.

"Let's start with one frame a second," Bill said. "Then use the left side. Pick out ten phosphenes that are low in current."

Steven listened intently and was scratching on his notepad at the same time. I guessed that when Bill said he didn't want us to give out details, he really meant he wanted to do it himself. Yet, in order to organize the stimulation parameters, there was really no choice unless we all talked a different language.

"The left side gave me the seizure yesterday," I said. "Wouldn't it be better to use the other side today?"

Bill sounded annoyed. "We're just picking out ten of the low-current ones. We're going to use both sides today." Bill was still talking about "low current" when all was recorded was voltage.

"One frame a second, left side, ten phosphenes," Jim repeated, verifying the settings on the screen of the laptop.

"How many pulses per frame?" Jim paused, then added, "Same as what we do for Jerry?"

Bill just grunted his agreement. I found out later it was five pulse trains being used.

"Edge detection on or off?"

"Leave it off for now," replied the genius. "Reverse of the image on or off?"

"What's that mean?" I asked. "Black turns white and white turns black?"

"Something like that, except . . ." Jim caught himself in time not to disclose information to Steven from *Wired* and waited for Bill's instruction.

"Turn it on."

I hooked up the cables. Steven from *Wired* thought it very interesting that I was putting the wires on by myself. "What's that feel like when you're doing that?" he said with all the curiosity of a child in his voice. It must have looked strange to the onlooker.

"Just like hooking up the VCR, I suppose." I struggled to find the words. I never thought this as a big deal. "Maybe like getting dressed, or stringing the belt through its loops, or something like putting on the glasses. Maybe even like putting in a hairpin, if you wore one."

Jim hooked up a diode block to the output of the stimulator to see if it made little flashes in its diodes when the camera was waved around the room. Steven looked at the block of diodes, eight grid of little red lights eight diodes wide and eight long.

"Is this what Jens will see?" Steven was hunched over the diodes, shielding them from the light so as to see better.

"Sort of," said Jim. "The diode locations aren't mapped the same as Jens's phosphene grid, so they're just going to light up all over the place."

"Ready to go?" asked Bill impatiently. I was impatient too as this was going to be the "big day" when the switch was to be thrown for my sight to come back.

"Just about," Steve unplugged the laptop from the outlet power so it had to run on its internal battery. This was done to prevent the possibility of household current flowing through my brain. That would mean another bad day like yesterday, or worse. Jim hooked the cables from my head to the stimulator. Then he placed a fresh 9 V battery in the power outlet of the camera. "Ready to go," he announced, and then, just when I was bracing myself for the big event, he added, "Oh, Bill, what about the multiplier?"

The multiplier was a factor by which all the threshold values were multiplied before being sent to the stimulator. Thus, a multiplier of 1 would not change the values. In the mapping program I had used when I had the seizure, the multiplier had been set at 1.25.

Bill hesitated, then said, "Given he had the seizure yesterday, we'd better start at.5 and work our way up."

Jim tapped the keys for an instant, then said, "All right, we're on."

There was no big "throwing the switch" ceremony as I had anticipated when first investing into this project. Even Steven seemed a bit disappointed as he said "is it really going now?" in a voice hinting on irritation for not having started the system with the fanfare it deserved.

"Yeah," said Jim.

"You probably don't see anything, do you?" said Bill. "We started the thresholds at half their required value to begin with."

I waved my head around with the glasses scanning the room. "What do you see?" asked Steven, pencil in hand.

"Nothing," I said in a flat tone.

"OK," Bill said, turning to Jim, "set the multiplier to.6" Jim fidgeted with the keys, then pushed the final button and said, "There . . ."

Again I waved around the glasses, pointing it in all directions.

"How's that?" Steven asked.

"Still nothing," I said, just blackness confronting me. Steve was observing the oscilloscope and remarked that it was indeed working. Everybody knew it was working except for me.

We repeated the procedure for multiplier values of.7 and.8, with no improvement. At the value of.9, I waved my head around again as if I wanted to see everything in the room. I saw a flash, then nothing.

"I saw a flash," I said, still moving my head. "There it is again, every time I point my head in the direction of that corner." I pointed toward the corner of the room beside the reporter. As I held the glasses still while pointing in that direction, it kept flashing, once a second.

"What do you see?" Steven from *Wired* was very serious about capturing the moment on paper when a man sees for the first time in eighteen years.

"I see a flash of light with no shape or size, just a flash once every second as if I saw someone's camera flashbulb go off somewhere out of the corner of my eye."

"Is that what he's supposed to see?" Steven asked Bill, who seemed pleased with the progress so far.

"We're only running a few phosphenes at one frame a second. Let's try it at two," he added, turning to Jim.

Jim shut the system off with his laptop and reopened the program. He fiddled for a few minutes and then started it again. Steven spoke up, "Can't Jens adjust that?"

"No, not this time. We need the laptop and program to do that." It looked like Steven had expected more than just an on–off switch as well.

At two frames a second, I saw a flash every half a second. I was astonished I could not determine the exact location of each phosphene as I could when the pulse trains were a full second long, as during thresholding and mapping. Here it was just a white flash, twice a second. I noticed it did not flash when I looked up at the florescent lights of the room, but it flashed without fail when I covered up the lens.

"I suppose with that 'reversal' setting, I can only see dark objects," I said, moving around my head in observation.

"That's right," said Bill. I pointed at a place right in front of me, beside the plant in the corner. "Are you wearing dark clothes, Steven?"

"Yes, I am too," he answered. "I guess that means you're looking right at me!" He seemed very pleased about it. "How do I look?"

"Like a flash of light every half a second," I replied. "Here, Jens, move your chair a little my way where the table is clear." Bill vaulted himself to my right, and I followed. The table in front of me was clear. Bill took the telephone, which was sitting at the edge of the table and placed it in front of me on the table. I could tell where it was by the sound, but I still moved my glasses around to find it.

"There's a phone in front of you somewhere. Try to find it." The telephone was dark, and the table was light colored, allowing the system to work as it should. I moved slowly so as not to miss the object, given that the frames were advancing at two a second. At one point, when pointing at the table, I could see flashes of light, which ceased as soon as I moved my head one direction or the other. I reached out in the direction the glasses were pointing, my hand landing immediately on the telephone. "There you go," said Bill proudly.

I saw the telephone, the reporter, and the plant all the first day. I pointed the camera at these objects, and light flashes went off in my visual field, which meant they were there. Steven, the plant, and the telephone all looked the same. I was looking at the telephone when suddenly all the phosphenes started to flash, regardless of what I did.

"It quit," I announced, waving my head around, trying to see a change in the flash pattern. I covered the lens and nothing changed. "It's not working now."

"I think the camera battery died." Jim was still looking at the laptop screen.

The battery was changed. It only lasted fifteen minutes before a new one had to be reinstalled. No wonder, I thought, they wanted to integrate the power supply for the camera with the power for the computer, which was a much larger battery.

"Let's try it at four frames," said Bill. Jim had to do some readjusting for that, taking a few minutes. The computer started up, flashes of light repeating themselves in an annoying rhythm in my visual field. I covered the camera, but that only made matters worse. I did not concentrate anymore on what I was trying to do—to see—but rather to get this to shut off. I looked desperately at the light once I remembered it was set to see the darker objects. Even then the residual phosphenes repeated themselves in a nauseating pattern. I started feeling faint, as if I was about to have another seizure. "Better shut it off now," I tried to keep a calm voice. "I'm feeling a bit sick from it." Jim hit a button on the laptop and it quit.

"It was always flashing, and before I knew it, the phosphenes were not going away," I said.

"You should have had phosphene fusion," Bill said. "Jerry had phosphene fusion when he had four frames a second." But I didn't; the phosphenes flashed just like a disco strobe, which drove me nuts even at the time I had my sight.

"We'll give it a rest for now, have a bite to eat and try a bit more this afternoon," Bill called Pat, who ordered a lunch for everyone and went into town to retrieve it.

That afternoon we went through a couple more 9v batteries when we tried the system once again. Four frames a second were still quite nauseating, but when Bill told Jim to switch it to seven, I could see better and not be as annoyed by the flashing.

"You shouldn't have any flashing now," Bill said, sitting beside me with his finger poised on the "off" button on the stimulator. This was the first time I really noticed him getting physically involved.

"I still see flashes, quite pronounced," I stated. "Also, the phosphenes of some electrodes are too bright, making them stick around even without stimulation, while others aren't bright enough." I was able now to move my head quicker without missing the objects. I saw less significant flashes of light when passing my camera over toward Jim and Steve. "What's all that?" I pointed at the table in front of them.

"It's a lot of electronic stuff," Steve said.

"What a mess!" I said jokingly.

I was not able to make out any shapes or sizes of objects when seeing them. I was using the camera as a visual cane rather than a device for assessing objects. It was even impossible to determine, when slowly sweeping the gaze from the "no object" zone until the object came into view, where the object lay, from which side of the visual field the phosphenes became visible. Moreover, lighter colored objects would be totally ignored by the camera. All the while, Bill was undeniably proud of himself as he demonstrated his success in making the blind see in front of the *Wired* magazine reporter, Steven.

That day, being a Friday, ended early, and we did not start in the morning again until well into 10:00 a.m. I should have brought something to do with me in the hotel room. Commack had no life other than that used to make money. There seemed to be no nightlife or anything to do other than listen to the cars roar by on the Motocross Parkway. Everyone was going somewhere else to do their living. I was glad to get back to the office, although it was duller than usual there as there was no one but Bill, Steve, Jim, and myself there during that weekend. There was no reporter now, making Bill not only less nervous but also a bit less worried whether or not I would be satisfied.

"Let's see if we can get both sides working together today, as well as use all the phosphenes," Bill suggested. I liked the sound of that, as this way, I'd get to see the potential of this thing. Jim and Steve got out the equipment, arranged it on the table, and got organized while I prepared myself for another session.

"I hope we aren't doing the painful ones again," I said to Steve. He quietly said to me, while Bill was in another room, "No, we're not going to touch those ones." That meant the day was going to be easier.

"How about we use the 'thresh-adjust program'?" suggested Jim. He turned to me, explaining the program, "With that program, we just use an up—or down key, starting the phosphene at its value determined from what we did two days ago, and refine the setting as it only changes the voltage by a small percentage at a time."

That was a very good idea, I thought. "If anything does cause pain that way, it would just be a slight tingle instead of an electrocution," I said.

"Exactly," Steve and Jim said almost in unison in a manner suggesting they would have liked to have been able to do this procedure in such a precautionary manner to begin with, had they had their way.

"First electrode," said Jim. "Now . . ."

I saw a flicker. "Down a bit," I said. Jim said "OK" and pressed it again. This time I barely saw it. "Good, right there," I said.

"Next," Jim said. I saw nothing. "No, nothing." I replied. He readjusted and tried again. "Now," followed by my "yes, right there," as I could barely see it. We went through quite a few before Bill wheeled himself awkwardly into the room, as there was no one but us to help him on the weekend. "What's going on?" he demanded.

Everyone in the room, including myself, astonishingly, tightened up inside, wondering if Bill was going to throw a wrench into the smooth, well-oiled routine Jim, Steve, and I had developed in the thresholding process.

"How are the thresholds?" Bill asked more specifically. "Some up, some down some," Jim said. We were all wishing Bill would just leave and let us finish as this wasn't a task one could rush.

"It's supposed to be like that though, right, Dr. Dobelle?" I inquired deliberately, forcing him to explain the absence of the adjustability of the system. "After all, Jerry's thresholds varied 20 percent daily, forcing him to readjust his thresholds every morning before using the system, according to your Journal 2000."

"I don't trust the patients with the adjustment of the phosphene thresholds." Bill paused and continued, "We saw what that did a couple of days ago."

There was nothing left to say on this issue. I'd just have to keep the thresholds the way they were set to begin with. Yet they could get worse and worse as the time went by, eventually rendering the equipment useless. I'd have to touch on it again before I left, as it seemed that Bill just wanted to blame everyone but himself for the seizure I had. First he blamed Steve, and now me for something that was no one's fault, and if there was fault, perhaps it should rest somewhat with him as well as he had the idea that larger electrodes would be better prior to extensive testing. It was under his instruction that the mapping program not only selected the multiplier of 1.25 over threshold, but also the duration of the stimulation of each phosphene during the process. At this point, I wondered what kind of information he had told the Wired reporter, Steven, as to who was responsible for the seizure. "I'll find out when the article comes out," I thought to myself.

We finished the thresh-adjust program on both sides within an hour, causing no pain in the process. We'd leave the mapping as it was, as it was impossible for me to criticize it until I could tell where each phosphene was precisely located when the camera was running. Jim started the program up again, this time using the two sides at the same time, according to Bill's instruction and my persistence. All the phosphenes were engaged. Bill did not sit with his finger poised on the "off" button of the stimulator this time; there was no reporter, so there was really no major concern. Nonetheless, I reached over the table until I had it within easy reach just in case.

"It's going now," stated Jim.

Bill had instructed a multiplier of.7 this time, speeding up the process by starting closer to the required value. I couldn't see anything.

"Try.8. Frames still at one per second."

I could see some remote, occasional flashes. "Still not more than the occasional weak flash," I said. Bill raised the threshold to.9. He didn't actually do it himself; Jim did. I still figured Bill should learn to use the program so there's a second person checking what values are entered; if Jim added an extra digit by accident, it would hurt, no doubt.

"Some good flashes now," I said. "But that's all. Just a flash a second when I look at something dark." I covered the lens. There were some brighter phosphenes and dimmer ones, but none could be used to make a picture. It was just like the same image was repeating itself over and over again if there was something dark, or nothing if I looked at something light.

"Let's use four frames a second," said Bill. The battery for the camera quit then, and we had to start over. It was very annoying that we couldn't just hit a button and change a setting while it was in action. Every time Jim was asked to readjust the equipment, it required the system be shut off for several minutes. I could not make proper comparisons like that. If a business presented a product in such a manner to the public, I said to myself, it wouldn't have a chance. But there were no competitors as there are in the business world; the four of us were all alone in this business.

We tried the four frames a second, and once again, I started to feel sick. "I'm just going to have a seizure at this frame rate," I pointed out, staring at the lights above me to stop the flickering. I continued to press my point. "I once read in a book that even traffic control lights are designed to avoid the —three—to four flashes per second rate for warning lights as that frequency of flashing can trigger seizures."

"Never heard of that nonsense," Bill grunted. "But if seven frames doesn't make you feel like that, we may as well use it. It's better anyway. I just don't understand why you see it as a flicker instead of a constant light like Jerry did." Bill had a lot to learn in this business—we all did.

We paused again while Jim readjusted the system. Then we had it: full speed frames of seven per second, all hundred phosphenes,.9 multiplier. I looked around the room, the flickering being annoying but not sickening. The results were identical to yesterday's with a bit more light present in my visual field from the extra phosphenes. There were one or two phosphenes on either side that would get brighter and brighter with every flash until they would keep blinking or even stay on permanently even though I was looking in a direction that did not cause stimulation. It would take several seconds before they'd go away so I could continue the experiment.

"I can locate black objects but have no idea what I am looking at. I cannot identify any objects at all. It seems like the flashing pattern of phosphenes is always the same."

Bill took the telephone and placed it again in front of me. "Find the phone," he instructed. I could do it without much thought. "See?" he said, totally convinced he had improved my quality of life. "You can see the phone now. You couldn't do that before." "True," I agreed, not at all contented by the results. "But this is far from the quality of vision you had promised. I sure hoped at least to tell a person from a tree. But right now I am looking at the chair across the room, which is just a flashing blob of light, and when I look at that plant," I pointed in the direction of the plastic plant in the corner of the room, "it's the same scenario. If you switched the two around now, I wouldn't know the difference."

There was a pause of silence in the room. Jim and Steve did not want to get involved. Bill finally said, "I'm surprised you're disappointed. What we'll do tomorrow is let you walk around a bit with it. Maybe that'll let you put it to use a bit more than just sitting in this room."

It was only early afternoon, and the engineers were packing up. I supposed that because Bill wanted them to come in on a Sunday, which was going to be the following day; he needed to let them have a bit of private time for themselves.

Steve wheeled Bill to the small car that Bill had rented for Steve and Jim to be able to drive back and forth to work. Steve put Bill in the front passenger seat, and I climbed in the back with Jim. They dropped me off at the Sheridan and took Bill home from there. I noticed by the odor in the car that Bill had sweated the day through again—marking the end of his stressful day. Tomorrow we'd walk with the system. I had asked Bill if I could take it to the hotel, seeing that we were quitting early, and experiment with it further.

"No," he had said. "I don't want you using it alone. Moreover, it won't run without the laptop attached right now. It needs some work to be independently operable."

I ordered dinner in the dining lounge and considered the course of the few last days. They hadn't been exactly what I had expected. There were only two young electronics engineers and a medical pioneer working on a project that merited far more in terms of expertise. The boss's physical fragility became more apparent by the day. The seemingly "crude" state of the vision technology was concerning and unexpected considering the sacrifices in money, health, and hope that the patients had made. My seizure from two days ago could have maybe been prevented if a medical expert had been present, hearing my description of how I seemed to even forget to breathe while not having feeling in body limbs during the mapping process—the first warning signs. But there was no medical expert in this company. They had all disappeared once they made their appearance in Portugal—the true term for "window dressing." But most distressing issue at the time was the thought that this vision is not going to give me the independence I had hoped for. How can seeing a few flashes of light when a dark object exists in front of me change my life? Or get me into a better job, like the land surveying job I craved to do again? How can I get back into downhill skiing, keeping on the correct trails, avoiding trees and other people, and then finding my way back into the lineup for the ski lift? What about those hopes I had to be able to participate in the sport of bicycling; the last time Lorri went out with the kids on their bikes, I had said, "Next time I'll be joining you on my bike . . ." There's no chance that will happen now. This vision system wasn't going to change my life at all except put more baggage around my body, along with all the wires, which would make me resemble a robot from outer space. I was going to have to make some major readjustments in my expectations—the expectations I had for the future, just like I had to when I lost my sight in the first place, then again after the failure in getting sight back in my left eye. Here we go again, I thought miserably. All that money and all that pain in Portugal for this? I picked at my supper, my tongue still smarting from the seizure. As I thought of what I was going to say to Lorri tonight, my mind drifted back to the first day when Dennis, with his problematic implant, just had to be sent back home. I've made it this far—right to where I started seeing some light on queue anyways, while he was still at his home, most likely very discouraged and anxious, I guessed. Then, what about the others? They were still far away, healing from the surgery, while I was moving forward. If I had called them tonight and told them of what happened so far, most likely they'd envy me for the bit I had seen so far. I thought again about what I'd say to Lorri and adjusted my mood somewhat before dialing.

The next day started late as well. It was a wonder Steve and Jim even came out to the office considering the negative connotations of the day before. But they came, seating themselves at the table cluttered with electronic marvels, awaiting Bill's commands.

"You should remap him today. Maybe we can get it to work better. Is there any way you can make this system portable?"

Jim thought it over and answered, "Yes, we do have a duffel bag that can hold the stimulator, battery, and computer, which Jens can carry in one hand while I walk behind with my laptop attached via longer cable. Then he'll be able to walk around if he goes slowly enough for me to keep up."

"We'll do that, then," said Bill. The mapping started up, easy now that I knew the routine. I noticed the phosphenes had a lot more color when increased to 1.25 of their normal threshold value. I had little to say to the engineers; I did not want them to get a full drift of my pessimism. I was sitting quietly in the chair when Steve suddenly said, "Jens!"

"What's wrong?" I responded, wondering about Steve's sudden outburst.

"I thought you were having another seizure," he confessed. It had been like this for the last few days ever since that Wednesday that I had it. I had to continue to make silly conversation of Lord knows what just to comfort the engineers I was all right. It must have taken a blow on them too; they were involved, and this was not part of the deal when they first applied for this job. I wondered if Steve knew that Bill had originally blamed him for the cause of the seizure.

"Two inches at 7:45 . . ." I repeated. Jim hit the next button. "Three inches at 6:30 . . ." the mapping was going good. I was able to concentrate on the points much more reliably than I did the first time.

"You know, Jim and Steve," I said, noting a difference in my concentration. "If we did this several times, and then took the average of each phosphene, we'd probably get a pretty good map."

"Tell the big man that, though," Jim said. Bill was not in the room; he was sleeping in his wheelchair in his large office, the last week taking its toll on him. Jim continued, "There are lots of good ideas with artificial vision and how to make it better. I just wish they'd be applied." We continued to work on the map, and within the hour Steve went to Bill's office to wake him up. He returned with the "big man" as we had come to refer to him. We all seemed to feel angry at him at times, but we also needed him a lot.

"Well, are you ready for a walk?" Bill sat in his chair while Jim and Steve busied themselves packing the duffel bag, which was like a gym bag with the two long handles on top. I put on the glasses while Jim, following me at the end of his six-foot cord, carried the laptop computer that controlled my system. I picked up my cane and looked around the room when Jim turned the system on.

"Coming through," I announced, waving my head from left to right, up and down in order to give the advantage to the glasses. I had to keep my eyes pointed straight forward or else the image would move from left to right, or in whichever direction I moved my eyes. I saw a barrage of dots in my visual field in front of me and stopped.

"Chairs," said Jim. I continued to walk, turning slightly right when seeing the object described as a "chair" by Jim. I stopped when I noticed there was no wall to my right. I had been following closely, noticing it by the echo as I always did, even as a young child playing in the dark. I looked around. There was an absence of dots in an area in front of me, but they would reappear when I cranked my head upward, to the left or right.

"This must be the doorframe," I said.

"Yeah, it is," said Bill, who was being pushed behind Jim by Steve. I walked through the cafeteria, noticing more chairs at the table that was there. For a fleeting moment I thought I saw the outline of the table, but I could not recreate the image. Yet I had the full impression it was there. I avoided the chairs again, looking around intently. I noticed an object to my left.

"What's that?"

Laughter broke out from Steve and Jim and the object. "It's me," said the object, identifying itself as one of the engineers from the breathing pacemaker department. He had been standing quietly by, watching intently, only to be noticed by his image, not by the sounds he was making. I wouldn't have known he was standing there unless I had hit him with my cane, had I not had this system. I could tell Bill was pleased, although he said nothing. I continued to walk, finding a doorframe again and walking through it. I could make out shapes, I began to discover, by noting how much my head had to turn or nod up and down in order to cover the object in my visual field. I could have done that with the cane too; however, that would not work past the range of the cane. Moreover, it would not have been polite or publically acceptable to scale the engineer, standing quietly by the wall, with a cane. But with this thing, it was perfectly acceptable.

As I came through the door, I advanced, avoiding the cabinets and chairs once again. This was Bill's office, which led me to a large plate-glass window. I could not see the window; there was nothing that set off the camera. I used my hearing again to tell I was close. I peered out the window and noticed a large object to my right, making the phosphenes light up in a random and unpredictable fashion. There must be something out there, I thought. Yet there was no knowing what it was; the phosphenes blinked as I moved my head around in that general direction.

"What is that out there?"

"That's a tree outside of the office window." Bill was as impressed as I was. Steve and Jim said nothing, but I knew they were feeling better about their jobs already.

"Let's go outside," Bill suggested, a half hour already passed without any hint of nausea in me. I tried to adjust to the rhythm of the flashing dots. It wasn't successful. "If we could just get them twice as fast yet, they may just fuse," I thought to myself.

Out we went, through the various rooms leading to the exit of the building. We did not strike any furniture, but I did discover a large couch in one of the front rooms I did not know was there before. I looked attentively around all the rooms, the clutter apparent in my visual field. I kept demanding a description from Jim and Steve as to what I saw. They filled me in on the details. I was out the door, trying to stay on the stretch of sidewalk. I saw the bush that was growing in a small plot of dirt between the sidewalk and the building. I turned my eyes to the left, and seeing the bush in front of me, I stepped to the left to avoid it, stepping off the sidewalk.

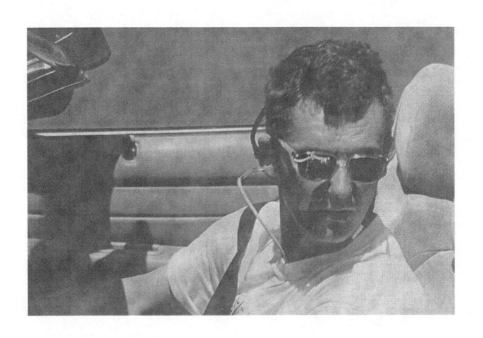

"I have to make sure my eyes are always straight forward," I commented to the audience. "That bush looked like it was in front of me because my eyes were turned to the left."

"You've got a bit to learn in this," Bill said. He did not have much to say while I was walking. He was watching intently. I approached an object at the end of the walkway.

"That is the car," said Jim. It was the car rented by Bill for Jim and Steve to commute between the city and Commack.

"Get in and take if for a drive on this lot," Bill challenged me in a manner suggesting there was nothing to it. I thought he was kidding.

"You mean it?" I looked at him, the blob of dots present from where I heard his voice. For a fleeting moment, once again, I thought I saw Steve, who was standing behind Bill while holding the handles of the wheelchair, move. It was like dots were blinking in my visual field even though I was not moving my head. They always blinked as a result of the pauses between the frames, but this time, the dots blinked out of pattern.

"Sure I do," said Bill. "Just get in." He then instructed Steve to grab the camera out of his office. I got in the car, Jim having to slide across the driver's seat in order to accommodate the cable joining the vision system's computer with the laptop he was holding. Jim gave me the ignition key.

I started the car. It was a better vehicle than I had ever driven before. I looked around me. Out the windshield I saw an object, large and obtrusive in my visual field.

"What's that?" I must have said that for the hundredth time in the last hour every time I saw the phosphenes rearranging themselves in my visual field.

"It's a large sign across the street advertising the other business."

I looked behind me, and after putting considerable effort in cranking my head around, as the camera was on the right lens, I saw the blob of phosphenes signifying the building.

"That's the building, right?" I wanted to make sure.

"You bet," said Bill. I saw him sitting there, a blob of phosphenes, and Steve beside him, a couple steps away, as his blob of phosphenes was a little oblong, requiring more vertical movement of my head to cover in my visual field.

"Here I go," I said, putting the shifter into first gear. I slowly let my foot off the brake, giving a slight amount of gas. How nice it would be to drive, all the way to Los Angeles.

I had been concentrating my vision on the blob signifying Bill, who sat quietly in his chair in the parking lot. Once he was out of sight, I stopped the car, placing it in reverse and backing up slowly until I saw him again in my visual field, taking care not to have my head too far up or down lest I miss his image. I roughly timed my time in reverse, making sure it wouldn't be much longer than the forward. All the time I was in the car, I took care to keep the steering wheel stationary as my vision quality was in no state to make complex maneuvers; just to go back and forth in the same track was enough for starters. I tried to look behind me, but the effort was hard on my neck, so I took off my glasses and held the camera out the window with one hand, the other on the wheel. Once the edge of the building came into view, signified by the blob of phosphenes which did not cease as I lifted my head vertically as the building was several feet high, I stopped the car.

Bill was still laughing from when he saw me take the glasses off and point them out the window. "That'll work too!"

Steve had been taking pictures all the while. I escaped the car, walking around the building. Steve and Bill followed, Jim close on my heels with the system.

"What's that?" I asked again. I was pointing to my left, following the wall of the institute on my right.

"That's a bunch of trees." They made the phosphenes light up randomly. They would blink in a slightly irregular pattern, not quite the same as looking at the wall of the institute.

"I never would have guessed you'd have so much nature in a New York industrial subdivision," I said. There had been no wind, and it was the effect of the wind rustling the leaves that could only mark the presence of trees or significant vegetation to the blind. Now I could see it. Not like trees before, but it was a start.

Suddenly the system quit. Two hours had come and gone since I first started walking. Jim must have rigged up a bigger battery for the camera as it outlasted the usual fifteen-minute duration by a good eight times.

"It's not working anymore," I said. The world was once again black. I needed the break but felt the remorse of the lack of sight creeping over me. Maybe next time they'll have it all in order and I'll be able to take it home, I hoped.

"Well, it was high time it was shut off," said Bill, looking at his watch. "That's more than two hours, and you had no seizure. You should be fine using it in the future."

"Yes, it did work out better than expected when I first tried it out. I could even get a feel for when I'd get the residual phosphenes, and at the first sign of a phosphene remaining on, I'd look at a place that wouldn't allow the stimulator to work, like up at the sky, and it would go away. After a while I did not even feel the possibility of passing out from this." I was praising the system, considering it was totally written off as a major disaster the day before. This needed some rethinking now.

"Steve will take you back to your hotel, and tomorrow Pat will drive you back to Canada. We'll call you next week and have you come down again in a couple of weeks. There's going to be an ASAIO meeting (American Society of Artificial Internal Organs) in Manhattan on June 13 that I want you to attend to show off the system. See you then."

I bade Bill and Jim good-bye and started getting into the front passenger side of the car. It would have been so nice to get in the driver's seat instead. But I was there—just for a moment—when would that happen again?

Pat drove me home in the Caddy the next day. I didn't sit in Bill's place in the back this time. How the thoughts were different in my head now compared to what they were a week ago! We did finally hit the magic button on the vision system, and now we knew what would happen. Or at least I thought I did. I remembered so clearly, on the way to Commack, how I joked to Pat I'd be helping him drive back up to Canada. That part was not such a surefire thing to expect; however, I did expect to see out of the window the American landscape rolling by as we progressed along the highways. Just like I had thought I'd be able to see coming back from the magic eye surgery in Toronto eighteen years ago, this was just a repetition of history; at least this time. How will I ever get out of this destructive cycle, a cycle of slavery to the prospect of eyesight, jumping recklessly at every opportunity, no matter how risky or costly it is? Here I had myself butchered a month ago in Portugal, forced now to carry these articles in my head, which left my scalp sore and weeping discharge continuously, the articles themselves being able to infect at any given moment, then was subject to a seizure last week, which left me scrambling to try to remember events gone by, signifying not only physical but now mental damage as well. How much further can I go? It couldn't go on like this; the human body and mind was just too fragile. The answer became quite obvious from the events gone by this past week. Yet, every time I tried to convince myself that enough is enough, the dreams would come at night, showing me exactly what it felt like being in the driver's seat and actually going somewhere, guided by no one except by my own decision. The teaser I had at the Dobelle Institute was enough to show me what I missed was real and not exaggerated in my imagination. This had to work, sooner or later—I had no choice but to continue with this project.

Once back home, the family had to readjust to the new reality. That was perhaps the easy part of the battle; we had yet to tell all the folk who helped us out the reassessment of the artificial eye and its potential. Ethel came by, wondering where my equipment was.

"Not at all ready yet. But I should be going down again in a couple of weeks to pick it up."

"You'd think with all the money you paid they'd be ready." She was sounding cross. "What's the problem anyways? If there were several people implanted, you being the first, why didn't they just give you the next person's to take home, and they could have repaired yours for that person when they did come? With all the others on the shelf ready to go, you should have been given one."

"Ethel, none of them were ready. They wouldn't even start or run on their own without an external control computer attached and an engineer to go with it."

Ethel, as did any of the other people I spoke to, shook her head in disbelief. These were supposed to be professionals, researchers working on one of the most sophisticated projects in the world located in one of the world's most glamorous cities.

"And we thought Napanee was backward," said one of my donors when they heard of this. "At least when you go to the local hairdresser, they have a pair of scissors that work!" It would have been great if artificial vision was as easy as a pair of scissors.

Janyce McGregor came by next, partially to pick up the pocket video camera belonging to CBC TV, including the video we recorded in Portugal, along with the curiosity of what we accomplished in Commack. Lorri and I had decided to erase the portion of the video where we had the testing procedure recorded. Dr. Dobelle had been strict about any information getting out where he had no control, and this would be a classic example. Janyce did have some very good shots of my head the first time the bandages were removed, our immediate environment and my recounts of what happened in Portugal on a daily basis. The filming of the testing in Portugal would have been valuable, but considering the circumstances once we got to know Bill, there had to be a change in plan. It was difficult to explain to Janyce that the man who was in charge was set in his mandate and protective of his invention to say the least. Thus, we became more and more vague with her, withdrawing somewhat from our former inviting manner, which must have annoyed her. We had to make this choice, however—the vision came first, the story comes later.

"Where is your equipment" I thought it would be issued to you in a matter of thirty days post surgery," she inquired, having hoped for a demonstration so she could get the story out first. I had learned quickly that that was a priority among reporters.

"Well, Dr. Dobelle ran into a few minor glitches, and we are going to have everything ready in the middle of June, when I go to New York, according to his schedule." I couldn't believe I was now making excuses for him. I should really have blurted out that Bill had overrated his accomplishments; the computers were far from ready, lacking enough manpower to accelerate the project to schedule. But no, I was protecting him. Just this one time, I hoped secretly. Just this one time. But then, as I reconsidered my position concerning Janyce, what did I owe her anyhow? I would have it just as soon that she drop the whole issue. Originally, the idea of her being involved was to gain publicity for my quest for vision in the hopes fund-raising efforts would go into high gear, but she wasn't going to air the subject until all was said and done. That was useless for us. Just to be on TV was simply not good enough. Maybe as a child it would have intrigued me, but now it did very little. I withdrew as much as I could from her, doing my best to remain diplomatic, principally for the sake of saving grace with Bill Dobelle. He needed control of the project, and as long as one made believe he had it, he'd be satisfied. Bill was convinced that media can cause him harm, but so far as what we were doing, I wasn't sure really how this could be, although there might have been more to the project than I knew at the time.

A week after returning home, I received a letter from the Dobelle Institute. Lorri walked in the house calmly that morning, inspecting the other envelopes that accompanied the letter from Bill. She wasn't ripping it open first thing the way she used to.

"A letter from Bill," she announced. Everyone crowded around the table to see. There was a letter along with a couple of pictures, one being of me driving a car, as well as one of me wearing the computer/stimulator/camera unit, both obviously taken by Steve as there was no one else there at the time with a camera.

> The Dobelle Institute (Portugal) Lda.
> Artificial Vision for the Blind
>
> May 20, 2002
> To: Mr. Jens Naumann RR6
> Napanee, Ontario K7R3L1
>
> Fr: Wm. H. Dobelle, PhD, Chairman & Chief Executive Officer
> Re: Totally Blind Man Drives a Car
>
> Based on testing last week on Dennis and Jens, I believe we should postpone testing of other patients for two (2) weeks, until May 31. This will give us time to "tighten" the software and will save innumerable hours with the other patients.

Both Dennis's and Jens's pedestals look good, although Jens was obviously a little ahead in the healing process. Most of our efforts concentrated on Jens, since Dennis can come here at any time. By the end of testing (late yesterday, Sunday, May 19), Jens was able to walk around the laboratory, avoid obstacles, and look out my office window and see the tree. Outside the building, he was able to walk freely and drive a small car (slowly and entirely on our property). I believe we can dramatically improve on this performance (see below) and, by the time of the ASAIO presentation, Thursday, June 13. I think it may be possible to videotape him slaloming the car around mannequins in the parking lot. In fact, several other patients may achieve this level of performance by the time of the June meeting. If so, we'll modify the press release accordingly. Meanwhile, I am attaching some photographs and the draft of the press release that I want you to read, mark-up, and fax back to me in New York (631-864-1610).

Jens only used the system about three hours total in five days. Most of our time was consumed by software problems. The system was originally written and tested by using the IBM Aptiva that plugs into the wall. With the Toshiba laptop (to eliminate the electrocution risk), the threshold programs—which we used in Portugal—worked perfectly, but 95 percent of the software did not. We need many changes so the software will run smoothly on the Toshiba (hence the two-week delay). However, each individual change is probably only a few lines of code.

1. Jens was easily able to connect and disconnect the system without help, using the four-inch "saver" cables. He was also able to connect and disconnect from the pedestal albeit with more difficulty. In Jerry's case, he can't connect or disconnect himself.

2. Jens sleeps easily with the extensions, although with his very short hair that look like "dreadlocks."

3. Stimulation suppresses background activity in the visual field. Post stimulation fields are entirely black.

4. The left and right visual fields are offset vertically probably due to the fact that one electrode was higher than the other. This appeared to be the case on the plane films taken in Portugal, but we have not yet gotten stereo X-rays.

5. Many of the phosphenes are brilliantly colored, but this color tends to disappear as one approaches threshold. In the future, pulse amplitude might be used to control color, but there is a complex in the relationship with brightness that will have to be studied.

6. In the conference room, Jens was easily able to detect people, the oscilloscope, and stimulator on the table—also, the ficus trees in the corner and a TV remote and small screwdriver on the tabletop. However, he is not yet able to recognize faces, at least in part because the mapping of phosphenes was relative and did not include any absolute values.

7. Attempts to insert absolute values from maps done in polar coordinates (clock face plus estimates of inches from the center of focus) were thwarted because phosphenes move with eye movements. After eighteen years of blindness, Jens does not yet have good control of his extra ocular muscles.

8. When we added Sobel edge detection, it helped slightly but was hindered by inaccuracies in the mapping. We need a program to "edit" the position and parameters for individual phosphenes.

9. Flicker fusion did not occur even at seven frames a second. We were not able to go faster because of limitations imposed by the band width of communication between the computer and stimulator. This band width problem can be rectified by going to a parallel interface and/or using the stimulators' on-board memory. However, no software has yet been written (Jerry "fused" at about five frames a second).

10. The more phosphenes used, the lower the threshold seemed to be for all of them. We started experiments with a global multiplier of 1.25 threshold and ended up at.9.

11. Most of the work was done with a TV camera with a 120ø acceptance angle. When this acceptance was narrowed (using the electric "zoom" feature), he had the same number of phosphenes for a smaller area and "saw better." We did not, however, test the opposite effect (e.g., "tunnel vision").

12. The camera ran on a standard 9 V battery, which it drained quickly. Because of the current draw, the camera should be interfaced with the main system's battery.

I shook my head in amazement. All the chaos in that office that had happened during my initial participation now was painted as a neat, scientific, and professionally handled, high-tech research/development effort showing its luscious fruits of success and promise. It sounded as good as the article I had read and reread for two years straight in anticipation of the surgery titled ASAIO Journal 2000.

"Hey, that's Dad in the car!" one of the kids commented. If only they had seen me when I was twenty, driving my motorbike through the Rocky Mountains of British Columbia, or crossing Canada with my old pickup, then they wouldn't think of it as such an unusual thing. This was a good start—their dad at the wheel, not holding a stick to guide him in one hand, but both hands on the steering wheel where they belong. How I wished we'd get this system going to the point where I'd get my driver's license back . . .

"I wonder what press release he's talking about," said Lorri.

"I have no idea. There was a reporter from the *Wired* magazine, but his report was to come out in late summer at best." I paused, remembering the day I drove the car. "The day I drove the car, Sunday, there was no reporter. Whatever did make it to the press would have been Bill's doing."

"Wait a minute." Lorri rifled the pages she was holding. "This must be it. Funny, though, as it seems this one is written in advance for June 13. I think Bill must have written this one himself, even though he quotes himself in it as a third person."

The Dobelle Institute (Portugal) Lda.
Artificial Vision for the Blind
Draft for Discussion Only
For Release: June 13, 2002
For Further Information Call: Louise Castagna (631) 864-1600 Ext. 212

Totally Blind Man Drives Car Using a New Electronic Artificial Eye

June 13: A totally blind man has been able to drive a car, using a new "electronic eye," like the glasses worn by Geordi La Forge, the "Chief Engineer" in *Star Trek*. "The patient drove slowly and entirely on private property " . . . cautioned Dr. Wm. H. Dobelle, addressing the 48th meeting of the American Society for Artificial

Internal Organs, today in New York." He added that, "as our technology improves, and becomes less costly, braille will become obsolete, the long cane will become obsolete, and the guide dog will become obsolete as surely as the airplane replaced the steamship."

His team, at the Dobelle Institute (Portugal) Lda. announced that their functional "artificial eye" for the blind was now available commercially. They reported eight cases from six countries. Two years ago, the same team reported implantation of a prototypes in "Jerry" and "Dan," the result of research which began in 1968.

The new systems, implanted in April 2002, cost $75,000 USD each, including all hospitalization, and surgical fees, plus free "updates" for five years. In several cases, foreign government insurance plans paid all or part of this cost, but the majority of the money was raised privately by each individual patient. Additional implants are scheduled to begin in June 2002. New systems will cost $98,000., including surgery and hospitalization but without updates.

A miniature television camera is mounted on the lens of sunglasses, sending its image to a microcomputer on the belt. This microcomputer processes the data and decides which electrodes to stimulate, controlling a stimulator—also worn on the belt. Cables from the stimulator enter the skull through a "percutaneous pedestal," which is like a tiny fire hydrant sticking through the skin. This connects to electrodes on the surface of the visual parts of the brain.

All of the patients lost their vision by trauma, and none of them were candidates for retinal implants. In fact, very few blind patients have an intact retina and are candidates for retinal implants. All sixteen bilateral implants in eight patients produced excellent displays of "phosphenes," which is the term for flashes of light created by stimulation of the brain. Four of the eight patients reported that their phosphenes were brilliantly colored—the first colored phosphenes reported by blind patients—giving hope that future prostheses will be in full color. The patients have just started to use the systems—the man driving the car was the first to have been implanted—and the remaining seven patients are now being trained. The device is primarily designed for mobility rather than reading. However, " . . . rapid advances provide the possibility that the patients will be able to scan the Internet and watch TV," said Dr. Dobelle. The patients had been blind from periods ranging from four to fifty-seven years at the time of surgery. One patient, blind from birth in one eye, lost the other at age forty-five. A second patient who was seventy-seven years old at the time of surgery lost both eyes in a mortar attack during World War II. Both patients saw "normal phosphenes." These cases suggest that neither patient age nor period of blindness is a contradiction for surgery.

All operations were performed at the CUF Hospital in Lisbon, Portugal, by Joao Lobo Antunes, MD, who is Chairman of the Neurosurgery Department at the University of Lisbon, along with John P. Girvin, MD, who is the Chief of Neurosurgery at the King Faisal Medical Center in Jeddah, Saudi Arabia. Both Dr. Antunes and Dr. Girvin have worked on the project for more than twenty-five years. They had collaborated on implanting Dan and Jerry, the successful prototype patient in 1979. They were assisted by Domingo Coiteiro, MD, a Portuguese neurosurgeon, and on some cases by Kenneth R. Smith Jr., MD who is director of the Division of Neurological Surgery at St. Louis University Health Sciences Center.

"Did you really drive that car?" One of my kids were inspecting the picture in which it showed Dad at the wheel.

"Ahead about twenty-five yards, and then backward the same distance at walking speed."

"Is that all?" By the looks of it, and by the sound of the letter, one got the impression that I drove for quite a distance, in perfect control all the way. I was sure Bill knew that, and now I came to realize why Bill had insisted I get in the car in the first place: in order to blow his own horn, yes, maybe, but also to make us all feel better. I couldn't rightly have refused either. I wanted to try it myself but had expected Bill to treat it as a joke rather than trying to make the world prematurely believe the blind were now driving thanks to his invention. What would Beth Seelig have said, considering her values where ethics were concerned, as seen in Portugal. But she was out of the equation now. Maybe this is why. It was only years later that I realized that ethics alone weren't going to make artificial vision work—it was about innovation, compromise, and sacrifice . . . to name a few.

"I hope the whole world doesn't get the wrong impression," Lorri said.

"I don't think this will be aired just like this on Bill's terms in any major media organization." I tried to downplay the situation. It was hard to do as I was directly involved. "Bill would have to invite a reporter directly from the news agency for the reporting, not make it up himself and expect news agencies to publish it. The vision system is good, but it's a long way from being used to drive a car." "I was going to have to be a little careful not to be talked into giving a wrong impression about the whole affair," I told myself.

"I imagine it'll be fun slaloming around the dummies in the parking lot," one of my boys said, reviewing the letter.

"If the battery dies in the middle of it, you'll see bits and pieces of plastic body parts flying all over the place." Everyone roared with laughter. I didn't think it was so funny, however. It was going to be a long time yet before the Internet or a TV screen was going to be scanned. The letter gave such a positive impression of the project. The reader was going to believe the vision I had allowed me to distinguish between a screwdriver on the table, an oscilloscope, a plant and a person, lacking only the minute details, preventing me from recognizing faces. In reality, a person was displayed to me by a few flickering dots, just as a plant was or the tree outside the office. I hoped that I'd get better with this system so this can eventually be a reality.

The letter made no mention of the seizure I had. Perhaps all the better, I thought. I hadn't mentioned it to my kids as I didn't think they really would have known what to do with this information. No one expected it, and no one wanted it to happen. It was best to leave it at that.

Klaus, the patient from Germany for whom I had translated, telephoned me. We had exchanged telephone numbers in Portugal.

"Jens!" His voice was filled with the enthusiasm of a child having received his favored wish for Christmas. "You were driving a car!"

I laughed lightly at this, then said, buying time to think of what to say about this. "Did you really have the operation?"

"Yes, I did. I was still thinking about it long after you left, and at the last minute, I decided to get it. But, man, did that hurt! When I came to, I was in the most awful pain. My head is still quite sore, and I have all this leakage around the jacks. There seems to be this stuff that builds up under my scalp, and when I push on it, a half a gallon of pus squirts out from around my jacks. Do you get that?"

That sounded disgusting, I thought. Bill's words written in his latest letter came back to me on that topic—"Both Jens's and Dennis's pedestals look good . . ."—the truth being that mine were perhaps OK for now, but Dennis had a way to go. Dennis's did not look good at all, as taken from the engineers who looked at them initially, with Bill most likely comparing their condition to that of much worse-case scenarios he may have seen in his past. But then again, I thought, maybe Dennis's jacks will heal over quickly now; time will tell.

"No, not like that at all. I do get pus oozing out over the course of the day and night, soiling my hair, and it is still somewhat sore around the jacks like it is a pimple, but not like you describe your head."

"I sure hope it heals soon," he continued, changing the subject, thinking again about the operation. "That automatic blood pressure sensor we had attached to our arm just about drove me nuts in intensive care unit in Portugal. But I guess it's all worth it if I will be able to drive a car just like you."

Back to that question. Diplomacy once again. I felt like blurting out that we got on the ship before it was time, that we got involved with an experimenter who himself was learning about the task at hand, that all I did really was drive forward and backward, which I could as well have done without the system if either Bill or Steve had made any noise, signaling me when to stop. But there were those few things I did see; the trees around the building, the silent engineer observing me in the cafeteria, the black sign of the other businesses across the road. I knew more about the area where I was, thanks to the precariously assembled equipment of Bill Dobelle than I would have in total darkness.

"It wasn't all that great for driving at that point. It was just a demonstration of its potential," I began, not pausing so as to make my point. "But I saw larger objects like trees, things on the other side of the road, furniture in the building that I never saw before. It's pretty crude at the moment, but with practice, and once their system is perfected, it may be better."

"Can you recognize faces?"

"No. Not a chance. You need really good vision for that."

"So what do you see right now?" asked Klaus. His tone had changed into one indicating slight deception.

"I don't have it yet. They weren't quite ready to give it to me as it takes some trial and error to figure out what a bilateral system needs. That's why I came down, to help them out." Not exactly, but I supposed one could say that was why I came down. They did figure out a better mapping process and also how to give a seizure. But I had no intention to share that with Klaus yet.

"Oh." Klaus was mulling it over. Being a German businessman, he was more than likely well organized and true to his word when making a deal with a client; all that Bill wasn't possibly able to do with a concept that is so early in its development process. He wouldn't have taken it too easily if I had told him what chaos the procedure in Commack was. I wasn't about to spill the beans. Just keep protecting Bill; he needed it . . . just as the rest of us did. But he'd better have it together in New York next month as he plans to invite everyone.

"I guess this letter says we get our equipment when we come down to New York," Klaus said, hoping his interpretation of English was correct.

"Not really written in the letter," I was rereading it with my computer/ scanner. "It just says we should all come down in June for the ASAIO meeting, a big deal for Bill. I would assume that it would be a waste of time and money, and moreover, bad publicity for Bill if we didn't get the equipment."

"It also says the price of the procedure jumped to $98,000 and the free updates would be dropped."

"Headaches are becoming more expensive by the minute!" I bade Klaus good-bye at that. I had no idea where a blind person, rejected from the workforce, thrown into a tumultuous cycle of depression and psychological fragility would ever find that kind of money. It had to make its stand soon with the medical service providers if this is to become accessible for all.

Another letter came a few days later, confirming my predictions. By now I had settled down a bit, viewing the process as one that may, if all went right, work out in the long run, even though the start had been rough. Lorri and I read the letter with minimal excitement, already having been conditioned to change our expectations as to the "big moment" when I'd bring home the system.

Dobelle Institute (Portugal) Lda.

Artificial Vision for the Blind
May 23, 2002

To: Mr. Jens Naumann
Napanee, Ontario K7R 3L1

Fr: Wm. H. Dobelle, PhD, Chairman & Chief Executive Officer

Re: Follow-Up on "Press Release"

Most people, including me, thought the press release was too much of a sales piece. Yes, Jens was actually driving a car on Sunday night, but I agree that we should not lead with this because it's too much like a piece in the National Enquirer.

Thinking about the matter, a more subtle professional approach is called for. Accordingly, on Tuesday, I hired Fred Spar: Kekst & Company who is a famous PR guy in New York. A former Brown University faculty member (his PhD is in Oriental languages from Harvard, I think) Fred handled the "Jerry" announcement a few years ago, which got more press than the AOL–Time Warner merger (which Kekst also handled).

I'm sure he will do as good–or even a better–job than last time. To give him ammunition, I hope to bring in all eight (8) patients for testing by the time of my presentation at ASAIO on Thursday, June 13, 2002.

Meanwhile, if you receive a phone call from Mr. Spar, feel free to speak openly with him.

"It looks like he got some negative feedback from his news release."

I somehow doubted it, though. It was hard to conceive anyone among the patients saying anything negative about the results, as they did not know anything about it other than what Bill provided them.

"More than likely," I commented regarding Bill's self-analysis. "Bill just couldn't resist sending everyone the article he had composed just to butter everyone up for that ASAIO meet. He wants everyone there, despite their own personal schedules so he can show everyone off to his counterparts in sight restoration research." I thought of what Bill had said about Richard Norman when I was in Portugal.

"So you figure he's trying to show them all up?"

"Just think of how difficult it would be to resist coming over, no matter what you had planned, upon reading that article. Driving a car, walking with no use of a blind aid, seeing people and tools and trees all in one day." I added the final note. "You'd be crazy not to cooperate with Bill."

"Well, let's hope he's got it in order this time and delivers with his promise."

We waited in anticipation for the next telephone call from the Dobelle Institute.

CHAPTER 10

Manhattan

It was Monday, May 27, 2002, when Dr. Dobelle called me again. I was comfortably resting on the back lawn at our home when I was told that Louise was on the telephone.

"Bill wants to talk to you about coming down." She informed me right off the bat.

"Well, why didn't he just phone himself?" was my question. "You know Bill," she replied quietly. I did know Bill by now. He probably felt more important this way. I didn't care, though, as all I wanted was my system. Louise was employed by Bill, and as an employee, just as I had been working for BCR and Alex Daniluk, you have to oblige to the request of your employer, however redundant the request may be. I was somewhat glad I didn't have to work for Bill Dobelle, although working with the team on artificial vision would be a dream too good to be true.

"Ready to come down in a couple of days?" Bill's voice was rusty and sounded haggard.

"I'm ready to go. I kind of wonder, though, why not drive down over the weekend and we'll have the week for work?" I was ready to go for a week again, even though it would probably entail the same amount of sitting around in the conference room as did the last time. I had not been able to get out for anything; I had been in either the office or the hotel room by myself.

"Pat doesn't want to drive through a weekend again," Bill began to explain. So that meant Pat wasn't the type Bill could push around too easily. "Maybe we need more people like that in the company," I thought recklessly. It was only years later when I ran my own company that I found out I was wrong about this.

Bill continued, "He's going to leave the day after tomorrow and pick you up on the thirtieth. Is that OK?"

"I suppose that's fine," I said in reply. "For another five days?"

"No, this time a couple of weeks. I need you on the ASAIO meet in Manhattan on June 13. You must have received my letter explaining that event."

My heart sunk. Two weeks in that dreary, quiet environment of the Dobelle Institute could give a person a lot of stress. Bill's voice sounded again at the other end of the line.

"I hope Lorri can come. It will be quite an experience, and you'll be more independent when we move from Commack to Manhattan halfway through your stay. You'll be staying at the Hilton right downtown Manhattan where the meet is."

I had no idea how Bill figured a blind man, denied his proper place in the workforce, raising eight children and just having spent money which could have sustained the family for years could afford just to quit work for a while. I began to explain the obvious as politely as possible.

"Look, Bill. We borrowed money not only from friends but from financial institutions that would repossess the house at the first sign of default, and we are obligated to repay the debts. I have lost many weeks already in my work with the firewood business, which I will not be able to make up as the work is very taxing. Lorri will have only one more month of pay as no one takes music lessons during the summer, and no one will watch the kids for free just so we can have a good time. I'm coming by myself."

There was a moment of silence on the other end of the line as Bill thought it over. I didn't think he really knew the depth of a financial crisis. More than likely, I thought, he had been propped up financially by his father, who had been a notorious surgeon in his time, and other family members, and never really had to work for mediocre gains. What he was doing at present certainly wasn't mediocre work for all he was contributing, for he appeared working for high stakes. It was the surgeons in Portugal and the engineers who did the grunt work in this project for mediocre gains. It was me, along with the other patients, who took the really unpleasant part of the task—the operations and their painful side effects.

"How about one of your kids?"

That idea sounded plausible, provided I could get some cooperation with the school board regarding the class work that had to be completed. There were the two smaller kids who lost more than two weeks of school during my initial stay in Portugal in April who would not come into question—they missed too much of the school year already. I really didn't want to have to take care of small children when engaged in this experimentation anyhow. It would have to be one of the older kids. The more I thought about it, the better the idea sounded. I certainly would be able to get out for walks with someone instead of sitting around in the hotel room.

"I'll have to make arrangements with the school as we are nearing the end of the year, and there are vital tests and assignments which need to be handed in. I'll let you know when Pat shows up. If I do that, though, it will be vital we return right after the June 13 event as these kids do need to pass their grade."

It was only after the trip that I realized the enormous, once-in-a-lifetime learning opportunity this chosen child would have from this decision.

Bill sounded relieved. "Well, that sounds all right. Let me know in advance so I can order a room with two beds for you."

I hung up the telephone, turning to Lorri who had been listening to my side of the conversation.

"That guy must think money grows on trees around here!" She was exasperated by the suggestion we could just drop all commitments and go to New York for a couple of weeks.

"I doubt he ever had a real job."

Lorri asked another question I had neglected to ask Bill, "Is the system going to be ready to take home?"

"I never asked." I really should have, I thought, as if it had not been I would just not come down until it was. "He had written in the letter he would, and most of all, he would have to have it ready considering the expense of the hotel stay, etc., and the publicity surrounding the ASAIO meet."

Lorri sighed, turning to the calendar hanging on the wall. "Another two weeks gone. Why would it take so long, anyways? I remember him saying the equipment was 'on the shelf and ready to go,' and the letter you received shortly before your operation, stating you would be visited by an engineer thirty days after your surgery so as to issue the equipment."

"Good question," I said, thinking about the initial expectations we had once had prior to the operation. We had imagined a large, sophisticated complex housing several dozen, if not hundreds, of employees working diligently on the project. "Let's hope this time all goes well."

There wasn't much more to say. Lorri was obviously worried about the possibility of another seizure, this one maybe not one from which one recovers. I was really going to have to be careful. We decided on Kyle, our fourth child, who was just completing his eighth grade at age thirteen, to accompany me to the States. He was perhaps the best choice as he not only was the easiest going of the bunch, but he also shared a keen interest in the field of electronics. Kyle was all excited to meet the "big man."

Pat arrived in the early morning of May 30. Kyle and I got in the back of the Stealth Stretch. I slid over to where Bill always sat when Pat drove him around and said to Kyle, "I'm the big doctor today—at least for the drive down!"

This was going to be an exciting trip for Kyle—better than school, that was for sure.

We had a good and uneventful ride down to Commack, this time taking the shorter route; we did not go into New Jersey or Pennsylvania this time. At 2:00 p.m., the car telephone rang.

"Where are you now?" The speaker on the telephone revealed an irritated voice of Bill Dobelle.

"About an hour to go." Pat had sounded upbeat during our ride down, but now his voice was more reserved.

"Good. Bring him right to the office. Let me talk to him." I wondered how Bill could keep forgetting the telephone had a loudspeaker despite the fact that he was always driven around with this same car.

"You sound like things are going rough, Bill," I said to introduce myself. Bill's tone of voice changed when he heard me, losing its gruff and bossy manner. Once again I was glad I wasn't his employee.

"Look, Jens," he began. "We're going to have you down here for some preliminary testing, then set the system up so it works good today and tomorrow. Then we'll have you do some filming with a camera crew that comes the following day, where you'll be driving a car, perhaps slaloming around obstacles in the lot. Dennis will be down here too, giving you a rest."

"Sounds good." I wanted to be upbeat about the idea but would rather first concentrate on just making the system work. "See you down there." The telephone connection was not too secure as we were going under bridges, leaving no room for discussion. Kyle and Pat both heard the conversation.

"You'll be driving a car?" Kyle was amazed, thinking about the picture in the latest letter of me driving a car.

"I don't get what he's talking about," I said out loud more to Pat than Kyle. Pat knew Bill, but Kyle would have a lot to learn these next two weeks. "I was lucky to see the presence of a telephone at an arm's length last time. You don't drive a car with that kind of vision, especially not in front of a camera crew!"

"The guy's nuts" was Pat's reply. The phrase hung in silence for a minute as I thought about it. Pat was right, to a point; but then again, people sometimes thought the same of me driving a car at home using just a tight-strung wire and stick . . . using the chain saw and wood splitter . . . not forgetting birthing my babies at home—one of whom was Kyle right there in the car with me . . . and most of all, one kind of had to be a bit "nuts" just to make this artificial vision work until the learning process was finished.

There wasn't much more to discuss for the rest of the ride. Pat was managing the traffic, and I was wondering what I'd be possibly doing for two weeks straight in this environment so contrary to the one I lived in. Why wouldn't Bill just call me down on the eleventh or the twelfth of June, give me the equipment and show up at the ASAIO meeting? I'd have to find out.

Kyle and I followed Pat up to the locked glass door of the Dobelle Institute. Pat unlocked the door with one hand, holding the suitcase with all of Kyle's and my belongings.

"Why, hello, how are you two?" It was Louise speaking, greeting us warmly. I introduced Kyle to the team, or at least those who were around the office area of the building.

"Come back here in my office," Bill said from another room. Kyle and I entered. Bill was still in the same wheelchair, his hand, arm, and shoulder as frail as the time before. "I'm just going to send you back to the engineers in the conference room to try to make your map a bit better, using our new mapping procedure, and then you can walk around a bit and get used to the system. I'm hoping to get some film of you driving this weekend."

The weekend was only two days away. I wondered at that point if I had maybe given Bill the wrong impression of my potential when using this system to drive the car two weeks ago, forward and then backward again. I thought at the time it was obvious that I had no directional control as I kept the steering wheel rigid. "I'd have to discuss this further with Bill at a later time," I thought to myself as I wandered over to the conference room.

Kyle and I seated ourselves at the table, my position being the same as two weeks ago, with the engineers on my left and a quantity of electronic wonders before me on the table. There was the noisy oscilloscope, two laptop computers, the vision system's computer and stimulator connected by a 25-pin communications cable. Both components were connected to a 16 V battery, and both were in turn connected by another communications cable to one of the laptops. The cover was off the stimulator, revealing its layers of circuitry. Kyle peered at it with interest. Steve and Jim sat in their usual places at the end of the table to my left as if they hadn't moved since the last time I was here.

"Didn't you get to go home yet?" I asked.

Steve stopped what he was doing and said in a serious voice, "Pardon?"

"I was just wondering if Bill let you go home yet, or if you'd been at it for the last two weeks nonstop as it seems to me like you're in the exact same chairs as last time I was here."

They looked at each other and finally laughed. "I guess you're right, we are."

"The perfect employees!" I chuckled. It was people like Steve, Jim, and Pat which made the day easy to bear.

"We've got instructions to improve your mapping some at first," Steve said, approaching me with a cable and screwdriver. "I see you still have your savers in."

I had taken them out upon returning home on May 20, seeing there was no need to have them in as my hair was still too short to hide them. I had put them in on the ride down to New York.

I took the cable from Steve and started to hook it up to the saver dangling from my head. I followed the cable back to the apparatus referred to as the stimulator in order to ensure its output jack corresponded to the designated side of my head.

"What we'll do," Jim explained, tapping on the keys of the laptop while talking, "is run the mapping program, which will allow us to adjust the thresholds of your phosphenes as they probably will be a bit different since the last time, plus allow us to remap your coordinates of each phosphene."

"I hear Bill has a new high-tech mapping method," I said. Steve handed me a pad of corkboard that measured about eighteen inches along each side. In the center of the board, I felt the head of a tack.

"There it is!" Steve announced the unveiling of the groundbreaking technology. "There's a grid marked on the surface. All you do is hold on the middle with one hand and point with the other to where you see the dot."

I hefted the corkboard in my hands in mock admiration. "That's quite a heavy investment of technology!" I held it up for Kyle to inspect. "Look at this beauty! Can you figure it out?" Kyle stared at it, wondering where the printed circuit boards would be.

"Now," said Jim, pushing a button on the keyboard of the laptop. I saw a faint flicker.

"Kind of dim, but should be all right." The light of the one-second duration phosphene was good to see once again. It would be even nicer if the voltage was higher, as that would add color and brilliance to the display. I knew better this time, however, and resisted the urge to ask Jim to modify the setting lest I have another seizure.

"I'll brighten it a bit for you for the mapping, and then we'll let it back to this value for threshold." Jim played a bit with the program, then said, "Ready?"

"Now," he said. I saw the phosphene slightly left of center and down two inches. I measured the distance using my fingers on the corkboard and pointed it out. Steve looked at it and said to Jim "negative 1/2, negative 2" marking the "X" and the "Y" coordinates of the phosphene.

We continued this procedure for four more phosphenes. I could not see this mapping technique being any more accurate than the last one as I was still forced to place a numerical value to the coordinates when first seeing them and then hoping I was accurate enough in pointing it out on the board. I felt more confident, however, that the software would be more apt to handle the direct coordinate value instead of translating the clock-position values at first.

I had no idea as to the mathematical background of Jim, who had apparently written the majority of the program. In the end we'd find out when I try to look at a straight line, I thought.

Tension mounted in the room as we all heard Bill's labored breathing as he vaulted himself in the direction of the conference room.

"How many have you done now?" he demanded in a tired voice. It had only been perhaps forty-five minutes since I had arrived.

"We've got five done so far," Steve said apologetically. "Do three on the other side now, and let's see how it works." I wasn't sure I was believing my ears. What good would that possibly do, I asked myself. I was getting quite involved in the decision-making process instead of allowing Bill to make his own plans. However, I remained quiet, and later that proved to be a good idea.

Obediently, Jim stored the values and switched sides on the program while I occupied myself connecting the other side. This wasn't going to be a good stay in New York, I thought to myself, reflecting on the possibility of stress caused by Bill's forceful manner. I heard Kyle rifling through a magazine at the end of the conference table opposite to that of Steve and Jim. At least, I thought, after this procedure I'll be able to get out for a bit tonight thanks to Kyle helping me.

"Now," Jim said.

"Good," I said, seeing a larger blotch of light to the right and top of my visual field. I pointed at the corkboard, making a small circle with my finger in its approximate location.

"That big?" said Bill, looking at my finger on the board. "They pretty well all are on this side," I said.

"When I was going to university, there was one room called the computer room in which there was one huge computer. I spent night after night working on phosphene programs and discovered that the larger phosphenes made the better images." Bill spoke with the conviction of a genius. I said nothing in reply, thinking all the while of how unbelievable the idea sounded, as the smaller phosphenes seemed to have an obvious advantage.

Jim managed to get in two more phosphenes on the left side when Bill suddenly announced, "All right, let's get him hooked up and walking with the system."

Jim fiddled with the keyboard while Steve retrieved a holder for the system. It was a belt a few inches wide, with two suspender-like straps attached to it. The belt had three pockets—one for the computer, one for the stimulator, and one for the battery. A heavy Velcro clasp at the back held it all on—the suspenders were far too stretchy to do any good. Steve placed all the equipment into its respective pockets, observing the finished product with dismay.

"We need a cable that is shorter for joining the stimulator and computer," he announced. The one we had was a couple of feet long and was awkward as it dangled between my legs, looking obviously out of place.

"Just get Russ to make a shorter one," Bill said from his chair. "Just use this for now."

A few minutes later, I was wired up and all was in its place. Right in front of my stomach, slightly below my navel sat the stimulator box with its two cables first drooping almost to the floor and then ascending toward the back of my head. The battery cable was attached to its left side and then to the battery, which sat in a pocket of the belt just above my left hip. The right side of the stimulator unit had the cable attaching it to the computer box, another protruding box situated above my right hip in its pocket. From its right side extended another cable, considerably thinner and shorter in length connected to the camera mounted within the right lens of the sunglasses I wore. I coiled up the excess cable and tucked it in the space between the belt and my stomach so as to prevent myself from tripping over them. Everyone in the room stopped what they were doing and looked at me. The presence of all the wire was obvious, as were the protrusions of the component boxes. I felt like a robot, perhaps the Terminator, ready for a mission.

"Quite the contraption," said Kyle, and everyone chuckled. "It's not too heavy, is it?" asked Bill.

"No, not at all," I said, lifting the belt somewhat for a more comfortable fit. "But I think we should cover it when I'm in town, especially since the panic of 911."

Bill said nothing for a minute, then reminded me, "We'll have the next update ready before the end of the year. This will do for now, it's just temporary." Then he turned to Jim and continued, "Jim, you might as well get it going, and we'll see what Jens can do with it right now."

I reached for the switch; the only control situated on the upper left corner of the stimulation unit. Jim halted me.

"Not yet, I first have to hook up the laptop." He lifted the computer box partially out of its pocket and connected a 9-pin communications cable to a port located at the bottom right side of the box, just under the cable attachment for the eyeglasses. I was wondering what all this was for.

"Is this thing still not ready just to turn on and use?" I turned to Bill as I asked the question.

"In the next couple of days it will be. You have two weeks down here, and we'll be doing the finishing touches on the system." Dr. Dobelle seemed to be squirming a bit uncomfortably in his chair.

Jim tapped away at the keys of the laptop, then reached over and turned on the computer on my belt. We waited a minute for it to boot up, and then Jim finished his tapping.

"We're ready to go. What multiplier to start?"

I knew Bill was in a hurry as it was not logical to map just eight of my phosphenes prior to trying out the system. We were already at 4:30 p.m., and the rest of the staff working for the breathing pacemaker company Avery Labs had all gone home a half hour ago. I hoped, nonetheless, that he wouldn't rush it either as I did not want another seizure, definitely not in front of Kyle.

"Try 0.7."

I waited for Jim to finish entering the value, then looked around the room. I saw nothing.

"Nothing," I stated.

Jim repeated the procedure for values of 0.8 and 0.9 and finally selected the value of 1.0—meaning the same value I saw the thresholds at.

Jim hit the key, and I started to see the rapid flashes of the seven frames per second phosphene images with a black interval between each flash. I instinctively covered the lens of the camera, but the flashing only persisted.

"Don't forget that we're in reverse format," Jim reminded me as he watched. "Darkness makes the phosphenes active."

"It would make more sense to have it the other way around," I said with a hint of irritation in my voice. Unlike the first time meeting with the Team where I was timid lest being labelled a "know-it-all", having had the seizure made me openly critical of anything that could harm me;

I was the employer and Bill, along with the rest of the gang, were my employees. Or at least that is how I felt at the time—I had to play the role of dad in control while Kyle was there, watching intently everything that unfolded.

I looked at the light on the ceiling of the conference room so as to stop the phosphenes. A couple of them had already developed into residual phosphenes, forcing me to wait until their incessant flashing stopped.

"What do you see?" said Bill, watching me move my head around once again as I attempted to make sense of the eight dots that flickered in my visual field every time the view range of the camera passed over a dark surface.

"A few flashing dots, maybe two when I look in that direction." I pointed my finger in the direction the camera was pointing. I was trying to get used to the flashing of the phosphenes, instinctively turning my head toward the ceiling every few seconds, afraid of another seizure. It would take some time before I would trust this system, I told myself.

"You know, Bill," I said as I tried again to locate the object that made the phosphenes appear. "The phosphenes look a lot better during mapping and thresholding than they do when they flash like this."

"We don't know what we'll do about that." Bill vaulted himself forward somewhat so as to clear a path for me to exit the room. "That was a chair you were pointing at. Why don't you go out and walk around a bit?"

"Let me disconnect the laptop now," Jim said, pulling the cable out of the computer box on my belt. "This will work good now until you shut it off."

I followed the wall on my right until I felt the doorframe. I looked in front of me in an attempt to avoid any obstacles that were dark in color. I could not locate the doorframes with the eight dots of light, but I could make out the odd object in front of me. Kyle told me later that the office chairs were mainly black, facilitating their easy location with this crude prosthesis. I pointed to a place where I could not see a single flash of light no matter where I pointed the camera.

"That's a window, right?"

"You see that, eh?" Bill was impressed.

"No, that's where I see nothing. It must be the light shutting off the phosphenes." I continued my way through the various rooms of the office leading to the exit door. I could tell I was close to it when I heard a passing car outside, probably the only one for the last hour as the street outside was very quiet. There were no phosphenes to be seen when looking at the glass door either.

"Maybe I'll try the sidewalk leading up to the door," I suggested.

"Go ahead," said Bill, following close behind as Steve and Jim maneuvered the wheelchair out the door. There was a sidewalk perhaps thirty feet long running parallel with the wall of the building, a narrow patch of dirt designated for a flower bed on my left between the sidewalk and the wall, the parking lot on my left. The sidewalk, the flower bed, and the parking lot pavement took turns lighting up the phosphenes. I shuffled my way along the path, feeling my way with my feet so as to avoid stepping off the walkway.

"It's kind of lighting up everywhere," I stated after unsuccessfully staying out of the flower bed.

"Yeah, the sidewalk has dark spots, the dirt of the flower bed is of uneven color, and even the pavement has discolorations." Jim was looking around, surveying the landscape with no suggestion to remedy the problem.

"Oh well, let's leave it at that." Bill sighed tiredly. "We'll go out, have dinner, and talk it over."

I disconnected the contraption back in the conference room, somewhat depressed at the turn of events. Nothing had changed since my last visit there two weeks ago. The system was still not ready; the manner in which the mapping was done was still crude, and the information that the system gave me regarding my environment would only be useful if the world was displayed as dark objects on a light background. Jim took the battery from my belt and plugged it into the charger on the conference room table. No one talked much as we all walked out to the parking lot, the engineers driving the small car I had driven two weeks ago, and Pat driving Kyle and myself along with Bill to the dining lounge in the Sheridan.

We all sat around a table and placed our orders. Bill was beside me in his wheelchair—I imagined he would have preferred the fancy restaurant chair as it looked more comfortable. I didn't mention anything about this, though, as I felt annoyed still every time someone drew attention to my loss of sight.

We started the discussion as we waited for the meals. "Eight phosphenes isn't enough to make a picture," I said, then added. "I also think that we need the patient able to adjust the system parameters. If I had been able to adjust the system's threshold of response as to when to light up a phosphene with regards to the shade of the surface observed by the camera, I may have been more successful in staying on the sidewalk."

Bill must have thought out a response for that scenario long in advance, considering he had once mentioned in his Journal 2000 write-up that Jerry had to readjust his thresholds every morning in order to make the system effective. "It's too dangerous to have the patient control the system. You saw what happened last time."

I paused, taken by surprise by the simplicity of the comment. The seizure had nothing to do with me running the system; it was entirely due to the 1.25 multiplier, the long pulse trains, all overcharging the grain thanks to the miscalculated idea of implanting three millimeter electrodes that I felt were responsible for the overstimulation. I tried again, feeling a bit like a father repeating himself before a small child who is unable to comprehend a simple principle of logic; I was really going on a power trip myself now.

"I did not say to have the patient change the designated voltage administered to each electrode. Rather, it is the conditions that set the camera off to cause stimulation that could very safely be adjusted by the patient. This would mean if there was a black object on a gray background, instead of the phosphenes lighting up no matter which one was observed, the patient could modify the behavior of the camera so only one of the two shades were . . ."

My explanation was interrupted by the waiter asking, "More coffee?" as if he was the most important person in the world at that moment. For Bill it was a saving grace as he could conveniently duck out of the discussion. Steve and Jim sat to my left, their cups rattling quietly in their saucers as they sipped their coffee. They were saying in their silence the same thing Louise had whispered over the telephone, "you know Bill . . ." I was getting to know him, all right. I was beginning to wonder how far a project like this could get in the hands of a man with such an attitude. Only later did I remember that our project was already rendering real vision to patients all the while the other artificial vision researchers were still pondering over their drawing boards.

The food came, and everyone started eating. Steve and Jim quietly accepted their dinner, so did Kyle as he ate with proper table manners as he was brought up to do. To my right was Bill, chewing somewhat noisily as if he was the one paying for the meal—good thing he was, I mused, as this restaurant seemed pricey, the splashing noises of the nearby water fountain a pleasant reminder of the cost the meals would be. Bill then started to talk.

"Tomorrow we'll give you more phosphenes and try the edge detection software. Last time things weren't quite ready, but this time it may improve the situation." Then he added rather smugly, "And we'll get you a nice car tomorrow too. I think we'll make it a convertible."

"We're kind of rushing into things a bit," I said, feeling uncomfortable at the prospect of driving a shiny, new car with all the obstructions around me. The possibility of me wrecking the car was very real.

"We'll help you along, don't worry." Bill continued with the noisy mastication of his dinner. I hoped he was enjoying it; he really deserved it.

At 7:20 a.m., Pat came by the following day to pick us up, apparently for a long, productive day's work. Kyle had been watching television until the early morning hours and would rather have stayed in bed for a few more hours. TV was new to him—we didn't have it back at the farm, and the seemingly endless selection of channels here in Commack seemed overwhelming for him. As for me, I didn't know what I wanted now. I spent a few hours awake the night before, worrying about the lack of progress in this sight-recovery venture. Dr. Dobelle's heart still seemed to be in it, but a shadow of doubt was now cast over his initial intentions—to bring back sight for the blind so they can be more content with their lives. Given he had already established that the blind would not be able to acquire a driver's license from this method of sight recovery, it made no sense to push the driving issue further in this venture, definitely not so early in its development, or so early in my introduction to this method of seeing.

He seemed, however, to be obsessed with the driving issue, going out of his way to make a film of the procedure. Was this going to benefit the blind, I asked myself. I didn't see how it could. It had to do with the upcoming ASAIO meet, there was no doubt. On the other hand, it was not beneficial either to criticize his motives openly, as they may be what forced him onward in the project. After all, I reminded myself, this technology of seeing phosphenes had been known for decades, ever since the experimentation of Jyles Brindley with his patients, and the idea had rested dormant for decades until Bill came along. Therefore, if his power-hungry attitude was what it took to make this work, why not let it happen and help him along in the process? Yet, all the while I cooperated, I felt like a pawn, at least during the over-publicized driving exercises that would face me that weekend. I hoped he wouldn't go too far.

"All ready for a day's hard work?" Bill greeted me in the office. "The engineers will be here any minute, and we'll map more phosphenes and then get a car for you. Dennis will be coming in the afternoon, and once he gets going, he'll be taking his turn on the car as well."

"How are his pedestals now?" I asked, remembering the mess they were two weeks ago.

"They'll be fine. He was just acting like a crybaby last time." Bill launched himself into his office, and Kyle and I went to our places in the conference room, awaiting Steve and Jim.

As Kyle and I waited in silence, I heard the telephone ring, and Dr. Dobelle was paged by Louise.

"Bill, Dillis Gore for you, line 1," she said as Bill struggled to the telephone in his office. He had left the door open, revealing his side of the conversation. I was eavesdropping as I knew her from Portugal, hoping things were going good over there.

"We already discussed your contract before. We're not changing it now," Bill said, and then there was silence as he listened for the answer. He continued, "No, I won't do that. That's it, that's my offer." Further silence, and then Bill finished the conversation. "Well then, you'll just have to resign." He slammed down the telephone. That was it; the last doctor was now out of the picture.

Two and a half hours later, the research/development team, the software development team, the hardware/electronics development team, the rehabilitation counseling team, and the medical consultation team walked into the conference room. Bill glared at them, obviously irritated at their tardiness. Kyle searched for more USA Today newspapers so he could continue killing time doing the word search puzzles.

"We got held up in traffic," Steve said apologetically. They skirted past Bill and into the room on the other side of the conference room table so as to begin hauling out all the electronic wonders designed to make the blind see again.

The mapping of more phosphenes began in full swing, as Steve and Jim knew about Dennis coming in the afternoon. When we switched to the left side (right visual field), I interrupted Jim.

"You're not going to do the painful ones again, are you?" I did not want torture today.

"No, we'll just leave them out. We already eliminated them, so you shouldn't have a problem this time."

395

With that we started on the left side, the phosphenes being large and not as useful-looking as the ones on the other side, but the distribution throughout my visual field was better. We were testing electrode no. 47 when I noticed an acute pain as Jim switched the voltage from 4 to 8. I never did think that was an appropriate jump in voltage.

"Sorry about that," Jim apologized. "I don't understand . . . this one was fine last time."

Bill came into the room, pushed by Pat who was about to get Dennis. "What's going on?"

Jim explained about the electrode that hurt now, but which had been fine the last time we tested. "Electrodes must be moving," he concluded. "Your encapsulating membrane must not be developed yet. There's no other explanation for that. How are we getting along anyhow?"

Jim explained that we had done the right side and now were on the left.

"Just do about twenty here on this side and then let's get going. We've got other patients coming later on this week, so I don't have too much time wasted on this. Get him hooked up afterward."

We continued with the work of mapping my left side as Pat pushed Bill back into the cafeteria section of the building. We all heard Bill's next words to Pat.

"Pat, I want you to go and pick up a car at that rental agency I was talking about earlier to you. Get that Chrysler convertible or something like that for the whole weekend. Here's the credit card."

Pat spoke up, "We can't get a car without a driver's license."

"Just use yours."

There was a pause, and then Pat said slowly, " . . . all right . . ." It was obvious he was not thrilled at all by that idea. As Pat walked out the door, I imagined the words he was whispering under his breath.

I was going to have to be even more careful not to smash the car lest Pat be implicated as well. More pressure was not what I needed at this point.

"Ready to go," Jim announced as we packed the equipment into the belt again. The laptop was hooked up, and we started right away with a multiplier of 1.0.

"Can we switch the color reaction of the camera to one that is light rather than for the dark objects?" I requested to Bill, who sat beside me, awaiting the results of our morning's work. We had just over sixty phosphenes mapped, about forty on the right side and twenty on the left.

"I suppose we'll try that," Bill agreed. It was a first, I thought to myself.

Jim got the camera rolling, and I could now cover the lens of the camera with my hand in order to control the stimulator output. I let myself get used to the flashes, which were set at the maximum of seven frames per minute.

"This is better," I commented, looking at the lights above the conference room table. I could count five in a row. "There are five lights, right?"

"Yup," Kyle said.

"There's nothing on the wall behind me, though." I had turned my head around and faced the wall that led to the door of the conference room. I kept moving my head around and noticed I couldn't pick up the office chairs either. Instead, the phosphenes appeared when I pointed the camera at the floor.

"That's because it's black," Steve said. I picked up my white cane, leaving it folded in half. I waved it slowly back and forth in front of my face like the windshield wiper of a car as I faced the black wall. To my amazement, I could actually see, for the first time, true motion as the row of vertical dots moved from one side of my visual field to the other. I watched this for several seconds when Bill asked, "What's the matter?"

"It's amazing," I said, continuing to wave the stick. The feeling of visual motion in my visual field was as refreshing as a cool shower on a hot summer's day. "I can actually see a line of dots moving across my visual field as I wave this thing. I think our mapping job was pretty good!"

I held the stick stationary in various places in front of the camera. In some instances, up to five phosphenes made a squiggly line, some of the phosphenes not exactly where they should be but close nonetheless, and when I moved the cane over an inch or two, there may be two, three, or even only one phosphene representing the cane. If I moved my head, however, I could see the whole scope of the picture as all different areas of phosphene groups were able to observe the same object. I turned the cane into a horizontal position. Now the line was sideways, represented by the phosphenes on the bottom, which were generally larger. They emitted a dull flashing glow as the dashboard lights of an automobile would when staring out of the windshield at night. As I lifted the cane, the line shut off and a few other phosphenes further toward the center of my visual field lit up instead. The line continued to advance upward, but when I reached the center of vision, suddenly the very top of the right visual field lit up while the center phosphenes on the left continued to light. The result was a line that was broken in the center and continued on a different level on the other side of the visual field.

"Jim," I said, holding the cane horizontally to the wall. "There is a mapping problem once I look directly at the cane. I think due to the fact that the very top of my phosphene group on the left visual field is lower than that on the right, it makes a crooked line at the top of my visual field at that level. Once the image is higher than center vision," I explained, "only the right visual field should be continuing the display of phosphenes, as no phosphenes exist in that region on the left side."

"Show me what it looks like," he replied, looking at my cane. I sketched with my finger the shape of the line I saw in relation to the cane. Jim came over and reconnected the computer to the laptop.

"Just give me fifteen minutes and I'll straighten that out. I think it's easy enough to balance the map."

Sure enough, Jim had it under control fifteen minutes later as Bill waited impatiently.

"Now let's get you out and walking. Soon Pat should be here with the car."

I tried not to think of the car. I was happy just to wave my cane around in front of my face for now, just like a person who is first fitted with an artificial limb is happy just to be able to take a few steps for starters. And speaking of that issue, I thought to myself, Bill had yet to get to that point after more than a year of having his amputation. It would have been great to be able to help him feel the way I just felt seeing the cane just then.

Back in the conference room, Bill's manner of rushing things was getting on my nerves.

I got up out of my chair after Jim disconnected the laptop and gave one last swing of the cane in front of my face to test the mapping. Sure enough, it was much better. It was not perfect yet, as the line was a bit crooked on the very bottom now but straight in the center. As I continued to lift the cane past center vision, only the right side represented the line with either one or two phosphenes. To see what that was, I'd have to move my head around to use a different section of my visual field, which was more populated with phosphenes.

Suddenly the system quit. There was no more output. "It quit," I announced flatly, moving my head around in the direction of the lights on the ceiling.

"What's wrong now?" Bill sounded annoyed.

Jim and Steve were frantically hooking up the laptop. "Don't know," they said after several minutes of fiddling. They checked the connection between the stimulator and computer units, which was now a very short wire—too short, in fact, which Russ, one of the engineers from Avery Labs, had made up to replace the one that was too long. But even that did not resolve the problem. "Back to the drawing board," I moaned silently. There was something about the idea of seeing that cane that made me miss the dots more now than ever.

Pat arrived with the car. "It's parked out back," he said simply, handing Bill the keys and credit card. Bill said nothing.

Dennis arrived with Nancy shortly after Pat's arrival with the car. I could hear Bill talking while Jim and Steve still sweated over the failed vision system.

"Yeah, we got a new convertible for you to drive!" he said to Dennis, expecting him to jump for joy. I had to admire Bill at that point for his ability to sound positive even amidst a pending crisis of a dead computer system.

"Yeah, right" was Dennis's reply, treating the matter a bit like a joke. "First we have to get those wires on my head. I think the skin's growing right over."

"We'll have to get them on somehow and leave the savers in so you can continue with the project," Bill said, preparing Dennis for the event. With a car parked outside for him to drive, and him not yet having the preliminary taste of the type of vision he would receive as I did, how could he not cooperate with Bill?

Bill came back in to the room where no progress was happening. "You may as well sit here and watch Dennis be thresholded and mapped," he said to Kyle and I. Then he turned to Jim. "Don't bother wasting time any more on this. Get the other system out and work on Dennis now. I hope to have him ready by three this afternoon. Just do enough phosphenes for now to get him going."

It was already past 1:00 p.m. That didn't leave much time, I thought. I heard Kyle sighing beside me, not having budged from his perch on the chair at the end of the conference room table since seven thirty this morning.

"Actually, Bill, I'm going out a bit with Kyle, and we'll be back in a couple of hours. We need to get out and move a bit."

"Oh no, you can't walk around here!" Bill reacted as if I was suggesting skydiving without wearing a parachute. "You'll get run over first thing. This is an industrial subdivision, you know. I'll have Pat take you back to the hotel, and he'll pick you up at around 3:00 p.m."

It was no sense arguing. As far as I was concerned, it was more dangerous in here being in the hands of Bill's overgenerous voltage increases to my visual cortex than it was being among the traffic.

"Once back at the hotel," I whispered to Kyle, "we'll go do what we want." This suggestion seemed to cheer him up.

Stretching our legs, moving around again and hearing the rhythm of the traffic, people walking and talking and the general sounds of life felt good once we escaped the tense atmosphere of the Dobelle Institute. There was a sidewalk along about a two-mile stretch in front of the Sheridan on Motocross Parkway that we walked in search of a cheaper place to eat. Each time we ate at the Sheridan, and it was not with Bill paying for it, even the simplest meal cost close to $50 US, translating to close to $80 Canadian. I couldn't possibly keep that up for two weeks without selling the house back in Napanee. This expense was not what I had expected when first buying into the project, that was for sure. We searched in vain and found nothing. There really wasn't much shopping to be done at this part of town, I thought.

"Perhaps we'll go the other way next time. Let's go up to the institute, as it's nearing three," I suggested.

"What about Dr. Dobelle's opposition to us walking there?"

"Too bad," I said, angry at the idea someone was telling me what I should do or not do, still puzzled by Bill's protective attitude. Maybe he was worried I'd get run over before the big media event could happen.

"Well, let's hope I don't get fired!" I said jokingly to Kyle.

We arrived at the office, the trip having been mundane at best. The three roads leading up to the office had no sidewalks, but all I had to do was listen for oncoming traffic and step up on the neighboring lawn until the traffic passed. It was a lot safer than cutting and splitting firewood, that was for sure. Bill said nothing about the issue when we arrived. Noticing Dennis was successful in being hooked up to the savers this time, I figured Bill was happy that the previous problem of Dennis's implants was solved.

"Ready to get the camera working on you?" he asked Dennis, who had been successful in retrieving fifty-five phosphenes on his right side and subsequently had them mapped. It was his first time through, as he did not even have a test for initial phosphene presence in Portugal as I did. I doubted his mapping would be very good as a result. Nancy got up and stood beside Dennis, just as excited about the big event as I was the first time Bill had suggested trying the camera with me.

"You bet," Dennis replied as Jim made the final adjustments.

"There it goes," Jim announced as he started the system. Dennis was quiet as he sat, very still.

"Move your head around," Bill said, watching from his wheelchair. "That way you can see the articles around you, as that makes the camera work."

Dennis kept sitting there, quiet for a moment longer, and then called out to his mother in a tone of distress.

"Mom! Where are you?"

Nancy rushed over and held onto his arm. "I'm right here beside you."

"Those beeps . . ." Dennis stammered uncertainly as he strived to describe the source of his anxiety. "Those beeps—they're driving me nuts!"

It was quiet in the conference room as the rest of us stared to hear the phantom beeps. The only sound was the hum of the oscilloscope ventilator fan. No beeps.

"It's flashes of light you're seeing, not beeps," I said quietly. The connection between Dennis's sense of hearing and that of sight must have been overlapping, I thought, even though I could not claim expertise in this field. The first time I saw the flickering frames, it was bewildering to me also, the constant flickering threatening to drive me crazy.

No one was saying anything as Dennis sat there at the table, motionless.

"It's got to be the visual input which is being translated into audio as it's been a while since we've seen." I spoke to Bill, who was dumbfounded by the situation and did not know how to proceed. "Remember that Dennis lost his sight at eighteen years of age, which means he may have developed better connections between his remaining senses than even me, who had another three years of light perception." This could have been a job for Beth Seelig, I thought. Where was she, along with the rehabilitation team, considering the importance and vastness of this project.

"Well, whatever it is, I don't like this. Shut it off." Dennis had had enough for the day. It wasn't hard to understand, considering that I had a lot more preliminary exposure to the phosphenes, then used the relative mapping program, and when being introduced to the camera output, it was drawn out over a period of days as the engineers fiddled with settings and computer problems. Bill had started with one frame a second, at a reduced multiplier, while Dennis just got mapped and hooked up to the camera at the full seven frames per second within a period of two hours. It somewhat predictable why Dennis had enough.

"Just shut it off and disconnect him." This was Dr. Dobelle's contribution to the situation for then. We all had so much more to learn.

"Pat will take you back to the hotel, and we'll work some more on it tomorrow."

That was Dennis's first big day. I couldn't help feeling sorry for him, Nancy, and for all the other patients who got involved in this project. It was going to be hard, just as hard as it was to go blind in the first place.

"Jens, you may as well come over, and we'll get the system going on you if we can get it going." Bill had a new plan to cheer himself up. "Then we'll take you out to the car." I was back in my electric chair at the side of the conference table. I hooked up as I heard Pat, Dennis, and Nancy leave. Steve and Jim fiddled more with the software so as to change the parameters in order to suit the new patient in the chair. We crossed our fingers as Jim fired up the system once again. I waited until I heard the two beeps coming from the vision system's computer module, signifying it had booted up successfully. I saw first one flash, then a sequence of seven per second. I covered my camera for an instant until I got used to the flashes, introducing them bit by bit until I was able to leave my camera lens totally uncovered.

"It works," I announced.

Bill beamed, then asked Jim, "What was it that made it quit before?"
"I really don't know."

Bill ignored the reply. All that mattered to him was that it worked now and we'd be able to go to the lot where the car was waiting. Jim packed the system in the belt again as I adjusted the belt and the shoulder straps. I tucked the excess from the cables going to my head into the belt and started to walk, white cane in hand, toward the door. The flashes from the phosphenes still became overpowering after a few seconds of continuous input, so I found places to look where no phosphenes would light, just to give me temporary relief from the irritating assault on my senses. The intervals of relief became increasingly shorter as I slowly ambled through the office rooms, and within fifteen minutes of use, it was no longer necessary to control the input. At that point, I lost all paranoia related to the possibility of having another seizure.

"It would be handy to have a control so I could reduce the thresholds for long enough to get used to this," I mentioned to Bill, who was following me in his wheelchair, pushed by Steve. Bill said nothing to my suggestion.

"Take him out to the car, Jim," Bill commanded. I followed Jim out the glass door, which was represented by a few dots now that the system had been readjusted to display light instead of darkness.

Once outside, the phosphenes appeared in a random pattern that did not seem to correspond at all with the environment. The only way to stop them was to look directly at the pavement in front of me. I remembered at that instant that Jim had said previously that only up to nineteen phosphenes would be lit at any one time per frame.

"Which nineteen phosphenes would the computer select if the picture took more than that to make?" I inquired as I followed Jim by the sound of his footsteps. I could not see much at all, as all the landscape was well lit by the sun, setting off many phosphenes in a chaotic pattern on my visual field.

"The first nineteen in the table of electrode numbers, which are randomly selected."

We arrived at the car. Bill was waiting silently for me to get in and drive it, demonstrating how good an invention this vision device was. But I just stood there, looking all around myself, trying to make sense of my environment. I felt the shiny, new metal under my hand as I held the clasp that would let me inside, let me in to sit upon the seat which had all the promises of freedom and adventure as the car would take me wherever I'd command it. I couldn't see any difference in looking beyond the car, looking to the right or left. Everywhere I turned, the phosphenes flashed in a wild and unorganized pattern, except for when I looked at the ground, when they would shut off.

"Are you going to get in?" Bill wanted to see action. "Everything looks alike to me right now." I took a few steps away from the car and looked toward it. There were no phosphenes to see in that direction either. When I looked to the left or right, the phosphenes reappeared, signifying the car's presence would be the lack of phosphenes.

"I suppose the car is almost the same shade as the pavement."

"Yes, it is," Jim said in reply. "It's dark blue."

"I don't see any phosphenes when looking at the car." I moved somewhat to my right, feeling the heat of the sun shining on the back of my neck. Suddenly, there was a full, powerful presence of phosphenes. "Except when I'm here. I suppose that would be the reflection."

"You're seeing quite a bit, then." Bill had been overhearing my conversation, convinced I could tell the color of the car, the color of the pavement, the location of the sun, along with the details regarding the reflection of the rays of light from the car. He just didn't seem to understand the problem. "Are you getting in now?"

I thought about Pat's name being on the rental agreement of this car, the newness of the vehicle and how it would be a shame if it got smashed up. But perhaps that's what it took to convince Bill that there was still work to do. I'd have to make sure no one got hurt. I got in the car. As I stared ahead, all I could see was the flashing randomly selected phosphenes.

"Kyle," I called to my son, who had been standing quietly behind me until the moment I got into the car. "Stand in front of the car and let me see if I can see you there."

"I'm right here," he said. He was right in front of the car, and I noticed no difference in the image. This would not do at all, I thought. I may as well not wear this thing at all.

"I can't even tell he's there," I said to Bill. "There's just not enough input for me to pull this off."

Bill sat quietly as I kept looking around. Suddenly everything went black.

"It quit again," I said. This time it had run for almost forty-five minutes.

"Well, let's just forget about it for today and go home," Bill spoke tiredly as we all marched back to the door of the Dobelle Institute, discouraged and drained, the useless electronics dangling about my waist.

We placed everything on the conference room table, hoping Steve and Jim could find the problem tomorrow. If not, I thought to myself, we could always use the system in half-hour intervals, seeing it restarted after its initial failure. That would mean, however, it wouldn't be ready to take home again. Once again, I thought of this possibility with dismay.

It was Bill and Kyle and I who dined at the Sheridan that night. Bill rambled on and on during the meal about his private life, his ex-wife who was trying to extract money from him, along with the expense of the private schools he was sending his children to. I tried to listen politely, and whenever I thought it not possible, I decided just not to listen. I listened more intently, however, when he began to talk about his financial situation surrounding the companies he owned.

"So are you still selling and servicing the various stimulators you claimed to have developed, such as the electronic pain controller?"

"No, not any more. They weren't bringing in enough, maybe a few hundred dollars at the most. I just couldn't be bothered. It's just the breathing pacemakers that bring in money as we sell them for about $60,000."

"And how many of those do you sell?" I was expecting a few hundred, or even thousand, per annum.

"Two or three a month," he said.

"That's not a lot at all," I said, imagining myself selling two or three cord of wood a month. We'd be in the poorhouse, I thought.

"No, it's not, but this vision will step in now." Bill chuckled to himself.

"Yeah, I guess so. I did notice the price went up."

"Don't you think it's worth it?" Bill was still eating, his mouth never stopping talking as he chewed. I struggled to find the right answer to his question without ruining my prospects in continuing to work on this project with Bill. I had no other choice now that my head along with my cash was invested. Just running from the Dobelle Institute would not solve a thing. Moreover, the taste of real vision I got from the feeling conjured up by watching my white cane waving before me in the conference room just made me crave for more.

"It's just too early to tell at this point," I started slowly, choosing my words carefully. "At this point, I have not seen enough of a result, and I don't think I will until I get to take the system home and experiment with it at my own leisure. It is, after all, a prosthesis that requires a certain time for one to get accustomed to." It was the most diplomatic answer I could find. Not even a well-honed politician could have done better under these circumstances, I thought to myself.

"You'll get to take it home, don't worry." Bill seemed happy with the answer, probably because it gave him more time to figure out what to do next. "Besides," he continued as more food was passed across the table, "I think your electrode array moved, as you had different electrodes, causing pain this time that didn't cause pain last time you were tested. Tomorrow we'll, providing we have time, go through all your electrodes to see which ones hurt this time."

What fun, I thought as I tried to eat my dinner. Tomorrow was going to be a bad day.

We didn't get to the office until 9:00 a.m. on Saturday, June 1, 2002. The Avery Labs team wasn't there, which meant there would be no morning conference ritual. As we sat and waited for the engineers to set up the equipment, I reminded Bill of yesterday's problems, hoping he'd forget completely about the idea of restimulating the painful phosphenes. I had worried about that all night, falling asleep into an uncertain slumber only after concluding that the best plan of action was to convince the engineers to advance the voltage slowly for those ones proven to be painful instead of following Dr. Dobelle's hasty "scientific" method of doubling the voltage with each augmentation. I prayed they'd go along with it.

"Yesterday I saw just a mess of phosphenes outside, probably due to the abundance of light. Maybe we should change back to the "reverse" imagery, wherein only the dark objects are displayed."

"We'll try the edge detection filter today." Bill was referring to the software that detected sudden changes in light reflections, displaying the edge as a line of phosphenes in my visual field.

"Before you put in the edge detection," Bill said, turning back to the engineers at work at the conference table, "run through Jens's painful phosphenes and let's see what's going on with that array." My heart sank at that. However, as Jim began to boot up the thresholding program in the laptop, Bill turned himself around and began going into another room, out of earshot. Here was my chance.

"Jim," I said, trying to sound as reasonable as possible. "You know these hurt a lot when they're overstimulated. Could you increase the power more slowly, say a half volt at a time? I'm sure we'll accomplish the same goal, but it won't hurt like that. I'd much rather feel a tingle than a wrenching zap in my brain." I had my fingers crossed that he would oblige.

"No problem," he said quietly. "I'll just jump a bit at a time, as all it involves is me punching each value in manually. Just don't tell Bill. If you don't, he'll never find out as he doesn't know that much about this particular computer program."

I sighed with relief. There was still humanity in this world, even in the Dobelle Institute. This day wasn't going to be so bad after all, I thought.

"Now," said Jim, pushing a button.

"No" was my reply, as all I saw was the black background of my visual field, much darker than it had been before we had started the experimentation at the Dobelle Institute. Jim entered a five-digit number and pressed the button again.

"Now," Jim said after the fifth time of changing the digits. I felt a slight but uncomfortable tingle.

"That one hurts a bit," I announced. It wasn't painful, but if it was stimulated seven times a second, I wouldn't be able to use the vision system as the pain would be too much.

"All right, that's a painful one. 4.5 V." Steve took note of the voltage and entered it on a sheet of paper.

"4.5 V?" I considered the situation. "I didn't feel it at four, nor did I see light, so the next step according to the 'genius' in the other room would have been eight."

"Ouch," said Steve. We continued with our testing in this manner, myself thanking fate for leaving Bill out of the conference room. When we were finished, we discovered that three of the phosphenes deemed as painful two weeks ago were actually useful. There was no saying, however, if these electrodes could have been useful had they had their voltage increased in smaller steps even at that time. When Bill reentered the conference room, he was all smiles about the success, yet not one of us mentioned why things went better this time. He wouldn't have been quite so happy then, I figured.

"Let's try the edge detection now." Jim was already in the process of installing it. We had been using the vision system hooked to the laptop all morning, and it still had not quit. I was amazed.

"Did you find the bug in the system?" I asked Jim. "No, not yet. It seems to only act up when it's running by itself." He added the finishing touches to his work and announced, "Ready for edge detection."

He pushed the last button, and once again the flashes started. I reached onto the table and retrieved my glasses that I had not yet placed upon my nose. I looked around the room as I had done many times before, this time noting a distinct difference. I once again could see the dots of phosphenes marking the black office chairs, but I could also see the lights on the ceiling. In the past it had been one or the other, depending upon the setting of the program. I turned to look at Bill.

"It seems to work better," I stated, explaining the success of the edge detection. "I can even see you in your chair." I scanned the glasses back and forth, noting the appearance of a tight group of phosphenes where the top of Bill's head would be. I turned to Steve, who was represented by a couple of dots where his face was, but no phosphenes lit up to mark the top of his head. I turned back to Bill. "Your head must be shiny as I see lots of phosphenes in that area."

Everyone laughed in the room except for Bill. Nonetheless, he was content with the success of the system. "You think that's better?" he asked.

I got out my white cane and waved it in front of me. It gave me the same line of phosphenes that marked its presence as it did the last time against a dark wall, but this time it was present even when the background was not entirely dark. There was no doubt that the edge detection software was doing its job. "Kyle, come over and hold this cane either sideways or vertically against the wall, but don't tell me how you're doing it."

Kyle put down his word search puzzle from *USA Today* and held the cane against the dark conference room wall. I moved away to a distance of about six feet, looking at Kyle holding the cane sideways on the wall. I determined its exact attitude after several seconds of sweeping my glasses first sideways and then vertically across the image, noting that when the cane was horizontal, sideways motion of my head was ineffective, but the vertical motion would allow the line to be displayed as a line of phosphenes in my visual field ascending and descending in my visual field corresponding with the motion of my head.

"Sideways," I said in full confidence. Kyle changed the location and asked, "How about now?"

Again I saw the same image. "Sideways still."

"Right you are," Bill said proudly.

Kyle moved the cane again, and this time, I could tell its vertical position only with the right side of my visual field as my left had no phosphenes present on the top half. The right side, however, had big, unevenly shaped phosphenes that gave a vertical line a shape like a bent lamppost having an oversized light bulb at the end of it. There were also a few black spots in between phosphenes, breaking up the image all the time as it flashed seven times a second. Still, the image was adequate for determining that the cane was at a vertical attitude.

"Vertical," I announced, and someone said "yup." Kyle moved the cane again and said, "Try it now."

I scanned first vertically, moving my head up and down, then horizontally, but in both cases, I got phosphenes lighting up randomly across my visual field. "Not too clear this way," I said, wondering if it was Kyle I was seeing.

"I'm holding it at an angle," Kyle said. I guessed that meant I needed more practice.

"Let's go out to the car," Bill suggested. I wondered what I'd be able to see out there this time around. I went back to my place at the conference table while Jim disconnected the laptop from the vision system computer. "I hope it keeps going this time," he muttered under his breath. This had been a stressful few days for the engineers. I felt under my chair for the cane, but it wasn't there. Kyle must not have put it back after doing the demonstrations on the wall with it. I moved my head around with my glasses pointing toward the dark conference room wall and suddenly saw a line of dots outlining a stick of some sort against the otherwise empty wall. I reached out and grasped the cane that had been leaned against the wall by Kyle. Kyle was watching and exclaimed, "Hey, you found your cane!" All of a sudden, I didn't feel blind any more.

"Ready to go," Jim said as he grabbed the handles of Bill's wheelchair, following me out of the room. I stopped at the doorframe, its shape crudely outlined with an image of different-sized flashing dots making a rough square shape in front of me, black spots in between the phosphenes like missing pieces in the center of a picture puzzle. It was the clearest I had ever seen the doorframe. I walked through it without bumping it. Three steps later, I stopped short as I stood in the cafeteria room, moving my head around until I thought I'd get dizzy. I pointed to my right.

"I never knew there was more than one table here!" The edges of the tables were outlined on my visual field. I moved my head to follow the lines, as the entire table did not fit in my visual field at once, and noticed the presence of another table ahead of the first. I knew about the first already, as I had bumped into it a few times when going to the bathroom, but had no idea of the presence of the second. Everyone stopped and watched as I actually "saw" for the first time. "This is a lot more useful than it had been before the implementation of the edge detection," I said to Bill, his shiny, bald head clearly displayed by several phosphenes.

"That's good," said Bill, meaning it. "We'd better get out and see what you'll be able to do with the photographers tomorrow."

"I thought they were coming today," I said.

"I delayed it until tomorrow as I wasn't sure if we'd have anything to film," Bill said, surprising me somewhat. I had expected he'd just ask me to fake it if it didn't work.

I hurried out, concentrating only on finding the other doorframes so I could get out as fast as possible. I remembered suddenly that perhaps the system would quit again and I'd never know how it worked outside. We stepped outside in the sunshine.

As I followed Steve along the sidewalk leading up to the front door, I noticed the same line of phosphenes as I saw when looking at the white cane held upright against the wall in the conference room. I tilted my head so as to look further down at the border of the sidewalk on either side of it. I lifted my cane and tried to walk between the two lines. I shifted my eyes to one side, which shifted the line in turn, making me step toward that side and into the flower bed beside the sidewalk.

"I really have to concentrate on keeping my eyes still or the sidewalk appears in a different location than it actually is," I pointed out to Bill, brushing the dirt off my shoes. Continuing once again along the sidewalk, a few phosphenes near the bottom of my visual field suddenly appeared, forcing me to halt as there could have been an object on the sidewalk I hadn't noticed before. I shifted my feet somewhat, noticing that the dots near the bottom of my visual field began to change place with other ones in that same area.

"Hey!" I exclaimed. "I can actually see my feet!" I moved my feet around a bit while watching them in wonder as if they never had been there before in my life.

The sidewalk ended suddenly when there were no more phosphenes portraying its border. All there was blackness when looking directly at the pavement beside the building of the Dobelle Institute. I turned to the right, noticing the line where the building intersected with the pavement and followed it. As I waved my white cane, as was taught by my first mobility instructor, a white line of dots waved back and forth near the bottom of my visual field. I was starting to ignore the flickering of the frames, seemingly developing a rhythm that corresponded to the rhythm of the frames, allowing me to concentrate only on the images. Maybe, I thought to myself, that is what Jerry, the first volunteer, did in his subconscious when he apparently achieved "phosphene fusion."

Once past the corner of the building, there was a large object in my way that had a flat and wide shape. I approached it, noting its location by what distance remained between my feet and the point where the object intersected the pavement. This area was black. "Is that the car?" I guessed, touching the metal for verification.

"Keys are in it," said Bill from behind me. I turned around to see a squat group of phosphenes outlined against the pavement, which indicated the presence of Bill. Slightly to the right, I saw a more vertical arrangement of phosphenes, where the outer ones flashed irregularly. That had to be Jim, whose voice came from beside Bill. I looked around, noting that the building was visible. I turned my head to the right, noticing a line about fifty feet away from the back of the building, running parallel.

"What's that there?" I pointed toward it, then walked toward it slowly.

"That divides our lot from the neighbor's," said Bill, following my gaze.

I touched the line when I reached it. It was a concrete curb perhaps six inches high. I would have to use that to guide the car, as the pavement in front of me did not make any phosphenes light up. If it had have, it would have resulted in confusion, as these phosphenes were too large to be used for identifying a material. I stood on the curb and looked back at the building. All of a sudden, the vastness of the world hit me. Here I was, for the first time in eighteen years, actually seeing the world again. The building was outlined against the sky, its squat vertical lines no higher than perhaps twenty feet, the roof sloping very slightly in an A shape while the width of the building displayed itself to me in full perspective. It was marvellous; I just stood there and stared.

"It's really something to see again," I said, still not believing the reality. It was coarse, more than likely written off as inadequate by the sighted populous, but for someone in the dark for a half a lifetime, it was beautiful. I noticed a small irregularity at the back of the building, close to the wall. I walked over to it and felt it. It made a buzzing noise, was made of concrete and was perhaps a half a meter in height.

"Is this an electrical service box?" I said, kicking it and noting its solidity. I would have to avoid that with the car. It would total it at best, I thought.

"Yes, it is," said Jim. Bill just watched, just as surprised at the improvement resulting from the integration of the edge detection filter as I was. I returned to the car, not floundering a bit in finding it, although I could not find the door handle visually, forcing me to feel for it.

I took my place in the driver's seat. It felt good to be there again, the steering wheel like an old friend within the clasp of my hands. It had only been a few days ago when I dreamed of sitting behind the steering wheel of my old '71 Ford, wondering why, why of all things, I was having such a terrible, unfulfilling existence when all seemed right. In my dream I had been able to see perfectly fine—the dotted white line stretching endlessly in front of me. It was only after I awoke, opening my eyes and seeing nothing, that the realization came to me. But now I was behind the wheel of this mechanical marvel, wide awake, and with the Dobelle Eye strapped to me as I had imagined it since my first encounter with the Web site of the Dobelle Institute. I looked out of the windshield.

I could see a few coarse dots near the bottom of my visual field marking the hood of the car. First it seemed like the camera was picking up the dashboard, but once I felt the dashboard with my right hand, it did not correspond with the place where I was seeing the row of dots. Just above the dots, when lifting my head a few degrees, I could pick up the concrete curb separating the two parking lots on my right. The windshield post was all I could see to the left, however, when I stuck my head slightly out the space where the rolled-down left window would be, I could pick up a broken line marking the intersection of the building of the Dobelle Institute with the pavement of the parking lot. I would have to stay a few feet from that wall in order to clear that electrical box, I concluded.

"Kyle," I called my son who had been observing my progress with interest. Maybe, I thought to myself, he would get the opportunity to see his real father in his rightful free state, not one held back for so many years, disguised as a blind man. "Stand in front of the car and let's see if I can see you."

Kyle moved in front of the car, stopping at about four feet from the front bumper. There he was, outlined by a handful of flashing dots that seemed to vary in brilliance now, perhaps as a result of incorrect threshold voltages assigned to each electrode. As I looked at him, the words of one of the people helping me fund-raise came back to me as we once discussed the merits of this procedure. "I bet the most touching moment would be when you first look at your kids . . ." she had said with all the confidence in the world for the Dobelle Institute as it appeared on the Web site. Now, looking at the few dots resembling Kyle, I was not moved at all by it. This image did not resemble a human being, let alone my own son. It could have been anything—a fire hydrant, telephone pole, or a telephone booth—and there was no being moved by the image. However, I reminded myself, today I could tell Kyle, or someone, was in front of the car, which would give me more confidence in driving it without thinking I was about to squash someone.

"Yeah, I can see you there. Move back slowly, counting your steps out loud, and I'll tell you when you disappear from sight." Kyle moved back, counting out loud. " . . . four, five, six . . ." He disappeared from view at number five, having been reduced to a mere single phosphene at number four. I would have to drive slow enough so I could react in time before hitting the end of the parking lot, and also to avoid hitting someone. I started the car.

"I'm just going to drive forward and back again," I said, placing the gear selector in first gear. This way I had some control as to the speed of the car as I could detect the slight whine as the low gear accelerated. In any other gear, it would simply switch into the next higher gear, giving no audible indication as to the speed. Since I could not actually see the pavement in front of me—it was signified by blackness—I wouldn't have any visual record as to my speed. I rolled forward slowly, keeping the motor at no more than at an idle, while I pumped the brakes ever so slightly at two-second intervals, using the car's reaction to the braking as another indicator of speed. Had I never had a driver's license and adequate driving experience in the past, this maneuver would be extremely dangerous with the limited vision I had.

I looked to my right, then to the left, and back to the right as I rolled parallel to the side of the Dobelle Institute's building. I cursed the rearview mirror stuck to the center of the windshield as it obstructed my view. I concentrated mainly on the building on the right, and when I noticed the vertical line marking the corner of the building, I stopped the car. There was still no indication there was something in front of me. I called to Jim.

"Is there any more space to drive?"

"Quite a bit yet," Jim replied, probably praying the system wouldn't conk out now. "You can keep going for several yards yet."

I continued at my walking speed until I saw the flickering phosphenes marking some bushes in front of the car. I stopped and put the car in reverse. I drove slowly backward again, using the wall again for the guidance of the automobile. I only felt comfortable once I was past that cursed electrical box. Stopping at the corner from where I started, I turned to Bill who was still sitting in his wheelchair at the side of the building. Steve had gone into the building to retrieve a camera, leaving Bill to his own fate. He must have had a lot of confidence in not only the system but also my driving as he would never have been able to move out of the way had I fouled up. "Try turning around," he suggested.

I knew that would be quite a bit more risky as I had to judge my environment much more precisely. Luckily, I had enough experience while driving on my farm using only a tightly strung wire for a guide to be able to judge how long to back up in order to turn the first ninety degrees, then cranking the steering wheel the opposite way, execute the other ninety degrees for the complete change in direction. I drove the car forward again to the far corner of the building, swerving it slightly to the right so I'd have more space on my left to allow the front of the car to swing around without striking the building. I backed up straight until I saw the corner of the building outlined by a few dots rising vertically. It was important to constantly move my head in order to take advantage of the more effective clusters of phosphenes in my visual field. I could not see a vertical wall with my left side as the top half had no phosphenes, forcing me to turn my head further in order to see the line with my right side. It was the left side with its small, tightly packed phosphenes, however, that allowed me to see the presence of smaller objects and properly judge the intersecting line of the building and the pavement. I threw the car in reverse and expertly backed up in an arc, turning the car ninety degrees. I did not look behind me, but rather to the left so as to make sure I was not striking anyone with the side of the car as it swung around. Behind me would be the curb, which was too low to damage the car.

Now I just had to make the second turn, but halfway through it, I was too close to the building for me to see the distance I was from it, as I judged that entirely by the intersecting line of the building and pavement. This area was now obscured by the right corner of the car's hood. I backed up a bit again, swinging the car more into a parallel position relative to the building, looking out my left side and lining myself up with the curb dividing the two parking lots. I used this line to drive the car back toward the other corner of the building where Bill was still sitting, watching closely my progress. I had to duck down so I could avoid the rearview mirror from obstructing my view of the corner of the building. I had to be able to see at least three phosphenes in a line in order to be able to assume that I was seeing it. I repeated this procedure a few times, sometimes asking Jim to warn me if I was about to hit something. He didn't have to do that even once. I was losing my nervousness and began to get a better feel for the automobile, even to the point where, once I was confident the car was pointed in a straight direction, floored the gas pedal, causing the powerful car to lurch forward, its tires squealing. It was a ball. Even if this vision was not safe for driving on the road, I concluded, one could set up a racecourse with brightly painted white lines on dark pavement, the contestant's cars painted with contrasting colors for easy view, facilitating blind people to once again participate in the domain of automobiles. That, no doubt, would be good advertising for artificial vision.

I stopped the car and checked my braille watch. The system had run for almost an hour and a half without shutting down. I looked around, suddenly aware of the entire layout of the property. I could see the flickering chaos of phosphene as I looked toward the trees on one side of the lot, my image substantiated by the slight audible rustling of their leaves. There was the lot divider behind, the car parked to one side of it. I looked toward the building and saw the outline of the roof, the sides, and the electrical box just a few feet away from the wall. The sighted world was beautiful. At this instant, I forgot all about the eccentricities of Bill, the problems of the company, the pain I had been subject to during the operation, and the seizure I had experienced just two weeks ago. I just stood and stared, and no one spoke. This was the feeling I had expected on the first day of the system being issued to me—the great unveiling I had hoped for, for so many years . . .

Then everything went black. I shuddered for an instant, not sure if I had been dreaming and now suddenly awake. Then I checked my watch again, which told me it had been an hour and a half.

"It quit," I said, hiding any emotion I may have felt. I wasn't sure what that emotion would have been. The darkness pressed around me like a huge angry cloud of black smoke engulfing my very soul.

"Well, it was time to go in anyways," Bill said, his part of the project having been accomplished. What was going on in my head at that instant did not matter the least to him. "Let's go in as I think Dennis is about to arrive, and we'll try to get him going again."

As Bill spoke, I walked with the usual uncertainty of a blind man toward the sound of Bill's voice, dragging my feet carefully so I wouldn't trip over any unseen objects. I couldn't see my feet now, not Bill, not the corner of the building. The trees now disappeared, along with the rest of the world. Just like when the metal got my last eye from that snow machine, with the exception that this time I'd still have a chance once the equipment was really mine, and once it worked. Jim would have to try harder.

Dennis was quickly run through the thresh-adjust program with the one side he had been tested on so far. He had been told about my driving the car, to which he said nothing. I said nothing either, wondering what would be the right approach in this situation. I remembered how I envied Jerry for being able to see the mannequins with his dots while I was in the dark—did Dennis feel that same envy toward me?

Then Bill instructed Jim to start the camera on Dennis at one frame a second. "Well, what do you see?" he asked.

Dennis turned his head this way and that, then answered in a frustrated voice. "I don't see anything. All there is are these flashes of light."

Bill grunted and said, "How can you say you don't see anything when you see the light?"

"Dennis," I tried to explain as no one else seemed to try. Steve and Jim just kept their tongues still when around Bill. "It is the pattern of phosphenes that you see during the flash that makes the picture. In other words, when you try to find an object on the table and there is a flash on the very right of your visual field, it means the object is there. Move your head a bit to the right and wait for the next flash, and you'll find the flashes more toward the center of your visual field. At that point you know it's in front of you."

An object was placed in front of Dennis, probably a spare battery from the vision system as its color was contrasting to that of the tabletop. Dennis moved his head around a bit, then reached for the battery. Whether he found it by accident or actually saw it, I couldn't tell.

"See, you saw it that time," Bill said. Dennis was not so convinced.

"I wouldn't call that seeing. It's just a flash of light, that's all. It could have been anything."

"Well, we'll leave it at that for now," said Bill, sensing the obvious discontentment of Dennis. "Tomorrow we'll get you set up and behind the wheel of the car." I had no idea what that was supposed to do for Dennis. But that didn't seem to matter to Bill.

That night I called home to Lorri and the family, sharing the good news of the day's events.

"It certainly isn't like the vision we had hoped for," I said, remembering my high hopes of driving, even if illegally, along relatively quiet roads in the country. "But when it comes to walking, I sure can pick up more of my environment than I can totally blind. I think this thing will help us a bit, anyways."

I didn't share the total awed feeling of seeing the scene at the back of the Dobelle building; I had to mull over it for a while before I could put this into the right words.

"Will you get it to take home?"

"I sure hope so. Bill said that all should be ready to go by the time I leave." I wished I could really believe this would happen.

The next day, Sunday, started at nine thirty in the morning. Right away we were introduced first to Dr. Dobelle's son Marty, a cute kid of perhaps eleven years who was having a ball playing video games on one of the office computers. He was to accompany me while I drove the car. Next was the photography team. There was a man named Charlie who did the still shots and Enrico who did the video along with his assistants. Enrico had a very strong foreign accent, making him difficult to understand.

"All right, we'll fire the system up and you," Bill said, nodding in my direction, "will drive the car for the crew to photograph." I remembered the phosphenes' variations in brightness that occurred yesterday, figuring it was time to readjust the thresholds. Some of them had been so bright they occasionally gave me a residual phosphene, which made the task of driving more precarious than it already was.

"I think I need my thresholds checked first," I said to Bill. "Yesterday even they were in need of readjustment."

Bill grunted in disapproval. "We don't have time for that now. Dennis is coming this afternoon as well for the filming, and these guys," he said, motioning to the film crew, "want to get going. We'll just skip it for now."

It was obvious at this point where Bill's priorities lay; it wasn't with the patient, that was for sure. I would just have to put up with the imperfections of my thresholds for now. I entered the conference room and started to collect up the vision system components Jim had already laid out for me.

I was halfway through the process of connecting one wire when both Enrico and Charlie halted me. "Can you disconnect that and reconnect it again?"

I did as they asked. Once Charlie asked me to hold still while I had the two cable ends, the one for the saver and the one for the stimulator in my hands for him to take a picture. When I finally was connected, ready to hit the "on" button, Enrico said, "Oh dear, it looks like the lighting in here is not quite right. Jens, come out into the room here," he said, stepping into the cafeteria room, "and reconnect again."

I disconnected all the wires, laid the belt with its components on the first table in the cafeteria, and restarted the procedure of connecting myself. It took another hour before the photographers were satisfied.

Then it was outside where the next routine was repeated. Enrico, Charlie, and all the assistants darted every which way while I tried to control the automobile. I must have repeated the same stretch of road twenty times while Marty fidgeted in the passenger seat. It was difficult to concentrate on the task as all the people blocked my view of the building, forcing me to use the curb on the right for orientation.

"Squeal the tires!" begged Marty. I was in no mood to take chances.

"Not unless we want another hole in the building beside us," I said as I eased the car to the end of the stretch of parking lot. I sighed with relief when Enrico asked me to halt. I got out of the car and walked over where Bill and the photography team converged, their presence not only audible but indicated by the groups of dots showing me where I was.

"I think we'd better do it again," I heard Enrico say. I protested. "But wait a minute! This system is only good for maybe another half hour of running time! What's the problem anyway?"

Enrico pointed at the car. "We left the license plates on.

The rental company could get ugly about it. I'll just pull them off and start again."

A screwdriver was retrieved by one of the engineers, and the plates were pulled. I walked to the car, its shape now more familiar as it was portrayed by the crude vision system. I got in and started all over again.

"Squeal the tires!" Marty begged. I did. The phosphenes were not as badly out of adjustment today as they had been yesterday, so I did not have any residual phosphenes after the first fifteen minutes of driving. All went smoothly until the system quit suddenly a half hour into the second run of filming as predicted.

"It stopped working," I announced as I stopped the car. Enrico was not satisfied yet. "Just follow the sound of my assistant for one more run, OK?" he said. I did as I was told as it was easy to hear the assistant calling me from the other side of the lot as there was no roof on the car, allowing me to have directional hearing. "Don't worry," Enrico said as he continued to roll the film, "I'll let you know if you're about to hit something." I cooperated despite the darkness closing in on me, obediently directing the car toward the yelling assistant who was strategically positioned out of the view of the camera. My only concern now was to get these photographers satisfied so they would leave us alone to continue working on the vision system, perfecting the phosphene adjustments, the map, and most of all, allowing Jim to install the necessary software so the system will start on its own rather than having to be booted up with a laptop. It was vital that this was done before any of us patients would be able to take the vision system home.

After the last pass across the parking lot, I followed the voices to the corner of the building, brandishing, once again, my white cane. My heart sank as I approached within earshot.

"No, we can't have that in there," Enrico agreed, still holding the license plates of the Chrysler. "I wonder where we could go."

"What's the problem now?" I asked curtly. If these guys were professionals, I thought, they sure weren't acting like that today.

"The garbage dumpsters are in the film," Kyle informed me, having heard the entire conversation. "They figure that won't look good."

"Who owns that over there?" It was Charlie speaking, gesturing to the other side of the concrete curb that separated Dobelle's lot from the neighbors. "Think they'd mind?"

"There's a lot more room there," Enrico agreed, "and considering it's Sunday, I doubt there'd be any notice of us."

Bill vaulted himself forward somewhat with his one foot to see past the building of the Dobelle Institute. "That'll do, if you make sure none of the buildings are in the picture. No one will ever know that lot was used."

"Well, I hope you're going to restart my system first," I protested, "as right now it's right off." I did not like the idea of there being much more room as I had limited range with this vision system. If the building and the curb weren't as close as they were, I wouldn't be able to orient myself. I'd have to wait and see, I thought. Then again, I mused, perhaps they really didn't care if the device worked or not, as long as I was wearing it and sitting behind the wheel of a moving car.

"Yeah, we'll get it restarted. We'll also get Dennis going with the other system, and you both will take turns with the filming. Let's first have some lunch," Bill spoke as Charlie pushed him back toward the front entrance.

Dennis was fitted with his equipment, being subject to the same level of interest by the photography team as I was. Once accomplished, he was led out to the car. I had no idea what he saw with the system, but it couldn't have been very much as he made no reference to anything he passed by as he was led out the door of the building. With the camera crew, and Bill outside, the office was once again peaceful. I took my place at the conference room table, and Jim hooked the system back up to the laptop, and since I had not turned it off yet, he hoped he'd be able to find the bug in the software that kept shutting it off. But he had no luck, and a half hour later, he gave up.

"We'd better get you going with this thing so you can go out there again," he said as he prepared the system for another hour and a half of service. I had nothing to say in return as Jim, an employee of Bill, had no real right to comment negatively on the proceedings. I hooked up the cables to my savers, adjusted the belt, and Jim started the stimulator. The light reappeared, cheering me up as the world was visible once again. I followed Kyle out the door, marveling at the fact I could see the doorframes as I passed through them. I followed Kyle across the parking lot, stepping over the barrier separating the two lots when I saw it approaching. My cane was still folded up in my hands. Had the ground been rougher, I would have used it as the system would never show drop-offs very reliably, but knowing this lot was flat, I could do away with it. It felt strange, but so, so good not to use the cane.

Several yards into the neighboring lot, I heard the voices of Enrico, Charlie, and the assistants shouting at Dennis as he drove.

"This way . . . this way . . . this way . . . —now turn right, keep going . . . OK . . . turn left and reverse . . . yeah, that's far enough . . . now this way . . . this way . . ." I approached the blob of phosphenes that indicated Bill, parked out of the way of the cameras in his chair. "You're next," he said.

I approached the car as Dennis had left it. I'd have to turn it around before driving it the other direction. There was a line of grass beside the lot that I could use as a guide, but in areas it was too dried up, and the color of the pavement blended in with the color of the sand, giving no phosphene image.

The concrete curb and the side of the building at the other lot had been much clearer to see with this system. I would be able to see the grass well enough on my left side, but when turning around the car to go the other direction, I'd have nothing to look at to guide me. This wasn't going to work very well at all.

"There's nothing to guide me on the way back," I told Enrico, interrupting his list of instructions he wanted me to follow, "as there's nothing on that side to look at. I had the building for one way and the curb for the return at the old place."

Enrico shrugged it off. "No problem, we'll help you get back."

I turned the car around, using part of the grass. Once the grass line was on my left, I started to go forward as they filmed. Occasionally, I looked out the windshield to make sure no one was standing in front of me. About a hundred yards later, I reached the assistant who was stationed, out of the view of the camera, to guide me into a turning-around procedure. He gave me directions just like they had done with Dennis. I could not use the system on the way back as the grass line, being on the passenger side of the car, was too far away for the vision system to react. I prayed this film would not be used on any media channel as blind people would line up by the thousands for this operation just to find out the truth afterward. Or maybe, I hoped, we'd get the software refined so we'd have accessible magnification and other goodies by that time so this can be pulled off with confidence the next time around, justifying this show of success.

"Now let's have a picture of both of you in the car," Enrico suggested, meaning Dennis and I as we wore our vision systems. He positioned himself at the side of the car so he'd get film of both of us looking at the camera. "Now when I say 'go,' just go ahead about twenty feet and stop. Don't worry, it's all clear for at least a hundred feet in front of you."

Dennis got at the wheel of the Chrysler and I in the passenger seat. Enrico was changing a battery for his camera when I asked, "Dennis, do you see the grass line we have to follow?"

Dennis turned to me and stated in a voice bordering on anger, "I can't see nothing! Nothing at all."

"Not even the outline of the windshield?"

"Nothing."

Enrico was ready and started the film. "In five seconds, just say something like 'good-bye' and go, all right?" Dennis did as he was asked, gunning the Chrysler as it lurched forward out of the view of the camera, giving an excellent impression that we were really going somewhere. I felt kind of dirty inside as if I had committed a crime that could hurt someone.

But then again, I did see that grass, even if Dennis didn't—with only thirty or so electrodes working at that time—Dennis just needed more rehab and adjustment with his system to do the same. There was so much potential with this system, and my impatience got the better part of me more often than not.

We were done filming, all of us now standing around in the parking lot, about a hundred or so yards from the institute building. I heard the trees on the right, and looked to see them. With the afternoon sun shining behind me as I stood there in the middle of the lot, the entire world behind me lit up with astonishing clarity. The institute building's roof and walls were outlined against the sky, the trees with their chaotic phosphene patterns on my left, the divider of the two lots as clear as can be. I must really be getting used to the system now, I thought as I looked at the world unfolding before me. Normally I'd have no idea where I was when stranded in the middle of an asphalt field, as there was no sound clue coming from the building. I was learning to move my head in such a manner to make a better picture out of the unevenly dispersed phosphene map I had. Even though the entire picture was not visible at first glance, a couple of seconds of moving my head around, scanning the landscape, and the picture materialized itself in what seemed like absolute clarity in my visual field. I stood there like a prisoner just released after decades of incarceration—I couldn't move—I was just awed by the size of the world before me. I didn't have to stand here now; I was free. Free to go wherever I wanted, and right now I wanted to go inside the building. I began to walk, first with uncertainty, then with absolute certainty, toward the building.

I paid close attention to the sounds coming from behind me as I stepped over the curb dividing the lots. Good. No one noticed I was going away. I felt like a dog, kept on a short leash forever, but this time, the master had neglected to fasten the clip. How far would I get before someone would notice and intervene? I approached the building until I saw the intersecting line between its walls and the pavement and proceeded to walk around it, heading to the front door. I saw the electrical box and at this point used my cane for reassurance as I knew there was a staircase coming up which was recessed for entering the basement. Then I heard the shouts and the running footsteps toward me. I cursed.

"Careful! There's stairs coming up!" He grabbed my arm as I strained to control myself from pushing the man right out of my path. What right did he have to destroy that magic moment of freedom? This man had no business in New York, let alone the United States, which supported a culture of personal rights and freedom. I turned on him in anger.

"Will you get out of here and mind your own business? What would you do if I grabbed at you with every step you took because I thought you were too stupid to walk by yourself? How do you figure I've made it through eighteen years of life and still survived? I had a mother once, and I moved out of home. I certainly don't need you as a replacement!" Although his face was represented by only a few dots, he must have had a look of utter astonishment on his face by my reaction. There was a moment of silence as he struggled for words. I probably would have been more forgiving had Kyle not been there, but to be humiliated like this in front of my own son was more than I could bear.

"I was just trying to help, you know," Charlie stammered. I hated that excuse. "You know, the stairs were there and I thought you might fall down them."

"I don't need anyone to save me," I said quietly, continuing my trek around the building, the magic gone from the experience of freedom.

The others had already left, perhaps because they understood, or perhaps because they just didn't know what to say. Charlie didn't get it, though. I could tell. He wasn't the only one, though, who thought that once one's eyesight went, their pride would go along with it. I'd have to try this again, I thought to myself. When all the Charlies have gone to bed, that is. Once again, I was reminded why I chose to hike in the forest alone at night—there were no Charlies out then as they would be too scared to enter a dark forest. But this was different again. Here I could see, but someone got it in their head that I should still not be allowed to function independently. When I was a child growing up, there were certain things I knew I could do alone, but had to wait until no one was looking lest someone would stop me with the idea that I was "too young"—now this feeling came back to me—only now I was undermined by someone even younger than me.

June 3 came with all the hopes of some good productivity arriving at the office of the Dobelle Institute. However, at 7:30 a.m., Bill informed me we wouldn't get picked up until 10:00 a.m. Kyle and I explored the hotel and found it had an indoor swimming pool and a fitness room as well. At 10:00 a.m., Pat came to get us with the Caddy.

"I want you to show Jerry D., one of the patients along with Ken, how the equipment looks when you have it on." Dr. Dobelle was ready for new patients, it seemed. In a few minutes, Jerry, who had travelled alone, as well as Ken and his wife Gene from England, introduced themselves. Jerry D. spoke in his Louisiana accent.

"I remember I met you in Portugal just before I had my operation," he said, his voice familiar to me.

"You're right there," I said, recalling the conversation. "At that time you said you never had a headache in your life. Did you have one after the operation?"

"Not so much from the operation, but the night after they tried to stimulate me, I had the most terrible headache. I never had that before."

"Well, let's hope that's the last one you get," I replied. I was now finished attaching all the equipment to my head, the glasses and the battery. "Take a look at all this stuff now," I said to Jerry. He came over and felt the computer box, stimulator box, glasses, and battery, asking questions about them each time he found a new component. The he pulled on the shoulder straps of the belt, stretching them a couple of feet longer without any effort.

"How are these supposed to do any good?" he asked. I shrugged. "It looks like that part needs improvement for the next time around. For now, the belt seems to hold it all."

Next it was Ken from England who introduced himself. He was in his late sixties and had lost his sight when using acid to clear a clogged drain in preparation for his retirement party. The story was horrible when Gale recounted it. But then we all had horrible stories, as Dennis crashed a car at high speed, causing his loss of sight, and Jerry D. had been serving with the military during World War II when a mortar went off too close to him. There was no such thing as a good story when recounting how one went blind.

Ken inspected all the equipment I was wearing, asking questions about it just like Jerry did. Bill then spoke up, causing even more excitement among the new patients.

"Jim, get Jens going, and then we can work with Ken and Jerry. Jens," he said, turning to me as if he accomplished something very important, "I had Jim install a two-hour timer so you can't overstimulate your visual cortex. You can go out and experiment with it for a while this morning."

I did not know what to say. Why would Bill waste Jim's time installing a timer if the darned thing quit anyways after an hour and a half? Moreover, when the camera crew was there, overstimulation of my visual cortex seemed to be the least of Bill's concerns.

"All right," I said flatly. This was no time for a confrontation. "I'll give you a call when the timer runs out." Jim hit the switch, not readjusting the thresholds. It hadn't been done for days, even though Bill had written in his Journal 2000 that they should be done every morning before using the system. Now, for some reason, it didn't matter. As Jim started the machine, the frames began to flicker, displaying the outline of the table with flickering phosphenes. I followed it until I reached the doorframe, and as I walked out bade good-bye to Ken and Jerry D. They answered me cheerily, "Yeah, see you later!" The poor guys, I thought, they really think they'll be up and running and seeing everything the world has to offer in a couple of hours. It wasn't going to be that simple.

Pat dropped us off at the hotel. The first thing we did was head straight to our room to retrieve my spring jacket, which I used to cover up the equipment around my waist. I had already pulled my shirt over it temporarily just to gain access to the hotel without causing general panic. Once I had my jacket, I closed the zipper while tucking all the wires and cables underneath. Even the cables coming from my head went straight down into my collar. I now resembled more an overweight man rather than a robot.

There was a fair amount of confusion at the front door from which Kyle and I tried to start our walk, with me insisting I try to find my own way. Since my ability to see a line like that of a grass line was limited to less than ten feet, I had trouble crossing the parking lot. I kept following the lines designated for marking the parking stalls and finally abandoned the idea and instead followed the sound of the traffic of the Motocross Parkway. I looked down while listening, hoping to intersect the sidewalk and finding the curb. But I never did, and when I was sure I was at the side of the busy road, I turned to Kyle.

"I can't see any curb here," Kyle answered by pointing out the on-ramp for the cars was on either side of the lot, making it impossible to see the line.

"Well, let's find the sidewalk and try it again." I followed Kyle out to the area of the sidewalk where there were no more ramps leading into parking lots. There was a good stretch of sidewalk in front of us, having grass on either side. It was perfect for experimenting as pedestrian traffic was low and there was no threat of stepping out on the road.

I walked along beside Kyle, trying to avoid using the cane, but I had trouble picking up the intersecting line between the sidewalk and the grass.

"The sidewalk is gray in the middle but slowly darkens toward the edges," Kyle explained the image we were trying to see with the vision device. "Then the grass is a bit trampled near the edge, so it starts in a gradual greening toward the center of the turf."

"In other words, there are no edges." I was discouraged at this, as the edge detection was what rendered useful the vision system in the first place. In real life, however, with the environment not being perfect, the system was having serious problems.

Well, if I can't do that, let's see if I can see the buildings and count them. Perhaps that would help me find specific houses when walking down the street." I was trying to think of how this device could be useful in my life. I walked along the sidewalk with my cane and looked to my left where the buildings were. All I could see were many phosphenes blinking in a chaotic fashion, making no sense at all. After a few minutes, I halted in frustration.

"I can't see a single building!"

Kyle looked over and pointed out, "That must be because there are trees planted in front of them, all along the sidewalk. They look pretty, and they really don't stop anyone from finding the building, but I guess it's not working for that vision system."

We came to an area where the grass was untrampled and the sidewalk was all the same color. I saw the borders and could walk for several steps without using the cane. I felt a little more encouraged. The traffic roaring by us on my right gave me another idea.

"Let's see if I can see oncoming cars," I suggested. I had been taught to cross the road safely by listening to the traffic, but that was at times inconvenient as the noise of a car already passed by would mask the probability of other cars coming after it, and even if there weren't any other cars, one would have to wait until the street was perfectly quiet before crossing it. Worst yet, as I had grown up with eyesight, I couldn't help feeling uncomfortable even with the street perfectly quiet to cross it without first looking right and then left for reassurance. I hoped this device could do it. I stepped out to the curb and looked in the direction of an oncoming car. I saw a couple of phosphenes blinking, and after the car whizzed past me, I still saw them. I tried again but with no more luck than the first time. I looked straight in front of me across the street and saw the outline of a roof from a building on the other side. As a big delivery truck lumbered by, one extra phosphene lit up for an instant as it passed in front of me.

"Does it work?" asked Kyle.

"I'd be dead three times over if I depended on this thing to see me through crossing the street in the last minute," I said discouragingly I thought of how Dr. Dobelle had claimed the volunteer Jerry had been "using the New York subway system regularly . . ." and the impression that sentence had given me for what to expect as far as personal mobility was concerned. Surely we'd be able to walk down a simple sidewalk and find a building larger than a barn; we had thought upon reading the accomplishments of the volunteer. Something needed improvement here.

"Well, I can see the roof of the building across the street," I pointed out to Kyle, trying to hide my feelings of disappointment, which was unjustified considering I wouldn't have known it was there had it not been for the system. I looked around for anything else there was to spot when the system suddenly died. We trudged home together, as I once again depended on my white cane. I was sweating profusely as the system had heated up to the point where neither the computer nor the stimulator could be touched by the naked finger without being scalded. Moreover, it was far too warm outside to wear a coat. Yet I didn't dare take it off.

Once in the hotel room, I phoned the Dobelle Institute. I discovered I did not have the means to disconnect the cables from my head, forcing me to continue to wear it even though it did not work anymore. We couldn't go anywhere, being stuck in the hotel room until someone would show up with the 1/16" allen wrench. It wasn't until three hours later that Mario showed up with a package containing a small wrench.

"Oh, that's rather cruel to be stuck with that thing all this time." He chuckled as he handed me the wrench. But it was the blindness, not the system, that was cruel. The system was just a problem when it didn't work. I kept a wrench in my wallet ever since.

Even though we were ready to go to the office at 7:30 a.m. on June 4, I didn't get picked up until 10:00 a.m. Steve said he had been hung up in traffic. He arrived alone as Jim was nowhere to be seen or heard. Ken, his wife Gale, and Jerry D. were already in the conference room. I wondered for an instant if they had even gone home for the night the day before, or if they simply became cemented in place on these chairs while the engineers fiddled with the precarious equipment.

"Steve, I want you to spend no more than a half hour with Jens to get him set up and then get to work with Ken and Jerry." It was Bill talking as he lumbered his chair into the conference room, the carpeted floor giving him additional mobility problems. If Bill had a wheelchair with bigger wheels, or even an electric chair, he may be able to get around better, I thought.

Bill left the room at that, not even greeting any of us. I wondered if he had a problem with Jim that made him so moody.

Steve turned to me as I placed the equipment on the table. "What do you think we should do in that half hour?" he asked me uncertainly. It wasn't really my business. I wasn't the inventor of this system. I was a patient. How many patients are asked by a surgeon what procedure to follow during an operation? Steve was twenty-one, fresh out of college and really didn't have a lot of experience to draw from.

"Yesterday I couldn't see oncoming cars. Maybe we can funnel the vision somewhat, like put in a zoom. Is there such a feature?"

"Yeah, I think that's the size factor. Let's see what it is now and maybe change it." Steve fiddled with the computer and then had the menu. He changed the size factor from 80 to 20. "The size factor dictates the number of camera pixels used per phosphene," Steve explained.

"Well, since we still have a bit of time, let's run through the thresh-adjust and even them out some," I suggested. Steve started the program, and we worked diligently. Steve was increasing or decreasing the voltage of each phosphene in small increments while I responded to each change until I could just see the phosphene appear. This way I would have no residual phosphenes, yet be able to use it to make an image. Jerry D. and Ken waited patiently. Neither of them were looking at me with their new equipment the way they had anticipated the day before. Neither did they say "see you soon" when I left the office this time. This time it was Louise who drove me to the hotel in her car as Pat was out getting more patients to be fitted with their equipment. Jim had better come over soon, I thought, as there was quite a shortage of manpower in the office presently.

I was already dressed up with my coat on when Louise dropped us off at the sidewalk. I didn't bother trying to find it from the front of the hotel as this time I concentrated on any improvement the size factor may have contributed to. Immediately I could find the turf line at a distance of up to twenty feet where the line was relatively clear. In some areas, it was not evident, but after only a few steps, it would reappear. I was also able to locate the trunks of trees up to fifty feet away, depending upon how well the background contrasted with the color of the trunk. I stepped up to the curb of Motocross Parkway once again and tried to see oncoming traffic. This time a few dots blinked out of place as cars approached, the blinking dots beginning to appear when the car was still almost hundred feet away from me. It was an improvement over yesterday's results for sure, but still far from sufficient for a safe crossing. I'd still have to depend on my ears for this task, I thought.

"Kyle, try standing in the middle of the sidewalk in front of me and let's see if I can avoid pedestrians with this thing." Kyle went out to in front of me and stood quietly as I came up from behind. The first time I saw him well as he stood in such a way that his light-colored clothing was outlined against the darker grass. From a distance of a few feet, he still looked like a tree trunk, just a line of dots vertically arranged. The second time he stopped in front of me, however, he was in front of a tree and I was not able to distinguish his dots from those in the background.

I checked my watch and noticed it had been almost an hour since starting the system. Knowing it would quit in a half hour, we decided to turn back. I could follow the sidewalk using my cane only occasionally until we reached the unshaded area of the Sheridan. The sun was on my face now, rendering the camera useless. I had to follow Kyle with my white cane in order to get into the building.

For the first time I had this system up and running while inside of the building. The electric lighting did not interfere at all with the camera, and the straight lines of the furniture made the system work well. I saw the row of dots signifying the counter at the reception area on the other side of the foyer, as well as the outline of the doorframe leading into the hallway where our room was. I could count the doors leading to each room without touching them as we walked toward our room. Once inside, I noticed the electric lights on the walls and tabletops as plain as day, each being represented by several phosphenes. They would disappear when I turned off the switch. It had been a long time since I could appreciate electric light. Looking around the room, there was not much to see.

"This thing isn't picking anything up in here," I said to Kyle. He laughed and answered, "That's because the light is off now. I can't see much either."

We turned the light back on, and everything began to make sense. The beds were outlined, along with the desk and the bathroom door.

"I wonder if you could see a line on a piece of paper," Kyle suggested as he found the hotel's pen on the small desk that held the television. He got out a piece of paper from inside.

"Try it and we'll know. But you had better hurry as this thing isn't going to last much longer." Kyle drew a line and gave it to me. I held the paper perhaps ten centimeters from my glasses and slowly moved it around. Suddenly, I saw a line of phosphenes blinking and moving rapidly upward. I stopped and searched the paper again. "There it is, horizontal." I pointed to the line. We tried the same trick four more times, and every time I succeeded.

"This is quite handy to tell if the computer printer is working!" I said. It was not, however, even close to being good enough to read technical diagrams. Then the system quit as predicted. I disconnected the cables from my head and called Louise.

Steve didn't show up until 4:00 p.m.

"How are things going at the office?" I asked him as he tiredly trudged into the room.

"Oh, every time I try to map Jerry D. or Ken, the system crashes. And to top it off, Bill's got more patients coming tomorrow."

"Did Jim finally make it?" Kyle asked. Jim, after all, was the pro in the field of software. Steve was just learning.

"Jim got . . . well . . . he just quit," Steve said. That evening when Kyle and I were dining in the lounge of the Sheridan, I heard the unmistakable voice of Jerry D. speaking in his Louisiana accent. Kyle and I got up and joined him as he was walking into his room, led by Pat.

"Hey, Jerry, if you want some company this evening, I brought some braille playing cards." I could have used a change from this dull routine.

"Sure, come on up!" Jerry sounded cheery in spite of the circumstances. He gave me his room number.

That night, while Kyle watched a movie on television, I went over to Jerry's room. I had called him via telephone just before leaving, asking him to stick his head out in the hallway and listen for me. He did just that, and as he heard me approaching, he called, "That you, Jens?"

He was the nicest guy I had ever met. As we played cards and chatted, I could not help but think of how he lost his sight fighting the people of my country of birth, the war being a gesture of madness that made no sense at all. Then I brought up the subject of artificial vision.

"So what do you think of the progress in the office of the Dobelle Institute so far?"

"Well," Jerry D. tried to sound positive despite the circumstances, just like I always did. "They're certainly having their problems, that's for sure. I never thought they'd be so understaffed. Heck, there was just one young guy doing all the work today."

"Yeah, that's right," I said sympathetically. "We used to have two, but Jim just quit. At least I think he quit. He was the pro with the software, and now Steve is trying to take over."

Jerry shuffled the cards and sighed. "I've been sitting around for two days now, and it looks like that won't change seeing that Dr. Dobelle is getting more patients coming over tomorrow. What really surprises me is, OK, the equipment Steve is trying to use to do us isn't working, why then doesn't he just get another box? He should have all of them ready for all the patients. That way he can fiddle with the one that doesn't work and have it fixed for the last patient that's coming."

"Let's hope the others are indeed ready," I said, but doubting that really was the case. So far Bill hadn't admitted to it, but it was quite possible that they weren't even close to ready. Now with Jim gone, it was unlikely the systems would be improved so they could start up by themselves without the aid of the laptop. The more I thought of it, the angrier I became.

June 5, 2002: Kyle and I made it to the office first thing in the morning where I met Steve who finally figured out that the stimulator he was using yesterday had a loose connection, causing the mapping problems. Pat made a second trip and retrieved Ken, Gene, and Jerry D. as well. We were all sitting around the conference room table, listening to Steve shuffling around at the other end of it, when Bill, who was still referred to as "Dr. Dobelle" by Ken and Jerry, rolled expertly into the room.

"After we get Jens going," he began in a labored voice, indicating stress was taking a hold of him, "Pat will move you all to the Howard Johnson hotel just on the other side of Morland Avenue." Bill turned to me as I connected the cables to my head. "By the way, Jens, I just finished talking to CNN—they were wondering if you'd drive a car downtown Manhattan for them to film." Bill sounded serious as I tried to believe my ears. "Do you figure you can do that?"

Bill just didn't get it, I thought. All I could see was about ninety points of light at best, unevenly dispersed, indicating no gray area, rendering them useful for only the most basic of display tasks. I still could not identify a person from a lamppost, and here this guy was expecting me to contend with New York traffic? No one with even the slightest sense of logic would suggest such absurdity. "Dr. Dobelle," I began, then thought of a better strategy. "It would be illegal. I don't have a driver's license, to begin with, and have not had enough experience driving again. It would be dangerous."

"Yeah, all right then." Bill seemed slightly disappointed. "We'll just have to give them the film we took last Sunday." My heart skipped a beat when I heard that. If they select the film of my driving in the neighboring property, it would be a bit of an exaggeration, as most of the time I was oriented by the voices of the cameramen; however, I figured if I had had these new zoom adjustments to my system Steve just finished making, I'd have been fine driving the car without help in that setting too.

"Are the threshold values still all right?" Steve interrupted my thoughts as he connected the laptop to the computer of the vision system, which was already in the belt around my waist. I quickly attached the remaining cable to my left saver.

"Yes, they were good yesterday, and I guess this time they'll do. It would be so much more useful if I could adjust them myself." Steve said nothing as Dr. Dobelle was still in the room. He hit the last key, and the system sprang into life, the white dots dancing in my visual field. I could see the blobs of phosphenes representing the other patients sitting impatiently at the table, waiting their turn.

Pat came into the room and asked, "Ready to go?" We all crammed into the Caddy and were transported back to the Sheridan, where we each had a half hour to gather our stuff. "We won't have the weight room or the indoor swimming pool," commiserated Kyle as he packed. He had, so far, had a relatively unexciting stay in Commack. It sure hadn't gone as expected—Dad just didn't strap on the system and return back to the fully sighted world as he had hoped. Even he was scratching his head about the obvious lack of systematic order seen at the Dobelle Institute. Research and development is a difficult business, often lacking obvious structure.

Pat came back and hoisted our suitcase in one hand. "Follow me," he said.

We all stood at the front desk of the lobby as we waited our turn to check out. I could see the outline of the counter and a few flickering dots indicating the clerk at the other side as he battled it out with Bill Dobelle on the telephone. Judging from the conversation, it was obvious Bill owed the Sheridan money that wasn't getting paid. I watched the flickering phosphenes for a few more minutes, noting that I was able to tell visually when the clerk moved. It was the first time I could see someone really move like this. I was ecstatic with enthusiasm but couldn't share it with the clerk as he was quite noticeably upset about something to do with the telephone call. I turned around to see if I could find the exit door, as I had heard someone leave, the noise marking its location. But I could not see the door; it looked just like the windows, a bunch of white dots. This thing needed more work.

The system quit only about forty minutes after it had been started. I cursed it now that it wasn't functioning, yet I was forced to wear it until we got to our room at the Howard Johnson's. Once there, I met Keith, a patient from the United States, and Edmundo, a patient from Argentina who did not speak English or German, making it impossible for the two of us to talk. Keith and Edmundo, just like Jerry and Ken, had high hopes of being implanted. Edmundo must have gone through extremes to make it here for this big event. I felt pity for both of them as they had no idea how ill-prepared the Dobelle Institute really was at that moment to receive them.

Nothing else was done with my equipment for the rest of the day.

The next day started just like all the others had, with me being fitted first for the system so I could continue to practice with it. I figured by now that Bill was doing this deliberately so as to give hope to those patients who watched; that is, give hope to a somewhat hopeless situation. None of these patients, including the Italian woman who had just arrived with her son from Italy for her system, were going to get their systems to take home, that was now a fact in my mind. The others didn't know that, however, and sat patiently, awaiting their turn. Once my system was up and running, the flashing dots keeping me company, Steve tried, once again, to map Ken. The procedure went on for hours while the system kept failing. Ken was becoming more and more agitated by the process.

In the meantime, Kyle and I walked around the office building, avoiding the heat of the increasingly upset patients in the conference room. No doubt that among us all, I was the lucky one. I asked Kyle to try the white cane test against the wall again. This time he held it at either a vertical, horizontal, or a diagonal attitude. I was able to tell every direction except the one where the left corner of the cane was high, as the upper left quadrant of my visual field had no phosphenes to represent an image. I noticed as well that when the cane was diagonal, with the right side being up, it would resemble a picture resembling more an inverted bottle at an angle as the phosphenes on my upper right quadrant were much larger and coarser than the fine dot-like phosphenes found on my bottom left quadrant. After some more experimenting, I decided to go outside to walk around the building some, but the minute I went out the door, the system quit again.

"I think my head is swelling up," I heard Ken say to Steve as I walked into the conference room. Kyle had found Marty, Bill's son, and they were playing on a computer somewhere else in the building. "I can feel it puffing up." Ken did not sound happy. His mapping was still unsuccessful as the program had quit again. Steve was surprisingly patient for such a young man, considering the stress he was under. He simply kept restarting the program and trying again.

Everybody turned to Dr. Dobelle, who sat in his chair not far from Ken. He was the doctor, so everyone thought he had all the solutions too. But I knew better—we were all in this together, pioneers in a risky business, with the potential fruits of our efforts briefly displaying themselves in the moments I see the world revealing its full beauty before me when all the conditions are met to make this crude system shine at its best.

"Your head's fine," he said. "You're just getting tired. Steve, disconnect Ken and get Jerry D. going on mapping, will you?" I had no idea why Bill would assume the problem wouldn't arise with another patient. To me, Dr. Dobelle's suggestion seemed as ludicrous as changing the type of goods to be hauled in order to resolve a mechanical problem with a malfunctioning delivery truck. On the other hand, however, he could be just buying time, I thought to myself as there really wasn't much to do in the office, so the patients think there is really movement in this project. There was no doubt that Jim's absence had thrown a wrench in Bill's plans.

Jerry D., who had been sitting quietly at the conference room table for four days straight by now, moved over to the chair just to the left of Steve. Steve hooked up his cables and went back to his laptop, changing files so as to organize the data for all the patients. Steve had very little time now to look at details such as current draw displayed on the oscilloscope every time an electrode was stimulated. In the past, even though the current was never recorded during stimulation, Steve would watch the current reading while Jim had run the stimulation program.

"Now," said Steve, warning Jerry he was stimulating the randomly selected electrode with the intention of finding the threshold.

"No," Jerry said. Steve increased the voltage and tried again. "Now," he said.

"Yeah," said Jerry. "It's kind of orange in color." Jerry D. ended up with over thirty phosphenes that were good for making a picture and reported them all as being orange. "Maybe it's because the last thing I saw was that orange flash from that mortar," he said. It was a sad thing to hear. That moment of his life was the last thing he should have been reminded of, I thought.

Next came Jerry's mapping. Without it mapping, it was impossible to relate a section of the camera with a corresponding area of one's visual field. Steve asked Bill who had been watching, with nothing to say.

"Should we use the relative mapping? It might work rather than this other program that has been giving nothing but problems."

"Sure," said Bill. He had no concrete idea about the computer's program, so he couldn't help much. He, along with us patients, was now at the full mercy of Steve, who was, in turn, at the mercy of his own lack of knowledge about the programs used in this system.

The telephone rang, and Bill was paged by Louise. He was pushed by her into the office, and a minute later, she came to get me.

"Jens, I want you to meet Fred Spar, our media organizer." Fred was an energetic, polite man who probably could have been a lot more fun to work with than Bill had he known as much about artificial vision. He shook my hand warmly. We engaged in some small talk when he asked, "Jens, could you walk for us in Manhattan without a cane?"

I was not too impressed with the request. "Fred, let me remind you, I just received this system after eighteen years of blindness. I have only an hour or so each day to use it, and that's not much. Your request is just like asking someone just fitted with an artificial leg to walk the tightrope over the Grand Canyon!"

"Yeah, yeah, I guess you're right." Fred accepted my answer as if he expected it but was hoping I'd try anyways. After all, I reminded myself, if I happened to get squashed flat in the middle of the street, it would still make a good story, if not a better one. I would have to be careful that these guys don't try to push me too far. I was here principally to receive my already-paid-for vision system, not to act on television.

I returned back to the conference room and sat down beside Gene. She leaned over to me and whispered, "That woman from Italy has been sitting here all day, and she looks mad."

I whispered back to her, "Tell me who isn't?"

Ken overheard and joined in the conversation, "I can't believe how haphazard this whole process is. I had expected some sophisticated outfit here, not this circus."

The mapping was not going well for Jerry D., even with the other program. Instead of the computer selecting different phosphenes to compare to one another in the mapping process, it selected the same pattern over and over. When Jerry said, for the twelfth time, "Upper left," indicating that phosphene number 1 was to the bottom right of phosphene no. 2, which lit a second after the first, Steve came to the conclusion it wasn't working either. He kept fiddling with it while Ken, Gene, and I talked quietly amongst ourselves to pass the time.

Bill rolled in, smelling of sweat and general stress.

"Will you guys shut up!" he said to Gene and Ken in the most forceful manner I had ever heard from Bill. Gene was obviously shocked. I wanted to comfort her by telling her that Bill was kind of a difficult person when under stress and had been like that for all the time I'd dealt with him, but that would only make matters worse as he constituted our big investment of our heads and our money. Moreover, just suggesting that the leader of the project was under stress would indicate a loss of control, only adding to the concern of the already concerned patients.

"He was looking right at me when he said that!" she whispered to me in disbelief. Steve continued to fiddle uncertainly with the mapping program, and the rest of us just sat and sat. "Even my first day here was better than it is turning out for the others," I thought sadly for the others. I was fine with the matter for now as I knew what this was all about, the development, the frustration, and most of all the taste of the eventual success. As I sat there, listening to the struggles of Steve, I knew he wouldn't be able to solve the problem of my system shutting off by himself.

The next few days followed an identical pattern of events in the Commack office of the Dobelle Institute. It was, in fact, worse for me as my equipment now was being used for stimulating the other patients. Steve had no luck in getting the second one to work so the engineers of the Avery Labs division were looking it over, trying to find the problem in the small amount of time that remained before we were to go to Manhattan. I was now out of the picture for experimentation as Steve struggled to spend at least a bit of time with each of the other patients. His luck was limited by the awkwardness of the language differences with the foreign patients. Marina, the woman from Italy, had no luck communicating, as even her guide did not know English. She had been only hooked up briefly and then abandoned, led back to her chair where she had been sitting for a few days now, as Steve could not tell when she actually saw the phosphene.

A similar problem arose when Edmundo was attempted to be mapped. His guide had interpreted incorrectly Steve's request of telling which phosphenes were too big, thus when the mapping was attempted, Edmundo could not locate the phosphene on the corkboard, as some of them filled half of his visual field with light. He would have to be thresholded again.

Keith, an American citizen, was mapped successfully. He was briefly given the camera to use, but knowing from my previous experience, the first time with the camera is not very encouraging. It had taken me a few days of using the camera a couple hours a day before I could begin to appreciate fully the crude vision this device offered. Keith did not have a chance, however, to do the same, as a half hour later, he was asked to give up the equipment so another patient could be tested. It must have been very discouraging for him as this was supposed to have been his "big moment" when the switch would be turned on and the world would appear before him.

Jerry D. still posed a problem in mapping. For a so far unknown reason, his pattern of phosphenes on his visual field threw a wrench into the relative mapping software, causing it to lock up on a certain display pattern.

"Upper left," Jerry would say to Steve for the tenth time in a row. When I later brought up the problem of Jerry's mapping to Dr. Dobelle, he shrugged it off and said, "I think he just lacks the common sense to figure out what he's supposed to do." It looked like this was the best that was offered by the patient support and rehabilitation department presently in full force at the Dobelle Institute.

That evening Bill must have sensed the dissatisfaction of the patients as he suggested we all get taken out to Chinese food. "You can wear the system to go out," he said to me. He wanted me to give some hope to the other patients, I supposed. I hoped the restaurant was air-conditioned as I'd have to wear my coat again. Steve set it up and got it going for me. I checked my watch to see how long it would work this time.

It felt good to see again, even though I had to get used to the flashing frames all over again, given I hadn't had the system for three days to use. While the rest of the blind patients fumbled around for their chairs around the table in the restaurant, I could see the one that was empty as the table and chairs contrasted in color with the carpeting. I looked around and could see at least three of the other tables surrounding us. When the waiter came and took the orders, I could see a moving group of phosphenes coming toward me and actually could "look" at him before he spoke. Usually, as a blind person, it was necessary the other person make the first sound so he can be located by sound. I could also see when he left; knowing he wasn't there any longer helped as I didn't keep talking to an empty space like I would at times when totally in the dark.

It took a while for the orders to be prepared. I spoke some to Keith's wife, who was interested in what I could see. I pointed out the light fixtures, describing as best as I could the picture it made. But it didn't take long for the system to quit. I checked my watch as I was plunged back into darkness. Seventy-eight minutes was all I got.

June 10 was our last day in Commack before being carted to the Hilton in Manhattan. Only three days remained before the ASAIO conference, the annual meeting of the American Society of Artificial Internal Organs in which Dr. Dobelle had planned to demonstrate his accomplishments in the quest for artificial vision through cortical stimulation. Steve's struggles did not pay off as everything seemed to fail. Ken, the patient from England, was just taking his place in the chair beside Steve, being subject to the stimulation process, when suddenly he gasped and grabbed at his head.

"Ow! Something's going wrong here! I felt a really sharp zap in my head!"

Steve had noted the sudden spike in the current draw on the oscilloscope and halted what he was doing. He had only entered a very low value of 3 V, yet it seemed to give out 16.

"That's odd," he said, looking over the software. "Do you already have his other side thresholded?" was Bill's question.

"Yes, I do," Steve said.

"Well, we're pressed for time here." Bill really was in a bind, that was for sure. "Just try running the camera with the side you have done already."

I was already concerned at the turn of events as the system that was failing was that which I had been using all this time. Now Bill, seemingly having forgotten all about my seizure three weeks ago, decided to use a system on Ken that just gave a warning that something was wrong—something that could cause brain damage if let continue. Steve did as he was told and connected the camera to Ken. I had been chatting quietly with his wife Gene up to this point, but now that the "big moment" was about to materialize for Ken, she sat bolt upright, observing the unfolding of events with unwavering interest.

"Here's a multiplier of 0.7," Steve announced, not waiting for Bill to tell him what the multiplier was going to be. I suspected Steve had done this deliberately lest Bill tell him just to start with the 1.0 multiplier.

Ken looked around uncertainly, still not trusting the stimulator. He had moved the box within his reach and sat poised with one finger on the "off" button.

"Is it running?" he asked. It was obvious it wasn't working. Steve increased the multiplier first to 0.8, then 0.9, then to 1.0. Ken kept moving his head around and finally announced.

"I only see about two dots."

He had over fifty good ones on the side now activated by the camera, but all he saw was a couple. Bill was losing his patience once again. Ken did not do much talking, seemingly lacking the words to fully describe the problem. I guessed he simply had expected it to work without having to have an in-depth knowledge of all its possible problems.

"Just disconnect him and get it connected to Keith." That was Bill's solution. "Keith saw a lot of phosphenes yesterday, so we may as well try it with him instead."

Steve obediently disconnected the cables from Ken's head. Gene led him back to a chair beside her as Steve reconnected Keith. Ken sighed but said nothing, neither did Gene. His big moment was a difficult one to bear as well. No one spoke as Keith was connected. Bill must have hoped Keith would prove his theory—that Ken was the problem rather than it being the equipment. The possibility was there that Keith could be zapped by the 16 V maximum inadvertently, considering the stimulator had just malfunctioned with Ken. But somehow this had to work out—I imagined Bill just hoped everything would work out and the stimulator would cooperate long enough to show off to ASAIO.

Steve entered the new values of Keith's stimulation parameters for a few minutes while we waited. Then he pushed the last button on the laptop. "Up and running," he announced.

Keith looked around for only a few seconds before saying, "About two or three phosphenes is all I see."

"Let me put the diode box on it," said Steve as he disconnected the cables from the stimulator and connected the block of red diodes that simulated the visual field of a blind person. He waved the camera around at the lights while he looked closely at the diodes. Only two lit up.

"Something's wrong with this stimulator," Steve said. It was late in the afternoon, and everyone was tired. Bill decided to try to cheer up the situation with a bit of damage control.

"Let's all go out for steak dinner," he said as if nothing at all was going wrong, as if the real, underlying reason for all the patients' voyage over to Commack was just to eat steak dinner with Dr. William H. Dobelle. It worked, as everyone politely obliged to his suggestion, even though they must have been seething inside.

The next day, Bill had a limo company bring us all over to Manhattan with a small bus. Pat helped us get our suitcases on board while I chatted with the secretary, a young Portuguese woman called Sheila. She had flown from Lisbon to New York at Bill's request just to take part in the ASAIO meeting.

"I have no idea why I am here, or what I am supposed to do," she attested. The she added, to my dismay, "I heard you are going to show the world how this vision system works. Maybe even drive a car for them!"

"Right now, Sheila," I began to inform her, "we have seven patients, eight when Klaus arrives from Germany tomorrow, who came here to get their vision systems and also to show the ASAIO guys what it can do, but suddenly not a single system works. Moreover, it doesn't work nearly as well as originally promised by Bill—at least not right away—I can't tell what it can do in a few more months."

"You have got to be kidding," she said after a brief moment of silence.

Two hours later, we were unloaded in front of the Hilton, right in the middle of Manhattan. The noise of the city was the first thing I noticed after stepping away from the idling bus. It was like a constant roar that echoed off the high walls of the buildings lining each street. Once entering the lobby of the Hilton, however, the noise disappeared behind me as the door closed. The lobby consisted of a huge room that seemed mainly empty except for the reception desk at one side. We all trudged behind the squeaky wheelchair of Bill Dobelle, none of us in the mood for arriving at the desk before him in case we'd be expected to pay the bill. Just the sound of the marble flooring under my feet as our footsteps echoed throughout the high-ceilinged room made this place seem very expensive.

Kyle and I stood a little away from the confusion at the front desk as Bill rifled for the fifth time through his stack of credit cards. Then I heard him turn to each one of the patients.

"Keith, do you have a credit card? They won't take mine for your room, but don't worry," he said consolingly, "I'll reimburse you as soon as possible."

This question was posed to each one of us in turn. Some of the patients obliged and pulled out their own credit card. My heart skipped a beat as I absorbed the situation. Kyle had edged up to see one of the invoices made out to one of the patients and returned quickly and whispered, "It's $255 per night plus tax!" That meant $40,000 in Canadian funds just to play Bill's game and not even come home with the vision system at the end of it. We'd be better off just to take the next Greyhound home, I thought. I had lost enough already.

"What about you, Jens. Do you have a credit card?" I was the last in line to be asked. Yes, I did have a card, but that was none of his business. Had I said that, however, it wouldn't have gone over too well as our relationship was already frail.

"My card is all Lorri has been using back home to pay the bills as I'm not working at the moment, so no, I don't have a card I can use." My mother always had said I shouldn't lie, but this time it was acceptable. It was, after all, possible that the card would have to feed us if I didn't stumble across an opportunity to make more money than that offered by the sale of firewood. I had gambled on this vision system allowing me to find better employment as a result of the eyesight gained, but that was out of the question now. Either they figure something out at the front desk, I thought, or we're going home.

Fortunately, they did figure something out and finally accepted Bill's card. Kyle and I were assigned to room 1437, a room on the fourteenth floor at the end of a corridor that seemed as long as a football field. When we entered the room, there was already a message on the telephone for us to meet Bill after lunch in the conference room on one of the lower floors.

Kyle and I found a restaurant on the bottom floor of the hotel. I felt pretty cheap when I asked Kyle to look at the menu for the cheapest meal, which consisted of a bowl of spaghetti with some sort of sauce straight from the can. Even this cost us over $50.00 US or $80.00 Canadian considering the exchange rate between the two currencies at that time. It took a while before Kyle and I found the right room for the meeting as only certain elevators in the building covered certain floors. We entered just when everyone else had arrived, everyone else except for Steve. I hoped he didn't quit as well. In this business, I thought, one can never predict what will happen to whom.

"Well, we've got this room until Friday, which will see us through more testing and also some news conferences with some big-shot agencies around here." Bill was full of good news. "Jens, you're going to do the brunt of the demonstrations for these agencies, and Steve will keep testing the rest of you. Today, however, he telephoned in sick, so we're going to start tomorrow at 9:00 a.m."

One of the patients spoke for all of us by asking, "So what are we going to do today?"

"Nothing." Bill didn't like that question. "Tonight at six, I'll take you all out for supper here in the hotel on the bottom floor. In the meantime, enjoy New York." He whispered something to one of the secretaries who proceeded to push him out the door of the conference room. I turned to Kyle, breaking the silence that had set into the room.

"How does one enjoy New York without spending a bunch of money we don't have?"

"You mean, money we don't have anymore!"

We all started to disband, going in our own directions with nothing much to say at all. There was a thick atmosphere of deception in the room as we left.

That night we made our way back to the hotel restaurant. We were both glad it was Bill who was paying this time. It was really us who were paying, I thought as I entered the room, except with the money we had given to Bill. I took my seat beside Ken, the Englishman. Jerry T, the first volunteer who was first implanted in 1978, was sitting across from us.

It did not take long for Ken to speak his mind. "You know, Jerry, this is turning out to be a real disaster. I've been here for almost a week and no one yet is able to see. And from what I did get to see, those few dots, is never going to help me get independent again as Dr. Dobelle had promised. I'm thinking of asking for my money back."

Jerry listened, then replied without mincing his words, "Look, I've dealt with Bill for twenty-five years now, and this kind of bullshitting around is just his way of doing things. He is disorganized and works in a spontaneous fashion, and quite often overestimates his success. And as far as getting the money back . . . it's spent. It's all gone. There is nothing to take back now. The best you can do is cooperate just for the sake of being able to give something to humanity for the future." He repeated bluntly, "The money is all gone."

There was no further discussion on that topic. Ken and Gene ate in silence. I was even more glad I hadn't given out my credit card for this room; perhaps I'd never see the money again.

The next few days in Manhattan were just as unproductive as was the week in Commack before that. Steve did manage to get one of the systems working again, although I once had it on just to demonstrate to a news agency its merits when suddenly I got some powerful jolts in my brain. The back of my head tingled, and I quickly covered up my camera. It had been set on "reversal of image" to "off," meaning that covering the lens actually did stop the stimulation.

"Steve," I said as I tried to recover from the pain, "this thing is putting out far too much. Try it with a voltmeter." Steve connected a voltmeter on the output and confirmed its malfunction.

"It's pumping out 16 V even when I just ask for half a volt!" he said unbelievingly. He shook the stimulator, tapping it on the table when it just as quickly resumed normal function. It was just in time, too, as just then another news agency came in for another interview and demonstration. This time they photographed me seeing if the cane held against the wall was horizontal, vertical, or diagonal. Steve did not have the time to reset my thresholds, and I prayed I would be able to put on a good show.

"Can you and your son walk out of the room now so we can photograph you leaving?" was one request. I started to leave the room, led by Kyle, when I decided to play a joke just to add to the humor of the otherwise dull day. "Kyle," I whispered in his ear as we walked, "take this cane and pretend you are the one who can't see and that I'm leading you."

Kyle took the cane, but what I didn't count on was that he'd close his eyes. I had not expected him to do that, and before we knew it, we were tangled up in a plant on the side of the room. I hoped the camera crew didn't film that.

I reentered the room and found Dr. John Girvin had arrived. He must have arrived just to give professional merit to the whole scheme as the question would surely arise during the numerous interviews as to Bill's medical background. I looked over where he sat and saw him with about two of my phosphenes.

"John, you're represented by two phosphenes back there!"

"Jens, I thought I was worth more than that!" he said jokingly. All the patients seemed somewhat relieved to have John back in the picture, but I doubted this would really last. He did not play any role in the decisions surrounding the stimulation or the design of the equipment. He inspected every one of the patient's implants, but that was all.

I lost the equipment as soon as the interview with the media was over so that Ken could be stimulated again. Bill preferred working with Ken, Keith, and myself. He was not taking Jerry D. very seriously as he thought Jerry was difficult to map, and he seemed to avoid the foreign patients as they wouldn't be able to talk to the media in English about the merits of the system. Most of the patients just sat around in the room and did nothing.

Steve hooked up Ken, and immediately Ken slid the stimulator box toward him and felt for the switch. "I want to make sure I can kill this thing if it zaps me again," he said. Steve entered the values for Ken's stimulation parameters and started. A few electrodes were tested when Ken said, "Ow. That one smarts." Steve hit a button when all of a sudden I heard Ken crash to the floor just as Gene, his wife, screamed and ran up to the table where her husband lay. Steve had pulled himself across the large table and turned the switch of the stimulator off, but it was too late. I could hear Ken groaning as he lay on the floor, making sounds I had never heard before. I was not sure if John Girvin was there at the time, but I was aware that there was no media representative—this one would be easy to cover up, no doubt. The cables were disconnected as Gene helped her sixty-nine-year-old husband to his unsteady feet. He sat in a chair, saying nothing as his wife was overcome with concern. Bill vaulted up in his chair.

"What the hell did you do, Steve?" he said accusingly as the young man trembled from the experience. He stammered and replied, "I had him at 8 V and he was hurting, so to stop it, I hit a button to cut the voltage in half, but in my haste I hit the one that doubled it instead."

It was Bill's incessant "scientific method" that did it, I thought. If the program had been designed to increase the voltage by a half a volt at a time, this never would happen. But there was no sense telling Bill; he just wouldn't change it, at least not for now.

Bill turned to Gene and Ken and said as I listened with disbelieving ears, "I hope you can forgive Steve for his mistake. He's really got to be more careful with what he's doing. But don't worry, he'll be all right." Then he said directly to Gene, "Just take him up to his room and let him rest for a while. I'll see you for dinner tonight."

Out of sight, out of mind, and definitely out of the range of the camera of the media. Ken was brought to his room just like I had been after my seizure in May, but he didn't have the full seizure, nor was he going to be alone with his troubles as Gene was there with him. "He'll be all right," I thought.

"Next," said Bill to Steve as the next patient in line for stimulation took his place where Ken had just sat a minute ago. "And Steve, be careful!" he added. As Bill left, I went over to Steve.

"Steve, I think you should just enter the values manually in the future. In fact, use the 'thresh-adjust' program that allows you to change the value by

10 percent at a time whenever possible. Remember, you're the one who has to live with the thought that you hurt someone, not Bill." I spoke quietly and expected no answer from Steve. I knew he listened, however, as the pattern of keystrokes were different the next time he stimulated a patient.

That night there was a message on my telephone in my hotel room. It was Klaus, who had luckily been given my hotel room number by the hotel staff. He was here with his son Robert, neither of whom spoke a lot of English. I telephoned him and immediately went to visit him in his room. He was not a happy camper by any means.

"I can't believe it," he said angrily. "I go through all this trouble, putting my business transactions on hold just to accommodate Bill's schedule, but when I arrive here, there is no representative at all for the company. If it wasn't for you, Jens, I wouldn't even know where to go to find him, and I'd never get my vision system."

I had no idea how to convey to him the reality of the state of the vision system. I'd have to wait on that one, I thought. We chatted some about Germany over a few drinks of rum, all the while Klaus still being perturbed by what he referred to as the unprofessional conduct of Bill Dobelle's Manhattan project.

The following day, Klaus said nothing to Bill about yesterday's outrage. He cooperated fully as I translated for Steve and Bill what Klaus was saying. Klaus's situation was different from the other patients; he had been born blind in one eye and then lost the sight of the other in his late forties. This fact was evident when he was mapped: The side of his visual cortex that corresponded with the visual field he had for more than forty years reacted normal as the phosphenes extended from center vision up to ten inches to the once-functioning side. However, the other side produced phosphenes that mapped only two inches or so in the other direction of center vision, with many of them present in the visual field represented by the other electrode array. None of the other patients had a similar scenario whereby one electrode array overlapped the phosphenes of the other. Klaus was very efficient with his mapping and thresholding, and Steve could connect him to the camera within a few hours.

Bill wasted no time and started out at seven frames per second right away. There wasn't much time to waste at this point. Klaus sat very still, holding his hand in front of the camera, the background being a carpet of contrasting color. He moved his hand back and forth a few times and stared at it.

"Hey, I can see my hand," he stated. "The dots change places with each other as I move my hand, making it look like it's moving." He looked around the room, spotting the window. He did not complain of the flashing of the frames, indicating that perhaps he achieved the "phosphene fusion" that Jerry, the volunteer, had. Bill was very pleased that at least one other patient succeeded in seeing some with his invention. A few minutes later, Klaus was disconnected and plunged again into the darkness as the day was over.

The day before the greatly anticipated ASAIO meeting, Bill had a wild idea to try something with me.

"Steve, so far Jens has all his phosphenes stimulated by five pulses. See if he can see them at one pulse like Jerry can." The idea was interesting if it was done right, no doubt. Presently, five pulses with a duration of one millisecond each (0.5 ms negative, 0.5 ms positive) was used to make a dot of light. Up to nineteen electrodes were used to make a single frame. In order to allow all nineteen electrodes to appear simultaneously stimulated, all nineteen electrodes received the first 1-ms pulse before the second 1-ms pulse was administered again in the same fashion. Thus, up to twenty phosphenes in theory could be stimulated in a matter of one-tenth of a second (100 ms) to make a frame. Only nineteen were possible due to slight delays in the computer/stimulator arrangement. This use of one-tenth of a sec per frame allowed in theory ten frames per second, but due to hardware and software constraints, principally the manner in which the camera provided the image information through a serial port, only seven frames per second was possible. However, if I could see less than five pulses to make a phosphene, that allowed the possibility of either adding more than nineteen electrodes per frame, or better yet, speeding up the frames per second.

"Now," said Steve as he gave me one pulse at the threshold already set for fifty pulses. I saw a flash that occupied the entire visual field.

"No, it's just a flash, not a point."

"Now," said Steve again, having increased the pulses to two. I still only saw a flash, but occupying about one half the visual field this time. "No, still just a flash, but smaller this time."

"Try three," said Bill. Steve reset the parameters on the laptop and said, "Now."

"Almost," I said. The point was not as small as with five pulses, but almost good enough to make an image. "I bet with four pulses, it will be adequate," I added.

"Look, let's just give it up." Bill lost interest suddenly.

I protested, "But if it works with four instead of five, we'd be able to increase the frame rate by 20 percent, maybe even accomplishing the "phosphene fusion" you had been talking about last week." I thought that made sense, but Bill just gave up.

"Look, skip it. It really doesn't matter." That was all he had to offer to improve the project's future. I felt frustrated but hoped the opportunity would arise again to resolve this—a quicker frame speed would make for a better picture, no doubt.

On the morning of the thirteenth, everyone was keyed up for the ASAIO meet. I had already engaged in various interviews from many leading news agencies, including one where I was to go to a building close to the Hilton and be interviewed live. That morning, not one of the systems worked. One system had a faulty computer, the other a faulty stimulator. Steve was already overworked, out of ideas as to what to do. Claire Dobelle, Bill's wife, was there as well, pushing Bill around in his chair and saying, under her breath, "After this you are going to go to rehabilitation and learn to walk for yourself . . ." She was an energetic woman who seemed rather concerned at the problem facing us. She turned to me and said, "I could have killed Bill when he said he fired Jim! Now what are we going to do?"

I thought it over and suggested, "We should just switch the working computer and hook it to the working stimulator. We really don't have time for anything else."

"That might work," said Steve.

Bill groaned. "Look, just give it up. There is nothing we can do now. This will never work."

I was shocked at the sudden outburst of despair from Bill, who had been the strong pillar of solutions, even those tactics used just to calm the patients—all these days I've been with him through similar tense moments. I didn't like this at all; I preferred the Bill who pretended to have everything under control even in the face of a major crisis. Pessimism about the success of the project was definitely not what I needed to hear this close to an important presentation.

Claire said sternly, "Bill, just let them do it. If you let them make some decisions, it just might work. After all, you are out of ideas for a better solution."

In no time, it worked again. I looked at my braille watch. "Steve, we have to go as there's only a three-quarter hour to go."

"But I don't have the parameters set in your computer yet!" He was just assembling the components into the belt.

"Just bring it along and maybe we can do it in the taxi," I suggested. Louise grabbed Bill's chair and pushed quickly along as Steve and I followed.

The taxi was waiting for us outside the hotel, and we all helped Bill in the front seat beside the driver. Steve, Louise, and I sat in the rear. I pulled the computer box partially out of my belt as Steve attempted to hook up the cable leading to his computer. He tried for a minute, then looked at the cable end.

"Oh no," he said despairingly. "A pin is bent. You wouldn't have anything pointed for me to straighten it out?"

Louise rummaged in her purse and pulled out a comb. "This is all I've got."

Steve grabbed it and managed to straighten out the pin. Quickly, he connected the system to his laptop and began to enter the parameters for my vision system. He was still typing when we arrived at the studio. Louise got out the right rear door of the cab, passed the driver the money owing, and wrestled Bill into his chair while Steve and I made our escape out the left rear door, still connected together with a wire. I used my cane expertly as I followed the squeaking wheels of Bill's chair as Louise pushed him at breakneck speed toward the studio entrance.

Steve and I were still connected when we entered the elevator. Steve had the laptop cradled in his left arm while he typed with the right, most of his view blocked by the laptop's screen. We both prayed it would get going without a hitch in the next few minutes.

We were in the filming/interviewing room when the system started to work. "Amazing!" I informed Steve, who was still not sure if this would actually work. "I can see pretty good, believe it or not." I looked around and saw the table in front of me, along with the crack to my left that indicated another table was pushed against the one I was sitting at. A few dots represented each spotlight. The room was well lit, with not only spotlights shining at my face, but the person interviewing me would have lights from behind me shining on his face as well. It was going to be the perfect lighting condition for this thing to work.

"We'll start in two minutes . . ." the voice said in my small earpiece, which was to let the recording staff give me advice without it being recorded on the film. I turned to Steve, who was sitting on the side in the studio.

"Steve, I think I'm going to have a seizure in a few minutes, right in the middle of the interview," I joked.

Steve was not amused. "My god, if you do that, I'll come over and hit you!" But just as Steve started talking, the voice in my earpiece informed me that recording had begun. I hoped the words of Steve wouldn't be broadcast.

The interview went better than anticipated. The interviewer's questions were the usual ones associated with how I lost my sight, what I could see now, and how I felt about wearing the system. No questions were asked about the way the company was run, allowing me to stay relatively free of possible controversy. No questions were asked about the other patients either. Within an hour, we were out of the studio and, while waiting for the taxi to retrieve us, my system suddenly quit. The outline of the sidewalks, the moving dots signifying the pedestrians, the outlines of the buildings just suddenly disappeared into blackness—back to the dingy drabness of darkness—for now anyways.

That afternoon, Kyle and I found ourselves taking our seats in the large conference room of the Hilton along with hundreds of other scientists, doctors, and researchers from all across the world. There were a few speeches and presentations by various teams working on artificial limbs and hearing. Then came Bill's turn.

He was wheeled to the front of the room where he spoke softly in the microphone. He spoke in simple vocabulary, concentrating upon the success of the eight implanted patients.

"Our medical team implanted eight patients of various backgrounds in April, and now they all can see good phosphenes. We have a video clip of one of our patients demonstrating the driving of a car."

There was a hush as the clip was displayed on a large screen in front of the room. I heard a person close to me whisper to his companion, "He has to feel for the handle . . ." indicating the film was just starting as I approached the car. I remember all I could see was the blob of phosphenes representing the car, and as I approached, it was the line of the top of the door that I could see. I would have had to feel for the handle.

The film continued as I drove the car in the neighboring parking lot of the Dobelle Institute. There was no sign of the cameraman's assistant calling me at the end of the lot so as to direct me. Bill really should have stuck to the film clip of me driving between the building and the curb behind the Dobelle Institute, as that one was really done with the use of the system at its best, as it showed how I could avoid hitting some obvious obstacles like the building and the divider. It was also unfortunate that Bill was somewhat unprepared to communicate to the crowd of scientists the exact manner in which this system worked. I could easily have prepared illustrations comparing normal vision to that of what I saw when looking at simple objects for all to see on the overhead projector, but Bill just seemed to worry about giving away too many secrets about the project—perhaps it was for the better—I wasn't sure. We sat through the rest of the presentations, listening with interest at the new developments, yet more informed as to their claims versus reality. After all, just thinking of how the blind population would view that Dobelle Institute's vision program compared to its function in its first few days was a sobering thought. The adjustment period would have to be emphasized more, I thought, in order to avoid the initial disappointment when the system is turned on for the first time.

The rest of ASAIO went well but without very notable projects I found interesting. The vision project was perhaps the most exciting—for sure for me, who already had a few moments of seeing it shine. I wished those moments would become the norm in my life soon.

Finally, my stay in New York was coming to a close. A limousine service came to pick me and Kyle up the next morning, and we were heading back to Canada, empty-handed, with the exception of the images in my mind—all that I had seen while in Commack and Manhattan.

Bill had given us no indication as to when he'd be done with the systems. I had the better end of the deal when comparing myself to the other patients—I had at least the chance to see with the system, even though only part-time. With the exception of Klaus who had a couple moments looking at his hand, nobody else accomplished anything in the days they spent in Commack and Manhattan; they returned to their homes in what I believed was disappointment at its worst. Yet they had to believe, somehow, that this would eventually work for them, as it was working for me at times, and that was more than what any of us had before we even heard of Bill Dobelle.

CHAPTER 11

Waiting for the Equipment

I returned home with no idea when the system would be ready for delivery. It was obvious that Steve would have to learn the entire software package, the thousands of lines of code written by Jim in order to even begin to figure out what was wrong. The best I could do was concentrate on my work, as there were a lot of bills to pay. When walking in town, I was bombarded by the usual questions regarding my vision system, with a few people having seen me on the CNN broadcast, driving a car. I did not downplay the event too much as this was what the donors really wanted to say. It was difficult, however, to answer the question as to when my system would be ready for me. It was practically impossible for anyone to believe that the Dobelle Institute was such a small company, now down to one engineer, with limited ideas of how to really run a research project as complex as this one.

Janyce McGregor from CBC TV was especially up-to-date with my appearances on television and wasted no words as I answered to her telephone call.

"I see other news agencies got a head start on us," she said, not sounding happy at all about it. What did she expect, I asked myself. I was not being paid by CBC to give them exclusive coverage, and Bill Dobelle certainly wouldn't accept my reason for refusing to cooperate with his newscasts on the grounds that CBC had it first.

"I really didn't have any choice," I stated, looking for a polite way out. "I really wasn't in the position to refuse to cooperate with Dr. Dobelle. All I did was try out the car using the new vision, never even knowing this clip would appear on CNN."

"When will you have the system so you can demonstrate here how it works?" she asked.

Here again I had to be careful. I really began to detest this question, which I was sure all the other patients had come to hate as well. Once again I would have to downplay the internal challenges within the Dobelle Institute for the benefit of the project. Janyce sounded like she could inadvertently reveal the project in a negative tone, but then again, I wasn't sure. "There are just a few minor problems to straighten out," I said, giving an excuse. "I'm sure it won't be long. Considering the merits of these efforts, I figure it best to be patient." What a great answer, I thought. I should be hired on as media representative to the company. Luckily, Janyce was happy with my answer.

It did not take long to dig up the CNN article composed during the ASAIO meeting in Manhattan.

Could Bionic Eye End Blindness?

June 13, 2002

By Dr. Sanjay Gupta and Kristi Petersen (CNN)—Artificial vision for the blind was once the stuff of science fiction—Lt. Geordi La Forge's visor on *Star Trek* or the bionic eye of "The Six Million Dollar Man."

But now, a limited form of artificial vision is a reality—one some say is one of the greatest triumphs in medical history. "We are now at a watershed," Joseph Lazzaro, author of *Adaptive Technologies for Learning and Work Environments*, told CNN. "We are at the beginning of the end of blindness with this type of technology."

Any scientific advance would have broad implications. According to statistics from Research to Prevent Blindness, Inc., 1.1 million people in the United States are legally blind, while worldwide 42 million people are without sight.

The Dobelle Institute is among several institutions trying in essence to create a new cornea through technology. The cornea allows light into the interior of the eye.

Dobelle is using a digital video camera mounted on glasses to capture an image and send it to a small computer on the patient's belt: the images are processed and sent to electrodes implanted in the patient's visual cortex. The electrodes stimulate the brain, producing a pattern of bright spots that form an image.

"With this device, you don't lose anything. You actually have a fifth sense restored, and that is what I just absolutely adore with this device," said one of the first eight implant patients to test the technology, a man who asked to be identified only as Jens.

"You are no longer blind. You might be blind to some objects, some situations, but you are not totally blind."

A Canadian farmer and father of eight, Jens lost his sight eighteen years ago in an accident. Now he's able to navigate through rooms, find doors, and even drive a car to some degree. "I was able to very carefully drive and look from my left side to my right side, making sure I was between this row of trees on the right and the building on my left," he says. "When I got near any obstruction, I would see that there was an obstruction. I would also see the lack of obstructions, knowing I wasn't going to run over anybody . . . It was a very nice feeling."

The black-and-white image Jens sees is not solid, but it resembles a dot matrix pattern. It's like looking at a sport scoreboard with different light patterns illuminated to show different scores.

The miniaturization of equipment and more powerful computers have made this artificial vision possible, but it's not cheap: the operation, equipment, and necessary training cost $70,000 per patient.

All eight of the experimental surgeries were performed in Portugal: FDA regulations still prohibit the procedure in the United States.

But Dr. Bill Dobelle, of the Dobelle Institute, says the technology has broad potential.

"It may not work for people blinded as children or as infants, because the visual cortex did not develop normally," he says. "But I would say (it will work) for the vast majority of the blind—98 to 99 percent."

Other researchers are focusing on new technology to replace damaged retinas, the part of the eye that converts light into electrical impulses that are sent to the brain to be turned into images.

Optobionics Corporation of Wheaton, Illinois, says six blind or nearly blind people can now see light and some can see shapes after having the company's artificial retina implanted. Optobionics hopes to have the artificial retina on the market in five years, but critics say it will take years of independent testing to prove it helps the blind.

NASA hopes to begin human testing this year on ceramic detectors that could be implanted in the retina to take over the job of damaged retinal cells. And the Office of Naval Research goes one step further—it says it is on the way to developing a chip that would replicate the entire nerve center of the retina. With all the new research developments coming into view, Jens says he's glad he's been able to catch a glimpse of the future of blindness.

"I could see that there was real potential for some really good life coming ahead of me," he says. "It was like, I would say, throwing back the curtains in the morning when you get up and letting in sunshine. I would equate it to that feeling."

There was no doubt that the entire project had gone over well with the press. CNN had set the stage for the other press releases, which proved to be of the same positive atmosphere. I had to chuckle at the quote wherein I said, "With this device, you don't lose anything . . ." as this made no reference to the discomfort of the jacks in my head, the pain of the operation, or the possibility of seizures. But then again, I reminded myself, I had been able to see 2/120 in acuity when I approached the Toronto St. Michael's Hospital only to lose the rest of my sight. So far, none of us really lost anything but the money, not counting our patience with Bill's tardy schedule. And speaking of which, it took only a few days to receive his usual "about to be delayed" date set for further progress on the development of the system.

Dobelle Institute (Portugal) Lda.
Artificial Vision for the Blind
June 24, 2002
To: Mr. Jens Naumann
Napanee, Ontario K7R 3L1

Fr:
Wm. H. Dobelle PhD, Chairman & Chief Executive Officer

Re: Update

Thank you for your patience under pressure during your visit to New York. Testing had gone fairly smoothly with Jens and Dennis, and we did not properly anticipate the problems we encountered with you. While we managed to get some very important information during our testing sessions with you, more work is clearly needed.

Don Kiefer has been working on the myriad small "teething" problems that cumulatively posed an almost insuperable barrier during your visit. During the past week, five of the eight systems have been modified. However, there is an underlying electronic "noise" problem in all units that needs to be resolved. One of the analog power lines is close to a digital lead, and, at higher amplitudes, may cause the system to inadvertently switch. Also, I want to "burn" in and test all systems thoroughly before releasing them to you.

All of these problems should be resolved shortly, and I will be in touch with you again about July 15 to arrange to stimulate you. We will give you the equipment when we visit.

If you have any questions in the meantime, I can always be reached here at the office or at my home.

Thanks.

"That'll be next month," Lorri said, reading the letter with interest. We all wanted the equipment for the summer holidays so we could go places. I had my doubts that this would really happen.

"Do you really think Dr. Dobelle knows what an analogue and digital line really is?" Kyle asked. He had seen with his own eyes that Bill Dobelle had stayed away from any electronic equipment as if they were scalding hot potatoes.

"No. Probably not. I bet that one of the breathing pacemaker engineers had said something to that effect, and that had been typed up by Louise. He wouldn't be worrying about these things himself." It was time to stop kidding ourselves, I thought. Bill Dobelle and electronics just did not mingle, but there were enough people to hire for that—it was his ability to pull this whole thing off that was his forte

July 15 came and went without any correspondence from the Dobelle Institute. Then, at the start of August, Dr. Dobelle called.

"Jens, would you like to come down to pose for the picture on the front cover of *Wired* magazine?" Here I had been hoping for the issue of the equipment. Bill continued, "They want you on the front cover of their September issue."

I couldn't imagine sitting in the car for an entire day to go down, another day to pose and the next to return. I really had better things to do. But maybe, just maybe, the equipment was ready for me to take. After all, I thought, what good was it to *Wired* if the thing didn't work?

"I really have lots to work on here at the moment," I started, trying to sway Bill from the idea that I'd be doing anything just to be on camera. I had found out early enough in this venture that being on camera does not pay the bills. "I don't really want to spend all that time just sitting in a car just to pose for a picture. However, if the equipment is ready, I'll certainly come down."

Bill had it all planned out. "Look, I already told them they'd have to charter you down in a private plane so you don't have to stay here overnight. We'll find an aircraft for you in Kingston."

On that morning, I took a taxi to Kingston and boarded a small twin-engine airplane that took my son Brandon and myself down to Commack in less than two hours. Pat picked me up at the airport, and I was in the Commack office before noon. I met the *Wired* crew, which was armed to the hilt with cameras. Immediately, I was taken to the conference room where I must have sat for over an hour while they took their pictures. Brandon looked in awe as they used, in spite of all the technological advances having been made in the past decades, a glass-plate film camera from the 1930s as, according to the cameraman, it produced a picture of an unmatched quality. Then Bill handed me the belt loaded with the vision system. My heart sank as Bill said to the camera crew, "He'll pose with this on, but he won't be able to turn it on. It needs a few weeks yet of work on it."

"No problem," said the crew representative. "So long as he can wear it, it's no problem." We all got in their van and went to a slightly wooded area where another ten rolls of film were shot of me wearing a dead, nonfunctional artificial vision system. As I stood there, I couldn't help but wonder how they would write about the seizure I had in May, in the full presence of their reporter. Surely, he couldn't just pretend it never happened.

We returned to the office, with still an hour to spare, where Dr. Dobelle introduced me to Tony, the new engineer just recently hired to work exclusively on the vision project, not only to repair the existing systems but to design the new ones. Tony, a Portuguese native in his late forties, had an impressive background and understanding of electronics, which was like a breath of fresh air amidst the haze of uncertainty in the vision project. I described all I could about my experience with the existing system as he listened intently and tried to understand the problems that had to be overcome. Steve was still working for Bill, to my surprise, but then informed me he would be leaving soon. "Back to one engineer again," I thought dismally.

"You've got a lot of work ahead of you," I said to Tony. "Jim wasn't done with the software when he was ejected from the project, and now it looks like you've got to review it all."

"It is quite a cumbersome program," Tony commented, looking at the 236 MB of disk space it occupied. "I'm sure it could be simplified."

"Have you ever thought of using EEPROM technology?" I suggested, hoping we'd be able to cut the size of the boxes so it wouldn't look so threatening to the casual observer.

"That's what I've been thinking all along!" Tony was pleased that there was support for his idea. "I have been trying to convince Bill that's a better idea." That would be a challenge, I thought. Trying to convince Bill as to what was required on the electronic front to improve the project would probably be Tony's greatest feat.

We continued to discuss the options for adjustment for the next system.

"In order to prevent unnecessary delays in designing the next equipment, I want to stay with the existing software for the next system but have it smaller and more adjustable for the patient." I liked what Tony was saying. "What do you think should be adjusted?" Tony asked.

I jumped at the opportunity as if I were writing up a wish list for Christmas. "Definitely the threshold multiplier needs to be accessible to the patient," I started to list the possibilities. "If the zoom had two or three settings, we could zero in on smaller objects far away, like the divider between grass and pavement at a greater distance. Also, it would be handy to adjust camera sensitivity to changes in brightness."

Tony made notes as I spoke. I wondered if other research institutes even bothered to ask their clients who would use the systems what they could do to improve them. I hoped Tony would stay with the company for a while.

When I returned home, there was another letter on its way from the Dobelle Institute. I guessed it was just another one to buy some time, and I was right.

> Dobelle Institute (Portugal) Lda.
> Artificial Vision for the Blind
> August 23, 2002
>
> To: Mr. Jens Naumann
> Napanee, Ontario K7R 3L1
>
> Wm. H. Dobelle, PhD, Chairman & Chief Executive Officer
> Re: Scheduling Delivery of Transmitters
>
> Steve Diamond and Tony Martins, our new senior engineers, have been diligently working on the software for the new systems. They have made substantial progress in many areas, but some problems remain. Obviously, because of the effort and expense involved in visiting each of you, I don't want to try this with any known imperfections.
> I will set a new date and contact you.
> Thank you for your patience.

It was nearly September now. The summer holidays had come and gone just like the last twenty had, again with nothing to see. It was difficult to know exactly what was going through the minds of the other patients. I was still the lucky one; having insider information not only through my frequent correspondence with the Dobelle Institute as to the problems and what was involved, but also had a good idea as to the difficulty of the tasks ahead. But for those just waiting, not knowing the depth of the problem, while being in another country on another continent, speaking a different language, the uncertainty must have been depressing.

Summer was nearly over, the kids preparing for another year in school, when the *Wired* magazine came out with its article. A few of my friends bought copies, as did my eldest daughter, who read the article with interest. It was her father on the front cover, after all.

Vision Quest
A Half Century of Artificial-Sight Research Has Succeeded. And Now This Blind Man Can See.
Steven Kotler

I'm Sitting Across from a Blind Man—Call Him Patient Alpha—at a long table in a windowless conference room in New York. On one end of the table, there's an old television and a VCR. On the other end are a couple of laptops. They're connected by wires to a pair of homemade signal processors housed in unadorned gunmetal-gray boxes, each no bigger than a loaf of bread. In the corner stands a plastic ficus tree, and beyond that, against the far wall, is a crowded bookshelf. Otherwise, the walls are white and bare. When the world's first bionic eye is turned on, this is what Patient Alpha will see.

Our guinea pig is thirty-nine, strong and tall, with an angular jaw, bold ears, and a rugged face. He looks hale, hearty, and healthy—except for the wires. They run from the laptops into the signal processors, then out again and across the table and up into the air, flanking his face like curtains before disappearing into holes drilled through his skull. Since his hair is dark and the wires are black, it's hard to see the actual points of entry. From a distance, the wires look like long ponytails. "Come on," says William Dobelle, "take a good look." From a few steps closer, I see that the wires plug into Patient Alpha's head like a pair of headphones plugged into a stereo. The actual connection is metallic and circular, like a common washer. So seamless is the integration that the skin appears to simply stop being skin and start being steel.

"It's called a percutaneous pedestal," Dobelle tells me. All I can do is stare. The man has computer jacks sunk into both sides of his skull.

On the far side of the pedestal, buried beneath hair and skin, is the wetware: a pair of brain implants. Each one is the size of a fat quarter, a platinum electrode array encased in biocompatible plastic.

Dobelle has designed a three-part system: a miniature video camera, a signal processor, and the brain implants. The camera, mounted on a pair of eyeglasses, captures the scene in front of the wearer. The processor translates the image into a series of signals that the brain can understand, then sends the information to the implant. The picture is fed into the brain and, if everything goes according to plan, the brain will "see" the image.

But I'm getting ahead of myself. The camera's not here yet. Right now the laptops are taking its place. Two computer techs are using them to calibrate the implants.

One of the techs punches a button, and a millisecond later, the patient rotates his head, right to left, as if surveying a crowded room.

"What do you see?" asks Dobelle.

"A medium-sized phosphene, about five inches from my face," responds the patient.

"How about now?"

"That one's too bright."

"OK," says Dobelle, "we won't use that one again."

This goes on all morning, and it's nothing new. For almost fifty years, scientists have known that electrical stimulation of the visual cortex causes blind subjects to perceive small points of light known as phosphenes. The tests they're running aim to determine the "map" of the patients' phosphenes. When electrical current zaps into the brain, the lights don't appear only in one spot. They are spread out across space, in what artificial-vision researchers call the "starry-night effect."

Dobelle is marshaling these dots like pixels on a screen. "We're building the patient's map, layer by layer," he explains. "The first layer was individual phosphenes. The next layer is multiples. We need to know where his phosphenes appear in relation to each other so a video feed can be translated in a way that makes sense to his mind."

Some phosphenes look like pinpricks or frozen raindrops. Others appear as odd shapes: floating bananas, fat pears, lightning squiggles. Of course, the use of the word *appear* is misleading, since the phosphenes appear only in the patient's mind. To the sighted, they are completely invisible.

Dobelle sits in a wheelchair beside the patient. His left leg was amputated a year ago after an ulcerated infection in his big toe spread out of control. Because being in a wheelchair makes it hard to dig into his pants pockets, he favors T-shirts—"the good kind"—with a chest pocket to carry his keys, a couple of pens, his wallet. His shirt is so weighed down that it sags from his neck, drooping cleavage-low. He has a patchy, unkempt gray beard. His forehead is high and wrinkled, and his glasses are thick and wide.

"Are we ready for multiple phosphenes?" asks one of the techs. Dobelle nods his head.

So smoothly has the morning been going that while we're talking, the techs allow the patient to take control of the keyboard and begin stimulating his own brain. This isn't standard operating procedure, but with the excitement, the techs don't stop him and the doctor doesn't notice.

Suddenly, the color drains from the patient's face. His hand drops the keys. His fingers crimp and gnarl, turning the hand into a disfigured claw. The claw, as if tethered to balloons, rises slowly upward. His arm follows and suddenly whips backward, torso turning with it, snapping his back into a terrible arch. Then his whole body wrenches like a mishandled marionette—shoulders tilting, neck craning, legs twittering. Within seconds, his lips have turned blue and his deadened eyes roll back, revealing bone-white pupils, lids snapping up and down like hydraulic window shades. There's another warping convulsion, and spittle sails from his mouth. Since the doctor's in a wheelchair and the techs seem hypnotized, I rush over and grab him. "Call 911!" one of the computer techs shouts.

But the doctor yells back, "No!"

"Lie him down," cries the other. "Get him some water!"

"No!"

My arms are under his, trying to steady the weight. His head snaps toward mine, and I take it on the chin with the force of a solid right cross. We're now close enough that I can count the wires going into his head. I can see a faint scar where a surgeon's saw cut a hole in his skull and removed a chunk of it like a plug from a drain. Finally, the techs move to action. They're up and struggling to unhook the patient from the seeing machine—but really, what can they do? It's in his brain. I'm pretty sure he's going to die in my arms.

William Dobelle Likes a Good Wright Brothers' Story.

Like how the first plane the Wright brothers built didn't have a steering mechanism, that it merely went up and down and straight. Or if you look at a plane these days, you won't see their names on the side. Instead, there's Boeing or Airbus, but even so, you know these makers are merely historical recipients of the Wright stuff, just as you know that your voting privileges are somehow owed to Thomas Jefferson.

Of all the Wright brothers stories, Dobelle likes the one about Lt. Tom Selfridge the best.

The Wright brothers ran low on money. They built their airplane, but they needed more cash for further experimentation. A lieutenant from the US Army showed up for a demonstration, and after watching Orville pilot around for a little while, he said, "That's great, now take me for a ride." So Orville strapped Selfridge into the passenger seat, took off, and promptly crashed. Crashed! The plane was wrecked, Orville was in the hospital for months, and Selfridge was killed—yet they still managed to land a contract for a military flier. The doctor treats this story like a talisman. Its moral—with great risk comes great reward—has been an inspiration for him during the past thirty years, since 1968, when he began working on an artificial-vision system to restore sight to the blind. The moral was there in the 1970s, when he went under the hot knife of surgery and had his own eye slit open to test the feasibility of a retinal implant. It was there when he looked over the work that had been done on the visual cortex and realized the only way to create a visual neuroprosthesis was to slice through the skull and attach an implant to the human brain. It was there two years ago, when he decided to skirt the Food and Drug Administration by sending his patients to a surgeon in Lisbon, Portugal, because he knew there was little chance the US government was ever going to give him permission to experiment on humans in America. There was one lab rat, however. In 1978, shortly before the FDA passed the last in a series of medical device amendments that would outlaw testing a visual neuroprosthesis on a human, Dobelle installed his prototype into the head of a genial, big-bellied, blind Irishman from Brooklyn named Jerry.

"When my grandkids meet a blind guy with a brain implant," says Jerry, explaining his participation in Dobelle's experiments, "I want them to be able to say, 'Let me tell you about my grandfather.'"

For years, the prototype sat in Jerry's occipital lobe, largely unused. Back then Dobelle's concerns were infection and biocompatibility. When neither turned out to be a problem, he edged the research forward. Over the years, Jerry's visual field was mapped, but his implant never produced true "functional mobility."

Functional mobility is a bit of jargon defined as the ability to cross streets, take subways, navigate buildings without aid of a cane or a dog. For the past forty years, this has been the goal of artificial-vision research. But Jerry's not there, instead caught halfway between sight and shadow.

When hooked up to a video camera, he sees only shades of gray in a limited field of vision. He also sees at a very slow rate. It helps to think of film. Normal film whirls by at twenty-four frames per second—but Jerry sees at merely a fifth of that speed. The effect, Dobelle tells me, is a bit like looking at snapshots in a photo album through holes punched in a note card.

Patient Alpha, on the other hand, has the full upgrade: the Dobelle Institute Artificial Vision System for the Blind. Because the system has yet to be patented, the doctor is cagey about specifics. He won't say how many electrodes are inside the patient's head, though by my count the number is around hundred. Other changes have been made as well. Instead of Jerry's one implant, the patient has two, one in each side of his head. Materials, as well, have been updated, and the power pack and signal processor has been made portable. But the biggest difference is that it took Dobelle twenty years to work Jerry up to any sort of vision. Patient Alpha got out of surgery a month ago.

William Dobelle was born in 1941 in Pittsfield, Massachusetts, the son of an orthopedic surgeon. Ask Dobelle how he got into this game and he'll say: "I've always done artificial organs. I've spent my whole life in the spare parts business. I just inherited it from my father. By age eight, I was doing real research."

Which sounds like hooey, until you check the records. He applied for his first patent, on an artificial hip improvement, at age thirteen. He was into college at fourteen and hooked on the artificial-vision challenge by eighteen. He dropped out of Vanderbilt to pursue independent research on visual physiology, supporting himself as a Porsche mechanic.

Bulky and expensive, early systems took twenty years to work up to any sort of vision. Patient Alpha got out of surgery a month ago. In 1960, he returned to school, earning an MS in biophysics from Johns Hopkins. This time he covered costs by selling scientific ephemera: iguana gall bladders and whale hearts he collected in South America. He finished his PhD in physiology from the University of Utah and became the director of artificial organs at Columbia-Presbyterian Medical Center. By 1984, he had a lab of his own.

Located in Hauppauge, New York, near the center of Long Island, Dobelle's lab sits inside one of the largest industrial parks in America. All around are the offices of high-tech whatevers—Aerostar, Gemini, Forest Labs, Nextech, Bystronic—housed in grim, squat warehouses accented only by trim lawns and odd awnings. Most of the buildings have them, these decorous afterthoughts: green shingles attached to aluminum siding, Spanish tile against cold stone. "We don't have an awning," notes Dobelle, proud of his austerity.

Walk inside and you'll see a carpet so thin it could be cement. The furniture in the front offices looks anonymous, wood-veneered, bought by the pound. Behind the offices is a larger workshop—the home to the breadwinners of the operation. During his tenure as a spare-parts man, Dobelle built hiccup suppressors and erection stimulators and pain inhibitors. Right now, there are fifteen thousand people running around the world with his inventory inside their bodies. The workshop is currently used to build lung, spinal cord, and deep-brain stimulators. Since he's never wanted to be beholden to anyone and thus never accepted venture capital, these devices pay the rent so Dobelle can pursue his real goal: artificial sight. The first person ever to receive this bill was Patient Alpha. His given name is Jens—pronounced "Yens." Twenty-two years ago, at age seventeen, while nailing down railroad ties, an errant splinter took his left eye. Then, three years later, this time fixing a snowmobile, a shiv of clutch metal broke free and took out his right.

He lives in rural Canada, where the winters are brutal. He makes his living by selling firewood. Working alone, he splits logs with the largest chain saw currently available in the market. During the high season, he manhandles twelve thousand pounds of wood in a day. He helped his wife deliver six of his eight children at home, without a physician or midwife. Jens dismisses the whole hospital birthing process as rapacious big business. Starting from scratch and without the aid of sight, Jens designed and built a solar—and wind-powered house and pulled his family off the grid. In his spare hours, he programs computers, tunes pianos, and gives the occasional concert. For a blind man to give a classical recital requires memorizing whole scores—a process that can take nearly five years. To cover his surgery, Jens gave quite a few recitals.

Back in the Lab, I'm Still Supporting Jens's Weight. He's Panting and Jerking.

Every pore on his body leaks sweat. His neck has gotten too slippery to hold, so I've jammed my right hand into his armpit. I can feel the throb of his axillary artery. His heart is beating. Thankfully, he's still alive. Over the next five minutes, the gasping subsides. Respiration returns to normal. The full-body twitch stills to the occasional flutter. Soon the grim rigor of his hand relaxes, his fingers merely stretching now, as if reaching for the far notes on his piano.

Dobelle's glaring at the techs.

"What happened?" he demands.

"He was overstimulated."

"Yeah, I know that."

Beside him, Jens's head bobs once and then again. Slowly, motor control returns. He stretches his arms as if waking from a long sleep.

"What happened?" echoes Jens, his voice a low, percolating gurgle.

"You had a seizure," says Dobelle.

"I wha . . ."

"A seizure. Jerry never had one, but it was always a possibility."

"I wha . . ."

"You'll be fine," says Dobelle.

"For what I paid . . ."

"What?"

"For what I paid, I better be."

"OK," says Dobelle, "I think we're done for today."

Later That Night, Dobelle Calls to Explain. His Voice Is Balmy, Preternaturally Pacific.

"My surgeon is the world's foremost expert on epilepsy. When someone's having a seizure, you don't lie them down or give them water—they could choke. I knew he would be OK." And the next morning, when I walk into the lab, Jens is OK. He's back at the table, amid another round of testing. He doesn't remember much of the seizure, but he remembers seeing the phosphenes.

"It was wonderful," says Jens. "It is wonderful. After eighteen years in a dark jail, I finally got to look out the door into the sunlight."

"Are you ready for a little more?" asks Dobelle. In his hand is a pair of oversized tortoiseshell glasses. The left lens is dark, and affixed to the right is a miniature video camera: black, plastic, and less than one inch square. The wires that yesterday ran from the laptops are now plugged into the camera. It's time to see if Jens can see.

"Are you ready?" repeats Dobelle.

"I've been ready for twenty years."

Jens slides the glasses onto his face, and the techs power up the system. I am sitting across the table from him. As it turns out, when the world's first bionic eye is turned on, Jens sees me. "Wow!" says Jens.

"Wow what?" I ask.

"I'm really using the part of my brain that's been doing dick-all for two decades."

"And that's only one implant," says Dobelle. "We still have to integrate the other side, and we haven't installed the edge-recognition software yet. The image is going to get better and better." Jens turns away, and we clear all objects off the conference table. Dobelle picks up a telephone and puts it down on the far corner. Jens turns back around. The camera is sending data down the pipe and to the implant in his brain at one frame per second. So when he first scans the table, his head swivels, robotic and turtle-slow. It takes him nearly two minutes to find the phone—but he finds the phone. Then we do it again. Fifteen minutes later, Jens can pick up the receiver in less than thirty seconds. Within a half hour, it takes him less than ten. They gradually work the frame speed up until there's nothing left to do but strap the signal processor and power pack to Jens's hips, like guns in their holsters. Then Jens heads out back, where he climbs inside a convertible Mustang. The top is down. The wind is in his hair. He fires up the ignition. Dobelle doesn't let him tour the freeways, but he has his way with the parking lot.

"The next version," Dobelle tells me, "may have enough resolution to use while driving in traffic."

In fact, since this is only a simple camera we're talking about, one could imagine the addition of any number of superhuman optical features: night vision, X-ray vision, microscopic focus, long-range zoom. Forget the camera even; there's no reason you couldn't jack directly into the Net. In the future, the disabled may prove more abled; we may all want their prostheses.

Public Discussion of Electricity's Effect on Vision dates to 1751, when it was addressed by Benjamin Franklin following his celebrated kite-and-key experiment. Despite some advocates, the idea of treating blindness through electrical stimulation did not catch on.

The human eye occupies a weird place in history. For more than a century, creationists, staring down Darwin's evolutionary barrel, claimed sight as proof positive of God's existence. The eye was too complicated for anything as seemingly accidental as natural selection. By extension, curing blindness was the sole province of faith healers. "It used to be a religious miracle," says Tom Hoglund of the Foundation Fighting Blindness, "but now it's a scientific miracle."

On June 13, Dobelle addressed the annual meeting of the American Society of Artificial Internal Organs in New York. He told the stunned, packed house that about eight patients of his had had the surgery, with Jens the first to have his implant turned on. Then he showed a tape of Jens driving. "I got the most applause," Dobelle told me, "but I don't think anyone really knew what they were seeing."

In fact, to most of the artificial-vision community, Dobelle's breakthrough came out of the blue. For years he had been merely a footnote, known mainly for his early work in phosphene stimulation. People had heard of Jerry, but because the testing was done privately, outside of academia, many felt the work suspect.

Dobelle leads one of a dozen teams spread out over four continents, racing ahead with all sorts of artificial-vision systems. There are teams working on battery-powered retinal implants and solar-powered retinal implants, teams growing ganglion cells on silicon chips, and teams working on optic-nerve stimulators. And there is Dick Normann, the former head of the University of Utah's Department of Bioengineering, who, up until Dobelle's success, was among the front-runners.

Like Dobelle, Normann is working on a visual neuroprosthesis. I was the first to tell him that the race was over: he lost.

"That's fantastic," Normann says.

"You're not even mad?"

"Fantastic, fantastic, fantastic"—and then he pauses—"if it works."

"What do you mean? I was there. I saw it work."

"But what do you mean by work? If a patient sees a point of light and it moves, is that sight? I need to know what the patient sees."

"OK. But what does it mean for your research?"

"Mean? It doesn't mean anything. We're going to keep going like we were going. Normann also envisions a three-part system—implant, signal processor, camera—but with a critical difference. While Dobelle's implant rests on the surface of the visual cortex, Normann's would penetrate it.

Normann's implant is much smaller than Dobelle's—about the size of a nail's head and designed to be hammered into the cortex, sinking to the exact spot in the brain where normal visual information is received. According to Normann, the implant is so precise that each electrode can stimulate individual neurons. "The reason this matters," he explains, "is that the cornerstone of artificial vision is the interaction between current and neurons. Because Dobelle's implant sits on the surface of the visual cortex, it requires a lot of current and lights up a whole bunch of neurons. Something in the one—to ten-milliamp range. With that much juice, a lot can go wrong."

Tell me about it.

"With penetrating electrodes, we've got the current down to the one—to ten-microamp range. That's a thousandfold difference." Lowering the amperage lowers the risk of seizure, but that's not all. Decreasing the amount of current also allows an increase of resolution: "The lower the current, the more electrodes you can pack on an implant," explains Normann. "We're not there yet, but with my electrodes, there's the chance of creating a contiguous phosphene field—that's exactly what you and I have—and that's just not possible with Dobelle's surface implant."

Which is the way things go when what was once a land of mystics becomes a field for engineers. Just like every other new technology, like operating systems and Web browsers, artificial vision is heading toward a standards war of its own.

Now that it's not faith healing, it's Beta versus VHS.

To Really Try to Understand What Jens Sees.

I Head to USC in Los Angeles, where Mark Humayun has his lab. Like the competition, Humayun uses eyeglass-mounted video cameras and signal processors to generate an image, but unlike Normann's and Dobelle's neuroprostheses, his implant sits atop the retina. It's designed to take the place of damaged rods and cones by jump-starting the still-healthy ones and then use the eye's own signal processing components—the ganglion cells and optic nerve—to send visual information to the brain.

There's a wash of light. Suddenly, things become clearer. "Did you up the resolution?"

"No, that's your brain learning to see."

"It's a limited approach, aimed at a limited number of pathologies, but it has its advantages," says Humayun. "We thought it was a better idea to operate on a blind eye than on a normal brain."

Humayun's Retinal Prosthesis Lab runs out of USC's Doheny Eye Institute. The room is small and square. Piles of electronic gear sit atop counters of maroon plastic—the same hue that offsets the bright yellow on Trojan football jerseys. Lab-coated technicians hunch over computers, barely registering my arrival. James Weiland, an assistant professor at the institute, helps me into an elaborate headdress: wraparound goggles cover my eyes, and black, light-blocking cloth hangs down over my ears. Plastic straps secure a miniature camera to the middle of my forehead, and wires run down my back and to a laptop computer to my left. The camera moves where my eyes move and then projects that image onto the "screen" of the goggles. The device, called a Glasstron and built by Sony, turns my normal eyesight into a pixelated version of itself.

With the power shut off, the view is complete darkness. Weiland flips a switch and asks me what I see.

"Vague gray shapes. Big dots. Blurry edges."

"Can you see the door? Could you walk to the door?"

"Yeah, I could, if you want me to trip over things and fall down."

"That's a 5-by-5 display. Hold on," says Weiland, "I'm going to up your pixel count to 32 by 32."

It's Weiland's belief that a 32-by-32 array, 1,024 pixels, should satisfy most vision needs. This is probably ten times the count on Dobelle's implant and much closer to Normann's design. Beside me I can hear Weiland futzing with the computer. There's a sudden wash of light, like viewing the Star Wars jump to hyperspace through a waterfall.

"Can you see now?"

"Not really."

"Give it a minute, let yourself adjust."

"OK, I've got blobs and edges and motion." Suddenly, things become clearer. What moments ago was attack of the Jell-O creatures has become doorways and faces. "What happened?" I ask. "Did you up the resolution again?"

"No," says Weiland, "that's your brain learning to see."

It's a weird feeling, watching my brain reorganize itself, but that's exactly what's happening. Beside me the fuzzy edge of the counter becomes a strong line, and then the computer atop it snaps into place.

I take one last glance around. Weiland is still not visible. Then there is a subtle shift in color. A drizzle of gray firms up, and I can see the white plane of his forehead offset by the darkness of his hair. I look around: door, desk, computer, person. So this is what a miracle looks like.

If Steven really didn't exaggerate the description of the seizure, I couldn't help but think that it would have been horrible had one of my children, or Lorri, been there to witness this. Considering he had neglected to mention my temporary memory loss after the seizure, it was unlikely he exaggerated the rest of the descriptions.

"Interesting, isn't it?" I said quietly to the family as they finished reading the article. "First Bill blames it either on me or the engineers, and then is the first to oppose the suggestion of calling 911. Just imagine what that would have caused if a medical team came in, along with the ensuing police investigation!"

"He'd probably go to jail," Lorri said.

"Yeah, and that would be the end of the project. No one else would touch this project with a ten-foot pole, and we'd all be stuck with this stuff in our heads and have no more use for it." But there could always be another investigation, I thought, taking into consideration the range of publicity this article will get. If it came down to a police investigation, there was no doubt I'd have to cover Dr. Dobelle one way or another.

"Bill really is made to look like a smart and knowledgeable man in this article," one of the boys who saw the real thing in Commack said. "Is he really the one behind the fifteen thousand implanted medical devices?"

I scratched my head at that question. I had been told by Bill that currently all that they were selling was the breathing pacemaker. "I'd have to look into that," I said, vowing to ask someone who had been with the company for a while next time I was down in Commack.

I received one more letter from Dr. Dobelle in October that year.

Dobelle Institute (Portugal) Lda.
Artificial Vision for the Blind
October 21, 2002
To: All Blind, Surgically Implanted Patients

Fr: Wm. H. Dobelle, PhD, Chairman & Chief Executive Officer
Re: Update on Artificial Vision

1. We have now implanted twelve (12) patients, including four that could not be scheduled during April. There are ten men and two women, and the primary cause of their blindness is trauma.

2. We have completely revised staffing on the project. Don Kiefer, a senior engineer, with more than a decade of experience, has been transferred from breathing pacemakers to vision. He has been joined by Tony Martins, a senior hardware/software engineer and Dr. Tim Dyer, who has a master's in biomedical engineering and is also a surgeon. Jie Song, who has a master's degree in computer science from Columbia will write software. We are still recruiting a fifth full-time person to serve as an electrode fabrication technician, under Mario D'Angelo's supervision.

3. This dramatic increase in manpower has been phased in so that we have completely revamped the hardware and software for the device. This includes many features ("auto start") etc. that were anticipated in June. We have also found and corrected the limitations imposed by the earliest software.

4. Don Kiefer has gone through the hardware in detail, and there are many changes to make it more reliable. This includes battery monitoring circuitry and software.

5. For the last several weeks, the systems have been sitting here in Commack while the crew attended to other details. Also, as you know, I have been almost totally incapacitated by shingles.

Arrangements will be made next week to begin distributing the systems. I had originally anticipated doing this at your home, but I am not sure that I will be able to travel very easily in the next couple of months. I do not want to delay the project even further. Hopefully, at least some of you can visit us in Commack or Lisbon (as our guests, of course).

Back in Napanee, for the past few weeks, the questions as to the state of my vision system were once again bombarding me, forcing me to either stay at my home or, if going out, going to Kingston as it was at least a half hour from our town, allowing me to shake the curious populous. Even Janice McGregor was asking me about it.

"Do you have your computer system yet? I need you to come down to Ottawa soon so we can film the conclusion. This show has to air by the new year." I wished she'd just drop the whole idea as Bill wanted control of the press. I had to remind myself that Bill was my employee as I originally hired him to resolve my blindness.

"I'm hoping for the word from Bill for me to come down any day and pick it up." I tried to explain, even though I had no idea how much longer it would be. Already precious time was being lost sitting around in the dark when I could be seeing some.

The latest letter was reread at the dinner table as it seemed more interesting than the others had been for some time.

"I can't believe it," I said, shaking my head. "Bill hired a real doctor! That's amazing! He must really be sick with those shingles to do something like that." After the disappearance of Dr. Beth Seelig, Dr. Dillis Gore, and the hands-off approach of Dr. John Girvin, the introduction of Dr. Dyre seemed rather refreshing. Now, I figured, there'd be less of a threat of having another seizure. It was the first item, however, that caught Lorri's attention.

"What on earth is he doing? How can he possibly justify implanting four other patients when nothing has been accomplished so far? Now we have twelve patients rid of their money, put through the wringer in the operating room with nothing to show for it."

I nudged her arm and reminded her, of one of the previous letters. "Remember, though, that the new price is $98,000. There's another $300,000 at least in his company's pocket to advance the project now that the hospital fees are paid. Let's hope that it's all worth it in the long run. I'm hoping Dr. Dyre, Tony, Don, and Jie will run the show and that guy just keeps in the background, running the business end of things. That way things might work out faster."

Shortly after receiving this last letter, I was hauled to Ottawa by CBC TV for my final cut for the documentary they were attempting to air even though I had no equipment yet. Even they had expected the progress to be somewhat faster than this. Janyce had bought clips from other news networks of me wearing the system in order to at least have some film of the result of my struggles. "We're airing this just after New Year's Day," she informed me. I figured Bill would disapprove strongly when he found out, but I really didn't owe him any apology about this. If I was working for him, I reasoned, that would be a different story.

"Ready to come down and get your system?" asked Bill's rusty voice as I pressed my ear disbelievingly against my ear. It was obvious that his shingles were tiring him out more than he already was. But I was ready to go, and on this late November day, I wasn't about to turn down the offer.

"Right away," I said willingly while thinking of the details of my leaving the business and family. "I'll have to come alone, however. Lorri has work and has to be here to take care of my business as well."

I had promised one of my friends from whom I had borrowed money I'd pay him back $4,000 US by Christmas, so the sale of firewood was vital. I would have liked to take along one of the kids, considering that the idea of having another seizure was out of the question now that we knew what caused it. Their school term, however, was about to come to an end, and they really needed to attend.

"That's all right," said Bill. "I'll send up a limo to pick you up."

The New York stretch limo driver, a middle-aged man by the name of Richie, pulled up to the house in the morning two days after my conversation with Bill. As I got into the huge car, Richie chuckled and said, "You should have seen all the heads turning as I drove through town. I bet everybody thought I had Avril Lavigne in the back!"

"I'd better lock my door then," I replied. "Just imagine if we stopped for a red light and a mob of young men, crazed at the thought of Avril being in here, mobbed the car."

Richie burst out laughing. "Won't they be in for a disappointment!" Then he turned serious. "So what are you going to do for the border?"

Richie was a limo driver, not a New York cop like Pat. Things may not go quite so smooth this time. I felt for my passport and tried to think it out. It was so hard to predict what the guards were looking for. I had to be careful as well about the idea that I was a patient of Dr. Dobelle. They could, after all, give me a hard time if they found I was pursuing a procedure not accepted by the FDA.

"What did you tell them when you came over?" I asked Richie. "Just that I'm picking up a client in Ontario and that I'll be back in New York the next day. Nothing about you at all."

That was good, I thought. Now it was up to me to decide on the story, rehearse it with Richie, and hope it flew. It was too bad it had to be that way between two countries so free and democratic. I always found it difficult to imagine having to do the job of a border guard. I braced myself as we approached the innocent little building, an idling police cruiser parked behind it, more than likely loaded with munitions for the purpose of destroying human life. Richie rolled down the windows and gave his driver's license to the guard, a woman I judged to be in her thirties.

"I'm just bringing him back," I heard Richie say. She came to my window next.

"And what are you going to do here in the United States?" There was a hint of sarcasm in her voice. At this point, had I mentioned the real reason for entering "her" country, she would probably have pointed to the larger building to the back of the hut, saying, "Bay 1," and we'd have spent the rest of the day there under interrogation. Richie would have been all right; he was a citizen and had rights, but I had none.

"I'm coming down for a few days to visit a friend, Dr. Dobelle."

"Kind of going in luxury, aren't you?" She was getting nasty. What did I do to her anyways? I held out my passport to ward her off. My white cane was visible to her as I had extended it in plain view as it may aid in my appearance as not a threat to this nation, now in fear since the September 11 bombings. "Lord, help me when I have to return with the vision equipment," I thought as I faced the guard.

"As a blind person, I obviously cannot drive myself. Moreover, a taxicab from Napanee wouldn't know his way around New York either. Believe me," I said, getting a little daring, trying to hide my anger, "I'd much rather see and drive a rusty little Volkswagen than being driven around in the dark."

"Have a good trip," she said curtly, returning the passport. Richie stepped on the gas and rolled up the windows.

"If she didn't have that gun strapped to her side, or those goons in the squad car behind the building, she'd have had to be more polite."

"Yeah, I heard what she said," said Richie, having to talk loudly in order to be heard as the car was very long. "I have no idea what gets into these people sometimes."

We arrived in Commack before 4:00 p.m., leaving just enough time to meet the new team in the office. Richie carried my suitcase as I followed him up to the door of the now-familiar Dobelle Institute on Mall Drive.

"Good day," said Louise warmly, shaking my hand. "I hope you had a great ride down here."

"With that car, how can I not?" was my reply. Not that many people in Canada ever get the luxury to be driven in a car like that.

"Come in here and meet the new team," said Bill from the cafeteria. I noticed right away he was still in his chair. Claire's plans of him receiving rehabilitation must not have worked out. I shook Bill's hand, which was even frailer than before. "Good to be back, Bill." I bent the truth somewhat for the second time that day. What I really wanted was the equipment, not the visit.

"Are you up and walking yet?"

"Forget it, these damned shingles hurt too much." He quickly changed the subject. "Meet the new team for the vision project."

I shook hands again with Tony and Don, both of whom I already knew. Tony had managed to straighten out the software problems that now allowed the system to self-start. Don and Tony worked on the electronic bugs that caused the system to be unreliable, as well as having finished the other systems that had been far from "on the shelf and ready to go . . ." as described by Bill eight months ago. Now they were actually ready to go.

"Jesse is working on the software and will do most of the computer work," Bill said as a young woman with a soft voice approached me. She had recently immigrated to the United States and was still a little uncertain of our slanged manner of speaking the English language. "Pleased to meet you," she said as she shook my hand. She was shy and polite, probably too timid to be working for someone like Bill, considering how I already witnessed his gruff treatment toward his employees. I'd have troubles being one of them, I thought.

"And finally, here's Dr. Dyre," Bill said as a man shook my hand in a firm and reassuring manner. "Glad to have you here," he said in a voice suggesting he had a lot to offer to this project. Just to hear he was a medical doctor was a great start. There was no one else; Steve had already left.

"Tomorrow we'll start setting your system up for you to take home," Bill said. "You should be out of here in a few days once we're sure all the bugs are out." I couldn't wait. With this team, I thought, all will work out. I was brought by Pat to a new hotel called the Hampton Inn, where I'd await tomorrow with great anticipation. It had been too long since I'd seen my last phosphenes.

It was Wednesday, December 4, 2002, when I entered the conference room late in the morning as the "morning conference" routine was already out of the way. Pat had picked me up after he had already brought Bill to the office. Jesse and Tony sat in the same seats once occupied by Jim and Steve, both manning a laptop computer. Tim Dyre sat to my left, taking notes. Jesse opened my file of parameters last used by Steve. She turned to Tony.

"When they say 'left' and 'right' side, what do you think they meant? Visual cortex or visual field?"

Tony looked at the computer screen of Jesse and then at the papers upon which the voltages and electrodes had been recorded.

Tim sat up and cautioned, "We don't want those mixed up."

"Yeah," I agreed, recalling the differences in stimulation parameters between the two sides. "Those 3 mm electrodes in my left side really don't use the high voltage that the right does, but their current draw was a lot greater."

"The current draw was never recorded," Tony said, looking over the notes made by Steve.

"We should be doing that," Tim said, adding, "and since we really don't know what's what, let's just start from scratch and reset Jens's threshold voltages. That's the safest measure."

I was supporting Dr. Dyre's decisions all the way. "Considering we're supposed to set the thresholds every morning, and since I hadn't been done since the start of . . ." I never got to finish.

Bill interjected, "Just hook it up and let's get it going!"

There was a moment of silence from the end of the table where everyone sat. "You mean, forget about the protocol we had discussed before stimulating any patient?" Dr. Dyre was speaking, taking orders instead of giving them.

"Yes. Just cut the nonsense. Left side is left, right side is right. Let's go."

Tim said nothing as Jesse made the final adjustments and said, "Ready?" That was the last I heard of her, or anyone, for a while.

There was a sudden, violent, searing pain tearing through my skull as if a machete had been stuck through both my temples and twisted while a bright, colorful display of red and orange with purple flashed through my visual field. The pain was excruciating as I screamed and covered up the camera with my right hand in vain—the computer had been set to display darkness instead of light. Before I realized my mistake and could shut off the system by turning the camera to the lights above me, I lost consciousness.

I awoke a while later, sprawled out on the conference room floor as Dr. Dyre fussed over me. For several minutes, I heard only murmurs, resembling no language at all, and then slowly it turned into English, yet I had no idea who the people were or where I was. It took a long time to recover that day. When I did, my back hurt immensely, and there was a nasty cut across the middle of my bruised tongue, a now familiar feeling.

Dr. Dyre spoke again, this time being understood. He sounded like he was trying to control his emotions, changing his voice especially for me, having just been very angry at someone in a heated argument. "Do you want to go to your hotel room for a bit to get some rest?" His voice indicated he himself did not agree with that idea.

"Oh no, no, not that isolation again," I said pleadingly. "Believe me, Tim, last time this happened, I almost didn't make it in there. Human interaction, talking, and activity all around me is what I need to get over this. Just give me a bit, and I'll be all right."

Tim agreed, sitting with me as we talked of our lives somewhat, trying to forget about the screw-up of the day. We both knew it could have been prevented. Tony was at the laptop, working away and occasionally joining in on the conversation. Jesse had left for a while, either to the back rooms of the building or gone home.

"She didn't take it too well when that happened to you," Tim explained quietly. "She pushed the button, which made this happen. She feels kind of responsible." Bill had gone off to another room, leaving us free to talk. Tony leaned over to me and said:

"You wouldn't believe it, but when you passed out, Bill turned to Jesse and snarled 'What did you do?!' as if it was she that was responsible. I wouldn't be surprised if she just quit right now."

Oh no, I thought, there we go again. Bill, once again, is scaring away the good workers necessary for the success of this project. I'd have to warn the others.

"Tim, Tony," I addressed my companions. "Let me tell you this. Bill is kind of quick to blame someone when things go wrong. When I had my first seizure, he blamed Steve for it. Yet Steve had nothing to do with it. I've been trying to convince him to increase the voltages, for example, for threshold testing in smaller increments, but he'll have none of it. He is too quick in taking risks, and I think I've figured it out. Do either of you recall the *Wired* magazine article?"

Both Tim and Tony had read it. I continued making my point. It was important they knew this much as it was the only way to prevent more disasters. "Not only did Bill draw a parallel with his project and that of the Wright brothers, but he seems to capitalize on the idea that a lieutenant was killed, no rather, according to Bill, *had* to be killed, to bring merit to the project."

There was a moment of silence as Tim and Tony absorbed the idea of having such a difficult boss. I had no qualms of them changing their mind about working here; they appeared to have their heart in the very idea of restoring sight to the blind, judging from their having already put up with Bill for a few months.

Tim spoke finally, "We had already discussed a specific procedure to follow before any patients are stimulated. Had we followed it, this never would have happened. We've got to be more careful, no matter what the Big Man says."

After lunch I felt better somewhat, even though my back was aching furiously and my tongue had been almost too sore for me to be able to eat. The hidden monster in me, the one which had almost had its way following my previous seizure, did not even show itself this time. I got back into the same chair I had been in first thing this morning and connected the cables to the savers. To my surprise and relief, Jesse once again took her place in front of her laptop. She said nothing to me. Bill also came vaulting into the conference room.

"Ready to try it again?" he said as if I'd just said the wrong answer during a math quiz.

"Yes, I am. We'll start slow, threshold each phosphene carefully and do it right. Also, we won't even try to stimulate the painful ones from June, given what already happened this morning."

The manner with which I addressed Bill left no room for argument. He knew at this point he had to cooperate; he knew it was also a luxury I didn't fit the description of a typical patient who is only too happy to launch a lawsuit and the big stink that goes with it. The vision quest had to succeed. There was no doubt left in the fact that Bill was overly determined, but that's what it seemed to take to get this project rolling. Unfortunately, his ambition not only translated into courage and daring, which set him apart from the rest of the researchers, but it also translated into an underestimation of the consequences of certain risks, posing an obviously dangerous scenario. It was therefore up to the rest of the team to control that negative side effect of working with a "genius."

Tony and Jesse started the stimulation program. "Now," Jesse said shyly. I saw nothing.

"No, nothing," I said. Jesse increased the voltage to the next level: 1.0 V.

"Now," she said. Tony read the oscilloscope for the second's worth duration of the pulse emissions.

"No, not yet." Jesse increased the voltage to 2.0 and tried again.

"Now," she said. I still did not see anything.

"No," I said, then added quickly, "3 V next." Bill just sat in his chair and said nothing as I overruled the "scientific" method. This was my head.

"Now," said Jesse. I saw a small flicker lasting for a second under the center point of my vision. Somehow the really good feeling associated with seeing phosphenes had left me for the day. Unlike my first seizure during which I had felt no pain, seeing a phosphene now reminded me of the sensation that my brain was being wrenched out of my head.

"Ya," I said. "Keep going down until I can't see it." I certainly did not want any more overstimulation.

We did only one side that day and decided to do the rest the following morning. By no means did we want to hurry. The process took longer this time as Tony was carefully reading the current readings coming from the oscilloscope while Tim was recording them. Tony looked over the notes from the previous recording of voltages from Steve and Jim.

"They're not that far from the previous ones," he observed. "Still about fifty to sixty on the left visual field—right visual cortex—that seem like you think they're useful." I was glad that hadn't changed. It was the phosphenes that made this thing work.

The following morning, my back still sore but slightly better since the many hot baths I had during the night, we were at it again in the conference room. This time it was the right visual field—left visual cortex—which was stimulated. I cautioned Jesse and Tony of the sensitivity of the three-millimeter electrodes.

"Considering that the average voltage per electrode on my right cortex is higher than that of the left, it's safe to assume that when the sides became mixed up yesterday it was the fact that the left side was overstimulated. Once again, it's those darned big electrodes."

Tim turned to me and said, "Yeah, it was figured out that those electrodes weren't a good idea after all, and the next four patients implanted since the initial 8 in April 2002 only received the small electrodes on both sides."

So I was now stuck with them, having proven the obvious—that if large surfaces of the brain are stimulated at once, the dots are big and useless, and other regions of the brain will receive stimulation inadvertently, causing negative side effects. I was in no mood, however, to have them exchanged.

"Don't worry," Bill spoke up from his wheelchair. "We'll pull them out next year anyways and give you something better—the larger electrode array." Bill sounded very tired, his voice slurring as if he had drunk too much, something I knew for a fact he never did. He needed a long rest. The rest of us went back to work, myself trying my best not to think about getting my head opened up again next year.

I ended up with thirty to forty electrodes on my left visual cortex—right visual field. The phosphenes hadn't changed since the last time I had been stimulated in June as I recognized the shapes of most of them. Even though the voltages were lower than those of the other side, Tim noted that the current readings were more than twice as high with the larger electrodes. Tony and Tim finished the transfer of the computer information onto a hard paper copy, but did not give the paper to Bill as usual. As they worked, I heard a soft snoring noise from the direction of Bill.

"He's not sleeping, is he?" I asked Tim in astonishment, gesturing in the direction of the genius.

"Oh yeah, he's out of it, all right." He seemed somewhat surprised I noticed. "He's just been taking too much pain medication for the shingles." Bill really didn't need that complication in his life as well. I had heard once that shingles were brought on as a result of extreme stress and wondered if it wasn't our past weeks in Manhattan that were responsible. But for now, he could rest as we seemed to know what to do to make things work for my vision system.

"Well, what's next?" Tony asked as the thresholding was complete. I was the only one who really knew now as the genius was taking a break from it, and the rest of the crew was new at this.

"Now we need to map it. But it really isn't critical to my health," I reminded the team of experts in their fields as they listened, "as wrong mapping will only give me a bad picture, not overstimulation."

"We might as well do it again and compare it to the old coordinates," Tony suggested. There was a lot of time of the day remaining, so we proceeded. I sat in front of the corkboard, which was equipped with a tack in the middle for me to feel. Tim suggested that I mount it on the wall and sit in front of it with the tack being at the same height as my line of sight. We tried this, and the result was probably slightly more accurate as I was more directly in front of the board than I would have been with it sitting on the tabletop in front of me, where I'd be looking at it from an angle. I also had more freedom to move my arms in this position.

"Only problem is, Tim, my arms get tired after a while of holding them up," I said as I sat back from the board after mapping about a dozen phosphenes.

"Just take a break. We have lots of time."

"Imagine how long it would take to map and threshold five hundred points, that being the count of the proposed new system's electrode arrays," I mused out loud.

Tim agreed, "Yeah, that would take quite a while. Probably a couple of weeks."

The mapping was almost completed when Bill awoke from his slumber. He groaned and shifted in his chair and then realized again where he was and what he was supposed to be doing.

"I'm just going to go in my office for a bit." He spoke as if he had been coordinating the progress of setting up the system all this time. "Let me know when you're ready for the camera." As he attempted to move himself toward the door of the conference room, Tim got out of his chair and helped him toward his office. All the better, I thought to myself, sure that the others thought the same, as now we can actually get the work done right while Bill freshens up for the next stage, which may need his help. Bill got the project this far, I thought, and we can figure out the minor details on our own.

"X is at—5.5, Y at—1," Tony said as he stood to one side of me, looking over my shoulder to see where the last coordinates were as I pointed them out on the corkboard. Jesse entered the values into the laptop and then said, "Finished!" I swiveled myself toward the table, resting my arms from the ordeal. Jesse continued tapping on the laptop when it occurred to me that we still had to balance the two maps, the one for the right with respect to the one on the left.

"Jim had to fiddle with the two maps for a bit until they were both on the same horizontal level," I said. "We did this as the top of the left visual field is much lower than the top of the right."

"That was fixed," Tony announced proudly. "We modified the program so the two sides make one big map."

Next, the image reversal feature was set to off, the size factor set to twenty, and the pulses were reduced to five per frame. All we needed was the genius.

"Well," sighed Dr. Dyre, standing up after Tony and Jesse indicated they were done for the second time, "I guess I'll get him now." He trudged out of the room to retrieve the doctor. I turned to Tony and Jesse.

"We'll start with a multiplier of 0.5 and go up in tenths, OK? The frame count isn't a problem, but try to avoid four frames per second. That speed seems to affect me."

We all heard Bill's lumbered breathing before he arrived, pushed by Tim until he reached his usual place beside me on my right as Tim sat back down on my left.

"Did the mapping go better this time?" Bill asked, referring to the idea of pasting the corkboard on the wall.

"I think it was a good idea," I said, knowing it would cheer Bill up. I really didn't want to be on his bad side as he was the only one who would try something like artificial vision on people. The corkboard idea had been all right, but far from my expectations coming from a high-tech, New York research firm.

"Well, let's start it up," Bill said. The value of 0.5 for a multiplier had already been entered into the computer. We started right away with seven frames per second.

"Now," said Jesse. I looked around but saw nothing.

"Nothing," I said. Jesse went back to the keyboard as Tim said, "0.6."

"Now," Jesse said again. I looked around again. Tony watched the oscilloscope, confirming the system was working.

"Nothing," I said again. It was a good sign as it indicated our thresholding was set properly.

"What are you doing, changing the multipliers?" Bill was suddenly conscious again, aware of what we were doing.

"Yeah. We're raising them slowly and carefully," Tim replied curtly.

At a multiplier of 0.9, I could see most of the phosphenes, although dimly. Theoretically, I should have only seen them at 1.0, as when we set the thresholds, we adjust the voltage for the absolute minimum required to see them. However, when several electrodes were used at once, it seemed like the brain responded at a lower voltage.

"I'm not sure I'm seeing them all, but most of them are there." I looked around the room. The front edge of the conference table showed up as a rough line of three or four larger, oddly shaped phosphenes near the bottom of my visual field. I confirmed this by quickly ducking down my head for an instant, noticing the line being replaced by another line of different phosphenes further toward the center of my visual field. The sensation of motion that moving line caused made me feel fresh and renewed inside, as if I just awoke from a long sleep. I sat, motionless, allowing the sensation to absorb itself into my light-deprived soul.

"Jens!" Tony shouted suddenly, vaulting out of his chair and shutting off the vision system. The line disappeared as quickly as it had materialized.

"What's wrong?" I asked, puzzled at his sudden attack of panic. He paused, then restarted the system. "I thought you were having another seizure," he explained sheepishly. "You just sat so still and weren't talking."

"I'll make sure I keep talking next time," I said. I wasn't making people around me feel comfortable, that was for sure. Last time I was here, Charlie, the photographer, had the impression I was about to fly down the nearest staircase, and now the Dobelle engineering team thought I was going to go into fits of convulsions any second.

Tony restarted the system, and this time, we went up to a multiplier of 1.0. The world was in better view now, the long, florescent lights above the conference room table clearly displayed by jagged rows of dots in my visual field. Only two could be seen at one time, necessitating the degree of motion of my head to fully gauge the span of the lights as they occupied the ceiling. I looked to my right, past the more distinct figure of Bill in his chair and noticed a few horizontal lines evenly spaced on the wall.

"What's that on that wall? Those lines, I mean." I pointed.

Bill followed my gaze and said, "Those are bookshelves. Is this the first time you saw those?"

"I can't remember seeing them before. It looks like my horizontal mapping is better than ever, judging by the shelves and the table's edge. I need a straight edge to check it the other way." As I spoke, I noticed two of my phosphenes continuing to stay lit in spite of the fact that I had looked at something, which wouldn't be using them. I covered my camera on my right lens of my sunglasses.

"Are you all right?" Tim suddenly asked. I quickly replied, explaining the residual phosphenes lest he think I was having another seizure.

"Maybe we should turn it back down," he suggested. I didn't want to lose phosphenes, so I suggested a threshold of 0.95. All this while Bill just sat and watched, or at least I hoped he did. Tim left the room and immediately returned with a ruler, which he placed into my hands. "Try this to check your vertical mapping."

I cleared the tabletop in front of me and looked directly at the empty space in front of me. No phosphenes were lit. Slowly, starting from the extreme left of my visual field, I started to move the ruler, holding it in a "6:00–12:00" position as I slid it across the tabletop. My farthest left phosphene lit first, flashing a glow near the periphery of my vision. Next three others lit in a row about six inches to the left of center vision at arm's length. The vertical line progressed to the right, new phosphenes replacing the old ones as the ruler's journey across my visual field continued, the line every time changing slightly in shape and appearance until it progressed to my extreme right side, causing only a dim glow of the extreme right phosphene, marking the end of its presence in my line of sight. Everyone watched silently as I then moved the ruler rapidly back and forth in front of me, observing with satisfaction the adequate mapping job.

"Considering the phosphenes have different shapes and sizes, one could never accomplish a perfect line," I said to Bill and the engineers. "I think this is as close as we'll get to perfect."

Bill grunted with approval. "I wish they'd all be this easy to map," he said as he looked toward the engineers. "We may as well get the thing set so he can wear it."

"You mean, so I can start it up myself?" I had been hoping for this. "This is the fourth time I'm down here, you know, so I can take home the system."

Tony laughed as he worked diligently at the alterations with Jesse. "Of course. You'll be taking it home. You've got the experts at it now!"

The belt was brought out and the stimulator, computer, and battery was placed inside. I had disconnected from the system as the preparations were made. The computer and stimulator were connected together with a 9-pin communications cable four inches long, then a one-foot long battery cable connected the battery to the stimulator. Two of the wires in the cable connecting the computer to the stimulator served to carry power from the battery to the computer and glasses, which connected as well to the side of the computer. I hoisted the belt, now loaded with equipment, to my waist and closed the Velcro catch, then adjusted the shoulder straps.

"Once you're connected to it," Tony said, "just press the rocker switch on the side of the stimulator and wait. You'll hear four beeps, then a pause, then two more. After the second one, it's ready to go." I connected the cables to my savers, double-checking to ensure they weren't mixed up. The jack on the left side of the stimulator was for my left jack in my head. I knew now from experience the consequences of a mix-up of the cables. I tried to be as careful as possible with the cable ends as Steve had once told me they were worth over a thousand dollars apiece. There were seventy-two delicate pins protruding from the male end, which could be easily sheared off by attempting to find the jack alignment while pressing the cable ends together. Once completed, I put the glasses on my nose and plugged them into the side of the computer. Then I pushed the button.

I was standing at the end of the conference room table as I counted the beeps: first four, then silence, then two more. I noticed the boxes made a buzzing noise as I stood there, now that the noisy oscilloscope was not in the vicinity.

"You put fans in these?"

"Yeah, the power supplies were getting too hot once I connected the camera as well. That camera draws a lot." Tony then added, "We won't have those cameras in the next system. Those ones are now obsolete, believe it or not."

The second beep sounded after the first four, and suddenly, the world transformed itself from a void of blackness into a mirage of white and gray dots. Their incessant flashing became background noise I tried my best to ignore as the full scope of the room came into view. I saw the jagged outlines of the table's edges and was able to follow them around the entire span of the table, noting the lumps of dots angled, marking the backs of the office chairs surrounding the table. I saw the dotted arrangements, which appeared to move as I regarded Tony and Jesse at the other end from where I stood. Small blobs of chaotically arranged phosphenes marked the junk on the table near Tony's end, while the doorframe accessing the back rooms of the building was silhouetted on the back wall. A square-shaped blob of phosphenes marked the conference room telephone just a couple of feet from my right hand, the same telephone I was first looking for when connected to the camera for the first time. In spite of the broken lines, the flashing dots of different sizes, this was a real picture of the world. If I could forget about all that had happened before this, it would be justified to say, I thought to myself as I stood there, that this is the magic moment where I pressed the "magic button" on the vision device I had once wanted so much for the past two decades.

Tony, Tim, and Jesse watched silently as I walked around the building, looking carefully for the doorframes as I checked out the office building. The system worked better now than it ever had. It was evident that my brain had not lost its gains it had made six months ago in adjusting to seeing with phosphenes. I was outside the door of the Dobelle Institute, walking carefully up and down the sidewalk and staying successfully out of the flower bed when Tim spoke to me.

"Do you want your cane?" He was holding out the white cane, forming a broken row of dots in my visual field, clearly visible as it contrasted against the darker background of the building wall. I reached for it.

"Since I can't see drop-offs, it probably is a good idea. Up to now I've been taking extra high steps just to keep from tripping." I walked around for another hour, then checked my braille watch. It had been over two hours since starting up the equipment. I made my way back into the building and found Tony, a flickering blob of phosphenes in one of the cafeteria room chairs.

"Amazing," I started as Tony ate his lunch, his lunch hour being long overdue. "This thing has gone for over two hours and still didn't quit!"

"Like I said, the experts were at it!"

There was no doubt in my mind that the team was good. Then a thought came to me, something I had meant to ask before.

"Tony, who are the four new implanted patients?"

"Let's see," started Tony, "there's a middle-aged man Tom, Kirk, a young man who was blinded just two years ago, there's Kim, and there's Ben, a boy of fourteen years who lost his sight at, I think, three years old. Ben wasn't promised any sight, but Bill had said there was a chance that if he received stimulation regularly, maybe he'd start seeing. His parents wanted to try anyways."

"I'm anxious to see what happens with Kirk," I said, "considering he is so freshly blinded, maybe he'll have a different learning curve. Ideally, this implant would be made available for people the same time they were blinded." Then I had to add, "But without all the chaos and mistakes we made in the past eight months." Just then I heard Bill calling from his office.

"Jens, come here for a minute," he said. "Here, push my chair over to Linda's room." Linda was the company's accountant and rarely showed her face out of her office. I had never met her and did find it bizarre a company as small as Avery Labs and Dobelle Institute needed a full-time accountant. I shook hands with Linda, a middle-aged woman with a strong New York accent, and took my seat in a chair beside Bill. Bill began to speak as I listened disbelievingly.

"What do you make right now in your wood-vending and piano-repair business?" he asked. I was surprised he even remembered what I did.

"Why do you ask?" I asked after I disclosed the unimpressive amount of my present salary.

"I'll match that and maybe add on a bit if you'll care to work for me. Patient representative would be your title. You'd be responding to all media inquiries, explaining the function of the system to potential patients, and aiding in the rehabilitation process as blind patients learn to use the system."

The offer was just too good to refuse. Yes, I'd be working for an occasionally cantankerous doctor who sometimes verbally reprimanded his employees, but that was no match to the contributions made to the fight against blindness. I'd be working in Portugal, New York, and who knows where other offices would arise, aiding in the research, sharing my ideas for the improvement of the new systems as they came about, "test driving" each one of them as I encouraged the blind patients to practice with their new systems and get back on their feet. In contrast, there could be another one thousand feet of piled logs waiting for me as I faced them with chain saw in hand, wondering why one had to suffer so just to be able to put bread on the table. I didn't even have to spend a second to consider my options.

"That would be my pleasure, Bill," I said quickly and directly, leaving no room for doubt. "I'll do whatever I can to ensure the world can see what I can see now instead of being stuck in the dark." I looked around and saw the outline of Linda's desk, the shelves on the wall, and the outline of the television monitor of her computer. We'd have to have many more, and smaller, dots before I'd be able to read the screen, I figured, but this was so much better than seeing nothing. Moreover, I'd be able to influence directly the progress of the vision project now that I was directly involved as an employee. Bill shook my hand, a gesture as final as signing the contract. I never felt this good about the Dobelle Institute as I did at that moment.

CHAPTER 12

Finally the Dream Comes True

Richie and I left in the stretch about midafternoon—the eight—to nine-hour trip ahead of us by now being very familiar to both of us. As the first hour or two of the stop-and-go traffic of New York City had Richie occupied, I took the time to reflect on the past week's trials and errors. The seizure on the first day should never have happened, and I still wondered if I'd feel consequences from this kind of abuse of my brain on a later date. It must never happen again, I vowed, it won't. I needed far more control during the testing sessions. When wearing the machine, I had the switch in my hand—ruling out the possibility of this happening when using the machine alone. However, at the institute, I was at the mercy of the engineers, who had known better than to just recklessly throw the switch, yet their cautious approach was overridden by the "master." Moreover, this last seizure was far more violent than the previous one, and I had been helpless to stop it even though I knew it was coming. So I once said I'd never want to work for Bill, yet here I was, a contract signed to stop my home businesses, instead dedicating my time to Bill Dobelle. Oh, but I couldn't refuse—the salary was good and steady, the teamwork with those great people down in Commack by far beat working alone, and the thrill of the travel and the idea of helping make people see was just what I needed to once again have a job comparing to that of the time I was a surveyor nineteen long years ago.

"What's the first thing you want to look at when you get home?" Richie's voice reminded me of what was supposed to be the big excitement of the day.

"Oh, you mean with that contraption?"

483

"Yeah, of course. You're going to be able to look at all the members of your family, your home, friends, and all that now that you can finally take this thing home."

I imagined walking in the door of my home and trying to see all of that, scanning up and down with the glasses, and hoping to see movement with the few dots offered by the implants. I knew it was going to be disappointing to the family given the high hopes we had to recognize faces, drive a car, and to return to the work of surveyor. I, personally, had already readjusted my expectations of the system, but the family hadn't. Would it be a good idea to put it on before getting out of the car?

"I think I'll just leave it for today and fool with it in the morning." Maybe Richie was surprised by this, or maybe he had a good idea what had been going on, but we didn't talk any more about seeing again. Instead, I thought long and hard about the new reality of having a job with Bill Dobelle at the famed Dobelle Institute. Just a couple of years ago, when hearing of the Dobelle Institute, I couldn't have imagined this would ever happen to me—not only being the first implanted patient to see with the system, but then to get a job there as well.

We mentioned nothing about the vision system as we crossed the border—it wasn't like we were lying either as the only question asked by an obviously overtired border guard was: "Do you have any alcohol or tobacco to claim?"

So we left it at that, listening to music from Richie's disk selection as the final one and a half hours passed and we pulled into the familiar driveway of my home.

Everyone was asleep, so I entered in the back door and unlocked the front for bringing in my suitcases, and of course, the new machine. Lorri by now had awoken and greeted me, not showing either surprise or disappointment regarding the absence of the equipment about my waist. I hadn't yet spoken to her since Bill offered the job, so this news I needed to share with her.

"Guess what—I got a job from Bill."

"Good, I hope it pays lots . . ." She motioned to the outdated family van parked in our driveway. "The van is getting tired, and we need to buy that, and yes, all those debts. What's the job?"

"Patient rep," I answered, trying to think of what I really had to do. "I am to work here mostly, as well as go to Portugal and to other functions to demonstrate the equipment, as well as work with patients to help understand how everything works."

"Sounds good—but does it really work?"

I wasn't sure how to answer. I wasn't sure at all what to say in all honesty. "I'll have to try it for a week or two around here, where we know how life was before, and just find out for myself."

Nervously, I assembled the equipment the next morning while the kids were still asleep. I found myself suddenly very self-conscious about wearing this machine. They really didn't need to watch me screw these wires to my head. I was still their dad, not a robot. I hadn't felt this at all down in New York. Everyone there was new, they didn't know me as dad, or a friend, or anything about my past, and to them, I was just another person on the sidewalk—maybe looking a bit weirder than most, but still not so weird that you'd get scared. That is, provided I covered the machine up with my coat. But here, at home with the kids who knew me from the very beginning of their lives as I comforted them, taught them, and struggled through difficulties together with them, the idea that my head, body, and face were suddenly going to be different made me worry. I retrieved a heavy sweatshirt from the bedroom, hoping Lorri was still asleep and not looking at all the wires and boxes strung around me as I slipped the shirt over my head, hiding the wires as best as I could in my curly hair and draping the shirt over the boxes. The stimulator, computer, and battery pack lost their shapes below the shirt, and now I looked like a man with a few pounds too many around the waist. I once had disapproved of looking overweight and out of shape, but this time it was a comfortable compromise.

I went back into the kitchen and then turned on the only switch that the machine had—the on–off switch. Immediately, the two ventilator fans—one each in the stimulator and computer—whirred to life with their high-pitched whine. "Wait two minutes, then twelve beeps, wait another minute and two more beeps, and then it should work . . ." Tony had told me before packing up the equipment into my suitcase back in Commack. I waited.

Suddenly small dots of light started to dance before my eyes, each one of the dots with their particular size, shape, and characteristics now familiar to me as they tried to display the presence of the windows in the kitchen. Moving around my head, as if looking around, the glasses repositioned the camera to display the lines where the windows and wall met, and in a few seconds, I could count the windows of the kitchen, living room, and adjoining rooms. I looked for the outline of the doorframes and found them, perhaps because I saw them or perhaps because I knew where they were in respect to the room. The floor tiles in the kitchen were white with a bluish pattern, a fact I knew only from once being told, now threw off the effectiveness of the vision system as it tried to make patterns of dots out of the patterns on the floor, giving the impression there were things on the floor that really weren't there. But the kitchen chairs, being made of plain wood, arrested the confusion and gave a jagged, broken dotted line where they were located. Looking around some more, I made out the shape of the white refrigerator against the wall as well as where it sat relative to the rest of the floor. I strained to look out of the window and then heard the kids coming downstairs. Forgetting about my appearance, I greeted them as they peered with interest at the glasses.

"Where is the rest of it—under the shirt?" I picked up the bottom of the sweatshirt, revealing the mess of wires and boxes, the hum from the fans now louder. I could see my kids as groups of a handful of dots moving about, the group blinking with the movement corresponding to the movement of the kids. I saw two dots located near the bottom of my visual field suddenly light up as one of the boys reached out their arm to touch the computer on my waist.

"Does it work now?" Brandon had only seen his dad in Commack wearing a defunct machine while *Wired* magazine photographers clicked away nine rolls of film—father and son finally reunited in a world they can now both share, the long and hard years of Dad's blindness now permanently behind him.

"Yeah, it kind of does." Moving around, I pointed to the windows in the living room, now visible as lines of dots indicating their borders. "I see dots where the sharp contrasts are. But we can't expect the world all at once, you know." Here I was reducing the kid's expectations in a positive light, yet it was me who had to live with the consequences of having been misled by Bill's original promises.

"Can you see anything outside?" I walked back to the window where I had been before everyone descended the stairs and peered out. I could not see the field beside the garden, nor the ditch at the side of the highway, nor the neighbor's house as it was in a valley on the other side of the road. I saw only one horizontal line where the van was parked, its roof outlined against the sky. I saw a long string of dots forming a vertical line.

"What's that?" I pointed.

"A telephone pole."

"Well, that and the van is all I can see." The snow was covering the ground, seemingly throwing the camera into a state of overload and just not able to reveal everything.

"Maybe the light's too bright," suggested Kyle as he had to squint just to look out. "You know, like overexposure in a film." It really could be the problem, I thought, as I looked back inside and more of the kitchen revealed itself—the desk with its usual clutter in the corner—the clutter portrayed as a barrage of dots similar to those produced by looking at the top of a tree—as well as the shelves mounted on the wall now familiar since having seen those at the Dobelle Institute in Commack.

"Can you regulate camera aperture?" Kyle peered at the computer under my shirt as I revealed the only control I had of the system. "I can turn it on and off."

"Yeah, but you're in the company now, so maybe you can make suggestions on how to build the new machine that's to come out in six months . . ." Maybe six months, but with Bill's reputed opposition to patient self-empowerment, I thought it would be more like three years.

"Yeah, if I had more knobs and dials, I could do some performance customizations that could alleviate the problem. But let's wait around for the night and see what happens then."

Lorri had been making breakfast and then informed me of the day's plans.

"I have a recital planned for this afternoon." A recital meant that a couple dozen of families of her students were coming over to play their prepared songs on the piano in our large rec room as we all socialized afterward and had refreshments. Many students enjoyed the chance to play for others, making this event an important part of Lorri's business. I looked at her as her movements caused different groups of phosphenes to flash on an off with the lines of both the kitchen counter and that of the cupboards in the background. The florescent lights located under the cupboards had been turned on, giving me the impression that many things of different sizes and shapes were on the counter. Slowly, I reached out to feel one interesting shape that seemed round as I moved around my head. It was a plate.

"Can you see that?" Lorri had been watching me as I felt around, verifying the shape of what I saw.

"Sort of, yes. The cups are a blob of dots, and the plates are round." A whole circle was not possible as I could not see dots out of the upper left quadrant of my visual field. I cleared off a section of the counter and gave her a plate and a cup.

"Put one or the other down and I'll tell you."

The kids had come to watch as Lorri did, and without a mistake, I could tell the difference. She had to be careful to put them down very quietly as I already knew the sound of either being placed on the table.

"Are you wearing the system for the recital?" I had not thought this over yet. I had felt self-conscious when first thinking about the family seeing me like this, but now that feeling had gone away with the first time I pointed at something I saw and shared it with the kids, feeling like I was now in their world of shapes and light in spite of the limitations of the technology. Could I do this with the students? They weren't my own family who together with me endured the problems of Dad not seeing, especially when we were trying to have fun together.

"I don't know yet."

Lorri had set the table, and as I sat down in the chair in my place, I saw the plate before I touched it. Looking around carefully, I saw the plates of the other kids, this time not round as I was looking at them from an angle, but a few dots of light in the direction of each child was enough for me to know that we were ready to eat. I heard each one get in their chairs, and the backs of the chairs, once visible as dotted lines, now changed to reveal a glob of dots that moved. This is what my kids looked like—their faces only two or three phosphenes as they faced me. But it was better than nothing.

A pancake landed on my plate, and I peered at it from only a few inches away. I could tell its borders and where it sat on the plate. I reached for the fork and waved it around in front of my face, a line of dots similar to the first time I saw my moving arm now visible. As the fork was lowered to the food, I could coordinate the two to meet without having to feel around first.

"Where's the butter and syrup?" I asked in my usual manner and then saw the hand of Joel, one of my boys sitting beside me, reach out and take a hold of a glob of phosphenes I saw in the middle of the table which couldn't have been anyone's plate.

"Hmmm. I guess I was already looking at it." It was such a new feeling to see I had forgotten I was actually now in this world again. I peered up and saw a group of dots on the ceiling I hadn't noticed before.

"Is the light on?"

"Yes. You can see it too?"

The light had been responsible for more clearly displaying the objects on the table, offering a contrast not normally on the table. I had not been using lights for nineteen years, and now here I was turning on the light to see better. Dobelle must have done something right, despite the problems. Or at least that is what I thought at the time.

The effort required to see with this device was more than I had anticipated. My head ached, and concentration on making out what the dots meant in actually became nearly impossible by the time lunch was served. I was watching the flickering light produced by the flames of the woodstove when the alarm sounded on the computer that it was time to change the battery. I took a last look around at the windows and furniture, which by now I could relate to by their particular shapes of dots and clicked off the machine. The whirring stopped, and the darkness closed in. I instinctively glanced in the direction of the door exiting the large rec room and then realized—yes, now I have to once again feel for the wall first for orientation. Only an hour remained before Lorri's students and their respective families would show up for the recital, and this was a good time to decide whether or not to leave the system hidden in the bedroom and just attend the function as I had the past several years—in the dark, moving slowly among the crowd so as not to rudely bump into anyone, asking my kids to fill my plate of refreshments because, after all, it wouldn't have been polite to feel around for food destined for everyone to eat. I went back to the kitchen where I'd left the suitcase and got out another battery.

"You are wearing it during the recital?"

"Yeah, I figure it would make life easier." I didn't need to mention that the darkness during the battery change had already made up my mind.

"That'll make the students' parents who gave money for this really happy."

I hadn't yet thought of that, but she was right. Everyone had tried to help out—Bill Summer's family had our two youngest kids for the eighteen days we were in Portugal, and many of the students' parents had given some money for the payment of this contraption. I owed it to them.

Ryan was watching as I plugged in the battery charger for the now-exhausted battery of the system. He looked it over and said, "This thing has a light that shows when the battery is charged, and another one for when it's charging." Then he added, "Can you see them?"

Lights on equipment was no longer a thing in my life and hadn't been since I remembered looking at my first CB radio when I was sixteen, its little red "transmit" light and its shiny little signal strength meter giving off a pretty glow, especially at night with the lights out. Now it was all just sound, and I often spent time thinking of how lonely life would be if that, too, one day quit as had my sight.

"I don't know . . ." I picked up the charger and held the surface where the lights were just millimeters from my camera of the glasses and saw a display of one lonely phosphene. I had to cup my hands over the charger to prevent other light from hitting the camera.

"Yup." I hadn't expected this. It was a bonus.

I helped the rest of the family move all chairs and sofas over to the rec room, finding the task physically more difficult because of the bulk of the equipment about my waist, yet, for the first time in years, I could aim for the doorway even though both hands were occupied carrying the chairs. It felt good to have this control. By now, the incessant flashing of the seven-frames-per-minute stimulator output had become background noise to me; it seemed my vision was getting to ignore the times there was no output and just concentrated on the times that there was. I could actually participate in the layout of the furniture of the room, noticing where the piano was in relation to the groups of chairs. The floor in the rec room had no design, and the walls were barren white, providing good contrast for any objects within. From any distance of more than ten feet, the chairs just resembled blobs of dots, but these were not there if there were no chairs, and any tables or larger objects actually looked a little like their real shape.

The students started to arrive, and I started to feel self-conscious about the equipment again. I pulled down my sweatshirt to make sure it was covering everything as well as roughing up my hair so as to make a better disguise over the wires. Some of the students had an idea what I was in for while in Portugal, others had started with Lorri for the first time the past September and knew nothing. There wasn't much time to explain the events of the past couple of years with everyone, but my most used single-sentence explanation went something like:

"I'm trying out this new artificial vision system to see if it can help a blind person . . ."

Bill Summers arrived with his family and seemed happy to see me with the system. I had to raise my shirt for them to see the entire system, then Bill asked, "What all can you see? Like, can you see my fingers?"

He raised up his arm, and I saw a couple dots raising up in my visual field, but there was no way I could have seen how many fingers he was holding up. His hand was represented by only a single dot.

"I wouldn't be able to count your fingers unless I was really close—like a few inches away." The idea hit me then that if it was possible somehow to change the magnification on the fly, I could have counted the fingers once locating the hand without having to move up close. I'd have to make note of that and discuss it with Bill.

One by one, the students presented their numbers for the recital. I was sitting near the front of the group of chairs when I heard a child behind me whisper, "Wow . . . see those wires coming out of his head?"

The hair really didn't cover up enough for my liking. We really need to work on a system that doesn't use wires.

It came to my turn to play a song. The usual routine was that Lorri would introduce me and then come to help me to the piano. I knew the direction of the piano by its sound, the layout of the room, and normally I'd just go up and not be worried about veering off course a bit as it was my house, but when I was among these students, I'd rather not look clumsy, so Lorri would assist me as much as she could not to look too much in control at the same time. But today was different—the dark wood of the piano and bench was starkly contrasting with the white wall, and I could make out the section of the keyboard from where I sat. I got up and walked over to it, scanning for the location of the bench which, too, was visible beyond guessing. I took my place on my left as Lorri sat down beside me. I glanced down to my right and saw the telltale dots of light telling me she'd placed her hands on the piano and was ready to start our duet. I didn't even have to ask her if she was ready as I normally would in this situation. I couldn't see more than a row of phosphenes for making out the keyboard—it was all feel and touch to orient myself to the keys—but it was great to see even this much—the bottom row of dots in my visual field lighting up as I moved my hands about on the keys. This was reality.

Following the performing of our pieces, everyone moved over to the ping-pong table we had set up against the wall opposite the piano. I could see its outline from where I was sitting, but now it was obscured by all the people around it. As the people cleared a bit, I walked, watching for the chairs in my way. My cane was folded up in my hand as in this room—light plain concrete floor with white walls—I could see far more than I could in the other rooms with various designs and color patterns making up the decor. Once at the table, I could make out the various plates set randomly, yet had no idea what was on them. Rather than asking for help, I just took a pair of tongs and selected some of every plate and accepted what I had.

It was before five as the light from the windows became less and less visible that the battery once again ran out of juice. No contemplation this time—I wanted to see what this thing could do at night. By now my head was throbbing from the stress of seeing again—I guessed—it could have been from the electrical bombardment coming from the electrodes, but I wasn't going to give up. Taking a flashlight and turning on the outside light of the house, I went out into the cold winter night. Looking around, I could see the light coming from the neighbor's house on the other side of the street. I could walk over there now, if I wanted to without getting lost, and find my way back as well as I could see our light just as clearly. Walking back in the yard, I could see nothing as it was not lit. Using the flashlight, I found it difficult to coordinate the beam from it and have the camera pointed in the right direction as well. I finally succeeded to shine the beam on the top of the shed roof at the same time as looking at it—the camera of my glasses was only using a narrow field of vision to coincide with the limited amount of phosphenes I had. What I succeeded in seeing was that the shed was actually much higher than was the house—even though I'd been on it several times to repair the roof, I still hadn't a good perspective of its height until now.

The month of December was one of light and happiness, despite the throbbing headache that every day of using the system left me with. I had the rec room set up with new phone lines and bought a new computer so I could start my new job with the Dobelle Institute. This job was going to be interesting—it would be impossible to find boring, considering the merits and success of the artificial vision project. Representing this initiative in a positive light was going to be a breeze and come perfectly naturally to me. Or so I thought.

I talked to Bill a few times per day about the plans of the future.

"We're going up to Portugal around the middle of January," he informed me. "We have a patient—the first diabetic patient—who wants the system, and we're going to have a host of press agencies up there to deal with. You're going to be busy showing it off, explaining it, and helping Karen, our new patient, get informed about everything. Moreover, Klaus will be there to get fitted with his system, and I need you to translate."

"More press should be a good thing this time," I thought. No having to fake something that doesn't work and no more having to talk highly of a project that was in the charge of a couple of young, inexperienced engineers. I was not so confident about Bill's physical stamina holding out for such a strenuous assignment, yet with Dr. Dyre, Tony Martins, Don Keefer, and Jesse's knowledge on the software, all will be under control nonetheless.

"Oh, I can't wait to show this thing off. It's really working great—I can see a bit more every day from practicing."

"Good. Just remember, in February, before going back to Canada after the trip, you and Jerry are going to show the system off to Morley Safer from *60 Minutes.*"

Jerry was the oldest patient we had—he had the operation just the day after I left back for Canada in April 2002. He had said he never had a headache in his life, and we figured this time he'd have one for sure. I made a note of calling him to see how he was doing.

I talked to Karen that week to give her a taste of what she was in for. Karen was a special case for Dobelle as she had diabetes, and Bill was concerned that this would lead to problems of infection or healing, which could be complicated and result in the removal of the electrodes if not resolved. I shuddered at the thought of having to have the head opened a second time within the same month just to remove the electrodes. Despite the success of this system, I was far from ready to get a new system of electrodes should there be one as I just couldn't stand another brain operation. At the same time, as we worried about Karen's possible complications, success would mark a milestone as a large number of prospective patients had diabetes—a health problem often leading to total blindness after reaching adulthood. These people wanted to see again really bad.

I had nothing but good to say about the system to Karen. Yet, I reminded her, it will not be like in some of the letters I had received from Dobelle—the idea of recognizing faces was just too far from the truth, I told her. I recounted some of the things I could do now and see now, and she became more convinced this was what she wanted, and we both hoped it would be successful.

I decided to call Jerry down in Louisiana to see how things were going for him.

"How did the operation go for you? I left for Canada the day before you were slated to go under," I started out the conversation.

"I was OK. I didn't really have much pain, but for the first time, I had a headache in my life from the first time they tested me." He recounted how he had been tested five days after the operation, then as he went back to his hotel room, he suddenly got a splitting headache for a few hours. "But I could see thirty-seven good phosphenes, so Bill figures it's a success."

I thought about how I had ninety-six, and how I'd feel ripped off if I only had thirty-seven as it would be hard to make a good picture from that.

"What are you doing with it?" I wondered if he was getting something out of all this expenditure of time, health, and cash.

"Yeah, I am. Every afternoon I strap it on and use up one battery charge—about four hours of use. I go outside and usually go for a two-hour walk, then stop at the Legion and have a beer or two before heading back home. I find in some places I can look down where the grass and sidewalk meet and walk without using my cane. And for the first time I notice trees when I walk along the park route—I can see their trunks from about six feet or so."

I could see trees from further away—his magnification must be set wrong. He continued, "But what I like most about having this thing is looking at the small ceramic Christmas tree I have. It has lights and decor, and it just makes those phosphenes dance and sparkle. Really pretty."

I told Jerry about the things I have been doing here, but I said nothing about working for Dobelle as I didn't want him to think I was treated any different from the other patients. I was satisfied he was doing good with his system—it was going to be fun at Morley Safer's interview. Or so I thought.

On December 9, I got up in the morning as usual and strapped on the machine only to find I could not see all the phosphenes. I had fatigue around my eyes and a headache, and then wondered if this system was not a step backward from the first volunteer's original system—Dobelle himself had said in his Journal 2000 that every morning the patient himself needed to adjust his thresholds for each electrodes before using the system. "The values of thresholds can vary as much as 25 percent from day to day," he had said after years of experimentation. Yet this system had an on–off switch and nothing more. I discussed this with Tony.

"Hang on, we're working on the design of the new system, and it will have these adjustments. Can you think of any others?"

I replied I'd make a list this month and send it to him via fax. I felt better that this was the problem surrounding the disappearance of the electrodes—tomorrow some of the lost ones would return and others may be gone, but the idea that I was going to eventually lose all the phosphenes was not one I could stand to think about at this time. This was just too good to go away now. Losing my sight in one eye, then the other, and a third time when attempted repairs were made on the first eye was more than enough of a loss—losing phosphenes permanently at this stage of the experiment would be like losing sight all over again. The thought was unthinkable, yet that situation would be all too familiar just the same. For nineteen years following the last eye operation I had at St. Michael's Hospital on September 14, 1984, the curse against my sight was in its full glory. But now, there was something to lose once again.

Lorri had a day off during the week, and we decided to go into town for lunch. I was glad to see that the following day of the loss of the phosphenes, I had regained them. I hadn't been drinking coffee that morning and associated this with the change of phosphenes and reported this to Tony right away. Then, leaving for town, I looked out the side window and saw a few shadows of things passing by. I tried to compensate for the speed of the vehicle so the camera would be able to pick up at least a couple of frames looking out of the side window. This allowed me to see where there were trees, and at times, I could make out a house. Where there was nothing, there was obviously a field, although it could have been a large parking lot or lake for that matter—but it was nice to see some things and point them out, asking Lorri about more details of what I was looking at.

Arriving at the restaurant, I was about to open my door when I noticed the shape of a car very close to me, and without further thought only opened my door a crack to squeeze out so as to keep from damaging the car with my door. Once out, I was about to call Lorri to see where she was heading when I realized I could see her moving about—a blob of a few phosphenes with moving dots where her arms and legs were—and followed her to the door, which soon became outlined against the wall. Before entering, I scanned the building, getting a picture of the rough shape of the building that I had imagined a little different all these years before. We entered, no longer worrying about the looks of my wires coming out of my head as I looked around for an empty table. I could make out the tables, their location with respect to the windows of the building, but was not sure if they were yet occupied.

"That one next to the one in front of you," Lorri said as I saw it and pointed to it.

"That one?"

"Yup." It was just about like old times, the time we were stopping our bikes at the restaurants and taking our coffee and cheesecake breaks, our lives ahead of us filled with the promise of adventure and beauty. Lorri just seemed to accept my newfound vision as if I had had it all along—never slipping once by forgetting that I now could see. Life was only going to get better. Or so I thought.

The waitress came over to our table as I saw her group of dots advancing, identifying her as she spoke from her voice. She spoke briefly and disappeared. I was about to say more to her when I noticed she had gone. Normally this situation would result in my talking to a person who was no longer there—a potentially embarrassing situation.

We ate and then sipped on our coffee. The waitress came back with a coffeepot, asking Lorri if she wanted more.

"Want more coffee?" she asked Lorri.

"Sure, I really need some today." Assuming Lorri's coffee would be filled up first, I reached out to finish off my own coffee so the waitress could fill my cup too. I stopped short of yanking my cup out from under the pouring coffee when I saw she was already filling up my own cup, avoiding a potentially messy situation. Neither the waitress nor Lorri seemed to take special notice of what happened. It just seemed like everything was the way it was supposed to be.

December 14 was a snowy day, but also a day of no work for either of us, so we decided to visit Ryan in Picton, a small town where he worked on a farm just a half hour south of Napanee. I walked up to the van, which was becoming more visible lately as I seemed to be getting more used to the phosphenes and the patterns created by certain objects. I still only had the ninety-five or so phosphenes to work with but learned that if I used the scattered groups of dots in my visual field to a higher advantage, by slightly altering the position of the glasses while looking at an object, I could use the next frame display to see a different part of the same object, therefore learning to paste the differing images together and forming a larger overall picture. A faster frame speed would have greatly improved this method of observing details, so I made note of it to tell Tony next time we spoke. We pulled out of the driveway and headed out of town, the moving objects on the side of the road more visible lately as I looked for the trees, houses, and the railing of the approaching bridge. This was a lot better than sitting in the dark. I could see approaching cars a second before they zoomed past us and could make out the signs of a tailgater in the rearview mirror.

We arrived at the farm where Ryan worked; already it was late afternoon. We spoke with his friends and boss, the blobs of moving phosphenes representing human beings, but yet easier to talk to than just a void. I could stray from the house where Ryan stayed and explore, seeing the trees that by now took on a special shape and became easier to recognize. I could always see the house behind me; I couldn't get lost anymore.

We wanted some refreshments, so Lorri and I decided to visit the corner store just a minute's drive away. I could see the dashboard lights out of my left side.

"I guess it's getting dark."

"Yeah, can you still see anything? I looked around and saw more than I had all day. The Becker's sign of the corner store was bright and obvious, although I could only make out the shape of the first letter's left side from this distance. Cars were driving around with their headlights and taillights clearly visible. We left the van and walked to the store, holding hands because we wanted to—not because I needed to be guided. Just like the old times were coming back. This couldn't be taken away from me now.

The snow had stopped falling as we headed back in the night. Snowplows had pushed the snow to the side, spreading salt on the highway, which melted any remaining snow. I looked at the taillights of the car in front of us as Lorri drove, the white snowbanks on the side providing stark contrast to the road. If we could have driven slower, I was sure I could have driven and even kept in my lane as the dotted line in the center was visible up to two dots in front of the van. I couldn't help thinking that just maybe I'd get the next system with the five hundred electrodes, if I could get over the fear of opening up the head just one more time, and if the system could be designed without jacks in the head.

It was December 17 when I noticed that something was going wrong. I got up in the morning and as usual strapped on the machine, but to my dismay only saw about a quarter of the phosphenes. There was a nagging slight zapping sensation in my right eye with every frame the system displayed, but this sensation was not associated with any phosphene. The family was getting ready for the day's events—school for the kids and work for Lorri. I could not tell them what was going on. I'd have to discuss this with Dr. Dobelle—hoping he'd be able to come up with something—maybe Dr. Dyre, as neither Tony nor Don would be able to help as the machine was working normally. Maybe if I had adjustable phosphenes, it would be avoided, but the truth remained that I could already feel the current, and cranking it up any further would only result in pain. With only some of the phosphenes working, I did not see much—I could scan the tabletop and find my coffee mug only represented by one or two dots.

As the first hour progressed, the phosphenes began to appear one by one until I could once again see as I should. Relieved, I spun around the mug on the table and found to my surprise that for the first time I could tell where the handle was from an arm's length distance. Forgetting about the morning's problems, I went about the house and saw the newly erected Christmas tree—its lights and tinsel producing a rewarding barrage of phosphenes I could detect from the other side of the house.

December 18 started out with seeing none but one or two phosphenes. I was near a state of panic when I remembered yesterday and just settled down and waited, praying this would pass and all will be well. I said nothing to the family, although they must have noticed my subdued mood. Luckily, it took only a few minutes before some of the other phosphenes appeared, and within an hour all was well. That's when I decided to give my friend Jerry a call.

I dialed the number and said the usual greetings, then got to the meat of the conversation.

"How is your system working now?" I had to ask without first talking about mine and its problems.

"Well, now that you ask," he started, looking for a good way to explain. He was quite old—seventy-nine years, but he was just as sharp as a college student, "I have been noticing few phosphenes lighting up when looking at the same Christmas tree, or even when looking at the curtains with the sun shining through them. I seem to be missing some as I can remember them all and some are just not appearing."

"Even if you wait a bit, they don't appear?"

"Yeah, I wait the full four hours and still nothing changes. I follow exactly the same routine every day and now I see less." He thought a bit and added, "I figure it just needs readjusting."

"Well, you know about that interview we have with Morley," I reminded him, "I am sure Bill will have the system readjusted beforehand so it works fine during the demonstration."

"Yeah, I'm looking forward to having it readjusted. I really miss those phosphenes."

The conversation left me confused and worried. Could it be the problem—just rethreshold and all will be well? I did not really believe it in my heart although every part of me wanted to. If this was really the case, some of the phosphenes I can see would be too bright now—out of adjustment the other direction with too much voltage instead of too little. Moreover, what about the pain during stimulation? That day I took the system off early, at four thirty in the afternoon, as I needed to go to a blood donor clinic and this thing would be kind of awkward during the process.

To my pleasant surprise, the next morning I could see all the phosphenes right away. Maybe this was the problem, I don't know.

"Wow, I can actually see all the phosphenes right away this morning," I said to Lorri as we had our coffee.

"What, you couldn't the other mornings?"

"Just lately now. It took an hour or so before I could, but last night, I took it off before supper, and this morning it is good."

"Mmmm, but you see so much at night with the electric lighting and all that. You will always take it off at night now?"

I then remembered that Jerry, too, was losing phosphenes and he had been using his system for only four hours a day. I wanted this thing all day, every day, and did not want to be in the dark anymore.

The week before Christmas was always an exciting one since we made last-minute shopping trips for the kids' presents, and Lorri would receive tokens of appreciation from her students. My system worked more or less fine—even though there was the usual delay in the morning before seeing all the phosphenes, but as the day progressed, I'd be seeing just like I should. One of the presents Lorri received from a student was a shiny brass candleholder with a long curvy stand. I waited the usual way as I heard the wrapper get removed, waiting my turn for Lorri to hand it to me afterward so I could inspect it. However, when I glanced over at the jumble of moving dots I could now use to distinguish Lorri and her package from the background, I found myself looking at the candleholder with almost perfect form—the shiny surface was what the camera liked to give me a dancing and sparkling image of the brass surface. I'd been so used to not being able to see that I almost forgot to look.

On December 21, Lorri announced that she was invited to a Christmas staff party for her colleagues. It was going to start at 7:00 p.m. and probably go on for quite some time afterward. I had vowed to disconnect the system every early evening just to preserve my phosphenes, but since talking to Jerry, I was no longer sure if I was doing the right thing. For the first time, I started wondering if I was going to lose the phosphenes no matter what, so may as well use them before they were all gone . . . I could not think much more on this—Christmas was around the corner, the world was beautiful, and we needed to get to this party. I packed an extra battery and watched as the houses decorated with Christmas lights went by us as we drove to the house where the party was.

"Is that where the door is?" I pointed at the light coming from the house, noticing the part of the doorframe lit by the porch light.

"Yup," replied Lorri, "brace yourself as everyone will want to see your new gadget."

We entered the house, and I looked around. There was a table on my right and a couple couches, a doorway to another room on the left. Sure enough, a lot of people, who had known about this system since my fund-raising efforts in year 2000, looked the components over carefully and asked, "Is it what you wanted?"

"It's not as detailed as I would like the image to be," I explained, then pointed out the obvious, "but it sure is good. I really need to get out of the dark for quite a while, and this provides relief, that's for sure." I walked over to the refreshment table and tried some without needing any help.

The night went on, and we all had fun—I could walk around the house and not worry about bumping into the furniture, being able to spot couches and chairs in other rooms as I now could see them. The phosphenes all seemed to work, or at least most of them, and the image was good. I still had the system on as we drove home, the white dotted line of the road blinking, the dashboard lights lighting the phosphenes of my bottom left side, the Christmas lights on the houses looking as pretty as could be. The battery died just as we pulled into the driveway. My head hurt, but it had been worth it.

Throughout the entire Christmas holidays, I had no work—everyone had gone home for the season at the Dobelle Institute, and I was free to experiment. The phosphene situation, although rough first thing in the morning, seemed to be stable and not get any worse. I felt as though I was participating fully in the festivities, being able to see the movements of the kids, the beauty of the tree, the decorations, and when we got out the traditional sparklers, I could even light my own as the flame of a match was clearly visible, and the sparklers themselves provoked a dazzling display of phosphenes. I found myself getting better at using the blob of closely spaced small phosphenes on my left bottom side to make out more detail. I had, at the start of December, written large letters on blank paper and had little luck reading them, but now I could read with moderate success letters four inches in height. "If I had variable magnification," I thought, "I'd be able to read smaller letters as well."

I found myself regretting the day we had to toss out the tree that was losing all of its needles by the time January hit.

"There's always next year," Lorri had said, but something nagged in my head that did not believe it fully.

"Hopefully," I couldn't help saying.

January 9, 2003, only worsened my suspicions. I could not get the phosphenes to appear—only a few made it out, and the situation did not improve much during the day; a couple of hours later, I still only had twenty or so. Just four days prior, Janyce McGregor's *Out of the Dark* was aired on CBC TV, but I did not watch it—I was just too worried about the situation at hand. However, Bill Dobelle heard about it and wasted no time calling me.

"Look, Jens," he started in an annoyed voice. "I heard about this CBC thing on the vision system. I did not authorize you to do this!"

"Bill," I really didn't want to be fired only a month into this job, "This had been filmed long before I started to work for you. It was a part of our fund-raising effort from two years ago."

"I don't care what it was." He didn't seem to comprehend what I said, "I want you to ask me before any such newscast is made, is that clear?"

What was I to say, I asked myself. But CBC was the only news agency that had filmed me and not yet aired its program until now, so this really wasn't going to happen again.

"OK, Bill, sorry." It was ridiculous to say this, but I wasn't talking with a normal person; one has to accommodate a genius in such times normally deemed to rationalization.

"Bill, the phosphenes are disappearing rapidly. Today I can only see a few, that's all."

Bill didn't even take the time to think about it. "Yeah, we haven't adjusted it yet, so just unhook it and bring it down with you next week, and we'll work on it in Portugal. We'll tweak it up, then you got work to do."

He explained how I had to show the system first to Karen and her husband, then to another prospective patient from Argentina who had already paid in full the $100,000 for the system. I hoped all would go well. All of me wanted to believe just adjusting the system would solve everything.

Before Bill hung up, he had a couple of tasks for me.

"Right now we are fitting a few of the American patients with their systems before heading out to Portugal. We have one guy here we implanted in October—John M., who is right now in his hotel room, quite dissatisfied with the outcome of his system." Bill went on, "I don't know his problem—he has over 110 phosphenes, all small and evenly spread over his visual field—in other words, a lot better than yours, and he claims he can't see anything."

"Well, I couldn't either at first," I said, adding how I could only see the handle of my coffee mug a couple weeks after using the system every day, "so I'll talk to him."

"Good," said Bill. "I also want you to write a manual for the system and have it ready for when you come down. But," he reminded me, "make sure you don't give out any secrets on how it works for other researchers to gain from."

Great, I thought, write a manual for a machine that has only an on–off switch, and don't get into details so other's can't copy the idea.

But first I was to call John, who was unhappy at present with his system, just like I was when I received it—the promise to see faces and detailed images quickly reduced to one of seeing flickering dots of light attempting to resemble the object seen. I understood this feeling and hoped John would give it time.

"For the love of me, Jens, there is no way I can tell the difference between a bottle, a cup, or a book on the table." John sounded frustrated as he continued, "I put a lot of money into this, went through the hassle of the operation, and all I see is a group of dots, no matter what I look at."

"You just got the system, John," I reminded him, "I couldn't see more than a glob of dots for the first three days, and then I finally could see my arm moving around in front of my face. Give it time, use the system lots, and don't expect too much right away."

"What can you see now?"

"I can now see that there is a handle on the side of a cup, that there is a definite difference between a plate, fork, and cup, and that a bottle is tall and thin and outside—well, that's where the system shines. There, you can't reach out and touch the roof of your neighbor's house, or the top of a tree, so anything you see with this thing is a bonus."

John asked more questions, mostly about the progress of my learning to use the system, and then admitted he may be expecting too much. I hoped he'd be happy to have more phosphenes than I had. I bade him good-bye, not knowing if he'd actually practice with the machine or just leave it in a box and forget about it.

I decided to call another patient, Kieth, who had been implanted at the same time that I was in April 2002. Kieth had been one of the very disappointed patients in Manhattan—yet, like all of us patients, had maintained his cool enough not to blurt everything out to the press who would have just loved to hear about the internal problems of the Dobelle Institute's research project. It was Kieth who answered the phone.

"Have you had any luck with your system?" This question left room for a one-word answer if he didn't.

"Yeah, I guess so." Kieth sounded tired. "I use it every day, but so far can't get outside because the weather's rather bad here. But I can see the cup, fork, and plate on the table when it's set, and often sit in front of the TV and see some of the motion on it."

"Any problems with phosphenes?"

"Yeah, I have large, sometimes too-dim-to-see phosphenes in the morning when first starting up." Kieth said. "But I sure look forward to a system we can adjust on our own."

I had to ask, "Is this thing making your life any better?"

"Yeah," he admitted, "it is better than being in the dark, that's for sure."

Richie came up the following week with the limo, and I climbed in, with the system secure in my suitcase. I had been using it after talking to Bill—on the day after some of the phosphenes had recovered and I could more or less use the system with a degraded image. Back at home, we were all concerned but also were confident that all we needed was to readjust the thresholds.

I thought some on the last telephone call I had made to John just prior to leaving. I figured on checking up on his progress, but he was madder than ever.

"This thing is just not giving any definition whatsoever. Neither inside or out. I think that Dr. Dyre who mapped me did it all wrong. Moreover," he had added, "they had two days of just fooling around with equipment problems before I even got tested. I really don't like this monkey-business setup."

I hadn't the heart to tell him that I already had a few weeks of equipment problems while being down there. I would have to talk this over with Bill, if it was possible.

I entered the office where everyone was gearing up for the trip. I was wearing jeans and a T-shirt for comfort on the trip.

"Jens," Bill said, looking me over from his seat in the wheelchair, "you have better clothes with you?"

"Yeah, my suitcase has some brand-new pants and button shirts just for the press appearances."

"Good," Bill retorted. "Claire also bought me a couple new shirts." Then he went on, "I want you to wear the system during the flight—we won't have problems at customs as this is a medical device."

I was suddenly speechless. To enter Kennedy International so fresh after what happened on September 11, 2001, with this thing strapped about my waist, was just like strapping a bull's eye target to my shirt.

"Bill," I protested, "this thing looks like a bomb. They aren't going to let me in, let alone on the plane." I heard Pat muttering something about possibly being shot on sight.

I didn't know what else to say. Bill spoke no more of it as if my protest went unnoticed. I worried all night long about this in the hotel room, getting very little sleep as I imagined spending the rest of my life in that USA concentration camp in Cuba—people were there who claimed to have no substantial evidence against them, and I was certainly going to have more than that against me. It was a toss-up, I decided against having this job or going back to my home business. But wait, if I quit, I probably would be put on the back burner regarding my vision system—Bill just wouldn't include me in the updates, or analyze my problems with the system after that. I felt trapped—my sight at stake.

Pat picked me up in the morning, and I couldn't help bringing up the subject of my worries.

"He actually thinks I should wear that system in the airport."

"I talked to him this morning driving him to work. I told him he was nuts."

"Thanks, Pat," I thought, "I need that help."

"You can leave the system with Don, and he'll pack it in the case with the other systems for Karen and Klaus," Bill informed me as I entered and greeted him. I was relieved. I'd make it to Portugal after all.

"Did you finish the manual for the system like I had asked?"

I reached into my briefcase and pulled out the twelve typed, single-spaced pages. Bill looked it over without reading a word.

"Is this all?" He seemed disgusted. I had actually written the manual twice as the first time I only came up with five pages.

"I still have to put in the diagrams . . ." I replied, wondering from how many angles one can take a picture of a single rocker switch—the only control on the machine.

Quickly, I brought up the subject of John.

"Bill, I phoned John just before leaving. He's upset that he still has no definition and figures the mapping was not done right."

"Don't worry about it, Jens," drawled Bill. "John is just a chronic complainer. Nothing can get him happy."

I wondered how he'd have made it through the psychological examination prior to acceptance for this project. It may have all been in the $100,000 check that mattered or, perhaps, John did all he could to get in the project with the thought that all will be fine once it is done.

It was five of us going—Bill, Tony, Don, Dr. Dyre, and myself. Bill distributed a list of the news agencies he had invited to come to Portugal to see the system work, principally by my demonstrations, as well as the procedure of Karen's implantation. There were over a dozen interested agencies, from Germany to France to London, all the way around the world. Everyone wanted a piece of the pie following the CNN clip of me driving the car in Manhattan.

I was in the dark again for a few days during the trip to New York, then during the hassle of getting out and during the flight. I would have liked to have had the system, but the system needed adjustment, which was only going to be done in Portugal. According to the USA laws, Bill was not allowed to do any testing or adjusting on patients while in the USA. The FDA had made it clear to him shortly after *Wired* run their article about what happened in his Commack office. I had been in the dark long enough to wait this one out, and after all, it would have been impossible to use the system in the airport/airplane, considering security issues. I thought about the conversation I had had with Klaus before Richie came to get me. My responsibility was to arrange all the flight and accommodations as we spoke the same language.

Klaus's first question was: "So is this actually going to work this time?" He sounded suspicious. "I say that because last time in Manhattan, we were paraded around just to give glamour to Bill's cause, but he had nothing ready for us to take home. I was very mad about that. I have work to do and things to do, and I cannot just go to his functions for his own agenda. I want my system, and if it isn't ready, don't waste my time."

I assured Klaus that the system was ready, that I already had mine, and that he was going to be happy. At least, I hoped he'd be happy. But we had two extra systems if one didn't work, I assured him, so surely he'd bring one home with him.

Portugal was beautiful as ever—the cold of Canada left behind as a light jacket was all one needed here in the middle of winter—the people chattering in their language that I regretted not being able to understand. "I'd have to learn it soon," I thought. "If this job from Dobelle pans out, maybe we'll all move over here. Portugal always had good food and wine, and a pleasant atmosphere in Lisbon—my home for the next three weeks."

The first day in the office in Lisbon, where I had once sat with Lorri talking to the big chief Dobelle for the first time, I now oriented myself as an employee. It had seven rooms in total, the largest of which was used for testing. Two large tables in the center of the room held the equipment for Klaus, Karen, Ken—a patient from England also coming there for set-up—and an extra system just in case one blew. Near the end of the day, I mentioned that the next day I'd have to demonstrate my system to Karen and to the prospective patient from Argentina, so hurriedly, Tony and Don increased the multipliers by 10 percent, which meant all pulses would be 10 percent higher than present. I hoped it would work.

Bill met us in the lobby of the hotel the next day as he was being pushed around in his chair by Sheila, the secretary for the Portuguese office since hired following the April 2002 operations. Sheila could speak Portuguese, Spanish, and English and was always there to help out either with Bill or with us, organizing the mess of journalists as best as she could for the days to come. The patient to meet first was the man from Argentina—he could already see light and could locate a window but was devastated by going blind and not seeing the whole world. I heard him walk into the lobby.

"It's him and his father and brother, I think," whispered Tony to inform me. The patient was about forty years old guided by his father who spoke briefly to Tony, as Tony was translating, then came to me.

"They want to see the machine. Just stand up and I'll explain," Tony said.

I stood up and opened my light jacket, which had been hiding the equipment. Hands reached out as the patient felt the boxes, then withdrew suddenly and made a sound as if he was shocked. His father urged him to feel up where my head was, and he touched the cable and jack in a manner that appeared to disgust him. There was no further inspection of the equipment.

"His father wants to know what you see now," Tony asked me after chattering to him. I had turned on the machine and braced myself for the new voltage settings, which smarted, and still I couldn't see all the phosphenes. I looked around and saw a light above me, a window in the distance and the outline of the table with its light-colored tablecloth in front of me.

"He said he can already see these things like light from the window and light from the electric lamps," Tony translated to Bill. Tony kept talking to the men as the blind man sobbed quietly from his chair at the table.

"Is he all right?" Bill said to Tony, pointing at the man who was beyond disappointed.

"Well," said Tony, "they said they had to ask family, friends, and sell a lot of properties in order to come up with this money. They need it back."

I knew about properties in Argentina—the salaries and prices are very different there—a property that could render a few hundred thousand dollars in the USA would only bring ten thousand dollars in the pocket over there in Argentina. For them to pay a hundred thousand would be like us paying a million or more.

"What's wrong?" demanded Bill. "What's wrong with the system?"

"They don't like the size and the looks. It's worse than being blind to walk around looking like this." Tony motioned to me. "They expected something much different and expected it to render sight that was like seeing before losing eyesight." Tony spoke to the father, who produced a picture of an artificial vision device illustrated in an Argentinian science magazine. There was a cutaway picture of a vision system with wires coming from glasses, going to a box similar in size to a cigarette package, then a fine wire entering the back of the patient's head. Far from what we had, that was for sure.

"Well, I'm sorry, but we never issued this picture," Bill said.

"They want to know when they can get their money back."

"Only $65,000 will be refunded. They can talk to Sheila who will make bank draft arrangements." Then Bill added, "The first $35,000 was already spent on developing and building the system for him to take home. We can't refund that as it is already used."

Bill had no choice in this matter as he did already spend probably more than that, according to my estimations, and having people hop on board without being able to tailor their expectations to that deemed a research project was going to cost them money. We had no idea why the patient's family didn't use the information given by Bill, describing the system, the jacks coming from my head, and all that was already shown by *Wired* and CNN, to name a few.

The patient group murmured quietly among themselves, then left without saying good-bye. It was hard being blind—and now, on top of that, they just lost $35,000, with nothing to show for it. I lost my appetite for supper that night. "Did I really look that bad?" I asked myself as I recalled what they had said about my system.

The following afternoon we found ourselves once again waiting in the lobby of the Marques de Pombal hotel, this time for Karen and her husband to show up and show the equipment. I was considerably more nervous, although I had already spoken to Karen previously in conference with Dr. Dyre so she shouldn't be quite as shocked about everything. I left the machine on for a bit, so I could get a few more phosphenes to work, and found that most of them were now working, some too bright however, as they wanted to stay on even though stimulation had stopped for that phosphene. I really needed it adjusted.

Karen appeared and embraced us all, a warm, friendly, and upbeat American who wasn't about to cry. We talked some as they shook Bill's hand—I thought they really thought highly of Bill as I did at first as well. As the great inventor looked on from his wheelchair, I unzipped my coat and revealed the equipment, with Karen's hands inspecting every component carefully. I watched and listened for her reaction—for the first time not taking for granted that a blind person would automatically accept it. I was learning more than ever that the onset of blindness affected every individual in its own unique manner; some would strengthen from it and others yet were forced to their knees. I wasn't sure where I stood on that scale—it would take others to tell me that.

"Just for now," I said, turning to Bill. "Bill's got a smaller one already in the making, right, Bill?" Bill grunted his approval, and Karen reached up to the jacks.

"Do they hurt?"

"Not now," I said, "but they itch at times. It's a little tender around the outside, and so far there's always something coming out of the junction. But I can sleep on it with a minimum of discomfort."

Karen sat down beside me, and I watched her as she spoke. Many times I saw her hand reach up and make gestures.

"Wow, you sure move your arms about when you talk," I said.

"You can see that?" She sounded very excited. She was sold on the equipment.

The following Monday was a confusion of journalists who all came to film the same thing—the cutting-edge technology of the Dobelle Institute with all the gadgets as well as the demonstrations from a blind person already fitted with the system, along with the shots of Karen's surgery and then the complex work of the engineers. We ate breakfast together in the lobby of the hotel as individually the cameramen and directors talked with me to plan our filming strategy. I was just as interested in making this a success as they were. But I couldn't make the major decisions; it was in the master's hands, I said as I motioned over to where Bill sat, relaxed in his wheelchair, munching on a cheese omelet, the insides of which dripped and stained the front of one of the new shirts Claire had just bought for him. One of the journalists was the correspondent of DZF, a TV station from Germany. Katherine, as she was called, spoke to me in German as I told her the bad news.

"I talked to Bill about you, and he is angry you came without asking him." She had tagged along with Klaus, a friend of his, not realizing the personality challenges of Bill.

Klaus sat beside her, already having heard about the sudden problems with Bill, feeling implicated and regretting having brought her out there.

"I thought he'd be glad I was coming." Katherine was concerned as she had bought over two crew members and was spending quite a bit of money. "Why would he mind anyways? I want to portray this as a good thing—not in any bad light whatsoever no matter how many difficulties you have."

"I'll talk to Bill," I told her. She already had told me earlier that she was afraid of confronting him.

I approached the man, who, by now, had a few people around him. They, all, were trying to deal with him as best as they could, trying to stay a lot more humble than I knew they really meant to be.

"Bill, Katherine from DZF is very sincere in portraying this vision quest in the best of light. She really understands well the possible complications, etc., and promises to cooperate fully. Can she stay and participate?" Then I added for good measure, "She's really afraid of having to go home and not being able to report on the vision breakthrough for all of Germany to see."

Bill must have changed his mood as he relented his stubborn stance. "All right, tell her she can do this show provided it is under my terms. I will tell her when she can film, which will start today."

I went over to her and conveyed the news. "I got the grouch to change his mind." Having to add some humor to the situation, I continued, "He's saying he'll be happy to let you film but only under his conditions, which he tells all of the reporters here, by the way."

She was elated and went over to Bill, spoke a few words of gratitude she knew in English, and shook Bill's hand, which was sticky from the breakfast.

I was back in the office with the team, reporters filing in as I tried out the system, and a few of the cameramen stopped to film me putting it on.

"Can you do that again?" I connected and disconnected the jacks from my head, a routine that had them especially mesmerized, several times as they changed angles and batteries in their cameras, cameras, and other gadgets as and all the while I had a few microphones stuck under my shirt.

"Now, to make it work, we hit this switch . . ." I revealed the switch and clicked it.

"We have to wait a few minutes for boot-up . . ." I waited as we all listened for the beeps.

"What's the processor that is inside?" one reporter asked.

"Not allowed to say," I said, knowing that to say it was a Pentium 166 would have been a joke, as even the computer I had bought along was 1.9G. I really wasn't allowed to talk about the details of the machine, and this was the easy way out.

I tried not to flinch as the first of the incessant zaps of excessive voltage hit my brain. My right eye hurt with every frame, and the phosphenes were big and splotchy while others were just barely visible after looking at an object for a small amount of time so a few frames could repeat the same phosphene.

"What do you see?" I pointed out a picture frame, which I knew was on the wall before seeing it, the edge of the table, and the window of that particular room. Then I pointed out where the lights of the cameras were—they were easy to see, with only half of the phosphenes working. All the while I worried about the phosphenes.

Bill allowed Discovery team to go out with me. Together with Tony, we drove over to the park outside of the hotel—a beautiful park with brick walkways and many flowers and benches to relax on. There was even a beer dispensary—we'd have to go there for sure.

"Look," I said to the reporter Lionel, "we haven't had the time yet to readjust my machine, and it really is working badly. Normally I can see lots, but today some dots are bright and others invisible. It's just in experimental stage, so we're going to have to keep it simple."

"Yeah, I understand," Lionel said, "what do you suggest we do?"

"Well, if Tony talks to me as I walk beside him, I can orient myself by his voice and footsteps, and you can decide whether or not to have Tony in the picture as I'll stay a little away from him."

Lionel went for that, and we did a few shots of me walking in the park, apparently looking at things that were hardly visible as some of my vital phosphenes just weren't appearing. Tony did well—walking with me and saying all he needed to keep me on track. Later we had a quick beer and returned to the office ten minutes later than Bill had allocated us time.

"Look," Bill was near shouting, "when I say be back by one, I mean it!"

Lionel was surprised by this outburst but kept his cool and pretended to be apologetic. Bill said nothing to me.

My next task was to go out with the crew from France. Bernardo, the cameraman, informed me he had a convertible just for me to drive around in Lisbon. I groaned silently and asked him to come with me to Bill.

"We saw him driving on CNN and want him to do that here," Bernardo explained. He sure got the wrong idea from CNN. Bill scrambled for an excuse.

"Well, he's got no driver's license, and his equipment is out of adjustment. It would take a day or two to rectify, and you really don't want to hang around here that long. But," he looked for a compromise, "you can sit him in the driver's seat once you park the car, as you are only taking still shots anyways, right?"

Bernardo nodded. It would be easy. I went out with them as they found a good place to park the car beside a busy roadway. They quickly got out, and I traded seats with the driver.

"Now look as if you are driving," were the instructions of Bernardo. I did as I was told, feeling very ill at ease but being a good employee. The film rolled on.

The situation did not improve the following day. Bill's mood grew grumpier, and he became more difficult to deal with as the day passed.

"Your time is up," he said harshly to a Portuguese cameraman who did not understand English, "now get out." The boss of the cameraman, a lady who had originally spoken to Bill before appearing, was in another room when she heard the shouting. The cameraman had not understood and walked by Bill to get a couple of final shots of vision equipment on display on a table.

"Get out!" Bill grabbed the pant leg of the cameraman and tugged as hard has his frail body would let him while the cameraman was as confused as ever.

"Look, he's not understanding!" his boss said to Bill. "Just let him go, and we'll go now." She spoke in Portuguese to the man, who wasted no time grabbing his equipment and getting out of that room. I quickly walked ahead to the exit of the office and met the boss.

"Sorry about what happened in there," I tried to apologize. "Bill is under a lot of stress, and sometimes he appears to becomes unreasonable. It's really a good project that can potentially help thousands of blind people, so I hope you don't have the wrong impression."

"Wow," she mused, "that poor cameraman was scared. He didn't have a clue what Bill was shouting about. But no," she assured me, "we'll treat this in stride, and we'll concentrate on the good."

A German independent crew—two men who really expected action—were next on the list of people to serve.

"I don't want the cane," one of them said as I started to follow them out of the door of the office. I left it behind, reluctantly, hoping my other senses would compensate. I did so good following them out of the building, down the elevator and all, until I forgot about the raised flower bed located just a few steps out of the office, separating the office exit from the rest of the sidewalk. I did not see it either, and just as the cameraman had turned to roll a film of me walking out of the building and in the sun, I hit that flower bed and fell smack into it.

I swore under my breath as I brushed off my hands and tried to straighten the squashed flowers. The cameraman said nothing but stared. If this wasn't a nightmare, I said to myself, then what is?

On the day before Karen's surgery, the reporters and cameramen wanted to capture her anxieties, apprehensions, and other thoughts going through her head before the big day. My task was to show her all the individual components of the computer system as the cameras rolled. She was so enthusiastic about the whole deal that I wished from the bottom of my heart that this would work for her. I made little mention of the loss of phosphenes, as I wasn't sure if this information would help her at this point. I didn't have any answers, neither did Bill or anyone. Following my demonstrations of the equipment, Dr. Domingo, Dr. Dobelle, and Karen were filmed in a room together as Domingo interviewed Karen, describing the entire surgery and assessing if she was indeed ready for this operation. A couple of cameramen were there, expecting to share their footage with the other media agencies once the filming was over. Don watched the procession through the glass window that looked into the room. I heard him silently curse.

"What's up?" I asked.

"Bill fell asleep in his chair. His head is lolling forward, and—yes, there goes a cameraman filming him." Bill was certainly stressed out, and the shingles medication didn't help matters any, and the camera crews seemed to be looking for juicy stories to film. In the meantime, Domingo and Karen kept on talking.

January 30, Klaus was on the list of people to threshold, map, and send home after some press work. Katherine had exclusively come for this event, my ability to speak German being a bonus. Tony, Don, Dr. Dyre, and I sat around the table while Klaus received instruction, translated by myself for assuring good results. We started with his one side that never had sight, and there were only two phosphenes visible. Each electrode was taken to 16 V just to make sure he couldn't see them.

His good side came next, and about five electrodes into the work, he suddenly gasped with pain.

"I can see a phosphene which isn't going away." He received this discomfort just at the 16 V mark.

We waited a bit, and then Dr. Dyre spoke, "We should stop now as this stress is more than he should get at one time."

"Keep going," overrode Bill from his chair where he was stationed beside me. Tony kept up the stimulation, Don recorded, while I recorded as a backup and kept translating.

We went through the rest of Klaus's good side, and he saw no more phosphenes, his speech slowing and his general attentiveness suffering.

Dr. Dyre spoke again, "I think he has had a small seizure with that very painful phosphene and we really need to stop."

The camera crews invited into the testing room had their cameras trained on Klaus, the engineers, and at times Bill, their microphones set to record anything spoken in the room. Klaus's son, Robert, a bright young man of nineteen years, sat a little apart but watched intently. He hadn't understood Dr. Dyre's words.

"Keep going," Bill repeated. Klaus had no more phosphenes. Just two. I checked my records from the past where in Manhattan he had had over fifty.

"Let's all take a breath and try something else after" was Bill's suggestion. Camera crews started to file out of the room, engineers shut down the equipment, and Robert came to his father's side to help him out. Klaus tried to get up, then lost his balance and hit the floor. His son, Robert, a strong young man now very scared, stuttered in his limited English, "Help . . . need a doctor . . ."

Dr. Dyre came over in a hurry and kneeling by Klaus's side looked closely and tried to comfort Klaus, who lay shuddering uncontrollably, strange noises escaping from his mouth. Some reporters were trying to get past Bill, who had been lodged with his chair in the doorway. Bill waved them back.

"What's going on in there?" asked one reporter, speaking for all. The door slammed shut.

Supported by his son on one side and Dr. Dyre on the other, a few moments later, Klaus was helped out of the building.

"Bring him to the hotel," Bill instructed. Dyre led Robert and Klaus to the hospital.

Later that night, Klaus was brought back to his hotel room. I went up to visit him.

"I hope you're better." I couldn't say more.

"That was really scary," he began recounting to me his experience, "my mouth was just blabbering, my whole body was shaking, and I could do nothing to stop it."

"I blacked right out during my seizures," I told him, "then would wake up a half hour later and not know who I was or where I was."

"It sure is frightening to lose control of one's own mind," Klaus said. "Also, I am very worried about the loss of phosphenes. I want this thing to work."

"Dr. Dyre said that you most likely had a seizure with that one phosphene that hurt and that shut the visual cortex down from seeing the others. If that's true, you'll see more tomorrow, if you're in for it."

"I sure hope so. That Dr. Dyre is a good person to have around. He knew I was in trouble, and we should have listened to him first thing."

"Yeah," I agreed. "He knows medicine. He has a medical degree."

"Yeah, so Bill does too, right?" Klaus asked.

"No, he is a doctor of biophysics. From the 1960s."

"Then he should listen to Dr. Dyre," Klaus said.

But the next day, he was ready for testing. And sure enough, he did see phosphenes. Before testing, however, Dr. Dyre, Tony, Don, and I had a meeting.

"We are going to have to be more careful," I started. "Bill's all success-focused and doesn't worry about seizures too much, but I know they're bad."

"Yeah, it can kill you under the right circumstances," Dyre said. "He's not listening to us, so what can we do?"

"Look, if you say the patient is in danger from any more stimulation, Tony and Don are just going to have to jimmy around on the computer and say they're giving out 16 V but only keep it way down."

"Good idea," we agreed.

We were careful with Klaus. Once past 10 V of stimulation, we increased the voltage little by little instead of taking that jump to sixteen. Klaus could see fifteen phosphenes in total. A far cry from fifty, I thought. We mapped what we could and sent him off with the system to experiment in the hotel corridors.

"Dr. Dobelle, what is your opinion about what happened yesterday?" One of the reporters asked during a group conference later that day.

"Well, it's really nothing. Just a minor inconvenience."

Wendy, a young woman from *60 Minutes* scouting out the situation with us, asked me to show off the machine by identifying the large plastic mannequins once used by the first volunteer Jerry, written about in Bill's famed Journal 2000. The mannequins were in a separate room: a tall one, a shorter one, and a little one. I tried my machine and only saw a few phosphenes. I had kept it off all day, hoping it would somehow solve the problem, but no dice. Wendy rearranged the mannequins for me to point out, but other than with the really tall one, I had no luck. I only saw the window.

"What's going on, Jens?" Bill was watching from the doorway.

"It's just not producing any phosphenes anymore."

"Look, Wendy, we'll adjust it in the morning, and then you can do this again. It's just that we hadn't done this yet."

That night I received a telephone call in my hotel room as did Don, Tony, and Dr. Dyre. It was Claire Dobelle, sounding upset and angry and somewhat hysterical.

"I hear that Bill is being really bad there and really difficult. I feel sorry for you guys to have to put up with him, but I cannot come over," she apologized. "So I am sending a good friend—Andy—out to help and set him straight. Andy will know what to do."

I hoped she was right. I tried to downplay Bill's stress problems. "Well, Bill has been trying to deal with lots of problems, and his health really isn't that good. He tends to fall asleep in inopportune moments. But I did talk to the press, and they assured me they are not here to cause problems or to discredit the vision project."

The next thing Claire said threw me off guard. "Jens, I can't see what this is all about anyways. You patients are just walking around wearing this thing, going through all this pain and trouble, and this isn't doing anything for you. I really think this should be stopped! Enough is enough."

Had Karen heard this coming from the mouth of the spouse of the great inventor, let alone any of the other patients already implanted, it could have triggered disaster in their lives and hopes. With my phosphenes giving me trouble, the fact that Jerry, too, was losing them, the fact that no one yet was resuming a normal life as it was before losing eyesight, told me what she was suggesting had some truth to it. But no, I couldn't let it get to me—I did see the Christmas lights on the houses back in December, the Christmas tree, the road before me that night of the snowstorm, didn't I?

"Claire, this is a good project. I had a few weeks of relief from the pressing darkness as I saw crude outlines of what was in front of me, but it was worth it, and it is worth it to continue." Then I had to add, a comment she probably knew was coming. "But I think we will need someone else besides Bill running it. His health is just too much of an issue for him to be able to concentrate on anything else much."

I felt uncomfortable after our conversation. Claire's support for her husband's project was vital for the success of this project, as even without her direct involvement, she was inevitably involved in the risk and expense associated with such a vast undertaking.

February 1 came, and there was little success in thresholding my phosphenes. Only a few lit up at excessive voltages. We did all we could, but I felt demoralized. How will I face the rest of the reporters?

Karen's operation had gone well—at least according to Dr. Antunes and Domingo, but they had said that too about mine. "Gone well" had nothing to do with how the patient felt afterward—I often wondered at what point in time the doctors would admit to the operation to have not gone well—perhaps if the patient died? Three reporters were allowed in the operating room to film the operation. I heard one of them, Larry, talking to colleagues in the office.

"You look kind of pale, Larry," commented someone.

"Yeah, and no wonder." Larry started to recount what he saw, heard, and smelled. "I already felt quite queasy when the cutting and pulling down of the scalp started. It was gross—it made quite an awful sound, but I hung on. But then, they got out the drill. They drill four holes at each corner of the plate of skull they want to take out, and seeing them holding that drill and then hearing that whine, smelling the burning bone, I just about lost it."

I remembered how the doctors had offered to allow Lorri to watch my operation back in April. Luckily, she had refused—it would have been impossible for her to ever be the same after seeing this done to her own husband. I felt a pang of guilt thinking of Karen's suffering while I was not able to see my own phosphenes only nine months after the operation. But, I wondered, what could I have done? Abandon the project the first time things go wrong? Had Dr. Brindley given up at the first sign of trouble, we still wouldn't know what a phosphene was. I, for sure, wouldn't.

The next day, I did not leave my hotel room until going out for dinner. From the higher voltages I had been using the past few days, I had noticed the back of my head bubbling out—liquid had built up around the ground plane—the metal foil under my scalp. I had a headache and felt unhealthy. Bill didn't want me seen like this with the cameras rolling. When going out with Tony, Domingo, and a few other colleagues for dinner that night, Tony informed me that a patient who had been implanted in April was coming from Italy to receive her equipment—Marina. I remember the times she was in the office in Commack—the equipment failing and as Steve and Jim fiddled with it for days, Marina just sat in a chair with no one to talk to in her language. The same problem arose in Manhattan—but Manhattan was bad for everyone. Maybe this time things will work out—although I was worried about her phosphene count as well.

"Bill wants you to meet her and show her the equipment and your success so far before she gets tested." Tony's voice carried a disappointed edge as he realized my problem.

"I have no idea what to say to her." I thought a bit, then said, "Except for the truth. I lost my phosphenes." Then I added, more to comfort myself, "For now, anyways."

On February 3, both Discovery and National Geographic wanted to have shots of the testing of Marina, but my problem had to be solved first. I was hooked up, and Tony and Don were trying to threshold the phosphenes, but to no avail. Slowly the voltage was increased for each, but when we hit 13 V, we decided to stop—any more and I'd be paying for it. We did not, however, tell Bill where we were stopping—he'd have it go past the normal limitations set by Mother Nature just in the name of science. I was not interested in either a bad headache or a seizure, or both.

"May as well do Marina," Bill grumbled. He was surprisingly calm about the whole thing.

It was around this time that the savior sent by Claire, Andy G., showed up at the office, greeting us warmly. Andy was a slick-talking lawyer of about my age, occupying himself by pushing Bill around in the wheelchair. He talked a lot with Bill in private, only making small talk with us. In no time we concluded that one of his tasks was to look in on us.

"I was digging around in the small equipment room with Tony, looking for some part of a stimulator, quietly talking amongst ourselves, when I suddenly turned to get out of the almost-closed door, and there was Andy, eavesdropping on us," recounted Don. From then on, we didn't trust him.

Marina was in the chair now, cameras trained on her and microphones strained to hear her responses. Communication was strained by none of us really knowing Italian very well, so we did our best. She had a guide with her who spoke some English, so we were better off this time than that time in Manhattan. Don screwed the cables to her jacks as the film rolled. Tony typed at the laptop that was connected to the computer of the vision system. Dr. Dyre and I had our laptops to take notes on the stimulation parameters.

First, we tried the left side but had a series of electrodes once producing phosphenes not producing any. We did a half dozen of these, and Bill told us to start over. Then he left with Andy to another room, and we started over. The first nine produced nothing, then some appeared. Where once forty-three had worked, now twenty-nine produced phosphenes. We then started on the other side, where things were going relatively well. We took advantage of Bill's absence, as that gave us the ability to follow preset protocols, carefully increasing the thresholds and carefully observing the reactions of Marina so as to minimize discomfort.

"Tim, come over here into my office." I heard the strained voice of Bill from the corridor. Tim got up to leave, and Don took over making notes on his computer. We never saw Dr. Dyre again. Later, we questioned Bill, and all he said was that Dr. Dyre was asked to go as he was causing problems.

"And how will we handle the medical problems which can arise?" I asked, already feeling the loss. Dyre had given the project an air of authenticity, which was now void.

"Don't worry about it." Bill didn't really want a doctor. "There are good doctors just in the hospital across the street." Now, in the absence of Tim and in full view of the international press, we looked like a group of electricians playing doctor—meddling in people's brains where we didn't belong.

Late that day, we received news from CUF Hospital that Karen had run into trouble with her diabetes. Apparently, one of the hospital workers had administered too much insulin, and now she was in a bad state of health. But I wasn't sure about the details as we no longer had a medical man on our team. We all hoped for the best.

Bill called a meeting in the conference room with all of us attending, all of us except for Dr. Dyre. Bill started the discussion, with Andy by his side.

"As you know, the surgery with Karen went well, and things now look like we can implant any diabetic patients who are interested," he waited a second and then added, "and can afford it." One of us made reference to the current problem with Karen's health.

"Oh, that's quite a mess up in the hospital, that's for sure . . . but she'll get over it. They have to be more careful there." Bill then unveiled the new plan.

"Back in the office in Commack, Mario is working with good success at the new 266 electrode version, up from seventy-two currently used," he continued, "the only problem we are having is that the jack has to force together 266 connections at once, and when that center screw is used, the jack tends to buckle from the pressure."

"How big is that jack?" was my question.

"Oh, just a bit bigger than what you have. Moreover, as we had problems with the jacks of patients with thicker scalps growing over, we increased the height of the jacks somewhat to make up for the thicker scalps."

I felt my jacks already protruding from my head by a few millimeters. I sure didn't need any more height to mine—short hair was already out of the question for me.

One of the engineers made a reference to the failure of my seeing phosphenes, starting the discussion taking a different direction.

"I think Jens just overstressed his visual cortex while he was at home and he needs to rest. That's all I can think of at the moment," said the expert of artificial vision. Then he changed the subject.

"We are going to aim for April to start new implants of perhaps five patients using the 266 electrode arrays. I think that you, Jens, should be the first patient to update yours at that time as well."

I felt tight inside as if the judge in the courthouse just had banged his gavel on the table and pronounced a long sentence of suffering for a crime I had not committed. I could not respond. I thought later on that Bill must have taken my silence as a yes. The rest of the meeting was just a dull murmur of words entering my ears as I thought about my future. I had just received my first salary payment, and now I was asked to sacrifice my health on a major scale just to stay in the employee roster. Dr. Dyre went fast for lord knows what, but whatever he did would not compare to my refusal to get a second implant as patient representative. I thought of my businesses at home and how I could get them going again. Yet I needed to see with this system, once again, so I could continue to enjoy the new freedom I had for such a short time just a couple of weeks ago.

The mapping of Marina went well, so we strapped on the equipment and threw the switch. The big moment was about to take place with her, but when the machine booted up and was ready for use, she suddenly complained of pain and a headache. She was not looking around at the new world—just sitting in the chair and holding her head.

"All I can see is white clouds, even with the system turned off." Quickly, we shut the system off. Dr. Dobelle was absent as he seemed to need long naps during the day now. Don unscrewed the cables from her head. Tony said, "Perhaps she has had enough stimulation just doing the mapping." We agreed quickly to let her walk around some and continue the experimentation in the morning. Her guide helped her to a restroom, then her guide came back and announced that Marina was feeling dizzy and faint. Our hearts sank. With only Tony, Don, and I there, we really couldn't do much at all. Whatever we did wouldn't be right—we weren't doctors. Don hurried out of the building to look for a doctor in the hospital next door. Neither Tony nor I even had the right to enter the restroom, where she could be having a seizure by now. Silently, we cursed Dr. Dobelle's haste in firing Dr. Dyre.

The next few days in Portugal I spent parading around with dead equipment—just like I had done back in Commack for *Wired* magazine. Several more news agencies, such as Bob Jennings from Australia, an independent named Oliver, as well as two ladies from a Portuguese press—Lina Grilo and Rita Bravo—had spoken to Tony. "They want the system working," he informed me. We had to think of a plan. They wanted to film me walking around the building, which I knew quite well by now.

Lina and Rita stood before me in the testing room, asking questions that Tony translated and I responded, tony translating the responses back into Portuguese. One of the questions made reference to the appearance of the system.

"Oh yes, it is not very sensitive to current international security problems," I explained. "But we must remember this system was already designed prior to the 9/11 attacks, and now we have to use them, being careful not to use them in high-security settings such as airports. Soon we'll have a new system that is much smaller." I wished I could believe it myself. This system hadn't yet been started, and I have already been implanted for ten months.

Next the ladies wanted to film me walking around. I sensed the door opening of the testing room with the absence of sound reflection. I had the machine going—the fans whirring inside their little boxes. I saw only a few phosphenes, not enough for independent mobility. I stepped out of the door, looking up and down and sideways as if I could see. In fact, I was trying to see a phosphene. Don was down the hall a bit, not taking part in the interview, and made a soft coughing sound as he saw me. I walked toward him, and as I approached the corner of the corridor, Don walked quickly ahead, dragging his feet slightly, and I followed, looking from left to right—almost like I had done for CNN when I drove the car on camera—the parking lot being far too large for me to use the system but following the voices of the cameramen. This would be on TV, as well, with millions of eyes watching and then describing the miracle to their loved ones who had been wishing for their eyesight back ever since going blind.

My conscience burned as I wondered if I'd ever be forgiven.

Marina tried the equipment the next day. I had just come back from shooting pictures with a Paris agency when Tony halted me in the corridor. "Careful, Marina is using the equipment."

"She is feeling better?"

"Yes, we dropped the multipliers to 0.8 and 0.9 for the left and right side, so she's been using the system for an hour without a headache yet."

I followed her movements as she carefully ambled down the corridor, pointing at things she spotted on the wall as her companion told her what she was looking at. She was smiling and suddenly stopped and pointed at me.

"That's Jens," Tony said. I approached her and shook her hand.

We packed up the equipment for her to take home. Trying our best to teach her companion how to hook up the wires to the jacks in the head, we hoped she wouldn't break the cable ends first thing. The equipment was somewhat difficult to connect, and people with little dexterity had major problems. The cable ends were very easy to break, and once broken, they had to be replaced for $1,000 US. This money came directly out of Bill's pocket as the system had a five-year warrantee. The project continued—working presently for Marina, somewhat for Klaus, but not for me.

Bill's health became worse as he made fewer appearances in the office. During the stimulation and mapping of Ken from England, Bill either slept in his chair or was just in his hotel room. A nurse named Liz was flown over by Claire to tend full time to Bill's needs as Andy could not do this anymore. I once overheard Andy urging Bill to use the prosthesis for his foot. I had been in an adjoining room that had no door as Andy said, "Gone on, Bill, I'll help you out of your chair and just try to walk a bit. Come on, let's go . . ." but Bill protested, refusing flatly to leave his chair. I couldn't imagine how he would be able to stand the prosthesis digging into his leg when he already had the shingles to contend with. Andy finally gave up.

The thresholding of Ken revealed he still had fifty good phosphenes, not significantly different from his original count. He had been implanted at the same time I was. His challenge was that he had real problems with the mapping. Every time we mapped him, his map was entirely different, and, subsequently, he could not see straight lines, but rather scattered groups of dots, when looking at a straight edge. This challenge was one we had expected—it was a relief to work with a problem not related to phosphene loss. As I worked with Ken, trying different techniques for the procedure, I couldn't help thinking about the truth of the project—as long as people like Ken and Marina could see phosphenes, the project had legitimacy and had to continue, even if I was out of the picture.

Karen was out of the hospital, now having recovered somewhat from the insulin problem. She slowly was led to a chair in the testing room as she carefully lowered herself into it. She was hurting, a feeling that I can remember very well. Her speech was slow as she recounted her hospital stay.

"Oh, that operation—it was sure a lot more dramatic than I had thought it would be . . ." But she was ready for testing. We just wanted to make sure the electrodes responded by testing a handful of electrodes, we told her. She was in no shape to do all the phosphenes today.

Karen's electrodes worked fine—out of eleven we tested, we had nine producing a phosphene. The appearance of the first phosphene had Karen ecstatic with surprise and excitement. "There it is! There it is!" She perked up in her chair as she looked at that little dot that appeared for only a second. I couldn't help but think of the time in April when I, too, had sat in that chair, Jim at the controls, Bill cleaning his teeth with the screwdriver used to attach the cables to my head, and John Girvin looking on. "Where will this end with Karen?" I thought.

We flew back to New York on February 9, Tony and Don sitting beside me as Bill was in the first class section while we were in economy class. We noticed the absence of Dr. Dyre but said nothing. Tony began to mention new improvements to future artificial vision systems, and together we discussed what could be added.

"First of all, we need to adjust our own thresholds in the morning," I said. Then adding, "Remember that the first volunteer had to adjust his every day as it varied by 25 percent up or down. This means perhaps I received too high stimulation in some cases and maybe that's why the phosphene count is so far down."

"I don't really know, but yes, let's adjust phosphenes. Not everyone will be able to do that, though." Don and Tony had a point there. The procedure was complicated, and we were already having trouble getting most patients to hook up their own wires to their heads, and this procedure will be almost impossible to teach people who had never used a computer. We needed to elaborate more on this.

"A zoom control would effectively increase the acuity if we could toggle between high zoom and normal vision at moment's notice," I suggested. We'd have to think more on how to make the switch accessible without using hands. Tony suggested, "We could have the system voice controlled." I didn't agree, as this could make us appear less human and more robotic as we chatted with our machines. Social integration remained our biggest challenge when dealing with issues of blindness, and this wouldn't help a bit. As we discussed our options, I tried to forget the loss of my phosphenes—perhaps a new machine with many controls and gadgets would solve my problem.

February 11 came, the day to meet with Morly Safer, and I was brought into the Commack office by Pat. He was concerned about the new turn of events, wondering what I am going to do.

"I am going to talk to Bill." I couldn't think of anything else. "Perhaps the phosphenes came back." I hadn't used the system for some days now. After all, once I had a problem with phosphenes not appearing in the morning back in December, and just by shutting the system off at 4:30 p.m. the night before seemed to solve the problem the next day as all the phosphenes appeared.

But that was not the case at all. I sat in the chair where I first sat back in May, Tony increasing the voltages bit by bit, until, suddenly, I saw a huge nasty splotch of light where once appeared a small phosphene some weeks ago. Don observed the oscilloscope.

"Wow, never saw this before. One minute there is practically no current flow, and then when you increase the voltage just a bit more, suddenly the current jumps over 20mA as if we were looking at the breakdown voltage of a zener diode." Most electrodes did nothing as I didn't dare allow Tony to go to 16 V, as sudden conductivity could be dangerous at the least. In the end, we only had a handful of phosphenes working, sort of, as it took several frames for the phosphenes just to appear. This would have to do, we agreed.

Bill heard the news, and so I asked what to say to Morley, who was by now on his way.

"Just tell them how it is. You'll just have to tell him what you could do, and that this is in an experimental stage and we can't just expect things to work all the time." I wasn't sure if Morley was coming down just for that. "But now here comes Jerry, and if he's good, we'll use him to do the demonstrations."

But Bill didn't have the ace he thought he had. I spoke briefly to Jerry from Louisiana as he took his place with Tony. With every stimulation attempt, all I heard was "No. No. No . . ." as Jerry indicated he was seeing nothing. Once all over, he had but three phosphenes, all useless, for their size was bad. Bill was at a loss. Then Morley's crew came into the office and began setting up lights and cameras and rearranging the furniture.

"All set up!" One of the camera crew personnel announced as Jerry muttered something about hoping that the Lord was with us today. We ambled over toward the direction of their voices in the conference room, which by now had all its familiarities voided by the rearrangement of the furniture.

"Sit down right here." It was the voice of Morley, who was already sitting across from the two chairs which were side by side in front of the bookshelves I had once been able to see with my system. Jerry and I felt around for the chairs as silence fell in the room. I didn't know if Jerry had decided to wear his system, and now I wasn't about to ask. We found the chairs, but it wasn't as smooth as it would have been if we had seen them.

Morley asked a run of questions regarding our interest in seeing again, briefly the history of our eye problems, and then predictably asked why we appeared not to be able to see very much at all.

I tried to defend the system. "This is the first such machine issued to people to take home. I could see nothing before getting this thing, and now I can see some of the lights of the cameras," I paused and pointed out a couple of the lights producing the odd phosphene, "and moreover, we are dealing with problems that we didn't know we'd have, as we haven't, nor has anyone else, done this before." I continued talking about some of the benefits I had had shortly before Christmas when I had taken home the equipment for the first time.

"But can you even see my arm?" Morley lifted his right arm, his crisp new suit making a crinkling sound, giving away the position of his arm. I did see one extra phosphene appear a second after he lifted his arm, but it was the telltale sound of his suit I was using for verification.

"Yeah, it's your right arm, and it is up."

Claire congratulated me later, saying in Bill's presence that she had been there to listen in, and I had answered the questions in a professional manner given the circumstances. But Bill still complained, almost like it was mine and Jerry's fault as to what happened.

Morley stormed into my office afterward and said, "What the hell are you doing, Bill, these guys can't see anything!"

But I wasn't sure if Morley really had said that or if Bill was only trying to make us feel personally responsible for the failure of the system. If so, he certainly succeeded.

We were only at midday, so Bill ordered Louise, the secretary, to phone Richie to take me home. I wanted to go home, as three weeks away from Lorri and my kids was enough, and these days had been anything but easy.

Then Bill spoke, "You and Jerry are leaving the machines here with us. We need to run some tests on them."

I looked around for the last time. Some of the dots had by now reappeared, almost as if mocking the situation with Morley Safer. But I was still missing lots, and those that reappeared would only do so after looking at the same object for a couple of seconds. I switched it off, disconnected the wires, and gave the system to Don. I knew there was nothing to test. They were both working fine—the problem was with the electrodes, or with our visual cortex, or something getting between there. Don and Tony both knew that too. Perhaps Bill did too and was only stalling to buy time.

I shook Jerry's hand and bade him good-bye, struggling to find words. There was just nothing to say. We were going home empty-handed, back to our only too-familiar worlds of feeling around and making the best of it—both of us having to not only deal with our personal loss, but facing also the many questions coming from those who had helped us and encouraged us to go through with this operation.

I returned home once again in the middle of the night. This time, no machine was in my suitcase. The following morning, we got up as usual and ate breakfast together. I felt around for my coffee cup, just like I had done for so many years. I thought of how my two eyes first served me seventeen years, then the one-eyed vision only three, yet once the left eye recuperated somewhat, that vision only lasted a few months, and now this artificial vision only served me a few weeks.

No one spoke of artificial vision as we sat together. The dream had ended, but we were still far from being able to admit to it openly. Even though the curse had its way once again, something in us kept hoping for my phosphenes to return.

CHAPTER 13

From Bad to Worse

I heard nothing from Commack for the next few days and didn't really want to either. I imagined Bill was not even in the office and that the rest of the staff, now void of Dr. Dyre, were scratching their heads wondering what was going to happen next. A lot of high hopes had been banked on this media blitz just gone by, and things just had to go wrong right in the middle of it. I had no idea what the media reporters were going to make up for a story and didn't really want to know either. I just wanted to forget about artificial vision for a while.

But that couldn't be quite so easy. The telephone rang, and I answered the call from Joe Lazzaro from Boston.

"How's everything working out with the vision system?"

I had to figure out how to stall this one, as I really didn't know except that my precious dots of light, along with those of Jerry D's, had suddenly disappeared.

"Well, Joe, the phosphenes I've been seeing have kind of given me some trouble and want too much voltage to show—but I am not sure what it could be other than perhaps fatigue . . ." I am not sure if this was going to make Joe have reservations for his planned eventual implant of the system. Joe worked in a technical aids outlet for the blind, and he was rather interested in receiving one of these systems to demonstrate its usefulness, as this would, as he put it, be the ultimate aid for the blind.

"What does Dobelle say about it all?" This was a question I found very hard to deal with. I was going to have to be careful what to say about Bill, as his bad health and difficult disposition had to be kept a secret if this vision project was going to go anywhere.

"Nothing much at the moment," I stalled again. "We're trying to figure it all out, and we'll have to work on it to get the answers." I promised Joe I'd call him once we had some answers.

However, to get some sort of answer about the loss of phosphenes, I decided to write to Dr. John Girvin. There was no way I'd get much satisfaction talking with Dobelle. In my e-mail, I mentioned to John the present condition of Bill, his bad decision to fire Dr. Dyre, and the loss of the phosphenes from both Jerry and my visual map. John replied in short time, addressing his letter to his son Doug, who was presently working at Queen's University in neighboring Kingston.

> My main reason for writing is to find out if Jens is using the prosthesis and how much help it is providing him. I have had two million US dollars put into a fund here in Jetta, from two independent individuals (of who I have no knowledge) for the initiation of a program here. Even though the hospital wanted me to start the program last fall, I indicated that I would have nothing to do with it until I have heard from the eight individuals upon whom we operated in Portugal, regarding the usefulness of it.
>
> I can understand Jens's concerns if indeed there are any as I have worked with Bill and his various colleagues over the course of thirty years. I have had concerns, which, other than being irritating, were minor until Portugal. Behind the scenes, there were lots of problems and I took the lead, by consensus and with the wishes of the others, to try to rectify them. By the way, this is the first time I would consider the concerns major. I would be glad to talk to Jens at any time.

The hospital in Jetta was also jumping to the conclusion that the artificial vision project was a guaranteed success. It was just too easy to be fooled by the overly-optomistic over-positive nature of the media reports from the past. There were blind people waiting and dreaming, all over the world, just for their chance to see again . . .

Dr. Dobelle telephoned me in my now very quiet office. He started out with pleasantries, which I was hoping would lead to something affirmative, such as a new plan of experimentation for the vision system. Instead, all he talked about was the snowstorm hitting the Eastern States, and how that may impede his trip to Washington where he was scheduled to have dinner with Dr. Kolff. I was hoping he'd go and perhaps share the present problems of phosphene disappearances with Dr. Kolff in quest of possible answers.

The telephone line designated to the Dobelle Institute in my house did not make a sound for the following two weeks. The only mail I received from Commack was a quick mention about the phosphene situation, which I assumed was to inform the other patients of the concerns regarding phosphene loss—something that none of the others besides Jerry and I knew about.

Mar-03-2003
12:08 p.m. From-Avery Laboratories Inst

Dobelle Institute
March 3, 2003
To: Jens Naumann
Fax: 613 354-1528

Overstimulation may cause some problems. However, we don't really know where to draw the line with how much time the system can be used.

Consequently, please stop using your system until I have had a chance to check things further.

Thanks.

Dr. Bill Dobelle

The Dobelle Institute (Portugal) Lda.

Dr. Dobelle told us to just shut it off and forget about it for a while. It was supposed to be easy. But I had to be blind again—the neighbor's outside light no longer visible to me, neither was the furniture, the open road nestled between its snowbanks—everything just disappeared, and I was left alone with the memories. I put the papers upon which I had drawn the ten-centimeter high letters and put them in the bottom drawer of the desk. My mind craved the phosphenes—seeing the windows, the outlines of the trees outside—the flames in the woodstove, but no dice. The following weekends we didn't go out much or even cared to go anywhere. I certainly did not want to spend much time in Napanee facing up to the donors who'd be disappointed that I wasn't wearing their investment. And I couldn't blame them for their disappointment.

I phoned the office in Commack after the first week of March and was told that Kirk had been re-thresholded and now could see his phosphenes again that he had used to make the system function for him. When I talked to him, he said that when first being issued the equipment, he had been able to walk in some instances without a cane down the sidewalk, but his "walking phosphenes" had disappeared. Now, with the news that he had them back, I felt like there may be some hope yet that I'd get my system back and be able to use it.

Dobelle telephoned me the following day on March 10 and wasted little time to get to the heart of the discussion.

"Well," he began with his usual sigh, "I e-mailed John Girvin, Ken Smith, and Dr. Antunes for a discussion on the subject of phosphene loss." He continued, "It was Ken Smith who got back to me first and said he'd had instances where silastic material—the plastic substrate presently used in the implants to mount the electrodes—can have reactions to the brain when in contact with it."

I asked, "Jerry T. and the former experimental patients didn't have this problem?"

"No, they had a straight teflon implant. No silastic for them."

"Then why didn't you use teflon for us?"

"Silastic is easier to handle. It's flexible, whereas the teflon is kind of rigid." Bill took a breath and continued in his now very familiar voice. "But, Jens, don't worry. In the next eight months or so, I figure, you should get over to Portugal and have another operation. We'll pull that stuff out and put in the new system."

I winced and said nothing. A quick calculation told me that next Christmas wasn't going to be so good. Bill continued to tell me that Tony was coming up March 24 to set up at my house and try thresholding me. Before Bill hung up, he informed me that Kieth was having some pain on the outer electrodes that were situated on the perimeter of his implants. He summarized by saying, "It seems his implants are bubbling up in the middle, as the center electrodes have no contact and the outer edges are consequently stressing his brain membrane. If this keeps up we may have to open him up."

"Just like opening the hood of a car," I thought as I hung up the phone; as if Keith hadn't enough problems on his plate already. Now we all need to get back in the hospital and get our heads opened again. What a mess! The term "guinea pig" for the first time came to me by itself. Sure, there had been many people who, in their initial attempts to dissuade me from pursuing the operation as it may not have been yet confirmed to work, would refer to the experimentation as a mere exercise fit for laboratory animals. I had vehemently dismissed this unjust categorization of my involvement as comparing it to a guinea pig, because, after all, previous volunteers had already agreed to be test specimens on a smaller scale so as to confirm that the implants do produce phosphenes reliably, for a time span of twenty-five years at least. But the situation was different now, as Dobelle admitted to implanting in my head an untested combination of material.

Tony arrived late in the afternoon on March 24, together with Richie in the long limousine. He said he'd been held up at the border for seven hours because he had told the border patrol that he had a medical device with him. Richie was quite exhausted and irritated.

"Just tell them you have neither guns, drugs, or alcohol and nothing else to claim," I suggested. Richie agreed, saying that such a tactic always succeeded with us.

Tony wasted no time setting up the stimulator, his laptop, and the vision system's computer for the testing session that took place in my office. Here there was no FDA to worry about.

Surprisingly enough, I could see almost all of the lost phosphenes. Some of them hurt, but I bore it and continued, reveling in the success of phosphene recovery. I asked Tony if the threshold values were far off the originals, but he replied he didn't have my previous data with him.

We contacted Dobelle, who sounded obviously pleased at the recuperation of the phosphene count. I was more pleased yet about the fact that I wouldn't have to go to get another operation after all. Tony and I passed the rest of the evening discussing improvements we could incorporate on the new system. I had meant to do this earlier, but the disappearance of my phosphenes had me discouraged to the point where I wanted to think of artificial vision as little as possible. Tony had been concentrating his efforts on making a more efficient system that would operate all day on one battery charge, and I had been thinking of what needed improving the most for ease of use of the system.

"Bill said he wants Jesse to incorporate a timer that shuts the system off after an hour of use per day."

"Then, I guess there's no use worrying about building a system that lasts fourteen hours," I thought it over with dismay. "What good is an hour of sight a day? Better than nothing, but really useless," I thought. I reflected on what I did with my system when I had it here—there was no time other than during in-the-house experimentation where I could have been out for just one hour. Even Lorri's music concert was two hours. It wasn't going to be practical at all.

"Maybe you can put on a standby mode that we can use when there's nothing interesting to see, then we can toggle between that and seeing so we make the most of that one hour," I suggested dismally. Tony agreed, then asked for any other ideas.

"A zoom control would work as we're far from utilizing all the pixels in the camera." Tony noted this as we discussed how the zoom would be activated. Bill had mentioned once in the office in Commack that one could incorporate voice commands, but I opposed that idea as we'd appear to be mentally unstable if we just started talking to our machine.

Bill had Louise send out another letter to all patients shortly afterward. The letter opened with strong Republican overtones, which offered little comfort to any of the patients. After all, to compare the vision project to the assault on Iraq served nothing as things weren't going all that well in Iraq either.

The Dobelle Institute (Portugal) Lda.
Artificial Vision for the Blind
March 27, 2003

To: All Artificial Vision Staff, Patients, and Surgeons

Fr: Wm. H. Dobelle, PhD, Chairman & Chief Executive Officer

Re: War Plan: Confidential

Now that it seems that deleterious effects of stimulation can be treated with the tincture of time, an orderly plan to take the program to the next level is needed. Obviously, this plan, like the one for the war in Iraq, may have to be changed as early as tomorrow.

I.   Thirteen (13) 140 electrode systems

1.   Try to clean electrode surfaces (reverse polarity, etc.)
2.   Improve cables and connectors
3.   Program a "timer" that will absolutely prohibit patients from exceeding fixed amounts of stimulation in any twenty-four-hour period.
4.   Complete a program to plot the visual results onto the electrode array.
5.   Complete "auto-restart" programs for thresh adjust, screen thresh, and mapping.
6.   Stimulate Karen to see if reliable phosphenes can be produced.
7.   Retest all twelve of the other patients. Videotape results and begin routine stimulation May 1, 2003.
8.   Prototype "temporary off" switch to prolong stimulation.
9.   Prototype hardware and software to allow the patients to control threshold, but "block" for the time being.

10. Prototype hardware and software to allow the patients to control "zoom."
11. Prototype hardware and software to allow the patients to control certain edge detection parameters.

II: New 512 channel stimulator

1. Recruit new foreign patients.
2. Develop techniques to fabricate ground plane electrodes with teflon backs so that a minimal amount of silastic (primarily the annuli around each electrode, and the edges of the implant) are in contact with dura. Also, make the electrode somewhat stiffer and more resistant to buckling.
3. New camera.
4. Prototype new pedestal and cable connectors for new, larger system, based on experience with the smaller system.
5. Prototype hardware and software for the new system, including control of threshold, "zoom," and edge detection.
6. Select mix of new and existing patients for implant (or reimplant at our expense) starting around October 1, 2003.

In this letter, Bill was openly admitting to the possible culprit in phosphene instability stemming directly from the implanted material, which did not correspond with the material used in Jerry T's and other previous volunteers' heads. I wondered if any of the other patients would question this.

Bill called me several times during April so I could get new patients signed up for more implantations. He was really positive about the whole affair now that I had my phosphenes back.

"We want a few patients for implanting in July," he told me after Louise faxed me several sheets of phone numbers of people who had already inquired in the past. "Seeing you and Kirk are back to normal, it's time to move on."

"How do my voltage and current thresholds compare to the previous ones before we had the trouble?" I asked.

"They are pretty well the same. Not only for you, but for Kirk also," Dobelle told me.

I felt comforted by this and turned to the task of telephoning the potential patients.

The next time Bill phoned was at the start of May. He insisted I come down to Commack for a few days for testing, re-thresholding, and to have my equipment returned to me to take to Canada. My spirits were high as I rolled in the limo with Richie on May—this date was special as it marked Lorri and my twentieth wedding anniversary, which was now being sacrificed for vision. I had thought it would be worth it. I was wrong.

The same day I arrived, I once again sat down in the conference room, facing the big table, the cables attached to my head as Tony and Don fiddled with the computer equipment, their cooling fans whirring the usual concert.

"Now," said Tony, signaling he was commencing stimulation on my first phosphene. I thought back to what seemed a long, long time ago when Jim had said the same word just before administering 0.5 V to my first phosphene—at that time, the little gray dot immediately greeted me with all its associated excitement. But this time, nothing happened.

"No," I stated.

Tony raised the voltage. "Now . . ." he'd say, over and over, as I continued to reply "no."

Some of the electrodes had to be abandoned as they hurt the minute any voltage was applied, while others allowed for a dim, splattered phosphene to appear at a near-maximum voltage. I insisted we increase the voltage by small increments only—I felt scared of the system by now and did not want to get hurt any more than possible. Tony agreed, reading the volts he'd administer for the test before activating the stimulator, which gave me the capacity to veto it if I wanted to. Yet when we heard Bill advancing toward the room, we both fell silent. Bill would probably not approve of our method—making the patient as comfortable as possible during testing was not part of his first priority. We stopped the testing after only one side was completed, hoping for a miracle the next morning.

Yet the next day only brought more worries. The other side of my visual cortex had no better results—just a dozen or so of unreliable, unclear phosphenes requiring very high voltages. These few that did work seemed to be accompanied with a time delay of a fraction of a second before reacting to the current.

"I don't understand why the phosphenes had been so good and at such low voltages just six weeks ago when you came to my house, and now they just disappeared," I said in frustration. With these phosphenes I had left, I thought, I'd never be able to take the system home.

"I have no idea as yet," said Tony as he looked at the charts of voltages and current of previous testings. "But remember, the time I was at your house, the voltages required were typically 2–3.5 times higher than they had been back in December."

I remembered that Bill had told me the voltages compared with the original values. He had said both mine and Kirk's were back to normal.

"And Kirk's?" I asked. Tony said that both of us had the same problem. Kirk's threshold voltages, also, had increased two to four times their original value. Bill must have misread the data, or maybe it was Tony; the fact remained that now I couldn't see the phosphenes reliably once again.

Bill had no explanation for the loss of phosphenes. He did not seem particularly worried either. He instructed Don to show me the new, larger jack that would accompany the future implants of 484 electrodes. He explained how he'd have had 512 electrodes, but the hole in the middle of the jack had to be of a larger diameter due to the stress required to keep the jack together. Don arrived with the jack.

At first I thought it was a container in which the jack would be stored. But I was wrong. Don noticed what I was trying to do—open it up to look inside—and said, "No, that's it. You're holding it . . ." I was shocked. The jack resembled the end of a large-diameter bottle; the diameter of the part that would protrude from my scalp was at least 3 cm, and the height of the jack would make it protrude more than 1.5 cm from my scalp. I would look like a monster with horns. I shook my head. Bill was watching me.

"Wow! This is far too large for me. This would be too difficult to live with. Why," I continued, imagining how I'd look, "if I walked in the front door of my family's house, the wife and kids would run away out the back door in fear!"

"Naa, you've got a good shock of hair. That'll cover it," replied Bill. "How about we call it a day and you have dinner with us, and we'll talk more."

The day was over. Don packed my vision system for me in my suitcase. I was to take it home and wear it for one hour every second day. It now had a timer built in, limiting its use to one hour per day. I had no idea what I'd do with a few foggy phosphenes even for that hour every two days. Maybe the phosphenes will come back, I hoped.

We went to a diner and had a decent meal. The food was always good in New York. Richie had instructions to pick up Marty and the three of us would dine and Richie would pick us up when we called him. Marty broke the silence while we ate.

"So, Jens, are you going to have that operation to install the new system?"

"No," I explained, speaking loud enough for Bill to hear. "First of all, the jacks are far too bulky and will cause constant discomfort, as I already have some continuous infection signs with my present implants. They stick out far, and if I choose not to wear extra long hair, I will look undesireable for all. Moreover," I continued, "we are having problems with these present implants. If we cannot figure out exactly what is going wrong with these, then I won't have that operation, be subject to all that agony, just to have a repeat of these problems."

I stopped short of referring to the present implantation procedures as a procedure more fit for guinea pigs—I'd probably lose my job if I did that, and I had lots of bills to pay.

Bill mumbled something about the system working just fine and there being no major problems. But I wasn't so sure.

"What is best for me to do," I continued, softening my stance for the preservation of peace at the dinner table, "is wait until a few of the next implanted patients have theirs. If they have no problems with the new teflon-covered implants, and if they can see better than I could when my system worked, it will be a possibility in the future."

Bill seemed to accept this explanation. "You'll be surprised what they will be able to see. With 484 phosphenes, their vision should be good enough to recognize faces . . ." I thought back of when he had said that to me about the 140 electrode systems. As we talked, Bill gave the waiter a credit card to pay for the meal, which promptly bounced. He gave the waiter one after another, rifling through his stack of credit cards as a gambler would a deck of cards. Bill hoped I wouldn't notice. I thought of our paychecks back at the office being delayed—Linda the accountant said there wasn't enough money yet to pay us. All that money paid by the patients was gone. We needed more money—which exclusively came from the pockets of new patients—just to keep this project going.

I arrived home and in only a few short days received another letter from Bill. It sounded good when I read it with the scanner, but the content was more and more reflective of an experiment rather than a clinical procedure.

Dobelle Institute (Portugal) Lda.
Artificial Vision for the Blind
May 13, 2003

To: Mr. Jens Naumann RR#6
Napanee, Ontario Canada. K7R 3L1

FR:
Wm. H. Dobelle, Ph. D. Chairman & Chief Executive Officer

Re: Resumption of Stimulation

I am pleased to report that stimulation can resume, but only on a very, very conservative basis until we develop more information.

This means not more than one (1) hour per day, every other day. If we encounter no problems, I will slowly increase this. For example, the next step would be one hour every day, then two hours per day and so on.

If, however, you have any indication that the phosphenes are "fading," you should:

1:     Stop stimulation immediately

2.   Contact me. My New York office phone is (631) 864-1600, fax is (631) 864-1610. My home is (516) 921-5747. Or e-mail me at: whd@dobelle.com.

I realize this restricted schedule is frustrating, but we have to be careful.

Regards!

Avenita Infante Santo 34, 7th Floor
Lisbon 1350-179 Portugal

On May 16, I took the system out of the suitcase and tried it out. I saw two phosphenes only. Any extras I had in Commack I could not use. I shut it back off. Two days later, I tried again, but this time I saw nothing. I told Bill, who told me to just give it a rest.

June started out to be a month of planning for another trip to Portugal in July. I looked forward to it—this time there'd be no media—just work with patients and possibly a couple of implants. A few patients, including Klaus, needed their systems checked out, as well, we had to honor the resolution we had made on the previous letter regarding regular testing of patients starting in May.

On June 2, Bill asked me to try the system again. This time I could see bright phosphenes numbering over twenty, rendering functional the system, although I was cautious to shut it off after a few minutes lest I have another seizure. The thresholds had changed again, and both Bill and I were pleased by the change. Bill suggested I try it every week and report to him every time to share the results.

On June 10, I was back down to two phosphenes. I could not do anything useful with them no matter what I tried. I had the same delay back in the appearance of the phosphenes as well, just as there was back on May 7.

On June 17, I had no phosphene at all. I was arranging the patient's flights and activities once in Portugal and hoped that they'd have better success than I with their systems.

On June 17, I tried to see phosphenes but to no avail—I even wore the system for its full hour. I felt the pulses in my head but saw nothing. Just to confirm the machine was working, I placed my tongue on the jack, which normally is connected to my head. The output of the stimulator smarted my tongue painfully. This strong current was going straight to my brain, I realized. I conveyed the lack of phosphenes to Bill, who didn't know what to say and quickly changed the subject, concentrating only on our scheduled trip to Portugal.

Then, on June 23, when I expected to see nothing once again, the phosphenes appeared in full brilliance, their rainbow colors in full shine as I quickly had to shut off the system to keep from having another convulsion. It was hard to believe how quickly everything changed. This condition was the same on June 30, with the brilliance of the phosphenes slightly less vigorous, but I still could see them. My last check was on July 7, when again I returned to one or two phosphenes.

I received the schedule for our planned trip to Portugal. It was going to be full, with possibly many sleepless nights as there was room for trouble. Four patients already implanted—Karen, Marina, Ken, and Klaus—were going to have their equipment reset, their performance assessed, while two new patients were going to be implanted with the new 484 electrode systems. There was going to be some media presence as they wanted a follow-up from Karen's implantation in January so they could photograph the results as she was issued her system.

Don, Tony, and I were back on the airplane, the eight-hour flight to Lisbon going quickly as we sipped on the tiny bottles of wine and discussed the three weeks facing us. With my phosphenes being as unreliable as they had been the past few weeks, it was only a good guess whether or not I'd be able to demonstrate the merits of the system to the two potential patients when we meet them for the first time. We also got word of a couple of scientists from Ohio University who were going to be present during our testing sessions.

The day we arrived—July 12—we scrambled to set up my system for demonstration. Luck was with us, and I saw enough phosphenes for seeing some of the furniture in the Lisbon office, which was a layout now very familiar to me. I'd be all right tomorrow, provided I'd still see the phosphenes, to show Lino and Paul—the two new patients—the merits of this project.

As my system had the same one-hour timer built into it, we waited in the lobby of the hotel until at least one of the potential patients arrived before I turned on the system. I waited with the usual combination of trepidation and hope as I listened to the beeps of the machine. When I saw the first few phosphenes, it was clear it would work this time. They seemed normal enough as I scanned the table and the windows, picking out the light fixtures on the ceiling as well. However, there was a delay in the appearance of some of the dots, requiring a fraction of a second extra before appearing. Paul, a man about my age from Austrailia, liked the machine and did not seem deterred by its size or its performance, assuming that his system with more electrodes would provide better resolution. Lino, a man from Italy, was not able to speak with us, so his grandson did the interpretations as we explained not only the system, but that it would be issued some weeks, or months, following the implant. This concerned Lino a lot, as he had thought he'd be able to take it home with him following the operation.

"We have to build each system according to your individual needs," began Bill as he explained something he had to make up as he went along, yet at the same time reflected the harsh reality of a voyage through unchartered waters. "An artificial vision system isn't something you can just slap together like a radio or TV." The truth was, Don, Tony, and I knew that Bill was scrambling to figure out how to make the stimulator that would accommodate the 484 electrodes. Presently, the systems already designed could only handle 144 channels, and to introduce extra channels was more complicated than first thought. It could be a while, I figured, before these patients would really be using their 484 electrodes. However, it would be possible to use the existing systems and use 144 of the most strategically located electrodes available in order to fabricate a phosphene map superior to that of what I had with only ninety-six haphazardly located phosphenes.

The following day, Dr. Domingo consulted with the two of them individually in the office, explaining the surgical procedure, giving details of what would be cut first, then next, tracing the planned areas of surgery over Lino and Paul's heads with his finger so they would get a sense of the size of the cuts. Right from the back of one ear, over the top of the head and down the other side to end at the back of the other ear, was the route followed by Dr. Domingo as he added that because these implants were larger, there would be an expected extension of the healing time compared to the smaller, previous implants such as what I had in my head. Lino, the patient from Italy, was an older gentleman of perhaps seventy-five, and I was worried of how this operation would affect him.

"Did it hurt?" one of the patients asked me as I sat and listened.

"Yes." Then I added, "The headache was terrible. It was gone at about three weeks, provided I didn't shake my head too much."

"Are you getting this update?"

"No." I had to think of how to put the rest of the explanation. This wasn't the same as sitting at the dinner table with Bill and Marty. "There's just that much my head can take. I have to wait for a while."

It was set. Both patients agreed to the operation, signed the hospital's consent forms, and were admitted.

Our next job was to threshold Karen. She had had some tentative phosphene stimulation just after her operation but had been too fatigued to do the complete routine of her 140 implanted electrodes. She, being our first patient with diabetes, had endured the past six months with the implants without any infection—or at least, without enough of an infection to warrant the removal of the implants. My own implants were still causing leakage around the pedestals, and several times a day, I'd have to clean the surrounding area and make sure none of my hair was in the crack between the scalp and the pedestal or it would hurt and become sore and itchy, the scalp around the pedestal bubbling up and feeling like a giant, nasty pimple. I imagined all the patients had this to some degree—Klaus had complained of this a lot as it seemed he had it worse than I; he said he'd have to apply an antibiotic cream daily to the area in order to control the discomfort. John Girvin had told me a while back that this would not rectify through time. "This is as good as it's going to get in terms of healing . . ." he had said. Yet, neither Jerry T. nor Dan, the two volunteers who received the experimental sixty-eight-electrode teflon implant with the pedestal made of carbon composite, had this problem.

We connected the equipment to Karen as she took her place in the testing room in front of the large table. The mood in the Portugal testing room was considerably more cheery and upbeat than the one in Commack, despite the fact that we were doing the same kind of work. In Commack, the testing room had no windows as it was an inside room surrounded by walls, leading to other rooms within the building. The Commack office lay in an obscure, quiet area of Commack with very little traffic and no surrounding activity. In contrast, the Portugal office had a few large windows overlooking a busy street lined with shops, businesses, while people chattered above the noise of the traffic as they headed yet for more excitement in this vibrant city. The windows were always wide open as there were no mosquitos and only a few, occasional flies at the most. Even in winter, this room was pleasant to be in.

Don attached the cables to Karen's head, and Tony fired up the stimulator. Her husband took a seat at the table, and the camera crew headed by Larry entered and started taking shots as Karen replied "yes" to most of the "now . . ." gestures from Tony, indicating a good turnout of phosphenes at fairly low voltages. The two scientists from Ohio University entered as well, taking their seats near the back of the room, avoiding Larry's camera. Lastly, Bill entered, his folding wheelchair pushed by Sheila. Bill sounded rough, straining to breathe, greeting us with a weak mumble. We knew he was sick again.

The thresholding was done after a few hours. Karen insisted we do the mapping so she could see what she would see with the machine. We had a quick break. The two scientists approached us, and we talked some about the system and its merits. They were obviously impressed by the proceedings so far with Karen's thresholding.

"How do you judge things are going so far?" One of them asked politely. We talked a bit about the low-voltage values, the good phosphene turnout we had and that very few didn't have connectivity, signifying a good contact with the visual cortex. The scientists left then, promising to come back later when the mapping was almost finished. Karen and her husband left for a quick lunch break, and the camera crew left to recharge their batteries for their equipment. That's when Bill spoke.

"You guys better watch what you are saying," he stated, referring to what we had said to the scientists.

I tried to recall what we had said. Just some general knowledge about the vision parameters, nothing else.

Bill continued, "No technical information whatsoever to these guys. Understood?" He sounded like a mother scolding her youngster who just tried to pocket a chocolate bar in a store.

I explained, "Look, Bill, we mentioned only those parameters and details you personally had already posted on the Internet in your Journal 2000. There, you specifically wrote about Jerry's stimulation parameters, such as frequency, voltages, . . ."

"Don't mention anything to these guys!" Bill was trying to shout in his frail, weak voice. I recalled hearing him shouting like this in a room adjacent to the conference room at Jim. This must be what he does just to feel like a boss. It didn't have to make any sense. Maybe, I thought, he didn't think that the scientists from Ohio knew how to look things up on the Internet, and therefore never would be able to read his latest published journal.

I gave up, and so did Tony and Don, who never even tried. They knew Bill better than I did. Bill continued his rambling, "No details to these guys. They are here just to pump you, you hear? Just to pump you for information about this. Keep quiet about what we are doing." Then he added his line I heard he had used on countless other occasions when he needed to reinforce his authority. "It's my way, or the highway."

Dr. Dyre went fast enough the last time we were in Portugal, so, I wondered, who would be it this time. I felt uneasy—I didn't think Tony or Don would be fired, as Tony was the only one now who knew how to run the program for the stimulator, and Don the only one who was fast at troubleshooting the hardware. But, I recalled with dismay, that hadn't stopped Bill last year from firing Jim, who had written the software in the first place.

"Yes, Bill, OK. Nothing more will be said. Sorry." That was the end of that.

Bill fell asleep during the mapping, breathing with difficulty in his chair as Karen pointed out the dots as she thought she saw them in her visual field. Larry had the sense and respect not to film Bill as he slept, concentrating on capturing Karen's obvious upbeat mood, which made the job easy and fun. Then she was ready for the camera.

Tony arranged the software while Don hooked up the camera and glasses. Karen put them on her face with stern conviction and high hopes. I remember when I first put those glasses on, I thought I was in for a miracle.

"Remember, Karen, I didn't see much to begin with but some splotches of light the first time I got my camera." I had to say this; I did not want Karen to go through that initial, disturbing, and demoralizing disappointment as I had in Commack.

Tony only let the stimulator begin by administering half the voltage used for the thresholds, a measure of precaution as at times the repeating frames can considerably reduce required voltages; or, if the voltage was set too high to begin with, then the repeating frames could provoke pain or even a seizure. Slowly, Tony increased the voltage in small increments until Karen said she could see her phosphenes.

Karen tried her best but did not succeed in picking things up off the table. Her husband kept reminding her not to move her eyes. Finally, she did admit seeing the edge of the table, but the dots were scrambled. We tried to get her to walk a bit as Tony followed with the attached laptop, but she did not make sense of the dots. The timer ran out on the stimulator, and we had to quit. It had been a long day.

On July 17, we tried it again with Karen. Bill was in his room, sick. Claire said he may have to go to the hospital. We mapped Karen again, and this time, her map was quite different. She was still rather upbeat and positive—the perfect patient. This time, she had no trouble picking things up off the table in front of her. Tony arranged the system's computer so it would run without the laptop, and she started to slowly walk in the halls of the office.

"Look for the baseboards," we urged her to look at edges to get an idea of what to go by to use this form of vision. She did that, and then pointed out a chair as well as a picture hung from the wall.

"I see that!" she announced as she pointed at the articles she noticed. She continued to walk around, using her cane very little, and noticed more things about the office until the timer ran out.

Karen was happy as she left for her home, with the equipment packed in her suitcase. We all felt really good about this, as did Claire when we told her. I felt a lot less uneasy about Lino and Paul having their operations now. Yes, I did not have good luck now with mine, as did some of the other patients, but Karen's enthusiasm and thrill when seeing again the little dots forming a picture was enough to say it wouldn't be fair to deny Lino or Paul the same chance. We spoke to Bill that night in his room as he had requested a meeting.

"Good work with Karen," he said as he lay in his bed. He sounded so weak I was truly worried. Without Bill, this show will not go on, I knew that.

"I am sick, guys, and I want you to phone Klaus and Ken and cancel their testing."

I didn't like the sound of that at all. Klaus, a businessman who traveled throughout Europe for the sale of specialty products, already was irritated at Bill's constant need to have to alter the schedule as he always received last-minute arrangements to come out, which often interrupted his work schedule. To call up and cancel now would make all hell break loose.

"Look, Bill," I began, "Klaus had said he went through great trouble to accommodate our schedule as it required a lot of rearranging his own schedule just to come out here." I hoped Bill would understand that people had to continue to prioritize their work and not just spend every day waiting to accommodate Bill's schedule alterations.

"Just tell him that it's tough luck!" Bill shouted.

"I can't say that to a patient." Claire tried to soothe him.

"Bill, stop . . . that's all OK, they can handle it on their own . . . we already bought him the plane tickets, so why not let them try . . . they did good with Karen, you know . . ."

We all knew Bill didn't mean what he said—he was very sick, and it was affecting his thinking at the time. It was sad to watch, and we felt sad for Claire as we sat in silence.

Bill groaned, "Then just do what you want . . ." His voice faded off in absolute resignation. It didn't make any of us feel better, but at least Klaus and Ken will have their systems readjusted. We thanked Bill and wished him a quick recovery. Claire thanked us and wished us a good night's sleep. It was time to go in town and get some good food, sit among the people in the great food square of Lisbon, and relax.

I followed Tony and Don, poking the borders of the sidewalk with my cane. A man speaking broken English stopped me.

"You know . . ." he began, then found more words. "Here, in Portugal, we have a cure for blindness." He must have been pointing at the hospital, which was still close to us. "They make you see, there, with a computer."

I didn't know what to say. I didn't have my computer on as the last time I tried it I only saw five points of light—not enough to do anything with. I fumbled for words.

"I know, it is good what they are working on . . . but . . ." Neither Tony, who knew Portuguese, nor Don helped me out to try to talk to this man about this issue. He had obviously seen everything on TV and believed it.

"Maybe I will get it some day. But it is a lot of money . . . and maybe it won't work with me, I don't know. Thanks."

I quickly left the scene. I must have seemed rather crazy to that man as I didn't immediately beg and plead for more information as if seeing again was my number one priority in life—as it once was.

I had more worries about Bill the next day, as I heard he'd been admitted to the hospital and was not cooperating with his medicine, and he was angry at the nursing staff as well. This was not like Bill, and I was then hoping for something that would guarantee some sort of continuation in Bill's absence. I thought he might have to retire soon, but I did not want to be stuck with these implants in my head, $130,000 out of my pocket, and nothing more to show for it. Something needed to give.

My answer came the next night. The day had been routine as we tested Ken and reset his equipment, and that evening, Claire came down to the bar to talk with us. She was obviously distressed about Bill, and I could tell she'd been crying. I wondered if she knew I shared her sentiments, yet, for different reasons, but for Bill's life just the same. I listened as she spoke, once our general discussion about Bill subsided.

"You know those two scientists are here as they represent the university that is interested in buying up this vision project so they can continue it."

The three of us had heard some unconfirmed talk of this before, but this time it was Claire who spoke. I wanted to know more.

"They are interested in perhaps investing into it and taking over. Dr. Kolff is connected with the university, and he is helping with the liaison. So I hope you guys can help out, make it all work, and keep the patients doing as best as they can."

We sat for some time at the bar, long after it closed, talking of Bill, his dreams for the vision project, and how great it would be to have a promising direction with the necessary funds to make this work. It was clear, very clear, that Claire was looking forward to Bill's retirement. She was not able to deal with this, and I did not blame her one bit. Bill was tough, really tough to deal with when he decided to be in a bad mood.

I thought more about the new turn of events the next few days. I had two perspectives to think of—one from that of a patient, and the other from that of an employee. The patient's perspective at first seemed very promising—more knowledge, more reason, and more money to help with the project. However, what about those big risks Bill was taking now—such as issuing patients equipment to take home? I realized before going to the Dobelle Institute that the normal procedure with new products is to implant patients, then only experiment with these products within the boundaries of the laboratory, then send the patients home empty-handed. Then, on the question of my employment with Dobelle, will I be kept on? I am a Canadian, and Canadians have a tough time generally to get work visas in the States. Dobelle pulled it off by subcontracting me out and having my office in Canada. I doubted that Ohio University would really do that, or would they?

The following morning, the three of us had to meet with Bill in the hospital where he was going to pick out the correct implants to use for Lino and Paul. Bill was laying on his back, his medication making him very drowsy. Tony held out the bag of electrode arrays as he fumbled through them. He selected a couple for Lino, then one for Paul, as Paul was going to start with just one implant. The head neurosurgeon, Dr. Antunes, then entered the room.

"These are the electrodes Bill wants to have implanted in Lino's head," Tony said to him as he held out those selected by Bill. Antunes looked them over, then rummaged more through the bag of arrays.

"It's not what he wants," he said as he gestured to Bill, who had already fallen asleep again. "It's what I want that matters here."

He continued to look for different arrays than those he had in his hand. He complained to us about the size of these implants, especially the heavy bundle of wire coming from the electrodes. 242 wires, even with a relatively fine gauge of thirty-six, translated to a heavy bundle that Antunes feared would not allow the skin covering the brain to heal and close off, or that the bulk of the wire will pull out the electrodes from their intended location on the visual cortex. When feeling the arrays through the bag, I could see his point. This seemed like such a primitive, archaic way of transmitting current to an electrode array.

Bill had to go home the following day. He had been so difficult in the hospital that he was told that he'd have to try to find a good hospital in the United States. Claire was urged to take him out while he was still able to travel. We were on our own.

Klaus came to be tested again. He said his system didn't work right and that he couldn't use it. Moreover, he said he was getting headaches ever since his seizure in January. He asked me how my system was doing.

"I have five phosphenes at the moment," I said. He sat in the testing chair, and we started the routine. In short time, we realized he had a problem—only about a dozen phosphenes, and no more. There wasn't much to map, and not much to test. Klaus was getting fed up.

"If this is all this thing has to offer, then I want my money back and you can keep this thing," he announced, not to my surprise. He took off the cables and placed the vision system on the table. "I don't even want to take this system home—just write me a letter that I left it here, and I'll go home and talk to Bill from there."

We called it a day, locking up the office and crossing over the footbridge that connected our office to the CUF Hospital to visit Lino and Paul before having dinner. We walked in odd silence as each of us had our own thoughts to deal with following Klaus's reaction. It was inevitable that this would materialize—it was possible all the patients eventually would ask for a refund and implant removal. With Bill's fading health, it was important that Ohio University jumped on board, but it was going to be a real challenge to make the project look as an appetizing investment while one patient is already having his system removed. And at this moment, we were going to greet two freshly implanted patients who were going to be in great pain from the operation, yet with high hopes on the project, equipped with the most positive of attitudes as we reinforced the positive attributes and merits of the system. We had no other choice either, as the possibility existed that these patients having the new teflon-covered arrays would have no problems at all.

I felt deeply for the patients as I entered their rooms. Paul was already sitting in a chair for a bit, complaining of a headache, but he had only received one implant, not two. Paul had another medical condition, which did not facilitate the implant of dual pedestals, so he had a good side to lay on when sleeping. Lino, however, was in rough shape. He spoke little except about the pain, and I didn't know how to respond.

We flew back to the United States at the end of the month. Paul had recovered enough in a few days that he could fly back to Australia, but Lino was in rough shape—still dizzy when on his feet, having a bad headache and no appetite.

Once home, I received a few phone calls from some of the patients—Kirk, Karen, and John—as their main concern was the health of Bill. I wanted to share the info about Ohio University possibly taking over but had been asked by both Claire and the scientists from Ohio to keep quiet, as, so far, nothing was written in stone. There remained a lot of work and convincing to be done yet, partially because our research notes were terribly disorganized, and partially because we all believed Bill was going to ask for a lot in return.

The next month seemed quiet enough as Bill did not talk to me at all—he was in a hospital in New York, and none of us really knew his exact condition. Klaus had sent a letter, formally requesting that his money be refunded in full and that his implants be removed. In his letter of request, he noted that his reasons were based on the fact that he was not receiving any functional vision, had complications with his health ever since his seizure in January, and that it appeared that no more real progress was being made on the further development of the system. Louise, the secretary of Dobelle Institute/Avery Labs in Commack, wrote a letter for me to translate to German as a reply in which Klaus was asked to wait until Bill came back from the hospital. None of us thought that Bill could ever refund any of the money—as Jerry T. had pointed out to us in Manhattan. We were all investors in a grand vision project, and the money was spent.

On August 28, my family and I decided to go have a meal at a restaurant. Once Lorri parked the van, I noticed a bright light beginning to form in my right visual field—so bright it resembled looking at a very bright lightbulb up close. The sides of this splotch of light had sharp corners similar to that of a broken piece of glass. As the light grew in size, I began to feel faint and dizzy—just as I had done just before having my first seizure. I waited, trying not to think of the light, taking deep breaths and praying I wouldn't have a seizure. I couldn't imagine how it would affect the kids who were with me in the van should I have a seizure right before their eyes. I couldn't even look away from the light—it was right in front of me, eyes closed or not, pointed left, to the right, or anywhere that light followed me wherever I looked. The light then slowly subsided and I felt better.

I said to Lorri, "We're going to have to be more careful in the future as to what I do to my brain."

"I know," Lorri replied, "but we never thought it would turn out like this."

On September 4, I was invited to go to the Kingston General Hospital in Kingston for an MRI. Dr. Girvin had been able to set this up through his influence and connections at the university, and I obliged but asked what was involved.

"As long as you have no steel or iron, it's fine . . ." I had been told long before going to a hospital for the MRI, but then I learned from the staff in Commack that the wires leading from the electrodes to the pedestal in the head of the patients were made of steel, not platinum. I recalled that Jerry T. had his wires made of platinum and had automatically assumed it was the same construction in my head. Not so, I was told first by the engineers, then confirmed by Bill albeit further on into the winter—they were all made of steel. These steel wires were directly welded onto the connectors of our electrodes. I did ask Bill about it once he did return from the hospital, and he explained by saying when he used platinum wires, they often broke as they offered little flexibility. When Tony and Don and I discussed this later, we came to a consensus that it was not a good idea to have done as the steel wire concepts had never been tested prior to our implantations. Did the welding of the wire change the purity of the platinum electrodes, we asked ourselves. This could add up to another reason why phosphenes were disappearing.

September rolled in, and Bill still was in the hospital. I spent my time in my office talking to the media about some previous details of their filming, all the while keeping quiet about the newest problems with our project. Patients who were already implanted called, one of them Kirk who insisted he get back his system and have it adjusted as he had to have it for his work program. It was difficult for the crew in Commack to authorize anything without Bill's consent, especially the testing of patients, so we tried to negotiate with Claire. This worked easier than expected, as Claire accepted our explanations and seemed to trust our judgment.

In early November, I received the following letter from Bill:

The Dobelle Institute (Portugal) Lda.
Artificial Vision for the Blind
To: All Recipients
Date: Nov. 4, 2003

Fr:
William H. Dobelle, PhD, Chairman and CEO

RE: I am Now Back in the Office

As you probably know, I was "air-lifted" from Lisbon to New York in July 2003 and have spent most of the intervening months in the hospital. I was never in any danger, but acute pain resulting from the shingles virtually incapacitated me.

I am pleased to report that a change in medication had a near miraculous effect, and I am now in the office on a regular basis. It will take a few weeks to get the artificial vision project moving again, and I appreciate your understanding and patience.

If you have any questions or problems that need immediate attention, please contact me by mail or telephone.

Regards,

Avenida Infante Santo 34, 7th Floor Lisboa 1350-179 Portugal Tel: +351 213 940 473, Answering machine: +351 213 940 536, Fax: +351 213 940 474 www.artificialvision.com

This letter was promptly followed by a very impressive summary of what Dr. Dobelle considered major breakthroughs in the further development of artificial vision. The two patients he made reference to were Lino and Paul. Lino had a difficult time with his implant recovery and spent subsequently almost three weeks in the CUF Hospital before being discharged.

The Dobelle Institute (Portugal) Lda.
Artificial Vision for the Blind
To: All Recipients
Date: November 4, 2003

Fr: William H. Dobelle, PhD, Chairman and CEO
Re: Status of the Latest Artificial Vision System

The first thirteen patients were implanted with a total of 136 electrodes each, but there were many technical problems that had to be overcome for larger systems. The final problem was whether or not the body would accept the larger system without infection because a greater area would be surgically exposed and there was a greater circumference to the incision.

Ultimately, we were able to build a refined system of totally 484 electrodes (242 on each side), but the question remained whether or not the electrodes would become infected.

Two new patients were implanted with these larger systems in July 2003, and I am very pleased to report that no problems were encountered. Systems in both patients have healed quite normally. All future implants, therefore, are expected to employ these new, larger electrode/pedestal combinations.

Meanwhile, our engineering team has been working on a new stimulator. The latest design, which is still under construction-, is slightly smaller than a standard VHS videotape. This small package encompasses a 484 channel stimulator, the computer to drive the stimulator, and battery power to permit twelve hours between recharges. The next series of implants with this new system is expected in January, 2004

If you are interested in being a patient, and have not talked to me or one of my colleagues in the last several weeks, please complete the questionnaire below.

Please fax to: 001 +631+ 864-1610 or mail to: 61 Mall Drive Commack, NY 11725-5703

Name: _____

Address:
City, State, Country_____
Telephone: Country Code: _____ Area Code:_____ Number:
Fax: Country Code: _____ Area Code:_____ Number:_____

Avenida Infante Santo 34, 7th Floor Lisboa 1350-179 Portugal
Tel: +351 213 940 473, Answering machine: +351 213 940 536,
Fax: +351 213 940 474 www.artificialvision.com

In the letter, the implants performed on Lino and Paul sounded more experimental than clinical, right from the words written by Bill. He had said during the January 2003 interviews that the program was now a clinical procedure, not an experimental one. Yet, he admitted to having no idea whether or not this massive implant would cause an infection in one of the most vital organs of the human body.

Bill called me and asked me to call all the people who had shown interest via the Web site's online application form. I spent days on end talking with interested men and women, some of them wanting the system more than anything in their lives, others more careful to jump to the conclusion that this type of vision would help. But the underlining problem at the end of the conversation was always the money. It just cost too much—US$100,000 was just too much for a person to accumulate while earning a normal wage. I found it difficult to convey to Bill the fact that people who went blind partially through life are stung hard by this fact alone and will seldom have the luxury to accumulate such a vast resource of cash. The project needed a cash injection coming from sources other than the already distraught patients, and this led us back to the high hopes we all had for Ohio University to take over. Everyone at the office in Commack discussed the possible takeover when Bill was absent. We all shared two major worries. First was the problem of the fading phosphenes. Klaus had obvious reason to be unhappy, and we hoped this matter would be handled as quietly as possible so as not to startle Ohio University and have them reconsider. But what if they asked for all the testing info, and upon reading it, lose interest because of the fading phosphenes? Secondly, we all knew Bill Dobelle very well by now. He was not the type to pass over any control to anyone without a fight. Thus, the idea that he was going to gracefully relinquish control and the future decision-making capacity to Ohio University was not something we believed possible. We prayed that some individuals within the deal would recognize this and give Bill some important presence in the project at least until the deal was signed so that he'd still feel he was being useful.

December came and Bill phoned me about having Klaus's implants removed. Bill sounded as if his change in medicine had revived him somewhat, but by now, I knew better than to believe he was fully cured and good to go for a few years.

"Have you talked to Klaus lately?" he asked. He had asked me before to try to sway Klaus's decision to remove the implants. He wanted me to ensure Klaus that there was still a lot of hope in this project working out for him.

"I did. But Klaus is determined to have the implants removed and to do no more experimentation. He complains of constant headaches and other discomfort from them, including the infection around the pedestals."

Bill elaborated for a few seconds on what I said and replied, "I figure he just wants out of the project. I don't think he's got any headaches at all."

"I don't know about that," I said, somewhat taken aback at this kind of diagnosis coming from the genius. "I had some trouble the other day—I started seeing large, bright light patterns in my visual field, and I felt like I was going to have a seizure myself. It is either from previous stimulations or from the seizures I have already had."

Bill reacted as if he didn't even hear what I said. "Did you have any luck contacting potential patients from that list I sent?"

"Lots of interest, but only a couple said they'd maybe be able to come up with the money. They figured on going public and asking for donors."

Bill became upset when I mentioned going public. "I don't want that! That's just asking for trouble—to have the media pry in our affairs without us inviting them first. Make sure you tell them not to do that!" As I listened to Bill, I thought again of the Ohio scientists and crossed my fingers and how much this project depended on them.

My task was to translate over the telephone the information Dr. Domingo in CUF Hospital wanted to convey to Klaus regarding the outcome of the operation for the removal of the implants. Klaus had been subject to the surgery for five hours as the doctors attempted to remove both implants, but only succeeded in removing one as most of the wires including the electrode array was stuck to the surface of Klaus's brain due to an excessive buildup of fibrous tissue. Once the first implant was removed, it was too risky to prolong the operation further with the removal of the second one, so the wires were clipped where they exited the dura, and the two pedestals were removed. Dr. Domingo said that the situation in Klaus's head would have probably been responsible for the headaches and other discomfort Klaus had been experienced up to the surgery.

I contacted Dr. Girvin via e-mail to update him on the present situation. He had not known about the possible takeover by Ohio and seemed to find this news interesting. We discussed the situation about Klaus losing his phosphenes, and he mentioned that no more implants should be performed until we have investigated why patients are losing phosphenes.

January 2004 started out with Bill asking me if I could go to Portugal that month. In fact, he wanted me down within the next couple of days for some testing, and then go directly to Portugal. There were four patients already lined up, with two having already paid and two others pending payment before their surgery. I came down fast with Richie and took my place at the table to be tested. But Tony led me to a small room beside the conference room, a little deeper yet into the center of the building. He explained to me that the FDA were starting to investigate what Bill was doing there, not surprising considering all the media coverage of the recent past. The FDA could make surprise spot checks there whenever they wanted, I was told, as it was forbidden to test patients in this manner without prior FDA approval. In this little room, referred to as the "Frankenstein" room, one could easily disconnect the system with the help from a call from the front desk before the FDA inspector could ever find it.

I noticed some stress as well as an air of excitement in the office. With Bill there, I couldn't really investigate, but before coming down, I had spoken to Tony who said that finally Bill announced to us that Ohio University was interested in signing a contract for the takeover of Dobelle Institute and Avery Labs and that now we'd have lots of money for the project. Bill hadn't yet said anything to me, so I had to pretend I didn't know a thing.

We tested my left visual field and found only two phosphenes working where I once had over fifty-five. My head was hurting, and I was starting to feel sick. I heard the sound of Bill's wheelchair being pushed into the Frankenstein room where I underwent the clandestine experimentation. Bill still hadn't acquired the energy to launch himself off his good foot like he used to. He seemed very frail.

"Just two working phosphenes on the left visual cortex," Tony announced to Bill's expectant expression. Bill didn't seem too disturbed by this; if he was, it didn't show. His coping skills were admirable.

"All right, we'll just not use his system to show off to the patients." He turned to me. "You'll just have to answer their questions, Jens, and forget about the demonstration."

I, the medical patient hoping to see from this experiment however, was disturbed by the absence of phosphenes. "These new implants that the patients in Portugal will receive are now coated with teflon, right?" I inquired. It would be fair enough to explain to the new patients the problem I was having and how they wouldn't have it because they had the material originally used in the implantations of the first volunteers.

"No," Bill replied indignantly. "That never had anything to do with it. Silastic material is used routinely in brain implants of different sorts without any problems."

I was stunned by this response. He had admitted only a few months ago in a letter issued to all of us patients that the new implants would be teflon coated to prevent the silastic material from touching the brain, yet now he was denying there ever was anything wrong. He was going to put exactly the same thing that I have in my head into the heads of the new patients. This could be problematic for the new patients, and I made it known to the others how I felt.

"We understand" was the reply, once Bill left the scene. "But Bill is his own ethical committee. We refer to him as the ethical committee on wheels."

We spent a few minutes experimenting with a small 1 channel stimulator Tony had built on the fly, which incorporated sine-wave style stimulation instead of square wave. For months we had been bugging Bill to relent and allow the stimulation of a different wave form, but he flatly refused, saying all had already been done. Yet, once Tony tried this sine wave on Karen, she was able to see phosphenes on electrodes that had suddenly stopped producing phosphenes. We tried it with my electrodes, using only one pulse. I never could see one pulse even when all went well back in December 2002. I asked Bill if we could try a five-pulse train, as that was what I needed since the first day of stimulation in order to see a phosphene. He refused, and we gave up the experiment.

"We'll have to try this once Ohio takes over . . ." I said, and Tony agreed.

Bill invited me to dine with him that evening. I took it he had a few things to discuss with me prior to going to Portugal. I was right.

The food was especially delicious following the eight-hour drive down from Canada.

Bill spoke, "I am selling the company."

I pretended to know nothing, as if I did, he'd have reprimanded the others at the office for spilling the beans. He, himself wanted to spill them instead.

"Are they competent people, who have the money to continue the project?" I asked innocently.

"Well," he grunted as he ate. "I don't know about the competent part as they don't know a hell of a lot about artificial vision." He continued eating and talking. "But there's lots of money there—probably around $200 million total they can stick into this project."

I ate a bit and nodded. Bill must have thought I'd be concerned that he wouldn't be making the decisions anymore. "But don't worry, Jens. I am going to continue to be in charge at least for another three years, and if they bankrupt the project, I get to keep the project and the money they're paying me as well."

"Money?" I asked curiously, expecting him to tell me to mind my own business.

"Yeah, they're giving me fifteen million." He said this as casually as if he was winning a free coke.

I continued eating my dinner. I had spoken to the two scientists once when they were still in Portugal, and they had never insinuated Bill would continue running the project. Bill then changed the subject to Klaus.

"I still think that Klaus was making up his pain."

"Dr. Domingo told me there was a high probability that the fibrous tissue buildup could easily have provoked a headache." I then added, maybe somewhat daringly, "At some point, it is important to believe the patient's testimony, even if it is negative."

There was a pause, and then Bill turned to me. "Are you getting yours removed?"

"I don't have plans to, no. I'd rather take part in the research and development, provided there is an opportunity and also provided the project is continuing. Once the project dies, I don't think there'd be much more use for them."

Bill laughed out loud and said, "Oh, don't worry, there's lots of life in me yet. We'll get this whole thing going after we iron out some glitches, and you'll be on your way with new implants." Then he added in a voice indicating he hadn't the slightest doubt about the eventual success of his project. "Just you wait until we test Lino and Paul, and with all their phosphenes, their vision will be enough for you to want this new implant too."

But it had to be smaller, I thought to myself as I finished dinner—much smaller. Tony, Don, and I had often discussed over a glass of wine the merits of implanting under the scalp a small multiplexer that would allow 242 electrodes to be selected by only seventeen wires. This would allow the implantation of a jack the size of the end of a pencil—much more comfortable and less apt to attract attention. Bill always insisted he didn't trust electronics and did not want to implant them. Understood, we had retorted, if the electronics were implanted within the skull, but if only under the scalp, service to it would be a minor skin operation that would not cause more than minor discomfort—able to be done with a mere local anesthetic. Yet, Bill did not budge. He had no logical explanation that could be used to argue our point. A miniature jack, I pointed out, would be the least difficult for a patient to tolerate, whereas the massive 3-cm diameter version used, in conjuction with the dual 244-lead cable having a diameter as that of a standard garden hose was obviously surpassing the limitations a person could be expected to adjust to. Patient discomfort, whether in the form of too large an implant or too high a price, or even to the degree of a seizure, however, was not a concern that affected the decisions Dr. Dobelle made for the further development of the project. We needed Ohio University more than ever. It was unlikely we'd encounter while working with Ohio the same barriers when attempting to press a point based on the humane treatment of patients, I assumed.

We flew to Portugal without the boss as Bill was still not sure he'd be able to go without getting sick. We did not mind by any means, as that meant we could concentrate on our tasks. First of all, we had three possible implant patients to meet before they'd be going to surgery. All the patients had already paid the new price—100,000 Euros, which was up from the previous $100,000.

The first patient we met was an older gentleman who had lost his sight suddenly a couple years ago. He was still frail from a sickness he had had. I answered his questions honestly; I was well beyond just trying to talk people into this for the sake of having more patients. I did feel more secure in my heart of what I was doing now that I knew Ohio University would run this project as it should be.

"Do you want to get the update?" Vincenzo asked me.

"No, I don't. I just had my head opened up a year and a half ago, and I am tired of hurting and hospitals. Moreover, I want to wait until the implants are smaller," I answered.

I then proceeded in explaining the sudden loss of phosphenes of some of the patients, and of Klaus having his pedestals removed. I explained this to all of the patients I met during this trip to Portugal. Interestingly enough, neither Vincenzo nor Cheri, the second patient who was a young American woman, swayed from their original decision to have the implant despite what I said. The third patient, Tatsa from Cameroon, was not going to show up until two weeks later, and if he wanted the operation, we would have to stay an extra ten days.

Dr. Domingo arrived at the office to talk to both Cheri and Vincenzo for his usual explanation of the operation, as well as assessing their health in preparation for the operations. Vincenzo was not ready yet, he was told, and should wait at least six months before going ahead with the surgery. Cheri was ready and was to receive her operation January 14.

Back in the office, Tony was busy testing Ken, when Ken's system failed. Tony resorted to his own engineer's system, commonly used as a backup or for testing when the patient had no system. It failed too. Jerry D. arrived next for testing and still did not get more than —three or four phosphenes. Kirk, in contrast, had jumped up in phosphene count again. He had originally lost a lot. Finally, Karen, who had been operated on a year ago during the media blitz, came in for testing. She lost most of her phosphenes—one side did not produce any at all. She was visibly sad, Tony had said, and she had asked Bill what it could be that made these phosphenes go away.

"I don't know just yet," he replied, then added, "just don't worry about it, go home, and I'll call you in a few days to discuss this with you."

Bill told Tony to stop testing as he had no more money in the company to bring in more patients. The tested patients went home empty-handed. They seemed used to it now, as they never complained out loud. Other than Klaus, the patients did not refuse any more testing. I understood why—they always came hoping Bill had things finally under control and that they'd go home seeing.

Once Vincenzo was told by Dr. Domingo about his required delay for the implantation, Vincenzo asked me for his money back. Shiela said she had to get permission from Bill before writing the check. I phoned Bill and told him the situation.

"Tell Vincenzo that the only way he's getting his money back is if I find another buyer for his machine. Make sure you tell him we already had to spend the money to make his machine."

I hung up the telephone and turned to Don in despair but didn't know what to say.

"There's a blind man in the next room—struck down by fate as he had that terrible sickness a couple years ago that even had taken most of his hearing, and now I am supposed to tell him that the vast quantity of money he had paid to see again is not going to be returned to him . . ." I needed advice desperately for what I had to do.

Don grabbed a copy of the contract that all patients signed prior to paying. As he read it out loud, I realized it hadn't changed from what mine was initially—money is refunded in full immediately if patient is found physically or mentally unfit for the surgery.

"He can't do that!" Don was as frustrated as I was. Yet, we couldn't say more—we knew why Bill was doing this. He had already spent all the money on the project such as the flights, development of the new system, paying off the new pedestal manufacturer, and more.

"If I did this, I'd feel like a crook," I stated. We decided that perhaps Vincenzo would accept that Dobelle Institute holds onto the money for six months, and if at that date the surgery still cannot be performed, he'd get an immediate refund. We approached him and presented this idea, which he eventually accepted. Lucky for us.

Cheri had her operation on January 14, and the next day, Don and I visited. She was sleepy, and in pain, yet in good spirits. She was ready to see again. I met Dr. Domingo on the way out of the hospital, and we talked for a bit as I described the problems we were having with the phosphenes. He did not realize that they were dropping at the rate that they were. When he asked which of the patients were presently using their system, I couldn't name anyone.

"I'll have to discuss this with Dr. Antunes," he said. "We have to investigate and find out whether we are helping the patients or whether we're hurting them."

Shiela announced the next day that Bill had gone to a dinner with Ohio University and received a good-faith payment from them. This news lifted our spirits.

The following day, Patient Tatsa showed up with his wife and one of his sons. They were tired from their flight but still wanted us to visit them in their hotel room. Don, Dr. Domingo, and I spoke with them, having to speak in French as they knew no English.

"I want to be able to tell my wife from another woman," Tatsa stated.

"Not possible," I said. I explained the type of image the vision using phosphenes actually rendered. Tatsa was disappointed as his wife and son shook their heads in disapproval. Don brought forth the jack and electrodes for them to see and Tatsa to feel.

Tatsa spoke up, "I can't run around with those things in my head! I am a businessman, and I can't look like that!

More questions were posed, and once Dr. Domingo described the details of the implantation procedure, Tatsa had had enough. "That's going to kill me!" he said. He changed his mind right then and there, and Shiela immediately handed him back his check.

I returned home on January 25. Cheri had still been in the hospital as she developed an infection and had to be reopened. I felt so sorry for her fate and all the pain that went with it. I telephoned the office in Commack regularly, as well as the one in Portugal, just to keep updated. Everyone was excited about the Ohio takeover and wondered what their new position would be. Apparently, info came down the grapevine that the takeover date would fall on the end of February. Then I received the letter in the mail that I found puzzling, as Bill seemed to be trying to say something in it I didn't quite understand.

The Dobelle Institute (Portugal) Lda.
Artificial Vision for the Blind

> February 3, 2004
> To: Jens Naumann
> From:
> William H. Dobelle, PhD, Chairman & CEO
>
> Subject: New Artificial Vision System
>
> As you know, we have been working on new electronics to support implanted systems with approximately five hundred electrodes, and we have now implanted arrays of 242 electrodes on each side (484 total).
>
> The design has undergone a number of major iterations, and the latest mock-up is depicted in the attached xerox. The

computer, stimulator, and battery supplies for the new system—484 electrodes—are combined in a single case smaller than a VCR videotape. The electronic architecture, however, is quite different from the existing 144 electrode systems. The new system can easily stimulate either of our electrode arrays (the smaller with 144 electrodes and the larger with 484 electrodes).

Total weight (including the battery) is about one pound, and the battery life is projected at eighteen hours. Implementation of this technology is presently being studied, and I will be back in touch with you in a few weeks with a tentative timetable.

Regards!

I asked myself, "Is he just trying to keep the implanted patients happy by stalling using the information tactic, or is he trying to demonstrate he'd be the boss of artificial vision no matter who bought him out?" The most puzzling was the line "I'll be in touch with you in the next few weeks . . ." as such a timetable would mean Bill would contact us even after Ohio took over.

I telephoned Sheila and asked how Cheri was doing—finally Cheri was starting to get better. She had been in the hospital a little less than a month now. When talking to Bill about it, he didn't seem worried.

"That's all part of this project—sometimes things just don't work out as well as they should. By the way, I had Jerry T., the original volunteer in here lately and he had thirty-eight good phosphenes still." Jerry T. was the one with the teflon implant. Kieth, however, did not fair so well—his phosphene count had gone down to just over a dozen, and most of them produced discomfort now. Bill also tried testing Dennis, but his scalp had never stopped growing around the implants; it just grew up and over, and he needed plastic surgery to cut the skin back before testing could be done. His savers were damaged but could not be removed because of the scalp. He must have been quite uncomfortable with those stuck permanently in his head. When talking to Bill, I did not hear him mention Ohio once. I was becoming worried as to the certainty of the takeover.

March was relatively uneventful except that Klaus was sending letters to pressure for the refund. He was beginning the threat with lawyers, and Bill then decided to commit himself for a refund, but he didn't know when. He must have received enough convincing however, perhaps directly to his office as Dobelle asked me to send a fax to Klaus confirming a deposit. A week later, Patient Marina from Italy called to say how angry she was with this company as she had to wait over a year for a cable and that she'd perhaps go to the media to talk about it. Bill told me to tell her if she did that, she would be ejected from the project. I mused at this—I never thought a patient could really be fired.

Hopes were fading in the Commack office regarding a takeover, but we tolerated the wait as Bill had gone on a cruise with his family and wasn't to return until early April. It was on April 8, 2004—exactly two years after my surgery that hurt so much, and had so many hopes attached to it—that I received one of the most concerning letters in my life.

The Dobelle Institute (Portugal) Lda.
Artificial Vision for the Blind

April 6, 2004
Fr: Pirn Kolff, MD, PhD, Dunwoody Village 3500 West Chester Pike A311 Newcown Square, Pennsylvania 19073
Friends and Advisors Re: Decision to Defer Selling Artificial Vision / Avery

Wm. H. Dobelle, PhD, Chairman & Chief Executive Officer
I think all of you know, I just completed a cruise from New York to Nassau, Bahamas, which was the first successful vacation that I have had with my family in almost five years. On all of the previous five attempts, I ended up in the hospital. In fact, it was rumored they had a "pool" going in the lab about whether or not I would make it this time. As a result of considerable thought (indeed I thought of little else during the cruise), I have decided to defer selling Artificial Vision / Avery, at least for the foreseeable future.

1. I feel quite well. Frankly, if I sold the business at this time, I would almost certainly be very unhappy. The buyers would do things differently from me, and I think that I would accept retirement rather poorly. Indeed, this may be the reason I accepted Ohio University's decision to back out with such equanimity.

2. We are now conducting an intensive study of the sixteen patients implanted since 2002 in Lisbon. As a result of this work, I believe we are on the verge of a number of critically important discoveries that will affect the future of Artificial Vision. Yesterday I accepted an invitation to present some of these new findings at the 50th Annual ASAIO Meeting in Washington, and a few weeks ago, I was notified that my early paper on vision and hearing (1974) had been selected as

" . . . one of the twenty-five most important papers in ASAIO history." Having invested my life in artificial vision over the last thirty-five years, this really isn't the time to quit.

3. Without false modesty, I think I know more about Artificial Vision than anyone else. I don't know how much is due to intellect and how much is due to having invested my life in the project This fact remains the same.

4. Based on our experience with Ohio University, I think I now understand what people really want (a sure thing with little or no risk). There is no way that I could keep a straight face in assuring prospective purchasers that this was the case with Artificial Vision / Avery.

I am sending copies of this memo to people in the United States and abroad who have chosen to take the "ride" with me, and I certainly welcome everyone's comments and suggestions.

Regards!
Avenida Infante. Santo 34, 7th floor Lisboa 1350 173 Portugal
c/o 61 Mall Drive, Commack, New York
Tel: +001 631 864-1600

I was not sure what the "intensive study on the patients" was all about, as all Bill did was some random testing as he saw fit. This letter was bad news for the patients and employees alike. Bill says he is feeling fine, but I can almost bet he'll be right back in the hospital the next month.

He had been going through bouts of serious illnesses ever since I received his first letter in August 2000, first with his heart bypass, then his diabetic ulcer, and more recently his shingles. Some of the comments in the letter were right out of place in the face of current problems, such as the first one that suggests we, the patients, are going to be satisfied by the fact that Bill would not have his pride harmed and thus feel unhappy should someone else take over the project. On separate occasions, Bill drew attention to his "expertise" and "experience" with artificial vision as if he was a one-of-a-kind genius. He was able to coordinate a risky project with his own skill, that was for sure, but he still needed some major help. Most peculiar of all, he still thought we, the patients, regarded him as infallible and without need of help from anyone else—especially from someone with a lot of money for the project. The fourth comment was by far the most significant that Bill's own expectations of the patients' success in seeing again was considerably modified from the first few letters we received from him. Only two years ago, he had suggested the surgery would be performed on an outpatient basis and that the patient should be able to recognize faces once fitted with the stimulator. Now he was reprimanding Ohio for expecting the vision system to actually function by restoring some sort of useful sight to the patients with little risk of failure. To me, however, it had been sold with those very promises.

I talked to Bill a couple of days later as he wanted myself and Tony to go to Portugal to test Lino and Paul. I wasn't sure if he was going to have the systems for them to take home, and neither was he. We all knew, though, that even though Lino and Paul had 242-electrode implants, we only had the archaic seventy-two-channel systems to give them. This meant that after testing, we could send them home with seventy-two randomly selected phosphenes, and no more. The new systems were far from finished—the company lacked money to pay for the electronics required. While talking to Bill, he explained that Ohio University got cold feet and that he didn't think they had any control of the money they thought they'd use for the purchase. I suspected there was more to it than that; from the way Bill had talked to me about Ohio previously, he had the idea he'd be able to control their assets available for this project as well as the project itself. The road was going to be rough from here on—as if it wasn't already. All of the employees knew it, as did those patients who already knew Bill.

The plans were in place for Tony and I to go to Portugal to first test Paul and then Lino. We knew it would take a lot more time than did the testing of the standard 144 electrode arrays as we had 3.5 times more electrodes to deal with. We allowed two weeks for Lino and another week for Paul, as Paul only had a single implant. Lino's family had sent an e-mail to Bill in which their concern was that Lino really wanted to be in front of Paul in the procedure for fitting him with the equipment. They did not want any further delays, and by the sounds of their letter, they expected that Lino would come home seeing. Bill seemed to show frustration when confronted with the letter.

"What do these people want? Don't they know everything takes time?" he asked us.

I thought that the request from Lino was simple—he served his period of suffering during the operation and subsequent healing time, he paid the vast amount of money to purchase the machine, and now he wanted to be rewarded with sight. He didn't want to be set on the back burner for experimentation.

I had been scheduled to go to Portugal with Tony in April for the stimulation of both Paul and Lino, but Bill canceled my ticket and asked Tony to go alone—it was a measure to save money. I was to come later for the testing of Lino. I talked to Tony on the telephone and discovered he had good success with Paul—that most of his phosphenes worked and that Paul could locate articles in the room. Once the testing and mapping was complete, Tony was faced with a very uncomfortable situation—he had to disclose to Paul that he did not have the right cable to be able to send him home with the equipment. Paul would have to wait, he was told, until someone came to his house in Australia with the cable from Dobelle. I could only imagine how Paul felt. He had to fly twenty-two hours in order to get to Portugal, and after all he paid and suffered, he had to go back empty-handed. Worst of all, neither Tony nor I was sure exactly when, or even if, the day would come where we'd be flying to Australia to issue the new equipment, or even just a cable. The treatment of the patients, we both concluded, was beginning to border on outright cruelty.

Pat picked me up in one of the Dobelle vehicles—a minivan from Claire that the babysitters often drove to cart the Dobelle children around. The private limo Bill once had was gone—apparently repossessed for some reason. Richie wasn't going to get me—I had already found out Bill owed money to the limo company and couldn't pay. I knew the problem was money—neither Sheila nor myself, along with the crew in Commack, had been paid for a few weeks. Tony and Don said that the development of the new system that Paul, Lino, and Cheri needed had come to a complete standstill as a result of lack of funds. To make things worse, Bill was once again hospitalized. It hadn't been two weeks when he attested feeling good, ready to lead the project of artificial vision to its next great step—involve himself in the intensive study of all the patients—and now he was once again in the hospital. None of us were surprised.

Testing Lino in Portugal was more difficult than we first thought. He started out seeing the phosphenes as he should, then suddenly we had ten in a row that did not react. I suggested out of interest's sake we would try some of the first ones to see if maybe the same situation was taking place as did once with Klaus—wherein suddenly he did not see any more phosphenes during testing. Sure enough, Lino did not see the first phosphenes he had seen only an hour ago. We decided to give it a rest—have lunch and a bit of relax time.

The pause seemed to help, and once again, Lino saw the phosphenes, but now we were more timid to stretch the day and try to do all phosphenes in the few days we had set aside. We were running behind schedule—the airline tickets had already been booked and paid for, and we had yet to do the mapping—when we did not get any reaction out of any electrodes in Lino's other side. Speaking with Dr. Domingo, he explained it was quite possible that the array folded up either during the surgery or shortly afterward—he said with all the attached wires it was very, very difficult to control them as the silastic material at the same time did not have any rigidity. So Lino was already minus one half his visual field. I heard his family translating the information to Lino. He listened and sat in silence and said nothing. He just had to accept it—there was no pity in this business.

Mapping Lino was a challenge on its own. He kept pointing on the same space when describing where he saw the phosphene, so we had to try a combination of four different methods before we could determine even tentatively where he was actually seeing the phosphene. I had to admit—I did find the mapping a challenge for myself as unlike during normal vision where you have the luxury to move your eyes to look at the two points you want to compare, with phosphene mapping you have to measure the distance and direction between the center of vision—the focal point—up to the point where you see the phosphene in—usually in the peripheral visual field. It would be as difficult as judging the height of a person in front of you by just looking at their feet.

Then the time came to make the major decision—what to say to the Lino family to keep them reasonably happy going home. They had already disclosed to us that Lino had fallen into a depression ever since the surgery and that now to say he couldn't take the system home would not be accepted. We only had one cable that had the 242 connector jack on one side and four of the seventy-two electrode jacks on the other end. This cable, costing a good two grand, was all we had to use the old stimulator systems with the new, large implants, allowing the old stimulator to stimulate the selected seventy-two electrodes that the selected jack happened to be connected to. If we gave this cable away, we'd have to get another one fabricated. I thought up the most convincing speech to share with Bill and set out to phone him.

Bill sounded weak and disoriented as he struggled to make out what I was saying. He explained briefly that he was back in the hospital from the rehab center because he had fluid in his lungs. I didn't like the sound of that at all. Tony began to explain to Bill the phosphene situation with Lino.

"What are you guys doing?" Bill asked feebly. "Are you in Portugal? Since when?"

We had to explain the trip from the beginning and how we had been asked by him to go. We hoped Bill would comprehend and be able to make a decision as we presented our case to allow Lino to take the system and cable home.

"I'll think about it and call you back later" was Bill's reply. We never did get the call back, and when trying to call him later, we couldn't get through.

Lino was inspected by Domingo, who said that the scalp appeared to be receding from the pedestals. There was an obvious gap between the metal pedestal and the scalp, and the Lino family explained the effort they made daily to clean the gap so it wouldn't infect.

"If the gap gets any bigger, he'll have to come in for surgery to correct this," Domingo announced. "More surgery," I groaned inwardly. I was feeling for the patients as if I was undergoing the same torture. My own pedestals still leaked fluid daily, and I was forced to clean around them a few times a day or they'd be caked in scabs. The idea of using this kind of metal—titanium—wasn't such a good idea. I then remembered that Bill had vowed, previous to the latest round of implantations, to coat the titanium with different material to alleviate this complication. It never happened.

Lino practiced for a half hour with his system, which only had twenty-five or so phosphenes active. We couldn't use more as the cable did not let us, neither did the stimulator. We could only select one of the four smaller jacks at the stimulator end of the cable, and this one was the best of them. He had a much bigger implant than I, yet was being sent home with far fewer active phosphenes. It wasn't a temporary thing either—Don hadn't even started the construction of the new stimulator in Commack. In fact, he, along with the others, was still waiting for his last two paychecks.

Lino, unaware of the mounting internal problems at the Dobelle Institute, practiced fastidiously as he started to make a correlation between the phosphenes and what was in front of him. He slowly reached out to the battery Tony had placed in front of him on the empty table, then moved it around somewhat while looking for the reaction of the phosphenes. And as I watched, my soul cringed as I realized the summary of my emotions—we were just four people—Don, Tony, and I, and a very sick, old man—who were trying desperately to make this work—to give sight to those who craved it the most—but we were slipping . . . we needed help . . . and for all that was happening that seemed unethical, there was no one to blame. No one at all.

We sent Lino home with the cable and his twenty-five phosphenes. We were thanked by the family, but I am sure they were disappointed. Dennis, one of the first implanted patients from April 2002, arrived to have plastic surgery on his scalp, as his scalp had grown over the pedestals. Dennis and Tony and I discussed the dismal state of affairs that the project was finding itself in, as Dennis already knew a lot of the details. None of us were using our systems for anything useful on a regular basis, and that was dismal enough. I asked Dennis if he wouldn't be better off just to get Domingo to remove the pedestals and repair the scalp, but to my surprise, Dennis hadn't even considered doing this.

"What? Take them out? I'd be out of the project then. No way," he said. Domingo looked at them, then later met with us as we discussed the present state of artificial vision. We talked of all the problems we were encountering, some of them foreign to Domingo who just didn't get the right information from Bill. No one had told him that one patient was losing his bone screws and had a problem as well of a receding scalp from the pedestals. Both he and Antunes had assumed that patients were seeing good phosphenes, that the thresholds were stable, and that some of the patients were actually using the systems to improve their lives. Finally, Domingo stated that he and Antunes were both catering to the patients when there were problems without charge—but he couldn't do the plastic surgery as he wasn't a plastic surgeon and that the plastic surgeon would have to be paid. Little did he know that we, too, were part of the volunteer crew at the moment.

Sheila received a phone call from Commack and passed on the information to us that Cheri was in a hospital in the United States as she had an infection under her scalp from the implants. Dr. Ken Smith was taking care of her, for which we all were grateful. Cheri was having it very rough in trying to recover from this operation. I winced with guilt as I thought of what all this suffering would lead to. If only I had known the Ohio deal was going to fall through, I'd never have supported Cheri's decision to go through with the operation.

I arrived back in New York, and Pat drove me back up to Canada. I never asked Pat if he was getting paid for this, but I was almost sure he was doing this on his own time. We listened to Neil Diamond as we cruised in the Dobelle van, all the while wondering if this would be the last trip. I had a terrible gut feeling things were going to change, and change fast, in the months to come.

John Girvin e-mailed me and asked if Bill was still able to make decisions, and if Claire was taking over the vision project. I tried to think positively about that suggestion, but I still remembered the initial phone call she gave us in January 2003, wherein she felt the project wasn't really helping anyone. I could not say whether or not she'd keep it afloat in the event that Bill couldn't. John also asked if any other implants were planned—a question I could not answer at that point. I was still receiving calls from inquiries about the project from interested patients, and I answered them as best as I could, describing the fact that some patients were having troubles maintaining their phosphenes, as well as what was planned for development. Tony informed me Bill was very weak, too weak to hold or dial even a telephone, but had composed the following letter distributed to all patients:

The Dobelle Institute (Portugal) Lda.
Artificial Vision for the Blind

To: Jens Naumann July 13, 2004
From:

Wm. H. Dobelle, PhD, Chairman & Chief Executive Officer

Re: Update on Artificial Vision Project

Tony Martins and Don Kiefer have continued to work on the new system, and the attached illustrations indicate their progress. The new camera, although much greater resolution than the one in the present systems, incorporates a real lens (not just a pinhole aperture). In addition, one-third of the circuitry—which had originally been planned for the computer/ stimulator box—is now further miniaturized and is mounted on the back of the lens in the glasses. This means the computer/stimulator box is even smaller and lighter.

Reviewing the result of the tests that we did earlier this year—before I went back into the hospital—I am reasonably confident that I know the cause for most of our problems to date. This has to do with the electrochemistry at the electrode-brain interface. The present system is restricted to square pulses and cannot correct for electrochemistry, but Tony built a small, single-channeled stimulator that had dramatic effects when tested on patients. While it is possible to retrofit the present 144-channel systems with the necessary hardware and software to control the electrochemistry, it would be an extremely difficult and time-consuming job (six to eight months). Also, the techniques for retrofitting the 144 channel systems would have little application for the new, second generation, 484-channel stimulators. Therefore, we will concentrate our efforts on producing the new hardware and software as quickly as possible. These new systems will be provided to each of you at "no charge" as soon as they are ready. We will provide 484-channel versions ("stopped down" to 144 channels) in case we wish to update your 144-electrode array in the future.

Meanwhile, I have been immersed in efforts to recruit a partner to join us in the project, and I think this effort is particularly urgent. Although I have no reason to believe that I am staring down the gun barrel of my own mortality, the fact is that my insurance bills for the last several years now total well over $860,000. The project will certainly be in trouble if I were to die or be incapacitated without having a partner in hand.

My research indicates that there are over a thousand possibilities, including medical device and pharmaceutical companies, venture capital pools, universities, and foundations. Because the number of prospective partners is almost overwhelming, I shall concentrate all of my time on this effort rather than diluting it with further efforts to test patients when I really don't have suitable hardware and software in hand.

While Tony, Don Keifer, etal are working on the hardware/software and I am working on "partnering," I would suggest that you use the existing systems sparingly, if at all. If you have any questions, please do not hesitate to contact me.

Thanks.

Sadness filled my heart as I read this letter—yes, Bill was trying desperately to make the project look like it was moving forward in leaps and bounds, but neither Cheri nor Paul had yet received their systems and already were instructed to use them sparingly or not at all. The idea to retrofit or manufacture from scratch stimulators for all the presently implanted patients in six to eight months—already a very long time to wait for a blind person waiting to see again—was absurd, considering the payroll for the employees was just starting to get caught back up. Bill also was still convinced that the patients with present 144-electrode arrays had the confidence in the project, despite the treatment they had endured the past several months, to agree to having another implantation with the larger electrodes.

The most disturbing sentence in the letter was the one of him staring down the barrel of his own mortality. He said he didn't think he was—but we weren't so sure.

CHAPTER 14

Back in the Dark

The Dobelle Institute (Portugal) Lda.
Artificial Vision for the Blind
To: Patients, Colleagues, and Friends

From: Claire L. Dobelle
Sub: In Memoriam—William H. Dobelle, PhD

It is with great sadness that we report the recent passing of the founder and chief executive officer of the Dobelle Institute (Portugal) Lda. William H. Dobelle, PhD, after a lengthy and debilitating illness.

Throughout his life, Dr. Dobelle sought to better the lives of his fellow man through implanted medical devices. He has served as associate director of the Institute of Biological Engineering at the University of Utah, the director of the Division of Artificial Organs at the Columbia-Presbyterian Medical Center, and is a founding fellow of the American Institute for Medical and Biological Engineering.

His pioneering research in intracochlear stimulation, the total artificial heart, and most notably artificial vision for the blind, has and will continue to benefit patients around the world.

Wm. H. Dobelle, PhD, 1941–2004

Understanding the importance of continuity in the artificial vision project, Dr. Dobelle devoted the last several months of his life in active pursuit of a partnership with universities and research centers.

Before his latest relapse, Dr. Dobelle made preliminary contact with several interested parties, and meetings have been scheduled in the upcoming months. To that end, we will continue to seek out a financial and research partner to secure the future success of Artificial Vision, ensuring that Dr. Dobelle's ultimate goal of sight for the blind becomes a reality.

We thank you for your continued patience through this difficult period and will keep you advised of our ongoing progress.

Avenida Infante Santo 34, 7th Floor, Lisboa 1350-179 (Portuaat
Tel: +351(213)940-473, answering Machine +351(213)940-536,
Tel: +351(213)940-474 www.artificialvision.com

The letter arrived in the mail on one crisp October morning, there in the very same mailbox at the end of our driveway where we discovered the first real ray of hope in August of 2000.

We had feared this letter—but thought we were well prepared as this was not a sudden death. The weeks leading up to Bill's death were sad—Bill had to go back into the hospital in August as he was having similar problems with his remaining foot as he had had with his left one back in 2001. I know Bill treasured that foot, and even though he never complained about the loss of his first foot openly to us, he did say that the loss was very inconvenient. Looking back at my similar circumstances in losing my eyes, I had complained much more vigorously about my loss once I lost my second eye, and I was certain that the loss of the remaining foot was going to hit Bill hard.

Shortly before the end of September, Linda, the accountant from Avery and Dobelle Institute, had called me and said I was being laid off. Just like that. The explanation was that Bill wasn't doing so well and the vision project was being delayed. We had just started to get the enormous personal debt load of ours incurred by the purchase of the vision system under control, and now my job was history.

"But what about these things in my head?" I asked. Linda assured me she'd have Tony compose a letter and tell me how the vision project would continue after this. I had hopes, at that point, that I'd be rehired.

Then the news came of Bill's death. I didn't know how to feel about it at first. Bill meant a lot to me as a cordial friend, an employer, and most powerfully, the one who made it possible for me to see again. And that was just me. I thought of Claire, who most likely had her frustrations with his situation, but equally wanted to help him succeed, her husband now a memory. Her name was on the letter, having composed such a beautiful letter without mentioning once her own pain in her loss. The children, whom I had met, now having to remember their father and his accomplishments, some of whom were so young and will most likely only understand the real impact of his accomplishments much later in their lives.

Then there were the patients. I remembered how Karen, having met Bill for the first time in Portugal, referred to him as her "hero." Her thrill of seeing the dots for the first time in using the system was not shared directly with Bill as he was sick and not in the office at the time she was first hooked up to the system. Now her hero was a memory. Cheri, just having been subjected to the operation while fighting infections, never having had the opportunity to meet Bill in person, upon hearing of his passing must have felt immense pain.

For us as a family, the layoff was more of a problem than I had first imagined—not only did I have a sudden lack of income from the Dobelle Institute, but I had simultaneously discontinued my firewood-processing and the piano-repair businesses, the clients long having found other resources for their needs. The churches and other institutions who made up my regular piano maintenance clientele no longer needed me, and as for the wood business, I didn't even have the thousands of dollars worth of raw material to process before even being able to win back clients with lowered prices.

Then for the vision project . . . I could not participate in the decision-making process of the future of the vision project. I no longer had a voice, the decision to lay me off came directly from Claire, I was told, partially to save money and also because there was just no more need to have a patient representative or a coach for patients using the vision system. It was over; but how serious the situation really was, I had yet to find out.

I had no idea how the other patients were taking this new development; I could only imagine how they would suffer. All that hope, and all that money. Gone.

Bill had not been able to afford the scalp repair for Dennis even in August, and Lino was having trouble with his implants just two weeks after going back home with his system and was scheduled to see the CUF team of surgeons. I could only wait patiently for the next letter to come from the Dobelle Institute, hoping for some sort of miracle whereby a new company took over and kept working on the project.

The Dobelle Institute (Portugal) Lda.
Artificial Vision for the Blind

June 1, 2005

Mr. Jens Naumann
RR6
Napanee, Ontario K7R3L1
Canada

Dear Jens:

I thought I would take the time to give you an update as to the progress being made with the artificial vision project.

I had a meeting recently at Stony Brook University's biomedical department. They are interested in the project and are looking to see if the university can take on the medical side of the project while private investors take on the financial side, so I will keep you posted.

Secondly, Dr. John Girvin (who started the project with Bill back in Utah) and I will be going to Stanford University the first week in June to present the vision project to their medical department.

Also, Dr. Girvin has been in contact with a researcher at Johns Hopkins University. The university, the City of Baltimore, and the State of Maryland are working together to come up with a "scientific research park" with local, state, and private money, so there is a possibility that they could find funding for the project.

So I'm working hard trying to find a new home for this project, although it's taking more time than I expected. I naively thought that several universities would contact us right after they read the letter that Claire Dobelle sent them. The fact is that universities are like big corporations, so it takes time to get to any decision.

This project is too important to be forgotten. I will keep on trying to achieve our goal.

With best regards,
Tony Martins

This letter was a long time coming. During the past year, I, along with my family, had to try to forget completely about the vision project and get back to doing what we had done before this even started.

But that was easier said than done. Trying to put aside my feelings about the extreme uncertainty of the future of the vision project, the first concern was getting back on financial track. I had a vast knowledge accumulated about the concept of artificial vision through cortical stimulation, including all the details in the processes from beginning to end. To find something in this field would have helped us in all ways. But since there isn't a definite job description in this field, I randomly searched all possible avenues of employment.

I was filling out my resume for the hundredth time, sending it off in response to the latest job description; my most recent recorded work experience being that of the Dobelle Institute, found on the www.artificialvision.com Web site. Just out of interest's sake, I decided to look at the site again to see if maybe there was more information added about new prospective investors. The site wouldn't open. Assuming I was having computer troubles, I telephoned a friend and asked him to open the site. But the message on the Internet server said the site was not to be found.

www.artificialvision.com was no more . . . gone—

It was then that the loss of Dr. Bill Dobelle hit home to me. My family had long since moved on, the old familiar dad with his way of feeling around for his way accepted as the norm, the brief interlude of his seeing the world not even spoken about. But as for me, it was different. On December 7, 1983, I lost my sight, plunged in total darkness . . . then on September 14, 1984, following the recovery of partial vision to my left eye and the subsequent botched retinal attachment surgery conducted by Dr. Fraser, I was again plunged into this unrelenting abyss. Then again, twenty years later, after a brief episode of seeing some dots—but dots of light forming an image of the world around me nonetheless; again, it was taken from me.

I thought of the pictures I had from the vision system. I had never seen Commack—neither the houses nor the streets with my biological eyes, and the times I was there before the system began to work, I only imagined what I may have seen, borrowing from sound queues, spacial indicators, such as the number of steps in a certain direction, and mostly imagination. But with the system, I had the rough shapes of the houses' rooftops, the trees, the layout of the landscape up to the range of the system's camera. Then there were all the places I visited once I had the system at home. I had lived there in Napanee for so many years and never seen the place. Yet, with the system under certain conditions, the world had opened before me in its dotted maze. There was the Christmas tree of 2002, the trips out to look at houses at night decorated with Christmas lights, the road home with the snowbanks outlining the road. There was the freedom—even if just for a moment—where I could read a four-inch high letter printed out on paper—the feeling that the light gave me when looking at the dancing flames through the glass door of the woodstove. Just like a dream, it, too, was gone.

August 2005: Five years after the first letter from Dr. Dobelle reached my hands—the one that was filled with promise and wonder and hope—I received this letter from Tony, who was now the only acting representative for Artificial Vision, although at times Dr. Girvin helped out with the medical side of it. I could not help feeling extreme dismay when I read the part about stopping the use of the systems. By that time mine had been in the cupboard so long that it was covered in a thick layer of dust.

The Dobelle Institute (Portugal) Lda.
Artificial Vision for the Blind

August 24, 2005

Update to Our Patients
Ladies and Gentlemen:

As you are aware, we are aggressively seeking universities and venture capital to secure the future of the vision project.

We have been in contact with such universities as Stony Brook, Johns Hopkins, and Stanford, as well as doctors from the National Institute of Health.

So as not to compromise the vision project as it is today, I would suggest that each of you stop using the system while we find a "home" for the project.

I will keep you posted as discussions progress. Thank you for your patience and understanding.

Sincerely,

Tony Martins
Director of Artificial Vision

I spoke to Tony who informed me that selling the project was more difficult than first thought. While Bill was alive, we had assumed it was his uncompromising demands that caused investors to steer clear of the project, but now, with the objective being just to have a new home for the vision system with no strings attached, luck in finding an investor was as yet difficult. It may be because of the fact that FDA didn't approve the implants, or perhaps from the risk of pending settlements for disgruntled patients in the future; we could only speculate. The fact remained that we had these things in our heads, spent a lot of money for them, and could not see nonetheless.

The doctors along with CUF Hospital offered to remove the implants from those patients who desired it. I was informed that two patients had already taken advantage of this offer. I asked myself if I should really go and have that done. No, I am resolved I wouldn't take out the electrodes—no more brain surgery for me. However, I really had a lot of discomfort with the pedestals—those two jacks sticking out of the back of my head—and removing them would have been minor surgery resulting in a lot of relief. But once out—that was it. I understood now why Dennis refused to have this done to himself when faced with a similar offer—we had put so much blood, guts, and tears into this effort and to pull out the implants now would be the ultimate gesture of absolute defeat.

I didn't receive any more letters from the Dobelle Institute. Sheila closed the office in Lisbon and was operating a telephone line from her own home instead, representing the Dobelle Institute for a few more months, until that, too, was closed. Claire, apparently to pay off debts incurred by Bill and his artificial vision project, had to sell the Commack building of the Dobelle Institute and Avery, and then rent back a smaller section from the new owner. Everything was disappearing and the thought of the vision project continuing, with myself having a voice and participation in its direction, became mere wishful thinking.

One day, in desperation, I was compelled to contact other vision research institutions. I wrote to a few I could find, scattered among the globe, and those who replied directed me to the Johns Hopkins institution in Baltimore—the head of the vision research being Dr. Richard Normann. I had heard of him many times while in conversation with Bill—they had known each other, and often Bill was critical of Richard's work as he did not agree with the principal of penetrating electrodes. I was in search of an institution interested in using my existing implants for further research, using differing pulse trains and wave patterns not yet tried during my work with Dobelle. By no means was I interested in the implantation of penetrating electrodes—it sounded all too much like a disaster waiting to happen. Perhaps, I thought, I'd go for it once a few hundred patients succeeded in having it work for them without brain damage. Seizures from overstimulation were hard enough to endure—I didn't need the possibility of brain damage resulting from penetration.

I wrote the following letter to Dr. Richard Normann in Utah:

Hello, Dr. Normann,

Please let me introduce myself as Jens Naumann, a former patient of Dr. Dobelle, who arranged my implantation of a bilateral arrangement consisting of 140 surface electrodes connected via two pedestals protruding from the back of my head—the electrodes contacting the surface of my visual cortex. I was the man demonstrating the driving of a car, among other things, during the mass media blitz of June 13, 2002, and again in January 2003.

As you may know already, not only has Dr. Dobelle died since October 5, 2004, but according to Dr. John Girvin's last e-mail, as well as the fact that www.artificialvision.com is rubbed off the Internet, it is obvious that all sixteen of the implanted patients, of which I'm one, are entirely on their own. My antiquated equipment I was first issued in 2002 is presently practically useless, given that any adjustments necessary must be done through a master computer operated by specific software, as well as replacement parts, even batteries, are no longer available. Claire Dobelle had made some efforts to sell the project to no avail, but I suspect her asking for any price as well as the possibility that any institute that purchases the remains of the Dobelle Institute also risks inheriting the grievances of the patients, who had been issued a contract upon payment for the service, which is now impossible to honor—is playing an important role in the lack of success in finding an investor.

However, I had vision restoration, even though crude in comparison to my former biological vision, for a few weeks during which I experienced a much better quality of life resulting from its limited function. Moreover, I have invested a great sum of money, my health, and many hopes in this venture. Realizing you are working on artificial vision yourself, and knowing you had once known Dr. Dobelle (Dobelle talked a lot about you during the time I knew him), I was wondering if you'd be interested in engaging me in further experimentation as you see fit. I had been working for Dr. Dobelle for two years as patient representative, participated in the testing of most of the other patients, and was the most tested patient simply due to my proximity to New York, and as a result of being an employee and readily available. All the electrode stimulation data collected I have retained in hard copy as I had requested this from the ex-engineer Tony Martins. I had also made careful notes at the time I was issued the equipment to take home, describing the merits and application of the crude vision.

Dr. Normann, I am presently at a crossroad: either I do something with what is still in my head, or I need to get it removed in time, especially the pedestals (as that won't require opening my skull), as it is uncomfortable to carry the pedestals, considering there is no reason to do so. However, having seen the improvement to my lifestyle upon using Bill Dobelle's experimentally assembled prosthesis, I'd like to contribute whatever possible to the quest of vision in the future. I had written to Dr. Mark Humayan, who in turn suggested I drop you a line on this issue.

In the arrangement I propose, I'd require a modest salary so as to be available at your institution's request; however, there would be absolutely no obligation to issue any equipment, or to restore my vision in any way or form. Details could be worked out provided you are interested, I have no doubt. I will not give up the search for further experimentation, even if I have to look outside of North America. As Bill Dobelle spent a lot of his last years following my implantation wrestling with his own survival, only a limited amount of innovation actually could take place in his laboratory. Therefore, many different possibilities of stimulation, mapping, etc., were never tried, even though there seemed to be a great potential remaining in improving the vision system.

Please consider my proposal. Thank you.

Sincerely,
Jens Naumann
RR 6
Napanee, Ontario (Canada)
K7R 3L1
E-mail:

I received the following reply in a few days—an answer I did not at all hope for.

Friday, 16 Dec 2005 12:53:58-0700
From: "Richard A. Normann" <Normann@m.cc.utah.edu>
Subject:
Human Experimentation
To: "jens naumann" <jen_snaumann@yahoo.ca>

Jens,

Sorry I have not responded sooner, but I have been a bit busy, and I also didn't know exactly how best to respond. I have seen you in the videos that described Dobelle's efforts and was quite impressed with how you have been able to deal with your vision loss. My colleagues and I have not started working with volunteers yet, but hope to do so in the next year or so. Based upon your experience with Dobelle's work, you would be a good candidate for our experimental work. As you know, we will be using penetrating electrodes (not the surface electrodes used by Dobelle). This should allow us to produce much more focal excitation of neurons in visual cortex than Dobelle's electrodes. Our work with human volunteers will be focused on basic research questions (does patterned electrical stimulation evoke patterned perceptions?). We intend to implant two to three volunteers for a three to four-week period, doing experiments on a daily basis, and then remove the implanted electrode arrays. So, if you were to become one of our subjects, we would fly you out to Utah, cover all your travel and living expenses for the month you were here, and fly you back home. Thus, we would not offer you a salary. You would not receive useful vision from this brief period of experimentation, but you would be helping us develop a vision prosthesis that may help restore functional vision to the blind community. Let me know if this level of involvement in our work might be of interest to you.

Cordially,
Richard A. Normann, PhD

I tried to summarize my emotions as I read the response. My existing implants were of no interest to him—he wanted them out and something from his department put in their place. I was to go to Utah, have an operation at least as massive as I had in Portugal, be experimented on within days of my surgery—for a two—to three-week period as I would hurt intensely from the pain of the operation, and just when the period of the beginning of relief from healing arrives three weeks later, just as it did when I started to feel better following Dobelle's operation, my head would be opened up again, the electrodes of Normann removed, and I'd be dropped off back at my home—totally incapacitated and in horrible pain—I couldn't see how I'd even survive this ordeal.

"You'd be helping us develop a vision prosthesis that may help restore vision to the blind community . . ." is the great reward I would be sacrificed for. Oh yes, I'd be fed and housed and transported for free, but I really wouldn't feel much like eating during that time, and to do all this without even a dime in my pocket so my family may pay the bills—were all the scientists working for free just to help the blind community restore vision—or was it just that because I was blind, naturally, I should give the most to this project and not receive a cent for it. I could not understand the thought behind this offer. I sent my letter of refusal the same day. "Forget about artificial vision for now," I thought to myself as I clicked on the "send" button on the Internet server.

Tony informed me a little while later that Stony Brook University had accepted to take over the project, but with similar arrangements as first discussed—money for the further development of the project had to come from other investors. I haven't spoken for a long time with the other patients, except for Klaus, but he was now out of the project as his implants wouldn't work since their partial removal. Upon speaking together, we didn't mention artificial vision any more. I think from time to time about Richard Normann's offer and wonder if he found volunteers yet. I am sure he will when he wants them—Bill and I found each other, after all.

Why is this so? I look for answers and could only conclude that once blinded, I was not only handicapped by the loss of vision, but even more so by my desire to see again, the obsession fueled by any publicized research on vision restoration. Since that first time I heard of the promises of artificial vision on CBC Radio in 1990, the quest for the promised land—the day I'd have my life return back to that of the good old days—began. From there the long wait started for the opportunity to jump on board of the project whose merits lay "just around the corner . . ." Considering all of the renowned newscasters involved, along with the prestigious country of origin for the vision project, little doubt remained as to the authenticity of the news reports. Adding to this is the pressure of friends and family equally believing the newscasts, the decision to pursue the operation would become a collective one rather than one based on the desire of the individual—after all, refusing outright to take advantage of such an opportunity would risk being viewed as a voluntary participant in the world of blindness.

It was Richard Normann's letter that marked the turning of a new page in my life. Vision had to rest on the back burner as I skimmed through the Internet searching for new opportunity. My children were getting older now, my youngest son already ten years old. I felt that my search for paradise had somehow stagnated the family as we were all caught up in the waiting game. Just to only return to the firewood business and wait for another miracle wouldn't do justice to the rest of the family. I felt I needed to play a leadership role in discovering new ideas for us all to be able to move on.

My answer came one afternoon in winter 2006 when Lorri read a small advertisement in the newspaper about volunteers wanted in Africa. The site, *www.iicd-volunteer.org*, was filled with exciting opportunities for international development in new countries and cultures not commony visited by Canadian folk. The process entailed a six-month rigorous training session in a school situated in Massachusetts, after which the participant stayed in their designated country where the project was located. As exciting as the opportunity appeared on the computer as it chatted its contents to me, I was again worried I'd be shut out due to my blindness. The school boasted of being inclusive to all who wanted to participate. I put them up to the challenge by writing an e-mail describing my disability along with all I thought I had to offer. I had nothing to lose.

The answer came back almost immediately. I couldn't believe my ears as the computer read the contents of the letter sent by the promotions manager of the Institute of International Cooperation and Development, M. Peterson. She described how Humana, the humanitarian agency for whom IICD trained volunteers for, were looking for teacher training college instructors at their new facility in Nhamatanda, Mozambique. The school, named Escola de Professores do Futuro, recruited both sighted and blind students who would graduate as certified elementary school teachers upon completion of a thirty-month program. M. Peterson continued by emphasizing that my skills acquired through living with no eyesight would be a definite asset for teaching at EPF as I'd be able to pass on my skills in teaching, reading braille, as well as the knowledge of using a computer with adaptive technology. Once again, I was faced with an offer too good to refuse, and this time, it didn't involve a medical operation nor having to collect a vast quantity of cash.

The ensuing schooling in Massachusetts, and then the experience I had in Mozambique pushed my quest for vision out of the list of priorities as my total immersion in this new culture altered my own conceptions as to what life was all about. The people of Mozambique mentored me, demonstrating a perspective on happiness which, similar to my experience in Morristown when retreiving my first guide dog, enriched my life to a height not experienced since before the loss of my second eye in 1983.

While in Africa, despite the hot weather, I kept my hair relatively long in order to cover the pedestals. They were increasingly irritated with infection, and when sleeping, I could no longer lie on my back as the back of my head was swelling and painful. My colleagues from Mozambique peered at them with interest as I tried my best to explain that this was not the norm for people to have in North America. They occasionally asked me why I would go to such extremes just to see a few dots of light.

Why did I do it?

I returned to Canada in April 2007, where the vast majority of visually impaired citizens remain unemployed and living off incomes well under the national low-income cutoff, where the thought of a totally blind schoolteacher being placed in charge of a primary school classroom is unheard-of . . . I was faced with the pressure to be able to drive a car as my home, being only a few miles out of town beside a busy roadway, was still without public transportation. Even the VIA Rail passenger train did not stop to pick up passengers in Napanee, so acquiring a job in Kingston or Belleville would entail paying a $100 taxi bill daily—maybe that was one reason—we *must* see to be accepted as a contributor in this highly expectant society of developed Canada.

Then there are the dreams of what I once did—the world that has passed by with its pictures and freedom. The beautiful mountains, the motorbiking and downhill skiing, watching expressions on the faces of those I love—the privilege of seeing my children learning to walk and growing up—I remember not only that what I saw with my own eyes, but now it's also that what I saw with the Dobelle vision system. The outline of the dinner table while walking into the house, the arm of my child reaching out to touch the system components on my belt—the taste of real freedom as I walked across the parking lot back to the institute back door without even using the white cane—where will these memories take me?

The recent opportunity to travel and live in another culture so different with its perspective on disabilities and abilities alike, along with the entire experience of working with Bill Dobelle, changed something in me that allowed for a much calmer, less emotionally charged reflection on the idea of artificial vision. I felt I could move forward now and make logical decisions in the path of new ventures. I felt refreshed, neither angry at the loss of sight nor disappointed at Bill's overrating of his invention; there was something at peace that materialized to the point where I could make the next necessary move.

It was on February 10, 2010, when I went to the Kingston General Hospital and had the pedestals—that is, the two jacks—taken out of my head. The wires still lie under my scalp, and the electrodes still rest on my visual cortex. But the jacks, made of titanium, were causing real health problems. By then, my scalp had been receding from the jacks, globs of infectious discharge oozing constantly out from around them, and I was feeling a constant irritation in my general mood. Later I found out that even people who had titanium joint replacements in the early 2000 had to have them removed as the titanium was dissolving into the bloodstream and bone marrow. Taking the jacks out once seemed like the final nail in the coffin of the artificial vision system, but now I wasn't so sure about that.

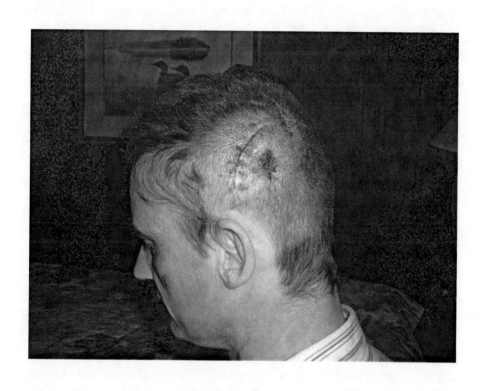

The fact remains that Bill's artificial vision concept did work. Mistakes were made, such as the substrate and pedestal material had been changed at the last minute from what was used with the original volunteer patients, and the introduction of the larger 3 mm electrodes proving to cause seizures. Many new possibilities remain to be tried; differing wave forms of stimulation, frequencies, electrode shapes, and other possible stimulation parameters have not yet been explored. Then there are the proposed changes to the new electronic system; the faster frame speed, gray area representation, instant magnification and brightness control, and even the standby option to protect the patient's brain from stimulation when he is in a familiar area not requiring sight.

But we never had the chance to implement these improvements with our existing implants. I was often frustrated with Bill's reluctance to listen to me and the engineers to try out new ideas while he maintained he would do whatever he saw fit in his own time; it seemed now that Bill thought he had lots of time left, but it was we around him that could see him deteriorating quickly. If he had lived another twenty years, he might have made it to the point of success with the vision project as was first outlined in his initial proposal sent to me back in August 2000.

I think a lot about the quest for my paradise—to see once again—this time my expectations tailored to that already seen with ninety-six points of light. Unlike the time I lost my final eye, upon finding out there was no such thing as an eye transplant—this time I know there is such a thing as visual cortex stimulation and that it does work. We have the knowledge, the computers, the cameras, the platinum, and the teflon for the implant. It is all there—all, that is, except for the leader of the project.

Who was that going to be?

Claire Dobelle had said in her letter that she was going to take all measures to ensure Bill's ultimate dream of restoring vision to the blind and that it would become a reality, just as Tony Martins stated that the project was too important to be forgotten. There have been no exciting reports coming from Stony Brook University since inheriting the project in 2005. The reason for this is not difficult to understand as no one who was directly involved with the project with Dobelle is on the team at Stony Brook. The leader for the continuation of this project would have to understand the various aspects of the system, from its initial installation on the visual cortex, the complications of the pedestals, the stimulation parameters and their effects, the quality of the vision and its merits, along with the details of phosphene mapping, patient rehabilitation and motivation. Additionally, a detailed knowledge of electronics and computer programming is required to guide the electronic systems development team. I hope to find this leader some day soon, and to be there to get the project back on track in accomplishing Bill Dobelle's—and my—ultimate goal.

ACKNOWLEDGEMENTS

To pull through the most difficult days of my life, I could not do it alone. My foremost tribute is dedicated to my parents Dietrich and Erika, who raised me not so much to be their friend, but to have the tools to survive and thrive under the most stressful conditions; my first wife Lorri, trusting me to fulfill my role of husband and father and giving me eight wonderful children: Danielle, Ryan, Leah, Kyle, Brandon, Joel, Jordan, and Aaron; my dearest friends Barb and Ken Sigsworth, who guided me to the positives when I could only see the negative; Angelina Estevao Mandlhate of Mozambique, introducing me to the beautiful world of social equality; and my dearest wife Yolanda along with our lovely daughter Ilta; you are my number one advocates and supporters. Many thanks additionally to all of my financial supporters helping me with the cost of this enormous project, including all participating churches and thoughtful, compassionate people of Napanee, Newberg, Deseronto, and surrounding area. Finally, I extend my admiration and thanks to William H. Dobelle and his lovely family, along with the staff of Dobelle Institute, for having tried so hard to make this project a success and to make my life a better experience.

I could not have come this far without any of you . . . Thank you.

CPSIA information can be obtained at www.ICGtesting.com
Printed in the USA
LVOW040358180912

299181LV00003BA/6/P